Inspected Hotels

Hotels
Great Britain & Ireland 2000

West One
PUBLISHING

Inspected Hotels
Hotels
Great Britain & Ireland 2000

The Saunton Sands Hotel, Saunton, Brend Hotels

West One Publishing • London

First published 1904

© West One (Trade) Publishing Ltd. 1999

ISBN 1-900327 38 4 paperback

A CIP catalogue record for this book is available from the British Library.

Cartography: © West One

Printed and bound in Slovenia.

Pictures reproduced with the kind permission of:
Ayrshire & Arran Tourist Board
(pp374-5, Girvan, Ayrshire);
English Heritage
(p58, Rievaulx Abbey, North Yorkshire);
Guernsey Tourist Board
(p499, St Peter Port, Guernsey);
Irish Tourist Board
(pp458-9, Glandore, West Cork);
The National Trust
(pp424-5, Joe Cornish, Rossili Beach, Swansea);
NMEC
(p29, The Millennium Dome)

Published by
West One (Trade) Publishing Ltd,
Kestrel House
Dukes Place
Marlow
Bucks SL7 2QH

Telephone: 01628 487722
Fax: 01628 487724
Email: sales@west-one.com

Managing Editor	Stan Dover
Production Manager	Liz York
Editorial Team	Sara Foster
	Matthias Thaler
	Jack Gough
Finance and Administration Team	Cathy Seabrook
	Alex Wilson
	Alan Pearson
Chief Executive Officer	Martin Coleman

Contents

Directory of Hotels

Momentum for the new millennium

Introduction by Graeme Potts
Group Managing Director
RAC Motoring Services

Writing the introduction to this guide gives me the opportunity to highlight a number of changes designed to serve our customers better as we begin a new century.

By the time you read this guide, one of the most significant developments in the history of the hotel industry will have been launched.

Unprecedented co-operation between the three main accreditation bodies – including RAC – has resulted in Harmonised Quality Standards, ending a confused situation where the consumer was often faced with several different ratings for the same property.

Clear definitions of the various types of accommodation and indications of the service quality which can be expected now provide the overseas and domestic guest with a framework for comparison- and a means of selecting the Hotel or Guest Accommodation which will best suit their needs.

With tourism a vital ingredient of the economies of both the UK and Ireland, this initiative will enable the hospitality industry to deliver a level of quality to match the consumers' expectations.

The aim of improving customer service was one of the principle reasons why Lex Service Plc bought RAC Motoring Services.

As part of a strong motor service based group, RAC can now offer a comprehensive service to its customers: Teaching learner drivers through BSM, providing an independent assessment of used cars, arranging lease or purchasing options as well as keeping vehicles on the road through servicing, repair and breakdown facilities. What's more, RAC Hotels and Travel services also help customers use their vehicle for the pleasurable things in life – like staying at RAC accredited properties.

Running a business like the new RAC group and running an Hotel or Bed and Breakfast shares an important aspect – satisfied customers are the ones who will tell their friends and neighbours – the best possible accolade.

This guide lists those properties which meet their guests' expectations and enjoy welcoming regular customers back.

I hope that you enjoy discovering them throughout Great Britain and Ireland and experiencing their own unique blend of quality and service.

A Swallow Hotels' Breakaway scores 4 out of 4

Short break or longer holiday, compare a Swallow Hotels' Breakaway with other hotel breaks and you'll be amazed at the sheer value for money.

1. Superb accommodation

2. A tasty breakfast

3. Unlimited free use of leisure clubs

4. Dinner each night

SWALLOW HOTELS
BREAKaways

All Swallow Hotels provide excellent accommodation, all provide use of a leisure club, and many of our restaurants have AA rosettes for fine dining. With the assurance of exceptional service and extra special touches like the Breakaway's welcome pack (often with free tickets to local attractions) you really will have made the right choice in <u>many</u> more ways than 4.

Telephone **0845 600 5 666** now for your brochure quoting ref: RA900

RAC Hotel Accreditation and Awards

New standards for the new millennium

To help tourists and business people identify the standard of accommodation they are looking for, Harmonised Quality Standards for all types of serviced accommodation have been launched.

Starting with extensive consumer research and with consultation within the hotel industry, the three main accreditation agencies – RAC, AA and English Tourist Council – have agreed a common set of inspection criteria to provide consistency for travellers looking for a place to stay.

Research shows that consumers are predominately interested in two main types of accommodation – Hotels, Guest Accommodation (which includes guesthouses, farmhouses, inns, small private hotels, restaurants with rooms and bed and breakfast properties).

New inspection criteria have also been introduced for two newly recognised types of accommodation – Townhouses and Travel Accommodation – thus recognising the growing diversity in accommodation styles demanded by today's customers.

Inspections for the Harmonised Quality Standards have been taking place since January 1998 to meet the deadlines to get the accommodation shown in this guide into the new format, new signage on properties and all other material in place for the new century, however with the scale and complexity of the operation means inevitably there will still be some work outstanding to complete this task.

Properties with a harmonised quality rating will be identifiable as follows :

Hotels:

1-5 stars, with signs in a new format to help distinguish them from the previous rating system

Townhouses:

4 and 5 star Townhouses

Guest Accommodation:

1- 5 diamonds

Travel Accommodation:

the description depicts this category

RAC Inspectors have been working with Hotel and Guest Accommodation proprietors, throughout the UK and Republic of Ireland, advising of the impact of this important new initiative to help the domestic and overseas guest select the type and standard of accommodation that best suits their needs.

The RAC supports the

BRITISH

Hospitality

ASSOCIATION

the effective voice of the hospitality industry

Harmonised Quality Standards explained

The different types of accommodation in the UK and Republic of Ireland have been categorised into four categories with differing levels, the requirements for each being :

Hotels – Stars

★ Star
Hotels in this classification are likely to be small and independently owned, with a family atmosphere. Services may be provided by the owner and family on an informal basis. There may be a limited range of facilities and meals may be fairly simple. Lunch, for example, may not be served. Some bedrooms may not have en suite bath / shower rooms. Maintenance, cleanliness and comfort should, however, always be of an acceptable standard.

★★ Star
In this classification, hotels will typically be small to medium sized and offer more extensive facilities than at one star level. Some business hotels come into two star classification and guests can expect comfortable, well-equipped, overnight accommodation, usually with an en suite bath / shower room. Reception and other staff will aim for a more professional presentation than at one star level, and offer a wider range of straightforward services, including food and drink.

★★★ 3 Star
At this level, hotels are usually of a size to support higher staffing levels, and a significantly greater quality and range of facilities than at the lower star classifications. Reception and the other public rooms will be more spacious and the restaurant will normally also cater for non-residents. All bedrooms will have fully en suite bath and shower rooms and offer a good standard of comfort and equipment, such as a hair dryer, direct dial telephone, toiletries in the bathroom. Some room service can be expected and some provision for business travellers.

★★★★ Star
Expectations at this level include a degree of luxury as well as quality in the furnishings, decor and equipment, in every area of the hotel. Bedrooms will also usually offer more space than at the lower star levels, and well designed, co-ordinated furnishings and decor. En suite bathrooms will have both bath and fixed shower. There will be a high enough ratio of staff to guests to provide services such as porterage, 24-hour room service, laundry and dry-cleaning. The restaurant will demonstrate a serious approach to cuisine.

★★★★★ Star
Here you should find spacious and luxurious accommodation throughout the hotel, matching the best international standards. Interior design should impress with its quality and attention to detail, comfort and elegance. Furnishings should be immaculate. Services should be formal, well supervised and flawless in attention to guests' needs without being intrusive. The restaurant will demonstrate a high level of technical skill, producing dishes to the highest international standards. Staff will be knowledgeable, helpful, well-versed in all aspects of customer care, combining efficiency with courtesy.

Townhouse Accommodation

This classification denotes small, personally run town or city centre hotels which afford a high degree of privacy and concentrate on luxuriously furnished bedrooms and suites with high quality room service, rather than public rooms or formal dining rooms usually associated with hotels, they are usually in areas well served by restaurants. All fall broadly within the four or five Star classification.

Guest Accommodation – Diamonds

The term Guest Accommodation comprises guest houses, farmhouses, small private hotels, inns, restaurants with rooms and bed and breakfast properties, which in the UK and Ireland offer a style and warmth of accommodation envied around the world.

The Guest Accommodation scheme assesses establishments at five levels of quality from one

MARSTON HOTELS

The Hythe Imperial, Hythe, Kent

Bridgewood Manor, Rochester, Kent

Coulsdon Manor, Coulsdon, Surrey

Stratford Manor, Stratford-upon-Avon

The Oxford Belfry, Nr. Oxford

The Hogarth, Kensington, London

Stade Court, Hythe, Kent

The Hampshire Centrecourt, Basingstoke

Flackley Ash, Nr. Rye, Sussex

The Crown, Lyndhurst, Hampshire

Stoneleigh Park Lodge, Nr. Warwick

DELIGHTFUL LOCATIONS

SUPERB LEISURE

For Further Information Telephone:

01303 269900

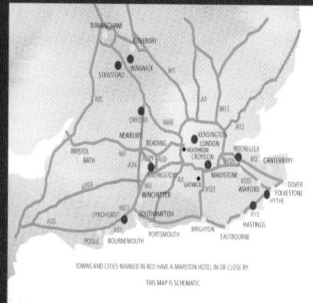

AWARD WINNING RESTAURANTS

CONFERENCES

CORPORATE ENTERTAINMENT IN OUR OWN WOOD

LEISURE BREAKS

GOLF & TENNIS

Marston Hotels

The Mews, Prince's Parade, Hythe, Kent CT21 6AQ

Tel: 01303 269900 Fax: 01303 263600

e-mail: info@marstonhotels.co.uk

web: http://www.marstonhotels.co.uk

INVESTOR IN PEOPLE

Harmonised Quality Standards explained

Diamond at the simplest, to five Diamonds at the luxury end of the spectrum.

To be recognised at all under the new Quality Standards, establishments must provide sufficient quality in all areas of operation covered under the following headings to merit a minimum score of 1 out of 5. If they do not achieve sufficient quality in one of these areas they cannot be awarded a quality rating at all:

Cleanliness and Housekeeping

Service and Hospitality (Guest Care)

Bedroom Facilities

Bathroom, Shower, WC and en suite Facilities

Food Quality and Service

Public Rooms

Safety and Security, Exterior and Interior Appearance and Up-keep (General Requirements)

The awards take into account the level of general cleanliness, the comfort and degree of style and quality of furnishings and decor throughout the establishment; the levels of service and hospitality displayed by owners and staff; the friendliness of the atmosphere; last but not least, the quality of the meals.

At all Diamond levels, cleanliness and good housekeeping are of the highest importance and the emphasis of the assessment for a Diamond rating is on guest care and quality rather than the provision of extra facilities.

The overall score in all areas of operation is then converted to a percentage, and this determines the quality rating awarded. The quality percentage bands at each level are listed below:

At 1 Diamond level:
Quality Percentage   20%-34%

At 2 Diamond level:
Quality Percentage   35%-49%

At 3 Diamond level:
Quality Percentage   50%-69%

At 4 Diamond level:
Quality Percentage   70%-84%

At 5 Diamond level:
Quality Percentage   85% plus

Travel Accommodation

This classification denotes budget or lodge accommodation suitable for an overnight stay, usually in purpose-built units close to main roads and motorways but could also include city centre locations. They provide consistent levels of accommodation and service, matching today's expectations.

Please Note
As Harmonised Quality Standards launches as this publication goes to print, direct comparison of properties with other inspection bodies may show some discrepancies as a result of different inspection dates.

The properties contained in this guide are accredited Hotels, Townhouses and Travel Accommodation, a full listing of Bed and Breakfast, Guesthouse, Inn, Farmhouse accredited properties can be found in 'RAC Inspected Guest Accommodation 2000', available at all good book stores.

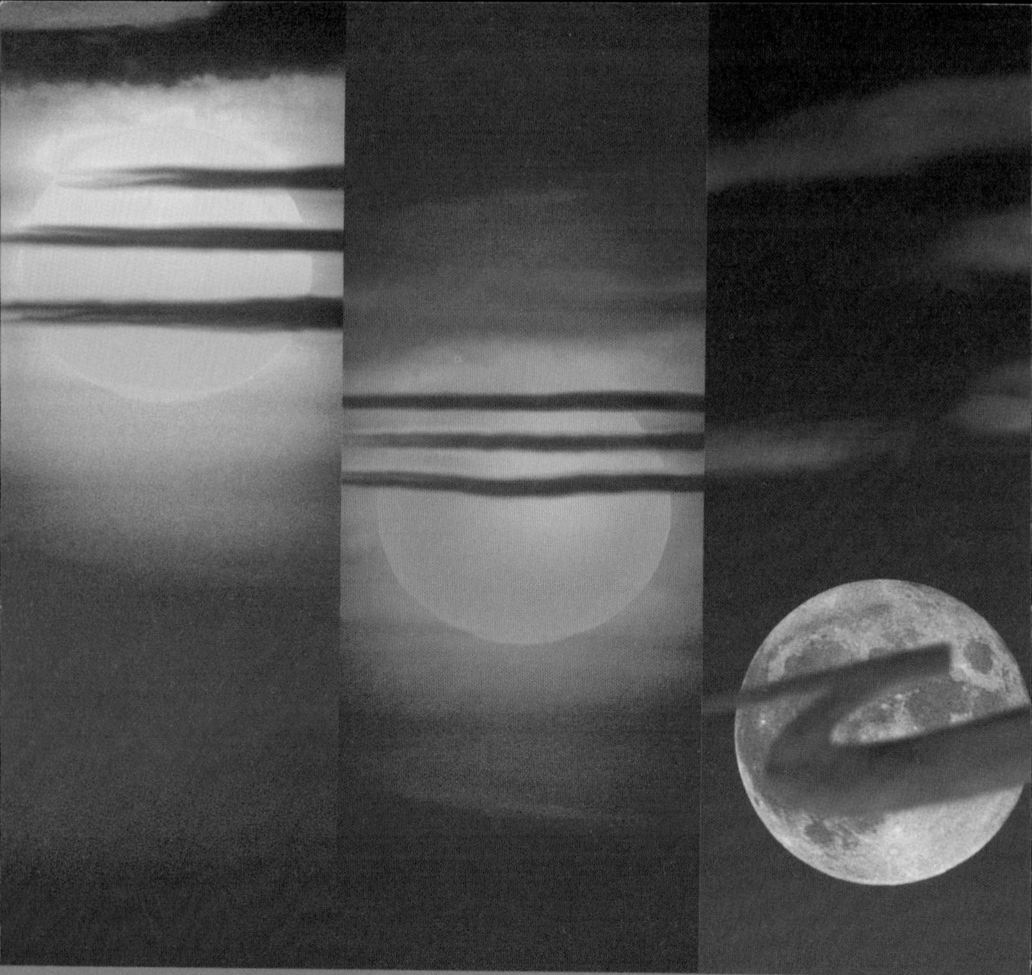

At the end of the day, make sure you're in the right hotel.

Whether you're looking for dependable comfort, reliable quality or something a little different, we can offer you a real choice.

We have over 80 hotels throughout the UK and Ireland (and another 350 in Europe), located everywhere from rural beauty spots to vibrant city centres. Great places to stay, great places to do business, great value. And all bookable through a single free telephone number or at our web site. At the end of the day what more could you ask?

Book from the UK on 0800 44 44 44. Book from Ireland on 1-800 500 600. http://www.choicehotelseurope.com

Depend on comfort.   Rely on quality.   Discover the difference.

New RAC Hospitality Awards

To reflect the increasing standards being achieved in the hotel industry, and to complement the new Harmonised Quality Standards, RAC has taken the opportunity to review its range of awards.

The range of awards celebrates excellence in both the Hotel and Guest Accommodation categories and a new award for dining recognises achievement at all that is good at all types of serviced accommodation.

Hotel Award

Gold Ribbon
For the past 13 years RAC has recognised excellence in hotel keeping with the RAC Blue Ribbon award. As hotel standards continue to rise, the best Blue Ribbon recipients are acknowledged by the introduction of the RAC Gold Ribbon accolade.

The new award is made to hotels who have raised their standards to even higher levels, continually demonstrating their commitment to superlative standards of customer care, service and accommodation.

Blue Ribbon
The RAC Blue Ribbon continues to stand for the high quality standards expected of the best in the industry. A Blue Ribbon award will only be presented to those properties who have achieved consistently high grades in all aspects of hotel keeping.

Both Gold and Blue Ribbon awards are made to Hotels in all classifications from 1 – 5 stars.

Guest Accommodation

RAC Little Gem
Now the highest accolade for Guest Accommodation, this award is presented to the best properties on a regional basis and recognises the all-round quality shown in hospitality, cleanliness, welcome and attention to detail that makes every stay memorable.

RAC Sparkling Diamond
This award is made to properties which achieve excellent standards of cleanliness, hygiene and attention to detail in their provision of guest comfort.

RAC Warm Welcome Award
Within the diamond scheme, only establishments that achieve excellent standards for hospitality and service in the overall inspection are put forward for this accolade.

RAC Dining Award

This new seal of quality assesses the entire dining experience at Hotel and Guest Accommodation, taking into account the quality of the cuisine as well as ambience, service and level of comfort.

The award reflects five levels of quality, starting at level one. The criteria for this award considers other guest meals available rather than purely concentrating on dinner and applies to both Hotel and Guest Accommodation categories.

16

The Bath
Tasburgh
Hotel

The Bath Tasburgh Hotel
Warminster Road, Bath BA2 6SH
Tel: 01225 425096 • Fax: 01225 463842
Email: reservations@bathtasburgh.demon.co.uk
Website: www.bathtasburgh.co.uk
RAC Merit Award for Hospitality, Comfort & Service

A Victorian mansion with beautiful gardens and extensive meadow land
stretching down to the Kennet & Avon Canal. Spectacular views. Charming
Ensuite Bedrooms (including Four-posters and Family room) individually
decorated and furnished. Elegant Drawing Room. Stunning Conservatory and
Garden Terrace. Evening meals with selective home-cooked gourmet dishes.
Licensed. Ample car parking. Personal and caring service. The Bath Tasburgh
Hotel offers the ideal base for combining stimulating sightseeing alongside
sought after country house comforts within a city setting.

RAC ★★

Types of Property

Country House Hotels

Country House Hotels offer a relaxed, informal atmosphere, with an emphasis on personal welcome. They are usually – but not always – in a secluded or rural setting and should offer peace and quiet regardless of their location.

Group Hotels

There are a number of hotel groups that operate throughout the UK and Ireland. Each group operates in different ways with some applying a consistent approach to each of the properties within their group, some operate under a number of different brands or styles while some run their establishments on an individual basis. Some of the groups in RAC accreditation are listed here:

Andrew Weir Hotels		**Millennium and Copthorne**	
Brend Hotels		**Novotel UK**	
Campanile		**Paramount Hotel Group**	
Choice Hotels Europe		**Peel Hotels Plc**	
Forte Heritage Hotels	Heritage HOTELS	**Principal Hotels**	
Forte Posthouse	Posthouse	**Savoy Group**	
Hanover International		**Scottish Highland Hotels**	
Jurys Doyle		**Shire Inns**	
Le Meridien	MERIDIEN	**Swallow Hotels**	
Marston Hotels		**Virgin Hotels**	

1999 Gold Ribbon Awards

England

★★★★	**Hartwell House, Restaurant & Spa** Aylesbury
★★★★	**Lucknam Park** Bath
★★★	**Buckland Manor** Broadway
★★★★	**Manor House** Castle Combe
★★★	**Gidleigh Park** Chagford
★★★	**Gravetye Manor** East Grinstead
★★★	**Summer Lodge** Evershot
★★	**Langshott Manor** Gatwick Airport
★★★	**Stock Hill Country House** Gillingham
★★★★	**Le Manoir aux Quat' Saisons** Great Milton
★★★★	**Hintlesham Hall** Ipswich
★★★	**Congham Hall** King's Lynn
★★★★	**The Athenaeum** London
★★★★★	**The Berkeley** London
★★★★	**The Capital** London
★★★★★	**Claridge's** London
★★★★★	**The Connaught** London
★★★★★	**The Dorchester** London
★★★★★	**Four Seasons** London
★★★★	**The Goring** London
★★★★	**The Halkin** London
★★★★★	**The Landmark** London
★★★★★	**The Lanesborough** London
★★★★★	**Mandarin Oriental Hyde Park** London
★★★★★	**The Ritz** London
★★★★★	**The Savoy** London
★★★	**Lower Slaughter Manor** Lower Slaughter
★★★	**Rookery Hall** Nantwich
★★★★★	**Chewton Glen** New Milton
★★★★	**The Vineyard at Stockcross** Newbury
★★★★	**Tylney Hall** Rotherwick
★★★★	**New Hall Country House** Sutton Coldfield
★★★★★	**Cliveden** Taplow
★★★	**Castle** Taunton
★★★	**Thornbury Castle** Thornbury
★★★	**Middlethorpe Hall** York

Scotland

★★★	**Kinnaird** Dunkeld
★★★★	**Inverlochy Castle** Fort William
★★★★★	**Turnberry** Turnberry

Wales

★★	**The Old Rectory** Conwy
★★★	**Bodysgallen Hall** Llandudno
★★	**St Tudno** Llandudno
★★★	**Ynyshir Hall** Machynlleth
★★	**Maes-y-Neuadd** Talsarnau

Republic of Ireland

★★	**Caragh Lodge** Caragh Lake
★★★	**Cashel House** Cashel
★★★	**Marlfield House** Gorey
★★★★	**Park Hotel Kenmare** Kenmare
★★★★	**Sheen Falls Lodge** Kenmare
★★★★★	**The Kildare & Country Club** Straffan
★★★★	**Mount Juliet** Thomastown

Channel Islands

★★★	**Chateau La Chaire** Jersey

1999 Blue Ribbon Awards

England

★★★	**Cavendish** Baslow
★★★★	**The Priory** Bath
★★★	**Queensberry** Bath
★★★★★	**The Royal Crescent** Bath
★★★	**Netherfield Place** Battle
★★★	**Devonshire Arms Country House** Bolton Abbey
★★★	**Farlam Hall** Brampton
★★★	**Old Vicarage** Bridgnorth
★★★★	**The Lygon Arms** Broadway
★★★	**Hotel on the Park** Cheltenham
★★★	**The Greenway** Cheltenham
★★★★★	**Chester Grosvenor** Chester
★★★	**Crabwall Manor** Chester
★★★	**Charingworth Manor** Chipping Campden
★★★	**Cotswold House** Chipping Campden
★★★★	**Crathorne Hall** Crathorne
★★★★	**Redworth Hall** Darlington
★★★	**Maison Talbooth** Dedham
★★	**The Mill at Harvington** Evesham
★★★★	**Ashdown Park** Forest Row
★★★	**Alexander House** Gatwick Airport
★★★	**Hob Green** Harrogate
★★★	**Sharrow Bay Country House** Howtown
★★★	**The George** Isle of Wight
★★★	**Island Hotel** Isles of Scilly
★★★	**St Martin's on the Isle** Isles of Scilly
★	**Swinside Lodge** Keswick
★	**Lansdowne** Leamington Spa
★★★★★	**One Aldwych** London
★	**South Lodge** Lower Beeding
★★★★	**Fredrick's** Maidenhead
★★★★	**Stapleford Park** Melton Mowbray
★★★★	**Donnington Valley Hotel & Golf Course** Newbury
★★★	**Hollington House** Newbury
★★★★	**Vermont Hotel** Newcastle upon Tyne
★★	**Oaks** Porlock
★★★	**The Rosevine** Portscatho
★★★	**Soar Mill Cove** Salcombe
★★★	**George of Stamford** Stamford
★★★	**Pear Tree at Purton** Swindon
★★★	**Calcot Manor** Tetbury
★★★	**Lords Of The Manor** Upper Slaughter
★★★	**Priory** Wareham
★★★	**Leeming House** Watermillock
★★	**Beechleas Wimborne** Minster
★★★★	**Lainston House** Winchester
★★	**Broadoaks Country House** Windermere
★★★	**Gilpin Lodge** Windermere
★★★	**Holbeck Ghyll Country House** Windermere
★★★	**Grange** York

Scotland

★★★	**Darroch Learg** Ballater
★★★	**Banchory Lodge** Banchory
★★★	**Norton House** Edinburgh
★★	**Old Manse of Marnoch** Huntly
★★★★	**Balbirnie House** Markinch
★★	**Ladyburn** Maybole
★	**Well View** Moffat
★★★	**Kirroughtree House** Newton Stewart
★★★	**Loch Torridon** Torridon

Wales

★★	**Tan-y-Foel Country House** Betws-y-Coed
★★★★★	**St David's Hotel and Spa** Cardiff
★★★	**The Lake Country House** Llangammarch Wells
★★★★	**Llangoed Hall** Llyswen
★★★	**The Portmeirion** Portmeirion

Republic of Ireland

★★★	**Gregans Castle** Ballyvaughan
★★★★	**Hayfield Manor** Cork
★★★★	**Glenlo Abbey** Galway & Salthill
★★★★	**Aghadoe Heights** Killarney
★★★	**Longueville House** Mallow
★★★	**Tinakilly Country House** Wicklow

Channel Islands

★★★★	**Longueville Manor** Jersey

RAC Hotel Services

Linda Astbury
Manager of Hotel Operations

This is the first guide using the new inspection criteria which takes the requirements of the guest as their basis.

This has meant that the RAC Inspection force underwent thorough and exhaustive re-training to allow them to assess each property to the new standards. Throughout the 19 month inspection process RAC Hotel Inspectors have been able to advise owners and managers of all styles of properties, of the requirements to ensure that consumer expectations are met at serviced accommodation throughout the UK and Republic of Ireland.

Of course each inspection is unique, with different styles of property serving differing clienteles and a major part of the Inspector's job is to take into account the individuality of each property. But, the bricks and mortar is only the beginning: in a service industry, it is the quality of the staff which makes the difference and that fact is reflected in the new Harmonised Quality Standards.

All Inspectors works incognito, observing the service received by other guests. The findings are discussed with the establishments and any areas for improvement are discussed. We believe that only in this way can RAC play its part in assisting properties to increase their standards on a constant basis.

Over the last few years we have noticed a marked improvement in the quality of properties in the RAC scheme. That fact, combined with the introduction of the Harmonised Quality Standards, has prompted us to review the range of our awards recognising excellence throughout the hotel industry.

We are particularly pleased to introduce the RAC Dining Award which acknowledges the quality of the dining experience not just at hotels but at Guesthouse, Bed and Breakfast and other Guest Accommodation where undoubtedly high standards are now abundant.

The award is not just about the food itself and recognises the atmosphere of the restaurant or dining room, the attention given to detail and service provided.

We hope that you will agree that the combination of a new rating scheme and new RAC awards will help you find the right property to suit your needs on every occasion.

Lancaster Hotel

Situated on the sea front within easy walking distance of the town centre.

From its public rooms can be seen the magnificent view of Oban Bay, with the islands of Kerrera, Lismore, and the more distant peaks of Mull in the background.

The hotel is readily distinguished by its attractive pseudo-tudor exterior.

The interior is appointed to a high modern standard and can offer guests a wide range of facilities:

INDOOR HEATED SWIMMING POOL
SAUNA BATH AND SPA
FULLY LICENSED
AMPLE CAR PARKING
RAC ★★
STB ★★

Esplanade, Oban, Argyll, PA34 5AD
Telephone: 01631 562587 • Fax: 01631 562587

General Information

Shortened hotel entries

Where no return was received from the hotel, all prices have been removed.

Maintenance of standards

All hotels listed in the guide are inspected regularly; nevertheless we welcome reports from readers on the standards being maintained. We are also glad to have reports about hotels which are not appointed by the RAC; such reports may enable the RAC to extend the number of hotels inspected.

Complaints

In cases of dissatisfaction or dispute, readers will find that discussion with the hotel management at the time of the problem/incident will normally enable the matter to be resolved promptly and amicably. Should the personal approach fail, the RAC will raise comments with the hotelier at the time of the next inspection.

Please write to RAC Hotel Services,
1.Forest Road
Feltham TW13 7RR

Please submit details of any discussion or correspondence involved when reporting a problem to RAC.

Cancellation of reservations

If you have to cancel a reservation of accommodation, you are advised to telephone the hotel at once, followed by a written confirmation of the cancellation. Please try to give the hotel as much notice as possible in order that they may have every opportunity to re-let the accommodation. If rooms which are reserved and not occupied cannot be re-let, the hotel proprietor may suffer loss and guests may be held legally responsible for part of the cost. This may also apply to table reservations in restaurants.

Arrival times

Small hotels and inns may close for part of the afternoon. It is wise to inform them of your expected arrival time when booking, and to telephone them if you are delayed, particularly after 6.00pm.

Information on towns

RAC Inspected Hotels is not a gazetteer and lists only those cities, towns and villages in which there are RAC Appointed (star rated) hotels.

Mileages

The mileages shown are computed by the shortest practical routes, which are not necessarily those recommended by RAC.

&. Facilities for the disabled

Hotels do their best to cater for disabled visitors. Some, in old or converted buildings, find it difficult to make the necessary alterations. Those hotels which are considered by their proprietors or managers to have suitable facilities are indicated in the guide by the usual symbol. Disabled visitors are recommended to contact the hotel direct and ascertain whether the hotel can provide for their particular requirements and to let the hotel know what they will need in the way of extra service or facilities.

How to use this guide

How to find a property

Town, county and map reference. ———————

ALDERSHOT Hampshire   4C3
Pop. 54,000. **EC** Wed **MD** Thu **see** Church with 15th
century tower **i** Military Museum, Queens Avenue
01252-20968

Hotel name, rating and contact details. ——————

★★★ Potters International
Fleet Road, Aldershot GU11 2ET
☎ 01252-344000 **Fax** 01252-311611

Short description with a picture of the hotel. ——————

A superb 97 bedroom hotel complex, with first class
accommodation, all ensuite, splendid restaurant,
health and fitness suite and extensive business,
conference and banqueting facilities.

Bedroom information and facilities. ——————
97 bedrs, all ensuite, ▣ ♀ ⚲ ☲ ☷ 400 **P** 200 ⊞ Rest
Resid **SB** £99-£115.50 **DB** £132 **L** £12.50 **L** ● **D** £17.50

Details of prices and credit cards accepted. ——————
D ● ✕ **LD** 23:00 Restaurant closed L Sat **CC** MC Visa
Amex DC JCB ▣ ▣ ▣ ▣ &

Notes

Properties in this guide are listed alphabetically by their
location within England, Scotland, Wales, Northern
Ireland, the Republic of Ireland, the Channel Islands and
the Isle of Man.

Properties are arranged by rating and then alphabetically
within the classification.

The final entries for each town list those few
establishments which, because of pressure of time, we
have been unable to complete an inspection for
Harmonised Quality Standards this year.

The Listing explained

Property Information

The listing for each property starts with its rating, followed by its name, RAC awards, address, telephone, fax number, e-mail address and details of any seasonal closing.

★   Hotel classification

❖   A small number of properties in this guide have a provisional classification denoted by this symbol. This means that we have been unable to confirm their new classification.

♔   Country House Hotel

Awards

Gold Ribbon (see page 18)
Blue Ribbon (see page 19)
Dining Award

Facilities at the property

&   Facilities for the disabled – see page 23
🐾   Dogs permitted
     No smoking anywhere in Hotel
     Lift
P   Parking
⋮⋮⋮   Conference facilities

Bedroom Information

4   Fourposter beds available
⌨   Socket for computer available
♀   Special rooms made available to women travelling alone

Other services

EC   Early closing day
MD   Market day

Meal Information

✕   Meal Information
LD   Last dinner
L   Lunch
D   Dinner

Licensing Information

⊞   Full licence
⊞ Rest   Restaurant or table licence. A licence whereby the sale of alcohol is restricted to customers taking meals
⊞ Resid   Residential licence. A licence whereby the sale of alcohol is restricted to residents at an establishment and to their friends entertained at their expense

Information on Charges

SB   Rate for Single Room & Breakfast
DB   Rate for Double Room and Breakfast
HB   Rate for Half board
Room   Rate for Room only
L   Price of table d'hote lunch
D   Price of table d'hote dinner
CC   Credit Cards
MC   MasterCard
Amex   American Express
DC   Diners Club
JCB   Japan Card Bank
Vi   Visa

The prices given range from that for standard rooms in low season to that for superior rooms in high season. Tariffs given in the guide are forecast by the hoteliers of what they expect to charge in 2000. It is always advisable to check with the property before booking. All prices quoted should include VAT where applicable, they may or may not include a charge for service.

Sporting Facilities

     Indoor swimming pool
     Outdoor swimming pool
     Golf course
     Tennis
     Fishing
     Squash
     Riding
     Gymnasium
     Billiards/snooker
     Sauna

 # Weddings

Where this symbol appears alongside the hotel entry, the hotel has informed us that they have a licence for weddings to take place at the hotel. Many will have a special room set aside, others will lay out a room in the same style as a registry office. The hotel will obviously lay on the reception and usually offer guests a bed and breakfast at a discounted rate. Contact the manager early for availability.

Symbols and Abbreviations

English	Français	Deutsch
★ hotel classification	Classification de l'hôtel	Hotelklassifikation
country house hotel	Hôtel/manoir	Landhaushotel
Gold Ribbon	'Gold Ribbon'	Gold Band
Blue Ribbon	'Blue Ribbon'	Blaues Band
facilities for the disabled	Aménagements pour handicapés	Einrichtungen für Behinderte
fourposter beds available	Lit a baldoquins	Himmelbett
EC early closing day	Jour hebdomadaire de fermeture anticipée	Tage mit frühem Geschäftsschluss
MD market day	Jour de marché	Markttag
dogs permitted	chiens acceptés	Hunde erlaubt
no smoking anywhere in hotel	Interdiction de fumer dans l'hôtel	Rauchverbot im ganzen Hotel
lift	ascenseur	Fahrstuhl
P parking	Parking	Parken
conference facilities	possibilité de conférences	Konferenzeinrichtungen
✗ meal information	Renseignements sur les repas	Informationen über Mahlzeiten
LD last dinner time	Dernière heure pour dîner	letzte Abendessenszeit
SB single room & breakfast	chambre d'une personne + petit déjeuner	Preis für Einzelzimmer und Frühstück
DB double room & breakfast	chambre pour deux personnes + petit déjeuner	Preis für Doppelzimmer und Frühstück
HB halfboard	demi-pension	Halb Pension
L lunch	Déjeuner	Mittagessen
D dinner	Dîner	Abendessen
₵ credit cards	Cartes de crédit	Kreditkarten
MC MasterCard	MasterCard	MasterCard
Amex American Express	American Express	American Express
DC Diners Club	Diners Club	Diners Club
JCB Japan Card Bank	Japan Card Bank	Japan Card Bank
Vi Visa	Visa	Visa

Sporting facilities

indoor swimming pool	Piscine couvert	Hallenbad
outdoor swimming pool	Piscine en plein air	Freibad
golf course	Terrain de Golf	Golfplatz
tennis	Tennis	Tennis
fishing	Peche	Angeln
squash	Squash	Squash
riding	Equitation	Reiten
gymnasium	Gymnase	Sporthalle
billiards/snooker	Billard	Billard
sauna	Sauna	Sauna

London

London Hotels

Because of the size of London, the Hotel Directory has been divided into seven regions for easy reference. These regions equate to groups of postal districts. The postcode map on page 32 will allow you to identify the area you wish to stay in and you can then look up the relevant part of the directory to find a hotel.

If you know the name of a hotel or guest house you wish to stay at, but are not sure where it is located, use the list below. This gives its postcode, position on the London Outer or Inner maps (pages 33 to 35) and also the page its entry appears in the directory.

22 Jermyn Street	SW1Y	Inner E3	41
Athenaeum	W1V 0BJ	Inner D3	41
Basil Street	SW3 1AH	Inner C3	50
Beaufort	SW3 1PP	Inner C4	51
Berkeley	SW1X 7RL	Inner C3	36
Berners	W1A 3BE	Inner D2	42
Bonnington in Bloomsbury	WC1B 4BH	Inner F2	52
Brown's	W1X 4BP	Inner D3	42
Cannizaro House	SW19 4UE	Outer B3	55
Capital	SW3 1AT	Inner C3	47
Cavendish	SW1Y 6JF	Inner E3	42
Chesterfield Mayfair	W1X 8LX	Inner D3	42
Clarendon	SE3 0RW	Outer E3	54
Claridge's	W1A 2JQ	Inner D2	36
Clifton-Ford	W1M 8DN	Inner D2	42
Cliveden Town House	SW3 2RP	Inner C4	50
Comfort Inn	UB3 1BL	Outer A2*	57
Comfort Inn Kensington	SW5 9QJ	Inner B4	51
Commodore	W2 3NA	Inner B2	50

Connaught	W1Y 6AL	Inner D2	36
Conrad International London	SW10 0XG	Inner B5	47
Copthorne Tara	W8 5SR	Inner B3	47
Covent Garden	WC2H 9HB	Inner E2	52
Cumberland	W1A 4RF	Inner C2	42
Delmere	W2 1UB	Inner B2	51
Dorchester	W1A 2HJ	Inner D3	36
Dorset Square	NW1 6QM	Inner C2	54
Durley House	SW1X 9PJ	Inner C4	41
Flemings Mayfair	W1Y 7RA	Inner C3	45
Forte Crest Heathrow	UB7 0JU	Outer A2*	57
Forum	SW7 4DN	Inner B4	48
Four Seasons	W1A 1AZ	Inner D3	38
Fox Club	W1Y 7PJ	Inner D3	47
Goring	SW1W 0JW	Inner D3	43
Halkin	SW1X 7DJ	Inner D3	43
Harrington Hall	SW7 4JW	Inner B4	48
Hogarth	SW5 0QQ	Inner B4	50
Jurys Kensington	SW7 5LR	Inner B4	48
Jurys London Inn	N1 1LA	Inner F1	54
Kingsway Hall	WC2B 5BZ	Inner F2	53
Landmark London	NW1 6JQ	Inner C2	54
Lanesborough	SW1X 7TA	Inner D3	38
Le Meridien Excelsior	UB7 0DU	Outer A2*	57
Le Meridien Grosvenor House	W1A 3AA	Inner C3	38
Le Meridien Piccadilly	W1V 0BH	Inner D3	38
Le Meridien Waldorf	WC2B 4DD	Inner F2	51
Leonard	W1H 5AA	Inner C2	45
London Bridge	SE1 9SG	Inner G3	54
London Marriott Grosvenor Square	W1A 4AW	Inner D2	38

Lowndes Hyatt	SW1X 9ES	Inner C3	43
Mandarin Oriental Hyde Park	SW1X 7LA	Inner C3	38
Mandeville	W1M 6BE	Inner D2	46
Master Robert	TW5 0BD	Outer A2*	57
May Fair Inter-Continental	W1A 2AN	Inner D3	40
Millennium Chelsea	SW1X 9NU	Inner C3	44
Millennium Britannia Mayfair	W1A 3AN	Inner D2	44
Millennium Gloucester	SW7 4LH	Inner B4	48
Montague	WC1B 5BJ	Inner E2	52
Montcalm Nikko	W1A 2LF	Inner C2	44
Novotel London West	W6 8DR	Outer B2	54
Novotel London Heathrow	UB7 9HB	Outer A2*	57
Novotel London Waterloo	SE1 7LS	Inner F4	54
Oki Kensington	SW5 0PG	Inner B4	51
One Aldwych	WC2B 4B2	Inner F2	52

Osterley Four Pillars	TW7 5NA	Outer A2*	57
Paragon	SW6 1UQ	Inner A4	51
Park Lane	W1Y 8BX	Inner D3	44
Pelham	SW7 2LA	Inner B4	50
Posthouse	NW3 4RB	Outer C1	54
Posthouse Ariel Heathrow	UB3 5AJ	Outer A2*	57
Posthouse Bloomsbury	WC1N 1HT	Inner E1	53
Posthouse Kensington	W8 5SP	Inner B3	51
Posthouse Regents Park	W1P 8EE	Inner D2	46
Quality	SW1V 1PS	Inner E4	46
Radisson Edwardian Berkshire	W1N 0BY	Inner D2	47
Radisson Edwardian Hampshire	WC1B 3LB	Inner E2	53
Radisson Edwardian Marlborough	WC1B 3QD	Inner E2	54
Regent Palace	W1A 4BZ	Inner D2	47
Rembrandt	SW7 2RS	Inner C4	48
Ritz	W1V 9DG	Inner D3	41
Royal Garden	W8 4PT	Inner B3	47
Royal Lancaster	W2 2TY	Inner B2	48
Rubens at The Palace	SW1W 0PS	Inner D4	45
Russell	WC1B 5BE	Inner E2	52
Saint George's	W1N 8QS	Inner D2	45
Savoy	WC2R 0EU	Inner F2	52
Sheraton Park Tower	SW1X 7RN	Inner C3	40
Sleeping Beauty Motel	E10 7EB	Outer D1	54
Sloane Square Moat House	SW1W 8EG	Inner C4	47
Stanley House	SW1V 1RR	Inner D4	47
Stanwell Hall	TW19 7PW	Outer A3*	57
Strand Palace	WC2R 0JJ	Inner F2	53
Swallow International	SW5 0TH	Inner B4	50
Washington Mayfair	W1Y 8DT	Inner D3	45
Westbury	W1A 4UH	Inner D2	45

National Code & Number Change

Telephone codes and numbers in London change in April 2000.

0171-XXXXXX becomes 020-7XXX XXXX
0181-XXXXXX becomes 020-8XXX XXXX

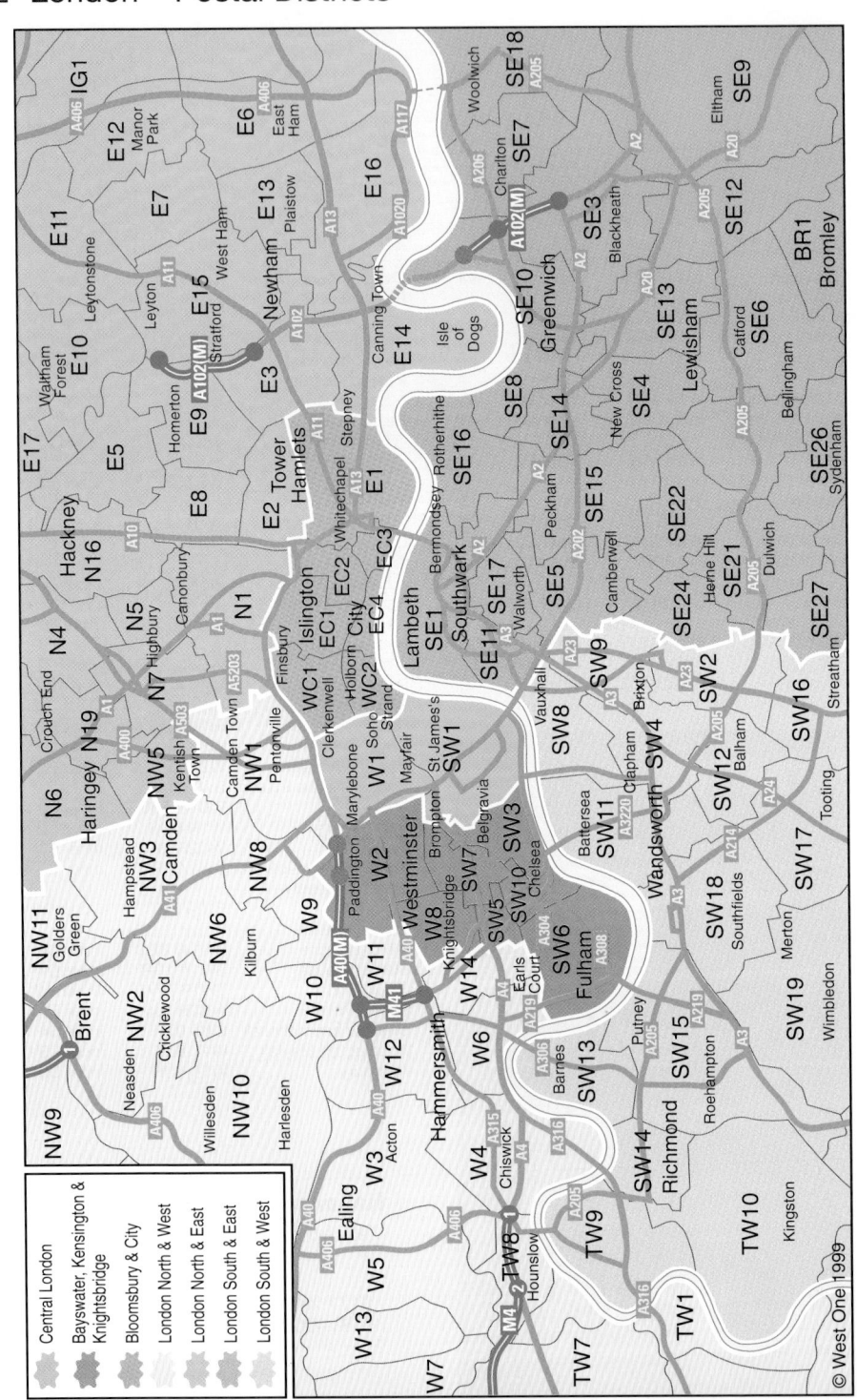

© West One 1999

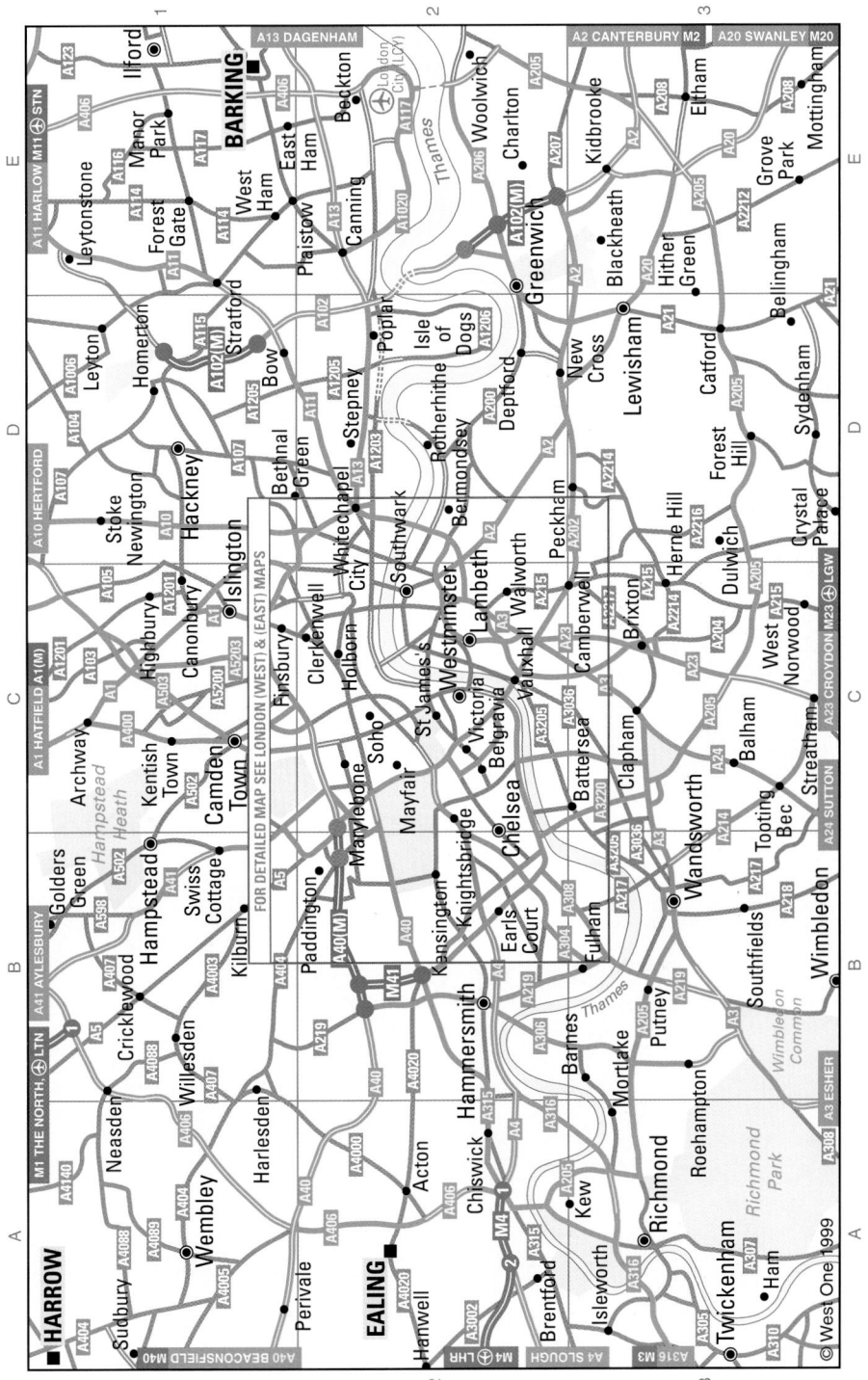

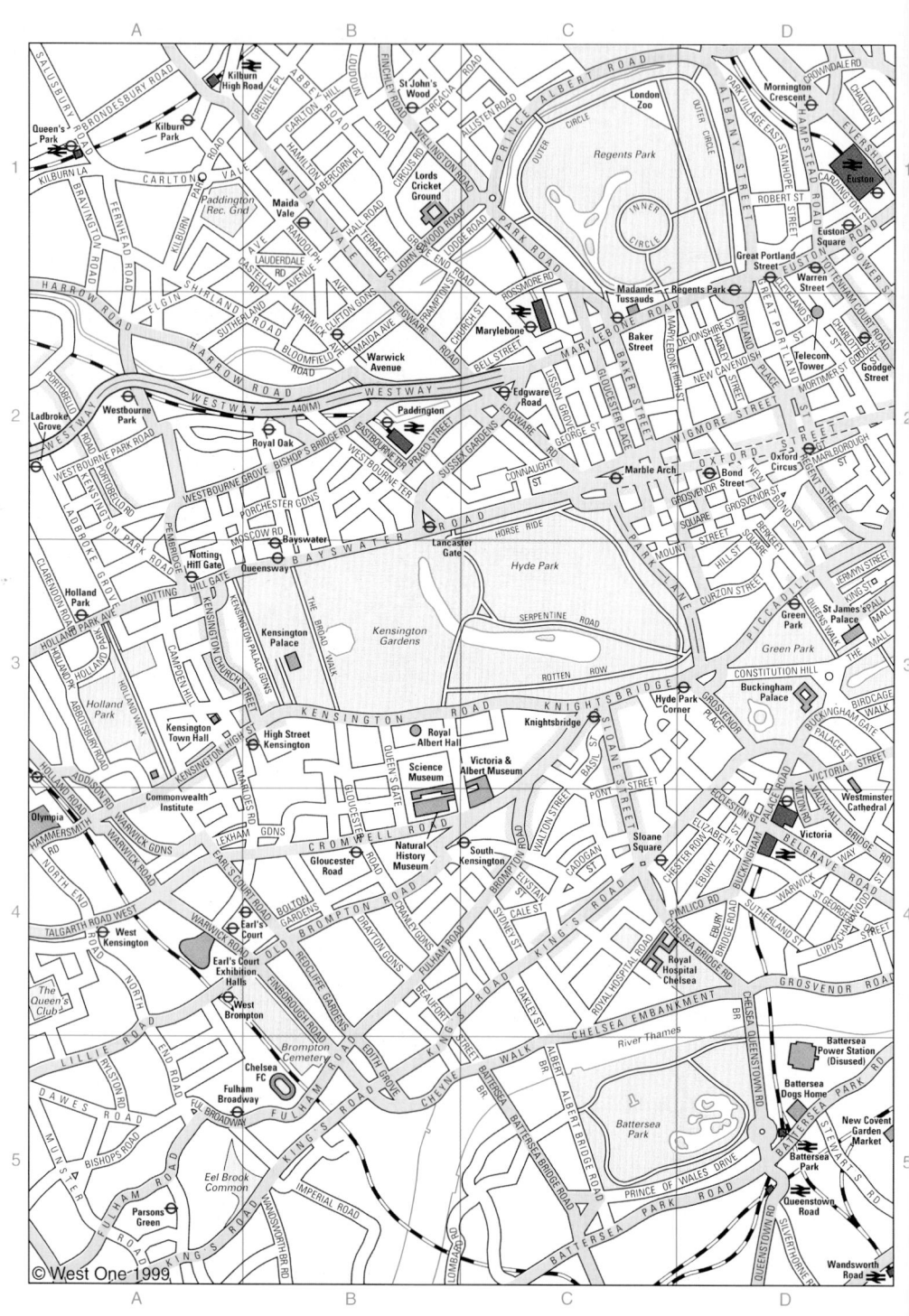

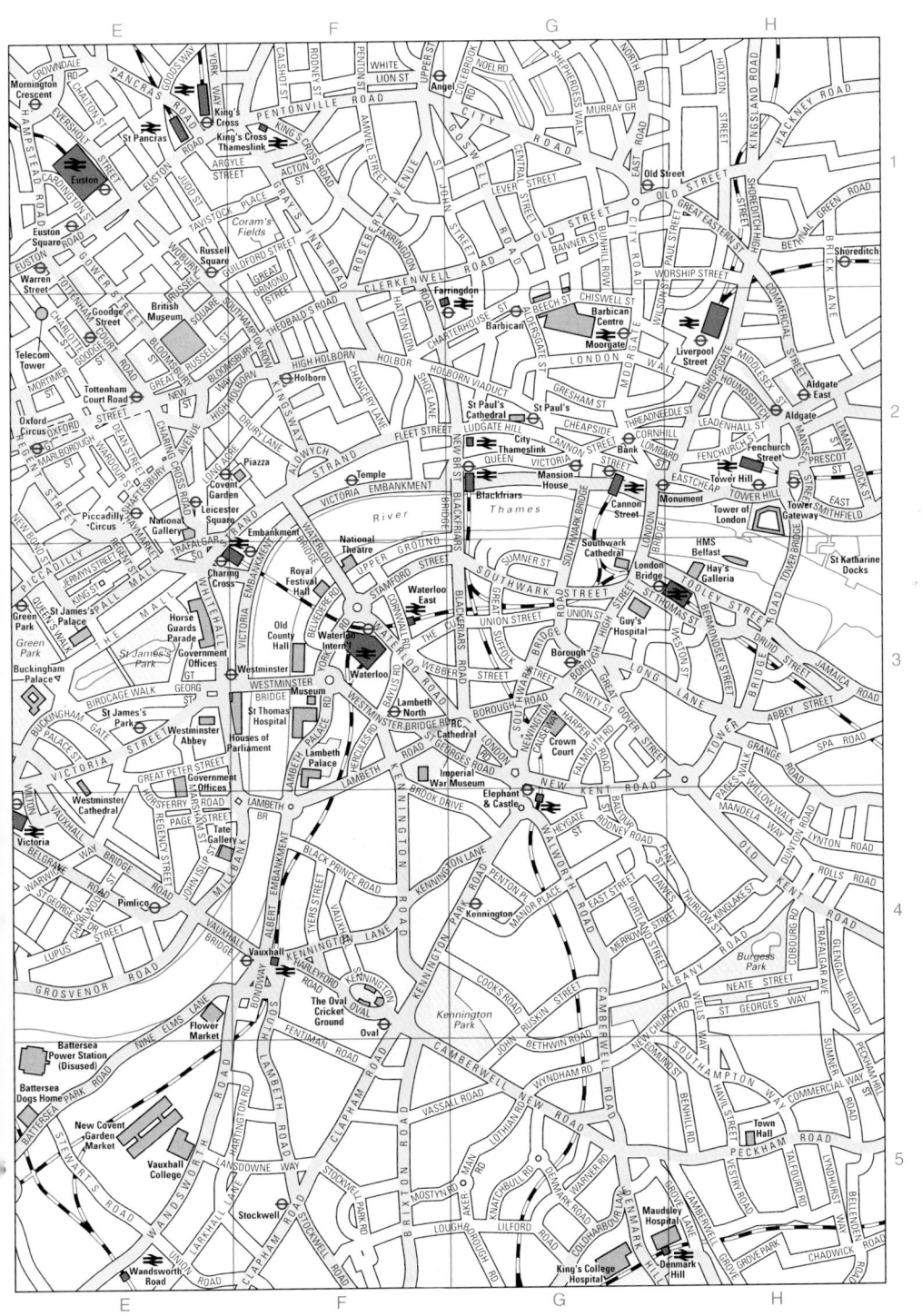

★★★★★ Berkeley 🎗 🎗 🎗 🎗
Gold Ribbon Hotel
Wilton Place, Knightsbridge, SW1X 7RL
📞 0171-235 6000 **Fax** 0171-235 4330
E-mail info@the-berkeley.co.uk

Perfectly placed for shopping in Knightsbridge, The Berkeley is a showcase for some of Englands leading interior designers. Facilities include the latest communications, in-room entertainment and roof-top swimming pool.
157 bedrs, all ensuite, ④ ⊟ ⊞ 250 **P** 50 ⊕ ⟪ MC Visa Amex DC JCB ☒ ☒ ▦

★★★★★ Claridge's 🎗 🎗 🎗
Gold Ribbon Hotel
Brook Street, Mayfair, London W1A 2JQ
📞 0171-629 8860 **Fax** 0171-499 2210
E-mail info@claridges.co.uk

Claridge's, with its stunning art deco restaurant, sophisticated bar and state-of-the-art health and beauty facilities, is London's most elegant hotel. Completely restored, the apartments are among the most exquisite and best-equipped in the world.
198 bedrs, all ensuite, ⊟ ⊞ 260 ⊕ ⟪ MC Visa Amex DC JCB ☒ ⟨

★★★★★ Connaught 🎗 🎗 🎗 🎗
Gold Ribbon Hotel
Carlos Place, Mayfair, London W1Y 6AL
📞 0171-499 7070 **Fax** 0171-495 3262
E-mail info@the-connaught.co.uk

In the heart of Mayfair, The Connaught is one of London's most distinguished addresses, providing supreme comfort, unobtrusive service and privacy. The Michelin-starred Restaurant and Grill Room specialise in classic French and English cuisine.
90 bedrs, all ensuite, ⊟ ⊞ 16 **P** 3 ⊕ ⟪ MC Visa Amex DC

★★★★★ Dorchester 🎗 🎗 🎗 🎗
Gold Ribbon Hotel
Park Lane, London W1A 2HJ
📞 0171-629 8888 **Fax** 0171-409 0114
E-mail info@dorchesterhotel.com

Consistently ranked one of the world's best, this opulent 1931 hotel offers the friendliest, almost telepathic levels of service, an outstanding choice of restaurants and glorious spa.
248 bedrs, all ensuite, ④ ⤢ ⊟ ⊞ 550 **P** 11 ⊕
SB £331.88-£355.38 **DB** £387.63-£422.88 **L** £29.50
L ⤢ **D** £39.50 **D** ⤢ ✕ **LD** 23:00 ⟪ MC Visa Amex DC JCB ☒ ▦ ⟨

The perfect location

In a unique location, with the most royal of parks on one side and London's finest shopping on the other, this famous hotel has been refurbished by Mandarin Oriental and must now rank amongst the most stylish in London.

A beautifully restored façade provides only a hint of what to expect. The informal elegance of the ground floor. One of the capital's most feted and beautiful restaurants. Luxuriously   appointed and individually designed guest rooms. And, of course, Mandarin Oriental's legendary service.

Whatever the occasion, Mandarin Oriental Hyde Park promises a visit to remember.

MANDARIN ORIENTAL
HYDE PARK
LONDON   SM

Mandarin Oriental Hyde Park
66 Knightsbridge, London SW1X 7LA, United Kingdom
Telephone: 020 7235 2000 Facsimile: 020 7235 4552
www.mandarin-oriental.com

★★★★★ Four Seasons 🏨 🏨 🏨
Gold Ribbon Hotel
Hamilton Place, Park Lane, W1A 1AZ
📞 0171-499 0888 **Fax** 0171-493 1895

With distinctive charm and warmth, set back from Park Lane, and in the heart of Mayfair overlooking Hyde Park, the Four Seasons Hotel is unrivalled in its service and setting. The result - a highly acclaimed hotel with handsomely appointed spacious rooms.
220 bedrs, all ensuite, ♀ ℘ ⊁ ⊞ ⠇ 500 **P** 55 ⊕
SB £260-£290 **DB** £305-£315 **L** £32 **L ♥ D** £30.50 **D ♥**
✕ **LD** 22:30 **CC** MC Visa Amex DC JCB ⊞ ♿

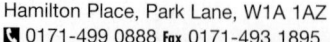

★★★★★ Lanesborough 🏨 🏨 🏨 🏨
Gold Ribbon Hotel
Hyde Park Corner, London SW1X 7TA
📞 0171-259 5599 **Fax** 0171-259 5606
E-mail info@lanesborough.co.uk

An exciting, recently developed hotel at Hyde Park Corner, occupying the building once housing St George's Hospital. The stately neo-classical exterior is matched by the beautiful Regency style furnishings.
95 bedrs, all ensuite, ④ ⊁ ⊞ ⠇ 90 **P** 38 ⊕ **CC** MC Visa Amex DC JCB ⊞ ♿

★★★★★ Le Meridien
Grosvenor House 🏨 🏨 🏨 🏨 🏨
Park Lane, London W1A 3AA
📞 0171-499 6363 **Fax** 0171-493 3341
E-mail 114475.1635@compuserve.com
584 bedrs, all ensuite, ℘ ⊞ ⠇ 1,500 **P** 80
⊕ **SB** £306 **DB** £350 **L** £24.50 **L ♥ D** £24.50
✕ **LD** 22:30 **CC** MC Visa Amex DC JCB
▣ ⊞ ▣ ⊞ ♿

★★★★★ Le Meridien
Piccadilly 🏨 🏨 🏨 🏨 🏨
21 Piccadilly, London W1V 0BH
📞 0870-400-8400 **Fax** 0171-437 3574
E-mail impiccres@forte-hotels.com
267 bedrs, all ensuite, ④ ⊞ ⠇ 250 ⊕
SB £364.13-£399.38 **DB** £416.88-£452.13
L £19.50 **D** £19.50 **D ♥** ✕ **LD** 23:00
CC MC Visa Amex DC JCB
▣ ⊞ ▣ ⊞ ♿

★★★★★ ❖ London Marriott
Grosvenor Square
Grosvenor Square, London W1A 4AW
📞 0171-493 1232 **Fax** 0171-491 3201
E-mail brenda.macdowell@marriott.com

Make this fashionable hotel your base while you take in a show, visit London's exceptional galleries and museums and shop for something special. Then return to the peaceful relaxation, dignified style and Marriot's distinctive warmth and hospitality.
221 bedrs, all ensuite, ℘ ⊞ ⠇ 900 **P** 65 ⊕ **SB** £260-£280 **DB** £275-£300 **L** £12 **D** £15 **D ♥** ✕ **LD** 22:30
CC MC Visa Amex DC JCB ⊞ ♿

★★★★★ Mandarin Oriental Hyde Park 🏨 🏨 🏨 🏨
Gold Ribbon Hotel
66 Knightsbridge, London SW1X 7LA
📞 0171-235 2000 **Fax** 0171-235 4552
186 bedrs, all ensuite, ④ ⊞ ⠇ 250 ⊕ **CC** MC Visa Amex DC JCB ⊞ ♿
See advert on previous page

THE RITZ HOTEL

RESTORED

HAVING RETURNED TO PRIVATE ENGLISH OWNERSHIP THE RITZ, LONDON HAS BEEN RESTORED & RENEWED. THE REVITALISATION HAS COMBINED MODERN TECHNOLOGY, TRADITIONAL ELEGANT SURROUNDINGS WITH SUBLIME SERVICE. THE NEW FITNESS ROOM & BUSINESS BUREAU COMPLETE THE PICTURE.

THE RITZ, LONDON
SIMPLY THE MOST FAMOUS.

AN RAC BLUE RIBBON HOTEL

THE RITZ HOTEL
150 PICCADILLY, LONDON W1V 9DG
TELEPHONE: (0171) 493 8181
FACIMILE: (0171) 493 2687
E-MAIL: ENQUIRE@THERITZHOTEL.CO.UK

★★★★★ ❖ May Fair Inter-Continental
Stratton Street, London W1A 2AN
☎ 0171-629 7777 **Fax** 0171-499 0531
E-mail mayfair@interconti.com

A small fashionable hotel in the heart of exclusive Mayfair. The hotel is within easy reach of Bond Street, the financial district and the theatres of London's West End. The hotel is traditionally British in style and has every modern facility.
290 bedrs, all ensuite, ▣ ⅲ ⬚ ((MC Visa Amex DC JCB 🔲 🔲 ⬚

★★★★★ Sheraton Park Tower 🛏 🛏 🛏
101 Knightsbridge, London SW1X 7RN
☎ 0171-235 8050 **Fax** 0171-235 8231
E-mail nielssherry@sheraton.com

Representing 'The Luxury Collection' in the heart of Knightsbridge, London, the Sheraton Park Tower provides travellers with a unique sense of luxury, peace and indulgence, as well as a boasting restaurant One-O-One, the city's finest fish restaurant.
295 bedrs, all ensuite, ▣ ⅲ 60 **P** 150 ⬚ **SB** £334 **DB** £358 **L** £40 **L** ⬚ **D** £40 ✕ **LD** 23:00 ((MC Visa Amex DC JCB

★★★★★ The Ritz 🍴 🍴 🍴
Gold Ribbon Hotel
150 Piccadilly, London W1V 9DG
📞 0171-493 8181 **Fax** 0171-493 2687
E-mail enquire@theritzhotel.co.uk
130 bedrs, all ensuite, ⊡ ⚟ 50 ⊞ ⊄ MC Visa Amex
DC JCB ♿
See advert on previous page

★★★★★ 22 Jermyn Street **Town House**
22 Jermyn Street, St James's, London SW1Y 6
📞 0171-734 2353 **Fax** 0171-734 0753
E-mail office@22jermyn.com
18 bedrs, all ensuite, 🏊 🐾 ⊡ ⚟ 20 ⊞ Resid
DB £264-£416 **L** £10 **L** 🍴 **D** £15 **D** 🍴 ✕ **LD** 00:00
⊄ MC Visa Amex DC JCB ♿

★★★★★ Durley House **Town House** 🍴
115 Sloane Square, London SW1X 9PJ
📞 0171-235 5537 **Fax** 0171-259 6977
E-mail durley@firmdale.com
11 bedrs, all ensuite, 🏊 ⊡ ⚟ 20 ⊞ Resid **SB** £294
DB £370.63-£535.13 **L** £10 **L** 🍴 **D** £10 **D** 🍴 ✕
LD 22:30 ⊄ MC Visa Amex 📷

★★★★ Athenaeum 🍴 🍴 🍴
Gold Ribbon Hotel
116 Piccadilly, London W1V 0BJ
📞 0171-499 3464 **Fax** 0171-493 1860
E-mail info@athenaeumhotel.com

Privately owned hotel combining traditional style
with the latest facilities. Situated in Mayfair,
overlooking Green Park, guests are assured of a
warm and friendly welcome.
157 bedrs, all ensuite, ⊡ ⚟ 55 ⊞ **SB** £240 **DB** £260
L £35.30 **D** £35.30 ✕ **LD** 22:45 Restaurant closed L
Sat & Sun ⊄ MC Visa Amex DC 🅟 📷

★★★★ Berners ♖
10 Berners Street, London W1A 3BE
📞 0171-666 2000 Fax 0171-666 2001
E-mail berners@berners.co.uk
217 bedrs, all ensuite, ♀ ♪ 🖃 ⊞ 180 ⊕ SB £174.95
DB £224.90 L £17 D £17 ✕ LD 22:00 ℂℂ MC Visa
Amex DC JCB ♿
See advert on previous page

★★★★ ❖ Brown's
Albemarle Street, London W1X 4BP
📞 0171-493 6020 Fax 0171-493 9381
E-mail brownshotel@brownshotel.com

Brown's, London's oldest and most established
town house hotel offers charm, comfort and unique
English hospitality in an enviable location next to
Bond Street and St James's.
118 bedrs, all ensuite, ④ ♪ 🖃 ⊞ 70 ⊕ SB £179-
£312 DB £199-£341 L £24 L ♥ D £45 D ♥ ✕ LD 22:00
Restaurant closed L Sat & Sun, D Sun ℂℂ MC Visa
Amex DC JCB ♿
See advert on previous page

★★★★ ❖ Cavendish   LONDON SIGNATURE HOTELS
Jermyn Street, St James,
London SW1Y 6JF
📞 0171-930 2111 Fax 0171-839 2125
255 bedrs, all ensuite, ④ 🖃 ⊞ 100 P 65 ⊕ ℂℂ MC
Visa Amex DC JCB

★★★★ Chesterfield Mayfair ♖ ♖
35 Charles Street, London W1X 8LX
📞 0171-491 2622 Fax 0171-491 4793
E-mail reservations@chesterfield.redcarnationhotels.com

A traditional, small, quiet friendly hotel with a club-
like interior, furnished with Chesterfield sofas and
large armchairs.
110 bedrs, all ensuite, ④ ♪ 🖃 ⊞ 100 ⊕ SB £155-
£205 DB £190-£375 L £10.50 L ♥ D £17.50 D ♥ ✕
LD 22:30 Restaurant closed L Sat ℂℂ MC Visa Amex
DC JCB ♿

★★★★ Clifton-Ford ♖
Welbeck Street, London W1M 8DN
📞 0171-486 6600 Fax 0171-486 7492
E-mail sales@cliftonf.itsnet.co.uk
200 bedrs, all ensuite, ♀ 🖃 ⊞ 120 P 19 ⊕ ℂℂ MC
Visa Amex DC

★★★★ ❖ Cumberland   LONDON SIGNATURE HOTELS
1a Gt Cumberland Place,
Marble Arch, London W1A 4RF
📞 0171-262 1234 Fax 0171-724 4621
900 bedrs, all ensuite, ♀ 🖃 ⊞ 800 ⊕
ℂℂ MC Visa Amex DC JCB

National Code & Number Change
Telephone codes and numbers in London
change in April 2000.

0171-XXXXXX becomes 020-7XXX XXXX
0181-XXXXXX becomes 020-8XXX XXXX

Don't forget to mention the guide
When booking direct, please remember to
tell the hotel that you chose it from
RAC Inspected Hotels 2000

★★★★ Goring
Gold Ribbon Hotel
Beeston Place, Grosvenor Gardens,
London SW1W 0JW
☎ 0171-396 9000 **Fax** 0171-834 4393
E-mail reception@goringhotel.co.uk

A family owned hotel in its third generation offering traditional standards of service and facilities to satisfy the demands of the international traveller. Situated in a quiet haven behind Buckingham Palace, convenient for the theatre and shopping. 75 bedrs, all ensuite, ✗ ☐ ⊞ 50 **P** 7 ⊞ **SB** £185-£208 **DB** £235-£260 **L** £27 **D** £35 **D** ➤ ✗ **LD** 22:00 Restaurant closed L Sat **CC** MC Visa Amex DC ♿

★★★★ Halkin
Gold Ribbon Hotel
Halkin Street, Belgravia, London SW1X 7DJ
☎ 0171-333 1000 **Fax** 0171-333 1100
E-mail sales@halkin.co.uk

Located off Hyde Park Corner in Belgravia, The Halkin offers the highest level of service and facilities in a striking and contemporary design. The award winning Stefano Cavallini Restaurant serves modern Italian cuisine.
41 bedrs, all ensuite, ✗ ☐ ⊞ 30 ⊞ **SB** £316.62-£398.88 **DB** £333.62-£415.88 **L** £25 **L** ➤ **D** £40 **D** ➤ ✗ **LD** 22.30 Restaurant closed L Sat-Sun **CC** MC Visa Amex DC JCB ♿

★★★★ ✦ Lowndes Hyatt
21 Lowndes Street, London SW1X 9ES
☎ 020-7823 1234 **Fax** 020-7235 1154
E-mail lowndes@hyattintl.com

A boutique hotel with bedrooms decorated in a true English country house style, located in the heart of Belgravia. The ideal place for business or pleasure. 78 bedrs, all ensuite, ♀ ✗ ☐ ⊞ 20 ⊞ **SB** £228.35-£255.40 **DB** £242.85-£270 **L** £18 **L** ➤ **D** £25 **D** ➤ ✗ **LD** 23:15 **CC** MC Visa Amex DC JCB ☐ ☒ ▦
See advert on this page

★★★★ Millennium Britannia Mayfair 🍴 🍴

Grosvenor Square, London W1A 3AN
☎ 0171-629 9400 **Fax** 0171-629 7736
E-mail britannia.res@mill-cop.com
341 bedrs, all ensuite, 4 🏃 ✝ 🖵 ⚙ 700 **P** 8 🅿
SB £160-£260 **DB** £215-£260 **L** £20 **D** £20 ✕ **LD** 22:30
《 MC Visa Amex DC JCB 🈷 ♿

★★★★ Millennium Chelsea 🍴 🍴 🍴
17 Sloane Street, London SW1X 9NU
☎ 0171-235 4377 **Fax** 0171-259 6973
224 bedrs, all ensuite, 🖵 ⚙ 120 **P** 12 🅿 《 MC Visa
Amex DC ♿

★★★★ Montcalm Nikko 🍴 🍴 🍴
Great Cumberland Place, London W1A 2LF
☎ 0171-402 4288 **Fax** 0171-724 9180
E-mail reservations@montcalm.co.uk
120 bedrs, all ensuite, 🏃 🖵 ⚙ 80 **P** 10 🅿
SB £242.12-£258.83 **DB** £288.52-£300.28 **L** £19 **D** £19
✕ **LD** 22:30 Restaurant closed L Sat & Sun, D Sun
《 MC Visa Amex DC JCB

★★★★ ✤ Park Lane
Piccadilly, London W1Y 8BX
☎ 0171-499 6321 **Fax** 0171-499 1965

Historic 1920's art deco hotel with recently renovated Palm Court lounge, fitness centre, business centre as well as bedrooms. 25 minutes from the financial district and ideal for exploring Mayfair.
305 bedrs, all ensuite, 🏃 🖵 ⚙ 500 **P** 50 🅿 Resid
SB £275 **DB** £315 **L** £15 **L** 🍷 **D** £25 **D** 🍷 ✕ **LD** 22:30
《 MC Visa Amex DC JCB 🈷 📺

★★★★ Saint George's
Langham Place, Regent Street,
London W1N 8QS
📞 0171-580 0111 **Fax** 0171-436 7997
86 bedrs, all ensuite, ⊷ ⊡ ⠿ 25 **P** 2 ⊕
《 MC Visa Amex DC 👍

LONDON
SIGNATURE
HOTELS

★★★★ The Rubens at The Palace ⌂ ⌂
Buckingham Palace Road, London SW1W 0PS
📞 0171-834 6600 **Fax** 0171-828 5401
174 bedrs, all ensuite, ⊞ ♀ ✍ ⊡ ⠿ 80 ⊕ **SB** £135-
£170 **DB** £145-£185 **L** £15 **L** 🍷 **D** £25 **D** 🍷 ✗ **LD** 22:30
《 MC Visa Amex DC 👍
See advert on opposite page

★★★★ Washington Mayfair
5-7 Curzon Street, London W1Y 8DT
📞 0171-499 7000 **Fax** 0171- 495 6172

Four star deluxe, located in heart of Mayfair,
minutes walk from Bond Street, Piccadilly,
theatreland, Leicester Square, Knightsbridge. All
173 rooms ensuite, Madison's Restaurant, lounge.
173 bedrs, all ensuite, ⊡ ⠿ 100 ⊕ 《 MC Visa
Amex DC JCB
See advert on this page

★★★★ Westbury ⌂ ⌂ ⌂
Bond Street at Conduit Street, London W1A 4UH
📞 0171-629 7755 **Fax** 0171-495 1163

Possibly the best address in London. Located in
the most exciting shopping street, the Westbury is
popular with guests from the world of Art and
Fashion.
244 bedrs, all ensuite, ✍ ⊷ ⊡ ⠿ 80 **P** 4 ⊕
SB £263.50 **DB** £297.85 **L** £16.50 **L** 🍷 **D** £17.50 **D** 🍷
✗ **LD** 22:00 Restaurant closed L Sat-Sun 《 MC Visa
Amex DC JCB 👍

★★★★ Leonard **Town House**
15 Seymour Street, London W1H 5AA
📞 0171-935 2010 **Fax** 0171-935 6700
E-mail the.leonard@dial.pipex.com
28 bedrs, all ensuite, ⊞ ✍ ⊡ ⠿ 15 ⊕ **SB** £212.25
DB £248.25-£296.37 **L** £13 **D** £13 ✗ **LD** 23:00 《 MC
Visa Amex DC JCB ⊞ ⊠ 👍

★★★ ❖ Flemings Mayfair
Half Moon Street, Mayfair, London W1Y 7RA
📞 0171-499 2964 **Fax** 0171-629 4063
E-mail sales@flemings-mayfair.co.uk
121 bedrs, all ensuite, ⊞ ✍ ⊡ ⠿ 55 ⊕ **L** £9.95 **L** 🍷
D £24.50 **D** 🍷 ✗ **LD** 22:30 《 MC Visa Amex DC JCB

★★★ ❖ Mandeville
Mandeville Place, London W1M 6BE
☎ 0171-935 5599 Fax 0171-935 9588
E-mail info@mandeville.co.uk

Modernised Victorian hotel conveniently placed just behind Oxford Street. Well-equipped rooms and 24-hour room service.
165 bedrs, all ensuite, ⚲ 🖭 ⋕ 35 🔌 🔌 Rest SB £85-£125 DB £115 L £12 D £12 ✗ LD 22:30 ℂℂ MC Visa Amex DC JCB
See advert on this page

★★★ Posthouse Regents Park **Posthouse**
Carburton Street, Regents Park,
London W1P 8EE
☎ 0171-388 2300 Fax 0171-387 2806
326 bedrs, all ensuite, ⚲ 🖭 ⋕ 320 P 80 🔌
SB £150.50-£170.50 DB £162-£182 L £12.95
D £12.95 D ☛ ✗ LD 22:00 Restaurant closed
L Sat-Sun ℂℂ MC Visa Amex DC JCB ♿

★★★ ❖ Quality
Eccleston Square, London SW1V 1PS
☎ 0171-834 8042 Fax 0171-630 8942
E-mail admin@gb614.u-net.com

The hotel has a traditional appearance and is located in a quiet 19th century square, with easy access to Victoria train and coach stations.
114 bedrs, all ensuite, ⌁ 🖭 ⋕ 150 🔌 SB £93-£114.25 DB £124-£128 L £14.50 D £14.50 ✗
LD 22:00 ℂℂ MC Visa Amex DC JCB 🔲

★★★ ✧ Sloane Square Moat House
Sloane Square, London SW1W 8EG
📞 0171-896 9988 **Fax** 0171-824 8381
105 bedrs, all ensuite, ⚑ ▣ ⌗ 40 **P** 3 ⊕ ⟪ MC Visa Amex DC

★★ ✧ Regent Palace

LONDON
SIGNATURE
HOTELS

Glasshouse Street, Piccadilly Circus, London W1A 4BZ
📞 0171-734 7000 **Fax** 0171-734 6435
950 bedrs, ▣ ⊕ ⟪ MC Visa Amex DC JCB

Fox Club **Town House Awaiting Inspection**
46 Clarges Street, London W1Y 7PJ
📞 0171-495 3656 **Fax** 0171-495 3626
Closed Christmas
9 bedrs, all ensuite, ⌿ ⚑ No children under 18 ⊕
Resid **SB** £144.50 **DB** £168 **L** £10 **L** ♥ **D** £12 **D** ♥ ✕
LD 22:00 ⟪ MC Visa Amex

Stanley House **Awaiting Inspection**
19-21 Belgrave Road, Victoria, London SW1V 1RR
📞 0171-834 7292 **Fax** 0171-834 8439
E-mail cmahotel@aol.com
44 bedrs, all ensuite, ♀ ⊕ **SB** £36-£45 **DB** £46-£60
⟪ MC Visa Amex DC JCB
See advert on opposite page

Radisson Edwardian Berkshire
350 Oxford Street, London W1N 0BY
📞 0171-629 7474 **Fax** 0171-629 8156

A haven of civilised service and English style, adorned with rich wooden panelling and fabrics, this hotel is located amid the shops on Oxford Street. Feast in our award-winning Ascots restaurant and enjoy some of the finest cuisine in London.
147 bedrs, all ensuite, ▣ ⌗ 45 ⊕ ⟪ MC Visa Amex DC JCB

★★★★★ Conrad International London ⍩ ⍩
Chelsea Harbour, London SW10 0XG
📞 0171-823 3000 **Fax** 0171-351 6525
160 bedrs, all ensuite, ⌿ ⚑ ▣ ⌗ 180 **P** 2,000 ⊕
SB £235 **DB** £258.50 **L** £17 **L** ♥ **D** £22.50 **D** ♥ ✕
LD 22:30 Restaurant closed L Sat ⟪ MC Visa Amex DC JCB ▣ ▣ ▣ ⚹

★★★★★ Royal Garden ⍩ ⍩ ⍩
Kensington High Street, London W8 4PT
📞 0171-937 8000 **Fax** 0171-361 1991
E-mail guest@royalgdn.co.uk
400 bedrs, all ensuite, ⚑ ▣ ⌗ 600 **P** 160 ⊕ ⟪ MC Visa Amex DC JCB ▣ ▣ ⚹

★★★★ Capital ⍩ ⍩ ⍩ ⍩
Gold Ribbon Hotel
Basil Street, Knightsbridge, London SW3 1AT
📞 0171-589 5171 **Fax** 0171-225 0011
E-mail reservations@capitalhotel.co.uk

The original luxurious town house in fashionable Knightsbridge, 50 yards from Harrods, with beautiful antiques and individually designed bedrooms.
48 bedrs, all ensuite, ⚑ ▣ ⌗ 24 **P** 13 ⊕ **SB** £195.50 **DB** £260 **L** £24.50 **D** £60 **D** ♥ ✕ **LD** 23:15 ⟪ MC Visa Amex DC

★★★★ Copthorne Tara
Scarsdale Place, Kensington, London W8 5SR
📞 0171-937 7211 **Fax** 0171-937 7100
E-mail tara.sales@mill-cop.com
831 bedrs, all ensuite, ⌿ ▣ ⌗ 400 **P** 90 ⊕
SB £172.75-£197.75 **DB** £200.50-£225.50 **L** £19 **L** ♥ **D** £19 **D** ♥ ✕ **LD** 22:30 ⟪ MC Visa Amex DC JCB ⚹

★★★★ Forum
Cromwell Road, London SW7 4DN
📞 0171-370 5757 **Fax** 0171-373 1448
E-mail forumlondon@interconti.com

Set in the Royal Borough of Kensington & Chelsea, The Forum Hotel London is near to London's most fashionable shopping areas, National Museum, major motorways and London Underground.
910 bedrs, all ensuite, 🖈 ⊡ ### 400 **P** 76 ⊕ **SB** £145 **DB** £165 **L** 🍽 **D** 🍽 **CC** MC Visa Amex DC JCB 🖾 &

★★★★ Harrington Hall ▤
5-25 Harrington Gardens, London SW7 4JW
📞 0171-396 9696 **Fax** 0171-396 1615
E-mail harringtonsales@compuserve.com
200 bedrs, all ensuite, 🖈 ⊡ ### 260 ⊕ **SB** £169.95-£173.95 **DB** £179.90-£187.90 **L** £20 **L** 🍽 **D** £20 ✕ **LD** 22:30 **CC** MC Visa Amex DC JCB 🖾 🖼
See advert on opposite page

★★★★ ✣ Jurys Kensington
109-113 Queensgate, South Kensington, London SW7 5LR
📞 0171-589 6300 **Fax** 0171-581 1492
E-mail bookings@jurys.com
Closed 24-26 Dec
172 bedrs, all ensuite, ♀ 🖈 ⊡ ### 80 ⊕ **SB** £184-£214 **DB** £198-£228 **L** 🍽 **D** £20 ✕ **LD** 21:45 **CC** MC Visa Amex DC

Short Breaks

Many hotels provide special rates for weekend and mid-week breaks – sometimes these are quoted in the hotel's entry, otherwise ring direct for the latest offers.

★★★★ ✣ Millennium Gloucester
4-18 Harrington Gardens, London SW7 4LH
📞 020-7373 6030 **Fax** 020-7373 0409

610 air conditioned bedrooms and suites, larger than the London standard, complemented by a choice of bars and restaurants. Superb location 100m from Gloucester Road underground served by 3 lines.
610 bedrs, all ensuite, ⊡ ### 500 **P** 110 ⊕ ✕ **LD** 22:30 **CC** MC Visa Amex DC 🖾

★★★★ ✣ Rembrandt
11 Thurloe Place, London SW7 2RS
📞 0171-589 8100 **Fax** 0171-225 3363
E-mail rembrandt@sarova.co.uk
195 bedrs, all ensuite, 🖈 ⊡ ### 200 ⊕ **Room** £165-£215 **L** £16.95 **L** 🍽 **D** £16.95 **D** 🍽 ✕ **LD** 22:00 **CC** MC Visa Amex DC JCB 🖾 🖾 🖼

★★★★ Royal Lancaster ▤ ▤ ▤
Lancaster Terrace, London W2 2TY
📞 0171-262 6737 **Fax** 0171-724 3191

In the heart of London overlooking Hyde Park, this deluxe hotel is ideally located with three fine restaurants serving the best of east and west cuisine.
416 bedrs, all ensuite, ⊡ ### 1,500 **P** 100 ⊕ **SB** £247 **DB** £290 **L** £23 **D** £23 ✕ **LD** 22:30 **CC** MC Visa Amex DC JCB &

★★★★ Swallow International
Cromwell Road, London SW5 0TH
☎ 0171-973 1000 Fax 0171-244 8194
E-mail info@swallowhotels.com
Closed 23-27 Dec

In Kensington, close to the National History Museum, the hotel has a cocktail bar, two restaurants with awards for fine food and an exclusive Swallow Leisure Club.
421 bedrs, all ensuite, 🛏 ▣ ♨ 200 P 60 ⊕
Room £130-£165 L £18 D £22.50 ✕ LD 23:45 ℂℂ MC Visa Amex DC ▣ ▣ ▣

★★★★ Cliveden Town House **Town House** ☗
26 Cadogan Gardens, London SW3 2RP
☎ 0171-730 6466 Fax 0171-730 0236
35 bedrs, all ensuite, ▣ 🛏 ▣ ♨ 12 ⊕ ℂℂ MC Visa Amex DC JCB ▣
See advert on previous page

★★★★ Pelham **Town House** ☗
15 Cromwell Place, London SW7 2LA
☎ 0171-589 8288 Fax 0171-584 8444
E-mail pelham@firmdale.com
50 bedrs, all ensuite, ▣ ⋀ ▣ ♨ 12 ⊕ SB £181.88 DB £228.63-£287.38 L £12.95 L ⬤ D £15.95 D ⬤ ✕ LD 22:30 Restaurant closed L & D Sat ℂℂ MC Visa Amex

★★★ ✣ Basil Street
Knightsbridge, London SW3 1AH
☎ 0171-581 3311 Fax 0171-581 3693

Situated in Knightsbridge - a few steps from Harrods, this 92 bedroom hotel offers a traditional style and service that draws people back time after time. Restaurant open every day.
92 bedrs, 86 ensuite, 🛏 ▣ ♨ 70 P 2 ⊕ ℂℂ MC Visa Amex DC JCB

★★★ ✣ Commodore
50 Lancaster Gate, Hyde Park, London W2 3NA
☎ 0171-402 5291 Fax 0171-262 1088
88 bedrs, all ensuite, ⋀ 🛏 ▣ ⊕ SB £88-£96 DB £110-£120 L £13.50 L ⬤ D £20 D ⬤ ✕ LD 22:00 Restaurant closed Sun ℂℂ MC Visa Amex DC JCB
See advert on this page

★★★ ✣ Hogarth
Hogarth Road, Kensington, London SW5 0QQ
☎ 0171-370 6831 Fax 0171-373 6179
E-mail hogarth@marstonhotels.co.uk
85 bedrs, all ensuite, ⋀ 🛏 ▣ ♨ 45 P 20 ⊕ SB £104 DB £130 L £10 D £20 ✕ LD 22:00 ℂℂ MC Visa Amex DC

★★★ ❖ Paragon
47 Lillie Road, London SW6 1UD
☎ 0171-385 1255 **Fax** 0171-381 4450
E-mail reservation@123paragonhotel.co.uk

A modern European hotel, newly refurbished and ideally situated within 2 minutes walk of Earl's Court Exhibition Centre and with easy access to explore Knightsbridge, Kensington and Chelsea.
501 bedrs, all ensuite, ★ 🖪 ⋕ 1,750 **P** 130 ⏏
SB £109 **DB** £129 **L** £14.50 **D** £14.50 ✕ **LD** 22:30
ℂℂ MC Visa Amex DC JCB

★★★ Posthouse Kensington   **Posthouse**
Wrights Lane, London W8 5SP
☎ 0171-937 8170 **Fax** 0171-937 8289
550 bedrs, all ensuite, ★ 🖪 ⋕ 180 **P** 70 ⏏ ℂℂ MC Visa Amex DC JCB 🖪 🖪 🖪 🖪 🖪

★★ Comfort Inn Kensington
22-32 West Cromwell Road, SW5 9QJ
☎ 0171-373 3300 **Fax** 0171-835 2040
E-mail admin@gb043.u-net.com

Situated on the Cromwell Road with easy access from the M4, the hotel is ideally placed for Earls Court, shopping in Kensington or Harrods and visiting museums. All rooms have air conditioning, TV and hospitality tray. Intimate restaurant and bar.
125 bedrs, all ensuite, ✐ 🖪 ⋕ 80 ⏏ **SB** £94.75-£107.75 **DB** £117.50-£130.50 **L** 🍷 **D** 🍷 ✕ **LD** 21:30
ℂℂ MC Visa Amex DC 🖪 ♿

★★ Delmere
130 Sussex Gardens, Hyde Park, London W2 1UB
☎ 0171-706 3344 **Fax** 0171-262 1863
E-mail delmerehotel@compuserve.com

Victorian town house hotel. All bedrooms are ensuite and are provided with satellite TV, tea and coffee making facilities and safes. This award winning hotel also features a restaurant and a bar.
38 bedrs, all ensuite, �4 🖪 **P** 2 ⏏ ℂℂ MC Visa Amex DC JCB

Beaufort **Town House Awaiting Inspection**
33 Beaufort Gardens, Knightsbridge,
London SW3 1PP
☎ 0171-584 5252 **Fax** 0171-589 2834
E-mail thebeaufort@nol.co.uk
28 bedrs, all ensuite, ♀ ⏏ **Resid SB** £199.75-£211.50
DB £235-£381.88 ℂℂ MC Visa Amex DC JCB

Oki Kensington **Awaiting Inspection**
25 Courtfield Gardens, London SW5 0PG
☎ 0171-565 2222 **Fax** 0171-565-2223
E-mail oki@oki-oki.demon.co.uk
72 bedrs, all ensuite, �4 ✐ ★ 🖪 ⋕ 15 **P** 4 ⏏
DB £99.88-£141 **L** 🍷 **D** 🍷 ℂℂ MC Visa Amex DC JCB

LONDON Bloomsbury & City

★★★★★ Le Meridien Waldorf 🏨 🏨   *Le*
Aldwych, London WC2B 4DD   **MERIDIEN**
☎ 0171-836 2400 **Fax** 0171-836 7244
292 bedrs, all ensuite, �4 ✐ 🖪 ⋕ 420
P 50 ⏏ **SB** £265 **DB** £318 **L** £20 **L** 🍷 **D** £22
D 🍷 ✕ **LD** 23:15 Restaurant closed L Sat
ℂℂ MC Visa Amex DC JCB

★★★★★ One Aldwych 🗟 🗟 🗟
Blue Ribbon Hotel
1 Aldwych, London WC2B 4BZ
📞 0171-300 1000

Poised where the City of London meets the West End, One Aldwych incorporates sleek contemporary design, cutting-edge technology and professional friendly service.

★★★★★ Savoy 🗟 🗟 🗟 🗟
Gold Ribbon Hotel
The Strand, London WC2R 0EU
📞 0171-836 4343 Fax 0171-240 6040
E-mail info@the-savoy.co.uk

Overlooking the River Thames, in the heart of London's theatre district, The Savoy remains one of London's famous landmarks. It offers guests highly personalised service, excellent cuisine, state-of-the-art fitness facilities and outstanding accommodation
207 bedrs, all ensuite, ⬛ ⠿ 500 P 58 ⊞ ℂ MC Visa Amex DC JCB ▣ ⊞ ▣ ♿

★★★★★ Covent Garden Town House 🗟
10 Monmouth Street, London WC2H 9HB
📞 0171-806 1000 Fax 0171-8061100
E-mail covent@firmdale.com

50 bedrs, all ensuite, ⬛ ⚲ ⬛ ⠿ 10 ⊞ SB £219.13 DB £262-£326.63 L £15 L ⬤ D £15 D ⬤ ✕ LD 23:00 ℂ MC Visa Amex ⊠

★★★★ ✦ Montague
15 Montague Street, London WC1B 5BJ
📞 0171-637 1001 Fax 0171-637 2516
E-mail reservations@montague.redcarnationhotels.com

Elegantly appointed and wonderfully equipped guest rooms and conference suites overlooking secluded gardens. Adjacent to The British Museum, convenient for the City and just a stroll to Covent Garden.
104 bedrs, all ensuite, ⬛ ⚲ ⚲ ⬛ ⠿ 120 ⊞ SB £110-£150 DB £140-£180 L £15.95 L ⬤ D £15.95 D ⬤ ✕ LD 23:00 Restaurant closed L Bank holidays ℂ MC Visa Amex DC JCB ⊠ ▣ ♿

★★★★ Russell
Russell Square, London WC1B 5BE
📞 0171-837 6470 Fax 0171-837 2857
329 bedrs, all ensuite, ✈ ⬛ ⠿ 650 ⊞ ℂ MC Visa Amex DC

LONDON
SIGNATURE
HOTELS

★★★ Bonnington in Bloomsbury
92 Southampton Row, London WC1B 4BH
📞 0171-242 2828 Fax 0171-831 9170
E-mail sales@bonnington-hotels.co.uk

In the heart of the capital, convenient for main rail termini, Heathrow (bus or Underground) and Gatwick (shuttle to Victoria). Close to shopping, theatres and major visitor attractions. Friendly, family owned. Lounge, buffet, Waterfalls restaurant.

215 bedrs, all ensuite, 🛏 ⊡ ⦂⦂ 250 ⊞ **SB** £80-£111
DB £120-£140 **L** £12 **L** 🍴 **D** £20.75 **D** 🍴 ✕ **LD** 22:30
Restaurant closed L Sat-Sun ‹‹ MC Visa Amex DC
JCB ♿

★★★ ✤ Posthouse Bloomsbury   **Posthouse**
Coram Street, Bloomsbury, WC1N 1HT
📞 0171-837 1200 **Fax** 0171-837 5374
284 bedrs, all ensuite, ♬ ⊡ ⦂⦂ 300 **P** 70 ⊞ **SB** £90-
£140 **DB** £90-£140 **L** 🍴 **D** £17 **D** 🍴 ✕ **LD** 22:30 ‹‹ MC
Visa Amex DC ♿

★★★ Strand Palace   LONDON **SIGNATURE** HOTELS
Strand, London WC2R 0JJ
📞 0171-836 8080 **Fax** 0171-836 2077
E-mail sue.verrent@forte-hotels.com
785 bedrs, all ensuite, ⊡ ⦂⦂ 180 ⊞ ‹‹ MC Visa
Amex DC JCB

Kingsway Hall **Awaiting Inspection**
Great Queen Street, London WC2B 5BZ
📞 0171-309 0909 **Fax** 0171-309 9696
E-mail kingswayhall@compuserve.com
170 bedrs, all ensuite, ♬ ⊡ ⦂⦂ 150 ⊞ **SB** £179-£189
DB £206-£216 **L** £20 **L** 🍴 **D** £20 **D** 🍴 ✕ **LD** 22:30
‹‹ MC Visa Amex DC JCB ▨ ▨ ♿
See advert on this page

Radisson Edwardian Hampshire
Leicester Square, London WC2H 7LH
📞 0171-839 9399 **Fax** 0171-930 8122

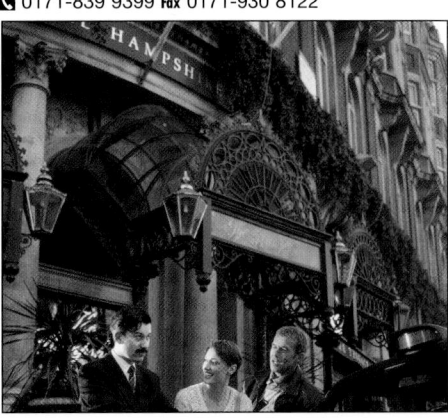

The very essence of English elegance, this hotel is
centrally located in a haven of tranquillity. The Apex
restaurant serves modern English cuisine with both
style and flair and is ideal for business or a
romantic dinner for two.
124 bedrs, all ensuite, ⊡ ⦂⦂ 145 ⊞ ‹‹ MC Visa
Amex DC JCB

Radisson Edwardian Marlborough
Bloomsbury Street, London WC1B 3QD
☎ 0171-636 5601 **Fax** 0171-636 0532

Immerse yourself in culture at The Marlborough Hotel, close to the British Museum, and at the heart of Bloomsbury. The hotel's first class amenities, include 24-hour room service, the international, Brasserie St Martin and the traditional Duke's Head Pub.
169 bedrs, all ensuite, ▣ ▦ 420 ⊕ ℭ MC Visa Amex DC JCB ㅎ

LONDON North & West

★★★★★ Landmark London ♔ ♔ ♔ ♔
Gold Ribbon Hotel
222 Marylebone Road, London NW1 6JQ
☎ 0171-631 8000 **Fax** 0171-631 8080
E-mail reservations@thelandmark.co.uk
298 bedrs, all ensuite, ④ ✎ ▣ ▦ 380 **P** 80 ⊕
SB £288-£326 **DB** £325 **HB** £270 **L** £26 **L** ♥ **D** £36.95
D ♥ ✕ **LD** 22:30 Restaurant closed L Sat, D Sun
ℭ MC Visa Amex DC JCB 🖪 🖾 🖫 ㅎ

★★★★ Dorset Square **Town House** ♔
39 Dorset Square, London NW1 6QM
☎ 0171-723 7874 **Fax** 0171-724-3328
E-mail dorset@firmdale.com
38 bedrs, 36 ensuite, 2 ⋔ ④ ✎ ▣ ⊕ **SB** £126.90-£135.13 **DB** £176.25-£252 **L** £14.95 **D** £17.95 ✕
LD 22:00 Restaurant closed L Sat-Sun, D Sat ℭ MC Visa Amex

★★★ Novotel London West
1 Shortlands, Hammersmith,
London W6 8DR
☎ 0181-741 1555 **Fax** 0181-741 2120
E-mail h0737@accor-hotels.com
629 bedrs, all ensuite, ♀ ✎ ⋔ ▣ ▦ 1,000 **P** 250 ⊕
SB £99-£126 **DB** £109-£143 **L** £13.95 **L** ♥ **D** £16.95
D ♥ ✕ **LD** 0:00 ℭ MC Visa Amex DC JCB 🖫 🖾 🖫 ㅎ

★★★ ✛ Posthouse   **Posthouse**
Haverstock Hill, Hampstead,
London NW3 4RB
☎ 0171-794 8121 **Fax** 0171-435 5586
140 bedrs, all ensuite, ⋔ ▣ ▦ 30 **P** 70 ⊕ ℭ MC Visa Amex DC JCB ㅎ

LONDON North & East

Jurys London Inn **Awaiting Inspection**
60 Pentonville Road, Islington, London N1 1LA
☎ 0171-282 5500 **Fax** 0171-282 5511
E-mail bookings@jurys.com
Closed 24-26 Dec
229 bedrs, all ensuite, ▣ ▦ 30 **P** 20 ⊕ **SB** £87-£92
DB £95-£100 **L** ♥ **D** £15.50 ✕ **LD** 21:30 ℭ MC Visa Amex DC ㅎ

Sleeping Beauty Motel **Lodge Awaiting Inspection**
543 Lea Bridge Road, Leyton, London E10 7EB
☎ 0181-556 8080 **Fax** 0181-556 8080
85 bedrs, all ensuite, ♀ ▣ **P** 75 No children under 4 ⊕ Resid **SB** £42-£45 **DB** £47-£50 ℭ MC Visa Amex DC 🖫 ㅎ

LONDON South & East

★★★★ London Bridge ♔ ♔ ♔
8-18 London Bridge Street, London SE1 9SG
☎ 0171-855 2200 **Fax** 0171-855 2233
138 bedrs, all ensuite, ▦ 85 ⊕ ℭ MC Visa Amex DC JCB ㅎ
See advert on opposite page

★★★ Novotel London Waterloo
113-127 Lambeth Road, London SE1 7LS
☎ 0171-793 1010 **Fax** 0171-793 0202
E-mail h1785@accor-hotels.com
187 bedrs, all ensuite, ✎ ⋔ ▣ ▦ 40 **P** 42 ⊕ **SB** £95-£134 **DB** £106-£165 **L** £17 **L** ♥ **D** £17 **D** ♥ ✕ **LD** 23:45
Restaurant closed L Sat-Sun ℭ MC Visa Amex DC 🖫 🖾 🖫 ㅎ

★★ Clarendon
8-16 Montpelier Row, Blackheath,
London SE3 0RW
☎ 0181-318 4321 **Fax** 0181-318 4378
198 bedrs, all ensuite, ④ ✎ ⋔ ▣ ▦ 200 **P** 60 ⊕
SB £59.50 **DB** £79 **L** £10 **L** ♥ **D** £15 **D** ♥ ✕ **LD** 21:45
ℭ MC Visa Amex DC ㅎ
See advert on next page

LONDON

LONDON BRIDGE HOTEL

Where History Meets Hospitality

- New, independently owned hotel, directly opposite London Bridge Station, appealing to both the business and leisure traveller.
- Close to the heart of the city and major tourist attractions.
- Easy access to Waterloo, London City and Gatwick Airports.
- 138 airconditioned bedrooms offering guests the perfect balance between traditional comfort and the latest facilities.

- Simply Nico Restaurant and Bar
- Hitchcock's City Bar
- Three two-bed serviced apartments for short and long term lets
- Curzons State-of-the-Art Gymnasium (opening October 99)

8-18 London Bridge Street, London SE1 9SG
Tel: 020 7855 2200 Fax: 020 7855 2233
Email: sales@london-bridge-hotel.co.uk
www.london-bridge-hotel.co.uk

LONDON South & West

★★★★ Cannizaro House ♖ ♖ ♖
West Side, Wimbledon, London SW19 4UE
📞 0181-879 1464 **Fax** 0181-879 7338

This Thistle country house hotel is an imposing Georgian mansion approached from the open spaces of Wimbledon Common and set in landscaped grounds of Cannizaro Park. Superb restaurant, luxurious bedrooms, meeting rooms and a licence for civil weddings.
45 bedrs, all ensuite, 🔳 ⫶⫶⫶ 80 **P** 90 ⊕ ⲥ MC Visa Amex DC JCB &

National Code & Number Change

Telephone codes and numbers in London change in April 2000.

0171-XXXXXX becomes 020-7XXX XXXX
0181-XXXXXX becomes 020-8XXX XXXX

Facilities for the disabled

Hotels do their best to cater for disabled visitors. However, it is advisable to contact the hotel direct to ensure it can provide particular requirement.

LONDON AIRPORT-HEATHROW 4C2
🛈 Underground Station Concourse 0839-123456

★★★★ Forte Crest Heathrow 🗟   LONDON SIGNATURE HOTELS
Sipson Road, West Drayton,
London UB7 0JU
📞 0181-759 2323 **Fax** 0181-897 8659
610 bedrs, all ensuite, 🖃 ⁑ 140 **P** 400 ⏚
SB £166.35 **DB** £166.35 **L** £18.50 **L** 💺 **D** £18.50 **D** 💺
✕ **LD** 23:00 《 MC Visa Amex DC JCB ♿

★★★★ Le Meridien Excelsior 🗟 🗟   *Le* MERIDIEN
Bath Road, West Drayton,
London UB7 0DU
📞 0181-759 6611 **Fax** 0181-759 3421
827 bedrs, all ensuite, ♪ ☈ 🖃 ⁑ 900
P 600 ⏚ **SB** £137.50 **DB** £160-£200
L £18.95 **L** 💺 **D** £18.95 **D** 💺 ✕ **LD** 22:30
《 MC Visa Amex DC JCB 🗟 🗟 🗟 🗟 ♿

★★★ Comfort Inn
Shepiston Lane, Hayes UB3 1BL
📞 0181-573 6162 **Fax** 0181-848 1057

This comfortable and welcoming hotel has been
extensively refurbished to offer guests modern well
appointed bedrooms, a sumptuous restaurant and
beautiful conservatory and bar. Easy reach of
motorways, Heathrow and a base for visiting
Windsor
80 bedrs, all ensuite, ⁑ 150 **P** 90 **SB** £94.95-£107.95
DB £120.90-£126.90 **L** £7 **L** 💺 **D** £16.95 **D** 💺 ✕
LD 22:15 《 MC Visa Amex DC

★★★ Master Robert
Great West Road, Hounslow TW5 0BD
📞 0181-570 6261 **Fax** 0181-569 4016
E-mail masterrobert@fullers.demon.co.uk
94 bedrs, all ensuite, ♪ ⁑ 150 **P** 150 ⏚ **SB** £102-
£104.50 **DB** £123-£125 **L** 💺 **D** 💺 ✕ **LD** 22:30 《 MC
Visa Amex DC ♿

★★★ ✣ Novotel London Heathrow
Junction 4, M4, Cherry Lane, West Drayton,
Heathrow UB7 9HB
📞 01895-431431 **Fax** 01895-431221
E-mail h1551@accor-hotels.com
178 bedrs, all ensuite, ☈ 🖃 ⁑ 250 **P** 160 ⏚
SB £109-£120 **DB** £109-£120 **L** £14.95 **D** £17.95 ✕
LD 23:59 《 MC Visa Amex DC 🗟 🗟 ♿

★★★ Osterley Four Pillars
764 Great West Road, Isleworth TW7 5NA
📞 0181-568 9981 **Fax** 0181-569 7819
E-mail enquiries@four-pillars.co.uk

A Tudor style hotel with 5 conference rooms,
restaurant, cocktail bar, conservatory, lounge,
restaurant, freehouse pub and large car park.
Piccadilly Line underground station 10 minutes
away; Heathrow 6 miles and central London 10
miles.
61 bedrs, all ensuite, ☈ ⁑ 250 **P** 100 ⏚ **SB** £55-£85
DB £60-£97 **L** £11.95 **D** £11.95 ✕ **LD** 22:00
Restaurant closed L Sat 《 MC Visa Amex DC

★★★ Posthouse Ariel Heathrow   **Posthouse**
Bath Road, Hayes UB3 5AJ
📞 0870-400-9040 **Fax** 0181-564 9265
186 bedrs, all ensuite, ☈ 🖃 ⁑ 50 **P** 120 ⏚
SB £59.50-£130 **DB** £69.50-£137 **L** £6 **L** 💺 **D** £14.95
D 💺 ✕ **LD** 22:30 《 MC Visa Amex DC ♿

★★ ✣ Stanwell Hall
Town Lane, Stanwell Staines,
London TW19 7PW
📞 01784-252292 **Fax** 01784-245250
19 bedrs, 18 ensuite, 1 🛏 ⁑ 20 **P** 50 ⏚ **SB** £65-£70
DB £90-£130 **L** £19 **L** 💺 **D** £19 **D** 💺 ✕ **LD** 22:00
Restaurant closed L Sat & Sun 《 MC Visa Amex
DC JCB

England

ABBERLEY Worcestershire 7E3
Pop. 589. Worcester 12, London 126,
Kidderminster 8, Ludlow 18, Bromyard 12 **see** Clock
Tower, Abberley Hill

Elms
Stockton Rd, Abberley WR6 6AT
☎ 01299-289954 **Fax** 01299-896804
E-mail info@swallowhotels.com

Built in 1710, this magnificent Queen Anne mansion
is set amidst 10 acres of lovely gardens. Antique
and comfortable furnishings adorn the public
rooms. All the bedrooms have their own character
with views across landscaped gardens and beyond.
25 bedrs, all ensuite, ◫ ⋕ 60 **P** 60 ◫ **SB** £90-£135
DB £140-£175 **L** £19.50 **D** £45 ✕ **LD** 21:30 **CC** MC Visa
Amex DC ▣ &

ABBOTS SALFORD Warwickshire 7F3
Pop. 1,300. Bidford-on-Avon 2, London 104,
Birmingham 24, Evesham 6, Stratford-upon-Avon
9½

★★★ ✤ Salford Hall
Abbots Salford WR11 5UT
☎ 01386-871300 **Fax** 01386-871301
Closed Christmas
34 bedrs, all ensuite, ◫ ✗ ⋕ 50 **P** 55 ◫ **SB** £85-
£115 **DB** £115-£150 **HB** £417-£510 **L** £15.95 **L** ☞
D £25 ✕ **LD** 21:30 Restaurant closed L Sat **CC** MC
Visa Amex DC JCB ▣ ▣ ▣

ABINGDON Oxfordshire 4B2
Pop. 28,500. Henley-on-Thames 21, London 56,
Faringdon 14, High Wycombe 29, Newbury 19,
Oxford 6½, Swindon 25, Wallingford 10 **EC** Thu
MD Mon **see** County Hall, 1677; containing Museum,
15th-18th cent Guildhall (portraits and plate), 14th
cent Abbey ruins, Almshouses, 13-15th cent St
Helen's Church, St Nicholas' Church ▯ 25 Bridge
Street 01235-522711

★★★ ✤ Abingdon Four Pillars
Marcham Road, Abingdon OX14 1TZ
☎ 01235-553456 **Fax** 01235-554117
63 bedrs, all ensuite, ✗ ⋕ 140 **P** 80 ◫ **SB** £49-£92
DB £56-£108 **L** £9 **L** ☞ **D** £13 **D** ☞ ✕ **LD** 21:30 **CC** MC
Visa Amex DC JCB &

★★★ Upper Reaches ▥ **Heritage** HOTELS
Thames Street, Abingdon OX14 3JA
☎ 01235-522311 **Fax** 01235-555182
31 bedrs, all ensuite, ◫ ♙ ⋕ 25 **P** 80 ◫ **CC** MC Visa
Amex DC JCB

ALDERLEY EDGE Cheshire 7E1

★★★ ✤ Alderley Edge
Macclesfield Road,
Alderley Edge SK9 7BJ
☎ 01625-583033 **Fax** 01625-586343
E-mail sales@alderley-edge-hotel.co.uk

Built in local sandstone in 1850, this country house
hotel is deservedly recognised for excellent food,
wine and service. Surrounded by picturesque
Cheshire countryside, yet ideally located for the
motorway network, Manchester Airport and
stations.
46 bedrs, all ensuite, ✗ ▣ ⋕ 100 **P** 80 ◫ **SB** £108-
£143.50 **DB** £132-£152 **L** £14.50 **L** ☞ **D** £23.95 ✕
LD 22:00 **CC** MC Visa Amex DC

ALDERSHOT Hampshire 4C3
Pop. 54,000. **EC** Wed **MD** Thu **see** Church with 15th
century tower ▯ Military Museum, Queens Avenue
01252-20968

★★★ Potters International
Fleet Road, Aldershot GU11 2ET
☎ 01252-344000 **Fax** 01252-311611

A superb 97 bedroom hotel complex, with first class accommodation, all ensuite, splendid restaurant, health and fitness suite and extensive business, conference and banqueting facilities.
97 bedrs, all ensuite, ⊞ ♀ ♗ ⊡ ⠿ 400 **P** 200 ⊕ ⊕ Rest Resid **SB** £99-£115.50 **DB** £132 **L** £12.50 **L** ⬤ **D** £17.50 **D** ⬤ ✕ **LD** 23:00 Restaurant closed L Sat **CC** MC Visa Amex DC JCB ▣ ▣ ▣ ▣ ㋧

ALFRISTON East Sussex	5D4

Pop. 700. Uckfield 16, London 60, Eastbourne 9½, Hastings 22, Hurst Green 24, Lewes 10, Newhaven 7½ **EC** Wed **see** 14th cent Clergy House (NT), 14th cent Star Inn, Market Cross House, Church, George Inn, Charleston Manor 1½ m S, Litlington Church

★★★ Star Inn ⌂   *Heritage* HOTELS
High Street, Alfriston BN26 5TA
☎ 01323-870495 **Fax** 01323-870922
37 bedrs, all ensuite, ⊁ ⠿ 30 **P** 34 ⊕ **CC** MC Visa Amex DC

George Inn
High Street, Alfriston BN26 5SY
☎ 01323-870319 **Fax** 01323-871384
E-mail george@coachinginn.freeserve.co.uk

Accommodation rooms from £60 including full English breakfast. Dine by candlelight in a beamed restaurant serving the finest a la carte food. The bar has a selection of fine ales.
8 bedrs, 6 ensuite, ⊞ ♀ ⊁ ⠿ 40 ⊕ **SB** £25-£40 **DB** £60-£80 **HB** £290 **L** £5.25 **L** ⬤ **D** £25 ✕ **LD** 21:30 **CC** MC Visa Amex ▣

White Lodge Country House
Sloe Lane, Alfriston BN26 5UR
☎ 01323-870265 **Fax** 01323-870284

ENGLAND

Elegant Edwardian building c1905, in an elevated position on the edge of the South Downs with 5 acres of gardens together with 17 bedrooms all of which have full facilities. The Orchid Restaurant offers fixed price and a la carte menus.
17 bedrs, all ensuite, ⊞ ⊁ ⊡ ⠿ 20 **P** 30 ⊕ Rest Resid **SB** £55-£85 **DB** £115-£140 **L** £14 **D** £19.50 ✕ **LD** 21:15 **CC** MC Visa Amex DC JCB ㋧

ALNMOUTH Northumberland	13F3

Pop. 300. Alnwick 4½, London 309, Corbridge 45, Newcastle 35 **EC** Wed **see** Alnmouth Bay

★★★ Famous Schooner
Northumberland Street, Alnwick, Alnmouth NE66 2RS
☎ 01665-830216 **Fax** 01665-830287
E-mail john@schooner.freeserve.co.uk

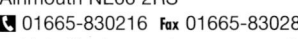

Listed 17th century coaching inn, only 100 yards from the beach, river and golf course. Renowned for superb cuisine and an extensive selection of real ales. Many rooms overlook hotel gardens, estuary or sea. Reputed to be haunted.
31 bedrs, all ensuite, ♗ ⊁ ⠿ 120 **P** 60 ⊕ **SB** £29.50-£37.50 **DB** £59-£69 **HB** £210-£276.50 **L** £7.50 **L** ⬤ **D** £12.95 ✕ **LD** 21:30 **CC** MC Visa Amex DC JCB ▣ ▣

ALSTON Cumbria 10B1
Pop. 1,900. Middleton-in-Teesdale 22, London 280, Brampton 19, Hexham 21, Penrith 19 EC Tue MD Sat
i Railway Station 01434-381696

★★ Lowbyer Manor Country House
Hexham Road, Alston CA9 3JX
🕿 01434-381230 Fax 01434-382937
12 bedrs, all ensuite, ⊶ ⚎ 20 P 14 ⊞ Rest Resid
SB £36 DB £72 HB £305 L ⬤ D £17.50 ✕ LD 20:30
《 MC Visa Amex DC

ALTON Hampshire 4B3
Pop. 16,500. Farnham 9½, London 48, Basingstoke 12, Fareham 24, Haslemere 16, Petersfield 12, Winchester 17 EC Wed MD Tue see Jane Austen's Home at Chawton ½m S *i* 7 Cross and Pillory Lane 01420-88448

★★★ Alton Grange
London Road, Alton GU34 4EG
🕿 01420-86565 Fax 01420-541346
Closed Christmas
30 bedrs, all ensuite, ⚎ ♀ ⌀ ⊶ ⚎ 80 P 40 No children under 4 ⊞ SB £67-£82.50 DB £82.50-£95
L £20 L ⬤ D £25 D ⬤ ✕ LD 22:00 Restaurant closed L Sat 《 MC Visa Amex DC JCB ⅄

ALTRINCHAM Cheshire 10C4
Pop. 32,600. Knutsford 7½, London 180, M56 (jn 7) 2½, Macclesfield 15, Manchester 8, Northwich 13, Stockport 8½, Warrington 11 EC Wed MD Tue, Fri, Sat see Dunham Park, St George's Church
i Stamford New Road 0161-912 5931

★★★ Cresta Court
Church Street, Altrincham WA14 4DP
🕿 0161-927 7272 Fax 0161-926 9194
138 bedrs, all ensuite, ⚎ ⊶ ▣ ⚎ 300 P 200 ⊞
DB £89.50 L £9 L ⬤ D £16.95 D ⬤ ✕ LD 21:30
Restaurant closed L Sat 《 MC Visa Amex DC ⊠ ⅄

★★★ Lodge at the Bull's Head
Wicker Lane, Hale Barns, Altrincham WA15 0HG
🕿 0161-903 1300 Fax 0161-903 1300

★★★ Quality
Langham Road, Bowdon, WA14 2HT
🕿 0161-928 7121 Fax 0161-927 7560
89 bedrs, all ensuite, ⚎ ⌀ ⊶ ⚎ 200 P 150
⊞ L £5.25 L ⬤ D £17.95 D ⬤ ✕ LD 21:45
Restaurant closed L Sat 《 MC Visa Amex DC ▣ ⊠ ▨ ⅄

★★★ ❖ Woodland Park
Wellington Road, Timperley, WA14 7RG
🕿 0161-928 8631 Fax 0161-941 2821
E-mail info@woodlandpark.co.uk

The Woodland Park is a delightful family owned hotel. 46 individually designed bedrooms, an elegant a la carte restaurant and facilities for conferences and weddings.
46 bedrs, all ensuite, ⚎ ⚎ 180 P 150 ⊞ SB £50-£80
DB £70-£140 L £12.95 L ⬤ D £16 ✕ LD 22:00 《 MC Visa Amex DC JCB

ALVESTON Avon 3E1
Pop. 2,500. M4 & M5 4, London 115, Bristol 10, Chepstow 9½, Gloucester 24 EC Wed see British Encampment, Tumuli, Church

★★★ Alveston House
Alveston BS12 2LJ
🕿 01454-415050 Fax 01454-415425
E-mail info@alvestonhousehotel.co.uk
30 bedrs, all ensuite, ⌀ ⊶ ⚎ 85 P 75 ⊞ SB £79.50-£89.50 DB £94.50-£99.50 L £11 D £17 ✕ LD 21:30
《 MC Visa Amex DC ⅄

AMBLESIDE Cumbria 10B2
See also GREAT LANGDALE, HAWKSHEAD and SAWREY.
Pop. 3,350. M6 (jn 36) 25, London 269, Broughton-in-Furness 16, Kendal 13, Keswick 16, Penrith 22, Windermere 5 EC Thu MD Wed see House on the Bridge, Stock Ghyll Force, Lake Windermere, Jenkin Crag (view point), Borrans Field (remains of Roman Camp), Rush Bearing ceremony July, White Craggs Rock Garden 1m W *i* Old Courthouse, Church Street 015394-32582

★★★ Nanny Brow Country House 🖥 🖥
Clappersgate, Ambleside LA22 9NF
☎ 01539-432036 **Fax** 01539-432450
17 bedrs, all ensuite, 🔳 ♀ ✗ ♀ ⅲ 30 **P** 25 ⊞ Resid
SB £55-£90 **DB** £110-£180 **HB** £475-£850 **L** £12.75
L ☞ **D** £30 **D** ☞ ✗ **LD** 20:45 《 MC Visa Amex DC
JCB 🖉
See advert on this page

★★★ Rothay Manor 🖥 🖥
Rothay Bridge, Ambleside LA22 0EH
☎ 01539-433605 **Fax** 01539-433607
E-mail hotel@rothaymanor.demon.co.uk
Closed Jan-early Feb

Elegant Regency manor house set in own gardens
on the edge of town. Friendly service and gourmet
food.
18 bedrs, all ensuite, 🔳 ⅲ 25 **P** 50 ⊞ Rest Resid
SB £75-£79 **DB** £120-£135 **L** £13.50 **L** ☞ **D** £24 ✗
LD 21:00 《 MC Visa Amex DC &

★★★ Salutation 🖥
Lake Road, Ambleside LA22 9BX
☎ 015394-32244 **Fax** 015394-34157

With its refurbished lounge bar, extended lounge
and restaurant the Salutation makes the ideal base
for a relaxing holiday with good food served by
friendly staff. Guests enjoy free membership of the
nearby luxury leisure club.
40 bedrs, all ensuite, ✗ ⅲ 50 **P** 50 ⊞ **SB** £35.50-
£48.50 **DB** £71-£97 **HB** £301-£372 **L** ☞ **D** £19 **D** ☞ ✗
LD 21:00 《 MC Visa Amex JCB

ENGLAND

★★★ Skelwith Bridge 🖫 🖫
Skelwith Bridge, Ambleside LA22 9NJ
📞 01539-432115 **Fax** 01539-434254
E-mail skelwithbr@aol.com
Closed 11-26 Dec
29 bedrs, all ensuite, 🅣 🕭 ⁂ 40 **P** 60 🔁 《 MC Visa JCB

★★★ ✤ Wateredge
Waterhead Bay, Ambleside LA22 0EP
📞 015394-32332 **Fax** 015394-31878
E-mail info-r@wateredgehotel.co.uk
Closed mid Dec-mid Jan

Delightfully situated on the shores of Lake Windemere, with garden to the lake edge. Comfortable lounges overlook the lake. Log fires, cosy bar, oak-beamed dining room.
23 bedrs, all ensuite, 🕭 **P** 25 No children under 7 🔁 Rest Resid **SB** £48-£64 **DB** £74-£156 **HB** £390-£655 **D** £29.50 ✕ **LD** 20:30 《 MC Visa Amex JCB

★★ ✤ Fisherbeck
Old Lake Road, Ambleside LA22 0DH
📞 015394-33215 **Fax** 015394-33600
Closed Jan
18 bedrs, all ensuite, ⁂ 20 **P** 20 🔁 《 MC Visa

★★ Kirkstone Foot 🖫 🖫
Kirkstone Pass Road, Ambleside LA22 9EH
📞 015394-32232 **Fax** 015394-32805
Closed Dec-Jan

Everywhere peace - everywhere serenity and a

marvellous freedom from the tumult of the world. A country house atmosphere, peaceful secluded gardens, beautiful ensuite bedrooms, fine food and wine. May we look forward to your visit.
14 bedrs, all ensuite, 🅣 **P** 30 🔁 Resid **SB** £44-£48 **DB** £71-£79 **HB** £270-£367 **D** £23.50 ✕ **LD** 20:30 《 MC Visa Amex DC ঙ

★★ ✤ Queen's
Market Place, Ambleside LA22 9BU
📞 01539-432206 **Fax** 01539-432721
26 bedrs, all ensuite, 🅣 ⁂ 50 **P** 11 🔁 **SB** £25-£35 **DB** £50-£70 **HB** £257-£320 **L** £9 **D** £14 ✕ **LD** 21:30 《 MC Visa Amex DC

★★ Waterhead
Lake Road, Ambleside LA22 0ER
📞 01539-432566 **Fax** 01539-431255

A traditional hotel situated at the northern end of Windermere. The Waterhead's central location makes it an ideal centre for touring the Lake District.
28 bedrs, all ensuite, 🕭 ⁂ 50 **P** 50 🔁 《 MC Visa Amex DC JCB

AMERSHAM Buckinghamshire   4C2
Pop. 13,250. Denham 9½, London 26, Aylesbury 15, Dunstable 19, High Wycombe 7½, Rickmansworth 8, Slough 12 **EC** Thu **MD** Tue **see** Parish Church (brasses), 17th cent Almhouses, Market Hall (1682), 17th cent Bury Farm (Penn assns) Protestant Martyr's Memorial, Milton's Cottage 3m S 🎫 Broadway/High Street 01494-729492

★★★ Crown 🖫
High Street, Amersham HP7 0DH
📞 01494-721541 **Fax** 01494-431283
23 bedrs, all ensuite, 🅣 🕭 ⁂ 30 **P** 33 🔁 **SB** £48-£124.95 **DB** £96-£154.90 **HB** £149.95 **L** £9.95 **L** 🍽 **D** £20.95 **D** 🍽 ✕ **LD** 21:30 《 MC Visa Amex DC

Heritage HOTELS

ENGLAND

ANDOVER Hampshire 4B3

Pop. 32,500. Basingstoke 19, London 65, Amesbury 14, Devizes 27, Newbury 16, Romsey 17, Salisbury 18, Winchester 14 **EC** Wed **MD** Thu, Sat **see** Guildhall, 19th cent Church *i* Town Mill House, Bridge Street 01264-324320

★★★ Ashley Court

Micheldever Road, Andover SP11 6LA
☎ 01264-357344 **Fax** 01264-356755
35 bedrs, all ensuite, **‖‖** 200 **P** 100 **⊞ ℂℂ** MC Visa Amex ⊠ ⅙

★★★ Esseborne Manor ⓡ

Hurstbourne Tarrant, Andover SP11 0ER
☎ 01264-736444 **Fax** 01264-736725
E-mail esseborne_manor@compuserve.com

A Victorian country house hotel set in landscaped gardens high on the North Wessex Downs. Ideal location for exploring Salisbury, Winchester, Stonehenge and the south.
14 bedrs, all ensuite, ④ ⅄ **‖‖** 40 **P** 30 **⊞** Resid **SB** £88 **DB** £95-£135 **L** £13 **D** £18 **D ⏻** ✕ **LD** 21:30 **ℂℂ** MC Visa Amex DC ⊠ ⅙

★★★ White Hart

12 Bridge Street, Andover SP10 1BH
☎ 01264-352266 **Fax** 01264-323767
27 bedrs, all ensuite, ④ ⅄ **‖‖** 65 **P** 25 **⊞ SB** £70 **DB** £85 **L** £15 **D** £15 ✕ **LD** 21:45 **ℂℂ** MC Visa Amex DC ⊠ ⅙

APPLEBY-IN-WESTMORLAND Cumbria 10B2

Pop. 2,400. Brough 8, London 272, Alston 26, Hawes 26, Kendal 24, Kirkby Lonsdale 30, Penrith 13 **EC** Thu **MD** Sat **see** Castle (not open), St Lawrence's Church, St Michael's Church, Grammar School, High Cross, 16th cent Moot Hall, Bull Ring *i* Moot Hall, Boroughgate 017683-51177

★★★ ❖ Appleby Manor Country House

Roman Road, Appleby-in-Westmorland CA16 6JB
☎ 017683-51571 **Fax** 017683-52888
E-mail reception@applebymanor.co.uk
Closed Christmas

Relaxing and friendly country house set in wooded grounds overlooking Appleby Castle. Super indoor leisure club with small pool, jacuzzi, sauna and steam room. Magnificent lounges.
30 bedrs, all ensuite, ④ ⅏ ⅄ **‖‖** 28 **P** 50 **⊞ SB** £72-£82 **DB** £104-£146 **HB** £372-£434 **L** £12 **L ⏻ D** £22 **D ⏻** ✕ **LD** 21:00 **ℂℂ** MC Visa Amex DC JCB ⊠ ⊠ ⊠ ⅙
See advert on this page

★★★ ✦ Tufton Arms

Market Square, CA16 6XA
☎ 01768-351593 Fax 01768-352761
21 bedrs, all ensuite, ⚲ ⋕ 100 P 15 ⊞ SB £49-£90
DB £90-£145 HB £360-£525 L £9.50 L ♥ D £21.50
D ♥ ✕ LD 21:00 ℂℂ MC Visa Amex DC JCB ☑

★★ Royal Oak
Bondgate, Appleby-in-Westmorland CA16 6UN
☎ 01768-351463 Fax 017683-52300
E-mail m.m.royaloak@btinternet.com

A lovely genuine old inn, the Royal Oak in Appleby stands out for its good food and drink, and above all its atmosphere.
9 bedrs, 7 ensuite, ⚲ ⋕ 20 P 12 ⊞ SB £33-£35
DB £72-£76 L ♥ D ♥ ✕ LD 21:00 ℂℂ MC Visa Amex

★ ✦ Courtfield
Bongate, Appleby-in-Westmorland CA16 6UP
☎ 017683-51394
11 bedrs, 4 ensuite, ⚲ P 30 ⊞ Resid ♿

ARUNDEL West Sussex   4C4
Pop. 3,175. Pulborough 9, London 56, Bognor Regis 9½, Brighton 20, Chichester 11, Worthing 10
EC Wed see Castle, Maison Dieu ruins, Swanbourne Lake, 14th cent St Nicholas church, R.C. Cathedral, Wildfowl Trust ⛵ 61 High Street 01903-882268

★★★ ✦ Swan
27-29 High Street, Arundel BN18 9AG
☎ 01903-882314 Fax 01903-883759

Elegant Grade II Listed building, situated in the heart of historic Arundel, featuring attractive Georgian and Victorian architecture and decor. Completely refurbished in 1994 to a very high standard.
15 bedrs, all ensuite, ⋕ 25 P 20 ⊞ SB £50 DB £65
HB £300 L £8 L ♥ D £12 D ♥ ✕ LD 21:30 ℂℂ MC Visa Amex DC

★★ ✦ Comfort Inn

Junction A27/A284, Crossbush, BN17 7QQ
☎ 01903-840840 Fax 01903-849849
E-mail admin@gb642.u-net.com

Opened in spring 1997, this hotel offers comfort you need at a price representing value for money. The bedrooms are ensuite with all facilities and the conference rooms can take up to 80 people.
55 bedrs, all ensuite, ⋕ 80 ⊞ Rest Resid SB £50-£61 DB £57-£68 D £9.75 ✕ LD 22:00 ℂℂ MC Visa Amex DC ☒ ♿

Amberley Castle
Amberley, Arundel BN18 9ND
☎ 01798-831992 Fax 01798-831998

A 900-year-old castle set in the lee of the glorious South Downs. Over an acre of ornamental garden invites the guest through the portcullis and behind the 60 foot 'Curtain' walls.
20 bedrs, all ensuite, ④ ⋕ 40 P 50 No children under 12 ⊞ DB £145-£300 L £12.50 L ♥ D £35 D ♥ ✕ LD 21:30 ℂℂ MC Visa Amex DC

ASCOT Berkshire   4C2
Pop. 18,266. Staines 8, London 25, Bagshot 4½,
Reading 14, Windsor 6½ **EC** Wed **see** Racecourse
founded 1711 by Queen Anne, Royal Meeting in
June

★★★★ Berystede ⊠   **Heritage**
Bagshot Road, Ascot SL5 9JH   HOTELS
☎ 01344-623311 **Fax** 01344-872301
E-mail heritagehotels_ascot.berystede@fortehotels.com
90 bedrs, all ensuite, ④ ➔ ☰ ⚌ 120 **P** 240
⊞ **SB** £100-£145 **DB** £150-£175 **L** £15.95
L ⚊ **D** £22.50 **D** ⚊ ✗ **LD** 21:45 **CC** MC Visa
Amex DC JCB ⊰ &

ASHBOURNE Derbyshire   7F1
Pop. 6,000. Derby 13, London 139, Buxton 20,
Matlock 13, Stoke 22, Uttoxeter 12 **ℹ** 13 Market
Place 01335-343666

★★★ Callow Hall
Mappleton Road, Ashbourne DE6 2AA
☎ 01335-343403 **Fax** 01335-343624
Closed 25-26 Dec

Beautifully restored country house in close
proximity to the stately homes of Derbyshire. Good
Food Guide recommended restaurant complements
the friendly and unobtrusive personal service.
16 bedrs, all ensuite, ④ ✎ ➔ ⚌ 36 **P** 42 ⊞ Rest
Resid **SB** £80-£105 **DB** £120-£150 **HB** £735 **L** £18.25
D £37 ✗ **LD** 21:15 **CC** MC Visa Amex DC ▣ &
See advert on this page

Short Breaks
Many hotels provide special rates for
weekend and mid-week breaks –
sometimes these are quoted in
the hotel's entry, otherwise ring
direct for the latest offers.

★★★ Hanover International,
Ashbourne
Derby Road, Ashbourne DE6 1XH
☎ 01335-346666 **Fax** 01335-346549

Attractive purpose built hotel and leisure club at the
'Gateway to Dovedale' with the highest standards
of traditional comfort and warm friendly service.
50 bedrs, all ensuite, ♀ ✎ ☰ ⚌ 200 **P** 130 ⊞ **SB** £75
DB £90 **L** ⚊ **D** £17.95 **D** ⚊ ✗ **LD** 22:00 **CC** MC Visa
Amex DC JCB ▨ ⊞ ▩ ▣ &

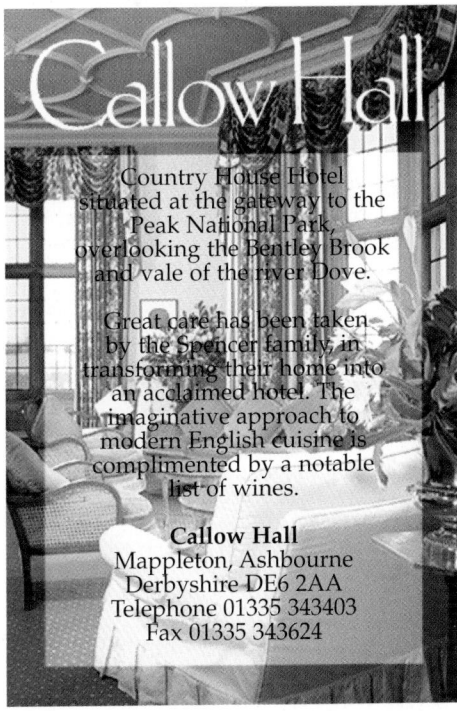

★★ Dog & Partridge
Swinscoe, Ashbourne DE6 2HS
☎ 01335-343183 **Fax** 01335-342742

Martin and Mary welcome you to stay at their country inn with rooms in the grounds. Good food, real ales, children and pets welcome. All special diets catered for.
30 bedrs, 28 ensuite, 🗟 ⊁ ⊞ 20 P 55 ⊕ ℂℂ MC Visa Amex DC 🔲 &

ASHBY-DE-LA-ZOUCH Leicestershire   7F2
Pop. 12,000. Hinckley 16, London 113, Atherstone 13, Burton-upon-Trent 9, Derby 14, Leicester 17, Loughborough 12, Nottingham 21, Nuneaton 17, Tamworth 13 ℂ Wed **MD** Sat ⚏ North Street 01530-411767

★★★ Fallen Knight ♞ ♞
Kilwardy Street, Ashby-de-la-Zouch LE65 2FQ
☎ 01530-412230 **Fax** 01530-417596
24 bedrs, all ensuite, 🗟 ⊁ ⊡ ⊞ 70 P 50 ⊕ **SB** £62 **DB** £79 L £15.95 L ⚐ D £22.50 D ⚐ ✕ **LD** 22:30 ℂℂ MC Visa Amex DC &

ASHFORD Kent   5E3
Pop. 55,000. Maidstone 19, London 56, Canterbury 14, Folkestone 16, Rochester 27, Tenterden 12, Tunbridge Wells 32 ℂ Wed **MD** Tue, Wed, Sat ⚏ 18 The Churchyard 01233-629165

★★★★ Ashford International
Simone Weil Avenue, Ashford TN24 8UX
☎ 01233-219988 **Fax** 01233-627708
200 bedrs, all ensuite, ⊁ ⊡ ⊞ 400 P 400 ⊕ ℂℂ MC Visa Amex DC 🔲 🔲 🔲 🔲 &

★★★★ Eastwell Manor ♞ ♞ ♞ ♞
Boughton Aluph, Ashford TN25 4HR
☎ 01233-213000 **Fax** 01233-635530
E-mail eastwell@btinternet.com

Millennium Experience 2000! House Party. Everything included in one payment. Three days of continuous celebration and entertainment, champagne all the way. Dancing every evening, gourmet dining, fun and fireworks, including first class Eurostar to Paris.
62 bedrs, all ensuite, 🗟 🖈 ⊁ ⊡ ⊞ 100 P 100 ⊕ **SB** £150-£310 **DB** £180-£340 L £15 L ⚐ D £28.50 D ⚐ ✕ **LD** 21:30 ℂℂ MC Visa Amex DC JCB 🔲 🔲 🔲 🔲 🔲 &

★★★ Posthouse   **Posthouse**
Canterbury Road, Ashford TN24 8QQ
☎ 01233-625790 **Fax** 01233-643176
103 bedrs, all ensuite, ⊁ ⊞ 120 P 130 ⊕ ℂℂ MC Visa Amex DC &

ASHTON-UNDER-LYNE Lancashire   10C4
Pop. 44,500. Buxton 22, London 181, Barnsley 30, Glossop 7½, Huddersfield 20, Manchester 6½, Oldham 4, Stockport 7½ ℂ Tue **MD** Daily (exc Tue) ⚏ 32 Market Street 0161-343 4343

★★ York House ♞
York Place, Richmond Street, Ashton-under-Lyne OL6 7TT
☎ 0161-330 9000 **Fax** 0161-343 1613
Closed 26 Dec

Situated in a peaceful tree-lined cul-de-sac, close to A635/A6017 junction, this very well maintained,

family owned and run hotel has been developed over the last 24 years. The hotel is set in award winning gardens.
34 bedrs, all ensuite, 🛏 🖉 ⟟ ⠇⠇⠇ 40 **P** 34 ⊞ Rest Resid **SB** £59 **DB** £70 **L** £8 **D** £15 ✗ **LD** 21:30 **CC** MC Visa Amex DC JCB

ASHURST Hampshire   4B4
Pop. 2,200. Winchester 16, London 81, Lyndhurst 3, Romsey 9, Salisbury 19, Southampton 6½
EC Wed

★★ Busketts Lawn
174 Woodlands Road, Woodlands, Ashurst SO4 2GL
📞 01703-292272 **Fax** 01703-292487
14 bedrs, all ensuite, 🛏 ⟟ ⠇⠇⠇ 130 **P** 50 ⊞ Rest Resid **CC** MC Visa Amex DC ⫨

ASPLEY GUISE Bedfordshire   4C1
Pop. 400. Dunstable 11, London 45, M1 (jn 13) 1, Bedford 12, Milton Keynes 6.

★★★ Moore Place 🛏 🛏
Aspley Guise MK17 8DW
📞 01908-282000 **Fax** 01908-281888

A Georgian mansion with a restaurant and bedroom extension at rear. Set in a small quiet village near Milton Keynes. Close to the M1 (jn 13).
54 bedrs, all ensuite, ⟟ ⠇⠇⠇ 50 **P** 70 ⊞ **SB** £45-£75 **DB** £65-£100 **L** £11.50 **L** 🍴 **D** £22.95 ✗ **LD** 21:45 Restaurant closed L Sat **CC** MC Visa Amex DC ♿

ASTON CLINTON Buckinghamshire   4C2
Pop. 3,250. Watford 19, London 36, Aylesbury 4½, Denham 22, Dunstable 11, High Wycombe 15, St Albans 19 **see** Roman remains, Parish Church

★★★ Bell Inn 🛏 🛏 🛏
London Road, Aston Clinton HP22 5HP
📞 01296-630252 **Fax** 01296-631250

A charming Listed 17th century luxury coaching inn. Individually styled spacious bedrooms and suites either in the main house, or in the courtyard with attractive gardens. Fine dining restaurant with speciality Aylesbury duck and excellent wine list.
20 bedrs, all ensuite, 🛏 ⠇⠇⠇ 20 **P** 200 ⊞ **CC** MC Visa Amex

---

AUSTWICK North Yorkshire   10C3
Pop. 485. Settle 4, London 233, Hawes 21, Kirkby Lonsdale 12, Lancaster 21

★★ Traddock
Austwick, Settle LA2 8BY
📞 015242-51224 **Fax** 015242-51224
9 bedrs, all ensuite, ♀ 🖉 ⠇⠇⠇ 50 **P** 20 ⊞ **SB** £40-£50 **DB** £80 **HB** £305-£375 **D** £21.50 **D** 🍴 ✗ **LD** 20:30 **CC** MC Visa

---

AVON Hampshire   4A4
Christchurch 4, London 98, Bournemouth 9½, Lymington 16, Ringwood 4½

★★★ Tyrrells Ford
Avon BH23 7BH
📞 01425-672646 **Fax** 01425-672262
16 bedrs, all ensuite, ⠇⠇⠇ 60 **P** 100 ⊞ **SB** £55-£65 **DB** £90-£100 **HB** £315-£372 **L** £14.95 **L** 🍴 **D** £21 **D** 🍴 ✗ **LD** 21:30 **CC** MC Visa Amex

---

AYLESBURY Buckinghamshire   4C2
Pop. 50,000. Watford 23, London 40, Bicester 16, Buckingham 16, Dunstable 15, High Wycombe 16, Oxford 22, St Albans 23 **EC** Thu **MD** Wed, Fri, Sat **see** 15th cent Church of St Mary, King's Head Hotel, Statue of John Hampden, Bucks County Museum, Prebendal House (home of John Wilkes) 🆔 8 Bourbon Street 01296-330559

★★★★ Hartwell House Hotel, Restaurant & Spa 🛏 🛏 🛏 🛏
Gold Ribbon Hotel
Oxford Road, Aylesbury HP17 8NL
📞 01296-747444 Fax 01296-747450
E-mail info@hartwell-house.com
46 bedrs, all ensuite, 🔳 ♀ ✎ ⊀ 🖃 ⠿ 60 P 90 No children under 8 ⊟ SB £108-£119 DB £165-£487
L £20.50 D £44 ✕ LD 21:45 ℂℂ MC Visa Amex 🖪 🖾
🖩 🖾 🗐 ♿

★★★ Posthouse   **Posthouse**
Aston Clinton Road,
Aylesbury HP22 5AA
📞 01296-393388 Fax 01296-392211
94 bedrs, all ensuite, ⊀ ⠿ 100 P 140
⊟ Room £95 L £12 L ⬤ D £15 D ⬤ ✕
LD 22:30 ℂℂ MC Visa Amex DC 🖪 🖾 🖩 ♿

★★ Horse and Jockey
Buckingham Road, Aylesbury HP19 3QL
📞 01296-23803 Fax 01296-395142
24 bedrs, all ensuite, P 60 ⊟ ℂℂ MC Visa Amex DC

★★★★★ Pennyhill Park Hotel
+ Country Club 🛏 🛏 🛏
London Road, Bagshot GU19 5EU
📞 01276-471774 Fax 01276-475570
E-mail pennyhillpark@msn.com

Luxuriously furnished manor house dating back to 1849, set in 120 acres of beautiful parkland, with a wide range of sporting facilities.
114 bedrs, all ensuite, 🔳 ♀ ✎ ⊀ 🖃 ⠿ 180 P 600 ⊟
SB £170.35-£188 DB £188-£199.75 L £17.95 L ⬤
D £32 D ⬤ ✕ LD 22:30 ℂℂ MC Visa Amex DC 🖪 🖾 🖸
🖾 🗐 🖾 ♿
See advert on this page

BAINBRIDGE North Yorkshire   10C2
Pop. 474. Leyburn 12, London 245, Hawes 4,
Leeds 54, Skipton 31 **EC** Wed **see** Old Inn, Waterfalls,
Semerwater Lake 1m W

★★ Rose & Crown ⬚
Bainbridge, Wensleydale DL8 3EE
📞 01969-650225 **Fax** 01969-650735
12 bedrs, all ensuite, ⬚ ⊁ ⠇⠇⠇ 36 **P** 65 ⬚ **SB** £32-£41
DB £52-£70 **HB** £207-£336 **L** £9 **L** ⬚ **D** £18 **D** ⬚ ✕
⬚ **LD** 21:30 Restaurant closed L Mon-Sat **CC** MC Visa
⬚

BALSALL COMMON West Midlands   8A3

★★ Haigs ⬚ ⬚ ⬚
273 Kenilworth Road, Balsall Common CV7 7EL
📞 01676-533004 **Fax** 01676-535132

Family run hotel recently refurbished to a high
standard with award winning restaurant. Ideally
situated 5 miles to NEC and hub of Midland
motorways. Close to Warwick and Stratford-upon-
Avon.
23 bedrs, all ensuite, ♀ ⬚ ⠇⠇⠇ 20 **P** 23 ⬚ Rest Resid
SB £59.50 **DB** £79.50 **L** £14.95 **L** ⬚ **D** £22 **D** ⬚ ✕
LD 21:30 Restaurant closed L Mon-Sat **CC** MC Visa
Amex JCB ⬚

Facilities for the disabled

Hotels do their best to cater for disabled
visitors. However, it is advisable to contact
the hotel direct to ensure it can provide
particular requirement.

BAMBURGH Northumberland   13F3
Pop. 423. Alnwick 16, London 324, Berwick 20,
Coldstream 26 **EC** Wed **see** Castle, St Aidan's Church,
Grace Darling Museum and boathouse, Farne
Islands (bird sanctuary)

Waren House Hotel

Traditional Country House Hotel on edge of Budle Bay overlooking Holy Island and just 2 miles from
Bamburgh Castle. Superb accommodation, excellent food complemented by over 250 reasonably priced wines.

No smoking except in Library, Children over 14 welcome. 2 miles from A1 on B1342. Floodlit at night.

Open all year. Short breaks available all week.

RAC ★★★

Waren Mill, Belford, Northumberland NE70 7EE

Telephone: 01668 214581   **Fax: 01668 214484**

www.warenhousehotel.co.uk

★★★ Waren House
Waren Mill, Belford NE70 7EE
☎ 01668-214581 **Fax** 01668-214484
E-mail enquiries@warenhousehotel.co.uk

Beautifully restored and refurbished country house on the edge of Budle Bay overlooking Holy Island. Professionally managed by resident owners.
10 bedrs, all ensuite, 🅰 ♀ ✦ ⅲ 30 **P** 20 No children under 14 ⊞ **SB** £57.50-£85 **DB** £115 **HB** £394-£546 **D** £25 ✕ **LD** 20:30 **CC** MC Visa Amex DC JCB
See advert on previous page

★★ Lord Crewe Arms 🖪
Front Street, Bamburgh NE69 7BL
☎ 01668-214243 **Fax** 01668-214273
Closed 31 Oct
20 bedrs, 18 ensuite, 2 ⌂ 🅰 ♀ ✦ **P** 15 No children under 5 ⊞ **SB** £50 **DB** £75 **L** ◗ **D** ◗ ✕ **LD** 21:00 **CC** MC Visa

---

BANBURY Oxfordshire   4B1
Pop. 39,500. Bicester 15, London 72, Buckingham 17, Chipping Norton 13, Coventry 27, Daventry 16, Oxford 23, Stratford-upon-Avon 20, Warwick 20 **EC** Tue **MD** Thu, Sat **see** 19th cent Cross in Horse Fair, 16th cent Calthorpe Manor House, 18th cent Church, Broughton Castle 2½ m SW. 🖪 Museum, 8 Horsefair 01295-259855

★★★ Whately Hall
Banbury Cross, Banbury OX16 0AN   **Heritage** HOTELS
☎ 01295-263451 **Fax** 01295-271736
73 bedrs, all ensuite, ♀ ✦ 🖃 ⅲ 120 **P** 60 ⊞ **SB** £45-£105 **DB** £53-£115 **HB** £60-£120 **L** £6.95 **L** ◗ **D** £21.50 **D** ◗ ✕ **LD** 21:30 **CC** MC Visa Amex DC JCB ♿

★★ Lismore
61 Oxford Road, Banbury OX16 9AJ
☎ 01295-267661 **Fax** 01295-269010
22 bedrs, all ensuite, 🅰 ✦ ⅲ 30 **P** 23 ⊞ **SB** £40-£75 **DB** £60-£95 **L** £8.25 **D** £16.95 ✕ **LD** 21:30 **CC** MC Visa Amex DC ♿

BARNET Hertfordshire   5D2

★★★★ West Lodge Park 🖪 🖪
Cockfosters Road, Hadley Wood EN4 0PY
☎ 0181-440 8311 **Fax** 0181-449 3698
55 bedrs, all ensuite, 🅰 🖃 ⅲ 70 **P** 100 ⊞ **CC** MC Visa Amex ♿

BARNSTAPLE Devon   2C2
Pop. 22,000. South Molton 11, London 193, Bideford 9, Crediton 33, Ilfracombe 11, Lynmouth 19 **EC** Wed **MD** Tue, Fri 🖪 Library, Tuly Street 01271-388583

★★★★ Imperial
Taw Vale Parade, Barnstaple EX32 8NB
☎ 01271-345861 **Fax** 01271-324448
E-mail info@brend-imperial.co.uk

Luxury refurbishment throughout 1999 has led to Barnstaple's premier hotel being awarded 4 star status. All rooms are ensuite, many with charming river views.
64 bedrs, all ensuite, ♀ ✦ ✦ 🖃 ⅲ 70 **P** 100 ⊞ **SB** £48-£75 **DB** £76-£180 **HB** £245-£560 **L** £12 **L** ◗ **D** £18 **D** ◗ ✕ **LD** 21:00 **CC** MC Visa Amex DC ▣ ♿
See advert on opposite page

★★★ Barnstaple
Braunton Road, Barnstaple EX31 1LE
☎ 01271-376221 **Fax** 01271-324101
E-mail info@barnstaplehotel.co.uk

ENGLAND

The Barnstaple offers a superb health and leisure complex, including magnificent heated outdoor and indoor pools, inviting ensuite bedrooms, a fine restaurant and the warmest of West Country welcomes.
60 bedrs, all ensuite, ♀ ⚲ ⊁ ⸬ 250 **P** 250 ⊞
SB £59-£64 **DB** £84-£94 **HB** £315-£490 **L** £9.50 **L** ➤
D £16.50 **D** ➤ ✕ **LD** 21:00 **CC** MC Visa Amex DC ☒ ⸾
☒ ☒ ☒ ⅋

★★★ Park
New Road, Barnstaple EX32 9AE
☎ 01271-372166 **Fax** 01271-323157
E-mail info@parkhotel.co.uk

With the whole of North Devon on your doorstep,

the Park Hotel combines luxury with wonderful value. Every bedroom has a bathroom ensuite, and all facilities including satellite TV.
42 bedrs, all ensuite, ♀ ⚲ ⊁ ⸬ 100 **P** 100 ⊞
SB £54-£59 **DB** £70-£80 **HB** £315-£462 **L** £10.50 **L** ➤
D £16.50 **D** ➤ ✕ **LD** 21:00 **CC** MC Visa Amex DC

★★★ Royal & Fortescue
Boutport Street, Barnstaple EX31 3HG
☎ 01271-342289 **Fax** 01271-342289
E-mail info@royalfortescue.co.uk

Extensive refurbishments have retained the hotel's coaching inn charm while adding fine modern facilities. A top class restaurant, elegant bars and beautiful bedrooms with private bathrooms.
50 bedrs, all ensuite, ♀ ⚲ ⊁ ⸬ ⸬ 25 **P** 40 ⊞
SB £54-£59 **DB** £70-£80 **HB** £315-£488 **L** £9.50 **L** ➤
D £16.50 **D** ➤ ✕ **LD** 21:00 **CC** MC Visa Amex DC ⅋

★★ Downrew House ⌘
Bishops Tawton, Barnstaple EX32 0DY
☎ 01271-342497 **Fax** 01271-323947
E-mail downrew@globalnet.co.uk
12 bedrs, all ensuite, ♀ ⸬ 40 **P** 20 ⊞ Rest Resid
SB £55 **DB** £80-£94 **HB** £367-£410 **L** £15 **L** ➤ **D** £22.50
D ➤ ✕ **LD** 20:45 **CC** MC Visa Amex ⸾ ☒ ☒

☾ ★ ❖ Old Rectory
Martinhoe, Parracombe, Barnstaple EX31 4QT
☎ 01598-763368 **Fax** 01598-763567
Closed Nov-Easter
8 bedrs, all ensuite, ☒ **P** 14 No children under 14 ⊞
DB £99 **HB** £441 **D** £28.50 ✕ **LD** 19:30 ⅋

BARROW-IN-FURNESS Cumbria   10A3
Pop. 60,000. Ulverston 8½, London 280, Broughton-in-Furness 14 **EC** Thu **MD** Wed, Fri, Sat **see** Parish Churches, Ruins of Furness Abbey, Piel Island and Castle, Two Nature Reserves on Walney Island, Biggar Village ⌕ Forum 28, Duke Street 01229-870156

★★★ Abbey House

Abbey Road, Barrow-in-Furness LA13 0PA
📞 01229-838282 Fax 01229-820403
28 bedrs, all ensuite, ▦ ⤚ ☲ ⁂ 120 P 100 ⊞
SB £48-£78 DB £68-£88 L £6 L ⬤ D £15 D ⬤ ✕
LD 21:30 Restaurant closed L Sat ⟨⟨ MC Visa Amex
DC ♿

BARTON ON SEA Hampshire	4A4

Pop. 21,000. Lyndhurst 13, London 97, Blandford
Forum 26, Bournemouth 11, Lymington 7,
Ringwood 12 ⟪ Wed

★★ ❖ Cliff House

Marine Drive East, Barton on Sea BH25 7QL
📞 01425-619333 Fax 01425-612462
9 bedrs, all ensuite, ☒ P 50 No children under 14 ⊞
⟨⟨ MC Visa Amex JCB ♿

BARTON-UPON-HUMBER Lincolnshire	11E

★★★ Reeds ⛾ ⛾

Far-Ings Road, Barton-upon-Humber
DN18 5RG
📞 01652-632313 Fax 01652-636361
6 bedrs, all ensuite, ▦ ⌕ ☒ ⁂ 200 P 200 ⊞ SB £52
DB £67 L ⬤ D £22 D ⬤ ✕ LD 22:00 ⟨⟨ MC Visa Amex
DC JCB ♿

BASILDON Essex	5D2

Pop. 103,000. Romford 13, London 30, Brentwood
9, Chelmsford 13, Dartford Crossing 14, Southend
12 MD Mon, Tue, Thur, Fri, Sat see St Martin's Church
'Basildon Christ' sculpture by T Huxley-Jones,
Gloucester Park, Fairytale Clock

★★★ Posthouse   **Posthouse**

Cranes Farm Road, Basildon SS14 3DG
📞 01268-533955 Fax 01268-530119
149 bedrs, all ensuite, ⌕ ☲ ⁂ 250 P 200
⊞ SB £118.95 DB £118.95 L £10 L ⬤ D £10
D ⬤ ✕ LD 22:30 ⟨⟨ MC Visa Amex DC ♿

Don't forget to mention the guide

When booking direct, please remember to
tell the hotel that you chose it from
RAC Inspected Hotels 2000

Campanile Basildon **Lodge**

A127 Southend Arterial Road,
Pipps Hill, Basildon SS14 3AE
📞 01268-530810 Fax 01268-286710

Campanile hotels offer comfortable and convenient
budget accommodation and a traditional French style
Bistro providing freshly cooked food for breakfast,
lunch and dinner. All rooms ensuite with tea/coffee
making facilities, DDT and TV with Sky channels.
98 bedrs, all ensuite, ⌕ ⁂ 20 P 98 ⊞ Rest Resid
SB £42.50 DB £47 L £5.75 D £10.95 ✕ LD 22:00
⟨⟨ MC Visa Amex DC ♿

BASINGSTOKE Hampshire	4B3

M3 (jn 6) 1½, London 47, Alton 12, Andover 19,
Farnham 15, Newbury 16, Reading 16, Salisbury
36, Winchester 18 ⟪ Thu MD Wed, Sat see 15th cent
Church, Museum, War Memorial Park, The Vyne-
early 16th cent house (NT) 3m N, Willis Museum
ℹ Old Town Hall, Market Place 01256-817618

★★★★ Audleys Wood ⛾ ⛾ ⛾

Alton Road, Basingstoke RG25 2JT
📞 01256-817555 Fax 01256-817500

A 19th century country mansion set in seven acres
of landscaped and lightly wooded grounds. A
superb restaurant, beautifully furnished
accommodation and meeting facilities make this a
luxury hotel.
71 bedrs, all ensuite, ⌕ ⁂ 40 P 100 ⊞ ⟨⟨ MC Visa
Amex DC JCB ♿

★★★ Posthouse **Posthouse**
Grove Road, Basingstoke RG21 3EE
☎ 01256-468181 **Fax** 01256-840081
84 bedrs, all ensuite, ⊶ ▦ 150 **P** 150 ⏣ ((MC Visa
Amex DC ♿

★★★ Red Lion
London Street, Basingstoke RG21 7NY
☎ 01256-328525 **Fax** 01256-844056
E-mail redlion@msihotels.co.uk
59 bedrs, all ensuite, ▦ ♀ ⌀ ⊶ ⊡ ▦ 40 **P** 65 ⏣
SB £45-£92.50 **DB** £65-£112 **L** ➽ **D** £10 **D** ➽ ✕
LD 21:30 ((MC Visa Amex DC ▨

★★★ Romans ☷ ☷
Little London Road, Silchester, Reading RG7 2PN
☎ 01189-700421 **Fax** 01189-700691
25 bedrs, all ensuite, ⊶ ▦ 60 **P** 40 ⏣ ((MC Visa
Amex DC ⤳ ▣ ▨ ▨
See advert on this page

Ringway **Awaiting Inspection**
Aldermaston Roundabout, Ringway North,
Basingstoke RG24 9NU
☎ 01256-320212 **Fax** 01256-842835
134 bedrs, all ensuite, **P** 240 ⏣ ((MC Visa Amex
DC ▣ ▣ ▨ ▨

BASLOW Derbyshire   8A1
Pop. 1,200. Matlock 9, London 154, Ashbourne 21,
Buxton 14, Chesterfield 9, Leek 22, Sheffield 12 **see**
St Anne's Church, 17th cent bridge, Chatsworth
(House, Garden and Theatre Gallery)

★★★ Cavendish ☷ ☷
Blue Ribbon Hotel
Baslow DE45 1SP
☎ 01246-582311 **Fax** 01246-582312
E-mail cavendish1@aol.com

Country hotel, originally an 18th century fishing inn,
set on the Chatsworth Estate in the Peak District.
Elegant decor and furnishings, many from the great
house. Fine art, open log fires, fresh flowers.
23 bedrs, all ensuite, ▦ ▦ 18 **P** 40 ⏣ **SB** £106
DB £147 **L** £30.50 **L** ➽ **D** £38.75 **D** ➽ ✕ **LD** 22:00
((MC Visa Amex DC ▨

BASSENTHWAITE Cumbria   10A1
Pop. 530. Keswick 7, London 292, Carlisle 21,
Cockermouth 8, Penrith 23 **see** Old Church by Lake

★★ Ravenstone
Bassenthwaite CA12 4QG
☎ 017687-76240 **Fax** 017687-76733
Closed Nov-Feb
20 bedrs, all ensuite, ▦ ♀ ⊶ **P** 24 ⏣ **SB** £32-£35
DB £64-£70 **HB** £294-£301 **D** £14.50 ✕ **LD** 19:30 ▨

BATH Somerset   3F1
Pop. 80,000. M4 (jn 18) 9, London 104, Bristol 12,
Chippenham 13, Chepstow 25, Devizes 19, Frome
13, Radstock 8½, Tetbury 23, Warminster 16, Wells
19 **MD** Mon, Wed **see** Abbey Church, Pump Room &
Hot Springs, Roman Baths, Assembly Rooms and
Museum of Costume, Royal Crescent, Pulteney
Bridge, The American Museum in Britain (Claverton
Manor) 2m E, Herschel House & Museum ⓘ Abbey
Chambers, Abbey Church Yard 01225-462831

ENGLAND

★★★★★ Bath Spa

Sydney Road, Bath BA2 6JF
☎ 01225-444424 **Fax** 01225-444006
E-mail fivestar@bathspa.u-net.com
98 bedrs, all ensuite, ⁴ ⌀ ☂ ⊡ ⋕ 140
P 160 ⊞ **SB** £153.75-£173.75 **DB** £198.50-
£238.50 **HB** £554.40-£778.40 **L** £25 **L** ☕
D £39 **D** ☕ ✕ **LD** 22:00 ⓒ MC Visa Amex
DC JCB ▦ ▦ ▦ ▦ ⅋

★★★★★ Royal Crescent ♜ ♜ ♜ ♜

Blue Ribbon Hotel
Royal Crescent, Bath BA1 2LS
☎ 01225-823333 **Fax** 01225-339401

Situated in the centre of one of Europe's finest
architectural masterpieces with individually
designed bedrooms, two superb restaurants and
The Bath House - a unique spa. UK free phone:
0800 980 0987, UK free fax: 0800 980 0876
45 bedrs, all ensuite, ⁴ ⚥ ⌀ ☂ ⊡ ⋕ 100 ⊞ **DB** £219
L £12 **L** ☕ **D** £28 ✕ **LD** 21:30 ⓒ MC Visa Amex DC ▦
⅃ ▦ ⅋

★★★★ Bath Priory ♜ ♜ ♜ ♜

Blue Ribbon Hotel
Weston Road, Bath BA1 2XT
☎ 01225-331922 **Fax** 01225-448276
28 bedrs, all ensuite, ⁴ ⌀ ⋕ 60 **P** 26 ⊞ **SB** £140
DB £210 **L** £15 **L** ☕ **D** £35 ✕ **LD** 21:30 ⓒ MC Visa
Amex DC ▦ ⅃ ▦ ▦ ⅋
See advert on opposite page

★★★★ Combe Grove Manor
Hotel & Country Club
Brassknocker Hill, Monkton Combe,
Bath BA2 7HS
☎ 01225-834644 **Fax** 01225-834961

An elegant 18th century manor house hotel with
21st century sports and leisure facilities. Set in 82
acres of gardens and woodlands with panoramic
views, just 2 miles from Bath city centre.
40 bedrs, all ensuite, ⁴ ⋕ 80 **P** 150 ⊞ **SB** £99
DB £99 **L** £16.50 **D** £24.50 ✕ **LD** 21:30 ⓒ MC Visa
Amex DC ▦ ⅃ ▦ ▦ ▣ ▦

★★★★ Lucknam Park ♜ ♜ ♜

Gold Ribbon Hotel
Colerne SN14 8AZ
☎ 01225-742777 **Fax** 01225-743536
E-mail reservations@lucknampark.co.uk

A magnificent 1720 Palladian mansion set in 500
acres of parkland, six miles from Bath. Beautifully
decorated and sumptuously furnished in period
style, graced by antiques.
41 bedrs, all ensuite, ⁴ ⋕ 40 **P** 100 ⊞ **SB** £140-
£180 **DB** £180-£650 **HB** £220-£730 **L** £5.50 **D** £40 ✕
LD 21:30 Restaurant closed L Sun ⓒ MC Visa Amex
DC JCB ▦ ▦ ▦ ▦ ▦ ▦ ⅋

★★★ Abbey
North Parade, Bath BA1 1LF
☎ 01225-461603 **Fax** 01225-447758
E-mail ahres@compasshotels.co.uk
60 bedrs, all ensuite, ⌀ ☂ ⊡ ⋕ 12 ⊞ **SB** £68
DB £110 **HB** £357-£468 **L** £11 **D** £17.50 ✕ **LD** 21:15
Restaurant closed L Mon-Fri ⓒ MC Visa Amex DC
⅋

The Bath Priory Hotel and Restaurant

The Bath Priory is a Country House style hotel with a warm friendly atmosphere resting in four acres of its own award-winning gardens. it was built in 1835 as a private residence and remains one of the finest examples of Gothic architecture of its time.

Now beautifully converted, The Bath Priory offers visitors comfort, peace and privacy as well as luxurious health spa facilities. The hotel boasts a beautiful indoor swimming pool, Jacuzzi, solarium, sauna and well equipped gym for residents use.

It is located in a quiet suburb of Bath, less than a mile from the city centre adjoining Victoria Park and the Botanical Gardens.

Not only have we been awarded the coveted Blue Ribbon Award for four stars, but have also been named as "Bath's Premier Hotel." Head Chef Robert Clayton offers a varied Modern French and Mediterranean cuisine in his award-winning restaurant.

Weston Road, Bath BA1 2XT

Tel: (01225) 331922 Fax: (01225) 448276 E-mail: 106076.1265@compuserve.com

★★★ Dukes
Great Pulteney Street, Bath BA2 4DN
☎ 01225-463512 **Fax** 01225-483733
E-mail dukeshotel@btinternet.com

With 24 newly refurbished bedrooms, all with ensuite facilities, this Grade I Listed townhouse is just a short stroll from the Roman Baths and the Abbey.
24 bedrs, all ensuite, ✦ ⅲ 20 ⊞ ℂℂ MC Visa Amex DC

★★★ Francis
Queen Square, Bath BA1 2HH
☎ 01225-424257 **Fax** 01225-319715
94 bedrs, all ensuite, 🔲 ✦ 🔲 ⅲ 80 **P** 45 ⊞ **SB** £94-£99 **DB** £128-£168 **HB** £398-£438 **L** 🍷 **D** £22.95 **D** 🍷 ✕ **LD** 22:00 ℂℂ MC Visa Amex DC JCB

Heritage HOTELS

★★★ Queensberry ⅲ ⅲ ⅲ
Blue Ribbon Hotel
Russel Street, Bath BA1 2QF
☎ 01225-447928 **Fax** 01225-446065
E-mail queensberry@dial.pipex.com
Closed Christmas

A luxury privately owned town house hotel in Georgian Bath. Minutes from the Royal Crescent, Roman Baths and Pump Rooms. Its restaurant, the Olive Tree, is nationally renowned for informal contemporary British cooking.
29 bedrs, all ensuite, 🔲 🖉 🔲 ⅲ 25 **P** 5 ⊞ Rest Resid **SB** £89-£110 **DB** £129-£210 **L** £14.50 **D** £24 ✕ **LD** 22:00 Restaurant closed L Sun ℂℂ MC Visa ♿

★★ Bath Tasburgh ⅲ
Warminster Road, Bath BA2 6SH
☎ 01225-425096 **Fax** 01225-463842
E-mail hotel@bathtasburgh.demon.co.uk

Victorian mansion with gardens stretching down to the canal. Spectacular views. Well appointed ensuite bedrooms. Elegant drawing room. Stunning conservatory. Evening meals. Licensed. Ample parking. Caring service.
12 bedrs, all ensuite, 🔲 🖂 ⅲ 15 **P** 15 ⊞ Resid **SB** £48-£58 **DB** £68-£90 **D** £19.50 ✕ **LD** 20:00 ℂℂ MC Visa Amex DC
See advert on opposite page

★★ ✤ George's
2-3 South Parade, Bath BA2 4AA
☎ 01225-464923 **Fax** 01225-425471
E-mail info@georgeshotel.co.uk
Closed 25-26 Dec

Grade I Listed building (1743) in city centre between Abbey and stations. Near to Roman Baths

and shopping areas and adjacent to public car park. Fully licensed. Short breaks available.
19 bedrs, all ensuite, 4 ♪ ∺ 35 ⊕ SB £45-£55 DB £55-£70 L £6.50 L ♥ D £10 D ♥ ✕ LD 23:00 ⓒ MC Visa Amex

★★ Limpley Stoke
Lower Limpley Stoke, Bath BA3 6HZ
📞 01225-723333 Fax 01225-722406

Bath's country hotel set in a village location overlooking the magnificent Avon valley. Large public rooms and tastefully decorated bedrooms. Relaxing informal atmosphere with attentive service.
67 bedrs, all ensuite, ☎ ∺ 120 P 70 ⊕ ⓒ MC Visa Amex DC ⊡ ▣

★★ Old Mill
Tollbridge Road, Batheaston, Bath BA1 7DE
📞 01225-858476 Fax 01225-852600

Beautifully located by the River Avon and only 1½ miles from the centre of Bath. All 27 bedrooms and the Waterwheel Grill Restaurant are newly refurbished. Pretty gardens lead to the river overlooked by the restaurant and relaxing conservatory bar.
26 bedrs, all ensuite, 4 ∺ 100 P 40 ⊕ SB £45 DB £60 L £8 D £12 ✕ LD 22:00 ⓒ MC Visa Amex JCB ⊡

BATLEY West Yorkshire   11D4
Pop. 41,300. M62 (jn 27) 2, Dewsbury 2, London 189, Bradford 7½, Halifax 11, Huddersfield 9, Leeds 7 **EC** Tue **MD** Fri, Sat **see** Ancient Church, Oakwell Hall, Bagshaw Museum

★★ Alder House ₰
Towngate Road, Healey Lane,
Batley WF17 7HR
📞 01924-444777 Fax 01924-442644

A Georgian house hotel set in delightful grounds, tastefully decorated with full facilities. Ideal for weekend breaks, within easy reach of the Royal Armories Museum and Bronte Country.
20 bedrs, all ensuite, 4 ⊢ ∺ 80 P 52 ⊕ SB £48.50-£58.50 DB £65-£75 L £8 D £16.50 ✕ LD 21:30 Restaurant closed L Sat, D Sun ⓒ MC Visa Amex DC

BATTLE East Sussex   5E4
Pop. 6,300. Hurst Green 7½, London 57, Eastbourne 15, Hastings 6½, Lewes 24, Tenterden 18, Uckfield 20 EC Wed MD Fri see Abbey ruins, 15th cent Pilgrim's Rest, St Mary's Church, The Deanery, Bullring, Windmill, Langton House Museum *i* 88 High Street 01424-773721

★★★ Netherfield Place ♟ ♟ ♟
Blue Ribbon Hotel
Netherfield, Battle TN33 9PP
☎ 01424-774455 Fax 01424-774024
E-mail reservations@netherfieldplace.co.uk

Attractive Georgian style country house set in 30 acres of oakland. Elegant furnishings, fresh flowers, log fires and a host of extras in the bedrooms add to the country house atmosphere.
14 bedrs, all ensuite, 4 ⋔ ⁂ 75 P 31 ⊞ SB £68 DB £120 L £16 L ⬤ D £28 D ⬤ ✕ LD 21:30 CC MC Visa Amex DC JCB ℙ ▨

★★★ Powder Mills ♟
Powdermill Lane, Battle TN33 0SP
☎ 01424-775511 Fax 01424-774540
E-mail powdc@aol.com
35 bedrs, all ensuite, 4 ⋗ ⋔ ⁂ 250 P 120 ⊞ Rest Resid SB £65-£75 DB £95-£150 HB £400-£500 L £15 L ⬤ D £25.50 D ⬤ ✕ LD 21:00 CC MC Visa Amex DC ♨ ▨ ♿
See advert on this page

BEACONSFIELD Buckinghamshire   4C2
Pop. 11,000. M40 (jn 2) 1, London 24, Aylesbury 20, Henley-on-Thames 16, High Wycombe 6, Reading 21, Slough 7½ EC Wed see Church, The Old Rectory, Bekonscot Model Village

ENGLAND

★★ ✧ Chequers Inn
Kiln Lane, Wooburn Common, Beaconsfield
HP10 0JQ
☎ 01628-529575 Fax 01628-850124
E-mail info@chequers-inn.com
17 bedrs, all ensuite, 4 ‖‖ 60 P 60 ⊕ SB £92.50
DB £97.50 L £17.95 L ♥ D £21.95 D ♥ ✕ LD 21:30
《 MC Visa DC
See advert on opposite page

BEANACRE Wiltshire   3F1
Chippenham 5, M4 (jn 17) 9, London 96, Bath 14,
Devizes 9½, Melksham 2

★★★ Beechfield House ⌁ ⌁
Beanacre, Melksham SN12 7PU
☎ 01225-703700 Fax 01225-790118

A comfortable privately owned country house hotel
and restaurant, set in eight acres of secluded
gardens and comprising 21 bedrooms, 2 drawing
rooms and a heated outdoor swimming pool.
21 bedrs, all ensuite, 4 ‖‖ 25 P 50 No children
under 10 ⊕ SB £75-£90 DB £95-£120 ✕ LD 21:00
《 MC Visa Amex DC ⅋

BEAULIEU Hampshire   4B4
Pop. 800. London 86, Lymington 6½, Lyndhurst
7½, Romsey 14, Southampton 13 see Beaulieu
Abbey, Palace House and National Motor Museum,
Exebury Gardens 3m SE, Maritime Museum at
Bucklers Hard

★★★ ✧ Beaulieu
Beaulieu Road, Beaulieu SO42 7YQ
☎ 01703-293344 Fax 01703-292729
E-mail information@carehotels.co.uk
18 bedrs, 17 ensuite, 1 ⋔ ⊨ ‖‖ 40 P 50 ⊕ SB £65-
£70 DB £110-£125 HB £345 D £21.50 ✕ LD 20:45
《 MC Visa Amex DC ⒊ ▣ &

★★★ Montagu Arms ⌁ ⌁
Beaulieu SO4 27ZL
☎ 01590-612324 Fax 01590-612188
E-mail enquire@montagu-arms.co.uk
24 bedrs, all ensuite, 4 ♪ ⊨ ‖‖ 45 P 86 ⊕ SB £72
DB £125 L £14.50 L ♥ D £25.90 D ♥ ✕ LD 21:30
《 MC Visa Amex DC
See advert on this page

BEDFORD Bedfordshire   4C1
Pop. 77,000. Luton 19, London 50, M1 (jn 13) 10,
Aylesbury 30, Biggleswade 11, Bletchley 16,
Cambridge 30, Dunstable 19, Huntingdon 21,
Northampton 22 E Thu MD Wed, Sat see Higgins Art
Gallery, Museum, Bedford School, Churches,
Bunyan Museum ⓘ 10 St Paul's Square 01234-
215226

★★★ Bedford Swan
The Embankment, Bedford MK40 1RW
☎ 01234-346565 Fax 01234-212009
110 bedrs, all ensuite, ♪ ⊨ ⊟ ‖‖ 250 P 90 ⊕
SB £79.25 DB £94 L £15.50 L ♥ D £15.50 D ♥ ✕
LD 21:30 《 MC Visa Amex DC ⒊

LAWS HOTEL

Situated just 8 miles from Bedford and Northampton, this superb country house hotel boasts 4-poster bedrooms, a Leisure Centre and award-winning cuisine!

HIGH STREET, TURVEY, BEDFORDSHIRE MK43 8DB
Tel: 01234 881213
Fax: 01234 888864

THE BLUE BELL HOTEL

Perfectly situated between Northumberland's magnificent coastline and superb National Parks, the Hotel offers delightful en-suite bedrooms, excellent cuisine in the three individual restaurants and merit awards for comfort, hospitality and service.

Short breaks for golf, birdwatching and walking are available all year round.

MARKET PLACE, BELFORD, NORTHUMBERLAND NE70 7NE
Tel: 01668-213543 Fax: 01668-213787
E-mail: bluebel@globalnet.co.uk

★★★ Woodlands Manor ⓡ
Green Lane, Clapham, Bedford MK41 6EP
☎ 01234-363281 **Fax** 01234-272390
E-mail woodlands.manor@pageant.co.uk

A secluded manor house set in gardens two miles from the centre of Bedford and within easy access of the M1/A1 an hour from London.
33 bedrs, all ensuite, 團 ♀ ⚓ ⚎ 40 **P** 100 ⊞ **SB** £75 **DB** £85 **L** £9.95 **L** ⚑ **D** £19.95 **D** ⚑ ✕ **LD** 21:45
Restaurant closed L Sat ₵ MC Visa Amex JCB

★★ Knife & Cleaver ⓡ
The Grove, Houghton Conquest, Bedford MK45 3LA
☎ 01234-740387 **Fax** 01234-740900
Closed 27-30 Dec
9 bedrs, all ensuite, ⚓ ⚎ 12 **P** 26 ⊞ **SB** £49-£59 **DB** £64-£74 **L** £12 **L** ⚑ **D** £20 **D** ⚑ ✕ **LD** 21:30
Restaurant closed D Sun ₵ MC Visa Amex DC JCB

★★ Laws
High Street, Turvey MK43 8DB
☎ 01234-881213 **Fax** 01234-888864
19 bedrs, all ensuite, 團 ⚎ 75 **P** 30 ⊞ ₵ MC Visa Amex DC ▣ ▣ ৬
See advert on this page

BELFORD Northumberland   13F3
Pop. 950. Alnwick 15, London 322, Berwick-upon-Tweed 15, Coldstream 20 ℻ Thu see St Mary's Church

★★★ ✢ Blue Bell
Market Place, Belford NE70 7NE
☎ 01668-213543 **Fax** 01668-213787
E-mail bluebel@globalnet.co.uk
17 bedrs, all ensuite, 團 ⚓ ⚎ 130 **P** 20 ⊞ **SB** £42 **DB** £84-£88 **HB** £315 **L** £7 **D** £21 ✕ **LD** 21:00 ₵ MC Visa Amex ৬
See advert on this page

BELLINGHAM Northumberland 13E4
Pop. 900. Corbridge 18, London 295, Brampton 33, Hawick 38, Newcastle upon Tyne 32 **EC** Tue, Sat **see** Kielder Forest and Water (largest reservoir in Britain) **i** Main Street 01434-220616

★★ Riverdale Hall
Hexham, Bellingham NE48 2JT
☎ 01434-220254 **Fax** 01434-220457

A stone-built 19th century mansion with a modern wing set in five acres of grounds alongside the North Tyne River.
20 bedrs, all ensuite, ⊞ ⟲ ⫲ 35 **P** 40 ⊕ **CC** MC Visa Amex DC ▣ ▣ ▣

BERKELEY Gloucestershire 7E4
Tetbury 13, London 111, M5 (jn 14) 2

★★★ Prince of Wales
Berkeley Road, Berkeley GL13 9HD
☎ 01453-810474 **Fax** 01453-511370

A privately owned hotel with welcoming friendly staff. Modern bedrooms, superb restaurant and the old Coaching Inn bar, which reflects its 100 year history.
43 bedrs, all ensuite, ⟲ ⫲ 150 **P** 100 ⊕ **SB** £56-£60 **DB** £72-£76 **L** ❦ **D** ❦ ✕ **LD** 21:30 Restaurant closed D Sun **CC** MC Visa Amex DC ▣

BERKSWELL Warwickshire 8A3
Coventry 6, London 100, M42 7, Birmingham 12, Kenilworth 7 **see** Church (Saxon and Normal crypts)

★★★★ Nailcote Hall ⫲ ⫲ ⫲
Nailcote Lane, Berkswell CV7 7DE
☎ 024-7646 6174 **Fax** 024-7647 0720
E-mail info@nailcotehall.co.uk

A beautifully refurbished and extended Elizabethan Hall, set in 15 acres of gardens, with a championship 9 hole par 3 golf course, leisure club, tennis courts and regular live entertainment programme. Just 10 minutes from NEC and motorway network.
38 bedrs, all ensuite, ⊞ ⟲ ⊡ ⫲ 100 **P** 170 ⊕ **SB** £135 **DB** £155 **L** £21.50 **L** ❦ **D** £29.50 ✕ **LD** 22:00 **CC** MC Visa Amex DC ▣ ▣ ▣ ▣ ▣ ▣ ▣ ⟲
See advert on this page

BERWICK-UPON-TWEED Northumberland   13E2
Pop. 12,000. Alnwick 30, London 337, Coldstream 14, Haddington 39, Lauder 32 **EC** Thu **MD** Wed, Fri, Sat *see* Elizabethan Ramparts, 18th cent Georgian Walls, Castle Remains, 17th cent Jacobean Bridge and modern bridges ⓘ Castlegate Car Park 01289-330733

★★★ King's Arms
Hide Hill, Berwick-upon-Tweed TD15 1EJ
☎ 01289-307454 **Fax** 01289-308867
36 bedrs, all ensuite, ④ ✠ ⦂ 160 ⊕ **SB** £60-£70 **DB** £80-£100 **L** £7 **L** ● **D** £13.75 **D** ● ✕ **LD** 22:00 ℂℂ MC Visa Amex DC
See advert on this page

★ Queens Head
Sandgate, Berwick-upon-Tweed TD15 1EP
☎ 01289-307852 **Fax** 01289 307852

Family run hotel situated near the town centre and adjacent to the historic town walls. Choice of two golf courses within easy reach.
6 bedrs, all ensuite, ✠ ⊕ **SB** £30-£35 **DB** £50-£55 **HB** £245 **L** £9 **L** ● **D** £15 **D** ● ✕ **LD** 21:00 ℂℂ MC Visa

---

BEVERLEY East Yorkshire   11E3
Pop. 23,000. Lincoln 46, London 179, Bridlington 22, Hull 8½, Malton 27, Market Weighton 10, Scarborough 33. **MD** Wed, Sat *see* Minster, 15th cent North Bar, Art Gallery and Museum, Market cross. ⓘ Guildhall, Register Square 01482 867430

★★★ Tickton Grange ⓡ ⓡ
Tickton, Beverley HU17 9SH
☎ 01964-543666 **Fax** 01964-542556
17 bedrs, all ensuite, ④ ✎ ⦂ 80 **P** 65 ⊕ **SB** £68.50 **DB** £92 **L** £15.95 **D** £25 **D** ● ✕ **LD** 21:30 ℂℂ MC Visa Amex DC

★★ Manor House ⓡ ⓡ ⓡ
Northlands, Walkington, Beverley HU17 8RT
☎ 01482-881645 **Fax** 01482-866501
E-mail derek@the-manor-house.co.uk
7 bedrs, all ensuite, ✠ ⦂ 20 **P** 50 ⊕ Resid **SB** £74 **DB** £93 **D** £18.50 ✕ **LD** 21:15 Restaurant closed D Sun ℂℂ MC Visa

---

BEWDLEY Worcestershire   7E3
Pop. 10,000. Kidderminster 3, London 126, Bridgnorth 15, Bromyard 19, Droitwich 13, Leominster 24, Ludlow 19, Worcester 15 **EC** Wed **MD** Tue, Sat *see* Forest of Wyre, St Anne's Church, old Tudor houses and inns, Georgian houses, fine bridge (1797, by Telford) ⓘ St. George's Hall, Load Street 01299-404740

★★ George
Load Street, Bewdley DY12 2AW
☎ 01299-402117 **Fax** 01299-401269
11 bedrs, all ensuite, ④ ⦂ 50 **P** 50 ⊕ **SB** £45 **DB** £62 **HB** £270 **L** ● **D** £9.50 **D** ● ✕ **LD** 21:30 Restaurant closed D Sun-Mon, L Mon ℂℂ MC Visa Amex JCB

BEXLEY Kent   5D2
Pop. 220,000. London 15, Dartford 3½, Sidcup 2½

★★★ Posthouse **Posthouse**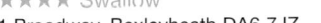
Black Prince Interchange,
Southwold Road, Bexley DA5 1ND
📞 01322-526900 **Fax** 01322-526113
105 bedrs, all ensuite, ⊶ 🖭 ⸬ 70 **P** 200 ⏢
SB £108.95 **DB** £118.90 **L** £7.95 **D** £10.75 ✕ **LD** 22:30
《 MC Visa Amex DC 🖾 ᜕

BEXLEYHEATH Kent 5D2

★★★★ Swallow
1 Broadway, Bexleyheath DA6 7JZ
📞 0181-298 1000 **Fax** 0181-298 1234
E-mail info@swallowhotels.com

This innovatively designed hotel is convenient for
London, the Channel Tunnel and ports. Luxurious
and air-conditioned throughout, it has two
restaurants and extensive leisure facilities.
142 bedrs, all ensuite, ⊶ 🖭 ⸬ 250 **P** 80 ⏢ **SB** £105
DB £130 **L** £14 **D** £19.75 ✕ **LD** 22:30 《 MC Visa
Amex DC 🖎 🖾 ᜕

BIBURY Gloucestershire 7F4
Pop. 524. Faringdon 14, London 84, Burford 10,
Cirencester 7, Cheltenham 17, Stow-on-the-Wold
14 **EC** Wed **see** Interesting Church, Arlington Row
(15th cent cottages), Arlington Mill Museum,
Wildfowl Reserve (NT), Trout Hatchery

★★★ Bibury Court ⩇ ⩇ ⩇
Bibury GL7 5NT
📞 01285-740337 **Fax** 01285-740660
Closed 21-30 Dec
19 bedrs, all ensuite, ④ ♨ ⊶ ⸬ 20 **P** 100 ⏢ **SB** £68-
£72 **DB** £95-£110 **L** ⬤ **D** £25 **D** ⬤ ✕ **LD** 21:00 《 MC
Visa Amex DC JCB 🖵
See advert on this page

BIDEFORD Devon 2C2
Pop. 12,200. Barnstaple 9, London 202, Bude 25,
Holsworthy 18, Okehampton 26 **EC** Wed **MD** Tue **see**

Royal Hotel (assoc. with Kingsley). Kingsley Statue,
Chudleigh Fort, Burton Art Gallery, St Mary's
Church, Victoria Park (Armada guns) 🖸 Victoria
Park, The Quay 01237-477676

★★★ Royal
Barnstaple Street, Bideford EX39 4AE
📞 01237-472005 **Fax** 01237-478957
E-mail info@royalbideford.co.uk

Enjoy unexpectedly fine dining in the Regency
restaurant, and always with a more personal touch.
Every bedroom has a private bathroom.
31 bedrs, all ensuite, ♀ ♨ ⊶ 🖭 ⸬ 40 **P** 60 ⏢
SB £54-£59 **DB** £60-£70 **HB** £315-£474 **L** £9.50
D £16.50 **D** ⬤ ✕ **LD** 21:00 《 MC Visa Amex DC

★★ Hoops Inn ⌇ ⌇ ⌇
Horns Cross, Clovelly, Bideford EX39 5DL
📞 01237-451222 **Fax** 01237-451247
12 bedrs, all ensuite, ⊞ ⋗ ✝ ⧈ 40 **P** 100 No
children under 10 ⊞ **SB** £40-£50 **DB** £60-£66 **HB** £300-
£315 **L** £8.50 **D** £19.50 **D** ⬤ ✕ **LD** 21:30 **CC** MC Visa
Amex DC JCB ▦

★★ Riversford
Limers Lane, Bideford EX39 2RG
📞 01237-474239 **Fax** 01237-421661
14 bedrs, all ensuite, ⊞ ✝ ⧈ 60 **P** 16 ⊞ **SB** £40
DB £60-£82 **HB** £266-£298 **L** £9 **D** £16 ✕ **LD** 21:30
CC MC Visa Amex DC JCB ♿

BIRKENHEAD Merseyside   10B4
See also WALLASEY
Pop. 99,500. Chester 15, London 197, M53 (jn 3) 3,
Liverpool 2, Queensferry 14 **EC** Thu **MD** Daily **see**
Priory ruins, Town Hall, Williamson Art Gallery,
Queen Victoria memorial (styled in form of an
Eleanor Cross) 🅸 Woodside Ferry Terminal 0151-
647 6780

★★ ✣ Riverhill
Talbot Road, Oxton, Birkenhead L43 2HJ
📞 0151-653 3773 **Fax** 0151-653 7162
16 bedrs, all ensuite, ⊞ **P** 25 ⊞ **CC** MC Visa Amex
DC ♿

BIRMINGHAM West Midlands   7F3
See also SOLIHULL and SUTTON COLDFIELD
Pop. 1,024,000. Coventry 18, London 111, A38(M)
1½, Bromsgrove 13, Droitwich 19, Kidderminster
17, Lichfield 15, Nuneaton 21, Sutton Coldfield 7,
Walsall 8½, Warwick 21, Wolverhampton 13 **EC** Wed
MD Daily **see** University Buildings, Art Gallery and
Museum, Town Hall, Museum of Science and
Industry, Engineering and Building Centre,
Botanical Gardens, Midlands Art Centre, Sarehole
Mill, Aston Hall (Jacobean), 16th cent Blakesley
Hall 🅸 National Exhibition Centre 0121-780 4321
and 2 City Arcade. 0121-643 2514

★★★★★ Swallow ⌇ ⌇ ⌇
12 Hagley Road, Birmingham
B16 8SJ
📞 0121-452 1144 **Fax** 0121-456 3442
E-mail info@swallowhotels.com

The Swallow is an elegant, five star, Edwardian
style hotel with a luxurious leisure club. The hotel
has awards for fine food. A gourmet's delight.
98 bedrs, all ensuite, ⊞ ✝ 🔲 ⧈ 20 **P** 70 ⊞ **SB** £150
DB £170 **L** £18.50 **D** £27 ✕ **LD** 22:30 Restaurant
closed L Sat **CC** MC Visa Amex DC ▥ ▦ ♿

★★★★ ✣ Burlington
Burlington Arcade, 126 New Street,
Birmingham B2 4JQ
📞 0121-643 9191 **Fax** 0121-628 5005
E-mail mail@burlingtonhotel.com

Long established as one of Birmingham's pre-
eminent hotels, the Burlington's central location
and proximity to the railway station allows
comfortable access to all the city's major tourist
and business venues.
112 bedrs, all ensuite, ⊞ ⋗ ✝ 🔲 ⧈ 400 ⊞
SB £132.50 **DB** £168 **L** £25 **L** ⬤ **D** £25 ✕ **LD** 21:30
CC MC Visa Amex DC ▦ ▩

★★★★ Copthorne
Paradise Circus, Birmingham B3 3HJ
📞 0121-200 2727 **Fax** 0121-200 1197
E-mail sales.birmingham@mill-cops.com
212 bedrs, all ensuite, ⋗ ✝ 🔲 ⧈ 180 **P** 80 ⊞
SB £142.75-£162.75 **DB** £175.50-£195.50 **L** £15 **L** ⬤
D £20 **D** ⬤ ✕ **LD** 23:00 **CC** MC Visa Amex DC ▥ ▦ ▩
♿

★★★ Great Barr
Pear Tree Drive, Newton Road Great Barr,
Birmingham B43 6HS
☎ 0121-357 1141 **Fax** 0121-357 7557
105 bedrs, all ensuite, ⚌ 120 **P** 175 ⊞ ⚌ MC Visa
Amex DC

★★★ Novotel Birmingham Centre
70 Broad Street, Birmingham B1 2HT
☎ 0121-643 2000 **Fax** 0121-643 9796
E-mail h1077@accor-hotels.com
148 bedrs, all ensuite, ♀ ⌁ ⊁ ▣ ⚌ 300 **P** 56 ⊞
SB £65-£115 **DB** £65-£125 **L** £14.50 **L** ⚌ **D** £16 **D** ⚌ ✕
LD 0:00 ⚌ MC Visa Amex DC ⊠ ▦ ⎈

★★★ ✦ Portland
313 Hagley Road, Edgbaston, Birmingham B16
9LQ
☎ 0121-455 0535 **Fax** 0121-456 1841
E-mail sales@portland-hotel.demon.co.uk
63 bedrs, all ensuite, ▣ ⚌ 80 **P** 80 ⊞ Rest Resid
⚌ MC Visa Amex DC

★★★ Posthouse   **Posthouse**
Birmingham City
Smallbrook, Queensway, B5 4EW
☎ 0121-643 8171 **Fax** 0121-631 2528
251 bedrs, all ensuite, ⊁ ▣ ⚌ 680 ⊞ ⚌ MC Visa
Amex DC ⊠ ⊠ ▦ ⊠

★★★ Posthouse Great Barr   **Posthouse**
Chapel Lane, Great Barr, B43 7BG
☎ 0121-357 7444 **Fax** 0121-357 7503
251 bedrs, all ensuite, ⊁ ▣ ⚌ 630 **P** 400 ⊞
SB £108.95 **DB** £118.90 **L** £12.95 **L** ⚌ **D** £17.25 **D** ⚌
✕ **LD** 22:30 ⚌ MC Visa Amex DC ⊠ ⊠ ▦ ⊠ ⎈

★★★ Quality
116 Hagley Road, Birmingham B16 9NZ
☎ 0121-454 6621
E-mail admin@gb605.u-net.com

Situated within easy reach of Birmingham city
centre on the A456, the Quality provides easy
access to the motorway network and Stratford, the

Cotswolds, the Severn valley and Warwick. With its
own leisure centre, its ideal for short breaks and
holidays.
230 bedrs, all ensuite, ⚌ 100
⊞ ⚌ MC Visa ⊠ ⊠ ▦

★★★ Quality
267 Hagley Road, Birmingham B16 9NA
☎ 0121-454 8071 **Fax** 0121-455 6149
E-mail admin@gb606.u-net.com

Set in its own gardens, only 2 miles from
Birmingham city centre and offering the
comfortable Edgbaston Bar and welcoming
Headingly Restaurant. Ideal for visting the famous
Cadbury World and National Sealife Centre or for a
weekend's shopping
210 bedrs, all ensuite, ♀ ⌁ ⊁ ▣ ⚌ 80
⊞ **SB** £80.75-£92.75 **DB** £102.50-£115.50
L ⚌ **D** £14.95 **D** ⚌ ✕ **LD** 21:15 Restaurant
closed L Sun ⚌ MC Visa Amex DC ⊠ ⎈

★★★ ✦ Quality Sutton Court
60 Lichfield Road,
Sutton Coldfield B74 2NA
☎ 0870-6011160 **Fax** 01543 481551
E-mail reservations@sutton-court-hotel.co.uk

Customer satisfaction, quality and friendliness are
key words at the Sutton Court hotel. Experience
excellent service and hospitality that is second to
none.
64 bedrs, all ensuite, ⊠ ⊁ ⚌ 100
P 90 ⊞ ⚌ MC Visa Amex DC

ENGLAND

Woodlands Hotel
and Restaurant

Ideal base for visitors to the Midlands.
Our Restaurant and Bar provides excellent cuisine
accompanied by fine wines.
All our rooms are tastefully decorated with en suite
facilities, colour television, radio alarm, telephone and
tea/coffee making facilities.
A full English breakfast is also included in our room rates.
Our Restaurant and Radmila Suite may be reserved for
conferences, sales meetings, luncheons or for those
special celebrations.
Your satisfaction is our future.
**379/381 HAGLEY ROAD, EDGBASTON,
BIRMINGHAM B17 8DL**
Tel: 0121 420 2341 Fax: 0121 429 3935
http://www.SmoothHound.co.uk/

★★★ Westley
Westley Road, Acocks Green, Birmingham B27 7UJ
☎ 0121-706 4312 Fax 0121-706 2824
36 bedrs, all ensuite, 4 ⊁ ♨ 250 P 200 ⊞
SB £49.45-£76.90 DB £57.40-£94.85 D £13.95 ✕
LD 22:00 ⊄ MC Visa Amex DC

★★ ✦ Bailey House
21 Sandon Road, Edgbaston, B17 8DR
☎ 0121-429 1929
15 bedrs, 6 ensuite, 5 ⋒ P 14 No children under 5
⊞ Resid SB £35 DB £50 ✕ LD 19:30 Restaurant
closed D Sun ⊄ MC Visa Amex

★★ Beechwood
201 Bristol Road, Edgbaston, B5 7UB
☎ 0121-440 2133 Fax 0121-446 4549
18 bedrs, 16 ensuite, ⊁ ♨ 100 P 30 ⊞ ⊄ MC Visa
Amex DC

★★ Norwood ⊟
87/89 Bunbury Road, Northfield, B31 2ET
☎ 0121-411 2202 Fax 0121-411 2202
E-mail norwoodhot@aol.uk
18 bedrs, all ensuite, ⊁ ♨ 24 P 11 ⊞ Rest Resid
SB £50-£77.50 DB £55-£82.50 D £17.50 ✕ LD 20:45
Restaurant closed D Fri-Sun ⊄ MC Visa Amex DC
JCB

★★ ✦ Woodlands Hotel
& Restaurant
379/381 Hagley Road, Edgbaston, B17 8DL
☎ 0121-420 2341 Fax 0121-429 3935
21 bedrs, 20 ensuite, 1 ⋒ ♀ ♪ ♨ 100 P 20 ⊞
SB £44-£50 DB £56-£64 L £8 L ♥ D £13 D ♥ ✕
LD 22:00 ⊄ MC Visa Amex JCB ⊠
See advert on this page

Clarine Lodge
229 Hagley Rd, Edgbaston, Birmingham B16 9RP
☎ 0121-454 6514 Fax 0121-456 2722
Closed Christmas-New Year

Clarine hotels comprise independent hotels
assuring you of a high standard of quality and
service during your stay. All bedrooms ensuite with
tea/coffee making facilities, DDT, TV and classic
French literature for your enjoyment.
27 bedrs, all ensuite, ♀ ♨ 14 P 30 ⊞ Rest Resid
SB £30-£45 DB £40-£58 L ♥ D £6.50 D ♥ ✕ LD 21:30
Restaurant closed L & D Sat-Sun ⊄ MC Visa Amex
DC JCB

Campanile Birmingham Lodge
Aston Lock South, Chester Street,
Birmingham B6 4BE
☎ 0121-359 3330 Fax 0121-359 1223

Campanile hotels offer comfortable and convenient
budget accommodation and a traditional French
style Bistro providing freshly cooked food for
breakfast, lunch and dinner. All rooms ensuite with

tea/coffee making facilities, DDT and TV with Sky channels.
111 bedrs, all ensuite, ⠿ **P** ⊕ ℂℂ MC Visa Amex DC ♿

BIRMINGHAM AIRPORT West Midlands   8A3
See also HAMPTON-IN-ARDEN
Coventry 11, London 105, Atherstone 15, Birmingham 7, Sutton Coldfield 11

★★★ ✧ Novotel Birmingham Airport
Birmingham International Airport, Birmingham B26 3QL
📞 0121-782 7000   **Fax** 0121-782 0445
E-mail h1158@accor-hotels.com
195 bedrs, all ensuite, ⋄ ⌁ ▣ ⠿ 35 ⊕ **SB** £63-£108.50 **DB** £73-£118 **L** £12.75 **D** £18.50 ✕ **LD** 0:00 ℂℂ MC Visa Amex DC ♿

★★★ Posthouse   **Posthouse**
Coventry Road,
Birmingham Airport B26 3QW
📞 0121-782 8141   **Fax** 0121-782 2476
141 bedrs, 14 ensuite, ⌁ ⠿ 150 **P** 200 ⊕ ℂℂ MC Visa Amex DC ♿

Helme Park Hall
Country House Hotel

Fir Tree (A68)
County Durham

Ancient country house, with spectacular views.
Superb reputation for food, hospitality and comfort.
Highly convenient location for the Businessman and Tourist.
The warmest welcome in the North.

FIR TREE
BISHOP AUCKLAND
CO. DURHAM DL13 4NW
Phone and Fax 01388 730970

BISHOP AUCKLAND Co. Durham   11D1
Pop. 26,000. West Auckland 3, London 251, Darlington 11, Durham 11, Middleton-in-Teesdale 19, Stockton 19 **EC** Wed **MD** Sat **see** 12th cent Church, Roman Heating Chamber at Vinovium (Binchester), Saxon Church (Escomb), Auckland Castle, residence of the Bishops of Durham, since 12th cent (Chapel viewable by arr) ⓘ Town Hall, Market Place 01388-604922

★★★ Helme Park Hall
Near Fir Tree, Bishop Auckland DL13 4NW
📞 01388-730970   **Fax** 01388-730970
13 bedrs, all ensuite, ⊞ ⠿ 150 **P** 70 ⊕ **SB** £41 **DB** £67 **D** £17 ✕ **LD** 21:30 ℂℂ MC Visa Amex ♿
See advert on this page

BLACKBURN Lancashire   10B4
Pop. 105,000. Bolton 13, London 208, Burnley 11, Bury 15, Chorley 10, Preston 10, Rochdale 18, Skipton 28, Whalley 7 **EC** Thu **MD** Wed, Fri, Sat **see** Cathedral, Museum and Art Gallery, Lewis Textile Museum ⓘ King George's Hall, Northgate 01254-53277

★★★ Mytton Fold Farm
Whalley Road, Langho, BB6 8AB
📞 01254-240662   **Fax** 01254-248119
E-mail mytton_fold.hotel@virgin.net

Set in 6 acres of beautiful gardens and surrounded by a picturesque 18 hole golf course (Par 72), the hotel is a friendly haven of peace. Built of local stone.
28 bedrs, all ensuite, ⊞ ♀ ⋄ ⠿ 300 **P** 150 No children under 5 ⊕ Rest Club Resid **SB** £43-£65 **DB** £70-£90 **L** £8.75 **D** £16 ✕ **LD** 21:30 ℂℂ MC Visa Amex ▣ ▩ ♿

★★ Millstone Hotel
Church Lane, Mellor, Blackburn BB2 7JR
📞 01254-813333   **Fax** 01254-812628
E-mail millstone@shireinns.co.uk
24 bedrs, all ensuite, ⌁ **P** 40 ⠿ 25 ⊕ **SB** £84-£94 **DB** £104-£114 **D** £20 ℂℂ MC Visa Amex DC

ENGLAND

BLACKPOOL Lancashire 10B3

Pop. 144,000. Preston 16, London 228, M55 (jn 4) 4, Lancaster 24 **EC** Wed **see** Tower (518ft), Winter Gardens, International Circus, Zoo Park, Model Village (Stanley Park), Art Gallery, Autumn Illuminations *i* 1 Clifton Street 01253-21623

★★★★ Imperial

North Promenade, FY1 2HB
☎ 01253-623971 **Fax** 01253-751784
E-mail imperialblackpool@paramounthotels.co.uk

PARAMOUNT
HOTEL · GROUP

Blackpool's premier Victorian hotel offers superb sea views. Leisure club with pool, sauna, spa bath, solarium, gym and steam room. Spacious lounge and bar areas. Executive rooms and suites with CD players, welcome tray, bathrobes and ironing boards. 181 bedrs, all ensuite, ♠ ▣ ⅲ 500 **P** 15 ⊞ **SB** £55-£99 **DB** £55-£125 **L** £10.95 **D** £21 ✕ **LD** 22:00 **CC** MC Visa Amex DC ▨ ▨ ▨ ₺

★★ Brabyns

Shaftesbury Avenue, North Shore, FY2 9QQ
☎ 01253-354263 **Fax** 01253-352915
25 bedrs, all ensuite, ♀ ♠ **P** 12 No children ⊞ Resid **SB** £25-£35 **DB** £45-£60 **L** £7 **D** £12 ✕ **LD** 19:30 **CC** MC Visa Amex DC

★★ Carlton

North Promenade, Blackpool FY1 2EZ
☎ 01253-628966 **Fax** 01253-752587

A warm welcome awaits you at the Carlton Hotel, which is set in the quieter northern end of Blackpool. All rooms ensuite, tea/coffee making facilities, direct dial telephone, Sea view restaurant,

residents' lounge/bar.
58 bedrs, all ensuite, ▣ ⅲ 100 **P** 45 ⊞ **SB** £20-£40 **DB** £40-£90 **HB** £210-£315 **D** £10 ✕ **LD** 20:00 **CC** MC Visa Amex DC

★★ Gables Balmoral

Balmoral Road, Blackpool FY4 1HR
☎ 01253-345432 **Fax** 01253-406058

The nearest two star hotel to Blackpool Pleasure Beach. All rooms with private facilities. Other facilities include swimming pool, jacuzzi and lounge bar. Five course buffet breakfast/dinner served. 63 bedrs, all ensuite, ♀ ♠ ▣ ⅲ 120 **P** 7 ⊞ **SB** £36-£49 **DB** £60-£74 **HB** £195-£234 **L** £8 **L** ● **D** £14 **D** ● ✕ **LD** 20:30 **CC** MC Visa Amex DC ▨ ▨
See advert on this page

★★ ✣ Headlands
New South Promenade, Blackpool FY4 1NJ
☎ 01253-341179 **Fax** 01253-342047
E-mail headlands@blackpool.net
Closed first two weeks of Jan
42 bedrs, all ensuite, ♪ ⟟ ▣ ▦ 40 **P** 38 ⊞
SB £29.50-£48 **DB** £59-£96 **HB** £277.50-£351.50
L £8.50 **L** ● **D** £13.50 **D** ● ✕ **LD** 20:30 ⟨⟨ MC Visa
Amex DC ▨

★★ Revills
192 North Promenade, FY1 1RJ
☎ 01253-25768 **Fax** 01253-24736
45 bedrs, all ensuite, ▣ ▦ 60 **P** 22 ⊞ **SB** £27.50-
£31.50 **DB** £45-£53 **D** £9 ✕ **LD** 19:30 ⟨⟨ MC Visa ▨

★★ ✣ Sheraton
54 Queen's Promenade, Blackpool FY2 9RP
☎ 01253-352723 **Fax** 01253-359549

Leading, family-run, seafront hotel with superb
facilities including wide choice menus, indoor
heated swimming pool, full complement of ensuite
rooms and lift to all floors. Families welcome.
113 bedrs, all ensuite, ▦ 200 ⊞ ⟨⟨ MC Visa ▣ ▨ ⟐

★★ Stretton
206 North Promenade, Blackpool FY1 1RU
☎ 01253-625688 **Fax** 01253-624075

The Stretton is highly recommended and is situated
opposite the North Pier. Close to all amenities, it
offers excellent cuisine and friendly, courteous
service.

50 bedrs, all ensuite, ⟟ ▣ ▦ 150 **P** 10 ⊞ Resid
DB £43-£59 **HB** £148.75-£217 **L** £5.95 **D** £7.50 ✕
LD 19:00 ⟨⟨ MC Visa Amex DC ▨

★★ ✣ Warwick
603 New South Promenade, Blackpool FY4 1NG
☎ 01253-342192 **Fax** 01253-405776
50 bedrs, all ensuite, ♪ ▣ ▦ 50 **P** 30 ⊞ **SB** £40-£46
DB £68-£78 **HB** £204-£276 **L** ● **D** £12.50 ✕ **LD** 20:30
⟨⟨ MC Visa Amex DC JCB ▣

Norbreck Castle
Awaiting Inspection
Queens Promenade, Blackpool FY2 9AA
☎ 01253-352341 **Fax** 01253-356833
363 bedrs, all ensuite, ▣ ▦ 3,500 **P** 800 ⊞ **SB** £60
DB £90 **L** £6.99 **L** ● **D** £12.50 **D** ● ✕ **LD** 20:30 ⟨⟨ MC
Visa Amex DC ▣ ▨ ▨ ▨ ⟐

PRINCIPAL
H O T E L S

BLAKENEY Norfolk   9E2
Pop. 978. Fakenham 13, London 125, Cromer 12,
East Dereham 22, Norwich 27. **EC** Wed **see** 15th cent
Guildhall, 14th cent Church with two towers,
Blakeney Point bird sanctuary (NT).

★★★ Blakeney ⟁
Quayside, Blakeney NR25 7NE
☎ 01263-740797 **Fax** 01263-740795

Traditional, privately owned, friendly hotel
overlooking National Trust Harbour, comfortable
lounges, bar, gardens, heated indoor pool,
billiards/games rooms. Ideal base from which to
explore Norfolk villages, countryside and coast.
59 bedrs, all ensuite, ▤ ⟟ ▣ ▦ 70 **P** 60 ⊞ **SB** £69-
£81 **DB** £138-£162 **HB** £503-£567 **L** £12 **D** £17.50 ✕
LD 21:30 ⟨⟨ MC Visa Amex DC JCB ▣ ▨ ▨ ▨ ⟐

Facilities for the disabled

Hotels do their best to cater for disabled visitors.
However, it is advisable to contact the hotel direct to
ensure it can provide particular requirement.

ENGLAND

★★ Manor
Holt, Blakeney NR25 7ND
☎ 01263-740376 Fax 01263-741116
Closed 3-23 Jan

A refurbished, 16th century, manor house with all modern facilities. Converted flint faced barns, stables and flanking, well kept gardens enhance the inherent period charm and character.
37 bedrs, all ensuite, 🅣 ⊁ ⧉ 12 P 60 No children under 14 ⊞ ⸨ MC Visa JCB ⟁

BLANCHLAND Northumberland   10C1
West Auckland 27, London 276, Durham 24, Hexham 10, Middleton-in-Teesdale 24, Newcastle 24 see Abbey Church (1165), Derwent Reservoir 3m NE

★★ Lord Crewe Arms
Blanchland, Consett DH8 9SP
☎ 01434-675251 Fax 01434-675337
19 bedrs, all ensuite, 🅣 ⊁ ⧉ 18 P 6 ⊞ SB £80 DB £110 L £14 L ⬤ D £28 D ⬤ ✕ LD 21:15 Restaurant closed L Mon-Sat ⸨ MC Visa Amex DC JCB

BLANDFORD FORUM Dorset   3F2
Salisbury 23, London 106, Bournemouth 17, Dorchester 16, Shaftesbury 11, Sherbourne 20, Wareham 14 EC Wed MD Thu, Sat see Parish Church, Georgian houses ⓘ Marsh & Ham Car Park, West Street 01258-454770

Short Breaks
Many hotels provide special rates for weekend and mid-week breaks – sometimes these are quoted in the hotel's entry, otherwise ring direct for the latest offers.

★★★ Crown
West Street, Blandford Forum DT11 7AJ
☎ 01258-456626 Fax 01258-451084
Closed 25-27 Dec

This original Georgian coaching hotel has been tastefully refurbished for today's discerning clientele, whilst retaining its yesteryear charm. Hospitality is our speciality.
32 bedrs, all ensuite, 🅣 ⊁ ⧉ ⧉ 200 P 140 ⊞ SB £58-£62 DB £70-£76 L £14 L ⬤ D £14 D ⬤ ✕ LD 21:15 Restaurant closed L Sat ⸨ MC Visa Amex DC
See advert on this page

ENGLAND

BLOCKLEY Gloucestershire 7F4
Moreton-in-Marsh 4, London 87, Banbury 22, Evesham 11, Stow-on-the-Wold 6½, Stratford-upon-Avon 15, Tewkesbury 20 see 12th cent Parish Church, 17th cent Porch House, Rock Cottage (home of Joanna Southcott)

★★★ Crown Inn
High Street, Blockley GL56 9EX
📞 01386-700245 Fax 01386-700247

Situated in the heart of one of the most unspoilt villages in the Cotswolds, this 16th century coaching inn has a unique aura of peace and tranquillity. The Brasserie Restaurant offers the best in English and French cuisine. Superb wine cellar. 21 bedrs, all ensuite, ♈ ⠿ 20 P 50 ⊞ ✕ LD 21:45 ℂℂ MC Visa Amex

BODMIN Cornwall 2B3
Launceston 22, London 233, Camelford 13, Liskeard 13, Newquay 19, St Austell 11, Truro 24, Wadebridge 7 EC Wed MD Sat see Parish Church of St Petroc, 14th cent chantry chapel ruins in churchyard, Guildhall, Respryn Bridge, DCLI Regimental Museum, Bodmin Beacon (obelisk), Lanhydrock House (NT) 2m SE 🚹 Shire House, Mount Folly Square 01208-76616

★★ Westberry
Rhind Street, Bodmin PL31 2EL
📞 01208-72772 Fax 01208-72212
21 bedrs, 15 ensuite, ♈ ⠿ 60 P 20 ⊞ SB £42 DB £50 HB £250 D £12 ✕ LD 20:45 Restaurant closed L Sat ℂℂ MC Visa Amex DC ▦ ▦

BOGNOR REGIS West Sussex 4C4
Pulborough 16, London 63, Arundel 9½, Chichester 6½, Haywards Heath 35, Littlehampton 7, Petworth 16 EC Wed MD Fri see Hotham Park (Arboretum, Mansion and Children's Zoo), RC Church, Dome House 🚹 Belmont Street 01243-823140

★★★ ✤ Inglenook
255 Pagham Road, Nyetimber, Pagham, Bognor Regis PL21 3QB
📞 01243-262495 Fax 01243-262668
E-mail inglenook@btinternet.com

Family owned and run 16th century hotel and restaurant. Cosy bar with inglenook fireplaces. Attractive restaurant overlooking and opening onto gardens. Car parking available. 18 bedrs, all ensuite, ▦ ♈ ⠿ 100 P 35 ⊞ SB £50 DB £90 HB £275 L £11.50 L 🌑 D £15.95 D 🌑 ✕ LD 21:30 ℂℂ MC Visa Amex DC ৬

BOLTON Lancashire 10B4
Manchester 112, London 195, M61 3, EC Wed MD Thu, Sat 🚹 Town Hall, Victoria Square 01204-364333

★★★ Beaumont
Beaumont Road, Bolton BL3 4TA
📞 01204-651511 Fax 01204-61064
96 bedrs, all ensuite, ▦ ♀ ♈ ⠿ 120 P 120 ⊞ SB £34-£78.95 DB £68-£88.90 HB £273 L 🌑 D £20 D 🌑 ✕ LD 22:00 ℂℂ MC Visa Amex DC JCB ▦

Egerton House
Bolton BL7 9PL
📞 01204-307171 Fax 01204-593030

Set in four and one half acres of tranquil gardens, with mouth watering cuisine and friendly service, you will be assured of a comfortable and relaxing stay. 32 bedrs, all ensuite, ☈ ⠿ 150 P 100 ⊞ SB £57-£86 DB £75-£104 HB £270 L £14 L 🌑 D £25 D 🌑 ✕ LD 22:00 Restaurant closed L Sat ℂℂ MC Visa Amex DC

Leeds 23, London 214, Harrogate 17, Keighley 11, Skipton 6 **EC** Tue **see** Bolton Priory (12th cent)

★★★ Devonshire Arms Country House 🛱 🛱 🛱
Blue Ribbon Hotel
Bolton Abbey, Skipton BD23 6AJ
📞 01756-710441 **Fax** 01756-710585
E-mail dev.arms@legend.co.uk

Traditional coaching inn dating back to 1753, now completely restored and refurbished to create a country house hotel with style and character, bedecked with antiques and pictures.
41 bedrs, all ensuite, 🖅 ⊁ ⚏ 150 **P** 150 ⊕ **SB** £110 **DB** £155 **L** £18 **L** ♥ **D** £37 **D** ♥ ✕ **LD** 22:00
Restaurant closed L Mon-Sat **CC** MC Visa Amex DC
◫ ⊞ ▦ ▩ 🗐 �&

Doncaster 44, London 208, Harrogate 10, Leyburn 26, Northallerton 19, Pontefract 31, Thirsk 12, York 17 **EC** Thu **MD** Mon **see** 'Devil's Arrows' - millstone-grit monoliths, Roman Museum at Aldborough
🖅 Fishergate 01423-323373

★★★ Crown 🛱
Horsefair, Boroughbridge YO5 9LB
📞 01423-322328 **Fax** 01423-324512

A 16th century former coaching inn.

42 bedrs, all ensuite, 🖅 ⊁ ⊡ ⚏ 200 **P** 60 ⊕ **CC** MC Visa Amex DC Ꮛ

★★★ Rose Manor
Horsefair, Boroughbridge YO5 9LL
📞 01423-322245 **Fax** 01423-324920

Elegant country house hotel, set in secluded ground, large private car park; within one mile of exit 48 for Boroughbridge on A1(M). Excellent conference and function facilities. See internet home page: http://www.smoothhound.co.uk/
20 bedrs, all ensuite, 🖅 ⋗ ⚏ 250 **P** 100 ⊕ **SB** £78 **DB** £103 **L** £11 **L** ♥ **D** £18 ✕ **LD** 21:30 **CC** MC Visa Amex

Keswick 6½, London 286, Cockermouth 16, Egremont 24 **see** Bowder Stone, Lodore Falls

★★★ Borrowdale
Borrowdale, Keswick CA12 5UV
📞 017687-77224 **Fax** 01768-777338
E-mail theborrowdalehotel@yahoo.com
33 bedrs, all ensuite, 🖅 ♀ ⋗ ⊁ ⚏ 20 **P** 100 ⊕ **SB** £49-£54 **DB** £110-£116 **L** ♥ **D** £14.95 ✕ **LD** 21:15 **CC** MC Visa JCB
See advert on opposite page

★★ Scafell 🛱
Rosthwaite, Borrowdale CA12 5XB
📞 017687-77208 **Fax** 017687-77280
Closed Jan-Feb
24 bedrs, all ensuite, ⊁ **P** 50 ⊕ **CC** MC Visa
See advert on opposite page

Launceston 18, London 229, Bude 14, Camelford 5 **see** Harbour, Willapark Point, Museum of Witchcraft

★★ Wellington
The Harbour, Boscastle PL35 OAQ
☎ 01840-250202 Fax 01840-250621
E-mail vtobutt@enterprise.net

Historic stone coaching inn, part dating to the 16th century, lots of atmosphere, log fires, beams, and Wellingtonia, Anglo/French cuisine. Near the harbour. 16 bedrs, all ensuite, ④ ✦ ⠇⠇ 20 P 20 No children under 7 ⊞ Rest Resid SB £32-£44 DB £58-£76 HB £281-£333 L £9.50 L ● D £17.95 D ● ✕ LD 21:30 C MC Visa Amex DC ⌖

BOSTON Lincolnshire   **9D2**
Spalding 16, London 117, Grantham 30, Horncastle 18, King's Lynn 34, Louth 30, Skegness 21, Sleaford 17 EC Thu MD Wed, Sat see 14th cent St Botolph's Church with 272ft tower - 'Boston Stump', 15th cent Guildhall ⓘ Blackfriars Art Centre, Spain Lane 01205-356656

★★ Comfort Inn
Bicker Bar Roundabout, Boston PE20 3AN
☎ 01205-820118 Fax 01205-820228
E-mail admin@gb607.u-net.com

Located in the heart of Fen Country. Good restaurant and bar. Ample free parking. All bedrooms offer ensuite facilities, TV, direct dial telephone, tea/coffee tray, alarm clock radio. 55 bedrs, all ensuite, ✦ ⠇⠇ 70 P 70 ⊞ SB £50.50-£61.25 DB £60-£68 L £6.95 D £9.75 D ● ✕ LD 22:00 C MC Visa Amex DC JCB ⌖ &

BOURNE Lincolnshire   8C3

Pop. 9,300. Peterborough 15, London 98, Boston 26, Grantham 18, Melton Mowbray 25, Sleaford 18, Spalding 11, Stamford 11 **EC** Wed **MD** Thu **see** Church (Abbey remains), School (1678), Elizabethan Red Hall and pleasure grounds, Roman Carr Dyke

★★ Black Horse Inn 🛏 🛏

Grimsthorpe, Bourne PE10 0LY
📞 01778-591247 **Fax** 01778-591373
E-mail blackhorseinn@saqnet.co.uk

Listed country inn (1717) nestling next to Grimsthorpe Castle offering traditional hospitality with a superb chef/proprietor run restaurant.
6 bedrs, all ensuite, ④ ⅲ 40 **P** 40 No children under 14 ⊕ Rest Resid **SB** £50-£59 **DB** £60-£95 **L** £10 **L** ☜ **D** £23 **D** ☜ ✕ **LD** 21:00 Restaurant closed D Sun
CC MC Visa Amex JCB

BOURNEMOUTH & BOSCOMBE Dorset   4A4

See also POOLE
Pop. 154,000. Ringwood 12, London 104, Blandford Forum 17, Dorchester 27, Lymington 17, Wareham 13 **see** Russell-Cotes Art Gallery and Museum, Winter Gardens, Pine Woods, Chines, Compton Acres Gardens 2m SW, Hengistbury Head ℹ Westover Road 01202-451700

★★★★ Norfolk Royale

Richmond Hill, Bournemouth BH2 6EN
📞 01202-551521 **Fax** 01202-299729

A deluxe country house style hotel located in the centre of town, with friendly, efficient staff. Bedrooms are beautifully appointed with all the amenities you would expect.
95 bedrs, all ensuite, ♀ ▣ ⅲ 150 **P** 80 ⊕ **SB** £95-£110 **DB** £100-£150 **HB** £330-£420 **L** £12.50 **L** ☜ **D** £25 **D** ☜ ✕ **LD** 22:00 **CC** MC Visa Amex DC ▣ ▦ ♿

★★★★ Swallow Highcliff

105 St Michael's Road, West Cliff, Bournemouth BH2 5DU
📞 01202-557702 **Fax** 01202-292734
E-mail info@swallowhotels.com

SWALLOW HOTELS

The Swallow Highcliff enjoys a breathtaking position overlooking Bournemouth beach, only minutes from the town centre. It has leisure facilities and air-conditioning in most areas.
157 bedrs, all ensuite, ⊱ ▣ ⅲ 500 **P** 115 ⊕ **SB** £85-£105 **DB** £130-£155 **HB** £295-£510 **L** £11.75 **D** £22 ✕ **LD** 22:00 **CC** MC Visa Amex DC ▣ ⊰ ▦ ▦ ▦ ▦ ♿

★★★★ Taurus Park

16 Knyveton Road, Bournemouth BH1 3QN
📞 01202-557374 **Fax** 01202-557374
42 bedrs, 40 ensuite, ▣ **P** 20 No children under 5 ⊕ Resid **SB** £20.50-£22 **DB** £41-£46 **HB** £140-£175 **L** ☜ **D** £6.75 ✕ **LD** 20:00 **CC** MC Visa

★★★ ✣ Bay View Court

35 East Overcliff Drive, East Cliff, BH1 3AT
📞 01202-294449 **Fax** 01202-292883

Personally managed by Cox family for the past 12 years. Many bedrooms boast panoramic views across the bay. Superb leisure complex includes

ENGLAND

heated indoor pool, spa bath, steam room and snooker room.
64 bedrs, all ensuite, ♪ ⊨ 🖃 ⅲ 170 P 56 ⊕ SB £41-£43 DB £82-£86 HB £280-£315 L £6.95 L ● D £16 D ● ✕ LD 20:30 ⓒ MC Visa Amex 🖃 🖼

★★★ ❖ Belvedere

Bath Road, Bournemouth BH1 2EU
☎ 01202-297556 **Fax** 01202-294699
E-mail belvedere_hotel@msn.com
61 bedrs, all ensuite, 🖃 ⅲ 80 P 55 ⊕ SB £37-£51 DB £58-£97 HB £227.50-£388.50 L £10.50 L ●
D £10.50 D ● ✕ LD 21:00 Restaurant closed L Mon-Sat ⓒ MC Visa Amex DC JCB ⅙

★★★ ❖ Burley Court

Bath Road, Bournemouth BH1 2NP
☎ 01202-552824 **Fax** 01202-298514
Closed 1-14 Jan
38 bedrs, all ensuite, 4 ⊨ 🖃 ⅲ 20 P 35 ⊕ Rest Resid SB £30-£41 DB £60-£78 HB £225-£305 L ●
D £16 D ● ✕ LD 20:30 ⓒ MC Visa ⇉ ⅙

★★★ Chesterwood

East Overcliff Drive, Bournemouth BH1 3AR
☎ 01202-558057 **Fax** 01202-556285
E-mail ehotel@aol.com
51 bedrs, all ensuite, 4 ⊨ 🖃 ⅲ 200 P 35 ⊕ SB £25-£55 DB £49-£93 HB £200-£309 L £8.95 L ● D £11.95
D ● ✕ LD 20:30 ⓒ MC Visa Amex DC ⇉ ⅙

★★★ ❖ Chine

25 Boscombe Spa Road, Boscombe, Bournemouth BH5 1AX
☎ 01202-396234 **Fax** 01202-391737
E-mail reservations@fjbhotels.co.uk
Closed 30 Dec-04 Jan

A traditional hotel with award winning cuisine, located in three acres of beautiful mature gardens, with direct access to the beach and pier.
92 bedrs, all ensuite, 4 ♪ 🖃 ⅲ 140 P 50 ⊕ SB £55-£70 DB £110-£140 HB £420-£540 L £14.50 D £18.50
✕ LD 20:30 Restaurant closed L Sat ⓒ MC Visa Amex DC 🖃 ⇉ 🖼

★★★ Cliffeside

East Overcliff Drive, Bournemouth BH1 3AQ
☎ 01202-555724 **Fax** 01202-314534
62 bedrs, all ensuite, 4 ♀ ⊨ 🖃 ⅲ 150 P 50 ⊕
SB £40.50-£52.50 DB £81-£105 HB £279-£357 L £8
L ● D £19 D ● ✕ LD 20:30 ⓒ MC Visa Amex DC ⇉ ⅙

★★★ Connaught

West Hill Road, Bournemouth BH2 5PH
☎ 01202-298020 **Fax** 01202-298028
E-mail sales@theconnaught.co.uk

Ideally situated just 5 minutes from the city centre, Bournemouth International Centre, pier and sandy beach. Outstanding food, friendly efficient service, clean comfortable environment. Magnificent indoor leisure centre and car park.
60 bedrs, all ensuite, 4 ♀ ⊨ 🖃 ⅲ 250 P 45 ⊕
SB £44-£65 DB £88-£110 HB £290-£357 L £9.25
D £19.50 D ● ✕ LD 21:30 Restaurant closed L Mon-Sat ⓒ MC Visa Amex DC 🖃 ⇉ 🖼 🖺 🖼 ⅙

★★★ Courtlands

16 Boscombe Spa Road, Bournemouth BH5 1BB
☎ 01202-302442 **Fax** 01202-309880

Situated on the East Cliff, 3 minutes walk from the sandy beaches, with free use of the local leisure centre, outdoor pool, jacuzzi, sauna and solarium.
58 bedrs, all ensuite, ⊨ 🖃 ⅲ 120 P 60 ⊕ SB £39-£49 DB £76-£90 HB £325-£369 L £8.20 D £13.50 ✕
LD 20:30 Restaurant closed L Mon-Sat ⓒ MC Visa Amex DC ⇉ 🖺

★★★ Cumberland
East Overcliff Drive, Bournemouth BH1 3AF
📞 01202-290722 **Fax** 01202-311394
E-mail hotels@arthuryoung.co.uk
102 bedrs, all ensuite, 4 ⊣ 🖃 ⋕ 140 **P** 51 ⊞ Rest Resid **SB** £29.50-£49.50 **DB** £60-£99 **HB** £210-£399 **L** £9.95 **L** ● **D** £18.95 **D** ● ✕ **LD** 20:30 ⊂⊂ MC Visa Amex DC ⍬

★★★ ✤ Durley Hall
Durley Chine Road, Bournemouth BH2 5JS
📞 01202-751000 **Fax** 01202-757585
E-mail sales@durleyhall.co.uk
Closed 28 Dec-4 Jan
81 bedrs, all ensuite, 🖃 ⋕ 200 **P** 150 ⊞ **SB** £50-£55 **DB** £100-£110 **HB** £294-£371 **L** £9.75 **L** ● **D** £16.50 **D** ● ✕ **LD** 20:45 Restaurant closed L Mon-Sat ⊂⊂ MC Visa Amex DC ⍖ ⍬ 🗆 🖾 ⍒

★★★ East Anglia
6 Poole Road, Bournemouth BH2 5QX
📞 01202-765163 **Fax** 01202-752949
70 bedrs, all ensuite, 🖃 ⋕ 120 **P** 70 ⊞ **SB** £44-£48 **DB** £84-£96 **HB** £300-£348 **L** £9.45 **D** £16.50 ✕ **LD** 20:30 Restaurant closed L Mon-Sat ⊂⊂ MC Visa Amex DC ⍬ 🗆 🖾

★★★ ✤ East Cliff Court
East Overcliff Drive, Bournemouth BH1 3AN
📞 01202-554545 **Fax** 01202-557456
70 bedrs, all ensuite, ⊣ 🖃 ⋕ 160 **P** 100 ⊞ ⊂⊂ MC Visa Amex ⍒ 🖾

★★★ ✤ Elstead
12 Kynveton Road, Bournemouth BH1 3QP
📞 01202-293071 **Fax** 01202-293827
50 bedrs, all ensuite, 4 ⊣ 🖃 ⋕ 70 **P** 45 ⊞ **SB** £45-£51 **DB** £70-£82 **HB** £275-£325 **D** £15.50 ✕ **LD** 20:30 Restaurant closed L Mon-Sat ⊂⊂ MC Visa Amex JCB 🗆 🗵 🖾 🖾 ⍒

★★★ Grosvenor
Bath Road, Bournemouth BH1 2EX
📞 01202-558858 **Fax** 01202-298332
40 bedrs, all ensuite, 4 🖃 ⋕ 80 **P** 40 ⊞ ⊂⊂ MC Visa Amex DC 🗆 🖾

★★★ Heathlands
12 Grove Road, East Cliff,
Bournemouth BH1 3AY
📞 01202-553336 **Fax** 01202-555937
E-mail info@heathlandshotel.com

Located on the exclusive tree lined East Cliff, within easy walking distance to sandy beaches, award winning gardens and town centre. Known for fine cuisine and friendly, professional staff.
115 bedrs, all ensuite, ♀ ⋒ ↰ ☲ ⁝⁝⁝ 270 P 95 ⊞
SB £33-£75 DB £42-£150 HB £252-£492 L £9.50 L ⬤
D £16.50 ✕ LD 20:30 ℂℂ MC Visa Amex DC ⋇ ☒ ▦
⛓

★★★ ✤ Hermitage
Exeter Road, Bournemouth BH2 5AH
☎ 01202-557363 **Fax** 01202-559173
80 bedrs, all ensuite, ☲ ⁝⁝⁝ 100 P 46 ⊞ ℂℂ MC Visa Amex ⛓

★★★ ✤ Hinton Firs
Manor Road, Bournemouth BH1 3HB
☎ 01202-555409 **Fax** 01202-299607
Closed Jan
52 bedrs, all ensuite, ☲ P 40 ⊞ Rest Resid ℂℂ MC Visa ☒ ⋇ ▦

★★★ Hotel Piccadilly
Bath Road, Bournemouth BH1 2NN
☎ 01202-552559 **Fax** 01202-298235
45 bedrs, all ensuite, ▣ ☲ ⁝⁝⁝ 120 P 38 ⊞ Rest Resid SB £48-£58 DB £76-£88 L ⬤ D £16.95 ✕
LD 20:30 ℂℂ MC Visa Amex DC

★★★ ✤ Marsham Court
Russell Cotes Road, Bournemouth BH1 3AB
☎ 01202-552111 **Fax** 01202-294744
E-mail reservations@marshamcourt.co.uk
86 bedrs, all ensuite, ▣ ☲ ⁝⁝⁝ 220 P 100 ⊞ SB £47-£56 DB £74-£92 HB £294-£343 L £6.50 L ⬤ D £17 ✕
LD 21:00 ℂℂ MC Visa Amex DC ⋇ ☒ ⛓
See advert on this page

★★★ ✤ Mayfair
27 Bath Road, Bournemouth BH1 2NW
☎ 01202-551983 **Fax** 01202-298459
40 bedrs, all ensuite, ☲ ⁝⁝⁝ 90 P 40 ⊞ SB £34-£35.50
DB £44-£58 HB £150-£230 L ⬤ D £12.95 D ⬤ ✕
LD 20:30 ℂℂ MC Visa Amex DC JCB

★★★ ✦ Miramar
East Overcliff Drive, Bournemouth BH1 3AL
☎ 01202-556581 Fax 01202-291242
45 bedrs, all ensuite, 🔲 ♀ 🖉 ➤ ⊡ ⦂⦂⦂ 200 P 80 ⊕
Rest Resid SB £55-£66 DB £100-£120 HB £399-£420
L £10 L 🐾 D £20 D 🐾 ✕ LD 21:00 Restaurant closed
L Sat ⊄ MC Visa Amex JCB ⅅ
See advert on previous page

★★★ ✦ New Durley Dean
Westcliff Road, Bournemouth BH2 5HE
☎ 01202-557711 Fax 01202-292815

Situated on the fashionable West Cliff, this elegant
Victorian hotel has easy access to seven miles of
sandy beaches, gardens, theatres and the BIC
conference centre.
121 bedrs, all ensuite, 🔲 ➤ ⊡ ⦂⦂⦂ 150 P 35 ⊕
SB £25-£59 DB £50-£118 HB £180-£273 D £15 ✕
LD 20:30 ⊄ MC Visa Amex 🔲 🔲 🔲 🔲

★★★ ✦ Pavilion
Bath Road, Bournemouth BH1 2NS
☎ 01202-291266 Fax 01202-559264
44 bedrs, all ensuite, 🔲 ➤ ⊡ ⦂⦂⦂ 100 P 40 ⊕ Resid
SB £25-£37 DB £50-£74 HB £224-£259 L 🐾 D £14 D 🐾
✕ LD 20:30 ⊄ MC Visa Amex DC JCB

★★★ Quality
8 Poole Road, Bournemouth BH2 5QU
☎ 01202-763006 Fax 01202-766168
E-mail admin@gb641.u-net.com

A comfortable, friendly hotel very much part of this

traditional resort. Situated on Bournemouth's West
Cliff, close to miles of sandy beaches, the Winter
Gardens and the new Oceanarium.
57 bedrs, all ensuite, 🔲 ⊡ ⦂⦂⦂ 90 P 60 ⊕ Rest Resid
SB £72.75-£83.75 DB £93.25-£104.25 L £5.75
D £14.50 ✕ LD 20:45 Restaurant closed L Mon-Thu
⊄ MC Visa Amex DC JCB

★★★ Queens
Meyrick Road, East Cliff, Bournemouth BH1 3DL
☎ 01202-554415 Fax 01202-294810
E-mail hotels@arthuryoung.co.uk
114 bedrs, all ensuite, 🔲 🖉 ➤ ⊡ ⦂⦂⦂ 200 P 80 ⊕
Rest Resid SB £40-£56.50 DB £80-£112 HB £275-£399
L £9 L 🐾 D £20 D 🐾 ✕ LD 20:30 Restaurant closed L
Sat ⊄ MC Visa Amex DC 🔲 🔲 🔲 🔲 ⅅ

★★★ Trouville
5 Priory Road, Bournemouth BH2 5DH
☎ 01202-552262 Fax 01202-293324
79 bedrs, all ensuite, ➤ ⊡ ⦂⦂⦂ 100 P 75 ⊕ Rest
Resid SB £45-£50 DB £90-£100 HB £330-£360 L £8.95
D £18.45 ✕ LD 20:30 ⊄ MC Visa Amex DC 🔲 🔲 🔲
ⅅ

★★ ✦ Arlington
Exeter Park Road, Lower Gardens, Bournemouth
BH2 5BD
☎ 01202-552879 Fax 01202-298317
29 bedrs, 28 ensuite, ⊡ ⦂⦂⦂ 55 P 21 No children
under 2 ⊕ Rest Resid ⊄ MC Visa Amex JCB

★★ ✦ Bourne Hall
14 Priory Road, Bournemouth BH2 5DN
☎ 01202-299715 Fax 01202-552669
E-mail info@bournehall.co.uk
49 bedrs, all ensuite, ➤ ⊡ ⦂⦂⦂ 25 P 32 ⊕ Rest Resid
⊄ MC Visa Amex DC 🔲

★★ Chinehurst
Studland Road, Westbourne, Bournemouth BH4
8JA
☎ 01202-764583 Fax 01202-762854
32 bedrs, all ensuite, 🔲 ➤ ⊡ 60 P 14 No children
under 2 ⊕ SB £22-£38 DB £44-£64 HB £140-£240 L £8
L 🐾 D £15 ✕ LD 20:30 ⊄ MC Visa Amex DC JCB ⅅ

★★ County
Westover Road, Bournemouth BH1 2BT
☎ 01202-552385 Fax 01202-297255
48 bedrs, all ensuite, ➤ ⊡ ⦂⦂⦂ 100 P 9 ⊕ SB £25-£46
DB £50-£96 HB £147-£252 L £5.95 L 🐾 D £12.50 D 🐾
✕ LD 20:00 Restaurant closed L Mon-Sat ⊄ MC
Visa Amex JCB

★★ ❖ Croham Hurst
9 Durley Road South, West Cliff, BH2 5JH
☎ 01202-552353 **Fax** 01202-311484
Closed 2 Jan-2 Feb
40 bedrs, all ensuite, ▣ **P** 30 ⊕ Resid ₵ MC Visa
JCB

★★ ❖ Durley Grange
6 Durley Road, West Cliff, Bournemouth BH2 5JL
☎ 01202-554473 **Fax** 01202-293774
50 bedrs, all ensuite, ▣ ⅲ 60 **P** 30 No children
under 5 ⊕ Resid ₵ MC Visa ▣ ▣

★★ Embassy
Meyrick Road, Bournemouth BH1 3DW
☎ 01202-290751 **Fax** 01202-557459
72 bedrs, all ensuite, ▣ **P** 100 ⅲ 150 ⊕ Resid
₵ MC Visa Amex ⅔

★★ ❖ Fircroft
Owls Road, Bournemouth BH5 1AE
☎ 01202-309771 **Fax** 01202-395644
50 bedrs, all ensuite, ★ ▣ ⅲ 200 **P** 50 ⊕ Rest
Resid **SB** £19-£28 **DB** £38-£56 **HB** £185-£235 **D** £14
D ● ✕ **LD** 20:00 ₵ MC Visa Amex DC JCB ▣ ▣ ▣ ▣

★★ Grange
Overcliffe Drive, Southbourne, BH6 3NL
☎ 01202-433093 **Fax** 01202-424228
31 bedrs, all ensuite, ★ ▣ **P** 37 ⊕ **SB** £30 **DB** £59
HB £195 **L** ● **D** £15.50 **D** ● ✕ **LD** 20:30 ₵ MC Visa ▣
&

★★ Hotel Riviera
West Cliff Gardens, Bournemouth BH2 5HL
☎ 01202-552845 **Fax** 01202-317717
Closed Jan-Feb

Situated in a quiet cul-de-sac with breathtaking
views of Bournemouth Bay and the golden sands;
our hotel has everything to offer for the ideal place
to stay. All rooms ensuite, with colour tv, radio,
telephone, tea-making facilities and central heating.
34 bedrs, all ensuite, ▣ **P** 24 ⊕ Rest Resid **SB** £25-
£35 **DB** £50-£70 **HB** £210-£260 **L** ● **D** £12.50 ✕
LD 19:30 ₵ MC Visa

★★ ❖ Russell Court
Bath Road, Bournemouth BH1 2EP
☎ 01202-295819 **Fax** 01202-293457
E-mail russellcrt@aol.com
56 bedrs, all ensuite, ★ ▣ ⅲ 80 **P** 40 **SB** £36-£45
DB £66-£74 **HB** £245-£299 **L** £5.95 **L** ● **D** £14.95 **D** ●
✕ **LD** 19:45 ₵ MC Visa Amex DC

★★ ❖ St George
West Cliff Gardens, Bournemouth BH2 5HL
☎ 01202-556075 **Fax** 01202-557330
Closed mid Nov-mid Dec, 2 Jan-Easter
22 bedrs, 20 ensuite, ★ ▣ **P** 10 ⊕ Rest Resid
₵ MC Visa &
See advert on this page

★★ Sun Court
West Hill Road, Bournemouth BH2 5PH
☎ 01202-551343 **Fax** 01202-316747
33 bedrs, all ensuite, ★ ▣ ⅲ 45 **P** 50 ⊕ Resid
SB £29-£43 **DB** £58-£86 **HB** £196-£294 **L** £73.45 **L** ●
D £16 ✕ **LD** 20:30 Restaurant closed L Mon-Sat
₵ MC Visa Amex DC ⅔ ▣

★★ ❖ Tower House
West Cliff Gardens, Bournemouth BH2 5HP
📞 01202-290742

A splendid hotel superbly positioned in West Cliff
Gardens, renowned for the professional yet friendly
relaxed atmosphere. The elegant restaurant highly
recommended. Seaviews. Fourposters available.
34 bedrs, 32 ensuite, 🛁 ➤ 🖥 P 38 🍴 ₵ MC Visa

★★ Ullswater 🛏
West Cliff Gardens, Bournemouth BH2 5HW
📞 01202-555181 Fax 01202-317896
42 bedrs, all ensuite, ➤ 🖥 ::: 40 P 10 🍴 Rest Resid
SB £27-£32 DB £54-£64 HB £161-£235 L £7.50 L 🍷
D £11 ✗ LD 20:00 Restaurant closed L Mon-Sat
₵ MC Visa Amex 🈺

★★ ❖ Westleigh
26 West Hill Road, Bournemouth BH2 5PG
📞 01202-296989 Fax 01202-296989
30 bedrs, 28 ensuite, 🖥 P 30 🍴 Resid SB £20-£35
DB £40-£70 HB £230 L £5.95 L 🍷 D £7.50 D 🍷 ✗
LD 19:30 ₵ MC Visa Amex DC JCB 🈺 🈺 🈺

★★ ❖ Whitehall
Exeter Park Road, Bournemouth BH2 5AX
📞 01202-554682 Fax 01202-554682
49 bedrs, 45 ensuite, ➤ 🖥 ::: 30 P 25 🍴 Rest Resid
SB £27-£30 DB £54-£60 HB £190-£265 D £12 ✗
LD 20:00 ₵ MC Visa Amex DC JCB

★★ ❖ Winterbourne
Priory Road, West Cliff, Bournemouth BH2 5DJ
📞 01202-296366 Fax 01202-780073
E-mail reservations@winterbourne.co.uk
41 bedrs, all ensuite, ➤ 🖥 ::: 80 P 31 🍴 Resid
SB £29-£39 DB £50-£70 HB £199-£288 L 🍷 D £10 D 🍷
✗ LD 20:00 ₵ MC Visa Amex 🍽 🈺 🍴

Pinehurst
West Cliff Gardens, Bournemouth BH2 5HR
📞 01202-556218 Fax 01202-551051

Just minutes from the West Cliff, yet this friendly
hotel is within a leisurely stroll of major shops,
theatres and Bournemouth International Centre.
73 bedrs, all ensuite, 🖥 ::: 80 P 40 🍴 ₵ MC Visa
Amex DC

Suncliff
East Overcliff Drive, Bournemouth BH1 3AG
📞 01202-291711 Fax 01202-293788

Located high on the East Cliff overlooking the sea
and noted for good food, friendly service and
entertainment. Rooms are tastefully decorated and
benefit from modern facilities. Superb extensive
leisure facilities.
94 bedrs, all ensuite, ➤ 🖥 ::: 100 P 70 🍴 ₵ MC
Visa Amex DC JCB 🍴 🈺 🍽 🈺 ♿

BOURTON-ON-THE-WATER Gloucestershire 4A1
Pop. 2,900. Burford 9, London 84, Cheltenham 16,
Cirencester 16, Gloucester 24, Stow-on-the-Wold
4, Tewkesbury 22 ₵ Sat **see** Model Village,
Aquarium, Birdland

★★ Chester House
Bourton-on-the-Water GL54 2BU
📞 01451-820286 Fax 01451-820471
E-mail juliand@chesterhouse.u-net.com
Closed Dec-Jan
22 bedrs, all ensuite, 🛁 ➤ ::: 16 P 20 🍴 Rest Resid
SB £54 DB £74-£102 HB £434.70-£543.90 L £10
D £17.75 ✗ LD 21:30 Restaurant closed L Thu
₵ MC Visa Amex DC JCB ♿

ENGLAND

★★ Old New Inn
High Street, Bourton-on-the-Water GL54 2AF
☎ 01451-820467 **Fax** 01451-810236
E-mail 106206.2571@compuserve.com
Closed 25 Dec

A Queen Anne hostelry. Traditional welcome with traditional standards. Log fires, three comfortable bars.
11 bedrs, 8 ensuite, ④ **P** 24 ⊞ **SB** £32-£40 **DB** £64-£80 **HB** £303-£359 **L** £10 **L** ● **D** £18 **D** ● ✕ **LD** 20:30 **CC** MC Visa
See advert on this page

⟨𝔒𝔩𝔡 **NEW INN**

A traditional country inn, with log fires, three bars, restaurant and residents lounge. An ideal location for touring the cotswolds.

**BOURTON-ON-THE WATER,
GLOS. GL54 2AF
Tel: (01451) 820467
Fax: (01451) 810236**

BOVEY TRACEY Devon　　　　　　　3D3
Pop. 4,500. Exeter 14, London 181, Ashburton 8, Okehampton 18, Tavistock 26 **EC** Wed

★★★ Edgemoor ⎾ ⎾
Lowerdown Cross, Haytor Road, TQ13 9LE
☎ 01626-832466 **Fax** 01626-834760
E-mail edgemoor@btinternet.com
Closed first week Jan

Wisteria-clad country house hotel, in a wooded setting with beautiful gardens, adjacent to Dartmoor National Park. See more pictures on www.edgemoor.co.uk
17 bedrs, all ensuite, ④ 🛏 ⁑ 50 **P** 50 ⊞ Rest Resid
CC MC Visa Amex DC JCB

★★ Coombe Cross
Bovey Tracey TQ13 9EY
☎ 01626-832476 **Fax** 01626-835298
23 bedrs, all ensuite, ♀ 🛏 ⁑ 60 **P** 28 ⊞ Rest Resid
SB £39-£45 **DB** £60-£70 **HB** £260-£308 **L** ● **D** £19 ✕
LD 20:30 **CC** MC Visa Amex DC JCB ▣ ▣ ▣ ⅙

★★ Riverside Inn
Fore Street, Bovey Tracey TQ13 9AF
☎ 01626-832293 **Fax** 01626-833880

Ten ensuite bedrooms all with colour TV, telephone, and tea and coffee facilities. Restaurant, bar and function room for 100. Open all year. Rooms from £29.50
10 bedrs, all ensuite, 🛏 ⁑ 100 **P** 100 ⊞ **SB** £30
DB £40 **L** ● **D** ● ✕ **LD** 21:30 **CC** MC Visa ▣

BOWBURN Co. Durham 11D1

Roadchef Lodge Lodge
Motorway Service Area, Thursdale Road, Bowburn
DH6 5NP
☎ 0191-377 3666 **Fax** 0191-377 1448
Closed 25 Dec-2 Jan
38 bedrs, all ensuite, ⋕ 8 **P** 130 **Room** £47.95 **CC** MC
Visa Amex DC ⅙

BRACKNELL Berkshire 4C2

Pop. 51,000. Staines 11, London 28, Bagshot 5,
Basingstoke 21, Henley-on-Thames 13, Reading
11, Weybridge 14, Windsor 9 **EC** Wed **MD** Fri, Sat
🛈 The Look Out, Nine Mile Ride 01344-868196

★★★★ Coppid Beech

John Nike Way, Bracknell RG12 8TF
☎ 01344-303333 **Fax** 01344-301200
E-mail coppid-beech-hotel-co.uk
205 bedrs, all ensuite, ♀ ✧ ✦ ☎ ⋕ 350 **P** 350 ⅊
SB £135 **DB** £175 **L** £17.50 **L** 🍷 **D** £22.95 ✕ **LD** 22:30
CC MC Visa Amex DC JCB ▣ ⊞ ▦ ⅙

BRADFORD West Yorkshire 10C3

Pop. 449,100. M606 2, London 196, Halifax 8,
Harrogate 18, Huddersfield 10, Leeds 9, Pontefract
22, Skipton 19 **EC** Wed **MD** Daily exc Wed **see**
Cathedral, City Hall, Cartwright Hall (Museum and
Art Gallery), 15th cent Bolling Hall (Museum), Wool
Exchange, Industrial Museum, National Museum of
photography 🛈 Museum of photography,
Pictureville 01274-753678

★★★★ Cedar Court 🛏 🛏

Mayo Avenue, Off Rooley Lane,
Bradford WF4 3QZ
☎ 01274-406606 **Fax** 01274-406600
E-mail sales@cedarcourt-hotel-bradford.co.uk

Cedar Court Hotel in Bradford is the city's first
purpose built hotel, conference centre and leisure
club for more than twenty years.

131 bedrs, all ensuite, ④ ♀ ✧ ☎ ⋕ 800 **P** 350 ⅊
SB £65-£109 **DB** £75-£119 **L** £13 **D** £19.95 ✕ **LD** 22:00
Restaurant closed L Sat **CC** MC Visa Amex DC JCB
▣ ⊞ ▦ ▥ ⅙

★★★ Midland

Forster Square, Bradford BD1 4HU
☎ 01274-735735 **Fax** 01274-720003
E-mail sales@penningtonmidland.co.uk

An owner-managed, city centre, 90 bedroomed
hotel restored to its former Victorian glory. The
hotel boasts two magnificent ballrooms, spacious
bedrooms 24 hour room service, friendly staff and
secure car parking. 7 meeting rooms for 6 to 400
people.
90 bedrs, all ensuite, ④ ✧ ☎ ⋕ 400 **P** 200 ⅊
SB £62-£85 **DB** £95-£105 **D** £23.50 ✕ **LD** 23:00
Restaurant closed L Sat **CC** MC Visa Amex DC JCB
⅙

★★★ Novotel Bradford

Merrydale Road, Bradford BD4 6SA
☎ 01274-683683 **Fax** 01274-651342
E-mail h0510@accor-hotels.com
127 bedrs, all ensuite, ✧ ☎ ⋕ 300 **P** 200 ⅊
SB £55 **DB** £72 **L** £10 **L** 🍷 **D** £13.50 **D** 🍷 ✕ **LD** 0:00
CC MC Visa Amex DC ⅌ ⊞ ⅙

★★★ Quality Victoria

Bridge Street, Bradford BD1 1JX
☎ 01274-728706 **Fax** 01274-736358
E-mail admin@gb654.u-net.com
60 bedrs, all ensuite, ☎ ⋕ 150 **P** 60 ⅊ **SB** £82.75-
£91.25 **DB** £107.25-£124 **D** £14.50 ✕ **LD** 22:00 **CC** MC
Visa Amex DC ⊞

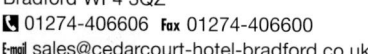

Facilities for the disabled

Hotels do their best to cater for disabled visitors.
However, it is advisable to contact the hotel direct to
ensure it can provide particular requirement.

★★ Park Drive
12 Park Drive, Bradford BD9 4DR
☎ 01274-480194 **Fax** 01274-484869

'It's like staying in the country!' This elegant Victorian residence in its delightful woodland setting offers delicious home cooking, friendly personal service and safe parking inside the grounds.
11 bedrs, all ensuite, ⊩ ⠇⠇⠇ 12 **P** 9 ⊞ Resid **SB** £30-£47 **DB** £48-£57 **HB** £243 **L** ☞ **D** £12 **D** ☞ ✕ **LD** 20:30 ⊄ MC Visa Amex DC

BRADFORD-ON-AVON Wiltshire   3F1
Pop. 8,900. Corsham 6, London 101, Bath 7, Melksham 5, Trowbridge 3, Warminster 13 ⓘ 34 Silver Street 01225-865797

◈ ★★★ ✥ Leigh Park
Leigh Road West, Bradford-on-Avon BA15 2RA
☎ 01225-864885 **Fax** 01225-862315

Bath-stone Georgian house in 5 acres of grounds with its own walled garden and vineyard. Lovely views.
22 bedrs, all ensuite, ⊞ ⊩ ⠇⠇⠇ 120 **P** 80 ⊞ ⊄ MC Visa Amex 🖾 🖾 &

BRAITHWAITE Cumbria   10A2
Pop. 500. Keswick 2½, London 288, Carlisle 30, Cockermouth 9½

★★★ Middle Ruddings
Braithwaite CA12 5RY
☎ 01768-778436 **Fax** 01768-778436
11 bedrs, all ensuite, ⊩ ⠇⠇⠇ 20 **P** 20 No children under 5 ⊞ ⊄ MC Visa

BRAMPTON Cumbria   10B1
Pop. 4,700. M6 (jn 43) 7, London 299, Alston 19, Carlisle 9, Gretna 15, Hexham 28 ⼕ Thu **MD** Wed **see** Church (Burne-Jones windows), Moot Hall, Stocks, Prince Charlie's House, Lanercost Priory 3m NE, Roman Wall ⓘ Moot Hall, Market Place 016977-3433

★★★ Farlam Hall ⫶ ⫶ ⫶
Blue Ribbon Hotel
Brampton CA8 2NG
☎ 016977-46234 **Fax** 016977-46683
E-mail farlamhall@dial.pipex.com
Closed 24-30 Dec

Personally owned by the Quinion & Stevenson families since 1975, this elegant manor house is a haven offering fine food, comfort and impeccable service.
12 bedrs, all ensuite, ⊞ ⊩ ⠇⠇⠇ 12 **P** 35 No children under 5 ⊞ Rest Resid **SB** £95-£105 **DB** £160-£180 **D** £30 ✕ **LD** 20:30 ⊄ MC Visa

BRANDON Suffolk   9E3
Pop. 7,400. Newmarket 18, London 81, Bury St Edmunds 15, East Dereham 24, Ely 22, King's Lynn 25, Swaffham 15, Thetford 6 ⼕ Wed **MD** Thu, Sat **see** St Peter's Church, 15th cent bridge

★★ Brandon House
High Street, Brandon IP27 0AX
☎ 01842-810171 **Fax** 01842-814859
15 bedrs, all ensuite, ⊩ ⠇⠇⠇ 20 **P** 40 ⊞ **SB** £55 **DB** £75 **L** £10 **L** ☞ **D** £10 **D** ☞ ✕ **LD** 21:00 ⊄ MC Visa Amex DC

ENGLAND

Pop. 72,800. Romford 6, London 22, Bishop's Stortford 23, Chelmsford 11, Dartford Crossing 13, Southend 21 **EC** Thu *see* 'White Hart' Inn (old Coaching House), 16th cent Moat House (once Hunting Lodge, now hotel), RC Cathedral *i* 14 Ongar Road 01277-200300

★★★★ Marygreen Manor
London Road, Brentwood CM14 4NR
☎ 01277-225252 **Fax** 01277-262809
E-mail info@marygreenmanor.co.uk

Located 2 minutes from junction 28 of the M25. Guests can choose from our air-conditioned Garden Suites, situated around the courtyard garden, or our new 'Country House' extension.
43 bedrs, all ensuite, 🔲 ♀ ⋟ ⠿ 55 **P** 120 ⊞ Rest Resid **SB** £117.50-£135 **DB** £129-£150.50 **L** £14 **D** £25 ✕ **LD** 22:15 **CC** MC Visa Amex DC ♿
See advert on opposite page

★★★ Posthouse **Posthouse**
Brook Street, Brentwood CM14 5NF
☎ 01277-260260 **Fax** 01277-264264
145 bedrs, all ensuite, ♀ ⌁ 🔲 ⠿ 120 **P** 200 ⊞
SB £118.95-£129 **DB** £128.90-£140 **L** £10 **L** ⚓ **D** £12
D ⚓ ✕ **LD** 22:30 **CC** MC Visa Amex DC 🔳 🔳 🔳 ♿

Lichfield 7, London 122, Burton-on-Trent 15, Stafford 9, Stone 15, Uttoxeter 12, Walsall 16, Wolverhampton 16

★★★ Cedar Tree
Main Road, Rugeley, Brereton WS15 1DY
☎ 01889-584241 **Fax** 01889-575823
30 bedrs, all ensuite, ⠿ 250 **P** 150 ⊞ **CC** MC Visa Amex DC 🔳 ♿
See advert on opposite page

Pop. 11,000. Kidderminster 13, London 137, Birmingham 25, Ludlow 19, Shrewsbury 21, Wolverhampton 14 **EC** Thu **MD** Mon, Sat *see* St Leonard's Church, St Mary's Church, 16th cent Bishop Percy's House, cliff railway, Town Hall 1652, Northgate Museum, remains of 12th cent Castle, Severn Valley Rly (steam engines) to Bewdley, Midland Motor Museum *i* Library, Listley Street 01746-763358

★★★★ Mill
Alveley, Bridgnorth WV15 6HL
☎ 01746-780437 **Fax** 01746-780850

A truly beautiful hotel, with first class facilities and luxurious accommodation, in a tranquil setting. Waterside Restaurant open daily.
21 bedrs, all ensuite, 🔲 ⋟ 🔲 ⠿ 200 **P** 200 ⊞
SB £67.50-£96.50 **DB** £86-£118 **HB** £609-£812
L £11.50 **L** ⚓ **D** £19.50 **D** ⚓ ✕ **LD** 22:15 **CC** MC Visa Amex DC 🔳 ♿
See advert on next page

★★★ Old Vicarage
Blue Ribbon Hotel
Worfield, Bridgnorth WV15 5JZ
☎ 01746-716497 **Fax** 01746-716552
Closed 22 Dec-3 Jan
14 bedrs, all ensuite, ⌁ ⠿ 20 **P** 30 ⊞ Rest Resid
CC MC Visa Amex DC ♿

Parlors Hall
Mill Street, Bridgnorth WV15 5AL
☎ 01746-761931 **Fax** 01746-767058
15 bedrs, all ensuite, 🔲 ⌁ ⠿ 30 **P** 25 ⊞ **CC** MC Visa
See advert on opposite page

ENGLAND

BRIDGWATER Somerset 3E2
Pop. 27,000. M5 (jn 23) 3, London 141, Bristol 32, Glastonbury 15, Taunton 10, Weston-super-Mare 18 **EC** Thu **MD** Wed, Sat **see** St Mary's Church, Town Hall (tapestry, Blake portraits), Admiral Blake House, Sedgemoor Battlefield (1685) 4m E *i* 50 High Street 01278-427652

★★★ Walnut Tree
North Pertherton, Bridgwater TA6 6QA
🔌 01278-662255 **Fax** 01278-663946
E-mail saleswalnuttree@btinternet.com
32 bedrs, all ensuite, ⊞ ⊞ 120 **P** 70 ⊕ **SB** £59-£65 **DB** £78-£84 **L** £7 **D** £15 **D** 👄 ✕ **LD** 22:00 **CC** MC Visa Amex DC JCB &

BRIDLINGTON East Yorkshire 11F3
Pop. 31,000. Beverley 22, London 201, Hull 30, Malton 28, Scarborough 17, York 41 **EC** Thu **MD** Wed, Sat **see** Bayle Gate (museum), Priory Church, Flamborough Head and Lighthouse *i* 25 Prince Street 01262-673474

★★★ Expanse
North Marine Drive, Bridlington YO15 2LS
🔌 01262-675347 **Fax** 01262-604928
E-mail expanseatbrid.demon.co.uk
48 bedrs, all ensuite, ⊞ ⊞ 40 **P** 31 ⊕ **SB** £29.50-£49 **DB** £55-£85 **HB** £207-£300 **L** £8 **D** £14 ✕ **LD** 21:00 **CC** MC Visa Amex DC

★★★ New Revelstoke
1-3 Flamborough Road, Bridlington YO15 2HU
🔌 01262-672362 **Fax** 01262-672362
E-mail revelstoke-hotel@compuserve.com

The Revelstoke Hotel is one of the finest hotels in the area ideally situated on Flamborough Road in Bridlington, only minutes walk from the sands and the Leisure World Complex.
25 bedrs, all ensuite, ⚲ ⊞ 250 **P** 14 ⊕ **SB** £38-£41 **DB** £65.50-£75.25 **HB** £245-£276 **D** £13.95 **D** 👄 ✕ **LD** 21:30 **CC** MC Visa Amex DC

★★ Monarch
South Marine Drive, Bridlington YO15 3JJ
🔌 01262-674447 **Fax** 01262-670060
Closed winter
40 bedrs, all ensuite, ⊡ ⊞ 30 **P** 10 No children ⊕ Resid **SB** £30-£32 **DB** £58-£62 **HB** £230-£250 **D** £11 ✕ **LD** 19:30 **CC** MC Visa &

★ Langdon
Pembroke Terrace, Bridlington YO15 3BX
🔌 01262-400124 **Fax** 01262-400124
27 bedrs, 24 ensuite, ⊡ ⊞ 42 **P** 3 ⊕ **SB** £23-£24 **DB** £46-£48 **HB** £172-£184 **D** £7.50

BRIDPORT Dorset 3E3
Pop. 7,900. Dorchester 15, London 137, Axminster 12, Crewkerne 13, Lyme Regis 10, Sherborne 26, Weymouth 19 **EC** Thu **MD** Wed, *i* 32 South Street 01308-424901

★★★ Haddon House
West Bay, Bridport DT6 4EL
🔌 01308-423626 **Fax** 01308-427348

300 yards from picturesque harbour, coast and golf course at West Bay. Renowned for fine cuisine and ideally situated for touring Dorset, Devon and Somerset.
12 bedrs, all ensuite, ⊞ 40 **P** 50 ⊕ **DB** £49-£75 **L** £9.50 **D** £17.50 ✕ **LD** 20:45 **CC** MC Visa Amex DC &

★★ Roundham House ⅎ
Roundham Gardens, West Bay Road, Bridport DT6 4BD
🔌 01308-422753 **Fax** 01308-421500
Closed Jan-Feb
8 bedrs, all ensuite, 🛏 ⊞ 12 **P** 12 ⊕ Rest Resid **SB** £35-£40 **DB** £60-£75 **HB** £280-£295 **D** £17.95 **D** 👄 ✕ **LD** 20:30 **CC** MC Visa JCB &

BRIGG Lincolnshire   11E4
Pop. 5,500. Lincoln 24, London 158, M180 1,
Gainsborough 20, Grimsby 21, Hull 20, Scunthorpe
8 **EC** Wed **MD** Tue, Thur *i* Buttercross, Market Place
01652-657053

★★★ Briggate Lodge Inn ⌘ ⌘

Ermine Street, Broughton,
Brigg DN20 0NQ
☎ 01652-650770 **Fax** 01652-650495

86 ensuite bedrooms. 27 hole championship golf
course with floodlit driving range. Bar meals (11am-
11pm), a la carte restaurant, banqueting suite.
Golfing breaks a speciality.
86 bedrs, all ensuite, ④ ♪ ⊡ ⫶ 250 **P** 300 ⊕
SB £69-£76 **DB** £78-£84 **L** £13 **D** £19.50 ✕ **LD** 22:00
℃ MC Visa Amex DC JCB ▣ ⌕ ▦ ▶ ⅊

BRIGHOUSE West Yorkshire   10C4
Pop. 29,700. Huddersfield 5, London 185, Bradford
7, Dewsbury 8, Halifax 4

★★★ Posthouse   **Posthouse**
Clifton Village, Leeds /
Brighouse HD6 4HW
☎ 01484-400400 **Fax** 01484-400068
94 bedrs, all ensuite, ⌁ ⫶ 200 **P** 155
⊕ **Room** £59-£99 **L** £10 **L** ⬤ **D** £11.95
D ⬤ ✕ **LD** 22:00 ℃ MC Visa Amex DC
▣ ⌕ ▦ ⅊

BRIGHTON East Sussex   5D4
See also HOVE
Pop. 142,300. Crawley 22, London 53, Arundel 20,
Haywards Heath 14, Horsham 23, Lewes 8,
Newhaven 9, Worthing 11 **EC** Wed **MD** Tue, Sat **see**
Royal Pavillion, Aquarium and Dolphinarium, St
Nicolas' Church, Booth Museum of British Birds,
Preston Manor Marina, St Peter's Church *i* 10
Bartholomew Square 01273-323755

★★★ King's

139-141 King's Road, Brighton BN1 2NA
☎ 01273-820854 **Fax** 01273-328120

The King's Hotel is a three star Grade II Listed
building, retaining all the character and elegance of
the Regency period. The hotel is located on the sea
front within easy walking distance of the town
centre and amenities.
85 bedrs, all ensuite, ④ ♪ ⊡ ⫶ 100 **P** 16 ⊕ **SB** £45-
£65 **DB** £70-£130 **L** ⬤ **D** £12 **D** ⬤ ✕ **LD** 21:30 ℃ MC
Visa Amex DC JCB

★★★ Old Ship

Kings Road, Brighton BN1 1NR
☎ 01273-329001 **Fax** 01273-820718
E-mail oldship@paramounthotels.co.uk

The hotel is perfectly situated at the heart of
Brighton overlooking the beach and promenade, a
stroll from The Lanes, famous antique shops, cafes,
bars and restaurants.
152 bedrs, all ensuite, ④ ♀ ♪ ⊡ ⫶ 150 **P** 70 ⊕
SB £70 **DB** £95 **L** £12 **L** ⬤ **D** £12 **D** ⬤ ✕ **LD** 22:00
℃ MC Visa Amex DC ⅊

★★★ Quality

West Street, Brighton BN1 2RQ
☎ 01273-220033 **Fax** 01273-778000
E-mail admin@gb057.u.net.com
138 bedrs, all ensuite, ♀ ⌁ ⊡ ⫶ 180 ⊕ **SB** £79.50
DB £100.50 **L** ⬤ **D** £14.75 **D** ⬤ ✕ **LD** 21:30 ℃ MC
Visa Amex DC JCB ⅊

ENGLAND

Lanes Awaiting Inspection
70-72 Marine Parade, Brighton BN2 1AE
📞 01273-674231

Brighton
145 Kings Road, Brighton BN1 2PQ
📞 01273-820555 **Fax** 01273-821555
E-mail bthotel@pavilion.co.uk

The Brighton Hotel is here to provide you with the friendliest service and the finest amenities that are the hallmark of this independently owned hotel. We are large enough to meet corporate needs and small enough to guarantee personal attention.
52 bedrs, all ensuite, 4 ⊡ ⠿ 100 **P** 18 ⊞ **SB** £55 **DB** £75-£120 **HB** £305 **L** ⍾ **D** £13.95 **D** ⍾ ✕ **LD** 21:00
((MC Visa Amex DC ▦

BRISTOL   3E1
Pop. 372,000. M32 (jn 3) 1, London 113, M5 (jn 18) 6, Bath 12, Chepstow 16, Tetbury 26, Wells 21, Weston-super-Mare 20 **EC** Wed **MD** Sun **see** Cathedral, Temple Church, Merchant Venturer's Almshouses, 17th cent Zoo, Observatory, Clifton Suspension Bridge and Avon Gorge, The Georgian House, Red Lodge, Church of St Mary Redcliffe, John Wesley's Chapel, 'SS Great Britain' 🛈 St Nicholas Church, St Nicholas Street 0117-926 0767

★★★★ ✧ Aztec
Aztec West, Almondsbury,
Bristol BS12 4TS
📞 01454-201090 **Fax** 01454-201593
E-mail aztec@shireinns.co.uk
128 bedrs, all ensuite, 4 ⌇ ⍭ ⊡ ⠿ 250 **P** 240 ⊞ **SB** £134-£154 **DB** £154-£174 **L** £16 **D** £20 ✕ **LD** 21:45 Restaurant closed L Sat, Sun ((MC Visa Amex DC ▦ ▦ ▦ ▦ ▦ ⅋

★★★★ ✧ Swallow Royal
College Green, Bristol BS1 5TA
📞 0117-925 5100 **Fax** 0117-925 1515
E-mail info@swallowhotels.com

This imposing Victorian building lies in the city centre, next to the Norman Cathedral. The restaurant has an award for fine food and the hotel has a luxurious leisure club.
242 bedrs, all ensuite, 4 ⍭ ⊡ ⠿ 300 **P** 200 ⊞ **SB** £120-£145 **DB** £135-£170 **L** £15 **D** £18 ✕ **LD** 22:30 ((MC Visa Amex DC ▦ ▦ ▦ ⅋

★★★ ✧ Avon Gorge
Sion Hill, Clifton, Bristol BS8 4LD
📞 0117-973 8955 **Fax** 0117-923 8125
76 bedrs, all ensuite, ⍭ ⊡ ⠿ 100 **P** 20 ⊞ **SB** £80-£85 **DB** £90-£95 **L** £11 **D** £15 ✕ **LD** 22:00 ((MC Visa Amex DC JCB

★★★ Berkeley Square
15 Berkeley Square, Clifton, Bristol BS8 1HB
📞 0117-925 4000 **Fax** 0117-925 2970

Bristol's most highly rated three star hotel is situated in a magnificent Georgian Square in the heart of the city and with just 41 bedrooms offers an exceptionally warm, friendly and personal service.
41 bedrs, all ensuite, ⌇ ⍭ ⊡ ⠿ 15 **P** 24 ⊞ **SB** £49-£96 **DB** £69-£117 **L** ⍾ **D** £15 ✕ **LD** 22:00 ((MC Visa Amex DC

★★★ Henbury Lodge ⯃
Station Road, Henbury, Bristol BS10 7QQ
📞 0117-950 2615 **Fax** 0117-950 9532
21 bedrs, all ensuite, ⍭ ⠿ 30 **P** 25 ⊞ Rest Resid **SB** £75-£85 **DB** £85-£95 **D** £18.50 **D** ⍾ ✕ **LD** 21:30 ((MC Visa Amex DC JCB ▦ ▦

★★★ ✦ Jurys Bristol
Prince Street, Bristol BS1 4QF
📞 0117-923 0333 **Fax** 0117-923 0300
E-mail bookings@jurys.com
191 bedrs, all ensuite, ♀ 🖂 ⚏ 360 **P** 400 ⊕
SB £124.50-£129.50 **DB** £134-£139 **D** £15.95 ✕
LD 22:15 ⓒⓒ MC Visa Amex DC ♿

★★★ Posthouse   **Posthouse**
Filton Road, Hambrook, Bristol BS16 1QX
📞 0117-956 4242 **Fax** 0117-956 9735
E-mail hotai05.brs01.fhi.com
198 bedrs, all ensuite, ⚲ 🖂 ⚏ 260 **P** 200
⊕ ⓒⓒ MC Visa Amex DC JCB ▨ ▨ ▨ ▨ ♿

★★ Arno's
470 Bath Road, Bristol BS4 3HQ
📞 0117-971 1461 **Fax** 0117-971 5507

This 18th century building boasts many original
features sensitively preserved alongside modern
amenities, with the unique Cloisters Restaurant
housed in a former chapel.
24 bedrs, 23 ensuite, 1 ⚱ ⚍ ⚏ 200 **P** 200 ⊕
SB £63.50 **DB** £73 **L** £10 **L** 🍴 **D** £10 **D** ✕ **LD** 22:00
Restaurant closed L Sat, D Sun ⓒⓒ MC Visa

★★ Chelwood House
Chelwood BS18 4NH
📞 01761-490730 **Fax** 01761-490072

Chelwood House is situated in an area of
outstanding beauty and enjoys an enviable location
between Bristol, Bath and Wells. Imposing 300 year

dower house with two reception lounges and a
conservatory restaurant.
11 bedrs, all ensuite, ⚍ ⚲ ⚏ 15 **P** 20 ⊕ Rest Resid
SB £49.50-£60 **DB** £82.50-£97.50 **D** 🍴 ✕ **LD** 21:00
Restaurant closed D Sun ⓒⓒ MC Visa Amex

★★ ✦ Clifton
St Pauls Road, Clifton, Bristol BS8 1LX
📞 0117-973 6882 **Fax** 0117-974 1082
Closed Christmas/New Year

Recently refurbished to an extremely high standard,
the Clifton is one of Bristol's most popular 2 star
hotels, home also to Racks, a lively wine bar and
restaurant.
60 bedrs, 48 ensuite, ⚲ 🖂 **P** 12 ⊕ **SB** £38-£64
DB £55-£71 **L** £15 **D** £15 **D** 🍴 ✕ **LD** 23:00 Restaurant
closed D Sun ⓒⓒ MC Visa Amex DC

★★ Glenroy
Victoria Square, Clifton, Bristol BS8 4EW
📞 0117-973 9058 **Fax** 0117-973 9058
E-mail admin@glenroyhotel.demon.co.uk
Closed Christmas
44 bedrs, all ensuite, ⚹ ⚲ ⚏ 45 **P** 16 ⊕ Resid
SB £56 **DB** £76 **HB** £350-£434 **L** 🍴 **D** £13 **D** 🍴 ✕
LD 21:30 Restaurant closed D Sat-Sun ⓒⓒ MC Visa
Amex DC ♿

★★ Rodney
Rodney Place, Clifton, Bristol BS8 4HY
📞 0117-973 5422 **Fax** 0117-946 7092
Closed Christmas

Town house forming part of a Georgian terrace. Sympathetically renovated and converted.
31 bedrs, all ensuite, ♥ ⅲ 14 ⊞ Rest Resid
SB £64.50 DB £78 L ● D £15 ✕ LD 22:00 Restaurant closed D Sun ⊄ MC Visa Amex DC

★★ Seeley's
17/27 St Paul's Road, Clifton, Bristol BS8 1LX
☎ 0117-973 8544 Fax 0117-973 2406
E-mail admin@seeleys.demon.co.uk
54 bedrs, all ensuite, ▣ ♀ ♪ ⅲ 70 P 30 ⊞ Resid
SB £60-£75 DB £65-£80 HB £504 L £10 L ● D £12 D ●
✕ LD 22:30 Restaurant closed D Sun ⊄ MC Visa Amex DC ☒ ▩
See advert on this page

Westbourne **Awaiting Inspection**
40-44 St Pauls Road, Clifton, Bristol BS8 1LR
☎ 0117-973 4214

BROADWAY Worcestershire	4A1

Pop. 2,100. Moreton-in-Marsh 8, London 92, Banbury 27, Cheltenham 15, Evesham 5, Stow-on-the-Wold 10, Stratford-upon-Avon 15, Tewkesbury 15 ⅡC Thu ▨ 1 Cotswold Court 01386-852937

★★★★ Lygon Arms ♔ ♔ ♔
Blue Ribbon Hotel
Broadway WR12 7DU
☎ 01386-852255 Fax 01386-858611
E-mail info@the-lygon-arms.co.uk

Set in the heart of the Cotswolds. The Lygon Arms combines the unique atmosphere of a 16th century coaching inn with 21st century refinements. The Inn's Country Club boasts a swimming pool, gym, saunas and extensive beauty treatments.
65 bedrs, all ensuite, ▣ ♥ ⅲ 80 P 150 ⊞ ⊄ MC Visa Amex DC JCB ☒ ☒ ▩ ▨ ☒ &

★★★ Buckland Manor ♔ ♔ ♔ ♔
Gold Ribbon Hotel
Buckland, Broadway WR12 7LY
☎ 01386-852626 Fax 01386-853557
E-mail buckland-manor-uk@msn.com

13th century manor situated in the heart of the Cotswolds, in glorious grounds. Superb food and wines in award winning restaurant. Luxury bedrooms with antiques and fourposter beds.
13 bedrs, all ensuite, ▣ ♀ ⅲ P 30 No children under 12 ⊞ SB £195-£335 DB £205-£345 L £28.50 L ● ✕ LD 21:00 ⊄ MC Visa Amex DC ⊰ ▩

★★★ Dormy House

Willersey Hill, Broadway WR12 7LF
☎ 01386-852711 **Fax** 01386-858636
E-mail reservations@dormyhouse.co.uk
Closed Christmas

Meticulously converted 17th century Cotswold farmhouse combining traditional charm with all modern comforts. Leisure facilities include a games room, gym, sauna/steam room, putting green and croquet lawns.
48 bedrs, all ensuite, ⊞ ♪ ⊁ ⠿ 170 **P** 80 ⊞ **SB** £73 **DB** £146 **L** £19.50 **L** ⬤ **D** £30.50 **D** ⬤ ✕ **LD** 21:30
Restaurant closed L Sat ‹‹ MC Visa Amex DC ⊠ ⊠ ⊠
See advert on this page

BROCKENHURST Hampshire   4A4
Pop. 3,300. Lyndhurst 4, London 88, Lymington 5, Ringwood 11 **EC** Wed **see** Parish Church (Norman features), yew tree reputed to be 1,000 years old

★★★ Balmer Lawn
Lyndhurst Road, Brockenhurst SO42 7ZB
☎ 01590-623116 **Fax** 01590-623864
55 bedrs, all ensuite, ⊁ ⊞ ⠿ 100 **P** 90 ⊞ ‹‹ MC Visa Amex DC ⊠ ⊰ ⊠ ⊠ ⊠ ⊠ ⊠ ⬤

★★★ ❖ Carey's Manor
Lyndhurst Road, Brockenhurst SO42 7RH
☎ 01590-623551 **Fax** 01590-622799
E-mail info@careys-manor.uk.

An elegant country house hotel located in the heart of the New Forest, just 90 minutes away from London. Full leisure centre with indoor pool.
79 bedrs, all ensuite, ⊞ ⊁ ⠿ 100 **P** 180 ⊞ ‹‹ MC Visa Amex DC JCB ⊠ ⊠ ⊠
See advert on opposite page

★★★ New Park Manor ⌘ ⌘ ⌘
Lyndhurst Road, Brockenhurst SO43 7QH
☎ 01590-623467 **Fax** 01590-622268

Escape from the crowds to one of the New Forest's finest country house hotels. A former hunting lodge, the building is Grade II Listed and dates back to the 16th century. Most of the individually decorated, ensuite bedrooms offer superb views.
24 bedrs, all ensuite, ⊞ ⠿ 75 **P** 50 No children under 7 ⊞ **SB** £85 **DB** £110-£185 **L** £14.95 **D** £27 ✕ **LD** 21:30 ‹‹ MC Visa Amex DC JCB ⊰ ⊠ ⊠

Careys Manor Hotel

An elegant Country House Hotel located in the heart of the New Forest, just 90 minutes away from London. The restaurant offers fine English and French cuisine. Bedrooms are elegantly furnished and the majority have a patio or balcony overlooking delightful gardens. Leisure Centre comprising an indoor swimming pool, jacuzzi, steam room, sauna, gymnasium, solarium and beauty treatment rooms.

**Brockenhurst, New Forest,
Hampshire SO42 7RH
Tel: (01590) 623551
Fax: (01590) 677299**

★★★ Rhinefield House
Rhinefield Road, Brockenhurst SO42 7QB
☎ 01590-622922 Fax 01590-622800
34 bedrs, all ensuite, ④ ♀ ⅲ 110 P 80 ⊕ SB £95-£105 DB £130-£140 HB £455 L £16 L ♥ D £25.50 D ♥ ✕ LD 22:00 ⲁ MC Visa Amex DC JCB ⊡ ⸬ ⊞ ⊠ ⊠ ⊞

♨ ★★★ ✦ Whitley Ridge Country House
Beaulieu Road, Brockenhurst SO42 7QL
☎ 01590-622354 Fax 01590-622856
E-mail whitleybridge@brockenhurst.co.uk
14 bedrs, all ensuite, ④ ✝ ⅲ 20 P 30 ⊕ Rest Resid SB £56-£60 DB £88-£98 HB £315-£343 L £13.50 L ♥ D £21.50 D ♥ ✕ LD 21:50 ⲁ MC Visa Amex DC JCB ⊠ �&

Don't forget to mention the guide

When booking direct, please remember to tell the hotel that you chose it from RAC Inspected Hotels 2000

★★ Watersplash ⚑
The Rise, Brockenhurst SO42 7ZP
☎ 01590-622344 Fax 01590-624047

Set in the New Forest, this family run country house hotel stands in 2 acres of secluded gardens and is noted for fine food and accommodation and friendly personal service. All rooms ensuite and fourposter room with double jacuzzi. Seasonal pool.
23 bedrs, all ensuite, ✝ ⅲ 60 P 25 ⊕ Resid SB £45-£48 DB £70-£80 HB £285-£299 L £10 D £18 ✕ LD 20:30 ⲁ MC Visa Amex ⸬ &

BROMLEY Kent   5D2
Pop. 65,700. London 11, Croydon 6, Sevenoaks 14, Sidcup 4, Westerham 11 ℇ Wed MD Thu see Church of SS Peter and Paul (memorial Dr Johnson's wife, Norman Font)

★★★ Bromley Court
Bromley Hill, Bromley BR1 4JD
☎ 0181-464 5011 Fax 0181-460 0899
E-mail bromley-hotel@btinternet.com
115 bedrs, all ensuite, ♀ ⊡ ⅲ 150 P 110 ⊕ SB £85-£90 DB £94-£98 L £9.50 L ♥ D £14.95 D ♥ ✕ LD 22:00 Restaurant closed L Sat ⲁ MC Visa Amex DC ⊞ ⊠

BROMSGROVE Worcestershire   7E3
Pop. 25,000. M42 (jn 1) 1, London 113, M5 3, Birmingham 13, Droitwich 6, Evesham 21, Kidderminster 9 ℇ Thu MD Tue, Fri, Sat see Church of St John the Baptist, Valley House, Fockbury (birthplace of A E Housman), United Reform Church ⓘ Bromsgrove Museum, 26 Birmingham Road 01527-831809

★★★ ✤ Pine Lodge
Kidderminster Road, Bromsgrove B61 9AB
☎ 01527-576600 **Fax** 01527-878981

Set in the beautiful Worcestershire countryside with easy access to the Midland's motorway network and only 20 minutes drive from Birmingham and the NEC, the Pine Lodge Hotel is the ideal venue for every occasion.
114 bedrs, all ensuite, 🖪 ♀ ⚲ ⊁ ☎ ⚑ ‖ 200 **P** 250 ⊞
SB £50-£105 **DB** £70-£120 **L** £15.50 **L** ● **D** £18.50
D ● ✕ **LD** 22:00 Restaurant closed L Sat ⟨⟨ MC Visa Amex DC 🖪 🗷 🖩 🗷 ⅼ
See advert on this page

Pine Lodge Hotel
Bromsgrove

- 114 En Suite Bedrooms • 2 Restaurants
- Lounge Bar • Health and Leisure Club/Snooker Lounge • 8 Meeting Rooms • Syndicate Rooms
- Banqueting Rooms • Free Car Parking for 250 Vehicles • Weekend Breaks – Families welcome.

Set in the beautiful Worcestershire countryside. With easy access to the Midlands motorway network and only 20 minutes from Birmingham and the NEC, the Pine Lodge Hotel is the ideal venue for every occasion.

To make your reservation please telephone:
01527 576600

Kidderminster Road, Bromsgrove, Worcestershire B61 9AB
Tel: 01527 576600 Fax: 01527 878981

BUCKDEN Cambridgeshire 8C4
Pop. 2,670. Biggleswade 16, London 62, Bedford 16, Huntingdon 4, Kettering 25 **see** Perp Church, remains of Palace of Bishops of Lincoln,

★★ Lion
High Street, Buckden, Huntingdon PE18 9XA
☎ 01480-810313 **Fax** 01480-811070

The Lion is a 15th century Grade II Listed building, offering open log fires, a beautiful oak panelled restaurant and individual accommodation. A warm friendly welcome awaits.
15 bedrs, all ensuite, 🖪 ⚲ ⊁ ‖ 12 **P** 20 ⊞ **SB** £60-£73.50 **DB** £75-£95 **L** £10.50 **L** ● **D** £16.75 **D** ● ✕
LD 21:30 ⟨⟨ MC Visa Amex DC JCB ⅼ

BUCKINGHAM Buckinghamshire 4B1
🄸 Old Goal Museum, Market Hill 01280-823020

★★★ Villiers 🍴
3 Castle Street, Buckingham MK18 1BS
☎ 01280-822444 **Fax** 01280-822113
E-mail villiers@villiers-hotels.demon.co.uk

A superbly renovated 400-year-old coaching inn with individually designed luxurious bedrooms set around an original courtyard. Quintessentially English restaurant, Italian bistro and a Jacobean pub.
38 bedrs, all ensuite, 🖪 ☎ ‖ 250 **P** 40 ⊞ **SB** £75-£95 **DB** £95-£110 **L** ● **D** £17.95 ✕ **LD** 22:00 ⟨⟨ MC Visa Amex DC 🖪 🗷 🖩 ⅼ
See advert on opposite page

ENGLAND

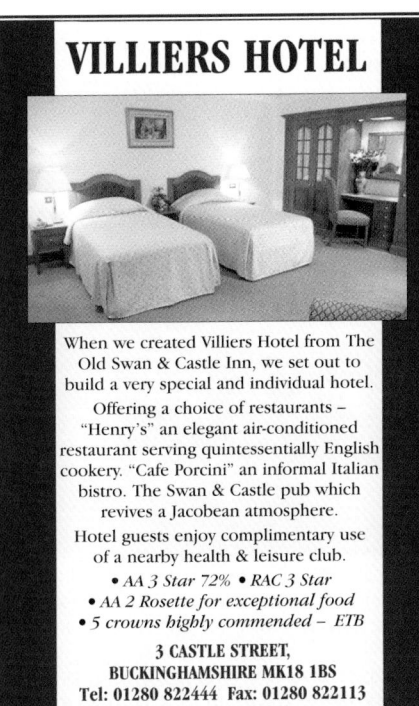

VILLIERS HOTEL

When we created Villiers Hotel from The Old Swan & Castle Inn, we set out to build a very special and individual hotel.

Offering a choice of restaurants – "Henry's" an elegant air-conditioned restaurant serving quintessentially English cookery. "Cafe Porcini" an informal Italian bistro. The Swan & Castle pub which revives a Jacobean atmosphere.

Hotel guests enjoy complimentary use of a nearby health & leisure club.

- *AA 3 Star 72%* • *RAC 3 Star*
- *AA 2 Rosette for exceptional food*
- *5 crowns highly commended – ETB*

**3 CASTLE STREET,
BUCKINGHAMSHIRE MK18 1BS
Tel: 01280 822444 Fax: 01280 822113**

BUDE Cornwall · 2B2

Pop. 7,700. Holsworthy 9, London 220, Bideford 25, Camelford 17, Launceston 18 **EC** Thu 🛈 Visitor Centre, The Crescent 01288-354240

★★★ Hartland
Hartland Terrace, Bude EX23 8JY
📞 01288-355661 **Fax** 01288-352664
Closed Nov-Mar ex Christmas/New Year
28 bedrs, all ensuite, ⊞ ➔ ☎ ⽕ 100 **P** 30 ⊞ **SB** £42-£47 **DB** £60-£76 **HB** £295-£363 **L** £13 **L** ● **D** £18 ✕ **LD** 20:30 ⬥ ⅙

★★ Camelot
Downs View, Bude EX23 8RE
📞 01288-352361 **Fax** 01288-355470

Overlooking Bude golf course and three minutes walk from either sandy beaches or the town centre. We offer fine food, comfortable rooms and friendly service. Golfing breaks a speciality.
21 bedrs, all ensuite, **P** 21 ⊞ Rest Resid **SB** £24-£28 **DB** £48-£56 **HB** £220-£255 **D** £15 **D** ● ✕ **LD** 20:30 **CC** MC Visa JCB

★★ Maer Lodge
Maer Down Road, Bude EX23 8NG
📞 01288-353306 **Fax** 01288-354005
E-mail maerlodgehotel@btinternet.com.
16 bedrs, all ensuite, ➔ ⽕ 60 **P** 20 ⊞ Rest Resid **CC** MC Visa Amex DC ⅙

★★ ⬥ St Margarets
Killerton Road, Bude EX23 8EN
📞 01288-352252 **Fax** 01288-355995

The hotel is situated in its own grounds on a quiet road, yet within minutes of the town centre, golf course and magnificent golden surfing beaches; and promises to provide everything to make your stay a memorable one.
10 bedrs, all ensuite, ➔ ⽕ 25 **P** 4 ⊞ Rest Resid **CC** MC Visa JCB ⅙

★ Meva Gwin
Upton, Bude EX23 0LY
📞 01288-352347 **Fax** 01288-352347
Closed Oct-Apr
12 bedrs, 11 ensuite, **P** 44 ⊞ Rest Resid **SB** £22-£24 **DB** £44-£48 **HB** £190-£200 **D** £9.50 ✕ **LD** 19:30 **CC** MC Visa

---

BURFORD Oxfordshire · 4A2

Pop. 1,150. Oxford 20, London 75, Cheltenham 22, Chipping Norton 11, Cirencester 17, Stow-on-the-Wold 10, Swindon 19 **EC** Wed **see** Church of St John, old Almshouses, small museum in 15th cent Tolsey, Old Houses, Cotswold Wild Life Park 2m S 🛈 The Brewery, Sheep Street 01993-823558

★★ ✣ Maytime
Asthall, Burford OX8 4HW
📞 01993-822068 Fax 01993-822635
6 bedrs, all ensuite, ♙ ☔ ⅲ 35 P 100 ⊞ SB £47.50
DB £57.50-£62.50 L ❤ D £6 D ❤ ✕ LD 21:30 ℂℂ MC
Visa Amex ♿

BURLEY Hampshire   4A4
Pop. 1,500. Lyndhurst 7, London 91, Bournemouth
13, Lymington 9, Ringwood 5 see Cricket Green

★★★ Moorhill House
Burley BH24 4AG
📞 01425-403285 Fax 01425-403715
E-mail information@carehotels.co.uk
24 bedrs, all ensuite, ☔ ⅲ 28 P 40 ⊞ Resid SB £65-
£70 DB £110-£125 HB £345 D £21.50 ✕ LD 20:45
ℂℂ MC Visa Amex DC ▣ ▨ ♿

BURNHAM-ON-SEA Somerset   3E2
Wells 17, London 140, Bridgwater 9, Bristol 27,
Glastonbury 18, Weston-Super-Mare 11 MD Mon see
St Andrew's Church with marble altarpiece by Inigo
Jones. Gore sands, Brean Down 🛈 South
Esplanade 01278-787852

★★ ✣ Royal Clarence
31 Esplanade, Burnham-on-Sea TA8 1BQ
📞 01278-783138 Fax 01278-792965
19 bedrs, 18 ensuite, ☔ ⅲ 300 P 18 ⊞ ℂℂ MC Visa
Amex DC

BURNLEY Lancashire   10C3
Pop. 91,000. Rochdale 14, London 206, Blackburn
11, Bolton 19, Bury 15, Settle 23, Skipton 18,
Todmorden 8, Whalley 8 ℂ Tue MD Mon, Thur, Sat see
St Peter's Church, 16th-17th cent Towneley Hall
(now Art Gallery and Museum) 🛈 Burnley
Mechanics, Manchester Road 01282-455485

★★★ Higher Trapp Country House 🖥
Trapp Lane, Simonstone,
Burnley BB12 7QW
📞 01282-772781 Fax 01282-772782
20 bedrs, all ensuite, ④ ⅲ 100 P 100 ⊞ SB £52
DB £75 L £10.50 D £15 D ❤ ✕ LD 21:50 ℂℂ MC Visa
JCB ♿

★★★ Oaks 🖥
Colne Road, Reedley, Burnley BD10 2LF
📞 01282-414141 Fax 01282-433401
E-mail oaks@shireinns.co.uk

53 bedrs, all ensuite, ④ ♙ ☔ ⅲ 120 P 110 ⊞
SB £92-£112 DB £112-£132 L £12 D £20 ✕ LD 21:45
Restaurant closed L Sat, Sun ℂℂ MC Visa Amex DC
▣ ▣ ▨ ▣

★★ Comfort Inn
Keirby Walk, Burnley BB11 2DH
📞 01282-427611 Fax 01282-436370
E-mail admin@gb608.u-net.com

Modern style hotel in centre of town. Good
restaurant and bar. Excellent touring base for
Granada Studios, Blackpool, Lake District and
scenic beauty of Northern England.
50 bedrs, all ensuite, ☔ ▣ ⅲ 300 P 60 ⊞ SB £53.50-
£61.25 DB £60.25-£68 D £10.75 ✕ LD 21:45 ℂℂ MC
Visa Amex DC ▣

Rosehill House
Rosehill Avenue, Burnley BB11 2PW
📞 01282-453931 Fax 01282-455628
E-mail rhhotel@provider.co.uk

Elegant stone built mansion standing in its own
grounds in a quiet residential area of Burnley.
Excellent touring base for Manchester, Blackpool,
Lake District, Rossendale Valley, Forest of
Bowland, Yorkshire Dales and Bronte Country to
the east.
30 bedrs, all ensuite, ④ ☔ ⅲ 50 P 60 ⊞ SB £27.50-
£40 DB £39.50-£65 D £13 ✕ LD 21:30 ℂℂ MC Visa
Amex DC JCB ▣

ENGLAND

The Queens Hotel & Conference Center

Behind the listed facade of this C16th hotel lies a true combination of tradition and technology. Our traditional service standards range from morning tea to washing your car. Combine this with in-house movies, ISDN data and "state of the art" conference facilities, including those in the famous Bass Museum of Brewing, and in the center of England you have our 3 star "special hospitality venue"

One Bridge Street, Burton upon Trent
Tel: 01283 523800
www.hermitagepark.com

BURTON-UPON-TRENT Staffordshire   7F2
Pop. 59,000. Ashby-de-la-Zouch 9, London 122, Ashbourne 19, Derby 11, Lichfield 13, Stafford 26, Tamworth 15, Uttoxeter 13 **MD** Thu, Sat **see** Parish Church, Abbey ruins ⓘ Octagon Centre, New Street 01283-516609

★★★ Queens
2-5 Bridge Street,
Burton-upon-Trent DE14 1SY
📞 01283-564993 **Fax** 01283-517556
38 bedrs, all ensuite, 4 ♀ ✗ 🖃 ∷ 100 **P** 50 ⊞
SB £42.50-£89.50 **DB** £49.50-£99.50 **L** £9.95 **L** ➡
D £12.50 **D** ➡ ✗ **LD** 22:00 Restaurant closed L Sat
CC MC Visa Amex
See advert on this page

BURY Lancashire   10C4
See also RAMSBOTTOM
Pop. 54,000. Manchester 8, London 192, M66 (jn 2) 1, Blackburn 15, Bolton 6, Burnley 15, Oldham 10, Rochdale 6 **EC** Tue **MD** Wed, Fri, Sat **see** Art Gallery and Museum, Regimental Museum, Statue of Sir Robert Peel ⓘ Met Arts Centre, Market Street 0161-705 5111

★★★ Bolholt
Walshaw Road, Bury BL8 1PU
📞 0161-764 3888 **Fax** 0161-763 1789
66 bedrs, all ensuite, 4 ✗ ➤ ∷ 200 **P** 250 ⊞ **SB** £64
DB £63-£79 **L** £9.50 **D** £14.50 ✗ **LD** 21:30 **CC** MC Visa Amex DC 🖾 🖾 🖾 🖾 🖾 ♿

BURY ST EDMUNDS Suffolk   9E4
Pop. 31,000. Sudbury 16, London 74, Ely 24, Harwich 41, Haverhill 19, Newmarket 14, Scole 22, Stowmarket 14, Thetford 12 **EC** Thu **MD** Wed, Sat **see** Cathedral Church of St James, St Edmund's Abbey, St Mary's Church contains tomb of Mary Tudor ⓘ 6 Angel Hill 01284-764667

★★★ Angel 🏨
Angel Hill, Bury St Edmunds IP33 1LT
📞 01284-753926 **Fax** 01284-750092
E-mail reception@theangel.co.uk
42 bedrs, all ensuite, 4 ➤ ∷ 150 **P** 40 ⊞ **CC** MC Visa Amex DC

★★★ Butterfly
A14 Bury East Exit, Moreton Hall, Bury St Edmunds IP32 7BW
📞 01284-760884 **Fax** 01284-755476
E-mail reception@butterflyhotels.co.uk

A modern, purpose built hotel providing polite and friendly service in an informal atmosphere. The pine furnished restaurant offers a la carte, daily specials and a buffet style self service. Bedrooms are light and well laid out with fitted furniture.
66 bedrs, all ensuite, ♀ ∷ 50 **P** 75 ⊞ **SB** £75
DB £82.50 **L** £15 **D** £15 ✗ **LD** 22:00 **CC** MC Visa Amex DC

BUTTERMERE Cumbria   10A2
Pop. 120. Keswick 8½, London 294, Cockermouth 10, Workington 16 **see** Crummock Water, Scale Force (120 ft fall)

★★ Bridge
Buttermere CA13 9UZ
☎ 01768-770252 **Fax** 01768-770215
22 bedrs, all ensuite, ☒ ⊁ ⊞ 30 **P** 60 ⊕ **SB** £39-£45
DB £78-£90 **HB** £355-£380 **L** ☻ **D** £20 ✕ **LD** 20:30
《 MC Visa

BUXTON Derbyshire   7F1
Pop. 20,797. Ashbourne 20, London 159, Chapel-en-le-Frith 5, Chesterfield 23, Congleton 17, Leek 13, Macclesfield 12, Matlock 20, Stockport 18 **EC** Wed **MD** Tue, Sat **see** The Crescent (18th cent houses, Pump Room), Pavillion Gdns, Peak Rail Steam Centre 🛈 The Crescent 01298-25106

★★★★ Palace
Palace Road, Buxton SK17 6AG
☎ 01298-22001 **Fax** 01298-72131
E-mail palace@paramount-hotels.co.uk

PARAMOUNT
HOTEL·GROUP

Beautiful Victorian hotel offering panoramic views over the spa town of Buxton. Relax in the leisure club with hair and beauty salon. Free car parking.
122 bedrs, all ensuite, ⊁ 📺 ⊞ 380 **P** 200 ⊕ **SB** £98
DB £115 **HB** £434 **L** £12.50 **D** £19.50 ✕ **LD** 21:30
《 MC Visa Amex ▣ ▣ ▣ ▣ ⅙

★★★ ✦ Buckingham
1-2 Burlington Road, Buxton SK17 9AS
☎ 01298-70481 **Fax** 01298-72186
29 bedrs, all ensuite, ☒ ⊁ 📺 ⊞ 40 **P** 30 ⊕ **SB** £65
DB £80 **HB** £320 **L** £10 **D** £16 ✕ **LD** 21:30 《 MC Visa
Amex ▣

★★★ ✦ Lee Wood
Manchester Road, Buxton SK17 6TQ
☎ 01298-23002 **Fax** 01298-23228
E-mail leewoodhotel@btinternet.com
37 bedrs, all ensuite, ⊁ 📺 ⊞ 120 **P** 50 ⊕ **SB** £70-£80 **DB** £92-£110 **HB** £365-£380 **L** £13 **D** £24.50 **D** ☻ ✕ **LD** 21:30 《 MC Visa Amex DC JCB

★★ Grove
Grove Parade, Buxton SK17 6AJ
☎ 01298-79919 **Fax** 01298-77906
21 bedrs, 11 ensuite, ⊞ 60 ⊕ **SB** £32.50 **DB** £65 **L** £6
L ☻ **D** £20 **D** ☻ ✕ **LD** 21:30 《 MC Visa JCB

★★ Portland
32 St John's Road, Buxton SK17 6XQ
☎ 01298-71493 **Fax** 01298-27464
E-mail brian@portland-hotel.freeserve.co.uk
22 bedrs, all ensuite, ☒ ⌀ ⊁ ⊞ 40 **P** 12 ⊕ ⊕ Rest
SB £48-£58 **DB** £65-£72 **L** £8.50 **L** ☻ **D** £20.95 **D** ☻ ✕
LD 21:30 《 MC Visa Amex DC

★ ✦ Hartington
18 Broad Walk, Buxton SK17 6JR
☎ 01298-22638 **Fax** 01298-22638
E-mail harthot@globalnet.co.uk
Closed Christmas-New Year

Detached former doctor's residence, built in the 1860s and overlooking the Pavilion gardens and lake. Established as a hotel in 1958 and remains in the same family ownership.
16 bedrs, 9 ensuite, ☒ **P** 15 ⊕ Rest Resid **SB** £30-£50 **DB** £50-£65 **HB** £250-£270 **D** £12.50 ✕ **LD** 20:00
《 MC Visa Amex ⅙

CADNAM Hampshire   4A4
M27 ½, London 82, Lyndhurst 4, Ringwood 12, Salisbury 14, Southampton 8

★★★ Bartley Lodge

Lyndhurst Road, Cadnam SO40 2NR
☎ 01703-812248 **Fax** 01703-812075
E-mail information@carehotels.co.uk
31 bedrs, 27 ensuite, 4 ⋒ ☒ ⊁ ⊞ 70 **P** 80 ⊕
SB £65-£70 **DB** £110-£125 **HB** £345 **D** £21.50 ✕
LD 20:45 Restaurant closed **L** Mon-Sat 《 MC Visa
Amex DC ▣ ▣ ▣ ▣
See advert on opposite page

ENGLAND

THE BARTLEY LODGE HOTEL

Grade II listed country house hotel set in 8 acres of grounds and gardens directly adjoining the New Forest.

31 delightfully furnished bedrooms, excellent cuisine, new indoor leisure with pool, sauna, fitness room and two hard surface tennis courts.

**CADNAM, NEW FOREST SO40 2NR
TEL: 01703 812248**

CAMBERLEY Surrey   4C3
Pop. 52,271. Bagshot 3, London 30, Basingstoke 17, Farnham 10, Guildford 12, Henley-on-Thames 18, Reading 15 **EC** Wed **see** St Michael's Church

★★★ Frimley Hall   **Heritage** HOTELS
Portsmouth Road,
Camberley GU15 2BG
☎ 01276-28321 **Fax** 01276-691253
E-mail gm1043@forte-hotels.com
86 bedrs, all ensuite, 🄰 ♪ ⊩ ▦ 70 **P** 100 🍽 **SB** £120-£145 **DB** £140-£161 **L** ♥ **D** £10 **D** ♥ ✕ **LD** 22:00 **CC** MC Visa Amex DC JCB

CAMBRIDGE Cambridgeshire   5D1
Pop. 101,000. M11 (jn 12) 1½, London 55, Biggleswade 22, Bishop's Stortford 27, Ely 16, Haverhill 18, Huntingdon 16, Newmarket 13, Royston 13 **MD** Daily **see** Colleges and Gardens, The Backs', Churches, Mathematical Bridge, Bridge of Sighs (St John's), Fitzwilliam Museum, King's College Chapel, Botanic Garden 🅸 Wheeler Street 01223-322640

★★★ Duxford Lodge
Ickleton Road, Duxford CB2 4RU
☎ 01223-836444 **Fax** 01223-832271
Closed 25-30 Dec

Comfortable country house hotel in beautiful gardens, ten miles south of Cambridge in 'Lovejoy Country', close to Duxford Air Museum. Featuring award winning 'Le Paradis' restaurant serving exquisite food.
15 bedrs, all ensuite, 🄰 ♪ ⊩ ▦ 30 **P** 35 🍽 **SB** £50-£80 **DB** £85-£100 **L** £20.50 **L** ♥ **D** £20.50 **D** ♥ ✕ **LD** 21:30 Restaurant closed L Sat **CC** MC Visa Amex DC

★★★ Gonville 🖫
Gonville Place, Cambridge CB1 1LY
☎ 01223-366611 **Fax** 01223-315470
64 bedrs, all ensuite, ♀ ♪ ⊩ 🖪 ▦ 200 **P** 80 🍽 **SB** £92 **DB** £110 **L** £13.50 **L** ♥ **D** £18.50 **D** ♥ ✕ **LD** 20:45 **CC** MC Visa Amex DC

★★★ Posthouse   **Posthouse**
Bridge Road, Impington,
Cambridge CB4 4PH
☎ 01223-237000 **Fax** 01223-233426
118 bedrs, all ensuite, ⊩ ▦ 60 **P** 200 🍽 **SB** £68.95-£108.95 **DB** £78.90-£118.90 **L** £10 **D** £15 ✕ **LD** 22:30 **CC** MC Visa Amex DC JCB 🖪 🖾 🖾 ċ

★★★ Royal Cambridge
Trumpington Street,
Cambridge CB2 1PY
☎ 01223-351631 **Fax** 01223-352972
E-mail royalcambridge@msihotels.co.uk
49 bedrs, all ensuite, ♪ ⊩ 🖪 ▦ 120 **P** 80 🍽 **SB** £81.50-£88 **DB** £99-£108.50 **L** £17.75 **L** ♥ **D** £17.75 **D** ♥ ✕ **LD** 21:30 Restaurant closed L Sat **CC** MC Visa Amex DC ċ

★★ Arundel House 🛏 🛏

Chesterton Road, Cambridge CB4 3AN
📞 01223-367701 **Fax** 01223-367721
Closed Christmas

Beautifully located overlooking the River Cam and open parkland, this elegant terrace hotel offers some of the best food in the area. Close to city centre.
105 bedrs, 102 ensuite, ▦ 50 **P** 70 ⊞ **SB** £45-£69 **DB** £65-£91 **L** £10.75 **L** ● **D** £15.95 **D** ● ✕ **LD** 21:30 ⓒ MC Visa Amex DC

★★ Centennial

63/71 Hills Road, Cambridge CB2 1PG
📞 01223-314652 **Fax** 01223-315443
Closed Christmas-New Year
39 bedrs, all ensuite, ♀ ⋟ ▦ 36 **P** 32 ⊞ Rest Resid **SB** £65-£70 **DB** £80-£88 **L** £13 **D** £15 ✕ **LD** 21:30 ⓒ MC Visa Amex DC
See advert on this page

CANTERBURY Kent	5E3

Pop. 39,000. M2 (jn 7) 8, London 58, Ashford 14, Dover 15, Folkestone 16, Maidstone 27, Margate 15 **EC** Thu **MD** Wed, **see** Cathedral (site of Becket's murder), St Martin's and other old Churches, Christchurch Gate, King's School, Eastbridge Hospital (Almshouses), Beaney Institute Museum, The Weavers, City Walls, Dane John Gardens ☑ 34 St Margaret's Street 01227-766567

★★★ Chaucer 🛏   Heritage
                            HOTELS

Ivy Lane, Canterbury CT1 1TT
📞 01227-464427 **Fax** 01227-450397
E-mail heritagehotels_canterbury.chaucer hotel@forte-hotels.com
42 bedrs, all ensuite, ④ ⌁ ▦ 110 **P** 45 ⊞ **SB** £66-£90 **DB** £124-£140 **L** £8.95 **D** £25 ✕ **LD** 21:30 ⓒ MC Visa Amex DC

★★ Canterbury
71 New Dover Road, Canterbury CT1 3DZ
☎ 01227-450551 **Fax** 01227-780145
E-mail canterbury.hotel@btinternet.com

Elegant hotel famed for the warmth of its welcome, its comfort, and its 'la bonne cuisine' won two rosettes, Good Food Guide 1998. 15 minutes walk from the city centre. Ample parking, bar and lift.
25 bedrs, all ensuite, ▦ ⊁ ▣ ⪢ 24 P 40 ⊟ SB £45-£48 DB £65-£72 L £12.95 L ⬤ D £15.95 D ⬤ ✕
LD 22:00 ℂℂ MC Visa Amex DC JCB

★★ Ebury ⏧
65-67 New Dover Road, Canterbury CT1 3DX
☎ 01227-768433 **Fax** 01227-459187
E-mail info@ebury-hotel.co.uk
Closed 15 Dec-15 Jan

An elegant Victorian building (c.1840) standing in three acres. All rooms ensuite. English restaurant, heated indoor pool and spa. Large car park.
15 bedrs, all ensuite, ▦ ♀ ⋄ ⊁ P 30 ⊟ Rest Resid
SB £45-£55 DB £65-£75 HB £250-£275 D £15 D ⬤ ✕
LD 20:30 Restaurant closed D Sun ℂℂ MC Visa Amex DC JCB ▣

County
High Street, Canterbury CT1 2RX
☎ 01227-766266 **Fax** 01277-451512
73 bedrs, all ensuite, ▦ ▣ ⪢ 180 P 40 ⊟ ℂℂ MC Visa Amex DC JCB ⅄
See advert on opposite page

Slatters
St Margaret's Street, Canterbury CT1 2TR
☎ 01227-463271 **Fax** 01227-764117
Closed Christmas

A warm welcome awaits you at Slatters Hotel in the heart of the historic city of Canterbury. Whether on business, shopping or exploring this fascinating city, Slatters provides the ideal base for a memorable visit.
31 bedrs, 27 ensuite, ⊁ ⪢ 100 P 18 ⊟ ✕ LD 21:30
ℂℂ MC Visa Amex DC

CARLISLE Cumbria   10B1
See also WETHERAL
Pop. 70,000. M6 (jn 44) 1½, London 294, Brampton 9, Cockermouth 25, Gretna 9, Langholm 20, Penrith 18 **EC** Thu **MD** Daily exc Thur, Sun **see** Cathedral and Monastic buildings, Castle (Border Regt Museum). Tullie House Museum and Art Gallery, 17th cent Market Cross, The Citadel ⅊ Old Town Hall, Green Market 01228-512444

★★★ ✦ Central Plaza
Victoria Viaduct, Carlisle CA3 8AL
☎ 01228-520256 **Fax** 01228-514657

Elegant, Victorian style, city centre hotel.
84 bedrs, all ensuite, ⊁ ▣ ⪢ 100 P 20 ⊟ ℂℂ MC Visa Amex DC

★★★ ✦ County
9 Botchergate, Carlisle CA1 1QP
☎ 01228-531316 **Fax** 01228-401805

This beautiful listed building underwent extensive
refurbishment in 1990. It now boasts all modern
amenities but keeps the original atmosphere and
decor of Georgian grandeur.
84 bedrs, all ensuite, ♀ ☷ ⅲ 180 **P** 80 ⊕ **CC** MC
Visa Amex DC JCB &
See advert on this page

★★★ Crown & Mitre
4 English Street, Carlisle CA3 8HZ
☎ 01228-525491 **Fax** 01228-514553
97 bedrs, all ensuite, ♀ ☷ ⅲ 400 **P** 45 ⊕ **SB** £79
DB £99 **D** £17 ✕ **LD** 21:30 **CC** MC Visa Amex DC ☒ &

★★★ Cumbria Park
32 Scotland Road, Carlisle CA3 9DG
☎ 01228-522887 **Fax** 01228-514796
Closed 25-26 Dec
47 bedrs, all ensuite, ④ ☷ ⅲ 180 **P** 40 ⊕ **SB** £71-
£87.50 **DB** £92.50-£117.50 **L** £12.50 **L** ♥ **D** £16 **D** ♥
✕ **LD** 21:45 Restaurant closed L Sun **CC** MC Visa
Amex DC JCB

★★★ ✦ Dalston Hall
Dalston, Carlisle CA5 7JX
☎ 01228-710271 **Fax** 01228-711273
E-mail info@dalston-hall-hotel.co.uk

Fifteenth century mansion, with a variety of high
standard rooms. Original 'Peel Tower', and Baronial
Hall dating back to 1065. Set in 7 acres of gardens.
13 bedrs, all ensuite, ④ ⌁ ⅲ 100 **P** 50 ⊕ **SB** £105
DB £135 **HB** £476 **L** £14.50 **L** ♥ **D** £19.95 **D** ♥ ✕
LD 21:30 **CC** MC Visa Amex DC JCB ▦ ☐ &

★★★ Posthouse   **Posthouse**
Park House Road, Kingstown, Carlisle CA3 0HR
☎ 01228-531201 **Fax** 01228-543178
127 bedrs, all ensuite, ⌁ ☷ ⅲ 120 **P** 150 ⊕ **SB** £36-
£89 **DB** £72-£99 **L** £17.50 **L** ♥ **D** £17.50 **D** ♥ ✕
LD 22:00 Restaurant closed (L) Saturday **CC** MC Visa
Amex DC ▣ ▨ ▦ &

★★★ Swallow Hilltop
London Road, Carlisle CA1 2PQ
☎ 01228-529255 **Fax** 01228-525238
E-mail info@swallowhotels.com

SWALLOW
HOTELS

Well situated for visiting the northern lakes, Borders
and historic Carlisle. The hotel has a newly

ENGLAND

refurbished leisure club.
92 bedrs, all ensuite, ⊷ ▣ ⠿ 500 **P** 350 ⊕ **SB** £75-£95 **DB** £95-£105 **L** £11.50 **D** £18.50 ✕ **LD** 21:30 ⓒ MC Visa Amex DC ▣ ▣ ▣ &

★★ Graham Arms
English Street, Longtown CA6 5SE
☏ 01228-791213 **Fax** 01228-791213
E-mail hotel@cumbria.com
14 bedrs, 12 ensuite, ▣ ⌀ ⊷ ⠿ 45 **P** 12 ⊕
SB £20.50-£29.50 **DB** £39-£49 **L** ▣ **D** £6.95 **D** ▣ ✕
LD 20:30 ⓒ MC Visa Amex

★★ Pinegrove
262 London Road, Carlisle CA1 2QS
☏ 01228-524828 **Fax** 01228-810941
Closed Christmas Day

A two star hotel offering a warm welcome and excellent home cooking, situated near the Lake District, golf courses, Hadrian's Wall, fishing and bowling greens.
31 bedrs, 29 ensuite, ▣ ⊷ ⠿ 120 **P** 50 ⊕ **SB** £46-£48 **DB** £58-£60 **L** ▣ **D** £14 **D** ▣ ✕ **LD** 21:00 Restaurant closed Sun ⓒ MC Visa Amex DC ▣ &

★★ Tarn End House
Talkin Tarn, Brampton, Carlisle CA8 1LS
☏ 01697-72340 **Fax** 01697-72089
Closed 8-28 Jan

Beautifully situated in own secluded grounds overlooking the Tarn. Renowned locally for quality of food and speciality meringues and afternoon teas. Excellent golf locally

7 bedrs, all ensuite, ▣ ♀ ⊷ ⠿ 30 **P** 40 ⊕ **SB** £39-£48 **DB** £55-£75 **HB** £253-£295 **L** £10 **L** ▣ **D** £16 **D** ▣ ✕ **LD** 21:00 ⓒ MC Visa Amex &

M6 (jn 35) 1, London 243, Kendal 15, Kirkby Lonsdale 10, Lancashire 7, Settle 24

★★ ✛ Royal Station
Market Street, Carnforth LA5 9BT
☏ 01524-733636 **Fax** 01524-720267
A traditional 19th century hotel situated in the centre of Carnforth, a small market town ideally located for visiting the Lake District. Comfortable ensuite bedrooms and a wide choice of home cooked food available in restaurant and lounge bar.
12 bedrs, all ensuite, ⊷ ⠿ 150 **P** 7 ⊕ ⓒ MC Visa Amex DC JCB ▣

CASTLE COMBE Wiltshire   3F1
Pop. 300. M4 (in 7) 6½, London 97, Bath 11, Bristol 18, Chippenham 6, Cirencester 22, Frome 22

★★★★ Manor House ▮ ▮ ▮
Gold Ribbon Hotel
Castle Combe SN14 7HR
☏ 01249-782206 **Fax** 01249-782159
E-mail enquiries@manor-house.co.uk
45 bedrs, all ensuite, ▣ ⠿ 40 **P** 100 ⊕ ⓒ MC Visa Amex DC ▣ ▣ ▣ ▣ &

★★★ Castle Inn
Castle Combe, Nr. Chippenham SN14 7HN
☏ 01249-783030 **Fax** 01249-782315
E-mail res@castle-inn.co.uk

At the heart of England's prettiest village, you will find hospitality and service that befits this bygone setting. Ideal base for exploring Bath and Bristol.
Website: http:// www.hatton-hotels.co.uk
11 bedrs, all ensuite, ⠿ 30 ⊕ ⓒ MC Visa Amex DC JCB

CATTERICK North Yorkshire   11D2

Pop. 2,800. Boroughbridge 22, London 230, Darlington 13, Leyburn 11, Northallerton 13, Scotch Corner 5, Stockton 23 **EC** Wed **see** River Swale, 14th cent Church

★★ Bridge House
Catterick DL10 7PE
☎ 01748-818331 **Fax** 01748-818331
E-mail bridge_house@hotmail.com

Good food, excellent wine and willing service is the hallmark of the Bridge House Hotel. It's the ideal centre for exploring the countless historic and scenic treasures of the North.

15 bedrs, all ensuite, 4 ⊁ ⅲ 150 **P** 70 ⊞ **SB** £40–£45 **DB** £60–£70 **HB** £315–£350 **L** £5.95 **L** 🍴 **D** £15 **D** 🍴 ✗ **LD** 21:30 **CC** MC Visa Amex DC 📷

CHAGFORD Devon   2C3

Pop. 1,400. Exeter 16, London 186, Ashburton 13, Crediton 14, Newton Abbot 16, Okehampton 11, Tavistock 20 **EC** Wed

★★★ Gidleigh Park ⍟ ⍟ ⍟ ⍟ ⍟
Gold Ribbon Hotel
Chagford TQ13 8HH
☎ 01647-432367 **Fax** 01647-432574
E-mail gidleighpark@gidleigh.co.uk
15 bedrs, all ensuite, ⊁ ⅲ 20 **P** 20 ⊞ Rest Resid
SB £170–£310 **DB** £270–£350 **L** £30 **L** 🍴 **D** £60 ✗
LD 21:00 **CC** MC Visa DC 📷 📷

Facilities for the disabled

Hotels do their best to cater for disabled visitors. However, it is advisable to contact the hotel direct to ensure it can provide particular requirement.

Three Crowns Hotel

A 13th century hostelry of character within Dartmoor National Park.
Centrally heated including four classic four poster beds. An ideal touring centre: close to Moretonhampstead, with riding, walking, swimming and fishing facilities.
Fully licensed, free house. Open all year.
Bar snacks and à la carte and table d'hôte menus.
Resident proprietors of local birth.
Weddings, conferences etc. catered for in our Cavalier Function Room.

HIGH STREET, CHAGFORD, DEVON TQ13 8AJ
Tel: (01647) 433444 Fax: (01647) 433117

★★★ Great Tree
Sandy Park, Chagford TQ13 8JS
☎ 01647-432491 **Fax** 01647-432562
E-mail nigel@greattree.softnet.co.uk

A delightfully quiet and secluded location in 25 acres of woods and gardens dedicated to nature conservation. A lovely unpretentious and homely atmosphere.

10 bedrs, all ensuite, ♀ ⊁ ⅲ 30 **P** 12 No children ⊞ **SB** £50 **DB** £79 **HB** £313–£383 **L** 🍴 **D** £21 ✗ **LD** 20:30 **CC** MC Visa Amex DC

★★★ Three Crowns
High Street, Chagford TQ13 8AJ
☎ 01647-433444 **Fax** 01647-433117

A 13th century, thatched, stone-built inn, situated opposite the ancient church in the village centre. 16 bedrs, 15 ensuite, ⍗ ⌀ ✈ Ⅲ 90 **P** 20 ⊞ **SB** £30-£45 **DB** £50-£65 **HB** £225-£270 **L** £10 **D** £19.50 ✕ **LD** 21:30 **CC** MC Visa DC ⌧
See advert on opposite page

Mill End
Sandy Park, Chagford TQ13 8JN
☎ 01647-432282 **Fax** 01647-433106

Charmingly converted flour mill, with working wheel on the banks of the River Teign. Set in delightful riverside gardens overlooked by Castle Drago. 17 bedrs, 15 ensuite, ✈ Ⅲ 30 **P** 17 ⊞ Rest Resid **CC** MC Visa Amex JCB ▣ ⧖

CHARMOUTH Dorset 3E3
Pop. 1,100. Dorchester 22, London 144, Axminster 6, Crewkerne 13, Lyme Regis 3

★★ Queens Armes ⌂
The Street, Charmouth DT6 6QF
☎ 01297-560339 **Fax** 01297-560339
E-mail peterm@netcomuk.co.uk
Closed Nov-mid Feb
11 bedrs, 10 ensuite, ⍗ ✈ **P** 20 ⊞ Rest Resid **SB** £30 **HB** £250 **D** £7 ✕ **LD** 20:00 **CC** MC Visa

---

CHATTERIS Cambridgeshire 9D3
Pop. 7,100. London 75, M11 (jn 14) 11, Huntingdon 16, Peterborough 21, Wisbech 17

★ Cross Keys ⌂ ⌂
16 Market Hill, Chatteris PE16 6BA
☎ 01354-693036 **Fax** 01354-694454
12 bedrs, 10 ensuite, ⍗ Ⅲ 90 **P** 12 ⊞ **SB** £21-£35 **DB** £35-£58 **L** ● **D** £15 **D** ● ✕ **LD** 14:00 Restaurant closed D Sun **CC** MC Visa Amex JCB

CHELMSFORD Essex 5D2
Pop. 92,479. Brentwood 11, London 33, Bishop's Stortford 18, Braintree 11, Colchester 22, Epping 17, Great Dunmow 12, Southend 19 **EC** Wed **MD** Tue, Wed, Sat ⓘ County Hall, Market Road 01245-283400

★★★★ Pontlands Park
West Hanningfield Road, Great Baddow, Chelmsford CM2 8HR
☎ 01245-476444 **Fax** 01245-478393
17 bedrs, all ensuite, ⍗ Ⅲ 45 **P** 120 ⊞ Rest Resid **SB** £98-£106 **DB** £126-£140 **L** £15.50 **L** ● **D** £21 **D** ● ✕ **LD** 21:45 Restaurant closed L Mon-Sat, D Sun **CC** MC Visa Amex DC JCB ▣ ⧖ ▣

★★★ County ⌂
29 Rainsford Road, Chelmsford CM1 2QA
☎ 01245-491911 **Fax** 01245-492762
E-mail sales@countryhotel-essex.co.uk
Closed 27-30 Dec
36 bedrs, all ensuite, Ⅲ 200 **P** 100 ⊞ **SB** £74 **DB** £84 **L** £20 **L** ● **D** £20 ✕ **LD** 21:30 **CC** MC Visa Amex DC

★★★ Ivy Hill
Writtle Road, Margaretting CM4 0EH
☎ 01277-353040 **Fax** 01277-355038
E-mail sales@ivyhillhotel.co.uk

A white walled Victorian mansion set in nine acres of beautifully landscaped gardens. 33 bedrs, all ensuite, ⍗ ⌀ Ⅲ 50 **P** 65 ⊞ **SB** £89-£95 **DB** £98-£148 **L** £22.95 **L** ● **D** ● ✕ **LD** 21:30 Restaurant closed L Sat, D Sun **CC** MC Visa Amex DC ⧖ ▣ ⧖

CHELTENHAM Gloucestershire 7E4
Pop. 85,000. Burford 22, M5 (jn 11) 3½, London 97, Cirencester 14, Evesham 16, Gloucester 9, Tewkesbury 9 **EC** Wed **MD** Thu **see** Art Gallery and Museum, St Mary's Parish Church, Rotunda, Mineral Springs ℹ 77 The Promenade 01242-522878

★★★★ Cheltenham Park
Cirencester Road, Charlton Kings, Cheltenham GL53 8EA

📞 01242-222021 **Fax** 01242-254880
E-mail cheltenhampark@paramount-hotels.co.uk

Georgian manor house set in its own gardens 2 miles from Cheltenham. Egon Ronay recommended cuisine. Leisure club with 15 metre indoor swimming pool, spa bath steam room, sauna, solarium, gymnasium. Free car parking.
144 bedrs, all ensuite, ♂ ⊢ ▣ ⠶ 320
P 200 ⊞ **SB** £99-£109 **DB** £128-£148
L £14.50 **L** ⬤ **D** £21.50 **D** ⬤ ✕ **LD** 21:30
Restaurant closed L Sat
《 MC Visa Amex DC JCB ▣ ▣ ▣ ᴋ

★★★ ✣ Carlton
Parabola Road, Cheltenham GL50 3AQ
📞 01242-514453 **Fax** 01242-226487

Situated in the heart of the town centre in a quiet tree lined road. Fashionable Montpellier, shops, theatre and gardens a two minute walk. An elegant hotel with excellent and friendly service. M5 two miles, BR station nearby, free car park.

75 bedrs, all ensuite, ▣ ⊢ ▣ ⠶ 225 **P** 85 ⊞ **SB** £45-£65 **DB** £70-£85 **HB** £315-£350 **L** £12 **D** £17 **D** ⬤ ✕ **LD** 21:30 《 MC Visa Amex DC JCB

★★★ Charlton Kings
London Road, Charlton Kings, Cheltenham GL52 6UU
📞 01242-231061 **Fax** 01242-241900
14 bedrs, all ensuite, ♂ ⊢ ⠶ 30 **P** 20 ⊞ Rest Resid
SB £59.50-£79.50 **DB** £89-£102 **HB** £329-£364 **L** £6.95
L ⬤ **D** £18.50 **D** ⬤ ✕ **LD** 20:45 Restaurant closed L Mon-Sat 《 MC Visa Amex JCB ᴋ

★★★ ✣ George
41-49 St George's Road, Cheltenham GL50 3DZ
📞 01242-235751 **Fax** 01242-224359
39 bedrs, all ensuite, ⊢ ⠶ 20 **P** 28 ⊞ **SB** £50-£55
DB £60-£75 **HB** £297.50-£367.50 **L** £9.95 **L** ⬤
D £14.50 **D** ⬤ ✕ **LD** 21 15 《 MC Visa Amex DC

★★★ Greenway ⚏ ⚏ ⚏
Blue Ribbon Hotel
Shurdington, Cheltenham GL51 5UG
📞 01242-862352 **Fax** 01242-862780
E-mail relax@greenway-hotel.demon.co.uk

A 16th century Elizabethan country house set in seven acres of gardens and parkland, nestled under the Cotswold hills, three miles from the town centre. The conservatory dining room looks out over the formal sunken garden and lily pond.
19 bedrs, all ensuite, ▣ ♂ ⠶ 24 **P** 50 No children under 7 ⊞ Rest Resid **SB** £95 **DB** £150 **L** £16 **D** £35
✕ **LD** 21:30 Restaurant closed L Sat 《 MC Visa Amex DC ᴋ

★★★ Hotel Kandinsky
(Formerly Savoy Hotel)
Bayshill Road, Montpellier, Cheltenham GL50 3AS
📞 01242-527788 **Fax** 01242-226412
48 bedrs, all ensuite, ♀ ▣ ⠶ 60 **P** 35 ⊞ **SB** £60-£70
DB £100-£120 **HB** £455 **D** £21.50 **D** ⬤ ✕ **LD** 21:30
《 MC Visa Amex DC JCB

★★★ Hotel on the Park 🛏 🛏 🛏
Blue Ribbon Hotel
38 Evesham Road, Cheltenham GL52 2AH
☎ 01242-518898 **Fax** 01242-511526
E-mail hotel@epinet.co.uk
12 bedrs, all ensuite, ⚃ ♀ ✗ ➤ ☷ 18 **P** 8 No
children under 8 ⊞ Rest Resid **SB** £84.75 **DB** £111
L £15 **L** ➍ **D** £22 ✗ **LD** 21:30 **CC** MC Visa Amex DC

★★★ Queens **Heritage** HOTELS
Promenade, Cheltenham GL50 1NN
☎ 01242-514724 **Fax** 01242-224145
79 bedrs, all ensuite, ⚃ ➤ ▣ ☷ 80
P 80 ⊞ **CC** MC Visa Amex DC JCB ♿

★★★ The Prestbury House Hotel
& Restaurant 🛏
The Burgage, Prestbury,
Cheltenham GL52 3DN
☎ 01242-529533 **Fax** 01242-227076

300 year old manor house hotel and restaurant
(open to non residents), set in five acres of
secluded grounds. Cheltenham centre is 1½ miles
away. Full conference and wedding reception
facilities.
17 bedrs, all ensuite, ⚃ ♀ ✗ ☷ 70 **P** 60 ⊞
SB £73.50-£75.50 **DB** £80-£98 **L** £25 **L** ➍ **D** £25 **D** ➍
✗ **LD** 21:00 **CC** MC Visa Amex DC ▨ ♿
See advert on this page

★★ Cotswold Grange
Pittville Circus Road, Cheltenham GL52 2QH
☎ 01242-515119 **Fax** 01242-241537
Closed Christmas
25 bedrs, all ensuite, ✗ ➤ ☷ 20 **P** 20 ⊞ Rest Resid
SB £48 **DB** £70 **HB** £400 **L** £6 **L** ➍ **D** £12 **D** ➍ ✗
LD 19:30 Restaurant closed Sun **CC** MC Visa Amex
DC

ENGLAND

CHENIES Buckinghamshire   4C2
Pop. 1,044. Rickmansworth 4, London 22,
Aylesbury 18, High Wycombe 12 **see** Church, Mill

★★★ Bedford Arms 🛏
Chenies WD3 6EQ
☎ 01923-283301 **Fax** 01923-284825
10 bedrs, all ensuite, ☷ 25 **P** 120 ⊞ **SB** £125.50
DB £141 **L** £22 **D** £22 ✗ **LD** 22:00 Restaurant closed
L Sat **CC** MC Visa Amex DC JCB

CHESTER Cheshire   7D1
Pop. 122,000. Nantwich 21, London 183, M53 2,
Birkenhead 15, Mold 11, Northwich 18,
Queensferry 6½, Wrexham 11 **EC** Wed **MD** Daily
see Cathedral, The Rows, City Walls, Gates and
Towers, High Cross, Roman amphitheatre, St.
John's Church and ruins ⅰ Town Hall, Northgate
Street 01244-317962 & Vicars Lane 01244-351609

★★★★★ The Chester Grosvenor 🛏🛏🛏🛏
Blue Ribbon Hotel
Eastgate, Chester CH1 1LT
📞 01244-324024 Fax 01244-313246
E-mail chesgrov@aol.com
Closed 25-26 Dec
85 bedrs, all ensuite, 4 ♉ 🖭 ☷ 220 P 500 🚪
SB £167.25-£184.88 DB £258.13-£293.38 L £22.50
L 🍷 D £40 D 🍷 ✕ LD 22:30 Restaurant closed L
Mon, D Sun ℭ MC Visa Amex DC JCB 🏧 📺 ⛵
See advert on this page

★★★★ Carden Park Hotel,
Golf Resort & Spa 🛏🛏🛏
Carden, Chester CH3 9DQ
📞 01829-731000 Fax 01829-731032
192 bedrs, all ensuite, 4 ♉ ♉ 🖭 ☷ 400 P 450 🚪
SB £120.95 DB £146.90 L £14.95 L 🍷 D £21.95 D 🍷
✕ LD 22:00 Restaurant closed L Mon-Sat ℭ MC
Visa Amex DC JCB 🎱 🏧 📺 🅿 🖼 🎣 ⛵
See advert on this page

ENGLAND

★★★★ Queen
City Road, Chester CH1 3AH
☎ 01244-350100 Fax 01244-318483
128 bedrs, all ensuite, ⊩ ⊡ ⦂⦂⦂ 280
P 100 ⊕ SB £85-£99 DB £95-£125
HB £425-£475 L £14 L ● D £17.95
D ● ✕ LD 21:30 Restaurant closed
L Sat ᙅ MC Visa Amex DC

PRINCIPAL HOTELS

★★★ Blossoms
St John Street, Chester CH1 1HL
☎ 01244-323186 Fax 01244-346433
64 bedrs, all ensuite, ⊞ ⊩ ⊡ ⦂⦂⦂ 80 ⊕ SB £50-£95
DB £70-£120 HB £400 L £5.95 L ● D £16 D ● ✕
LD 21:45 ᙅ MC Visa Amex DC JCB

Heritage
HOTELS

★★★ ✦ Broxton Hall
Broxton, Chester CH3 9JS
☎ 01829-782321 Fax 01829-782330
Closed 25 Dec
11 bedrs, all ensuite, ⊩ ⦂⦂⦂ 30 P 30 No children
under 12 ⊕ SB £60 DB £75-£105 L £12.90 D £25.50
D ● ✕ LD 21:30 ᙅ MC Visa Amex DC
See advert on this page

★★★ Crabwall Manor ♟ ♟ ♟ ♟
Blue Ribbon Hotel
Parkgate Road, Mollington,
Chester CH1 6NE
☎ 01244-851666 **Fax** 01244-851400
E-mail sales@crabwall.u-net.com
48 bedrs, all ensuite, 🖩 ⅲ 100 **P** 150 🚪 **CC** MC Visa
Amex DC JCB 🈲 ♿
See advert on previous page

★★★ Gateway to Wales ♟ ♟
Welsh Road, Sealand CH5 2HX
☎ 01244-830332 **Fax** 01244-836190
39 bedrs, all ensuite, 🖩 ⅲ 140 **P** 51 🚪 **SB** £65-£95
DB £90-£105 **HB** £437.50-£577.50 **L** £10.95 **D** £17.50
✕ **LD** 21:30 **CC** MC Visa Amex DC 🈲 🈲 🈲 🈲 ♿
See advert on previous page

Short Breaks
Many hotels provide special rates for
weekend and mid-week breaks –
sometimes these are quoted in
the hotel's entry, otherwise ring
direct for the latest offers.

★★★ Grosvenor-Pulford ♟
Wrexham Road, Pulford,
Chester CH4 9DG
☎ 01244-570560 **Fax** 01244-570809
E-mail enquiries@grosvenorpulford.co.uk

Converted farmhouse of Victorian origins but of
lovely Elizabeth design.
68 bedrs, all ensuite, 🖩 𝄞 ✝ 🖃 ⅲ 200 **P** 200 🚪
SB £60-£67.50 **DB** £75-£110 **L** £6 **L** 🍴 **D** £13 **D** 🍴 ✕
LD 22:00 **CC** MC Visa Amex DC 🈲 🈲 🈲 🈲 ♿
See advert on opposite page

★★★ Posthouse   **Posthouse**
Wrexham Road, Chester CH3 6AF
☎ 01244-680111 **Fax** 01244-674100
145 bedrs, all ensuite, ✝ ⅲ 100 **P** 150
🚪 **CC** MC Visa Amex DC JCB 🈲 🈲 🈲 🈲

𝕽𝖔𝖜𝖙𝖔𝖓 𝕳𝖆𝖑𝖑 𝕳𝖔𝖙𝖊𝖑

Formerly an 18th Century manor house but now a fine country house hotel renowned for its
informal welcome. Set at the end of a leafy lane in eight acres of award winning gardens and
grounds, and just a five-minute drive from the historic walled city of Chester. Extensive Health &
Leisure club comprising of indoor swimming pool, sauna, steam room, swim-in jacuzzi, dance
studio, fully equipped gym, and a full range of health & beauty treatments and tennis courts. The
Langdale Restaurant offers both traditional English and Continental cuisine, complemented by
a fine selection of wines.

Rowton Hall Hotel, Whitchurch Road, Rowton, Chester CH3 6AD.
Telephone Chester (01244) 335262 • Fax (01244) 335464

The GROSVENOR PULFORD HOTEL

Wrexham Road, Pulford, Chester, CH4 9DG
Tel: 01244 570560 Fax: 01244 570809
E-mail: enquiries@grosvenorpulford.co.uk
www.grosvenorpulfordhotel.co.uk

Ideally situated only minutes from Chesters' historic city centre & offering easy access to Wales and Snowdonia, this imposing hotel offers quality and excellent value for money.
68 well equipped rooms ranging from singles to luxury suites. The bar offers a fine selection of wines, spirits and traditional ales. Snacks and a la carte meals served daily. Wedding and conference facilities available for up to 250 people.
The Leisure club boasts a magnificent 18 metre Roman style swimming pool with whirlpool, aromatherapy steam room, sauna, solarium, snooker room, state of the art gymnasium, and hair and beauty salon.

★★★ Rowton Hall ⌖
Whitchurch Road, Rowton,
Chester CH3 6AD
☎ 01244-335262 **Fax** 01244-335464
E-mail rowtonhall@rowtonhall.co.uk
Closed 25-28 Dec
38 bedrs, all ensuite, ⌀ ⠿ 200 **P** 200 ⊞ **SB** £100-
£150 **DB** £110-£160 **HB** £560 **L** £13.50 **L** ⬤ **D** £21.50
D ⬤ ✕ **LD** 21:30 **CC** MC Visa Amex DC 🔲 🔳 🔲 🔲 ⅃
See advert on opposite page

★★ ✤ Brookside
Brook Lane, Chester CH2 2AN
☎ 01244-381943 **Fax** 01244-379701

Quiet residential area - 10 minutes walk from city centre. Relaxing character of The Brookside offers

ENGLAND

comfort and attentive service. Licensed bar and restaurant, International cuisine.
26 bedrs, all ensuite, ⠿ ⠿ 20 **P** 16 ⊞ Resid **SB** £37-
£38 **DB** £52 **D** £10.95 ✕ **LD** 21:30 **CC** MC Visa JCB 🔳
⅃

★★ ✤ Dene
95 Hoole Road, Chester CH2 3ND
☎ 01244-321165 **Fax** 01244-350277

A friendly welcome is guaranteed. The hotel is set in a peaceful location less than a mile from the city centre. Ample parking. Comfortable, well equipped bedrooms. 'Francs Restaurant' - French country-style cooking with flair.
48 bedrs, all ensuite, ⌀ ⠿ ⠿ 50 **P** 55 ⊞ Rest Resid
SB £42-£45 **DB** £55-£57 **HB** £219-£237 **L** £8.95
D £12.85 **D** ⬤ ✕ **LD** 22:00 Restaurant closed L Mon-
Sat **CC** MC Visa Amex 🔳 ⅃

★★ Eaton
29 City Road, Chester CH1 3AE
☎ 01244-320840 **Fax** 01244-320850
E-mail welcome@eatonhotelchester.co.uk

In the heart of Chester, with secure parking and convenient for the station, The Eaton offers traditional standards of service in a friendly atmosphere.
16 bedrs, all ensuite, ⠿ **P** 9 ⊞ Rest Resid **SB** £45
DB £57.50-£65 **HB** £250-£306 **L** ⬤ **D** £12.95 **D** ⬤ ✕
LD 20:00 **CC** MC Visa Amex DC JCB ⅃

GREEN BOUGH
——— HOTEL ———

Ideally situated, only 1km from the city centre, this is a homely and relaxing hotel, which provides a personal, professional, quality service and an excellent restaurant and wine list. Ground floor and non-smoking rooms are available.

**60 HOOLE ROAD, HOOLE, CHESTER CH2 3NL
Tel: 01244 326241
Fax: 01244 326265**

LLYNDIR HALL HOTEL

Set in some of the finest countryside, 10 minutes from the historic city of Chester, this delightful Strawberry Gothic country house has been lovingly restored and now provides the best in comfort and cuisine, also boasting excellent leisure facilities.

**LLYNDIR LANE, ROSSETT, NR. CHESTER
Tel: 01244-571648
Fax: 01244-571258**

★★ ✣ Green Bough
60 Hoole Road, Hoole, Chester CH2 3NL
☎ 01244-326241 Fax 01244-326265
19 bedrs, all ensuite, ▣ ♀ ⦂⦂⦂ 6 **P** 20 No children under 11 ⊞ Rest Resid **SB** £50-£60 **DB** £60-£95
L £12.50 **D** £16.50 **D** ♥ ✕ **LD** 21:00 Restaurant closed D Sun **CC** MC Visa Amex JCB ♿
See advert on this page

Llyndir Hall
Llyndir Lane, Rossett, Nr Chester LL12 0AY
☎ 01244-571648 Fax 01244-571258

A country house hotel five miles south of Chester, set in its own grounds with leisure and business facilities.
38 bedrs, all ensuite, ⦂⦂⦂ 120 **P** 70 ⊞ **CC** MC Visa Amex JCB ▣ ▣ ▣ ♿
See advert on this page

CHESTERFIELD Derbyshire   8B1
Pop. 73,500. M1 (jn 29) 5, London 149, Chapel-en-le-Frith 23, Derby 23, Mansfield 12, Matlock 10, Sheffield 12, Worksop 14 **EC** Wed **see** 14th cent Parish Church ('crooked' spire), Trinity Church
🛈 Peacock Information Centre, Low Pavement 01246-207777

★★ Portland ⫯
West Bars, Chesterfield S40 1AY
☎ 01246-234502 Fax 01246-550915
24 bedrs, all ensuite, ♀ ✗ ⦂⦂⦂ 70 **P** 40 ⊞ **SB** £44-£55
DB £55-£66 **L** £7.50 **L** ♥ **D** £12.75 ✕ **LD** 21:30 **CC** MC Visa Amex DC

CHICHESTER West Sussex   4C4
See also BOGNOR REGIS
Pop. 25,300. Midhurst 12, London 61, Arundel 11, Bognor Regis 6½, Cosham 13, Pulborough 17
EC Thu **MD** Wed, Sat **see** Cathedral, Market Cross, ancient Walls, Council House (Corporation plate), remains of Greyfriars Monastery, St Mary's Hospital Almshouses, Chichester Festival Theatre, 🛈 29a South Street 01243-775888

★★★ Millstream ⚑ ⚑

Bosham Lane, Bosham,
Chichester PO18 8HL
📞 01243-573234 **Fax** 01243-573459

Beautifully appointed country house hotel dating
from 1701, set in a picturesque sailing village. Bar,
sitting room, restaurant and a bedroom designed
for wheelchair access, all on ground floor. Locally
renowned award winning restaurant.
33 bedrs, all ensuite, 🅰 🐾 🐕 🏨 20 **P** 40 ♨ Rest
Resid **SB** £69-£72 **DB** £112-£115 **HB** £390-£438
L £13.95 **L** 🍴 **D** £20 **D** 🍴 ✕ **LD** 21:30 ℂℂ MC Visa
Amex DC ♿
See advert on this page

★★★ Ship

North Street, Chichester PO19 1NH
📞 01243-778000 **Fax** 01243-788000

Georgian hotel with stunning Adam flying staircase
and all rooms recently refurbished. 400 yards from
Festival Theatre and Cathedral. Award winning
cuisine. Free on site parking.
34 bedrs, all ensuite, 🐕 📧 🏨 70 **P** 38 ♨ ✕ **LD** 21:30
ℂℂ MC Visa Amex DC

CHINNOR Oxfordshire   4B2
M 40 (jn 6) 3, London 45, Aylesbury 10½, High
Wycombe 13, Thame 4 **see** Ridgeway Path

★★ Peacock ⚑

Henton, Chinnor OX9 4AH
📞 01844-353519 **Fax** 01844-353891

A beautiful 17th century thatched country inn,
extended to provide all modern conveniences.
Featuring candle-lit dining and outdoor, heated
swimming pool. Lovely rural setting at the foot of
the Chilterns.
26 bedrs, all ensuite, 🅰 🐕 🏨 14 **P** 55 ♨ ♨ Resid
SB £40-£60 **DB** £45-£78 **L** £12.50 **D** £16.45 ✕
LD 21:30 ℂℂ MC Visa Amex DC JCB ⚐ ♿

Pop. 2,000. Moreton-in-Marsh 6½, London 90, Banbury 22, Cheltenham 21, Evesham 9, Stratford-upon-Avon 12 **EC** Thu

★★★ Charingworth Manor
Blue Ribbon Hotel
Chipping Campden GL55 6NS
☎ 01386-593555 **Fax** 01386-593353

An idyllic setting for a stylish and relaxed visit where only the finest accommodation and cuisine will suffice. Elegantly decorated rooms enhanced with antiques and object d'art creating a stunning country house with award winning cuisine.
26 bedrs, all ensuite, ▦ ⫴⫴⫴ 40 **P** 50 ⊞ Resid
SB £105-£125 **DB** £140-£270 **L** £17.50 **D** £37.50 ✕ **LD** 21:30 **CC** MC Visa Amex DC ▣ ▣ ▣ ▣
See advert on opposite page

★★★ Cotswold House
Blue Ribbon Hotel
The Square, Chipping Campden GL55 6AN
☎ 01386-840330 **Fax** 01386-840310
E-mail reception@cotswold-house.demon.co.uk
Closed 24-26 Dec

An elegant and delightful town house with an attractive garden, situated on the sunny side of

Chipping Campden's historic High Street. The hotel maintains high standards of food, accommodation and service.
15 bedrs, all ensuite, ▦ ⫽ ⫴⫴⫴ 20 **P** 15 No children under 7 ⊞ **SB** £55-£75 **DB** £120-£150 **HB** £420-£595 **L** £12 **D** £22 **D** ⫴ ✕ **LD** 21:30 **CC** MC Visa Amex DC JCB
See advert on opposite page

★★★ Seymour House
High Street, Chipping Campden GL55 6AH
☎ 01386-840429 **Fax** 01386-840369
E-mail seymourhousehotel@btinternet.com

Renovated, 17th century Cotswold-stone building in town centre, with charming secluded garden.
15 bedrs, all ensuite, ▦ ⫴⫴⫴ 40 **P** 28 ⊞ **SB** £72.50 **DB** £95 **HB** £365 **L** £15.50 **L** ⫴ **D** £24.95 **D** ⫴ ✕ **LD** 22:00 **CC** MC Visa Amex

★★★ Three Ways House
Mickleton, Chipping Campden GL55 6SB
☎ 01386-438429 **Fax** 01386-438118

Charming Cotswold village hotel with 41 individually styled bedrooms, candle-lit restaurant and brasserie-bar. Conveniently situated for Hidcote Manor Garden and Stratford-upon-Avon. Seen on TV as home of the Pudding Club.
41 bedrs, all ensuite, ⫴ ⫴⫴⫴ 80 **P** 37 ⊞ **SB** £65-£70 **DB** £92-£115 **L** ⫴ **D** £21 **D** ⫴ ✕ **LD** 21:30 **CC** MC Visa Amex DC JCB ⸸

ENGLAND

Charingworth Manor

*An idyllic setting for a stylish
and relaxed visit where only
the finest accommodation and
cuisine will suffice.
Elegantly decorated rooms
enhanced with antiques and
objet d'art creating a stunning
country house with award
winning cuisine.*

CHIPPING CAMPDEN GL55 6NS
Tel: 01386 593555 Fax: 01386 593353

ESCAPE
TO THE PEACE AND TRANQUILLITY OF
THE COTSWOLD HOUSE
AN ELEGANT TOWN HOUSE IN UNCHANGING
CHIPPING CAMPDEN. JUST 15 VERY
INDIVIDUAL BEDROOMS, A RESTAURANT
WITH AN ENVIABLE REPUTATION AND QUIET
EFFICIENT SERVICE THAT YOU THOUGHT
HAD DISAPPEARED FOREVER.
CALL TODAY FOR OUR BROCHURE

Recommended by all leading Grades

RAC BLUE RIBBON AWARD

CHIPPING CAMPDEN, GLOUCESTERSHIRE GL55 6AN
TELEPHONE: (01386) 840330   FAX: (01386) 840310

CHITTLEHAMHOLT Devon   2C2
Pop. 170. South Molton 5, London 185, Barnstaple 10, Crediton 26, Torrington 11

★★★ Highbullen ₨
Chittlehamholt EX37 9HD
☎ 01769-540561 **Fax** 01769-540492
E-mail highbullen@sosi.net
37 bedrs, all ensuite, ⊞ 20 **P** 60 No children under 8 ⊕ Rest Resid **SB** £60 **DB** £95-£150 **L** ☛ **D** £20 ✕ **LD** 21:00 **CC** MC Visa 🗺 ⚲ 🖥 🖨 🖼 🎮 📺 🖼

CHOLLERFORD Northumberland   13E4
Hexham 5, London 285, Alston 24, Bellingham 11, Brampton 26, Corbridge 7½, Newcastle 22

★★★ Swallow George Hotel ₨ ₨
Chollerford, Nr Hexham NE46 4EW
☎ 01434-681611 **Fax** 01434-681727
E-mail info@swallowhotels.com

SWALLOW HOTELS

A country hotel with landscaped gardens overlooking the River Tyne, an excellent base for exploring Northumbria. Award winning restaurant and leisure club.
47 bedrs, all ensuite, 🈯 ✚ ⊞ 70 **P** 70 ⊕ **SB** £90 **DB** £112.50 **L** £15 **D** £24.95 ✕ **LD** 21:30 **CC** MC Visa Amex DC 🖥 🖼 🖨 🎮 ⅙

CHRISTCHURCH Dorset   4A4
Pop. 29,000. Lyndhurst 14, London 98, Blandford Forum 21, Bournemouth 5, Lymington 12, Ringwood 9 **EC** Wed **MD** Mon **see** Priory Church, Red House Museum, Hengistbury Head 🛈 23 High Street 01202-471780

Facilities for the disabled
Hotels do their best to cater for disabled visitors. However, it is advisable to contact the hotel direct to ensure it can provide particular requirement.

★★★ Waterford Lodge ₨ ₨ ₨
87 Bure Lane, Friars Cliff, Christchurch BH23 4DN
☎ 01425-272948 **Fax** 01425-279130

Waterford Lodge Hotel is close to the New Forest, Mudeford harbour and beaches. Relax in comfortable surroundings and enjoy the standards we set in hospitality, cuisine and cleanliness.
18 bedrs, all ensuite, ✚ ⊞ 100 **P** 38 ⊕ **SB** £87 **DB** £109-£139 **HB** £357-£417 **L** £15 **L** ☛ **D** £25.50 **D** ✕ **LD** 21:00 **CC** MC Visa Amex DC

★★ Fisherman's Haunt ₨
Winkton, Christchurch BH23 7AS
☎ 01202-477283 **Fax** 01202-478883
18 bedrs, 17 ensuite, 🈞 ✚ **P** 75 ⊕ **SB** £48 **DB** £64 **L** £8.95 **D** £11.75 **D** ☛ ✕ **LD** 19:30 **CC** MC Visa Amex DC JCB ⅙

CHURCH STRETTON Shropshire   7D3
Pop. 4,000. Bridgnorth 19, London 156, Ludlow 15, Newton 28, Shrewsbury 13 **EC** Wed **MD** Thu **see** Parish Church, The Long Mynd 5,000 acres (NT), Acton Scott Farm Museum 🛈 Church Street 01694-723133

★★★ ✣ Long Mynd
Cunnery Road, Church Stretton SY6 6AG
☎ 01694-722244 **Fax** 01694-722718
E-mail reservations@longmynd.co.uk
50 bedrs, all ensuite, 🈯 ✚ 🖃 ⊞ 100 **P** 100 ⊕ **SB** £50 **DB** £100-£120 **HB** £259-£350 **L** £7.50 **L** ☛ **D** £20 **D** ☛ ✕ **LD** 21:00 **CC** MC Visa Amex DC ⚲ 🖼 🖨 ⅙

★★ Mynd House ₨ ₨
Little Stretton, Church Stretton SY6 6RB
☎ 01694-722212 **Fax** 01694-724180
E-mail myndhouse@go2.co.uk
Closed Jan

Set in an idyllic rural hamlet where the Shropshire Highlands sweep down, many walks radiate from the door. Half an hour's drive to Ironbridge, Ludlow and Shrewsbury. Bargain short breaks available.
7 bedrs, all ensuite, ⊞ ♀ ✝ ⅲ 20 **P** 12 ⊕ Rest Resid **SB** £35-£55 **DB** £30-£65 **HB** £385-£595 **D** £26 ✕ **LD** 21:15 **CC** MC Visa Amex

Stretton Hall
All Stretton, Church Stretton SY6 6HG
☎ 01694-723224 **Fax** 01694-724365

Eighteenth century manor, now family run hotel, set in glorious Shropshire hills. Our attractions include cosy open fires, panelled rooms and Georgian style - award winning restaurant famous for its fine English/French cuisine.
12 bedrs, all ensuite, **P** 70 ✕ **LD** 21:30 **CC** MC Visa

CLANFIELD Oxfordshire   4A2

★★★ Plough at Clanfield 🍴 🍴 🍴
Bourton Road, Clanfield OX18 2RB
☎ 01367-810222 **Fax** 01367-810596
Closed 27-29 Dec
6 bedrs, all ensuite, ⊞ ⅲ 10 **P** 30 No children under 12 ⊕ **SB** £70-£90 **DB** £95-£125 **L** £19 **L** ➐ **D** £32.50 ✕ **LD** 21:30 **CC** MC Visa Amex DC JCB

CLAYTON-LE-WOODS Lancashire   10B4
Pop. 8,929. M6 (jn 28) ½, London 207, Blackburn 9 **EC** Wed **see** RC Church of St Bedes, Convent.

★★★ ✦ Pines
Preston Road, Clayton-le-Woods PR6 7ED
☎ 01772-338551 **Fax** 01772-629002
E-mail pineshotel@mywebpage.net
Closed 26 Dec
38 bedrs, all ensuite, ⅲ 200 **P** 119 ⊕ **SB** £70 **DB** £80 **L** £10 **L** ➐ **D** ➐ ✕ **LD** 22:00 **CC** MC Visa Amex DC JCB ♿
See advert on this page

CLEETHORPES Lincolnshire   11F4
Pop. 35,000. Louth 16, London 164, Grimsby 6½, Hull 34 **EC** Thu **MD** Thu (win) **see** Beacon, Leisure Park
✉ 43 Alexandra Road 01472-200220

★★★ Kingsway
Kingsway, Cleethorpes DN35 0AE
☎ 01472-601122 **Fax** 01472-601381
Closed 25-26 Dec
50 bedrs, all ensuite, ▣ **P** 50 No children under 5 ⊕ Rest Resid **SB** £58-£68 **DB** £84-£90 **HB** £357 **L** £14.25 **D** £17.95 ✕ **LD** 21:00 **CC** MC Visa Amex DC

ENGLAND

CLEOBURY MORTIMER Shropshire   7E3
Pop. 2,300. Kidderminster 11, London 134, Bridgnorth 13, Droitwich 20, Leominster 18, Ludlow 11, Worcester 20 **EC** Thu

★★★ Redfern ⬛
Lower Street, Cleobury Mortimer DY14 8AA
📞 01299-270395 **Fax** 01299-271011
E-mail jon@red-fern.demon.co.uk
11 bedrs, all ensuite, ▣ ♒ ⫶⫶⫶ 20 **P** 20 ⊟ Rest Resid
CC MC Visa Amex DC

CLEVEDON Somerset   3E1
Pop. 23,000. M5 (jn 20) 1, Bristol 12, London 126, Bridgwater 28, Radstock 27, Wells 24, Weston-super-Mare 14 **EC** Wed

★★★ ✤ Walton Park
1 Wellington Terrace, Clevedon BS21 7BL
📞 01275-874253 **Fax** 01275-343577

Imposing country hotel with pleasant gardens and magnificent views over the Severn Estuary. Good food and wine. Situated two miles from the M5 (jn 20).
40 bedrs, all ensuite, ♒ ▣ ⫶⫶⫶ 150 **P** 40 ⊟ **CC** MC Visa Amex DC &

CLITHEROE Lancashire   10C3
Pop. 13,700. Whalley 4, London 214, Settle 19, Skipton 18 **EC** Wed **MD** Tue **see** Castle Keep, Pendle Hill 1,830 ft, Sawley Abbey **i** 12-14 Market Place 01200-25566

★★★★ Clarion ⬛
Whalley Road, Billington, Clitheroe BB7 9HY
📞 01254-822556 **Fax** 01254-824613
E-mail admin@gb065.u.net.com
44 bedrs, all ensuite, ▣ ♀ ⌀ ♒ ⫶⫶⫶ 200 **P** 150 ⊟
SB £99.50-£104.50 **DB** £121-£134 **L** £7.50 **L** ♥
D £19.50 **D** ♥ ✕ **LD** 21:30 Restaurant closed L & D Sat **CC** MC Visa Amex DC ▣ ▣ ▣ &

COALVILLE Leicestershire   8B3
Pop. 30,700. M1 (jn 22) ½, London 113, Ashby-de-la-Zouche 5, Castle Donington 12, Hinckley 16, Leicester 20 **i** Snibston Discovery Park, Ashby Road 01530-813608

★★★ Hermitage Park
Whitwick Road, Coalville LE67 3FA
📞 01530-814814 **Fax** 01530-814202
E-mail hermitage_park_hotel@btinternet.com
25 bedrs, all ensuite, ♀ ⫶⫶⫶ 60 **P** 40 ⊟ **SB** £69.50
DB £74.50 **HB** £262.50-£313.25 **L** £5.95 **L** ♥ **D** £11.95
✕ **LD** 22:15 Restaurant closed L Sat **CC** MC Visa Amex ▣ &
See advert on opposite page

★★ Charnwood Arms
Beveridge Lane, Bardon Hill, Coalville LE67 1TB
📞 01530-813644 **Fax** 01530-815425

A country house converted into a comfortable hotel, with modern bedroom blocks built in an attractive mews development.
34 bedrs, all ensuite, ⫶⫶⫶ 200 **P** 150 ⊟ **CC** MC Visa Amex DC &
See advert on opposite page

COCKERMOUTH Cumbria   10A1
Pop. 7,200. Keswick 11, London 297, Carlisle 25, Egremont 15, Maryport 7, Workington 8½ **EC** Thu **MD** Mon **i** Town Hall, Market Street 01900-822634

★★★ Trout
Crown Street, Cockermouth CA13 0EJ
📞 01900-823591 **Fax** 01900-827514
30 bedrs, all ensuite, ♒ ⫶⫶⫶ 50 **P** 60 ⊟ **SB** £60-£65
DB £75-£90 **HB** £350-£405 **L** £12 **D** £19 ✕ **LD** 21:30
CC MC Visa Amex ▣ &

Hermitage Park Hotel & Restaurant

Close to East Midlands Airport and Donington Park, in the middle of the East Midlands Motorway network and the picturesque Charnwood Forest, the hotel is ideal for business, conferences and tourism alike. The Carvery restaurant enjoys a high reputation whilst its 25 rooms have every modern facility and our friendly service even includes washing our guest's cars

Whitwick Road, Coalville, Leicester

Tel: 01530 814814

www.hermitagepark.com

THE CHARNWOOD ARMS

- 35 en suite rooms • Close to Junction 22 M1
- Conference & Meeting facilities

All rooms with colour TV, Hair Dryer, Trouser Press, Direct Dial Telephone, Tea & Coffee making facilities. Originally a country house, in a commanding situation overlooking the landscape. Now tastefully converted to a hotel with bars and bar food area. The hotel rooms are arranged in an attractive mews style around the main building.

Beveridge Lane, (A50) Bardon Hill, Nr Coalville, Leicestershire

Tel: 01530 813644 Fax: 01530 815425

COLCHESTER Essex   5E1
Pop. 151,900. Chelmsford 22, London 56, Braintree 15, Clacton 15, Harwich 18, Haverhill 28, Ipswich 18, Sudbury 14 EC Thu MD Tue, Sat see Colchester and Essex Museum (incorp the Castle, Hollytrees mansion and All Saints' Church), St John's Abbey
🛈 1 Queen Street 01206-282920

ENGLAND

★★★ Butterfly

A12/A120 Junction, Old Ipswich Road, Colchester CO7 7QY
📞 01206-230900 Fax 01206-231095
E-mail reception@butterflyhotels.co.uk

Purpose built hotel in traditional style, modern coaching inn by the waters edge. Many of the rooms overlook the lake. Walts restaurant and bar offers a la carte daily specials and a buffet style self service. Lounge service available throughout the day.

50 bedrs, all ensuite, ⌁ ⁂ 80 P 75 ⊟ SB £57-£72.50 DB £69-£80 L £13 L ⬤ D £16 D ⬤ ✕ LD 22:00 ℂℂ MC Visa Amex DC JCB ♿

★★★ ✦ George

116 High Street, Colchester CO1 1DT
📞 01206-578494 Fax 01206-761732

A 500-year-old former coaching inn, now completely refurbished. Brasserie restaurant open for lunch and dinner. Lounge food available all day. Non residents welcome.

48 bedrs, all ensuite, ④ ⁂ 70 P 50 ⊟ SB £62.50-£110 DB £75-£120 L £10.50 L ⬤ D £15 D ⬤ ✕ LD 22:00 ℂℂ MC Visa Amex DC JCB

★★★ ✦ Marks Tey
London Road, Marks Tey, Colchester CO6 1DU
📞 01206-210001 **Fax** 01206-212167
110 bedrs, all ensuite, ⛵ ⦂⦂⦂ 200 **P** 160 ⊞ **SB** £75.75
DB £91 **L** £15.50 **L** ⬤ **D** £15.50 **D** ⬤ ✕ **LD** 22:00
℀ MC Visa Amex DC 🗗 🎬 🕮 📷 ♿

★★★ Posthouse   **Posthouse**
Abbotts Lane, Eight Ash Green,
Colchester CO6 3QL
📞 01206-767740 **Fax** 01206-766577
110 bedrs, all ensuite, ⛵ ⦂⦂⦂ 150 **P** 110 ⊞
SB £84.95 **DB** £94.90 **L** £8.95 **L** ⬤ **D** £12.95
D ⬤ ✕ **LD** 22:30 **℀** MC Visa Amex DC JCB
🗗 🎬 🕮 ♿

★★★ Rose & Crown 🍴 🍴 🍴
East Street, Colchester CO1 2TZ
📞 01206-866677 **Fax** 01206-866616
E-mail info@rose-and-crown.com

Experience the oldest inn in England's oldest town, recently refurbished and only a quarter of a mile from the Roman town of Colchester, the castle and the renowned Mercury Theatre.
29 bedrs, all ensuite, 🎬 🍴 ⦂⦂⦂ 100 **P** 50 ⊞ **Room** £65–£67.50 **L** £15.95 **L** ⬤ **D** £20 **D** ⬤ ✕ **LD** 22:00
Restaurant closed D Sun **℀** MC Visa Amex DC ♿

COLEFORD Gloucestershire	7E4

Pop. 5,000. M4 (jn 27) 14, London 124, Chepstow 13, Gloucester 20, Monmouth 5½, Ross-on-Wye 12 **E** Thu **see** Remains of 14th cent Church, Forest of Dean 🛈 High Street 01594-836307

★★★ Speech House 🍴
Forest of Dean, Coleford GL16 7EL
📞 01594-822607 **Fax** 01594-823658
20 bedrs, all ensuite, ⛵ ⦂⦂⦂ 40 **P** 40 ⊞ **℀** MC Visa Amex DC

Orepool Inn
St Briavels Road, Sling, Coleford GL16 8LH
📞 01594-833277 **Fax** 01594-833785

A mid 17th century inn with discreet modernisation, separate ensuite accommodation. Ideal base for exploring the Forest of Dean and surrounding areas.
10 bedrs, all ensuite, ⦂⦂⦂ 60 **P** 100 ⊞ ✕ **LD** 21.30
℀ MC Visa Amex ♿

COLESHILL Warwickshire	8A3

Pop. 6,470. M6 (jn 4) 2, London 106, Atherstone 10, Birmingham 9½, Coventry 12, Lichfield 15, Nuneaton 12, Sutton Coldfield 7½, Tamworth 10, Warwick 18 **E** Thu **see** Pillory, Whipping Post and Stocks on Church Hill, 14th cent Church

★★★ Grimstock Country House
Gilson Road, Gilson, Coleshill B46 1AJ
📞 01675-462121 **Fax** 01675-467646
44 bedrs, all ensuite, ♪ ⛵ ⦂⦂⦂ 100 **P** 100 ⊞ **SB** £75
DB £85 **L** £8.50 **L** ⬤ **D** £14.50 ✕ **LD** 21:15 **℀** MC Visa Amex DC 🎬

CORBRIDGE ON TYNE Northumberland	10C1

Pop. 2,900. West Auckland 31, London 280, Bellingham 18, Durham 25, Hexham 3½, Jedburgh 47, Newcastle 17 **E** Thu **see** St Andrew's Church, Market Cross, 17th cent bridge, ruins of Aydon and Dilston castles. Museum of Roman relics at Corstopitum 🛈 Hill Street 01434-632815

★★★ Lion of Corbridge
Bridge End, Corbridge on Tyne NE45 5AX
📞 01434-632504 **Fax** 01434-632571
14 bedrs, all ensuite, ⦂⦂⦂ 40 **P** 30 ⊞ **℀** MC Visa Amex DC JCB ♿

★★ Angel Inn 🍴
Main Street, Corbridge on Tyne NE45 5LA
📞 01434-632119
5 bedrs, all ensuite, **P** 34 ⊞ **℀** MC Visa Amex DC

CORNHILL-ON-TWEED Northumberland 13E3
Pop. 320. Newcastle 59, London 333, Berwick-upon-Tweed 13, Coldstream 1½, Kelso 10 **EC** Thu

★★★ Tillmouth Park
Cornhill-on-Tweed TD12 4UU

☎ 01890-882255 **Fax** 01890-882540

Tillmouth Park, a magnificent Victorian baronial mansion, set high above the River Till in 15 acres of secluded parkland, boasts 14 individually styled ensuite bedrooms.
14 bedrs, all ensuite, ▦ ⊀ ⸬ 40 **P** 60 ⊕ **SB** £90 **DB** £120 **D** £27.50 ✕ **LD** 21:00 **CC** MC Visa Amex DC ⊠
See advert on this page

A superb Baronial country mansion built in 1882 by renowned architect Charles Barry using stones from nearby Twizel Castle. Set in 15 acres of mature parkland high above the river Till, Tillmouth Park boasts 14 individually styled en-suite bedrooms, library dining room and informal bistro.

Tillmouth Park
Hospitality. Comfort merit awards.
Cornhill-on Tweed TD12 4UU
Tel: 01890-882255 Fax: 01890-882540

★★ Collingwood Arms
Cornhill-on-Tweed TD12 4UH
☎ 01890-882424 **Fax** 01890-883644
16 bedrs, all ensuite, ⊀ ⸬ 90 **P** 30 ⊕ **CC** MC Visa ⸝

CORSHAM Wiltshire 3F1
Pop. 12,000. Chippenham 4, London 95, Bath 9½, Bristol 21, Chepstow 31, Devizes 12, Frome 17, Westbury 14 **EC** Wed **MD** Tue

ENGLAND

★★ Methuen Arms ⸖
High Street, Corsham SN13 0HB
☎ 01249-714867 **Fax** 01249-712004
24 bedrs, all ensuite, ⌀ ⊀ ⸬ 100 **P** 60 ⊕ **SB** £50-£55 **DB** £60-£65 **L** ⬤ **D** £12.50 **D** ⬤ ✕ **LD** 21:45 **CC** MC Visa Amex DC JCB ⊠ ⸝

COVENTRY West Midlands 7F3
Pop. 304,000. Daventry 19, London 94, M6 (jn 2) 4, Banbury 27, Birmingham 18, Leicester 25, Nuneaton 8½, Rugby 12, Warwick 10 **MD** Daily exc Thu **see** Cathedral remains and new Cathedral, St Mary's Hall, Holy Trinity Church, Lady Godiva Statue, Herbert Art Gallery and Museum, City Wall and Lady Herbert's *i* Bayley Lane 01203-832303

National Code & Number Change
Telephone codes and numbers in Coventry change in April 2000.
01203-XXXXXX becomes 024-76XX XXXX
eg 01203-766222 becomes 023-7676 6222

★★★ Brandon Hall
Brandon, Coventry CV8 3FW
☎ 01203-542571 **Fax** 01203-544909
60 bedrs, all ensuite, ▦ ⊀ ⸬ 100 **P** 150 ⊕ **CC** MC Visa Amex DC ⊡ ⊠

Heritage
HOTELS

★★★ Brooklands Grange ⸖
Holyhead Road, Coventry CV5 8HX
☎ 01203-601601 **Fax** 01203-601277
E-mail lesley.jackson@virgin.net
30 bedrs, all ensuite, ⌀ ⸬ 18 **P** 54 ⊕ **SB** £90 **DB** £105 **L** £12.95 **D** £21.50 **D** ⬤ ✕ **LD** 22:00 Restaurant closed L Sat **CC** MC Visa Amex DC ⸝

★★★ ✦ Coventry Hill
Rye Hill, Allesley, Coventry CV5 9PH
☎ 01203-402151 **Fax** 01203-402235
180 bedrs, all ensuite, ⊀ ⊡ ⸬ 100 **P** 200 ⊕ **CC** MC Visa Amex DC JCB ⸝

★★★ ❖ Novotel Coventry
Wilsons Lane, Longford, Coventry CV6 6HL
☎ 01203-365000 **Fax** 01203-362422
E-mail h0506@accor-hotels.com
98 bedrs, all ensuite, ♪ ✝ ▣ ▦ 250 **P** 180 🏠
SB £73.50 **DB** £81.50 **L** £10.50 **L** ⬤ **D** £13.50 **D** ⬤ ✕
LD 0:00 **℠** MC Visa Amex DC ⤳ ઙ

★★★ Posthouse
Posthouse
Hinckley Road, Walsgrave, CV2 2HP
☎ 01203-613261 **Fax** 01203-621736
E-mail gm1412@forte-hotels.com
160 bedrs, all ensuite, ♀ ✝ ▣ ▦ 250 **P** 400 🏠
SB £59-£95 **L** ⬤ **D** £18 **D** ⬤ ✕ **LD** 22:00 Restaurant
closed L Sat **℠** MC Visa Amex DC ▣ ☒ ▦ ઙ

★★★ Quality Stonebridge Manor
Coventry
☎ 01203-403835 **Fax** 01203-403081
80 bedrs, all ensuite, ④ ♀ ♪ ▦ 120 🏠
SB £79.75 **DB** £99.50 **HB** £683.90 **L** £10
L ⬤ **D** £18 **D** ⬤ ✕ **LD** 22:00 Restaurant
closed L Sun **℠** MC Visa Amex DC ☒ ▦

★★★ Weston Hall
Weston Lane, Bulkington, CV12 9RU
☎ 01203-312989 **Fax** 01203-640846
40 bedrs, all ensuite, ④ ✝ ▦ 200 **P** 200 🏠
SB £69.50 **DB** £85 **L** ⬤ **D** £14.95 **D** ⬤ ✕ **LD** 21:30
℠ MC Visa Amex DC ☒ ▦ ઙ

Campanile Coventry North **Lodge**
4 Wigston Road, Walsgrave
(off junction 2, M6), Coventry CV2 2SD
☎ 01203-622311 **Fax** 01203-602362

Campanile hotels offer comfortable and convenient
budget accommodation and a traditional French
style Bistro providing freshly cooked food for
breakfast, lunch and dinner. All rooms ensuite with
tea/coffee making facilities, DDT and TV with Sky
channels.
51 bedrs, all ensuite, ✝ ▦ 30 **P** 51 🏠 Rest Resid
℠ MC Visa Amex DC ઙ

Campanile Coventry South **Lodge**
Abbey Road, Whitley, Coventry CV3 4BJ
☎ 01203-639922 **Fax** 01203-306898

A practical and efficient hotel, located within easy
distance of major motorways and on the outskirts
of the town centre. Grill restaurant.
50 bedrs, all ensuite, ✝ ▦ 20 **P** 50 🏠 Rest Resid
℠ MC Visa Amex DC ઙ

CRANTOCK Cornwall 2A3
Pop. 900. Bodmin 21, London 254, Newquay 3½,
Redruth 15, St Austell 17, Truro 12, Wadebridge 18
EC Wed **see** 12th cent Church, St Ambrose Well,
sandy beach

★★ Crantock Bay
West Pentire, Crantock TR8 5SE
☎ 01637-830229 **Fax** 01637-831111
Closed Dec-Jan
34 bedrs, all ensuite, ⚐ ⚏ 60 **P** 36 ⊞ ⟪ MC Visa
Amex DC JCB 🔲 🔲 🔲 🔲 🔲 🔲

CRATHORNE North Yorkshire 11D2
Thirsk 16, London 236, Darlington 12,
Middlesbrough 8, Stockton 8

★★★★ Crathorne Hall ☗ ☗ ☗
Blue Ribbon Hotel
Crathorne, Nr. Yarm TS15 0AR
☎ 01642-700398 **Fax** 01642-700814
E-mail hotel.reservations@virgin.co.uk

Impressive Edwardian mansion in classical style
with oak-panelled rooms and fine antiques. Set in
15 acres of wooded grounds.
37 bedrs, all ensuite, ⚐ ♀ ⚐ ⚏ 140 **P** 120 ⊞
SB £120-£150 **DB** £160-£235 **L** £14.95 **L** ⚐ **D** £27.50
D ⚐ ✕ **LD** 22:00 ⟪ MC Visa Amex DC JCB
See advert on opposite page

CROMER Norfolk 9F2
Pop. 7,200. Fakenham 22, London 133, Great
Yarmouth 34, Norwich 23 **EC** Wed **see** 14th cent
Church, Lighthouse, Lifeboat Stations and
Museum, Felbrigg Hall 3m SW ⓘ Bus Station,
Prince of Wales Road 01263-512497

★ Anglia Court ☗
5 Runton Road, Cromer NR27 9AR
☎ 01263-512443 **Fax** 01263-513104
30 bedrs, 26 ensuite, ⚐ ⚏ 30 **P** 18 ⊞ **SB** £18.50-£35
DB £37-£70 **HB** £320 **L** ⚐ **D** £10 **D** ⚐ ✕ **LD** 20:45
Restaurant closed L (low season) ⟪ MC Visa Amex
DC

CROYDE Devon 2C2
Barnstaple 10, London 203, Ilfracombe 9

★★ Kittiwell
St Marys Road, Croyde EX33 1PG
☎ 01271-890247 **Fax** 01271-890469
Closed Jan 3 weeks

Thatched 16th century building with considerable
character, fronted by a cobbled courtyard, walking
distance from sea. Twelve well appointed
bedrooms and an award winning restaurant. Golf,
walking, and riding available.
12 bedrs, all ensuite, ⚐ ⚐ **P** 20 ⊞ Rest Resid
SB £39-£46 **DB** £70-£78 **HB** £371 **L** £11.50 **D** £21.50 ✕
LD 21:00 ⟪ MC Visa JCB

CROYDON Surrey 5D3
Pop. 318,200. Thornton Heath 2, London 10,
Bromley 6, Epsom 8½, Mitcham 4, Purley 2½,
Westerham 12 **MD** Daily ⓘ Katharine Street 0181-
253 1009

★★★★ Coulsdon Manor ☗ ☗ ☗
Coulsdon Court Road,
Coulsdon, Croydon CR5 2LL
☎ 0181-668 0414 **Fax** 0181-668 3118
E-mail coulsdonmanor@marstonhotels.co.uk
35 bedrs, all ensuite, ⚐ ⚏ 180 **P** 200 ⊞ **SB** £104
DB £130 **HB** £360 **L** £16.50 **D** £25 **D** ⚐ ✕ **LD** 21:30
Restaurant closed L Sat ⟪ MC Visa Amex DC JCB
🔲 🔲 🔲 🔲 🔲

★★★★ Croydon Park
7 Altyre Road, Croydon CR9 5AA
☎ 0181-680 9200 **Fax** 0181-760 0426
211 bedrs, all ensuite, ♀ ⚐ ⚐ ⚐ ⚏ 300 **P** 147 ⊞
SB £99 **DB** £120 **L** £14.95 **D** £16.95 **D** ⚐ ✕ **LD** 22:15
⟪ MC Visa Amex DC 🔲 🔲 🔲 🔲 ♿

★★★★ Selsdon Park

Addington Road, Sanderstead,
Croydon CR2 8YA
☎ 0181-657 8811 **Fax** 0181-651 6171
204 bedrs, all ensuite, ⌗ ♀ ♪ ⊡ ⠿ 400
P 350 ⊕ **SB** £120-£180 **DB** £149-£179
L £19.95 **L** ⚬ **D** £24.95 **D** ⚬ ✕ **LD** 21:45
《 MC Visa Amex DC ⊡ ⚒ ⊞ ⊞ ⊡ ⊡ ⊡

★★★ Posthouse

Posthouse

Purley Way, Croydon CR9 4LT
☎ 0181-688 5185 **Fax** 0181-681 6438
83 bedrs, all ensuite, ⊶ ⠿ 100 **P** 70 ⊕ 《 MC Visa
Amex DC

★★ ❖ Hayesthorpe

48-52 St Augustines Avenue, Croydon CR2 6JJ
☎ 0181-688 8120 **Fax** 0181-688 8120
25 bedrs, all ensuite, **P** 10 ⊕ Resid **SB** £45 **DB** £55
D £7 ✕ **LD** 20:30 《 MC Visa Amex DC JCB

★★ Markington

9 Haling Park Road, Croydon CR2 6NG
☎ 0181-681 6022 **Fax** 0181-688 6530
E-mail rooms@markingtonhotel.ndirect.co.uk
Closed Christmas
29 bedrs, 28 ensuite, ⠿ 30 **P** 17 No children under
5 ⊕ Rest Resid **SB** £48-£55 **DB** £60-£87 **L** ⚬ **D** £7.50
D ⚬ ✕ **LD** 21:00 Restaurant closed D Fri-Sun 《 MC
Visa Amex
See advert on this page

★★ ❖ South Park

3-5 South Park Hill Road, Croydon CR2 7DY
☎ 0181-688 5644 **Fax** 0181-760 0861
19 bedrs, all ensuite, ♀ **P** 10 No children under 10
⊕ Resid **SB** £50 **DB** £60 **L** £8.50 **D** £10.50 ✕ **LD** 19:45
Restaurant closed Sat-Sun 《 MC Visa Amex JCB
⟁

CUCKFIELD West Sussex　　　　5D3

Pop. 4,000. Redhill 17, London 37, Brighton 14,
Crawley 9½, Haywards Heath 2, Horsham 11,
Worthing 22 **EC** Wed

ᚷ ★★★ ❖ Ockenden Manor

Ockenden Lane, Cuckfield RH17 5LD
☎ 01444-416111 **Fax** 01444-415549
E-mail ockenden@hshotels.co.uk
22 bedrs, all ensuite, ⌗ ⠿ 50 **P** 45 ⊕ Resid **SB** £99-
£150 **DB** £120-£250 **HB** £630-£980 **L** £18.50 **L** ⚬
D £29.50 **D** ⚬ ✕ **LD** 21:30 《 MC Visa Amex DC

CULLOMPTON Devon　　　　3D2

★★ Manor House

2/4 Fore Street, Cullompton FX15 1JL
☎ 01884-32281 **Fax** 01884-38344
10 bedrs, all ensuite, ⌗ ⊶ ⠿ 45 **P** 30 ⊕ **SB** £45
DB £59.50 **L** £7 **D** £13 ✕ **LD** 20:45 《 MC Visa

DARLINGTON Co. Durham　　　　11D2

Pop. 98,000. A66(M) 2, London 244, Barnard
Castle 19, Durham 18, Leyburn 24, Northallerton
16, Stockton 11, West Auckland 10 **EC** Wed **MD** Mon,
Thur, Sat ▮ 4 West Row 01325-382698

★★★★ Redworth Hall ▯ ▯

Blue Ribbon Hotel
Redworth, Newton Aycliffe DL5 6NL
☎ 01388-772442 **Fax** 01388-775112
E-mail rhh@scottishhighlandhotels.co.uk
100 bedrs, all ensuite, ⌗ ♀ ♪ ⊶ ⊡ ⠿ 300 **P** 300 ⊕
SB £124.50-£154.50 **DB** £157-£187 **HB** £556.50-
£661.50 **L** £13.50 **D** £21.75 ✕ **LD** 22:00 《 MC Visa
Amex DC ⊡ ⊞ ⊞ ⊡ ⊡ ⟁

★★★ Headlam Hall
Headlam, Gainford, Darlington DL2 3HA
📞 01325-730238 **Fax** 01325-730790
E-mail office@headlamhall.co.uk
Closed 25-26 Dec

Set in four acres of formal gardens and surrounded by the rolling countryside of Lower Teesdale. The hall boasts excellent cuisine and has extensive leisure facilities.
36 bedrs, all ensuite, 4 ♪ ✝ ⋕ 150 **P** 60 ⊞ **SB** £65-£75 **DB** £80-£90 **L** £13 **D** £22 ✕ **LD** 21:30 **CC** MC Visa Amex DC JCB ⬚⬚⬚⬚⬚⬚ ⟨

★★★ Quality Kings Head
Priestgate, Darlington DL1 1NW
📞 01325-380222 **Fax** 01325-382006
85 bedrs, all ensuite, ♪ ✝ ⬚ ⋕ 250 **P** 30
⊞ **SB** £75-£90 **DB** £95-£105 **L** ⬚ **D** £11.95 **D** ⬚ ✕
LD 21:30 **CC** MC Visa Amex DC JCB ⟨

★★★ St George
Teesside Airport, Darlington DL2 1RH
📞 01325-332631 **Fax** 01325-333851
59 bedrs, all ensuite, ✝ ⋕ 150 **P** 210 ⊞ **SB** £74-£85
DB £84-£95 **L** £9 **D** £17 ✕ **LD** 21:45 Restaurant
closed L Sat, D Sun **CC** MC Visa Amex DC ⬚⬚ ⟨

DARTFORD Kent	5D2

🏆 ★★★★ Rowhill Grange
Country House
Wilmington, Dartford DA2 7QH
📞 01322-615136 **Fax** 01322-615137
E-mail admin@rowhillgrange.com

With 9 acres of mature gardens and the finest health spa in the south, Rowhill Grange is ideal for business or pleasure - just 2 miles from the M25.
30 bedrs, all ensuite, 4 ⬚ ⋕ 150 **P** 120 ⊞
SB £109.95 **DB** £126.90 **L** £16.95 **L** ⬚ **D** £29.95 **D** ⬚
✕ **LD** 21:00 Restaurant closed Sat **CC** MC Visa Amex DC ⬚⬚⬚ ⟨

Campanile Dartford Lodge
1 Clipper Boulevard West,
Crossways Business Park, DA2 6QN
📞 01322-278925 **Fax** 01322-278948

Campanile hotels offer comfortable and convenient budget accommodation and a traditional French style Bistro providing freshly cooked food for breakfast, lunch and dinner. All rooms ensuite with tea/coffee making facilities, DDT and TV with Sky channels.
80 bedrs, all ensuite, ✝ ⋕ 40 **P** 80 ⊞ Rest Resid
CC MC Visa Amex DC ⟨

DARTMOUTH Devon	3D4

Pop. 5,500. Totnes 13, (fy 11), London 205, Kingsbridge 15, Plymouth 28, Torquay (fy) 10
EC Wed **MD** Tue, Fri **see** St Pryroc's Church, Butterwalk, Castle, St Saviour's Church (14th cent), Mayflower Stone, Newcomen Engine House
ℹ️ Engin House, Mayor's Avenue 01803-834224

★★★ Dart Marina ⬚ ⬚

Heritage HOTELS

Sandquay, Dartmouth TQ6 9PH
☎ 01803-832580 **Fax** 01803-835040
50 bedrs, all ensuite, ⛏ **P** 50 ⊟ **SB** £48-£64 **DB** £96-£128 **HB** £372-£492 **L** £9.95 **L** ♥ **D** £21.95 **D** ♥ ✕
LD 21:30 ⟨⟨ MC Visa Amex DC ⟨

★★★ Royal Castle ⬚

11 The Quay, Dartmouth TQ6 9PS
☎ 01803-833033 **Fax** 01803-835445

Two bars serving choice bar meals, ales and wines.
Adam room restaurant specialising in local seafood.
25 luxuriously appointed ensuite bedrooms to
choose from.
25 bedrs, all ensuite, ▦ ♪ ⛏ ⁙ 80 **P** 12 ⊟
SB £47.50-£62.50 **DB** £84-£99 **HB** £474-£546 **L** £10
L ♥ **D** £18.45 **D** ♥ ✕ **LD** 21:30 ⟨⟨ MC Visa Amex

★★★ Stoke Lodge

Stoke Fleming, Dartmouth TQ6 0RA
☎ 01803-770523 **Fax** 01803-770851
24 bedrs, all ensuite, ▦ ⛏ ⁙ 80 **P** 50 ⊟ **SB** £47-£53
DB £74-£88 **HB** £238-£371 **L** £11 **D** £17 **D** ♥ ✕
LD 21:00 ⟨⟨ MC Visa Amex ▣ ⟩ ▦ ▧ ▨

DARWEN Lancashire 10B4
Pop. 33,000. Bolton 9, London 204, Blackburn 4,
Preston 14 **EC** Tue **MD** Mon, Fri, Sat

★★★ ✤ Whitehall

Springbank, Whitehall,
Darwen BB3 2JU
☎ 01254-701595 **Fax** 01254-773426
17 bedrs, all ensuite, ⛏ ⁙ 80 **P** 60 ⊟ Rest Club
Resid **SB** £55 **DB** £90 **L** £10.50 **D** £16.95 **D** ♥ ✕
LD 21:30 ⟨⟨ MC Visa Amex DC ▣ ▦ ▧ ⟨

DAVENTRY Northamptonshire 4B1
M1 (jn 16) 9, London 78, Banbury 17, Leamington
Spa 18, Rugby 13 🅸 Moot Hall, Market Square
01327-300277

★★★★ Hanover International, Daventry
Sedgemore Way, Daventry NN11 5SG
☎ 01327-301777 **Fax** 01327-706313

Stylish and elegant, located in the Nene Valley
close to Silverstone, with a superb fully equipped
leisure club. The Waterside Restaurant overlooks
beautiful Drayton Water.
138 bedrs, all ensuite, ⛏ ▣ ⁙ 600 **P** 350 ⊟ ⟨⟨ MC
Visa Amex DC ▣ ▧ ▨ ⟨

DAWLISH Devon 3D3
Pop. 12,100. Honiton 26, London 179, Exeter 13,
Newton Abbot 9, Okehampton 30, Torquay 11
EC Thu 🅸 The Lawn 01626-863589

ENGLAND

★★★ Langstone Cliff
Dawlish EX7 0NA
☎ 01626-868000 **Fax** 01626-868006
E-mail reception@langstone-hotel.co.uk
67 bedrs, all ensuite, ♫ ★ ▣ ‼ 400 **P** 200 ⊕
SB £53-£60 **DB** £90-£98 **HB** £330-£360 **L** £12 **L** ●
D £15.50 **D** ● ✕ **LD** 21:00 **CC** MC Visa Amex DC ▣ ⌧
▨ ▨ &
See advert on opposite page

DEDHAM Essex   5E1
Pop. 2,100. Colchester 7, London 63, Clacton 17,
Harwich 15, Ipswich 11, Sudbury 14 **EC** Wed **see** 15th
cent Church, Castle House, Flatford Mill & Dedham
Vale

★★★ Maison Talbooth ◪ ◪ ◪
Blue Ribbon Hotel
Stratford Road, Dedham CO7 6HN
☎ 01206-322367 **Fax** 01206-322752

Victorian rectory set in three acres of gardens, in
the heart of Constable Country. Exquisitely
furnished.
10 bedrs, all ensuite, ‼ 70 **P** 10 ⊕ **SB** £95-£130
DB £115-£175 **L** £20 **D** £24 ✕ **LD** 21:30 Restaurant
closed D Sun **CC** MC Visa Amex DC

DERBY Derbyshire   7F1
Pop. 220,600. M1 (jn 5) 10, London 126,
Ashbourne 13, Ashby-de-la-Zouch 14, Burton-
upon-Trent 11, Loughborough 16, Mansfield 23,
Matlock 18, Nottingham 15 **MD** Tue, Thur, Fri, Sat **see**
Cathedral, St Werburgh's Church, RC Church of St
Mary by Pugin, St Mary's Bridge, St Peter's Church,
Sadler Gate **ℹ** Assembly Rooms, Market Place
01332-255802

★★★★ Mickleover Court ◪ ◪
Etwall Road, Derby DE3 5XX
☎ 01332-521234 **Fax** 01332-521238
E-mail enquiries@mickleovercourt.com
80 bedrs, all ensuite, ♀ ♫ ▣ ‼ 250 **P** 200 ⊕
SB £120 **DB** £145 **L** £16 **L** ● **D** £22 **D** ● ✕ **LD** 23:00
CC MC Visa Amex DC JCB ▣ ⌧ ▨ &

★★★ International
Burton Road, Derby DE23 6AD
☎ 01332-369321 **Fax** 01332-294430
62 bedrs, all ensuite, ★ ▣ ‼ 60 **P** 80 ⊕ Rest Resid
SB £40.50-£61.50 **DB** £45.50-£71.50 **L** £8 **L** ● **D** £15
D ● ✕ **LD** 22:15 Restaurant closed L Mon **CC** MC
Visa Amex DC

★★★ Midland
Midland Road, Derby DE1 2SQ
☎ 01332-345894 **Fax** 01332-293522
E-mail sales@midland-derby.co.uk
Closed Christmas Day & New Year
100 bedrs, all ensuite, ▣ ♀ ♫ ▣ ‼ 150 **P** 120 ⊕
SB £88.50-£106 **DB** £106-£123 **L** £14.26 **L** ● **D** £20 ✕
LD 21:45 Restaurant closed L Sat **CC** MC Visa Amex
DC JCB

★★★ Posthouse **Posthouse**
Pasture Hill, Littleover, Derby DE23 7BA
☎ 01332-514933 **Fax** 01332-518668
63 bedrs, all ensuite, ♀ ⚲ ⚹ ⚌ 90 **P** 150 ⚏
SB £89.95 **DB** £100.90 **L** £11 **D** £17 ✕
LD 22:30 **CC** MC Visa Amex DC ⚒

★★★ Risley Hall ⚘
Derby Road, Risley DE72 3SS
☎ 0115-939 9000 **Fax** 0115-939 7766
16 bedrs, all ensuite, ⚃ ⚲ ⚏ ⚌ 150 **P** 160 ⚏
SB £82.50-£102.50 **DB** £110-£130 **L** £11 **D** £16 **D** ⚑ ✕
LD 21:30 Restaurant closed D Sun **CC** MC Visa Amex
⚞ ⚟ ⚠ ⚒
See advert on previous page

★★ Hotel La Gondola
220 Osmaston Road, Derby DE23 8JX
☎ 01332-332895 **Fax** 01332-384512
20 bedrs, all ensuite, ⚌ 90 **P** 70 ⚏ **SB** £51 **DB** £56
L £6.90 **L** ⚑ **D** £11.90 ✕ **LD** 22:00 **CC** MC Visa Amex
DC ⚒

DEVIZES Wiltshire 4A3
Pop. 11,000. Marlborough 14, London 86,
Amesbury 18, Bath 19, Chippenham 11, Pewsey
12, Swindon 15, Warminster 15 **EC** Wed **MD** Thu, Sat
see Market Cross, St John's Church, Wiltshire
Archaeological Society Museum, Town Hall 🛈 39 St
John's Street 01380-729408

★★★ Bear
Market Place, Devizes SN10 1HS
☎ 01380-722444 **Fax** 01380-722450
Closed 25-26 Dec
24 bedrs, 22 ensuite, 2 ⚲ ⚃ ⚹ ⚌ 120 **P** 30 ⚏
SB £59 **DB** £86 **L** £10 **L** ⚑ **D** £16.95 **D** ⚑ ✕ **LD** 21:15
Restaurant closed D Sun **CC** MC Visa Amex JCB

DISS Norfolk 9E3
See also TIVETSHALL ST MARY
Pop. 5,500. London 97, Bury St Edmunds 19,
Ipswich 24, Scole 2½, Thetford 19 **EC** Tue **MD** Fri **see**
Diss Mere, St Mary's Church 🛈 Meres Mouth, Mere
Street 01379-650523

★★★ Cornwallis Arms ⚘
Brome, Eye IP23 8AJ
☎ 01379-870326 **Fax** 01379-870051
16 bedrs, all ensuite, ⚃ ♀ ⚹ ⚌ 40 **P** 60 ⚏ **SB** £67.50
DB £87.50 **L** £17.95 **L** ⚑ **D** £17.95 **D** ⚑ ✕ **LD** 21:30
CC MC Visa Amex DC JCB

DONCASTER South Yorkshire 11DF
Pop. 81,600. A1 (M) 2½, London 164, Barnsley 15,
Bawtry 9, Pontefract 14, Rotherham 11, Thorne 9½,
Worksop 16 **EC** Thu **MD** Tue, Fri, Sat **see** St George's
Church, Christ Church, Art Gallery, Mansion House
🛈 Library, Waterdale 01302-734309

★★★ Mount Pleasant
Great North Road (A638),
Rossington, Doncaster DN11 0HP
☎ 01302-868219 **Fax** 01302-865130
E-mail mountpleasant@fax.co.uk
Closed Christmas Day
32 bedrs, all ensuite, ⚃ ⚌ 100 **P** 100 ⚏ Rest Resid
SB £55 **DB** £84 **L** £10.50 **L** ⚑ **D** £19.50 ✕ **LD** 21:30
CC MC Visa Amex DC ⚒

★★★ Quality
High Street, Doncaster DN1 1DN
☎ 01302-342261 **Fax** 01302-329034
66 bedrs, all ensuite, ♀ ⚲ ⚹ ⚏ ⚌ 300 **P** 40
⚏ **SB** £57-£75 **DB** £77-£90 **L** ⚑ **D** £16.95
D ⚑ ✕ **LD** 21:15 Restaurant closed
L Mon-Sat **CC** MC Visa Amex DC ⚒

★★ Belmont
Horse Fair Green, Thorne, Doncaster DN8 5EE
☎ 01405-812320 **Fax** 01405-740508
E-mail belmonthotel@compuserve.com
Closed Christmas
23 bedrs, all ensuite, ⚃ ♀ ⚹ ⚌ 50 **P** 20 ⚏
SB £56.95-£63.95 **DB** £69-£95 **L** £11 **D** £11 ✕
LD 22:00 **CC** MC Visa Amex DC ⚒

★★ Regent
Regent Square, Doncaster DN1 2DS
☎ 01302-364180 **Fax** 01302-322331

A charming Victorian building overlooking a
secluded Regency park. The hotel is ideally
situated within easy reach of Doncaster's vibrant
town centre and only minutes away from the
historic race course.

50 bedrs, all ensuite, 🄴 🛏 🖭 ⅲ 100 P 20 🍴 SB £60-£75 DB £70-£85 D £10 ✕ LD 22:00 ⊄ MC Visa Amex DC JCB 🖳 ⅙

Campanile Doncaster Lodge

Doncaster Leisure Park,
Bawtry Road, Doncaster DN4 7PD
☎ 01302-370770 Fax 01302-370813

Campanile hotels offer comfortable and convenient budget accommodation and a traditional French style Bistro providing freshly cooked food for beakfast, lunch and dinner. All rooms ensuite with tea/coffee making facilities, DDT and TV with Sky channels.
50 bedrs, all ensuite, 🛏 ⅲ 20 P 60 🍴 Rest Resid ⊄ MC Visa Amex DC ⅙

DORCHESTER ON THAMES Oxfordshire   4B2
Pop. 900. Wallingford 4, London 50, Aylesbury 20, Burford 28, Farington 20, Oxford 9 see Abbey Church, Museum

★★★ ✜ George
High Street, Dorchester on Thames OX10 7HH
☎ 01865-340404 Fax 01865-341620
18 bedrs, all ensuite, 🄴 🛏 ⅲ 35 P 50 🍴 ⊄ MC Visa Amex

★★ White Hart 🖳 🖳
26 High Street, Dorchester on Thames OX9 8HN
☎ 01865-340074 Fax 01865-341082

A 16th century coaching inn, the White Hart has an unmistakable character and offers the best of English hospitality.
19 bedrs, all ensuite, 🄴 🛏 ⅲ 50 P 25 🍴 SB £65-£85 DB £75-£95 L £17.50 L 🍴 D £23 D 🍴 ✕ LD 21:30 ⊄ MC Visa Amex DC

DORKING Surrey   4C3
Pop. 23,000. Leatherhead 5, London 23, Crawley 13, Guildford 12, Horsham 13, Reigate 6 ᴇ Wed MD Fri see Old Inns, Parish Church of St Martins, Box Hill, Polesdon Lacey (NT) 2½ m NW

★★★★ Burford Bridge   Heritage HOTELS
Burford Bridge, Box Hill,
Dorking RH5 6BX
☎ 01306-887821 Fax 01306-880386
57 bedrs, all ensuite, ⌀ 🛏 ⅲ 300 P 100 🍴 SB £140-£150 DB £150-£160 L £18.50 D £21 D 🍴 ✕ LD 22:00 ⊄ MC Visa Amex DC JCB ⌁

★★★ ✜ Gatton Manor Hotel Golf & Country Club
Ockley, Dorking RH5 5PQ
☎ 01306-627555 Fax 01306-627713
E-mail gattonmanor@enterprize.net

An 18th century manor house set in 250 acres of beautiful parklands with its own 18 hole championship length golf course. Excellent food and accommodation. Gym and Health Club. Conference suites.
16 bedrs, all ensuite, 🄴 ⌀ ⅲ 60 P 200 🍴 SB £67.50 DB £105 L 🍴 D £15 D 🍴 ✕ LD 21:30 ⊄ MC Visa Amex DC 🖾 🖳 🖭 🖳 🖳

★★★ White Horse 🖳   Heritage HOTELS
High Street, Dorking RH4 1BE
☎ 01306-881138 Fax 01306-887241
69 bedrs, all ensuite, 🄴 🛏 ⅲ 60 P 72 🍴 SB £115-£120 DB £125-£135 L £8 D £19.75 ✕ LD 21:30 ⊄ MC Visa Amex DC JCB

DOVEDALE Derbyshire   8A2
Pop. 225. Ashbourne 4½, London 143, Buxton 17, Leek 13, Matlock 15, Stoke 21 **see** Dale (explorable on foot), Pike Pool (Beresford Dale), Thorpe Cloud, Lion's Head Rock, Ilam Hall

★★★ Izaak Walton
Dovedale DE6 2AY

☎ 01335-350555 **Fax** 01335-350539

A 17th century farmhouse where Izaak Walton regularly stayed to fish in the nearby River Dove. Now a luxury hotel, with views of Dovedale and the Derbyshire hills.
30 bedrs, all ensuite, ▣ ☂ ▥ 40 **P** 80 ⊞ **SB** £81-£99 **DB** £105-£135 **L** £14.25 **L** ❤ **D** £23.50 **D** ❤ ✕ **LD** 21:15 Restaurant closed L Mon-Sat **CC** MC Visa Amex DC JCB ▣

★★★ Peveril of the Peak ⌖   Heritage
Thorpe, Dovedale DE6 2AW   HOTELS
☎ 01335-350333 **Fax** 01335-350507
46 bedrs, all ensuite, ▣ ☂ ▥ 70 **P** 65 ⊞ **SB** £75-£85 **DB** £95-£105 **L** £11.95 **D** £21.95 ✕ **LD** 21:00 **CC** MC Visa Amex DC

DOVER Kent   5F3
Pop. 30,300. Canterbury 15, London 74, Folkstone 7, Margate 20 **EC** Wed **MD** Sat **see** Castle and Roman Pharos (lighthouse), Keep and underground passages, Church, Town Hall incorp 13th cent Maison Dieu, Museum, Bleriot Memorial, Roman Painted House ℹ Townwall Street 01304-205108

★★★ Churchill
Dover Waterfront, Dover CT17 9BP
☎ 01304-203633 **Fax** 01304-216320
68 bedrs, 67 ensuite, ⌀ ▣ ▥ 110 **P** 32 ⊞ **SB** £68 **DB** £97 **L** £13 **L** ❤ **D** £16 **D** ❤ ✕ **LD** 21:15 **CC** MC Visa Amex DC ♿

★★★ Posthouse   **Posthouse**
Whitfield, Dover CT16 3LF
☎ 01304-821222 **Fax** 01304-825576
68 bedrs, all ensuite, ☂ ▥ 55 **P** 92 ⊞ **SB** £68.95-£98.95 **DB** £78.90-£98.90 **HB** £329-£389 **L** £14 **D** £14 ✕ **LD** 22:30 **CC** MC Visa Amex DC JCB ♿

★★★ Wallett's Court Country House ⌖ ⌖
West Cliffe, St Margarets-at-Cliffe, Dover CT15 6EW
☎ 01304-852424 **Fax** 01304-853430
E-mail wallettscourt@compuserve.com
Closed 24-27 Dec

A 17th century manor with luxurious rooms, highly acclaimed restaurant and relaxing health spa with indoor pools, in a tranquil, rural setting. Fifteen miles from Canterbury in beautiful countryside on the white cliffs of Dover
16 bedrs, all ensuite, ▣ ⌀ ▥ 30 **P** 40 ⊞ Rest Resid **SB** £50-£70 **DB** £80-£130 **L** £17.50 **L** ❤ **D** £27.50 **D** ❤ ✕ **LD** 21:00 **CC** MC Visa Amex ▣ ▣ ▣ ▣

DOWNHAM MARKET Norfolk   9D3
Pop. 6,000. Ely 17, London 88, King's Lynn 11, Swaffham 15, Thetford 22, Wisbech 13 **EC** Wed **MD** Fri, Sat **see** St Edmund's Parish Church

★★ ✤ Castle
High Street, Downham Market PE38 9HF
☎ 01366-384311 **Fax** 01366-384311
12 bedrs, 10 ensuite, ☂ ▥ 50 **P** 40 ⊞ **CC** MC Visa Amex

DRIFFIELD, GREAT East Yorkshire   11E3
Pop. 9,600. Beverley 13, London 192, Bridlington 11, Malton 19, Scarborough 21, York 29 **EC** Wed **MD** Thu, Sat **see** All Saints Church, St Mary's Church (Little Driffield)

★★★ Bell ⚲
Market Place, Great Driffield YO25 7AP
☎ 01377-256661 **Fax** 01377-253228
16 bedrs, all ensuite, 4️⃣ ♀ ⚲ ▤ ▦ 200 **P** 18 No
children under 12 ⊕ **SB** £76-£86 **DB** £105-£115 **L** ⬝
D £15 **D** ⬝ ✕ **LD** 21:30 ℂℂ MC Visa Amex DC JCB ▣
▨ ▨ ▨ ▨ ♿

DUDLEY West Midlands   7E3
Pop. 187,400. Birmingham 8½, London 120,
Bridgnorth 17, Kidderminster 12, Walsall 7½,
Wolverhampton 6 **EC** Wed **MD** Daily **see** Castle ruins,
remains of 12th cent Cluniac Priory, Art Gallery,
Geological Museum, Zoo, Black Country Museum
ℹ 39 Churchill Shopping Centre 01384-457494

★★★★ Copthorne Merry Hill-Dudley
Level Street, Brierley Hill, Dudley DY5 1UR
☎ 01384-482882 **Fax** 01384-482773
138 bedrs, all ensuite, ⚲ ▤ ▦ 570 **P** 160 ⊕
SB £125-£150 **DB** £135-£160 **L** £16.95 **L** ⬝ **D** £18.95
✕ **LD** 23:00 ℂℂ MC Visa Amex DC JCB ▣ ▨ ▨ ♿

DUNSTABLE Bedfordshire   4C1
Pop. 35,900. M1(jn 11) 2½, London 34, Aylesbury
15, Bedford 19, Bletchley 12, Luton 5, St Albans 13
EC Thu **MD** Wed, Fri, Sat **see** Chew's Almshouses,
Dunstable Downs (NT), Whipsnade Zoo, Luton Hoo
ℹ Library, Vernon Place 01582-471012

★★★ Old Palace Lodge
Church Street, Dunstable LU5 4RT
☎ 01582-662201 **Fax** 01582-696422

Delightfully converted Victorian house,
sympathetically extended to offer 68 luxury
bedrooms. Award winning restaurant. Ample
parking. Close to Whipsnade, Woburn and other
attractions.
68 bedrs, all ensuite, 4️⃣ ⚲ ☂ ▤ ▦ 40 **P** 70 ⊕
SB £55-£105 **DB** £70-£125 **L** £14 **L** ⬝ **D** £19.95 **D** ⬝ ✕
LD 21:45 Restaurant closed L Sat ℂℂ MC Visa Amex
DC JCB

DUNSTER Somerset   3D2
Pop. 790. Taunton 22, London 165, Bridgwater 24,
Minehead 2, South Molton 24, Tiverton 26 **EC** Wed
see Historic Castle, Yarn Market, Church with 15th
cent font and rood screen, Dovecote (unique
revolving ladder), Nunnery (pantiled cottages), old
Grist Mill with double wheel, old Buttercross

★★★ Luttrell Arms ⚲   **Heritage** HOTELS
High Street, Dunster TA24 6SG
☎ 01643-821555 **Fax** 01643-821567
27 bedrs, all ensuite, 4️⃣ ☂ ▦ 20 **P** 3 ⊕ **SB** £35-£55
DB £70-£110 **HB** £315-£455 **L** £12.95 **D** £25 ✕
LD 21:30 ℂℂ MC Visa Amex DC JCB

DURHAM Co. Durham   11D1
Pop. 24,800. A1(M) 3, London 260, Corbridge 24,
Darlington 19, Newcastle 14, Stockton 19,
Sunderland 13, West Ackland 13 **EC** Wed **MD** Sat **see**
Cathedral, Norman Castle, St Giles and St
Margaret's Churches (both 12th cent), St Oswald's
Church, remains of 14th cent Almshouses, Art
Gallery, Gulbenkian Museum of Oriental Art and
Archeaology ℹ Market Place 0191-384 3720

★★★★ Swallow Royal County ⚲ ⚲
Old Elvet, Durham DH1 3JN   **SWALLOW** HOTELS
☎ 0191-386 6821 **Fax** 0191-386 0704
E-mail info@swallowhotels.com

The Swallow Royal County is one of the region's
premier hotels set on the banks of the River Wear
in the heart of the city. It has awards for fine food,
and a leisure club.
151 bedrs, all ensuite, 4️⃣ ☂ ▤ ▦ 140 **P** 80 ⊕
SB £95-£115 **DB** £130-£145 **L** £10 **D** £24.50 ✕
LD 22:15 ℂℂ MC Visa Amex DC ▣ ▨ ▨ ♿

★★★ Ramside Hall
Carrville, Durham DH1 1TD
☎ 0191-386 5282 **Fax** 0191-386 0399
82 bedrs, all ensuite, ☂ ▤ ▦ 400 **P** 500 ⊕ ℂℂ MC
Visa Amex DC ▣ ♿

★★★ Swallow Three Tuns ⌇⌇
New Elvet, Durham DH1 3AQ
📞 0191-386 4326 **Fax** 0191-386 1406
E-mail info@swallowhotels.com

Set in the heart of historic Durham, this former 16th century coaching inn offers traditional charm and an intimate atmosphere, with ancient beams and open fireplaces.
50 bedrs, all ensuite, ⊬ ⋕ 350 **P** 60 ⊟ **SB** £50-£115 **DB** £70-£125 **L** £11.25 **D** £19.25 ✕ **LD** 21:30 ⊄ MC Visa Amex DC

🌣 Hallgarth Manor
Pittington, Durham DH6 1AB
📞 0191-372 1188 **Fax** 0191-372 1249
23 bedrs, all ensuite, ⊬ ⋕ 250 **P** 300 ⊟ ⊄ MC Visa Amex DC JCB
See advert on this page

EAGLESCLIFFE Cleveland   11D2
Pop. 8,160. Thirsk 20, London 239, Darlington 9, Helmsley 28, Northallerton 16, Stockton 4, Whitby 35 **see** Preston Park

★★ Claireville
519 Yarm Road, Eaglescliffe TS16 9BG
📞 01642-780378 **Fax** 01642-784109
17 bedrs, all ensuite, ⊬ ⋕ 30 **P** 30 ⊟ Rest Resid ⊄ MC Visa Amex DC

★★ Sunnyside
580-582 Yarm Road, Eaglescliffe TS16 0DF
📞 01642-780075 **Fax** 01642-783789
23 bedrs, 21 ensuite, ⌁ ⊬ ⋕ 30 **P** 22 ⊟ Resid **SB** £35-£43 **DB** £40-£61 **D** £6 **D** ⬤ ✕ **LD** 20:00 ⊄ MC Visa Amex DC JCB

EAST GRINSTEAD West Sussex   5D3
Pop. 25,000. Godstone 10, London 30, Crawley 9, Lewes 21, Redhill 13, Reigate 14, Tunbridge Wells 13, Uckfield 13 **EC** Wed **MD** Sat

★★★ Gravetye Manor ⌇⌇⌇⌇
Gold Ribbon Hotel
East Grinstead RH19 4LJ
📞 01342-810567 **Fax** 01342-810080
E-mail gravetye@relaischateaux.fr

A picturesque ivy clad Elizabethan manor house, set in 30 acres of William Robinson's natural English gardens, surrounded by a 1,000 acre forest. 18 bedrs, all ensuite, ⊿ ⋕ 16 **P** 25 No children under 7 ⊟ Rest Resid **SB** £98-£145 **DB** £135-£290 **L** £29 **D** £38 ✕ **LD** 21:30 ⊄ MC Visa ▣

★★★ Woodbury House
Lewes Road, East Grinstead RH19 3UD
☎ 01342-313657 **Fax** 01342-314801
14 bedrs, all ensuite, 4 ♒ ☷ 40 **P** 45 ⊕ **SB** £60-£75
DB £75-£90 **L** £9.95 **L** ● **D** £16.95 **D** ● ✕ **LD** 21:30
CC MC Visa Amex DC

| EASTBOURNE East Sussex | 5D4 |

Pop. 83,000. Uckfield 19, London 63, Hastings 20,
Hurst Green 23, Lewes 16, Newhaven 12, **EC** Wed
MD Wed, Sat ⓘ 3 Cornfield Road 01323-411400

★★★★★ Grand 🛏 🛏 🛏
King Edwards Parade, Eastbourne BN21 4EQ
☎ 01323-412345 **Fax** 01323-412233
164 bedrs, all ensuite, ♒ ☰ ☷ 400 **P** 56 ⊕ **CC** MC
Visa Amex DC ☒ ⚿ 🖼 ⚿
See advert on this page

★★★ Chatsworth
Grand Parade, Eastbourne BN21 3YR
☎ 01323-411016 **Fax** 01323-643270
E-mail sales@chatsworth-hotel.demon.co.uk
47 bedrs, all ensuite, ✐ ♒ ☰ ☷ 100 ⊕ **SB** £40-£50
DB £65-£90 **L** £9 **D** £16 **D** ● ✕ **LD** 20:30 **CC** MC Visa
Amex DC

CUMBERLAND HOTEL

*A beautiful three star 72 bedroomed hotel
right on the seafront opposite the bandstand.
Large comfortable seafacing lounges.
Elegant dining room serving delicious cuisine.
Friendly, professional service.
Close to shops and theatres.*

**GRAND PARADE, EASTBOURNE,
EAST SUSSEX BN21 3YT
Tel: 01323 730342
Fax: 01323 646314**

ENGLAND

★★★ ✦ Cumberland
Grand Parade, Eastbourne BN21 3YT
☎ 01323-730342 **Fax** 01323-646314

Beautiful three star hotel right on the seafront, opposite the bandstand. Elegant dining room serving delicious cuisine. Friendly, professional service. Close to shops and theatres.
72 bedrs, all ensuite, ♀ ▣ ⦿ 200 ♨ **SB** £28-£37 **DB** £56-£74 **HB** £224-£287 **D** £12.95 **D** ♥ ✕ **LD** 20:30 ⦅ MC Visa Amex
See advert on previous page

★★★ ✦ Hydro
Mount Road, Eastbourne BN20 7HZ
☎ 01323-720643 **Fax** 01323-641167

This award winning hotel overlooks the sea from a unique garden setting and offers croquet, putting, swimming pool (May-Sept), gym, sauna, ample car parking and English cuisine. Established since 1895.
83 bedrs, all ensuite, ♀ ▣ ⦿ 150 **P** 50 ♨ **SB** £33-£55 **DB** £56-£99 **HB** £266-£434 **L** £8.95 **D** £15.95 ✕ **LD** 20:30 ⦅ MC Visa DC ⌇ ▣ ▨ ▨

ENGLAND

★★★ ❖ Lansdowne

King Edwards Parade, Eastbourne BN21 4EE
☎ 01323-725174 **Fax** 01323-739721
E-mail thelansdowne@btinternet.com
Closed 1-13 Jan

Traditional, privately owned seafront hotel, overlooking the Western Lawns. Spacious elegant lounges facing the sea. Attractive Regency bar and quality English cuisine. Golfing holidays all year.
121 bedrs, all ensuite, ⊢ ⊡ ⠿ 120 **P** 22 ⊕ **SB** £53-£61 **DB** £86-£106 **HB** £270-£511 **L** £10 **L** ⬤ **D** £17.95 **D** ⬤ ✕ **LD** 20:30 Restaurant closed L Mon-Sat
⸨ MC Visa Amex DC JCB 🌠
See advert on opposite page

★★★ ❖ Princes

Lascelles Terrace, Eastbourne BN21 4BL
☎ 01323-722056 **Fax** 01323-727469

Family-run hotel in an unspoilt Victorian terrace. Quiet area just off the seafront.
44 bedrs, 38 ensuite, 6 ⋒ ④ ⊡ ⠿ 60 ⊕ Resid
SB £34-£41.50 **DB** £58-£73 **HB** £248-£325.50 **D** £14 ✕
LD 20:30 ⸨ MC Visa Amex

★★★ Quality

Grand Parade, Eastbourne BN21 3YS
☎ 01323-727411 **Fax** 01323-720665
E-mail admin@gb610.u-net.com

Quality Hotel

A traditional 1920s seafront hotel overlooking the beach.
115 bedrs, all ensuite, ⊢ ⊡ ⠿ 200 ⊕ **SB** £72.75-£93.25 **DB** £102.75-£104.25 **D** £14.50 ✕ **LD** 20:30
⸨ MC Visa Amex DC JCB 🌠

★★★ Wish Tower

King Edward's Parade, Eastbourne BN21 4EB
☎ 01323-722676 **Fax** 01323-721474
56 bedrs, all ensuite, ⊢ ⊡ ⠿ 60 ⊕ ⸨ MC Visa Amex DC

★★ Congress

31-41 Carlisle Road, Eastbourne BN21 4JS
☎ 01323-732118 **Fax** 01323-720016
E-mail congresshotel@msn.co.uk
Closed Nov-Feb ex Christmas, New Year
60 bedrs, 58 ensuite, ④ ⊢ ⊡ ⠿ 20 **P** 16 ⊕ **SB** £29-£36 **DB** £58-£72 **HB** £225-£270 **L** ⬤ **D** £9 ✕ **LD** 19:45
⸨ MC Visa 🌠 ♿
See advert on opposite page

★★ Langham

Royal Parade, Eastbourne BN22 7AH
☎ 01323-731451 **Fax** 01323-646623
E-mail enquiries@seet6.org.uk
Closed Dec-Jan
87 bedrs, all ensuite, ⊢ ⊡ ⠿ 80 **P** 4 ⊕ ⸨ MC Visa Amex JCB

★★ ❖ Lathom

Howards Square, Eastbourne BN21 4BG
☎ 01323-641986 **Fax** 01323-416405
45 bedrs, all ensuite, ⊡ **P** 10 ⊕ Resid **SB** £25-£30
DB £50-£60 **HB** £200-£240 **L** £5.25 **D** £8.75 ✕
LD 19:30 ⸨ MC Visa Amex JCB

★★ ❖ New Wilmington

25 Compton Street, Eastbourne BN21 4DU
☎ 01323-721219 **Fax** 01323-728900
Closed Jan-Feb
40 bedrs, all ensuite, ⊢ ⊡ ⠿ 20 **P** 1 ⊕ **SB** £34-£40
DB £58-£70 **HB** £273-£315 **L** £6.25 **L** ⬤ **D** £13 **D** ⬤ ✕
LD 20:00 ⸨ MC Visa Amex

★★ ✤ Oban
King Edwards Parade,
Eastbourne BN21 4DS
☎ 01323-731581 **Fax** 01323-721994
Closed Jan-Feb
30 bedrs, all ensuite, ⚞ 🖪 ⚎ 40 **P** 10 ⊞ ℂℂ MC Visa
Amex DC JCB ♿

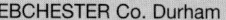

★★ ✤ West Rocks
Grand Parade, Eastbourne BN21 4DL
☎ 01323-725217 **Fax** 01323-720421
Closed mid Nov-mid Mar
45 bedrs, all ensuite, 🖪 ⚎ 30 No children under 3
⊞ Rest Resid **SB** £35-£45 **DB** £50-£80 **HB** £190-£374
L 🍴 **D** £12.50 ✕ **LD** 20 ℂℂ MC Visa Amex DC JCB ♿

★★ ✤ York House
14/21 Royal Parade,
Eastbourne BN22 7AP
☎ 01323-412918 **Fax** 01323-646238
E-mail yorkhouse@pavilion.co.uk
86 bedrs, all ensuite, ⋒ ⚞ 🖪 ⚎ 100 ⊞ **SB** £33-£40
DB £66-£80 **HB** £210-£329 **L** £9.95 **L** 🍴 **D** £12.50 ✕
LD 20:30 ℂℂ MC Visa Amex DC JCB 🔲 🈂 ♿

EBCHESTER Co. Durham   10C1
Pop. 3,800. Consett 3, London 246, Corbridge 10,
Durham 15, Newcastle 15

★★★ Raven Country
Broomhill, Ebchester, Consett DH8 6RY
☎ 01207-562562 **Fax** 01207-560262
E-mail enquiries@ravenhotel.co.uk

A delightful hotel in a rural setting, overlooking the
beautiful Derwent Valley. For a true breath of fresh
air, the hotel is ideal for a quiet stay of luxury. Close
to Beamish Museum, Hadrian's Wall, Gateshead's
MetroCentre, Newcastle and Durham City.
28 bedrs, all ensuite, ▣ ⋒ ⚎ 120 **P** 120 ⊞ **SB** £40-
£52 **DB** £55-£69 **HB** £300 **L** 🍴 **D** 🍴 ✕ **LD** 22:00
Restaurant closed D Sun ℂℂ MC Visa Amex DC ♿

EGHAM Surrey   4C2
Pop. 12,000. Staines 1½, London 18, M25 (jn 13)
½, Bagshot 8½, Reading 21, Weybridge 7, Windsor
6, Woking 10 **EC** Thu **see** Virginia Water, Runnymede
Memorials

★★★★ Runnymede 🛏 🛏 🛏
Windsor Road, Egham TW20 0AG
☎ 01784-436171 **Fax** 01784-436340
E-mail info@runnymedehotel.com

Privately owned on the banks of the River Thames
with extensive conference and spa facilities.
Modern hotel with a reputation for quality and
service.
180 bedrs, all ensuite, ⋒ 🖪 ⚎ 350 **P** 300 ⊞
SB £157.95-£177.95 **DB** £205.90-£230.90 **L** £17.95
D £26.75 ✕ **LD** 22:15 Restaurant closed L Sat, D
Sun ℂℂ MC Visa Amex DC 🔲 🈂 🈶 🈂 🈂 ♿

EGREMONT Cumbria   10A2
Pop. 6,300. Broughton-in-Furness 31, London 308,
Cockermouth 15, Keswick 25, Workington 13 🅹 12
Main Street 01946-820693

★★ Blackbeck Bridge Inn
Beckermet, Egremont CA22 2NY
☎ 01946-841661 **Fax** 01946-841007
22 bedrs, 20 ensuite, 2 ℗ ⚞ ⚎ 40 **P** 70 ⊞ ℂℂ MC
Visa Amex DC 🈂 ♿

ELLESMERE PORT Cheshire   7D1

★★★ Quality Chester
Berwick Road, Welsh Road,
Little Sutton, Ellesmere Port L66 4PS
☎ 0151-339 5121 **Fax** 0151-339 3214
E-mail admin@gb066.u-net.com
53 bedrs, all ensuite, ▣ ♀ ⋒ ⚞ ⚎ 300 **P** 150 ⊞
SB £84.50 **DB** £99.50 **L** 🍴 **D** £16.50 **D** 🍴 ✕
LD 21:30 Restaurant closed L Sat
ℂℂ MC Visa Amex DC JCB 🔲 🈂 🈶 ♿

ENGLAND

ELY Cambridgeshire 9D3

Pop. 11,900. Cambridge 16, London 71, Huntingdon 21, King's Lynn 28, Newmarket 13, Swaffham 26, Wisbech 23 ℻ Tue **MD** Thu see Cathedral, Bishop's Palace, Prior Crauden's Chapel and Ely Porta (King's School), 15th cent Monk's Granary, 13th cent St Mary's Church, Goldsmith Tower, Museums, Brass Rubbing Centre 🅸 Oliver Cromwell's House, 29 St. Mary's Street 01353-662062

★ Nyton
7 Barton Road, Ely CB7 4HZ
☎ 01353-662459 **Fax** 01353-666217

Comfortable family hotel in quiet residential area. Approximately 2 acres attractive gardens. Golf course adjoining. 10 minutes walk cathedral and city. Ample parking.
10 bedrs, all ensuite, ⊁ ⠿ 40 **P** 26 ⊕ **SB** £38 **DB** £60 **L** £15 **D** £15 ✕ **LD** 20:30 ℂℂ MC Visa Amex DC ⴵ

EMSWORTH Hampshire 4B4

Pop. 9,400. Petersfield 13, London 66, A3(M) 3, Chichester 7, Cosham 6 ℻ Wed see St. James's Church, Oyster beds.

★★★ ✦ Brookfield
Havant Road, Emsworth PO10 7LF
☎ 01243-373363 **Fax** 01243-376342
Closed 24 Dec-2 Jan
40 bedrs, all ensuite, ▦ ♪ ⠿ 100 **P** 80 ⊕ Rest Resid **SB** £58-£65 **DB** £80 **L** £15 **D** £15 ✕ **LD** 21:30 ℂℂ MC Visa Amex DC ⴵ

ENFIELD Middlesex 5D2

Pop. 109,000. London 12, Barnet 6, Epping 11, Hatfield 12, Hoddesdon 9, Woodford 6½ ℻ Wed **MD** Sat

★★★ Royal Chace ⍟ ⍟
The Ridgeway, Enfield EN2 8AR
☎ 0181-366 6500 **Fax** 0181-367 7191
E-mail royal.chace@dial.pipex.com.
Closed 25-26 Dec
92 bedrs, all ensuite, ▦ ♀ ⠿ 270 **P** 300 ⊕ **SB** £99.50 **DB** £115 **L** ♥ **D** £19.95 **D** ♥ ✕ **LD** 21:30 Restaurant closed L Mon-Sat, D Sun ℂℂ MC Visa Amex DC ⸓ ⴵ

EPPING Essex 5D2

Pop. 10,700. Woodford 8½, London 18, M11 (jn 27) 3½, Bishop's Stortford 13, Chelmsford 17, Hoddesdon 9 ℻ Wed **MD** Mon see Epping Forest

★★★ Posthouse **Posthouse**
Bell Common, High Road,
Epping CM16 4DG
☎ 01992-573137 **Fax** 01992-560402
79 bedrs, all ensuite, ⊁ ⠿ 80 **P** 100 ⊕ ℂℂ MC Visa Amex DC ⴵ

EPWORTH Lincolnshire 11E4

East Retford 21, London 167, M180 3, Scunthorpe 12 see The Old Rectory (Wesley's birthplace)

★★ Red Lion
Market Place, Epworth DN9 1EU
☎ 01427-872208 **Fax** 01427-875214
20 bedrs, 19 ensuite, ⠿ 70 **P** 40 ⊕ ℂℂ MC Visa Amex DC ⊠ ⴵ

ESHER Surrey 4C3

Kingston 3½, London 13, Guildford 15, Leatherhead 6½, Chertsey 6½ ℻ Wed

★★ Haven
Portsmouth Road, Esher KT10 9AR
☎ 0181-398 0023 **Fax** 0181-398 9463
20 bedrs, all ensuite, ⠿ 24 **P** 20 ⊕ Rest Resid ℂℂ MC Visa Amex DC

★★★ Summer Lodge ♟ ♟ ♟ ♟
Gold Ribbon Hotel
Evershot DT2 0JR
☎ 01935-83424 **Fax** 01935-83005
E-mail sumlodge@sumlodge.demon.co.uk

Elegant Georgian building in a charming garden set high up overlooking the quiet village of Evershot. Beautifully co-ordinated fabrics and furnishings enhance the country house atmosphere.
17 bedrs, all ensuite, ⚲ ⊬ ⋕ 40 **P** 40 ⊟ **SB** £125
DB £175 **L** £13.75 **L** ♥ **D** £37.50 ✕ **LD** 21:00 ℂℂ MC Visa Amex DC ⊰ ⊠ ⅄

Pop. 17,000. Moreton-in-Marsh 14, London 98, Birmingham 30, Cheltenham 16, Stratford-upon-Avon 14, Tewkesbury 13, Worcester 16 **EC** Wed **see** Abbey ruins, All Saints' Church, St Lawrence Church, Walker Hall, Abbey Almonry (now local history museum), Old Town Hall, Abbey Park and Gardens *i* Almonry Museum, Abbey Gate 01386-446944

★★★ Evesham
Coppers Lane, Evesham WR11 6DA
☎ 01386-765566 **Fax** 01386-765443
Closed Christmas
40 bedrs, all ensuite, ⊬ ⋕ 10 **P** 50 ⊟ **SB** £63-£72
DB £94-£100 ✕ **LD** 21:30 ℂℂ MC Visa Amex DC ⊡

★★★ Northwick
Waterside, Evesham WR11 6BT
☎ 01386-40322 **Fax** 01386-41070
30 bedrs, all ensuite, ⊡ ⚲ ⊬ ⋕ 200 **P** 90 ⊟ **SB** £62
DB £85-£110 **HB** £312 **L** £12 **L** ♥ **D** £17.50 **D** ♥ ✕
LD 21:30 ℂℂ MC Visa Amex DC JCB ⅄

★★ Mill at Harvington ⌂ ⌂
Blue Ribbon Hotel
Anchor Lane, Harvington, Evesham WR11 5NR
☎ 01386-870688 **Fax** 01386-870688
Closed 24-28 Dec

Tastefully converted beautiful Georgian house and former baking mill, set in acres of parkland on the banks of the River Avon, half a mile from the main road.
21 bedrs, all ensuite, ⚌ 15 **P** 55 No children under 10 ⊞ Rest Resid **SB** £61-£65 **DB** £84-£115 **HB** £360-£430 **L** £14 **L** 🍴 **D** £22 ✕ **LD** 21:00 **CC** MC Visa Amex DC JCB ⚹ ▣ ▨

EWEN Gloucestershire   4A2

★★ Wild Duck Inn
Ewen GL7 6BY
☎ 01285-770310 **Fax** 01285-770310
11 bedrs, all ensuite, ④ **P** 50 ⊞ **SB** £50 **DB** £70 **L** £5 **L** 🍴 **D** £10 **D** 🍴 ✕ **LD** 22:00 **CC** MC Visa Amex
See advert on opposite page

EXETER Devon   3D3
Pop. 103,800. Honiton 17, London 169, M5 3, Ashburton 19, Crediton 7½, Okehampton 22, Tiverton 15 **MD** Daily **see** Cathedral, Museum and Art Gallery, Northernhay Gardens, Southernhay (old houses and fine gardens), Customs House, Mol's Coffee House, Tucker's Hall, Rougemont, Castle ruins, Maritime Museum, Guildhall, ℹ Civic Centre, Paris Street 01392-265700

★★★★ Southgate ⌂   Heritage
                                        HOTELS
Southernway East, Exeter EX1 1QF
☎ 01392-412812 **Fax** 01392-413549
110 bedrs, all ensuite, ④ 🖉 ✝ ▣ ⚌ 100 **P** 130 ⊞ **SB** £70-£90 **DB** £80-£120 **HB** £336-£413 **L** £12 **L** 🍴 **D** £19.50 **D** 🍴 ✕ **LD** 21:50 Restaurant closed L Sat **CC** MC Visa Amex DC ▣ ▤ ▣ ⚹

★★★ Barton Cross ⌂
Huxham, Stoke Canon, Exeter EX5 4EJ
☎ 01392-841245 **Fax** 01392-841942

An early 17th century thatched hotel situated in beautiful countryside, just four miles from the historic city of Exeter. The charm of bygone centuries is combined with the luxury expected in the late 20th century.
9 bedrs, all ensuite, ♀ 🖉 ✝ ⚌ 20 **P** 35 ⊞ Rest Resid **SB** £65 **DB** £90 **D** £25 **D** 🍴 ✕ **LD** 21:30 **CC** MC Visa Amex JCB ⚹
See advert on this page

ENGLAND

★★★ Devon
Exeter By-Pass, Matford, Exeter EX2 8XU
☎ 01392-259268 **Fax** 01392-413142
E-mail info@devonhotel.co.uk

Luxurious standards of comfort, personal service and fine cuisine is everything you can expect from the Devon Hotel. Conveniently located within easy reach of the M25 and Exeter's city centre.
41 bedrs, all ensuite, ♀ ♪ ⟟ ⫙ 160 **P** 250 ⊕
SB £59-£64 **DB** £82-£92 **HB** £340-£490 **L** £10.50 **L** ●
D £15 **D** ● ✕ **LD** 21:00 **CC** MC Visa Amex DC

★★★ St Olaves Court ⊠ ⊠
Mary Arches Street, Exeter EX4 3AZ
☎ 01392-217736 **Fax** 01392-413054
15 bedrs, all ensuite, ▦ ♀ ♪ ⟟ ⫙ 45 **P** 15 ⊕ Rest
Resid **SB** £65-£85 **DB** £70-£100 **L** £11.50 **L** ● **D** £29
D ● ✕ **LD** 21:30 Restaurant closed L Sat & Sun
CC MC Visa Amex DC JCB

★★★ White Hart
South Street, Exeter EX1 1EE
☎ 01392-279897 **Fax** 01392-250159
59 bedrs, all ensuite, ▦ ♪ ⊡ ⫙ 70 **P** 60 ⊕ **SB** £46-
£61 **DB** £60-£94 **L** £10 **D** £12.50 ✕ **LD** 22:00 **CC** MC
Visa Amex DC

★★ Fingle Glen Hotel, Golf & Country Club
Old Tedburn Road, Tedburn St Mary, Exeter EX6
6AF
☎ 01647-61817 **Fax** 01647-61135

A delightful country hotel set within a 9 hole golf course. Ideally situated five miles from Exeter and close to Dartmoor. Seven ensuite bedrooms and a highly acclaimed bar and restaurant.
7 bedrs, all ensuite, ⫙ 200 **P** 200 ⊕ **SB** £39.50
DB £56.50 **D** £5.50 ✕ **LD** 19:30 **CC** MC Visa Amex DC
⊡ ⊡

★★ Great Western
St David's Station Approach, Exeter EX4 4NU
☎ 01392-274039 **Fax** 01392-425529
41 bedrs, 30 ensuite, ⟟ ⫙ 40 **P** 24 ⊕ **SB** £36 **DB** £52
L £6.95 **L** ● **D** £11.50 **D** ● ✕ **LD** 21:30 **CC** MC Visa
Amex DC

★★ Red House
2 Whipton Village Road, Exeter EX4 8AR
☎ 01392-256104 **Fax** 01392-435708

Family run hotel with licensed bar, carvery and restaurant. Bedrooms all have bathrooms, welcome tray, colour TV's and telephones. Large car park.
12 bedrs, all ensuite, ⟟ ⫙ 50 **P** 28 ⊕ **SB** £30-£35
DB £46-£50 **L** £7.50 **D** £7.95 ✕ **LD** 22:00 **CC** MC Visa
Amex DC ♿

★★ St Andrews
28 Alphington Road, Exeter EX2 8HN
☎ 01392-276784 **Fax** 01392-250249
Closed 24 Dec-2 Jan

St Andrews is a long established, family run hotel

offering a high standard of comfort and service in a friendly relaxing atmosphere. Excellent home cooking.
17 bedrs, all ensuite, ⚌ 12 **P** 20 ⊟ Rest Resid
SB £39-£45 **DB** £49.50-£61 **D** £12 ✕ **LD** 20:00 **CC** MC Visa Amex DC ♿

EXFORD Somerset   3D2
Dunster 11, London 177, Barnstaple 22, Lynmouth 14, South Molton 13, Taunton 35, Tiverton 22

★★★ Crown
Exford TA24 7PP
📞 01643-831554 **Fax** 01643-831665
E-mail bradleyhotelsexmoor@easynet.co.uk
17 bedrs, all ensuite, ♪ ✦ ⚌ 14 **P** 30 ⊟ **SB** £47.50-£75 **DB** £80-£116 **HB** £462-£535.50 **L** £15 **L** ☞
D £19.50 **D** ☞ ✕ **LD** 21:30 Restaurant closed L Mon-Sat **CC** MC Visa Amex JCB

EXMOUTH Devon   3D3
Pop. 28,319. Honiton 17, London 170, Axminster 26, Exeter 11, Lyme Regis 27 **EC** Wed **see** A La Ronde -18th cent house with Shell Gallery
ℹ Alexandra Terrace 01395-222299

★★ ✤ Manor
The Beacon, Exmouth EX8 2AG
📞 01395-272549 **Fax** 01395-225519
40 bedrs, all ensuite, 🖵 ⚌ 100 **P** 14 No children under 5 ⊟ **SB** £17.50-£32.50 **DB** £35-£60 **HB** £120-£215 **L** ☞ **D** £8.50 **D** ☞ ✕ **LD** 20:30 **CC** MC Visa

---

FAKENHAM Norfolk   9E2
ℹ Red Lion House, Market Place 01328-851981

★★ Wensum Lodge ⛉
Bridge Street, Fakenham NR21 9AY
📞 01328-862100 **Fax** 01328-863365
17 bedrs, all ensuite, 🖵 ♪ ⚌ 140 **P** 17 ⊟ **SB** £50
DB £65 **L** £14 **L** ☞ **D** £15 **D** ☞ ✕ **LD** 22:00 **CC** MC Visa Amex DC JCB 🖵

FALMOUTH Cornwall   2B4
Pop. 18,400. Truro 11, London 266, Helston 13, Redruth 10 **see** 16th cent Pendennis Castle, Charles I window in 16th cent Church ℹ 28 Killigrew Street 01326-312300

★★★★ Budock Vean Golf & Country House ⛉ ⛉
Mawnan Smith, Falmouth TR11 5LG
📞 01326-250288 **Fax** 01326-250892

Enjoy the quiet dignity of this splendid country house hotel set in 65 acres of spectacular parkland, with superb golf course, tennis courts, indoor heated pool and revitalising natural health spa.
58 bedrs, all ensuite, 🖵 ✦ 🖵 ⚌ 100 **P** 100 ⊟
SB £49-£85 **DB** £98-£170 **HB** £343-£595 **L** ☞ **D** £24.50 **D** ☞ ✕ **LD** 21:00 **CC** MC Visa DC 🖵🖵🖵🖵🖵 ♿

★★★★ Royal Duchy 🛏 🛏
Cliff Road, Falmouth TR11 4NX
📞 01326-313042 **Fax** 01326-319420
E-mail info@royalduchy.co.uk

Renowned cuisine is matched by the hotel's lavish accommodation. Every bedroom enjoys private bathroom ensuite, colour television with satellite reception and direct dial telephone.
43 bedrs, all ensuite, ♀ 🏊 🖿 ⚏ 100 **P** 50 ⏻ **SB** £58-£86 **DB** £108-£196 **HB** £315-£756 **L** £10 **L** 🍽 **D** £22 **D** 🍽 ✕ **LD** 21:00 《 MC Visa Amex DC 🖳 🖾 ⛍
See advert on previous page

★★★ Falmouth
Castle Beach, Falmouth TR11 4NZ
📞 0500-602030 **Fax** 01326-319533
E-mail falhotel@connexions.co.uk
Closed 23 Dec-3 Jan

Grade II listed Victorian seafront hotel in five acres of award-winning gardens, just a short walk from town. Self-catering apartments and cottages within hotel grounds with full use of hotel facilities.
69 bedrs, all ensuite, ⊿ 🏊 ⊁ 🖿 ⚏ 250 **P** 175 ⏻ **SB** £52 **DB** £70 **HB** £250 **L** £10 **L** 🍽 **D** £21 **D** 🍽 ✕ **LD** 21:30 《 MC Visa Amex DC JCB 🖳 🖾 🖾 🖾 🖾 🖾
See advert on this page

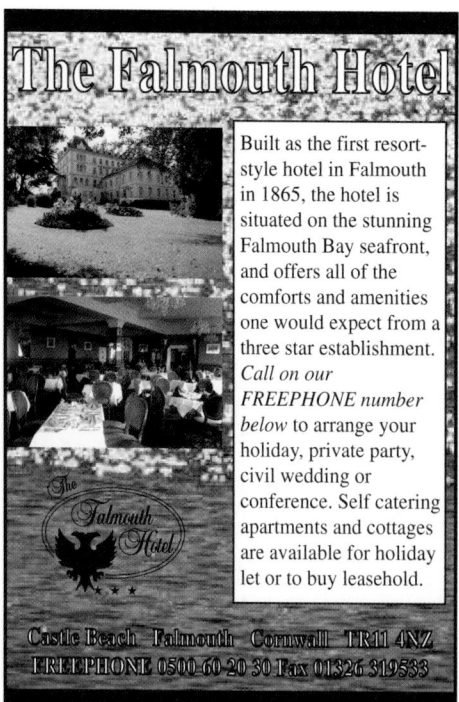

★★★ Green Lawns
Western Terrace, Falmouth TR11 4QJ
01326-312734 Fax 01326-211427
E-mail green.lawns@dial.pipex.com

Chateau style hotel set in prize winning gardens only a short stroll to the main beaches and town. A la carte restaurant and leisure complex. Some bedrooms and all public rooms are on the ground floor. 'Britain in Bloom' winner.
39 bedrs, all ensuite, 4 ⁂ 200 P 60 CC MC Visa Amex DC

★★★ Greenbank
Harbourside, Falmouth TR11 2SR
01326-312440 Fax 01326-211362

Falmouth's only harbourside hotel and restaurant with superb views to Flushing. All bedrooms luxuriously refurbished 1999. Most with harbour views. Terrace bar and bistro/seafood restaurant. Beauty salon, masseuse. Patisserie Bakery.
75 bedrs, all ensuite, ⁂ 200 P 64 SB £45-£150 DB £75-£180 L £12.50 L D £19.95 D LD 21:45 CC MC Visa Amex DC

★★★ Gyllyngdune Manor
Melvill Road, Falmouth TR11 4AR
01326-312978 Fax 01326-211881
30 bedrs, all ensuite, 4 P 25 SB £25-£50 DB £50-£100 HB £266-£400 L £9.50 D £16 D LD 21:00 Restaurant closed L Mon-Sat CC MC Visa Amex DC JCB

FAREHAM Hampshire 4B4

Pop. 84,200. Cosham 5, London 72, M27 (jn 10) 1, Alton 24, Portsmouth 9, Romsey 20, Southampton 12, Winchester 19 MD Mon see St Peter's Church. Titchfield Abbey 2m W, Portchester Castle, Church and Roman Fort 3m E, Titchfield Abbey 2m W
i Westbury Manor, West Street 01329-221342

★★★★ Solent
Rookery Avenue, Whiteley, PO15 7AJ
01489-880000 Fax 01489-880007
E-mail solent@shireinns.co.uk
117 bedrs, all ensuite, 4 ⁂ 250 P 200 SB £112-£122 DB £140-£160 L £14 D £20 LD 21:45 Restaurant closed L Sat, Sun CC MC Visa Amex DC

★★★ Posthouse **Posthouse**
Cartwright Drive, Fareham PO15 5RJ
01329-844644 Fax 01329-844666
125 bedrs, all ensuite, ⁂ 110 P 130 SB £64.95-£94.95 DB £74.90-£104.90 L £12 D £20 D LD 22:30 CC MC Visa Amex DC

FARINGDON Oxfordshire 4A2

Pop. 5,107. Wantage 9, London 70, Burford 12, Cirencester 18, Oxford 17, Swindon 12 EC Thu MD Tue see Gothic Church, old arcaded Town Hall (now Library), Folly Tower, Pusey House Gardens, Buscot Park i Pump House, 5 Market Place 01367-242191

★★ Faringdon
Market Place, Faringdon SN7 7HL
01367-240536 Fax 01367-243250

All rooms ensuite, equipped with remote control colour TV, direct dial telephone, tea/coffee facilities, hairdryer and some fourposter beds. Vintage lounge bar and cosy restaurant. Special diets catered for, home cooked food at reasonable prices.
20 bedrs, all ensuite, 4 ⁂ 25 P 5 SB £50 DB £60 D £10 LD 22:00 CC MC Visa Amex DC

ENGLAND

FARNBOROUGH Hampshire 4C3

Bagshot 7, London 34, M3 (jn 4) 3, Basingstoke 18, Farnham 5, Guildford 11, Henley-on-Thames 22, Reading 19, Woking 10 **EC** Wed **MD** Tue **see** St Michael's Abbey and Benedictine Monastery

★★★ Falcon

68 Farnborough Road, Farnborough GU14 6TH
01252-545378 **Fax** 01252-522539
30 bedrs, all ensuite, 20 **P** 30 Rest Resid
CC MC Visa Amex DC

★★★ Posthouse

Posthouse

Farnborough Road,
Farnborough GU14 6AZ
01252-545051 **Fax** 01252-377210
143 bedrs, all ensuite, 150 **P** 170 **CC** MC Visa Amex DC

FARNHAM Surrey 4C3

Pop. 37,000. Guildford 10, London 38, Alton 9½, Bagshot 12, Basingstoke 15, Hindhead 8½, Reading 25, Woking 14 **EC** Wed **see** 12th cent Castle Keep, 14th cent Church, 'The William Cobbett' (birthplace of William Cobbett) **i** Vernon House, 28 West Street 01252-715109

★★★ Bishop's Table

27 West Street, Farnham GU9 7DR
01252-710222 **Fax** 01252-733494
E-mail bishops.table@btinternet.com
Closed 29 Dec-3 Jan
17 bedrs, all ensuite, 15 No children under 11 **SB** £88 **DB** £105 **L** £21 **D** £21 **D** ✕ **LD** 21:45
Restaurant closed L Sat **CC** MC Visa Amex DC

★★★ Bush

Heritage HOTELS

The Borough, Farnham GU9 7NN
01252-715237 **Fax** 01252-733530
65 bedrs, all ensuite, 80 **P** 80
CC MC Visa Amex DC JCB

FELIXSTOWE Suffolk 5F1

Pop. 23,200. Ipswich 12, London 86, Aldeburgh 29, Saxmundham 25, Scole 36 **EC** Wed **MD** Thu
i Leisure Centre, Undercliff Road West 01394-276770

★★★ Orwell

Hamilton Road, Felixstowe IP11 7DX
01394-285511 **Fax** 01394-670687
58 bedrs, all ensuite, 200 **P** 100 **CC** MC Visa Amex DC

FERNDOWN Dorset 4A4

Pop. 16,500. Ringwood 6, London 99, Blandford Forum 14, Bournemouth 7, Dorchester 28, Wareham 15 **EC** Wed **see** Church

★★ Coach House Inn

579 Wimborne Road East, Ferndown BH22 9NW
01202-861222 **Fax** 01202-894130
44 bedrs, all ensuite, 180 **P** 100 **SB** £47-£53 **DB** £53-£60 **L** £6 **L** **D** £12 **D** ✕ **LD** 21:30
Restaurant closed D Sun **CC** MC Visa Amex DC

FILEY North Yorkshire 11F2

Pop. 6,000. Gt Driffield 21, London 213, Bridlington 10, Malton 23, Scarborough 7½ **EC** Wed **i** John Street 01723-512204

★★ Downcliffe House

The Beach, Filey YO14 9LA
01723-513310 **Fax** 01723-516141
Closed Jan
10 bedrs, all ensuite, 12 **P** 6 Rest Resid **SB** £31-£33 **DB** £62-£66 **HB** £301-£315 **L** £7 **D** £12 ✕ **LD** 21:00 **CC** MC Visa

★★ Sea Brink

3 The Beach, Filey YO14 9LA
01723-513257 **Fax** 01723-514139
E-mail seabrink@att.net
Closed Nov-Jan

Licensed seafront hotel with delightful ensuite rooms, many overlooking magnificent Filey Bay. Excellent food. Families and pets welcome. Open Feb-Oct. Ideal touring base. 3 nights dinner, B & B from £90pp low season.
9 bedrs, all ensuite, Rest Resid **SB** £30-£35 **DB** £50-£60 **HB** £218-£238 **L** £5.25 **D** £11 ✕ **LD** 20:00
Restaurant closed D Sun **CC** MC Visa JCB

Clifton Hotel
FOLKESTONE

80 bedroomed, elegant Victorian style cliff top hotel, views of the English Channel, ideal venue for seminars or conferences of 10-80 or relaxing breaks exploring Kent. Easy access M20 London, Le Shuttle and Sea Cat Terminal.

**THE LEAS,
FOLKESTONE CT20 2EB
Tel: 01303 851231
Fax: 01303 851231**

FINEDON Northamptonshire 8C4
Bedford 18, London 68, Kettering 6, Northampton 20, Thrapston 9

★★ Tudor Gate 🏠 🏠
High Street, Finedon, Wellingborough NN9 5JN
📞 01933-680408 **Fax** 01933-680745
27 bedrs, all ensuite, 🛏 ♀ ⚓ ⊞ 40 **P** 45 ⊕ **SB** £44-£80 **DB** £55.50-£100 **L** £14.50 **D** £14.50 ✕ **LD** 21:45 ⓒ MC Visa Amex DC ⚫

FLEET Hampshire 4C3
Pop. 27,400. Bagshot 10, London 37, M3 (jn 4) 6, Alton 12, Basingstoke 12, Farnham 6, Reading 15, Woking 14 **K** Wed **MD** Sat **see** Fleet Pond (nature reserve) 🅹 Harlington Centre, Fleet Road 01252-811151

★★★ Lismoyne
Church Road, Fleet GU13 8NA
📞 01252-628555 **Fax** 01252-811761
44 bedrs, all ensuite, 🛏 ⚓ ⊞ 130 **P** 80 ⊕ **SB** £40-£89.85 **DB** £65-£134.90 **L** £13.95 **L** 💮 **D** £19.50 **D** 💮 ✕ **LD** 21:30 ⓒ MC Visa Amex DC ⚫

FOLKESTONE Kent 5F3
Pop. 45,300. Ashford 16, London 71, M20 (jn 13) 2, Canterbury 16, Dover 7, Margate 26, Rye 25, Tenterden 23 **K** Wed **MD** Thu, Sun **see** Church of St Mary and St Eanswythe, Kingsnorth Gdns, The Leas, The Arts Centre (New Metropole) 🅹 Harbour Street. 01303-258594

★★★ Clifton
The Leas, Clifton Gardens, Folkestone CT20 2EB
📞 01303-851231 **Fax** 01303-851231
80 bedrs, all ensuite, ♀ ⚓ ⚓ ⊞ ⊞ 80 ⊕ **SB** £57-£72 **DB** £78-£96 **HB** £322-£490 **L** £10.25 **L** 💮 **D** £16.50 **D** 💮 ✕ **LD** 21:15 ⓒ MC Visa Amex DC JCB
See advert on this page

FORDINGBRIDGE Hampshire 4A4
Pop. 5,700. Romsey 15, London 91, Blandford Forum 21, Lyndhurst 13, Ringwood 6, Salisbury 10, Shaftesbury 23, Southampton 19 **see** Modernised 14th century bridge, EE and Dec Church, Augustus John statue. Breamore House 🅹 Salisbury Street 01425-654560

★★ Ashburn 🏠
Station Road, Fordingbridge SP16 1JP
📞 01425-652060 **Fax** 01425-652150
E-mail ashburn@mistral.co.uk
20 bedrs, all ensuite, 🛏 ♀ ⚓ ⚓ ⊞ 150 **P** 60 ⊕ **SB** £39.50 **DB** £74 **HB** £252 **L** £9.50 **L** 💮 **D** £15 **D** 💮 ✕ **LD** 21:30 Restaurant closed L Mon-Sat ⓒ MC Visa Amex DC JCB 🔔

FOREST ROW East Sussex 5D3
Pop. 3,800. East Grinstead 3, London 33, Haywards Heath 10, Lewes 17, Tunbridge Wells 12, Uckfield 10 **K** Wed **see** Ruins of Brambletye Castle

★★★★ Ashdown Park 🏠 🏠 🏠
Blue Ribbon Hotel
Wych Cross, Forest Row RH18 5JR
📞 01342-824988 **Fax** 01342-826206
E-mail sales@ashdownpark.co.uk
95 bedrs, all ensuite, 🛏 ⚓ ⊞ ⊞ 150 **P** 160 ⊕ **SB** £115 **DB** £145 **L** £23 **L** 💮 **D** £36 ✕ **LD** 21:30 ⓒ MC Visa Amex DC 🔔 🔔 🔔 🔔 🔔 ⚫
See advert under Gatwick Airport

FOWEY Cornwall 2B4
Pop. 2,000. Liskeard 18, London 239 (fy 236), Bodmin 8, Looe 19 (fy 10), St Austell 7½ **EC** Wed **see** Parish Church, Museum, Aquarium, St Catherine's Castle ruins, St Catherine's and St Saviour's Point (NT) 🖼 Post Office, 4 Custom House Hill 01726-833616

★★★ Fowey 🛆 🛆
The Esplanade, Fowey PL23 1HX
📞 01726-832551 **Fax** 01726-832125
23 bedrs, all ensuite, 🛪 ▣ ⅲ 100 **P** 24 ⊕ ℂ MC Visa Amex DC 🖂 ♿

★★ Cormorant 🛆 🛆
Golant, Fowey PL23 1LL
📞 01726-833426 **Fax** 01726-833426

Small family run hotel, all bedrooms enjoying spectacular views over the Fowey Estuary to timbered slopes beyond. Chef proprietor ensures highest quality food. Indoor pool. Log fire.
11 bedrs, all ensuite, 🛪 ⅲ 20 **P** 20 ⊕ Rest Resid **SB** £39-£58 **DB** £78-£92 **L** £6 **D** £19 ✕ **LD** 21:00 ℂ MC Visa Amex JCB 🖪

FOWNHOPE Herefordshire 7E4
Gloucester 21, London 125, Abergavenny 27, Bromyard 16, Hereford 6½, Ledbury 13, Ross-on-Wye 8, Worcester 24

★★ ❖ Green Man Inn
Fownhope HR1 4PE
📞 01432-860243 **Fax** 01432-860207
20 bedrs, all ensuite, 4 🛪 ⅲ 50 **P** 75 ⊕ **SB** £34.50-£35.50 **DB** £54.50-£56 **HB** £261-£278 **L** £10 **L** ♥ **D** £16 **D** ♥ ✕ **LD** 21:00 ℂ MC Visa Amex DC 🖪 🖾 🖾 🖾 🖂 ♿

FRIMLEY GREEN Surrey 4C3
M3 (jn 4) 1, London 32, Basingstoke 18, Farnborough 2, Reading 17, Woking 10

★★★ Lakeside International
Wharf Road, Frimley Green GU16 6JR
📞 01252-838000 **Fax** 01252-837857

Beautifully appointed, waters-edge hotel complex with all ensuite bedrooms, first class restaurant, health and fitness suite, and extensive business, conference and banquetting facilities.
98 bedrs, all ensuite, 🖉 ▣ ⅲ 120 **P** 250 ⊕ **SB** £50-£105 **DB** £70-£120 **L** £16.50 **L** ♥ **D** £16.50 ✕ **LD** 22:30 Restaurant closed L Sat ℂ MC Visa Amex DC 🖪 🖾 🖾 🖾 🖾

FROME Somerset 3F2
Pop. 32,800. Warminster 7, London 105, Bath 13, Chippenham 21, Devizes 18, Radstock 8, Shaftesbury 19, Shepton Mallet 11, Wincanton 15 **EC** Thu **MD** Wed 🖼 The Round Tower, Justice Lane 01373-467271

★★★ ❖ Mendip Lodge
Bath Road, Frome BA11 2HP
📞 01373-463223 **Fax** 01373-463990

Edwardian house with modern motel-style accommodation set in attractive grounds in a quiet location on the road to Bath.
40 bedrs, all ensuite, 🛪 ⅲ 80 **P** 100 ⊕ ℂ MC Visa Amex DC JCB ♿

★★ George
4 Market Place, Frome BA11 1AF
📞 01373-462584 **Fax** 01373-451945

GARSTANG Lancashire 10B3
Pop. 3,600. Preston 10, London 221, M55 (jn 33)
7½, Blackpool 15, Lancaster 10 **EC** Wed **MD** Thu
i Council Offices, High Street 01995-602125

★★★ Crofters ⚲
A6 Cabus, Garstang PR3 1PH
☎ 01995-604128 **Fax** 01995-601646
19 bedrs, all ensuite, ⚹ ♨ 200 **P** 200 ⊟ **SB** £44-£51
DB £56-£62 **L** £10 **L** ● **D** £15 **D** ● ✕ **LD** 22:00
Restaurant closed L Mon-Sat **CC** MC Visa Amex DC
JCB ⊠

★★★ Pickering Park ⚲
Garstang Road, Catterall, PR3 0HD
☎ 01995-600999 **Fax** 01995-602100
E-mail hotel@pickeringpark.demon.co.uk
16 bedrs, all ensuite, ④ ♀ ♨ 50 **P** 40 ⊟ **SB** £49.50-
£55 **DB** £70-£105 **HB** £308-£462 **L** £9.95 **L** ●
D £14.50 **D** ● ✕ **LD** 21:30 **CC** MC Visa Amex DC ♿
See advert under Preston

GATESHEAD Tyne & Wear 11O1
Pop. 91,893. Durham 14, London 272, Newcastle
1, Sunderland 11 **EC** Wed *i* Metrocentre, 7 The
Arcade 0191-460 6345

★★★ Swallow
High West Street, Gateshead NE8 1PE
☎ 0191-477 1105 **Fax** 0191-478 7214
E-mail info@swallowhotels.com

This friendly hotel, with leisure facilities and plenty
of free parking, is well placed to visit both the
Metro Centre and Northumbria's beautiful coastline
and castles.
103 bedrs, all ensuite, ⚹ ▣ ♨ 350 **P** 200 ⊟ **SB** £65-
£90 **DB** £95-£105 **L** £10.95 **D** £15 ✕ **LD** 21:45
Restaurant closed L Sat **CC** MC Visa Amex DC ▣ ⊠
▥ ♿

GATWICK AIRPORT West Sussex 5C3
i South Terminal Arrivals, 01293-560108

★★★★ ✦ Copthorne
Copthorne RH10 3PG
☎ 01342-714971 **Fax** 01342-717375
E-mail coplgw@mill-cop.com
227 bedrs, all ensuite, ⊞ ♪ ⊁ 🖃 ⊞ 110 **P** 260 ⊞
SB £142.95 **DB** £165.90 **L** £17.50 **L** 🍷 **D** £17.50 **D** 🍷
✕ **LD** 22:30 Restaurant closed L Sat, L & D Sun
《 MC Visa Amex DC JCB 🖪 🖪 🖽 🖪 🖪 🖪 &

★★★★ ✦ Copthorne Effingham Park
West Park Road, Copthorne RH10 3EU
☎ 01342-714994 **Fax** 01342-716039
122 bedrs, all ensuite, ♀ ♪ 🖃 ⊞ 600 **P** 500 ⊞
SB £85-£140 **DB** £95-£150 **L** £16.50 **L** 🍷 **D** £19.50
D 🍷 ✕ **LD** 22:30 《 MC Visa Amex DC 🖪 🖪 🖽 🖪 🖪 &

★★★★ Le Meridien
London Gatwick

North Terminal,
Gatwick Airport RH6 0PH
☎ 01293-567070 **Fax** 01293-567739
E-mail gm1096@forte.hotels.com
494 bedrs, all ensuite, ♪ ⊁ 🖃 ⊞ 300 **P** 140 ⊞
SB £155.95-£185.95 **DB** £166.90-£206.90
L £14 **L** 🍷 **D** £19 **D** 🍷 ✕ **LD** 23
《 MC Visa Amex DC JCB 🖪 🖪 🖽 &

★★★ Alexander House 🍴 🍴 🍴
Blue Ribbon Hotel
Fen Place, Turners Hill RH10 4QD
☎ 01342-714914 **Fax** 01342-717328
E-mail info@alexanderhouse.co.uk

Beautiful 17th century English mansion. 15 luxury
ensuite guest rooms including rooms with
fourposter beds. Free car parking and courtesy
transport to Gatwick Airport available for residents.
15 bedrs, all ensuite, ⊞ 🖃 ⊞ 60 **P** 75 No children
under 7 ⊞ **SB** £120 **DB** £155 **L** £22 **D** £28 ✕ **LD** 21:30
《 MC Visa Amex DC 🖪 🖪
See advert on opposite page

★★★ Posthouse Gatwick   **Posthouse**
Povey Cross Road, Horley RH6 0BA
☎ 01293-771621 **Fax** 01293-771054
210 bedrs, all ensuite, ⊁ 🖃 ⊞ 170 **P** 150 ⊞ 《 MC
Visa Amex DC &

🍴 ★★★ ✦ Stanhill Court
Stanhill, Horley RH6 0EP
☎ 01293-862166 **Fax** 01293-862773
E-mail stanhillct@aol.com

Experience the delights of this Victorian country
house of timeless elegance and grace, built in the
Scottish baronial style. Some fourposter rooms,
excellent food and 200 bin wine list.
14 bedrs, all ensuite, ⊞ ♀ ⊞ 180 **P** 100 ⊞ **SB** £99-
£110 **DB** £125-£160 **L** £21 **L** 🍷 **D** £25 **D** 🍷 ✕ **LD** 21:30
Restaurant closed L Sat 《 MC Visa Amex DC JCB
🖪 🖊

★★ Langshott Manor 🍴 🍴 🍴
Gold Ribbon Hotel
Langshott, Horley RH6 9LN
☎ 01293-786680 **Fax** 01293-783905
E-mail admin@langshottmanor.com

Peaceful Elizabethan manor house hotel,
authentically restored with beautiful gardens and
comfortable beds.
15 bedrs, all ensuite, ⊞ ♀ ♪ ⊁ ⊞ 12 **P** 30 ⊞ Rest
Resid **SB** £115-£175 **DB** £145-£195 **L** £25 **L** 🍷
D £37.50 **D** 🍷 ✕ **LD** 21:30 《 MC Visa Amex DC JCB

ALEXANDER HOUSE HOTEL

This magnificent 17th Century country house hotel is set in 135 acres of private parkland in the heart of the glorious Sussex countryside.

The hotel boasts luxury accommodation, including two four-poster suites, executive conference facilities and award winning cuisine.

Leisure facilities include tennis, snooker and croquet and the hotel also has a resident beautician.

EAST STREET, TURNERS HILL, WEST SUSSEX RH10 4QD
Tel: 01342 714914 Fax: 01342 717328

GILLINGHAM Dorset 3F2

Pop. 7,000. Shaftesbury 4½, London 108, Frome 15, Sherborne 14, Wincanton 7 **EC** Thu **see** St Mary's Church, Museum

★★★ Stock Hill Country House ⍨ ⍨ ⍨
Gold Ribbon Hotel
Stock Hill, Gillingham SP8 5NR
📞 01747-823626 **Fax** 01747-825628
E-mail reception@stockhill.net
9 bedrs, all ensuite, 🖥 ♨ 12 **P** 30 No children under 7 🍴 Resid **SB** £115-£145 **DB** £240-£280 **L** £25 **L** ⍢
D £35 ✕ **LD** 20:45 Restaurant closed L Mon **CC** MC Visa 🖼 🖼

Don't forget to mention the guide

When booking direct, please remember to tell the hotel that you chose it from RAC Inspected Hotels 2000

GLOSSOP Derbyshire 10C4

Pop. 25,300. Chapel-en-le-Frith 9, London 174, Barnsley 24, Huddersfield 19, Macclesfield 19, Manchester 14, Oldham 12, Sheffield 24, Stockport 11 **EC** Tue **MD** Thu, Fri, Sat **see** Dinting Rly Centre (steam trains), Saxon Cross, Snake Pass, Peak National Park 🛈 The Gatehouse, Victoria Street 01457-855920

★★ Wind in the Willows ⍨ ⍨
Derbyshire Level, Off Sheffield Road (A57), Glossop SK13 7PT
📞 01457-868001 **Fax** 01457-853354
E-mail twitwh@aol.com
Closed Christmas & New Year
12 bedrs, all ensuite, 🖥 ⍓ ♨ 12 **P** 20 No children under 8 🍴 Resid **SB** £70-£90 **DB** £87-£115 **L** ⍢ **D** £25
D ⍢ ✕ **LD** 19:45 **CC** MC Visa Amex DC

GLOUCESTER Gloucestershire 7E4

Pop. 97,000. Cheltenham 9, London 104, M5 (jn 11) 4½, Bristol 35, Chepstow 28, Cirencester 18, Ross-on-Wye 16, Tewkesbury 10 **MD** Daily **see** Cathedral (fine cloisters), St Mary de Crypt Church, Bishop Hooper's Lodging, St Oswald's Priory 🛈 St Michael's Tower, The Cross 01452-421188

★★★ Hatton Court 🛏 🛏

Upton Hill, Upton St Leonards,
Gloucester GL4 8DE
📞 01452-617412 **Fax** 01452-612945
E-mail res@hatton.court.co.uk

A 17th century Cotswold manor perched on an escarpment overlooking the Severn Vale. A more idyllic setting is hard to imagine. A perfect base for exploring the Cotswolds.
45 bedrs, all ensuite, 📺 ⅲ 60 **P** 70 🍴 **SB** £95 **DB** £110 **HB** £420 **L** £10 **L** 🍷 **D** £22.50 **D** 🍷 ✕ **LD** 22:00 **CC** MC Visa Amex DC JCB 🏊 🎾 🏌
See advert on this page

★★★ Posthouse **Posthouse**
Crest Way, Barnwood,
Gloucester GL4 7RX
📞 01452-613311 **Fax** 01452-371036
122 bedrs, all ensuite, 🏊 ⅲ 100 **P** 150 🍴 **SB** £85-£125 **DB** £104.90 **HB** £353 **L** £12 **L** 🍷 **D** £12.95 **D** 🍷 ✕ **LD** 22:30 Restaurant closed L Sat **CC** MC Visa Amex DC JCB 🏊 🎾 🏌 ♿

GOATHLAND North Yorkshire 11E2
Pop. 425. Pickering 14, London 227, Whitby 9
EC Thu **see** Church, Moors, Waterfalls, Roman Road.

★★★ Inn on the Moor
Goathland YO22 5LZ
📞 01947-896296 **Fax** 01947-896484
25 bedrs, all ensuite, 📺 🐾 ⅲ 50 **P** 50 🍴 **CC** MC Visa Amex ♿
See advert on opposite page

ENGLAND

GODALMING Surrey   4C3
Pop. 20,000. Guildford 4, London 32, Dorking 15, Farnham 9, Haslemere 8½, Hindhead 8, Horsham 18, Petworth 16 **EC** Wed **MD** Fri **see** Church, Church House, Winkwirth Arboretum 2m SE

★★ Kings Arms & Royal
High Street, Godalming GU7 1BZ
☎ 01483-421545 **Fax** 01483-415403
16 bedrs, 11 ensuite, 5 ☗ ∺ 40 **P** 40 ⊕ **CC** MC Visa Amex

---

GOMERSAL West Yorkshire   10C4
M62 (jn 27) 1, London 189, Bradford 7, Dewsbury 3, Leeds 8, Wakefield 9 **see** Oakwell Hall

★★ Gomersal Lodge
Spen Lane, Gomersal BD19 4PJ
☎ 01274-861111 **Fax** 01274-861111
9 bedrs, all ensuite, ♀ ∺ 10 **P** 50 ⊕ Rest **SB** £45.50-£50 **DB** £55 **L** ● **D** £9.95 **D** ● ✕ **LD** 20:30 Restaurant closed D Sun **CC** MC Visa Amex

---

GOOLE East Yorkshire   11E4
Pop. 18,300. M62 (jn 36) 1, London 190, Beverley 23, Hull 33, Pontefract 20, Scunthorpe 21, Selby 12, York 24 **EC** Thu **MD** Mon, Wed, Fri **see** Port

★★ Clifton
1 Clifton Gardens, Boothferry Road, Goole DN14 6AR
☎ 01405-761336 **Fax** 01405-762350
Closed Christmas
9 bedrs, 8 ensuite, ♫ ↑ ∺ 30 **P** 8 ⊕ Rest Resid **SB** £29-£42 **DB** £44-£49 **D** £7.95 ✕ **LD** 21:00
Restaurant closed L Sat-Sun **CC** MC Visa Amex DC JCB

GORLESTON-ON-SEA Norfolk   9F3
Lowestoft 8, London 125, Gt Yarmouth 2, Scole 32 **EC** Wed

★★★ Cliff
Cliff Hill, Gorleston-on-Sea NR31 6DH
☎ 01493-662179 **Fax** 01493-653617
39 bedrs, all ensuite, ↑ ∺ 160 **P** 70 ⊕ **SB** £69-£88 **DB** £97-£140 **HB** £290 **L** £16 **D** £16 ✕ **LD** 21:30 **CC** MC Visa Amex DC

PIER HOTEL
3* Crown Commended

Over 100 years old, the Pier Hotel is one of Gorleston-On Sea's landmarks combining its traditional features with modern conveniences.
Whether you plan to visit us as a business guest, a holiday maker, or for a very special party, we promise to welcome you warmly and to care about even the smallest details to bring you back again!

* ★ 20 bedrooms each with river, harbour or panoramic sea views
* ★ Single, twin, double and family rooms all with en suite facilities
* ★ Restaurant and bar food, including unique range of cuisine featuring fresh fish from the local area.

**HARBOURMOUTH, GORLESTON-ON-SEA
GREAT YARMOUTH, NORFOLK NR31 6PI
TEL: 01493 662631 FAX: 01493 440263**

★★ Pier
Harbour Mouth, Gorleston-on-Sea NR31 6PL
☎ 01493-662631 **Fax** 01493-440263
20 bedrs, all ensuite, ⚲ ⚏ 100 **P** 20 ⊞ **CC** MC Visa Amex DC
See advert on this page

See advert on this page

GOSPORT Hampshire 4B4
Pop. 76,500. Fareham 5, London 81, Romsey 23, Southampton 16 **EC** Wed **MD** Tue *i* Museum, Walpole Road 01705-522944

★★★ Belle Vue
39 Marine Parade East, Lee-on-the-Solent, Gosport PO13 9BW
☎ 01705-550258 **Fax** 01705-552624
Closed 24-26 Dec
27 bedrs, all ensuite, ⚲ ⚏ 140 **P** 55 ⊞ **SB** £56.45-£82.45 **DB** £65.40-£91.40 **L** £17.50 **L** ● **D** £17.50 **D** ● ✕ **LD** 21:45 **CC** MC Visa Amex ⚭

GRANGE-OVER-SANDS Cumbria 10B3
Pop. 3,700. Lancaster 24, London 259, Ambleside 19, Kendal 13, Kirkby Lonsdale 20, Ulverston 15 **EC** Thu **see** 12th cent Cartmel Priory Gatehouse, 1½m W Holker Hall 3m *i* Victoria Hall, Main Street 015395-34026

⚹ ★★★ ❖ Cumbria Grand
Lindale Road, Grange-over-Sands LA11 6EN
☎ 01539-532331 **Fax** 01539-534534

★★★ Graythwaite Manor ⚱
Fernhill Road, Grange-over-Sands LA11 7JE
☎ 01539-532001 **Fax** 01539-535549
Closed 5-19 Jan

A lovely family run country house set in extensive gardens and woodland overlooking bay and hills. Charming bedrooms, some ground floor, generous lounges with antiques and log fires. Excellent cuisine and wine cellar.
21 bedrs, all ensuite, ⚏ 25 **P** 34 ⊞ Rest Resid ✕ **LD** 20:30 **CC** MC Visa Amex JCB ▦ ▦ ⚭

★★★ ❖ Netherwood
Lindale Road, Grange-over-Sands LA11 6ET
☎ 01539-532552 **Fax** 01539-534121
28 bedrs, all ensuite, ⚲ ☲ ⚏ 150 **P** 160 ⊞ **SB** £50-£60 **DB** £100-£120 **HB** £420-£525 **L** £15.50 **L** ● **D** £23 **D** ● ✕ **LD** 20.30 **CC** MC Visa ▦ ▦ ⚭

GRANTHAM Lincolnshire 8C2
Pop. 32,800. Stamford 21, London 111, Boston 30, Lincoln 25, Melton Mowbray 16, Newark 15, Nottingham 24, Sleaford 14 **EC** Wed **MD** Thu, Sat **see** Market Cross, Isaac Newton statue, Belton House *i* Guildhall Centre, St Peter's Hill 01476-66444

★★★ Swallow
Swingbridge Road, Grantham NG31 7XT
☎ 01476-593000 **Fax** 01476-592592
E-mail info@swallowhotels.com

SWALLOW
HOTELS

Situated just off the A1, this friendly hotel has leisure facilities and is well placed for Lincoln, Spalding and Stamford.
90 bedrs, all ensuite, ♀ ♨ 200 **P** 117 ⊞ **SB** £90-£100 **DB** £105-£115 **L** £10.50 **D** £19.75 ✕ **LD** 22:00 ₵ MC Visa Amex DC JCB ⊞ ⊞ ⊞ &

GRASMERE Cumbria   10B2
Pop. 1,600. Ambleside 4, London 273, Keswick 12, Penrith 25 **EC** Thu **see** Dove Cottage and Wordsworth Museum, St. Oswald's church, graves of Wordsworth and Coleridge. Grasmere sports Aug
⚡ Redbank Road 015394-35245

★★★★ Wordsworth ⿻ ⿻
Ambleside, Grasmere LA22 9SW
☎ 01539-435592 **Fax** 01539-435765

Set in the heart of Lakeland, in magnificent surroundings, the Wordsworth Hotel has a reputation for the high quality of its food, accommodation and hospitality.
37 bedrs, all ensuite, ⊞ ♀ ✎ ✎ ♨ 100 **P** 60 ⊞ **SB** £65 **DB** £160-£220 **L** £18 **L** ● **D** £32.50 ✕ **LD** 21:30 ₵ MC Visa Amex DC ⊞ ⊞ ⊞ ⊞ &

★★★ Gold Rill ⿻
Red Bank Road, Grasmere LA22 9PU
☎ 01539-435486 **Fax** 01539-435486
Closed Jan
25 bedrs, all ensuite, ⊞ **P** 35 ⊞ **SB** £35-£57 **DB** £70-£114 **HB** £341-£910 **D** £18.50 ✕ **LD** 20:30 ₵ MC Visa ⿻ ▣ &

★★★ Grasmere Red Lion
Red Lion Square, Grasmere LA22 9SS
☎ 01539-435456 **Fax** 01539-435579

Offering a bright and airy conservatory and newly extended restaurant, we have a reputation for good food served by friendly staff. There's a choice of lounge or buttery bar plus a hairdressing salon and leisure facilities.
36 bedrs, all ensuite, ♀ ✎ ♨ 50 **P** 38 ⊞ **SB** £39.50-£52.50 **DB** £79-£105 **HB** £321-£396 **D** £19 **D** ● ✕ **LD** 21:00 ₵ MC Visa Amex DC ⊞ ⊞

★★★ Swan ⬚

Grasmere LA22 9RF
☎ 01539-435551 **Fax** 01539-435741
36 bedrs, all ensuite, ⊞ ☂ ⁂ 60 **P** 43 ⊕ **SB** £45-£105.45 **DB** £90-£130.90 **HB** £324-£444 **L** £15.75 ✕ **LD** 21.30 **CC** MC Visa Amex DC JCB

★★ Grasmere ⬚

Broadgate, Grasmere LA22 9TA
☎ 01539-435277 **Fax** 01539-435277
E-mail grashotel@aol.com
Closed Jan

A Victorian country house hotel situated in an acre of informal gardens running down to the River Rothey and close to the centre of Wordsworth's Grasmere.
12 bedrs, all ensuite, ⊞ ♀ ☂ ⁂ 20 **P** 20 No children under 8 ⊕ Rest Resid **SB** £35-£42 **DB** £70-£80 **HB** £180-£200 **L** ☕ **D** £15 **D** ☕ ✕ **LD** 19:30 **CC** MC Visa JCB ⬚

See advert on previous page

★★ Moss Grove

Grasmere LA22 9SW
☎ 01539-435251 **Fax** 01539-435691
E-mail martinw@globalnet.co.uk
Closed Dec-Jan
13 bedrs, all ensuite, ⊞ **P** 16 ⊕ Rest Resid **SB** £26-£45 **DB** £52-£90 **HB** £272-£370 **L** £6 **L** ☕ **D** £14 ✕ **LD** 20:30 **CC** MC Visa JCB ⬚

GRAVESEND Kent   5D2

Pop. 74,300. Dartford 8, London 24, Dartford Crossing 8½, Rochester 7, Sevenoaks 18 **EC** Wed **MD** Daily **see** Chapel of Milton Chantry, Princess Pocahontas Memorial Church and Statue ⬚ 10 Parrock Street 01474-337600

Tollgate

Watling Street, Gravesend DA13 9RA
☎ 01474-357655 **Fax** 01474-567543
E-mail tollgate@net.com.uk.co.uk
Closed 25-26 Dec

Ideal stopover hotel for travellers to and from London and Channel Tunnel/Ports and Gatwick Airport. Only 5 minutes from junction 2 of the M25. Excellent conference/meeting facilities.
114 bedrs, all ensuite, ☂ ⁂ 150 **P** 200 ⊕ **SB** £54.50-£64.50 **DB** £59.50-£69.50 **D** £12.50 ✕ **LD** 22:00 **CC** MC Visa Amex DC

GREAT BADMINTON Gloucestershire 3F1
M4 (jn 18) 5, London 111, Bristol 18, Chippenham 10, Chepstow 24, Swindon 26

★★★ Petty France ⚖
Dunkirk, Badminton GL9 1AF
☎ 01454-238361 **Fax** 01454-238768
E-mail hotel@pettyfrance.telme.com
20 bedrs, all ensuite, ④ ♪ ✝ ⚙ 25 **P** 50 ⊕ **SB** £69
DB £89 **HB** £330 **L** £21 **L** ● **D** £21 **D** ● ✕ **LD** 21:30
《 MC Visa Amex DC ♿

GREAT LANGDALE Cumbria 10B2
6 miles west of Ambleside, Windermere 9½, London 274, Coniston, Grasmere 4½ **see** Langdale, Langdale Fell & Pikes

★★★ Langdale Hotel & Country Club
Langdale Estate, Ambleside, Great Langdale LA22 9JD
☎ 01539-437302 **Fax** 01539-437694
E-mail info@langdale.co.uk

Modern hotel and country club in forest setting.
65 bedrs, all ensuite, ⚙ 90 **P** 100 ⊕ **SB** £105-£120
DB £140-£170 **L** £12.50 **L** ● **D** £18.50 ✕ **LD** 21:45
《 MC Visa Amex DC ▣ ▦ ▩ ▨ ▦ ▣ ▦
See advert on opposite page

♨ ★★ ♣ Eltermere
Elterwater, Ambleside LA22 9HY
☎ 01539-437207
E-mail colin@hersington.demon.co.uk
18 bedrs, 15 ensuite, ♀ ⚙ 12 **P** 22 ⊕ Resid **SB** £28-£41.50 **DB** £56-£83 **HB** £245-£322 **D** £18 ✕ **LD** 20:15
《 MC Visa ▶ ▨ ♿
See advert under Ambleside

GREAT MILTON Oxfordshire 4B2
M40 (jn 7), London 49, Abingdon 12, Oxford 8, Thame 5.

★★★★ Le Manoir aux Quat'Saisons ⚖ ⚖ ⚖ ⚖ ⚖
Gold Ribbon Hotel
Great Milton OX44 7PD
☎ 01844-278881 **Fax** 01844-278847
E-mail lemanoir@blanc.co.uk
32 bedrs, all ensuite, ④ ✝ ⚙ 40 **P** 60 ⊕ **SB** £230-£550 **DB** £230-£550 **L** £32 **L** ● **D** £72 **D** ● ✕ **LD** 21.45
《 MC Visa Amex DC JCB ♿

GREAT YARMOUTH Norfolk 9F3
See also GORLESTON-ON-SEA
Pop. 50,400. Lowestoft 10, London 127, Cromer 34, Norwich 18, Scole 34 **MD** Wed, Sat **see** The Rows', Old Merchant's House (museum), Nelson Monument, St Nicholas' Parish Church, restored medieval Tollhouse, 17th cent Fisherman's Hospital, Caister Castle ruins (with Motor Museum adj)
🛈 Marine Parade 01493-842195

★★★ Imperial ⓡ
North Drive, Great Yarmouth NR30 1EQ
☎ 01493-851113 **Fax** 01493-852229
E-mail imperial@scs-datacom.co.uk
39 bedrs, all ensuite, ⌁ ⌁ 🖭 ⦙⦙⦙ 140 **P** 41 ⦸ **SB** £60-£66 **DB** £80-£82 **HB** £269-£290 **L** £13 **L** 🖝 **D** £20 **D** 🖝 ✕ **LD** 22:00 Restaurant closed L Sat **CC** MC Visa Amex DC

★★★ Regency Dolphin
Albert Square, Great Yarmouth NR30 3JH
☎ 01493-855070 **Fax** 01493-853798
48 bedrs, all ensuite, ⌁ ⦙⦙⦙ 144 **P** 28 ⦸ **SB** £60-£65 **DB** £70-£85 **HB** £275-£300 **L** £10.95 **L** 🖝 **D** £16.95 **D** 🖝 ✕ **LD** 21:30 **CC** MC Visa Amex DC ⌁ ⌁
See advert on previous page

★★★ Star
24 Hall Quay, Great Yarmouth NR30 1HG
☎ 01493-842294 **Fax** 01493-330215
40 bedrs, all ensuite, ⌁ ⌁ ⌁ 🖭 ⦙⦙⦙ 140 **P** 24 ⦸ **SB** £66-£75 **DB** £82-£94 **HB** £280 **L** £6 **D** £9.75 ✕ **LD** 21:30 **CC** MC Visa Amex DC

★★ Burlington Palm Court
North Drive, Great Yarmouth NR30 1EG
☎ 01493-844568 **Fax** 01493-331848
E-mail burlipalm@aol.com
Closed Jan

The hotel is situated in its own grounds overlooking the sea and recreation grounds together with a large private car park, managed by the Delf family for 29 years.
72 bedrs, all ensuite, 🖭 ⦙⦙⦙ 140 **P** 72 ⦸ Rest Resid **SB** £45-£60 **DB** £60-£82 **HB** £230-£294 **L** £10 **L** 🖝 **D** £16 **D** 🖝 ✕ **LD** 20:00 **CC** MC Visa Amex DC ⌁ ⌁ ⌁ ⌁

★★ Sandringham
74-75 Marine Parade, Great Yarmouth NR30 2BU
☎ 01493-852427 **Fax** 01493-852336
Closed Easter to Oct
24 bedrs, all ensuite, ⌁ ⦙⦙⦙ 50 ⦸ **SB** £27.50-£37.50 **DB** £46-£64 **HB** £210-£260 **L** £11.50 **L** 🖝 **D** £12.50 **D** 🖝 ✕ **LD** 19:00 **CC** MC Visa Amex

★★ Two Bears
South Town Road, Great Yarmouth NR31 0HW
☎ 01493-603198 **Fax** 01493-440486
11 bedrs, all ensuite, ⦙⦙⦙ 30 **P** 75 ⦸ **CC** MC Visa Amex DC JCB ⓡ

Swanvale Awaiting Inspection
6 Standard Road, Great Yarmouth NR30 2EZ
☎ 01493-331442

GRIMSBY Lincolnshire 11F4
See also CLEETHORPES
Pop. 90,000. Louth 16, London 164, Hull 31, Gainsborough 36, Market Rasen 20, Scunthorpe 30
EC Thu **MD** Tue, Fri, Sat **see** Fish Docks, Market Hall, Churches ⓘ National Fishing Heritage, Alexandra Dock 01472-342422

★★★ Posthouse **Posthouse**
Little Coates Road, Grimsby DN34 4LX
☎ 01472-350295 **Fax** 01473-241354
52 bedrs, all ensuite, ④ ⌁ 🖭 ⦙⦙⦙ 300 **P** 250 ⦸ **CC** MC Visa Amex DC

GRINDLEFORD Derbyshire 8A1
Pop. 1,000. Matlock 13, London 158, Buxton 15, Chapel-en-le-Frith 14, Chesterfield 13, Glossop 20, Sheffield 10 **see** Padley Chapel

★★★ Maynard Arms ⓡ ⓡ
Main Road, Grindleford S32 2HE
☎ 01433-630321 **Fax** 01433-630445

A former Victorian inn, now a privately owned 'olde worlde' hotel set in lovely grounds with views over the Hope Valley.
10 bedrs, all ensuite, ④ ⌁ ⌁ ⦙⦙⦙ 120 **P** 70 ⦸ **SB** £63-£83 **DB** £73-£93 **L** £15 **L** 🖝 **D** £19 **D** 🖝 ✕ **LD** 21:30 **CC** MC Visa Amex
See advert on opposite page

ENGLAND

GUILDFORD Surrey   4C3
Pop. 61,600. Ripley 6, London 28, Bagshot 11, Dorking 13, Farnham 10, Haslemere 12, Horsham 19, Leatherhead 12, Woking 6½ *i* 14 Tunsgate 01483-444333

★★★ Posthouse   **Posthouse**
Egerton Road, Guildford GU2 5XZ
☎ 0870 4009036 Fax 01483-302960
158 bedrs, all ensuite, ♪ ✝ ∷ 200 P 200 ⊞
SB £139-£159 DB £139-£159 L £9.95 L ♥ D
£18 D ♥ ✕ LD 22:00 Restaurant closed
L Sat ℂℂ MC Visa Amex DC JCB ▣ ▣ ▣ க

HAILSHAM East Sussex   5D4
Pop. 20,100. Uckfield 12, London 56, Eastbourne 8, Hastings 17, Lewes 13 **MD** Wed **see** Restored Perp. Church, Michelham Priory 2m *i* Library, Western Road 01323-844426

★★ ✤ Old Forge
Magham Down, Hailsham BN27 1PN
☎ 01323-842893 Fax 01323-842893
Closed Christmas-New Year
8 bedrs, 1 ensuite, 5 ℞ ✝ P 12 ⊞ Rest Resid
ℂℂ MC Visa Amex DC

HALIFAX West Yorkshire   10C4
Pop. 84,500. **MD** Daily *i* Piece Hall 01422-368725

★★★ Holdsworth House ⊠ ⊠
Holdsworth, Halifax HX2 9TG
☎ 01422-240024 Fax 01422-245174
Closed first week Jan

Standing three miles north of Halifax in the heart of the West Yorkshire countryside, a lovely 17th century house offering individually designed bedrooms, polished panelling and open fireplaces, and set in two acres of landscaped gardens.
40 bedrs, all ensuite, ▣ ♀ ♪ ✝ ∷ 150 P 60 ⊞
SB £85-£115 DB £101-£130 L £10 D £22.50 D ♥ ✕
LD 21:30 Restaurant closed L Sat & Sun ℂℂ MC Visa Amex DC க

★★★ Rock Inn
Holywell Green, Halifax HX4 9BS
☎ 01422-379721 **Fax** 01422-379110

★★ Hobbit 🍴
Hob Lane, Norland, Sowerby Bridge HX6 3QL
☎ 01422-832202 **Fax** 01422-835381
E-mail david@hobbit-hotel.demon.co.uk

Sympathetically extended stone-built hotel at the side of a country lane, nestling into a rock and moorland bank, high up with panoramic views of the Calder Valley and moors.
22 bedrs, all ensuite, 4 ⋕ 60 **P** 100 ⊕ **SB** £35-£63 **DB** £50-£79 **HB** £266-£308 **L** 🍷 **D** £12.95 **D** 🍷 ✕ **LD** 21:45 **CC** MC Visa Amex DC

Shibden Mill Inn Awaiting Inspection
Shibden Mill Fold, Shibden, Halifax HX3 7UL
☎ 01422-365840 **Fax** 01422-362971

White Swan Awaiting Inspection
Princess Street, Halifax HX1 1TS
☎ 01422-355541 **Fax** 01422-357311
E-mail whiteswan@clara.net
50 bedrs, all ensuite, ♀ ⋔ 🛏 🖃 ⋕ 100 **P** 14 ⊕ **SB** £65 **DB** £89-£99 **HB** £425 **L** £7.95 **L** 🍷 **D** £14.50 **D** 🍷 ✕ **LD** 21:30 **CC** MC Visa Amex DC

HALLAND East Sussex	5D4

Pop. 780. Uckfield 3½, London 47, Eastbourne 15, Hastings 25,Hurst Green 17, Lewes 7½

Short Breaks

Many hotels provide special rates for weekend and mid-week breaks – sometimes these are quoted in the hotel's entry, otherwise ring direct for the latest offers.

★★★ Halland Forge
Halland, Nr Lewes BN8 6PW
☎ 01825-840456 **Fax** 01825-840773
E-mail hotel@hallandforge.co.uk

Charming fully licensed hotel. Excellent restaurant, lounge bar, coffee shop. Ideal touring centre for South East. On A22/B2192, 16 miles from Eastbourne & Brighton. Garden, woodland walks. Sports & attractions nearby.
20 bedrs, all ensuite, ⋔ ⋔ ⋕ 70 **P** 70 No children under 5 ⊕ **SB** £59.50-£62 **DB** £82-£85 **HB** £301-£315 **L** £9.95 **L** 🍷 **D** £14 ✕ **LD** 21:30 **CC** MC Visa Amex DC JCB ᴋ

HARLOW Essex	5D2

Pop. 71,000. Epping 6, London 25, M11 (jn 7) 3, Bishop's Stortford 6½, Chelmsford 18, Dunmow 14, Hoddesdon 8 **MD** Tue, Thur, Fri, Sat

★★★ Swallow Churchgate 🍴
Churchgate Street,
Old Harlow, CM17 0JT
☎ 01279-420246 **Fax** 01279-437720
E-mail info@swallowhotels.com

SWALLOW HOTELS

A Jacobean Chantry house set in its own landscaped gardens. The restaurant has an award for its fine food. The hotel also has a leisure club.
85 bedrs, all ensuite, 4 ⋔ ⋕ 170 **P** 120 ⊕ **SB** £72-£95 **DB** £98.90-£134.90 **L** £15 **D** £18 ✕ **LD** 21:45 Restaurant closed L Sat **CC** MC Visa Amex DC JCB 🎴 🎴 🎴

ENGLAND

HARPENDEN Hertfordshire 4C2
Pop. 28,800. St Albans 5, London 25, M1 (jn 9) 4½, Aylesbury 25, Baldock 17, Hatfield 8, High Wycombe 26, Luton 5½, **EC** Wed **see** Church with 15th cent tower, Luton Hoo 3m N

★★★ Glen Eagle ⍭
1 Luton Road, Harpenden AL5 2PX
☎ 01582-760271 **Fax** 01582-460819
50 bedrs, all ensuite, ⚏ 80 **P** 100 **CC** MC Visa DC

HARROGATE North Yorkshire 11D3
Pop. 69,300. Wetherby 10, Skipton 22, York 22 **MD** Daily **see** Valley Gardens, The Stray, Harlow Car Gardens, Pump Room Museum, Moor and Dales ⛤ Royal Baths Assembly Rooms, Crescent Road 01423-525666

★★★★ Balmoral ⍭ ⍭ ⍭
Franklin Mount, Harrogate HG1 5EJ
☎ 01423-508208 **Fax** 01423-530652
E-mail info@balmoralhotel.co.uk
21 bedrs, all ensuite, ④ ⚭ **P** 12 ⍟ Resid **SB** £70-£88.50 **DB** £85-£112 **HB** £385 **L** £6 **D** £12.50 **D** ● ✕ **LD** 22:00 Restaurant closed L Sat **CC** MC Visa Amex

★★★★ Cedar Court ⍭
Park Parade, Harrogate HG1 5AH
☎ 01423-858585 **Fax** 01423-504950

Historic Grade II Listed building dated back to 1671, carefully restored and offering 100 fully ensuite modern amenities, free car parking, international "The Queens" restaurant, overlooking the famous 200 acre stray parkland.
100 bedrs, all ensuite,

★★★★ Majestic
Ripon Road, Harrogate HG1 2HU
☎ 01423-700300 **Fax** 01423-521332
E-mail majestic@paramount-hotels.co.uk

PARAMOUNT
HOTEL·GROUP

Beautiful Victorian hotel set in 12 acres of gardens. Relax in the public areas decorated with marble columns and chandeliers. Leisure club offers pool, sauna and gym. Free car parking.
156 bedrs, all ensuite, ⌀ ⚭ ⚏ ⚏ 500 **P** 250 ⍟ **SB** £106.95 **DB** £153.90 **L** £10 **D** £20 ✕ **LD** 21:30 **CC** MC Visa Amex DC ⊠ ⊠ ⊠ ⊠ ⊠ ⊠ ⚿

★★★ Boars Head ⍭ ⍭ ⍭
Ripley, Harrogate HG3 3AY
☎ 01423-771888 **Fax** 01423-771509
E-mail boarshead@ripleycastle.co.uk

The Boar's Head, one of the Great Inns of England, is a luxury hotel at the heart of the Ripley Castle Estate renowned for friendly service and fine cuisine.
25 bedrs, all ensuite, ♀ ⚭ ⚏ 60 **P** 60 ⍟ **SB** £95-£115 **DB** £115-£135 **L** £13.50 **L** ● **D** £30 **D** ● ✕ **LD** 21:30 **CC** MC Visa Amex DC ⊠ ⊡ ⚿

★★★ Grants ⍭
3-13 Swan Road, Harrogate HG1 2SS
☎ 01423-560666 **Fax** 01423-502550
42 bedrs, all ensuite, ④ ⌀ ⚏ ⚏ 70 **P** 26 ⍟ **SB** £58-£99 **DB** £85-£110 **D** £18 ✕ **LD** 21:30 **CC** MC Visa Amex DC JCB ⚿

★★★ Harrogate Spa
West Park, Harrogate HG1 1LB
☎ 01423-564601 **Fax** 01423-507508
71 bedrs, all ensuite, ⚭ ⚏ ⚏ 120 **P** 40 ⍟ **SB** £81.50-£93.50 **DB** £98-£112 **L** £10.50 **D** £16.50 ✕ **LD** 21:30 Restaurant closed L Mon-Sat **CC** MC Visa Amex DC

★★★ Hob Green 🍴🍴
Blue Ribbon Hotel
Markington, Harrogate HG3 3PJ
📞 01423-770031 **Fax** 01423-771589

Hob Green, set in 800 acres of beautiful rolling countryside, is a charming and elegant hotel known locally for its excellent restaurant. The main rooms, furnished with antiques, enjoy a stunning view of the valley below.
12 bedrs, all ensuite, ④ ⊩ ⠇⠇⠇ 12 **P** 40 ⊕ Resid
SB £85 **DB** £95-£105 **HB** £140 **L** £13.50 **L** 📦 **D** £23.50
D 📦 ✕ **LD** 21:30 **CC** MC Visa Amex DC JCB

★★★ Imperial
Prospect Place, Harrogate HG1 1LA
📞 01423-565071 **Fax** 01423-500082
85 bedrs, all ensuite, ⊩ 🖹 ⠇⠇⠇ 200 **P** 40
⊕ **SB** £46-£85 **DB** £92-£110 **L** £7.50 **L** 📦
D £15.50 ✕ **LD** 21:30 **CC** MC Visa Amex DC

★★★ Swallow St George Hotel
1 Ripon Road, Harrogate HG1 2SY
📞 01423-561431 **Fax** 01423-530037
E-mail info@swallowhotels.com

An extensively refurbished Edwardian hotel, just a short stroll from Valley Gardens and the fine town centre, with a Swallow Leisure Club.
90 bedrs, all ensuite, ⊩ 🖹 ⠇⠇⠇ 200 **P** 63 ⊕ **SB** £95
DB £110 **L** £5.50 **D** £18.50 ✕ **LD** 21:30 **CC** MC Visa
Amex DC 🖼🖼🖼

★★ Ascot House
53 Kings Road, Harrogate HG1 5HJ
📞 01423-531005 **Fax** 01423-503523
E-mail admin@ascothouse.com
Closed New Year & early Feb
19 bedrs, all ensuite, ④ ⊩ ⠇⠇⠇ 80 **P** 14 ⊕ **SB** £49.50-£59.50 **DB** £72-£82 **HB** £282-£312 **D** £14.95 **D** 📦 ✕
LD 20:30 **CC** MC Visa Amex DC

★★ Bay Horse
Burnt Yates, Harrogate HG3 3EJ
📞 01423-770230 **Fax** 01423-771894

Charming olde worlde, ivy clad 18th century inn of character, set at the gateway to Yorkshire Dales with glorious views of Nidderdale. This friendly inn offers superb cuisine and best of Yorkshire hospitality.
16 bedrs, all ensuite, ⠇⠇⠇ 35 **P** 70 ⊕ **CC** MC Visa ♿

★★ Grafton
1-3 Franklin Mount, Harrogate HG1 5EJ
📞 01423-508491 **Fax** 01423-523168
17 bedrs, all ensuite, ♀ 🐾 ⠇⠇⠇ 16 **P** 3 ⊕ Rest Resid
SB £39-£45 **DB** £58-£75 **HB** £225-£280 **D** £17.50 **D** 📦
✕ **LD** 19:00 **CC** MC Visa Amex DC JCB

★★ Low Hall 🍴
Ripon Road, Killinghall, Harrogate HG3 2AY
📞 01423-508598 **Fax** 01423-560848

Charming, privately owned country hotel circa 1672. Modern, comfortable ensuite rooms. Private

gardens. Excellent restaurant and bar menus, extensive, affordable wine list. Harrogate two miles.
7 bedrs, all ensuite, ::: 90 **P** 40 ⊕ **SB** £49.50-£79.50 **DB** £59.50-£89.50 **D** £13.95 ✕ **LD** 21:00 **CC** MC Visa Amex DC ৬

Russell
Valley Drive, Harrogate HG2 0JN
☎ 01423-509866 **Fax** 01423-506185

Conference or holiday in floral Harrogate is a pleasure. The central location and 37 ensuite bedrooms, large restaurant and bars are ideal for family or business alike.
37 bedrs, all ensuite, ↟ ▣ ::: 180 ⊕ **CC** MC Visa Amex DC JCB 🖼

HARROW Middlesex　　　　　　　　　4C2
Pop. 189,000. London 10, Barnet 9½, Denham 8½, Ealing 5½, Hatfield 16, Rickmansworth 7½, St Albans 13, Uxbridge 8, Watford 7 **MD** Thu **see** Harrow School, St Mary's Church, 16th cent King's Head
🛈 Civic Centre, Station Road 0181-424 1103

★★★★ Grims Dyke
Old Redding, Harrow Weald HA3 6SH
☎ 0208-385 3100 **Fax** 0208-954 4560
E-mail enquiries@grimsdyke.com
44 bedrs, all ensuite, ④ ↟ ::: 300 **P** 100 ⊕ **SB** £115-£275 **DB** £140-£275 **L** £17.50 **L** ● **D** £21.50 **D** ● ✕ **LD** 21:30 **CC** MC Visa Amex DC
See advert on this page

★★★ ✦ Cumberland
St Johns Road, Harrow HA1 2EF
☎ 0208-863 4111 **Fax** 0208-861 5668
84 bedrs, all ensuite, ♀ ⊘ ::: 130 **P** 65 ⊕ **SB** £95 **DB** £105 **L** £9.95 **L** ● **D** £9.95 **D** ● ✕ **LD** 22:00 **CC** MC Visa Amex DC 🖼
See advert on this page

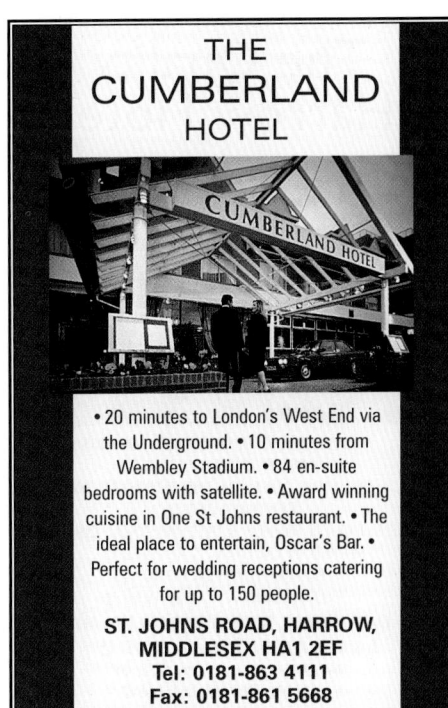

★★★ Quality Harrow
12/22 Pinner Road, Harrow HA1 4HZ
📞 0181-427 3435 **Fax** 0181-861 1370
E-mail info@harrowhotel.co.uk

In 1997, the Quality Harrow hotel proudly opened Lanfranc's restaurant serving International and French cuisine. Open 7 days a week for breakfast, lunch and dinner. Licensed to hold civil weddings. 50 bedrs, all ensuite, 🅰 🐾 ⅱ 200 **P** 60 ⊞
SB £79-£99 **DB** £104-£135 **L** £10.95 **L** 🍷
D £18 **D** 🍷 ✕ **LD** 22:30
⟨⟨ MC Visa Amex DC
See advert on this page

★★ Lindal 🛏 🛏
2 Hindes Road, Harrow HA1 1SJ
📞 0181-863 3164 **Fax** 0181-427 5435
19 bedrs, all ensuite, 🛬 **P** 17 ⊞ Rest Resid **SB** £48
DB £58-£60 **D** £12 ✕ **LD** 19:30 ⟨⟨ MC Visa DC

HARWELL Oxfordshire 4B2
Wallingford 9, London 5, M4 (jn13) 10 Newbury 22, Oxford 12, Wantage 5.

★★★ Kingswell
Reading Road, Harwell OX11 0LZ
📞 01235-833043 **Fax** 01235-833193
19 bedrs, all ensuite, ⅱ 35 **P** 80 No children under 7 ⊞ **SB** £78.50 **DB** £95 **L** £15 **L** 🍷 **D** £18 **D** 🍷 ✕
LD 22:00 ⟨⟨ MC Visa Amex DC ♿

HARWICH Essex 5F1
Pop. 15,000. Colchester 18, London 74, Bury St Edmunds 41, Clacton 16, Ipswich 22 **E** Fri **see** Guildhall, Redoubt (Napoleonic Fort), The Harwich Crane ℹ Parkeston Quay 01255-506139

★★ Cliff
Marine Parade, Dovercourt, Harwich CO12 3RE
📞 01255-503345 **Fax** 01255-240358
26 bedrs, all ensuite, 🛬 ⅱ 200 **P** 60 ⊞ **SB** £48
DB £58 **L** £11 **D** £14.95 **D** 🍷 ✕ **LD** 20:45 ⟨⟨ MC Visa Amex DC

★★ Pier At Harwich 🛏 🛏 🛏
The Quay, Harwich CO12 3HH
📞 01255-241212 **Fax** 01255-551922

6 ensuite bedrooms with TV, 'phone and beverage facilities, overlooking the Stour and Orwell rivers. Harbourside and Ha'penny restaurants plus extensive wine list and refurbished cocktail bar.
6 bedrs, all ensuite, ⅱ 50 **P** 12 ⊞ **SB** £52.50-£67.50
DB £75-£85 **L** £14 **D** £19.50 **D** 🍷 ✕ **LD** 21:30 ⟨⟨ MC Visa Amex DC

ENGLAND

Short Breaks

Many hotels provide special rates for weekend and mid-week breaks – sometimes these are quoted in the hotel's entry, otherwise ring direct for the latest offers.

★★ ✤ Tower
Main Road, Dovercourt, Harwich CO12 3PJ
☎ 01255-504952 **Fax** 01255-504952
14 bedrs, all ensuite, ▨ ⠿ 60 **P** 50 ⏣ **SB** £50 **DB** £60
L £10 **D** £10 ✕ **LD** 22:00 **CC** MC Visa Amex DC &

HASLEMERE Surrey   4C3
Guildford 12, London 41, Dorking 23, Hindhead 3½, Horsham 20, Midhurst 8, Petersfield 12 **EC** Wed
see Educational Museum, Dolmetsch Workshops (early musical instruments).

★★★★ Lythe Hill 🎗 🎗
Petworth Road, Haslemere GU27 3BQ
☎ 01428-651251 **Fax** 01428-644131
E-mail lythe@lythehill.co.uk

Set on the Surrey/Sussex border, this privately owned, 14th century house offers five oak beamed rooms including a fourposter. Web site lythehill.co.uk
41 bedrs, all ensuite, ▨ ⊶ ⠿ 60 **P** 200 ⏣ **SB** £109 **DB** £142 **L** £19.50 **D** £19.50 **D** ☕ ✕ **LD** 21:15 **CC** MC Visa Amex DC JCB ▨ ▨
See advert on this page

HASSOP Derbyshire 7F1

Pop. 100. Chesterfield 10, London 159, Ashbourne 20, Buxton 12, Chaple-en-le-Frith 15, Matlock 11, Shefield 14. see Church

★★★ Hassop Hall ⚑ ⚑

Bakewell, Hassop DE45 1NS
📞 01629-640488 **Fax** 01629-640577
E-mail hassophallhotel@btinternet.com
Closed Christmas

The ancient seat of the Eyre family, in a tranquil setting at the heart of the Peak District National Park.
13 bedrs, all ensuite, 🔲 ⛏ 🖭 ♨ 30 **P** 60 ⊞ Rest Resid **SB** £86-£149 **DB** £93-£159 **HB** £699-£1,133 **L** £14.95 **D** £26.75 ✗ **LD** 21:30 Restaurant closed L Mon, D Sun ℂℂ MC Visa Amex DC ▨

HASTINGS & ST LEONARDS East Sussex 5E4

Pop. 81,900. Hurst Green 13, London 63, Eastbourne 20, Hawkhurst 15, Lewes 29, Rye 11, Tenterden 20, Uckfield 26 **EC** Wed **MD** Wed, Sat see Ruins of Castle, Museum and Art Gallery, Hastings Historical Embroidery, Fisherman's Museum ⓘ 4 Robertson Terrace 01424-781111

★★★ Royal Victoria

Marina, St. Leonards-on-Sea, TN38 0BD
📞 01424-445544 **Fax** 01424-721995
E-mail reception@royal-vic-hotel.demon.co.uk

Tastefully furnished, situated on the seafront, this elegant Victorian hotel provides established standards of comfort and hospitality. All bedrooms are individually styled, with private facilities, and include suites and premier rooms. Superb restaurant.
50 bedrs, all ensuite, ♀ ⌀ ⛏ 🖭 ♨ 100 **P** 6 ⊞ **SB** £75 **DB** £85 **HB** £435 **L** ⚑ **D** ⚑ ✗ **LD** 21:30 ℂℂ MC Visa Amex DC JCB ⅊

HATFIELD Hertfordshire 4C2

Pop. 29,000. Barnet 9, London 20, A1 (M)2, Baldock 17, Enfield 12, Hoddesdon 11, Luton 13, St Albans 6. **EC** Wed, Sat see Church, Hatfield House

★★★ Quality Hatfield

Roehyde Way, Hatfield AL10 9AF
📞 01707-275701 **Fax** 01707-266033
E-mail admin@gb059.u-net.com
76 bedrs, all ensuite, ⌀ ⛏ ♨ 120 **P** 150 ⊞ **SB** £94.25-£108.25 **DB** £108.50-£127.50 **L** ⚑ **D** £15 **D** ⚑ ✗ **LD** 21:45 Restaurant closed L Sat ℂℂ MC Visa Amex DC ⅊

HATFIELD HEATH Essex 5D1

Harlow 5, London 30, M11 (jn 8) 8, Bishop's Stortford 5, Chelmsford 15½.

★★★★ Down Hall Country House ⚑

Hatfield Heath,
Bishop's Stortford CM22 7AS
📞 01279-731441 **Fax** 01279-730416
E-mail reservations@downhall.demon.co.uk

Mid Victorian stone mansion of notable historic interest. Set in 110 acres of own grounds - lawns, parkland and woodland.
103 bedrs, all ensuite, 🔲 ⌀ ⛏ 🖭 ♨ 250 **P** 110 ⊞ **SB** £125.95 **DB** £172.90 **L** £18.50 **L** ⚑ **D** £29.50 **D** ⚑ ✗ **LD** 21:45 ℂℂ MC Visa Amex DC ▨ ▨ ▨ ▨ ▨ ⅊

HATHERSAGE Derbyshire   7F1
Pop. 2,000. Matlock 19, London 163, Chesterfield
15, Glossop 18, Sheffield 11 **see** Iron Age Fort,
Norman Castle (earthworks), 14th cent Church,
assns with Robin Hood.

★★★ George
Main Street, Hathersage S30 1BB
📞 01433-650436 **Fax** 01433-650099
E-mail cavendishg@aol.com
19 bedrs, all ensuite, ▥ ⊞ 60 **P** 30 ⊟ **SB** £69.50
DB £99.50-£119.50 **L** ♥ **D** £20 ✗ **LD** 21:45 **CC** MC Visa
Amex DC

HAWES North Yorkshire   10C2
Pop. 1,100. Leyburn 16, London 250, Brough 21,
Kendal 26, Kirkby Lonsdale 23, Settle 22, Skipton.
EC Tue ℹ Countryside Museum 01969-667450

🏡 ★★ ✦ Simonstone Hall
Hawes DL8 3LY
📞 01969-667255 **Fax** 01969-667741
E-mail simon@simonstonehall.demon.co.uk

This 18 bedroom country house hotel overlooking
Upper Wensleydale has a unique atmosphere of
warm, relaxed friendliness with peace, tranquillity,
luxury and indulgence as its guiding principles.
Excellent traditional and classic cuisine.
18 bedrs, all ensuite, ▥ ⤙ ⊞ 22 **P** 50 ⊟ **CC** MC Visa
JCB

HAWKHURST Kent   5E3
Pop. 4,300. Tonbridge 16, London 50, Hastings 15,
Hurst Green 3, Maidstone 17, Rye 13, Tenterden
10, Tunbridge Wells 15 **EC** Wed **see** Church, Bodiam
Castle 3m S.

Queens Head **Awaiting Inspection**
Rye Road, Hawkhurst TN18 4EY
📞 01580-753577 **Fax** 01580-754241
8 bedrs, all ensuite, ⊞ 85 **P** 50 ⊟

HAWKSHEAD Cumbria   10B2
M6 (jn 36) 24, London 271, Ambleside 5,
Broughton-in-Furness 13, Kendal 17, Lancaster 36,
Ulverston 14 **EC** Thu **see** 12th cent Church, Court
House, Tarn Hows ℹ Main Car Park 015394-36525

★★ Grizedale Lodge ⍩
Grizedale LA22 0QL
📞 01539-436532 **Fax** 01539-436572

A comfortable and elegant former shooting lodge
tucked away in the heart of the magnificent
Grizedale Forest Park, midway between Coniston
Water and Windermere.
9 bedrs, all ensuite, ▥ ⤙ **P** 20 No children under 5
⊟ Rest **SB** £30-£37.50 **DB** £51.50 **HB** £295 **D** £23.50
✗ **LD** 20:00 **CC** MC Visa Amex ♿

★★ Highfield House Country ⍩
Hawkshead Hill, Hawkshead LA22 0PN
📞 015394-36344 **Fax** 015394-36793
E-mail highfield.hawkshead@btinternet.com
Closed Christmas & 3-31 Jan
11 bedrs, all ensuite, ⤙ **P** 15 ⊟ Rest Resid **SB** £42
DB £80-£90 **HB** £350-£385 **L** ♥ **D** £19 ✗ **LD** 20:30
CC MC Visa JCB

HAYDOCK Merseyside   10B4
Pop. 11,500. M6 (jn 23) 1½, London 194, Newton-
le-Willows 2½, St Helens 4½, Wigan 6.

★★★ Posthouse   **Posthouse**
Lodge Lane, Haydock WA12 0JG
📞 01942-717878 **Fax** 01942-718419
138 bedrs, all ensuite, ⤙ ▣ ⊞ 180 **P** 200
⊟ **SB** £39-£99 **DB** £78-£119 **L** £9 **L** ♥ **D** £12
D ♥ ✗ **LD** 22:30 **CC** MC Visa Amex DC
▨ ▨ ▨ ▨ ♿

HAYLING ISLAND Hampshire   4B4
Pop. 15,100. Petersfield 18, London 71, Chichester
14, Cosham 9 **EC** Wed ℹ Beachlands Seafront
01705-467111

★★★ ❖ Posthouse Havant   **Posthouse**
Northney Road, Hayling Island PO11 0NQ
☎ 01705-465011 **Fax** 01705-466468
92 bedrs, all ensuite, ♀ ♪ ⍦ ⅲ 180 **P** 200 ⊕
SB £58.95-£88.95 **DB** £68.90-£98.90 **HB** £35-£55
L £12.95 **L** ● **D** £16 **D** ● ✕ **LD** 22.30 《 MC Visa
Amex DC ⊡ ⊞ ▣

HAYWARDS HEATH West Sussex   5D3
Pop. 20,000. Crawley 9, London 40, Brighton 14,
East Grinstead 11, Lewes 13 **EC** Wed **MD** Tue, Thur,
Sun **see** Church, cattle market

★★ Hilton Park
Cuckfield, Haywards Heath RH17 5EG
☎ 01444-454555 **Fax** 01444-457222
E-mail hiltonpark@janus-systems.com
10 bedrs, all ensuite, ♀ ♪ ⅲ 30 **P** 50 ⊕ Rest Resid
SB £70-£85 **DB** £90-£105 **L** £11 **L** ● **D** £19 ✕ **LD** 21:00
《 MC Visa Amex DC JCB

HEBDEN BRIDGE West Yorkshire   10C4
Halifax 8, London 195, Keighley 11, Rochdale 12
🛈 1 Bridge Gate 01422-843831

★★★ Carlton
Albert Street, Hebden Bridge HX7 8ES
☎ 01422-844400 **Fax** 01422-843117
E-mail ctonhotel@aol.com
16 bedrs, all ensuite, 📺 ⍦ ☎ ⅲ 150 ⊕ **SB** £56
DB £75 **L** £11.50 **L** ● **D** £12.95 **D** ● ✕ **LD** 21:30
《 MC Visa Amex DC JCB

HELMSLEY North Yorkshire   11D2
Pop. 2,000. York 24, London 222, Malton 16,
Middlesbrough 28, Pickering 13, Thirsk 14 **EC** Wed
MD Fri **see** Castle ruins, Rievaulx Terrace frescoes 2m
NW, Rievaulx Abbey 3m NW 🛈 Town Hall, Market
Place 01439-770173

★★★ Black Swan ♟ ♟   *Heritage* HOTELS
Market Place, Helmsley YO6 5BJ
☎ 01439-770466 **Fax** 01439-770174
E-mail gavin.dron@forte-hotels.com
45 bedrs, all ensuite, ⍦ ⅲ 20 **P** 60 ⊕ **SB** £55-£88
DB £110-£176 **HB** £275-£440 **L** £15 **L** ● **D** £25 ✕
LD 21:00 《 MC Visa Amex DC JCB

★★★ Feversham Arms
1 High Street, Helmsley YO6 5AG
☎ 01439-770766 **Fax** 01439-770346

Warm, historic inn, elegantly modernised, built of
Yorkshire stone, with attractive patio, swimming
pool, tennis courts and walled gardens. Ground
floor and fourposter bedrooms. Bonanza Breaks all
year round.
18 bedrs, all ensuite, 📺 ⍦ ⅲ 24 **P** 30 ⊕ **SB** £55-£65
DB £80-£90 **L** £15 **L** ● **D** £20 **D** ● ✕ **LD** 21:00 《 MC
Visa Amex DC ⋛ ▣ ⅋

★★★ Pheasant
Harome, Helmsley YO6 5JG
☎ 01439-771241 **Fax** 01439-771744
Closed Dec-Feb
12 bedrs, all ensuite, ⍦ **P** 20 No children under 10
⊕ Rest Resid **SB** £35-£40 **DB** £60-£80 **HB** £364-£469
L £6 **L** ● **D** £20 ✕ **LD** 20:00 《 MC Visa Amex ▣ ⅋

★★ Crown
Market Place, Helmsley YO62 5BJ
☎ 01439-770297 **Fax** 01439-771595

A 16th century former coaching inn run by the
same family for 37 years with great character and a
warm and friendly atmosphere. Traditional country
cooking served in Jacobean dining room. Dogs
welcome.
12 bedrs, all ensuite, ⍦ ☎ ⅲ 25 **P** 14 ⊕ **SB** £30-£35
DB £60-£70 **HB** £285-£295 **L** £10.75 **L** ● **D** £16 **D** ● ✕
LD 20:00 《 MC Visa

★★ Feathers
Market Place, Helmsley YO6 5BH
☎ 01439-770275 **Fax** 01439-771101
Closed 25 December
14 bedrs, all ensuite, **P** 30 ⊞ **SB** £35-£45 **DB** £50-£140 **L** ♥ **D** ♥ ✕ **LD** 21:30 **CC** MC Visa

---

HELSTON Cornwall   2A4
Pop. 10,300. Truro 16, London 271, Falmouth 13,
Penzance 13, Redruth 10, St Ives 15 **EC** Wed
MD Mon, Sat **see** Furry Dance - held annually, 18th
cent houses ⚫ 79 Menage Lane 01326-565431

★★ Nansloe Manor 🛏 🛏 🛏
Meneage Road, Helston TR13 0SB
☎ 01326-574691 **Fax** 01326-564680
7 bedrs, 6 ensuite, **P** 30 No children under 10 ⊞
Rest Resid **SB** £42-£51 **DB** £80-£120 **HB** £385-£525
L £12 **L** ♥ **D** £25 ✕ **LD** 20:30 Restaurant closed L
Mon-Sat **CC** MC Visa JCB

HEMEL HEMPSTEAD Hertfordshire   4C2
Pop. 85,000. Watford 7½, London 24, M1 (jn 8) 2½,
Aylesbury 17, Barnet 16, Bletchley 22, Dunstable
12, St Albans 7 ⚫ Dacorum Information Centre,
Marlowes 01442-234222

★★★ Posthouse   **Posthouse**
Breakspear Way,
Hemel Hempstead HP2 4UA
☎ 01422-251122 **Fax** 01442-211812
146 bedrs, all ensuite, ♀ ☐ ☷ 60 **P** 200
⊞ **CC** MC Visa Amex DC JCB ▦ ▦ ▦ ⅄

HENLEY-ON-THAMES Oxfordshire   4B2
⚫ Town Hall, Market Place 01491-578034

★★★ Stonor Arms Hotel 🛏 🛏
Stonor, Henley-on-Thames RG9 6HE
☎ 01491-638866 **Fax** 01491-638863
10 bedrs, all ensuite, ♀ ☐ ☷ 16 **P** 26 no children
under 14 ⊞ **SB** £95 **DB** £115 **L** £18.50 **D** £30 ✕
LD 21:30 **CC** MC Visa Amex ⅄

HEREFORD Herefordshire   7D4
Pop. 48,400. London 132, Abergavenny 23,
Ledbury 14, Leominster 12, Monmouth 17, Ross-on-Wye 14, Worcester 25 **EC** Thu **MD** Mon, **see**
Cathedral, The Old House, Museum & Art Gallery.
⚫ 1 King Street 01432-268430

★★★ ✤ Belmont Lodge and Golf Course
Belmont, Hereford HR2 9SA
☎ 01432-352666 **Fax** 01432-358090
E-mail info@belmontlodge.co.uk
30 bedrs, all ensuite, ♀ ☷ 40 **P** 200 ⊞ **SB** £31.50-£49.50 **DB** £55-£70 **D** £13 ✕ **LD** 21:30 **CC** MC Visa
Amex DC ▦ ▦ ▦ ▦ ⅄

★★★ Green Dragon   **Heritage**
Broad Street, Hereford HR4 9BG   **HOTELS**
☎ 01432-272506 **Fax** 01432-352139
83 bedrs, all ensuite, ④ ♀ ☐ ☷ 200 **P** 55 ⊞
SB £68.75-£78.75 **DB** £87.50-£97.50
HB £434-£469 **L** £10.50 **L** ♥ **D** £18.95 ✕
LD 21:15 **CC** MC Visa Amex DC JCB

★★★ Pilgrim
Much Birch, Hereford HR2 8HJ
☎ 01981-540742 **Fax** 01981-540620
20 bedrs, all ensuite, ④ ♀ ☷ 45 **P** 45 ⊞ **SB** £49.50-£60 **DB** £47-£69 **HB** £297 **L** £10.50 **L** ♥ **D** £21.50 **D** ♥
✕ **LD** 21:30 **CC** MC Visa Amex DC ▦ ▦ ⅄

★★★ Three Counties
Belmont Road, Hereford HR2 7BP
☎ 01432-299955 **Fax** 01432-275114
E-mail dgptch@aol.com

Modern hotel with a relaxing atmosphere and
beautiful scenery on the outskirts of the city.
Bedrooms set by a quiet garden.
60 bedrs, all ensuite, ♀ ☷ 300 **P** 200 ⊞ **SB** £37.50-£60 **DB** £55-£79 **D** £16 ✕ **LD** 21:30 **CC** MC Visa Amex
DC ⅄

★★ Castle Pool
Castle Street, Hereford HR1 2NW
☎ 01432-356321 **Fax** 01432-356321
27 bedrs, all ensuite, ④ ♀ ☷ 40 **P** 14 ⊞ **SB** £39-£50
DB £59-£82 **HB** £350-£410 **L** £9 **D** £17 ✕ **LD** 21:30
CC MC Visa Amex DC

★★ Merton
Commercial Road, Hereford HR1 2BD
📞 01432-265925 **Fax** 01432-354983
E-mail sale@mertonhotel.co.uk

Georgian coaching inn with warm, comfortable atmosphere. Conveniently situated near the town centre.
19 bedrs, all ensuite, 🖪 📺 ⊞ 40 **P** 4 ◫ **SB** £45-£50 **DB** £60-£65 **HB** £400 **L** £14 **L** 🍷 **D** £14.20 **D** 🍷 ✕ **LD** 21:30 Restaurant closed D Sunday ₵ MC Visa Amex DC 🖼 🖼 🖼

SALISBURY ARMS HOTEL

Hertford's oldest Hostelry, retaining all the character of a bygone age.
Featuring a beam-work frontage, Jacobean staircase and a panelled dining room.
Single Occupancy: Mon – Thurs from £60.00 B&B
Fri – Sun from £35.00 B&B
Double Occupancy: Mon – Thurs from £75.50 B&B
Fri – Sun from £65.00 B&B

FORE STREET, HERTFORD SG14 1BZ
Tel: 01992-583091 Fax: 01922-552510

HERTFORD Hertfordshire 5D2
Pop. 22,400. Hoddesdon 4½, London 24, Baldock 17, Barnet 13, Bishop's Stortford 13, Epping 13, Hatfield 7, Royston 19 **MD** Sat **see** Municipal buildings (once castle), St Leonard's Church, All Saint's Church ℹ The Castle 01992-584322

★★★ White Horse
Hertingfordbury, Hertford SG14 2LB
📞 01992-586791 **Fax** 01992-550809
42 bedrs, all ensuite, 📺 ⊞ 60 **P** 43 ◫ ₵ MC Visa Amex DC JCB

Heritage HOTELS

★★ ✦ Salisbury Arms
Fore Street, Hertford SG14 1BZ
📞 01992-583091 **Fax** 01992-552510
29 bedrs, all ensuite, 🖪 🖉 ⊞ 30 **P** 30 ◫ **SB** £60 **DB** £75.50 **L** £7.50 **L** 🍷 **D** £13.95 **D** 🍷 ✕ **LD** 22:00 Restaurant closed Bank holidays ₵ MC Visa Amex DC JCB
See advert on this page

HEXHAM Northumberland 10C1
Pop. 10,500. West Auckland 33, London 282, Alston 21, Bellingham 17, Brampton 28, Corbridge 3½, Durham 27, Jedburgh 48. **MD** Tue, Fri **see** Abbey Church, 15th cent Moot Hall, Roman Wall, Housteads Roman Camp, Chelsters Roman Camp, Brunton Turret (Roman Milecastle), Vindolanda excavations, Kielder Water ℹ Manor Office, Hallgate 01434-605225

★★★ Langley Castle 🍸
Langley-on-Tyne, Hexham NE47 5LU
📞 01434-688888 **Fax** 01434-684019
E-mail langleycastle@dial.pipex.com
18 bedrs, all ensuite, 🖪 🖉 🖻 ⊞ 120 **P** 70 ◫ **SB** £84.50-£104.50 **DB** £105-£155 **HB** £425 **L** £14.95 **D** £26.50 ✕ **LD** 21:00 ₵ MC Visa Amex DC
See advert on opposite page

HEYWOOD Greater Manchester 10C4

★★ Birch
Manchester Road, Birch, Heywood OL10 2QD
📞 01706-366137 **Fax** 01706-621000
E-mail birchhotel@bhotel.freeserve.co.uk
30 bedrs, all ensuite, 📺 ⊞ 60 **P** 100 ◫ **SB** £55 **DB** £70 **L** 🍷 **D** £18 **D** 🍷 ✕ **LD** 21:30 ₵ MC Visa Amex DC JCB ♿
See advert on opposite page

ENGLAND

HIGH WYCOMBE Buckinghamshire   4C2
Pop. 61,500. London 30, M40 (jn 4) 1½, Aylesbury 16, Henley-on-Thames 12, Oxford 26, Reading 18, Rickmansworth 15 **MD** Tue, Fri, Sat *see* All Saints Church, Guildhall, Art Gallery and Museum, the Priory (now shops), Little Market House, Hughenden Manor, home and burial place of Disraeli (NT), West Wycombe Park *i* 6 Cornmarket 01494-421892

★★★ Posthouse   **Posthouse**
Crest Road, High Wycombe HP11 1TL
📞 01494-442100 **Fax** 01494-439071
106 bedrs, all ensuite, ♨ 200 **P** 300 ⊞ **SB** £98.95-£119.95 **DB** £108.90-£130.90 L £5.95 L ● D £10 D ●
✕ **LD** 22:30 Restaurant closed L Sat **cc** MC Visa Amex DC 🐾 ♿

HINCKLEY Leicestershire   8B3
Pop. 42,600. London 97, M69 (jn 1) 2, Alshby-de-la-Zouch 16, Atherstone 8½, Daventry 23, Leicester 13, Market Harborough 24, Nuneaton 4½, Rugby 15 **MD** Mon, Sat *see* Church (13th–14th cent), Bosworth Field 4m NNW *i* Library, Lancaster Road 01455-635106

★★★★ Hanover International, Hinckley
A5 Watling Street, Hinckley LE10 3JA
📞 01455-635370 **Fax** 01455-634536
E-mail hisland@webleicester.co.uk

Unique, friendly modern hotel and extensive leisure club set in lovely countryside, with easy access to Midlands attractions, the NEC and motorway connections.
349 bedrs, all ensuite, ♨ 🔲 ♨ 400 **P** 600 ⊞ **SB** £90 **DB** £100 L £16 L ● D £18 D ● ✕ **LD** 22:00 **cc** MC Visa Amex DC 🔲 🐾 📶 🐾 ♿

HINDON Wiltshire   4A3
Pop. 500. Amesbury 17, London 97, Frome 14, Salisbury 16, Shaftesbury 7½, Warminster 9½, Wincanton 14.

★★ Lamb at Hindon Hotel ⬚ ⬚
High Street, Hindon, Salisbury SP3 6DP
☎ 01747-820573 Fax 01747-820605
E-mail the-lamb.demon.co.uk

A small 17th century country inn with open log fires, situated in an attractive, unspoilt Wiltshire village with a wealth of local history.
14 bedrs, all ensuite, ④ ✦ ♨ 50 P 30 ⬚ SB £40-£45 DB £55-£70 HB £285-£305 L £11 D £19 D ➤ ✕ LD 21:45 ℂ MC Visa Amex JCB

HITCHIN Hertfordshire   4C1
Pop. 30,500. Hatfield 14, London 35, A1(M) (jn 8) 3, Baldock 5, Bedford 16, Hoddesdon 19, Luton 8, St Albans 16 MD Tue, Sat see Priory, St Mary's Church, The Biggin

★★ Redcoats Farmhouse ⬚
Redcoats Green, Hitchin SG4 7JR
☎ 01463-729500 Fax 01438-723322
E-mail sales@redcoats.co.uk
Closed 1 week after Christmas
14 bedrs, 12 ensuite, ♪ ✦ ♨ 50 P 50 ⬚ SB £75-£85 DB £85-£95 L £15 L ➤ D £30 D ➤ ✕ LD 21:30 Restaurant closed L Sat, D Sun ℂ MC Visa Amex DC

★ Firs Hotel
83 Bedford Road, Hitchin SG5 2TY
☎ 01462-422322 Fax 01462-432051

Close to town centre, Luton Airport, Bedford, Stevenage, A1 and M1. Family managed business, relaxed informal atmosphere. Rooms with ensuite facilities, ample parking. Licensed bar, restaurant.
30 bedrs, 24 ensuite, ✦ ♨ 40 P 33 ⬚ SB £32-£47 DB £52-£57 D £11 D ➤ ✕ LD 21:30 Restaurant closed D Sun ℂ MC Visa Amex DC JCB

HOCKLEY HEATH Warwickshire   7F3
M42 (jn 4) 2, London 104, Birmingham 10, Coventry 14, Redditch 9, Solihull 4, Warwick 10 see Packwood House (NT) 2m E

★★★ Nuthurst Grange ⬚ ⬚ ⬚

Hockley Heath B94 5NL
☎ 01564-783972 Fax 01564-783919
E-mail nuthurst-grange.co.uk.

Set in seven and a half acres, with award winning restaurant and 15 luxurious bedrooms, all ensuite with whirlpool baths.
15 bedrs, all ensuite, ④ ♀ ♪ ♨ 90 P 50 ⬚ Rest Resid SB £125 DB £140-£165 L £18.50 D £29.50 ✕ LD 21:30 Restaurant closed L Sat ℂ MC Visa Amex DC ♿

HODNET Shropshire   7E2
Pop. 1,400. Telford 13, London 180, Market Drayton 5, Shrewsbury 12, Whitchurch 10.

★★ ❖ Bear
Hodnet, Market Drayton TF9 3NH
☎ 01630-685214 Fax 01630-685787
8 bedrs, all ensuite, ④ ♨ 100 P 60 ⬚ SB £35 DB £55-£60 L £7 L ➤ D £14 D ➤ ✕ LD 21:30 ℂ MC Visa Amex JCB

ENGLAND

HOLFORD Somerset   3D2
Pop. 275. Bridgwater 11, London 152, Dunster 13,
Taunton 15, Tiverton 31

🛏 ★★ Alfoxton Park
Holford TA5 1SG
📞 01278-741211
Closed Dec-Feb
18 bedrs, all ensuite, **P** 20 ⊞ ((MC Visa Amex DC
⟆

★★ Combe House
Holford TA5 1RZ
📞 01278-741382 **Fax** 01278-741322
E-mail enquiries@combehouse.co.uk
16 bedrs, all ensuite, ⊞ ✔ ⫴ 20 **P** 15 ⊞ Rest Resid
SB £33-£44 **DB** £65-£97 **HB** £273-£339 **D** £19.50 ✗
LD 20:30 ((MC Visa Amex JCB ▣ ▨

HOLMES CHAPEL Cheshire   7E1
Newcastle under Lyme 16, London 165, M6 (jn 18)
1½, Chester 24, Manchester 23.

★★★ Old Vicarage ▯ ▯
Knutsford Road, Cranage, Holmes Chapel CW4
8EF
📞 01477-532041 **Fax** 01477-535728
29 bedrs, all ensuite, ♯ ⫴ 30 **P** 60 ⊞ **SB** £36.50-
£68.50 **DB** £55.50-£80 **L** £12.90 **D** £17 ✗ **LD** 22:00
Restaurant closed Bank holidays ((MC Visa Amex
DC ⴲ

HOLMROOK Cumbria   10A2
Pop. 300. Broughton-in-Furness 21, London 299,
Ambleside 21, Egremont 9 **E** Wed

★★ ✤ Lutwidge Arms
Holmrook, Holmrook CA19 1UH
📞 019467-24230 **Fax** 019467-24100
24 bedrs, all ensuite, ✔ ⫴ 50 **P** 50 ⊞ ((MC Visa
JCB ▨ ⴲ

HOLSWORTHY Devon   2C3

🛏 ★★ ✤ Court Barn Country House
Clawton, Holsworthy EX22 6PS
📞 01409-271219 **Fax** 01409-271309
8 bedrs, all ensuite, ✔ ⫴ 30 **P** 18 ⊞ Rest Resid
((MC Visa Amex DC JCB ▨ ▨

HOLT Norfolk   9E2
Fakenham 12, London 123, Cromer 10, East
Dereham 18, Great Yarmouth 40, Norwich 22 **E** Thu

★ Feathers ▯
6 Market Place, Holt NR25 6BW
📞 01263-712318 **Fax** 01263-711774
E-mail feathersholt@compuserve.com
15 bedrs, 12 ensuite, ⊞ ⫴ 100 **P** 10 ⊞ **SB** £44-£49
DB £61-£66 **L** £7.95 **D** £15.95 **D** ✆ ✗ **LD** 21:30 ((MC
Visa

HONITON Devon   3D3
Pop. 9,000. Ilminster 17, London 153, Axminster 10,
Crewkerne 13, Exeter 17, Taunton 18, Tiverton 19
MD Tue, Sat 🅸 Lace Walk Car Park 01404-43716

★★★ Deer Park
Weston, Honiton EX14 0PG
📞 01404-41266 **Fax** 01404-46598
Georgian mansion in 26 acres of beautiful
countryside 2½ miles west off A30.
24 bedrs, all ensuite, ⊞ ♀ ✔ ⫴ 70 **P** 60 ⊞ **SB** £40-
£90 **DB** £60-£145 **HB** £380-£500 **L** £16 **L** ✆ **D** £25 ✗
LD 22:00 ((MC Visa Amex DC ⟆ ▨ ▨ ▣ ▨ ▣ ⴲ

HOOK Hampshire   4B3
Pop. 6,200. M3 (jn 5) 1, London 41, Basingstoke 6,
Camberley 11, Farnham 11, Reading 13.

★★★★ Basingstoke Country ▯ ▯ ▯
Scures Hill, Nately Scures,
Hook RG27 9JS
📞 01256-764161 **Fax** 01256-768341
100 bedrs, all ensuite, ⊞ ♀ ♯ ✔ ▣ ⫴ 250 **P** 220 ⊞
SB £60.25-£113.95 **DB** £90.40-£132.90 **L** £13 **L** ✆
D £20 **D** ✆ ✗ **LD** 21:45 ((MC Visa Amex DC JCB ▣
▣ ▨ ⴲ

★★ White Hart
London Road, Hook RG27 9DZ
📞 01256-762462 **Fax** 01256-768351
21 bedrs, all ensuite, ⊞ ✔ ⫴ 30 **P** 60 ⊞ **SB** £43.50-
£75 **DB** £48-£81 ✗ **LD** 21:30 ((MC Visa Amex DC

HOPE COVE Devon   2C4
Pop. 110. London 209, Plymouth 23, Tavistock 33

★★ Cottage ▯
Hope Cove TQ7 3HJ
📞 01548-561555 **Fax** 01548-561455
Closed 2-30 Jan
35 bedrs, 25 ensuite, ✔ ⫴ 50 **P** 50 ⊞

★★ Sun Bay
Inner Hope Cove, Kingsbridge TQ7 3HS
☎ 01548-561371 **Fax** 01548-561371
Closed Jan
14 bedrs, all ensuite, ⚓ **P** 12 ⬚ Rest Resid ⟨⟨ MC
Visa JCB

HORNING Norfolk   9F3
Pop. 1,200. Norwich 10, London 122, Cromer 19,
Fakenham 32, Great Yarmouth 17 **EC** Wed **see** St
Benet's Abbey ruins.

★★★ Petersfield House
Lower Street, Horning NR12 8PF
☎ 01692-630741 **Fax** 01692-630745
18 bedrs, all ensuite, ⚓ ⚏ 50 **P** 50 ⬚ **SB** £58-£63
DB £75-£85 **HB** £346.50-£381.50 **L** £14 **D** £16 **D** ☛ ✕
LD 21:30 ⟨⟨ MC Visa Amex DC ▣

HORSHAM West Sussex   4C3
Pop. 38,600. Dorking 13, London 36, Brighton 23,
Crawley 8, Guildford 19, Haslemere 20, Haywards
Heath 13, Pulborough 12 **EC** Thu ▣ 9 Causeway
01403-211661

★★ ❖ Ye Olde King's Head
Carfax, Horsham RH12 1EG
☎ 01403-253126 **Fax** 01403-242291
42 bedrs, 41 ensuite, 1 ⌂ ▣ ⚓ ⚏ 40 **P** 40 ⬚ **SB** £70
DB £85 **L** £7 **D** £15 ✕ **LD** 22:00 ⟨⟨ MC Visa Amex DC ♿

HOVE East Sussex   5D4
Pop. 89,000. Brighton 1½, London 54, Arundel 18,
Pulborough 21, Worthing 9½ **EC** Wed **see** All Saint's
Church, Floral Clock, Brocke Scented Garden For
The Blind, King Alfred Leisure Centre, British
Engineerium, Hove Museum ▣ King Alfred Leisure
Centre, Kingsway 01273-746100

★★★ ❖ Courtlands
15-27 The Drive, Hove BN3 3JE
☎ 01273-731055 **Fax** 01273-328295

Situated in Hove's premier street, our ensuite
rooms are ideal for both business and leisure
visitors. Private car park and indoor swimming pool
are available.
75 bedrs, all ensuite, ▣ ⚓ ▣ ⚏ 150 **P** 30 ⬚ **SB** £45-
£55 **DB** £65-£75 **HB** £269-£330 **L** £9.95 **D** £13.95 **D** ☛
✕ **LD** 21:30 ⟨⟨ MC Visa Amex DC ▣ ♿

★★★ Langfords ⚑
Third Avenue, Hove BN3 2PX
☎ 01273-738222 **Fax** 01273-779426
E-mail langfords@pavilion.co.uk

Offering ensuite rooms, with all of today's modern
facilities, yet traditional hospitality. Situated close to
central Brighton and only minutes from Hove's
promenade.
65 bedrs, all ensuite, ▣ ⚓ ▣ ⚏ 300 ⬚ **SB** £45-£50
DB £75-£100 **HB** £330 **L** £12.95 **D** £12.95 ✕ **LD** 23:00
⟨⟨ MC Visa Amex DC

★★★ Princes Marine
153 Kingsway, Hove BN3 2WE
☎ 01273-207660 **Fax** 01273-325913

Seafront hotel with well equiped ensuite bedrooms.
Rooftop function suites, sea view restaurant and
bar. Large private car park. Situated close to all
attractions, bowling greens and the King Alfred
Leisure Centre. Open for Christmas and New Year.

47 bedrs, all ensuite, ▨ ⚲ ⊁ 🔲 ⊞ 90 **P** 20 ⊟
SB £40-£55 **DB** £60-£85 **L** ⚑ **D** £14.95 **D** ⚑ ✕
LD 21.30 Restaurant closed L MON-SAT **CC** MC Visa
Amex DC ♿

★★ ✦ St Catherine's Lodge
Sea Front, Kingsway, Hove BN3 2RZ
📞 01273-778181 **Fax** 01273-774949

A traditional seafront hotel, situated opposite the
leisure centre, with an abundance of character
throughout, particularly in the Regency restaurant,
Edwardian lounge and cocktail bar.
50 bedrs, 40 ensuite, ▨ 🔲 ⊞ 60 **P** 9 ⊟ **SB** £36-£55
DB £60-£75 **HB** £190-£280 **L** £6 **D** £14.50 ✕ **LD** 21:00
CC MC Visa Amex DC

Imperial Awaiting Inspection
First Avenue, Hove, Brighton BN3 2GU
📞 01273-777320 **Fax** 01273-777310
E-mail imperialhotel@pavilion.co.uk

Situated 100 yards from seafront, close to central
Brighton and amenities, with ample street parking.
Recently refurbished, to ensure your comfort and
enjoyment.
76 bedrs, all ensuite, ♀ ⚲ ⊁ 🔲 ⊞ 120 ⊟ **SB** £45-£78
DB £70-£98 **L** £10.95 **D** £14.50 ✕ **LD** 21:30 **CC** MC
Visa Amex DC

HOWTOWN Cumbria   10B2
Windermere 23, London 264, M6 (jn 40) 9, Keswick
22, Penrfith 8.

★★★ Sharrow Bay Country House 🍴🍴🍴🍴
Blue Ribbon Hotel
Ullswater, Howtown CA10 2LZ
📞 01768-486301 **Fax** 01768-486349
E-mail enquiries@sharrow-bay.com
Closed Nov-Feb
26 bedrs, 24 ensuite, ♀ ⊞ 12 **P** 28 No children
under 13 ⊟ Rest Resid **SB** £105-£200 **DB** £200-£270
L £36.25 **L** ⚑ **D** £46 ✕ **LD** 20:30 **CC** MC Visa JCB

HUDDERSFIELD West Yorkshire   10C4
Pop. 123,200. Sheffield 26, London 180, M62 (jn
24) 2½, Barnsley 17, Bradford 10, Halifax 7, Leeds
15, Oldham 18 **MD** Mon, Thur **see** Town Hall, Art
Gallery, Roman remains, Museum, Castle Hill
Tower, Kirklees Hall, Scarmmonden Dam 🛈 3
Albion Street 01484-430808

★★★ Bagden Hall
Wakefield Road, Scissett, Huddersfield HD8 9LE
📞 01484-865330 **Fax** 01484-861001
E-mail bagdenhall@demon.co.uk

Hidden away in 40 acres of beautiful, secluded,
parkland, yet only minutes from the M1.
17 bedrs, all ensuite, ▨ ⊞ 90 **P** 85 ⊟ **CC** MC Visa
Amex DC 🅿

Facilities for the disabled

Hotels do their best to cater for disabled
visitors. However, it is advisable to contact
the hotel direct to ensure it can provide
particular requirement.

ENGLAND

★★★ Briar Court
Halifax Road, Birchencliffe, HD3 3NT
☎ 01484-519902 **Fax** 01484-431812

Elegant and comfortable, the Briar Court offers excellent standards in all aspects. Choice of two restaurants, with Da Sandro Pizzeria Ristorante a recent recipient of an Accolade for Catering Excellence.
47 bedrs, all ensuite, ⊩ ⫼ 150 **P** 140 ⊞ ⟪ MC Visa Amex DC
See advert on opposite page

★★★ ✦ Durker Roods
Bishopsway, Meltham HD7 3AG
☎ 01484-851413 **Fax** 01484-851843
31 bedrs, all ensuite, ⊩ ⫼ 100 **P** 95 ⊞ **SB** £25-£35
DB £40-£60 **L** £10.50 **L** ⫰ **D** £14.50 **D** ⫰ ⟪ MC Visa Amex ⛉
See advert on this page

★★★ George ⫗
St Georges Square, HD1 1JA
☎ 01484-515444 **Fax** 01484-435056
60 bedrs, all ensuite, ⊩ ⊡ ⫼ 200 **P** 35 ⊞
SB £79-£84 **DB** £89-£94 **L** £9.95 **D** £15.95 ✕
LD 21:30 Restaurant closed L Sat
⟪ MC Visa Amex DC ⛉

P+B
PRINCIPAL
H O T E L S

★★★ Hanover International, Huddersfield
Penistone Road, Kirkburton, HD8 0PE
☎ 01484-607788 **Fax** 01484-607961

A former spinning mill full of charm and character, the Brasserie 209 offers contemporary cuisine in stylish surroundings. Ideally situated for 'Last of the Summer Wine' country.
47 bedrs, all ensuite, ④ ⊩ ⫼ 150 **P** 100 ⊞ **SB** £35
DB £69 **L** ⫰ **D** ⫰ ✕ **LD** 21:45 Restaurant closed L Sat
⟪ MC Visa Amex DC

★★★ Huddersfield
33-47 Kirkgate, Huddersfield HD1 1QT
☎ 01484-512111 **Fax** 01484-435262
E-mail enquiries@thehuddersfieldhotel.com
60 bedrs, all ensuite, ④ ⊩ ⊡ **P** 70 ⊞ **SB** £35-£55
DB £50-£70 **L** £7 **L** ⫰ **D** £11 **D** ⫰ ✕ **LD** 23:00 ⟪ MC Visa Amex DC JCB
See advert on next page

Facilities for the disabled

Hotels do their best to cater for disabled visitors. However, it is advisable to contact the hotel direct to ensure it can provide particular requirement.

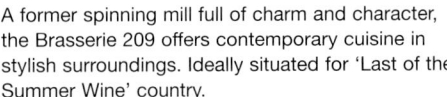

THE
HUDDERSFIELD
HOTEL & ENTERTAINMENT COMPLEX

Town Centre location. Award winning high security overnight parking. Renowned for friendliness. All day Continental Brasserie open 7 days and nights. Rosemary Lane Bistro serving Dinner every evening. Our own local style Pub, the Boy and Barrel Inn with entertainment most evenings. All rooms ensuite with all facilities.

HOSPITALITY MERIT AWARD

**KIRKGATE, HUDDERSFIELD,
WEST YORKSHIRE HD1 1QT
Tel: 01484 512111
Fax: 01484 435262**

HULL East Yorkshire   11E3

Pop. 245,000. Lincoln 42, London 175, Beverley 8½, Bridlington 30, Goole 33, Scunthorpe 26, Grimsby 31 **MD** Tue, Fri, Sat ℹ️ Library, Albion Street 01482-223344

★★★ Portland ⍨

Paragon Street, Hull HU1 3PJ
📞 01482-326462 **Fax** 01482-213460
106 bedrs, all ensuite, ✈ 📺 ⏚ 250 **P** 12 ⊕ **CC** MC Visa Amex DC

★★★ Posthouse   **Posthouse**

Ferriby High Road, North Ferriby, Hull HU14 3LG
📞 01482-164 5212 **Fax** 01482-164 3332
95 bedrs, all ensuite, ✈ ⏚ 100 **P** 150 ⊕
SB £68.75-£78.95 **DB** £78.90-£88.90 **L** 💺
D 💺 ✗ **LD** 22:00 **CC** MC Visa Amex DC 🖼️

★★★ ✤ Posthouse Hull Marina   **Posthouse**

Castle Street, Kingston upon Hull HU1 2BX
📞 01482-225221 **Fax** 01482-213299
99 bedrs, all ensuite, ✈ 📺 ⏚ 120 **P** 150 No children under 15 ⊕ **SB** £78.95-£118.95 **DB** £88.90-£128.90
L £12.95 **D** £16.95 ✗ **LD** 22:00
Restaurant closed L Sat
CC MC Visa Amex DC JCB 🖼️🖼️🖼️ ♿

★★★ Quality

Ferensway, Kingston upon Hull HU1 3UF
📞 01482-325087 **Fax** 01482-323172
E-mail admin@gb611.u-net.com

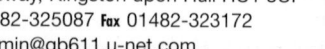

A splendid Victorian hotel, located in the city centre, with rail and bus connections adjacent to the hotel.
155 bedrs, all ensuite, ④ ♀ ⍟ ✈ 📺 ⏚ 450 **P** 128 ⊕
SB £84.75-£92.75 **DB** £109-£127 **L** £5.95
L 💺 **D** £9.95 **D** 💺 ✗ **LD** 22:00 Restaurant closed L Sat-Sun **CC** MC Visa Amex DC 🖼️🖼️🖼️ ♿

★★★ Rowley Manor ⍨

Little Weighton, Hull HU20 3XR
📞 01482-848248 **Fax** 01482-849900

A delightful Georgian country house set in lawns and rose gardens, boasting an excellent restaurant, with an extensive wine list and specialising in fresh produce.
16 bedrs, all ensuite, ④ ✈ ⏚ 150 **P** 80 ⊕ **SB** £70
DB £85 **L** £21.50 **D** £22.50 ✗ **LD** 22:00 **CC** MC Visa Amex DC ⍩ 🖼️

★★★ Willerby Manor ⍨

Well Lane, Willerby, Hull HU10 6ER
📞 01482-652616 **Fax** 01482-653901
E-mail info@willerbymanor.co.uk
Closed 25 Dec
51 bedrs, all ensuite, ♀ ⍟ ⏚ 500 **P** 300 ⊕
SB £41.50-£80 **DB** £67-£105 **L** £14.50 **L** 💺 **D** £17.25
D 💺 ✗ **LD** 21:30 Restaurant closed L Sat, D Sun
CC MC Visa Amex 🖼️🖼️🖼️

ENGLAND

★★ Comfort Inn
Anlaby Road, Hull HU1 2PJ
☎ 01482-323299 **Fax** 01482-214730
E-mail admin@gb631.u-net.com

Value for money accommodation and a cheerful informal atmosphere at this hotel. Parking front and rear. The lounge bar overlooks the city.
59 bedrs, all ensuite, ♀ ♒ 🖭 ⁑ 200 **P** 11 🍴
SB £53.50-£61 **DB** £60-£68 **D** £9.75 ✕ **LD** 21:30 **CC** MC Visa Amex DC 🖼

Campanile Hull **Lodge**
Beverley Road, Freetown Way,
Kingston-upon-Hull HU2 9AN
☎ 01482-325530 **Fax** 01482-587538

Campanile hotels offer comfortable and convenient budget accommodation and a traditional French style Bistro providing freshly cooked food for breakfast, lunch and dinner. All rooms ensuite with tea/coffee making facilities, DDT and TV with Sky channels.
48 bedrs, all ensuite, ♀ ♒ ♒ ⁑ 35 **P** 50 🍴 Rest Resid **SB** £39.50 **DB** £45.50 **HB** £47.50 **L** £5.75 **L** 🍷
D £10.85 **D** 🍷 ✕ **LD** 22:00 **CC** MC Visa Amex DC ઙ

HUNSTANTON Norfolk   9D2
Pop. 4,900. King's Lynn 16, London 115, Cromer 37, Fakenham 19, Swaffham 24. **MD** Wed **see** Church of Mary the Virgin, St Edmunds Chapel ruins, Lighthouse 🇮 Town Hall, The Green 01485-532610

★★ Caley Hall Motel
Old Hunstanton, Hunstanton PE36 6HH
☎ 01485-533486 **Fax** 01485-533348
29 bedrs, all ensuite, 🆓 ♒ ⁑ 80 **P** 70 🍴 **SB** £32-£35
DB £64-£70 **HB** £280-£301 **L** £14.75 **D** £14.75 ✕
LD 21:00 **CC** MC Visa 🖼 ઙ

★★ Lodge
Old Hunstanton Road, Old Hunstanton PE36 6HX
☎ 01485-532896 **Fax** 01485-535007
22 bedrs, all ensuite, 🆓 🏊 ♒ ⁑ 40 **P** 70 🍴 **SB** £30-
£46 **DB** £54-£84 **HB** £237-£350 **L** £10 **L** 🍷 **D** £18.95
D 🍷 ✕ **LD** 21:30 **CC** MC Visa Amex JCB 🖼 ઙ

HUNTINGDON Cambridgeshire   8C4
Royston 21, London 62, Biggleswade 20, Cambridge 16, Ely 21, Kettering 26, Peterborough 19, Stamford 27, Wisbech 33 **MD** Sat **see** All Saint's Church, Cromwell Museum, Town Hall, Bridge, Cowper's House 🇮 Library, Princes Street 01480-388588

★★★★ Swallow
Kingfisher Way, Huntingdon PE18 8FL
☎ 01480-446000 **Fax** 01480-451111
E-mail info@swallowhotels.com

SWALLOW
HOTELS

A magnificent, brand new four star hotel, just outside a charming market town. The hotel has a restaurant, lounge bar, drawing room and a luxurious Swallow Leisure Club.
150 bedrs, all ensuite, 🆓 🖭 ⁑ 250 **P** 200 🍴 **CC** MC Visa Amex DC 🎬 🖼 🎞 ઙ

HYTHE Kent   5E3
Pop. 12,900. Ashford 11, London 66, Canterbury 17, Folkestone 5, Rye 21 **EC** Wed **see** St Leonard's Church and Crypt, Romney, Hythe and Dymchurch Light Rly, Royal Military Canal, Port Lympne Zoo Park 🇮 En Route Travel, Red Lion Square 01303-267799

★★★★ ✦ Hythe Imperial
Princes Parade, Hythe CT21 6AE
☎ 01303-267441 **Fax** 01303-264610
E-mail hytheimperial@marstonhotels.co.uk
100 bedrs, all ensuite, 🔳 ♪ 🔳 ⅲ 200 **P** 200 ⊕
SB £95-£124 **DB** £130-£170 **HB** £450-£590 **L** £16 **L** 🍵
D £24 **D** 🍵 ✕ **LD** 21:30 Restaurant closed L Sat
CC MC Visa Amex DC 🔳 🔳 🔳 🔳 🔳 🔳 🔳

★★★ Stade Court 🔳
West Parade, Hythe CT21 6DT
☎ 01303-268263 **Fax** 01303-261803
E-mail stadecourt@marstonhotels.co.uk
42 bedrs, all ensuite, 🛏 🔳 ⅲ 60 **P** 12 ⊕ **SB** £72-£82
DB £101 **HB** £354 **L** £12.50 **D** £19.50 ✕ **LD** 21:00
Restaurant closed L Mon-Sat **CC** MC Visa Amex DC
🔳 🔳 🔳 🔳 🔳 🔳 🔳

ILFRACOMBE Devon	2C2

Pop. 10,600. Dunster 36, London 201, Barnstaple
11, Lynmouth 18 **EC** Thu **MD** Sat **see** Holy Trinity
Church, Museum, 14th cent Chapel of St Nicholas
on Lantern Hill 🔳 The Promenade 01271-863001

★★ Arlington
Sommers Crescent, Ilfracombe EX34 9DT
☎ 01271-862002 **Fax** 01271-862803
32 bedrs, all ensuite, 🛏 🔳 ⅲ 30 **P** 30 ⊕ Rest Resid
SB £26-£36 **DB** £52-£72 **HB** £190-£250 **D** £13 ✕
LD 20:30 **CC** MC Visa Amex ⌐ 🔳

★★ Elmfield
Torrs Park, Ilfracombe EX34 8AZ
☎ 01271-863377 **Fax** 01271-866828
Closed Nov-Easter excl Christmas
13 bedrs, all ensuite, 🔳 ♀ **P** 14 No children under 8
⊕ Rest Resid **SB** £35 **DB** £70 **HB** £230-£250 **L** £6
D £18 ✕ **LD** 19:30 **CC** MC Visa 🔳 🔳 🔳
See advert on this page

★★ Ilfracombe Carlton
Runnacleave Road, Ilfracombe EX34 8AR
☎ 01271-862446 **Fax** 01271-865379
Closed Jan-Feb

Well maintained Victorian hotel, centrally situated
adjacent to the beach, coastal walks and harbour.
Entertainment in season.
48 bedrs, all ensuite, 🔳 ⅲ 50 **P** 24 ⊕ **SB** £27.50-
£29.50 **DB** £50-£55 **HB** £205-£230 **L** 🍵 **D** £12.50 **D** 🍵
✕ **LD** 20:30 **CC** MC Visa Amex
See advert on opposite page

★★ ✦ St Helier
Hillsborough Road, Ilfracombe EX34 9QQ
☎ 01271-864906 **Fax** 01271-864906
Closed Oct
9 bedrs, all ensuite, 🛏 **P** 20 ⊕ Rest **SB** £26-£28
DB £48-£52 **HB** £200-£216 **L** 🍵 **D** £9 ✕ **LD** 20:00
CC MC Visa

★★ ✦ Tracy House
Belmont Road, Ilfracombe EX34 8DR
☎ 01271-863933
Closed Oct-Mar
11 bedrs, 9 ensuite, 🛏 ⅲ 11 **P** 11 ⊕ **CC** MC Visa
Amex

ENGLAND

ILFRACOMBE CARLTON HOTEL

Centrally situated hotel adjacent to beaches and coastal walks. Music for dancing during the season, also quiet lounge and non-smoking lounge. You are welcome at the "hotel with a smile".

RUNNACLEAVE ROAD, ILFRACOMBE EX34 8AR
Tel: 01271 862446

★ ✤ Cairn House
43 St Brannocks Road, Ilfracombe EX34 8EH
☎ 01271-863911 Fax 07070-800630

A comfortable small hotel set in its own grounds with superb views of the sea and surrounding hills.
10 bedrs, all ensuite, ⚓ P 10 ⊕ Resid SB £18-£20
DB £36-£40 HB £180-£190 L £7 L ⚑ D £10 D ⚑ ✕
LD 19:00 ℂℂ MC Visa ⚬

★ ✤ Torrs
Torrs Park, Ilfracombe EX34 8AY
☎ 01271-862334
Closed Feb-Nov
14 bedrs, all ensuite, ⚓ P 14 No children under 5 ⊕
Rest Resid SB £20-£24 DB £40-£48 HB £203-£224
L £7 D £8 ✕ LD 19:30 ℂℂ MC Visa JCB

★ Westwell Hall
Torrs Park, Ilfracombe EX34 8AZ
☎ 01271-862792 Fax 01271-862792

Quiet and secluded hotel situated in its own grounds with glorious views of the countryside and sea. Ample car parking. Adjacent to National Trust coastal walks.
10 bedrs, all ensuite, ④ ⚓ P 10 ⊕ Rest Resid
SB £22-£26 DB £44-£52 HB £219-£233 D £12 ✕
LD 19:00 ℂℂ MC Visa

ILKLEY West Yorkshire   10C3
Pop. 13,000. Leeds 16, London 207, Bradford 13,
Harrogate 17, Skipton 9½, Todmorden 26 ℝ Wed
ℹ Station Road 01943-602319

★★★ Rombalds Hotel & Restaurant ⛾ ⛾
West View, Wells Road, Ilkley LS29 9JG
☎ 01943-603201 Fax 01943-816586
E-mail reception@rombalds.demon.co.uk

Attractive early Victorian building situated on fringe of Ilkley Moor.
15 bedrs, all ensuite, ♀ ⚲ ⚓ ⯬ 70 P 22 ⊕ Rest
Resid SB £55-£99 DB £80-£119 HB £320-£435 L £8.95
L ⚑ D £12.95 D ⚑ ✕ LD 21:30 ℂℂ MC Visa Amex DC
JCB

ILSINGTON Devon   3D3
Bovey Tracey 2, London 183, Ashburton 6,
Moretonhampstead 8, Newton Abbot 6

★★★ Ilsington
Ilsington, Newton Abbot TQ13 9RR
📞 01364-661452 **Fax** 01364-661307
E-mail hotel@ilsington.co.uk

Set within Dartmoor National Park we are a family run and owned hotel priding ourselves on a friendly welcome and relaxed atmosphere. With excellent food and on site leisure facilities.
25 bedrs, 24 ensuite, 1 🕅 ➤ 🎬 ‖‖ 35 **P** 100 ⊞
SB £60 **DB** £90 **HB** £315 **L** £12.50 **L** 💷 **D** £22.50 **D** 💷 ✕
LD 21:00 **CC** MC Visa Amex DC 🗓 🖾 🖾 🖾

INGATESTONE Essex   5D2
Pop. 4,900. Brentwood 5, London 27, Bishop's Stortford 23, Chelmsford 6, Epping 15, Southend 21 **EC** Wed **see** 15th cent Church, Ingatestone Hall

★★★ Heybridge 🖥
Roman Road, Ingatestone CM4 9AB
📞 01277-355355 **Fax** 01277-353288

Offers guests deluxe hotel accommodation with extensive conference and banqueting facilities, and excellent restaurant offering international cuisine in a characteristic Tudor style setting.
22 bedrs, all ensuite, ‖‖ 600 **P** 220 ⊞ **CC** MC Visa Amex DC ♿

INSTOW Devon   2C2
Pop. 960. Barnstaple 6, London 199, Bideford 3 **EC** Wed

★★★ Commodore 🖥
Marine Parade, Instow EX39 4JN
📞 01271-860347 **Fax** 01271-861233
E-mail anyone@the-commodore.freeserve.co.uk
Closed 23-27 Dec

3 star hotel with award winning restaurant, set in its own grounds overlooking Taw and Torridge Estuaries.
20 bedrs, all ensuite, ‖‖ 280 **P** 150 ⊞ **CC** MC Visa Amex

---

IPSWICH Suffolk   5E1
Pop. 119,000. Colchester 18, London 74, Aldeburgh 24, Harwich 22, Saxmundham 21, Scole 23, Stowmarket 12, Sudbury 21 **MD** Tue, Wed, Fri, Sat 🗓 St Stephens Church, St Stephens Lane 01473-258070

★★★★ Hintlesham Hall 🖥 🖥 🖥 🖥
Gold Ribbon Hotel
Hintlesham, Ipswich IP8 3NS
📞 01473-652334 **Fax** 01473-652463
33 bedrs, all ensuite, 🗓 🗗 ➤ ‖‖ 80 **P** 100 ⊞ **SB** £89-£105 **DB** £115-£220 **L** £19.50 **D** £26 ✕ **LD** 21:30
Restaurant closed L Sat **CC** MC Visa Amex DC 🖈 🖾 🖾 🖾 🖾 🖾
See advert on opposite page

★★★ Marlborough
73 Henley Road, Ipswich IP1 3SP
📞 01473-257677 **Fax** 01473-226927
22 bedrs, all ensuite, ♀ 🗗 ➤ ‖‖ 50 **P** 80 ⊞ **SB** £75-£85 **DB** £85-£100 **L** £16.50 **L** 💷 **D** £21.85 **D** 💷 ✕
LD 21:30 Restaurant closed L Sat **CC** MC Visa Amex DC ♿

★★★ Novotel Ipswich
Greyfriars Road, Ipswich IP1 1UP
📞 01473-232400 **Fax** 01473-232414
E-mail h0995@accor-hotels.com
100 bedrs, all ensuite, 🗗 ➤ 🎬 ‖‖ 180 **P** 50 ⊞
SB £48-£85.50 **DB** £57.50-£95 **HB** £507-£770 **L** £13 **D** £15 ✕ **LD** 0:00 **CC** MC Visa Amex DC JCB 🖾 ♿

Hintlesham Hall

Hintlesham Hall is a prestigious 16th Century Manor set in 175 acres of peaceful rolling Suffolk countryside. The Hall offers 33 beautifully appointed guestrooms and is luxuriously furnished with antiques and paintings.

This is an ideal base for hunting out antiques, exploring Suffolk's 16th century wool merchants' villages, its pretty coast and 'Constable Country'. The delightful University City of Cambridge together with Newmarket, the headquarters of English flat racing, are under one hour's car journey away.

Leisure facilities at the hotel include an 18-hole championship length golf course, sauna, steam room, spa bath, fully equipped gymnasium, croquet and snooker.
Above all Hintlesham Hall is renowned for its excellent food and wines, its comfort and its tranquillity.

HINTLESHAM HALL, HINTLESHAM, SUFFOLK
Tel: 01473 652268 Fax: 01473 652463

ENGLAND

★★★ Posthouse — **Posthouse**
London Road, Ipswich IP2 0UA
☎ 01473-690313 **Fax** 01473-680412
109 bedrs, all ensuite, ⊱ ⠿ 110 **P** 200 ⊕ **SB** £76.95
DB £84.90 **L** £14.95 **D** £14.95 ✕ **LD** 22:30 Restaurant
closed L Sat **CC** MC Visa Amex DC ▦ ▦ ▦ &

★★★ Swallow Belstead Brook Manor ⍟ ⍟
Belstead Brook Park, Belstead Road,
Ipswich IP2 9HB
☎ 01473-684241 **Fax** 01473-681249
E-mail info@swallowhotels.com

A 16th century hunting lodge in 9 acres of
parkland. A charming hotel, with an award winning
restaurant, cocktail bar and leisure club.
76 bedrs, all ensuite, ⊱ ▣ ⠿ 200 **P** 150 ⊕ **SB** £80
DB £89 **L** £18.50 **D** £19 ✕ **LD** 22:00 Restaurant
closed L Sat **CC** MC Visa Amex DC ▦ ▦ ▦ &

★★ Claydon Country House
16-18 Ipswich Road, Claydon, Ipswich IP6 0AR
☎ 01473-830382 **Fax** 01473-832476

Small village on the outskirts of Ipswich, offering
country house charm and comfort combined with
excellent cuisine and friendly, personal service. The
perfect location to reach all of our local golf clubs.
14 bedrs, all ensuite, ▨ ⠿ 50 **P** 60 ⊕ Rest Resid
CC MC Visa Amex

ISLE OF WIGHT — 4B4
🛈 The Arcade, Fountain Quay, Cowes 01983-
280078

★★★ Bonchurch Manor
Bonchurch Shute, Bonchurch PO38 1NU
☎ 01983-852868 **Fax** 01983-852443
E-mail bonmanor@demon.co.uk
Closed Dec-Jan

Charming early Victorian manor house, with a
conservatory in style, set in three acres of gardens.
Spacious and elegantly furnished, the hotel has
superb Channel views and an aura of comfort and
warm hospitality.
12 bedrs, all ensuite, ⊱ **P** 11 No children under 7 ⊕
Rest Resid **SB** £48-£53 **DB** £96-£108 **HB** £302-£335
D £16 ✕ **LD** 20:30 Restaurant closed L Mon-Sat
CC MC Visa ▦

★★★ Brunswick
Queens Road, Shanklin PO37 6AM
☎ 01983-863245 **Fax** 01983-868398
Closed Nov-Jan
35 bedrs, all ensuite, ▨ ⊱ **P** 30 ⊕ Resid **SB** £34-£42
DB £68-£84 **HB** £295-£357 **L** ⍟ **D** £12 ✕ **LD** 20:00
CC MC Visa ▦ ▦ ▦ ▦

★★★ ✦ Burlington
Bellevue Road, Ventnor PO38 1DB
☎ 01983-852113 **Fax** 01983-853862
Closed winter
24 bedrs, all ensuite, ▨ **P** 20 No children under 3 ⊕
SB £28-£36 **DB** £56-£72 **HB** £245-£292 **D** £13 ✕
LD 20:30 **CC** MC Visa ▦

★★★ Country Garden ⍟
Church Hill, Totland Bay PO39 0ET
☎ 01983-754521 **Fax** 01938-754521
E-mail alan_smith@lineone.net
Closed Jan
16 bedrs, all ensuite, ⊱ ⠿ **P** 40 No children under
14 ⊕ Resid **SB** £44-£48 **DB** £88-£96 **HB** £335-£360
L £10.50 **L** ⍟ **D** £17.50 **D** ⍟ ✕ **LD** 21:00 Restaurant
closed L mid week **CC** MC Visa &

★★★ George ⌘ ⌘ ⌘
Blue Ribbon Hotel
The Quay, Yarmouth PO14 0PE
☎ 01983-760331 Fax 01983-760425
16 bedrs, all ensuite, ⌘ ⠿ 15 No children under 8
⌘ ⓒ MC Visa Amex JCB

★★★ Holliers
Church Road, Old Village, Shanklin PO37 6ND
☎ 01983-862764 Fax 01983-867134
33 bedrs, all ensuite, ⌘ P 40 ⌘ SB £40-£45 DB £66-
£90 L ⬤ D £15.25 D ⬤ ✕ LD 20:30 ⓒ MC Visa Amex
JCB ⌘ ⌘ ⌘ ⌘ ⌘

★★★ New Holmwood
Queens Road, Cowes
☎ 01983-292508 Fax 01983-295020
25 bedrs, all ensuite, ⓒ MC Visa Amex DC
See advert on this page

★★★ Sentry Mead
Madeira Road, Totland Bay PO39 0BJ
☎ 01983-753212 Fax 01983-753212
E-mail sentrymead@aol.com
Closed 20 Dec-2 Jan
14 bedrs, all ensuite, ⚓ P 10 ⌘ Rest Resid SB £25-
£35 DB £50-£70 HB £240-£320 D £15 ✕ LD 20:00
ⓒ MC Visa

★★★ Shanklin Manor House ⌘
Church Road Old Village,
Shanklin PO37 6QX
☎ 01983-862777 Fax 01983-863464

A majestic manor house standing in four and a half
acres of beautiful, secluded gardens. Offering many
leisure facilities.
38 bedrs, all ensuite, ⌘ ⠿ 60 P 50 ⌘ Rest Resid
SB £38-£42 DB £72-£82 HB £280-£325 L ⬤ D £15 ✕
LD 20:30 ⓒ MC Visa ⌘ ⌘ ⌘ ⌘ ⌘ ⌘ ⌘

ENGLAND

★★ Braemar ♐
1 Grange Road, Shanklin PO37 6NN
☎ 01983-863172 **Fax** 01983-863172
11 bedrs, all ensuite, ▦ ★ **P** 12 ⊞ Resid **SB** £19-£22
DB £38-£44 **HB** £170-£204 **D** £10 **CC** MC Visa

★★ Clarendon Hotel & Wight Mouse Inn
Newport Road, Chale PO38 2HA
☎ 01983-730431 **Fax** 01983-730431

The Clarendon Hotel is a delightful 17th century coaching inn with excellent food, sea views, hospitality and accommodation. The White Mouse Inn has open fires, 365 whiskies, 6 real ales and entertainment nightly. Children are most welcome.
9 bedrs, all ensuite, ★ ⦂ 60 **P** 200 ⊞ **SB** £25-£39
DB £50-£76 **HB** £195-£325 **L** £10 **D** £12 ✕ **LD** 22:00
CC MC Visa JCB ⊡ ⊡ ⛬

★★ Farringford ♐
Freshwater Bay PO40 9PE
☎ 01983-752500 **Fax** 01983-756515
19 bedrs, all ensuite, ★ ⦂ 30 **P** 150 ⊞ **SB** £32-£50
DB £64-£100 **HB** £234-£370 **L** £10 **L** ⬤ **D** £16 **D** ✕
LD 21:30 Restaurant closed L Mon-Sat **CC** MC Visa
Amex DC ⊡ ⊡ ⊡ ⊡
See advert on previous page

★★ Fernbank
Highfield Road, Shanklin PO37 6PP
☎ 01983-862790 **Fax** 01983-864412
24 bedrs, all ensuite, ★ **P** 22 No children under 7 ⊞
SB £27-£37 **DB** £54-£74 **HB** £245-£294 **D** £12 ✕
LD 20:30 **CC** MC Visa ⊡ ⊡ ⊡ ⛬

Don't forget to mention the guide
When booking direct, please remember to tell the hotel that you chose it from RAC Inspected Hotels 2000

★★ Hambledon
11 Queens Road, Shanklin PO37 6AW
☎ 01983-862403 **Fax** 01983-867894
E-mail hambledon@netguides.co.uk

Our licensed hotel offers you personal attention and an informal atmosphere within which to enjoy your visit. All bedrooms ensuite with TV, radio and beverage facilities. Choice of menu. Free use of nearby indoor leisure facility. Open all year
12 bedrs, all ensuite, ★ ⦂ 20 **P** 9 ⊞ Resid **SB** £21-£25 **DB** £42-£50 **HB** £170-£215 **D** £9 ✕ **LD** 18:30
CC MC Visa JCB

★★ ✤ Keats Green
3 Queens Road, Shanklin PO37 6AN
☎ 01983-862742 **Fax** 01983-868572
Closed Oct-Mar
33 bedrs, all ensuite, ★ **P** 30 ⊞ Resid **SB** £25-£30
DB £50-£60 **HB** £210-£260 **D** £12 ✕ **LD** 20:00 **CC** MC Visa JCB ⊋

★★ Luccombe Hall
Luccombe Road, Shanklin PO37 6RL
☎ 01983-862719 **Fax** 01983-863082
29 bedrs, all ensuite, ▦ ★ ⦂ 50 **P** 26 ⊞ Rest Resid
SB £30-£50 **DB** £60-£100 **HB** £268-£405 **L** ⬤ **D** £20
D ⬤ ✕ **LD** 20:30 **CC** MC Visa JCB ⊡ ⊋ ⊡ ⊡ ⊡ ⊡ ⊡ ⛬

★★ ✤ Malton House
8 Park Road, Shanklin PO37 6AY
☎ 01983-865007 **Fax** 01983-865576
15 bedrs, all ensuite, **P** 16 ⊞ Rest Resid **SB** £22-£25
DB £40-£46 **HB** £140-£182 **D** £9 ✕ **LD** 20:00 **CC** MC Visa

Short Breaks
Many hotels provide special rates for weekend and mid-week breaks – sometimes these are quoted in the hotel's entry, otherwise ring direct for the latest offers.

ENGLAND

★★ ✦ Melbourne Ardenlea
Queens Road, Shanklin PO37 6AP
☎ 01983-862283 **Fax** 01983-862865
Closed Nov-Feb

Long established, family run hotel in pleasant gardens, giving personal service. Centrally situated in peaceful area, yet close to all of Shanklin's amenities.
56 bedrs, all ensuite, ♒ ☲ P 28 ⊕ Rest Resid
SB £24-£37 DB £48-£74 HB £196 £308 D £13 ✕
LD 20:00 ⟨⟨ MC Visa Amex JCB

★★ ✦ Monteagle
Priory Road, Shanklin PO37 6RJ
☎ 01983-862854

★★ ✦ Montrene
Avenue Road, Sandown PO36 8BN
☎ 01983-403722 **Fax** 01983-405553
E-mail info@montrene.co.uk
Closed Jan
40 bedrs, all ensuite, ④ ♒ ⦿ 40 P 35 ⊕ SB £33-£39
DB £66-£78 HB £265-£308 L ☕ D £10 ✕ LD 20:00
⟨⟨ MC Visa

★★ Orchardcroft
53 Victoria Avenue, Shanklin PO37 6LT
☎ 01983-862133 **Fax** 01983-862133
Closed 3 Jan
16 bedrs, all ensuite, ④ ♒ P 12 ⊕ Rest Resid
SB £23.50-£27.50 DB £47-£54 HB £221-£256 D £12
D ☕ ✕ LD 20:00 ⟨⟨ MC Visa

★★ Sandpipers Country House
& Fat Cat Bar
Coastguard Lane, Freshwater PO40 9QX
☎ 01983-753634 **Fax** 01983-754364
E-mail sandpipers@fatcattrading.demon.co.uk
10 bedrs, all ensuite, ♀ ♪ ♒ ⦿ 50 P 24 ⊕
SB £21.95-£24.95 DB £21.95-£24.95 HB £230-£255.80
L ☕ D £6.99 D ☕ ✕ LD 20:45 Restaurant closed L
Mon ⟨⟨ MC Visa

★ ✦ Villa Mentone
11 Park Road, Shanklin PO37 6AY
☎ 01983-862346 **Fax** 01983-862130

Magnificent views of the English Channel make the Villa Mentone a special place to stay. Direct access to cliff walk with beach lift close by.
27 bedrs, all ensuite, P 15 ⊕ Resid SB £26-£28
DB £52 HB £238-£258 D £12.50 ✕ LD 19:30 ⟨⟨ MC Visa

ISLES OF SCILLY 2A3
ℹ Porthcressa Bank, St Mary's 01720-422536

★★★ Island ♜ ♜ ♜
Blue Ribbon Hotel
Tresco TR24 0PU
☎ 01720-422883 **Fax** 01720-423008
E-mail islandhotel@tresco.co.uk
Closed Nov-Feb
48 bedrs, all ensuite, ♀ ⦿ 50 ⊕ SB £88-£130
DB £176-£260 HB £585-£855 L £17 L ☕ D £33 ✕
LD 21:30 ⟨⟨ MC Visa Amex

★★★ St Martin's on the Isle ♜ ♜ ♜ ♜
Blue Ribbon Hotel
St Martin's TR25 0QW
☎ 01720-422092 **Fax** 01720-422298
Closed Nov-Feb
30 bedrs, all ensuite, ④ ♀ ♒ ⦿ 60 ⊕ SB £70-£85
DB £140-£200 L ☕ D £35 D ☕ ✕ LD 22:00 ⟨⟨ MC Visa
Amex DC ⟨⟨ &
See advert on next page

★★ Godolphin
St Mary's TR21 0JR
☎ 01720-422316 **Fax** 01720-422252
E-mail hotelgodolphin@sallyonline.co.uk
Closed 1 Nov-mid Mar
31 bedrs, 28 ensuite, ⊕ DB £76-£100 HB £336-£420
L ☕ D £18 ✕ LD 20:00 ⟨⟨ MC Visa

ST MARTIN'S ON THE ISLE
St Martin's, Isles of Scilly

Escapes in the British Isles rarely come more romantic than on St Martin's, one of the five inhabited islands in the Isles of Scilly. The variety of landscape is the stuff of children's adventure books; heather, endless sun-bleached beaches, gin-clear waters, seabird colonies, and scarcely another soul in sight, even at the height of summer. St Martin's on the Isle, the island's only Hotel, is a truly secluded hideaway, as well as being the highest rated Hotel and Restaurant in Scilly. The transfer launch from St Mary's deposits you on to the Hotel Quay, the welcome from Keith Bradford, General Manager is friendly, and the rooms well appointed. For 'foodies', the sea is the larder, and, whether you are tucking into a creamy white Scillonian Crabmeat Salad for lunch or a Cornish Tournedos for dinner, the sea-facing Restaurant is the perfect place.

Visitors can choose to explore, go fishing for crab and mackerel, or just watch the world go by (it moves slowly in these parts). With double rooms from £85 per person, including dinner, bed and breakfast, St Martin's on the Isle offers remarkably good value.

For further information on how to get here and reservations, contact:
St Martin's on the Isle, St Martin's, Isles of Scilly, TR25 0QW
Tel. 01720 422090, Fax. 01720 422298

★★ Tregarthen's
Hughtown, St Mary's TR21 0PP
☎ 01720-422540 **Fax** 01720-422089
Closed Oct-Mar
33 bedrs, all ensuite, No children under 5 ♨ **SB** £60-£68 **DB** £104-£124 L ❦ **D** £22.50 ✗ **LD** 20:30 **CC** MC Visa Amex DC
See advert on this page

IVYBRIDGE Devon   2C4
🛈 Leonards Road 01752-897035

★★ Sportsmans Inn
Exeter Road, Ivybridge PL21 0BQ
☎ 01752-892280 **Fax** 01752-690714

South West Devon's premier eating house. Beautiful ensuite rooms with special weekend breaks and extensive day and evening menus. Close to Cornwall, Plymouth, Torbay and Exeter.
10 bedrs, all ensuite, **P** 40 ♨ **SB** £39.95 **DB** £49.95 L £8.95 L ❦ **D** £8.95 **D** ❦ ✗ **LD** 21:30 **CC** MC Visa Amex ♿

KEGWORTH Leicestershire   8B2
Pop. 3,500. Loughborough 6, London 116, M1 (jn 24) 1, Ashby-de-la-Zouch 11, Derby 11, Melton Mowbray 18, Nottingham 11

★★ Kegworth
Packington Hill, Kegworth DE7 2DF
☎ 01509-672427 **Fax** 01509-674664
E-mail kegworth@kegworth-hotel.co.uk

The Kegworth Hotel is ideally situated on the A6 in a quiet village setting only 500 metres from M1 motorway and M42. The hotel offers 60 ensuite bedrooms, extensive conference facilities and leisure complex which comprises of swimming pool, sauna & gym.
60 bedrs, all ensuite, ♀ ✝ ⚏ 300 **P** 150 ♨ **SB** £60-£75 **DB** £65-£90 L £11.50 L ❦ **D** £11.50 **D** ❦ ✗ **LD** 21:30 **CC** MC Visa Amex ▨ ▨ ▨

KEIGHLEY West Yorkshire   10C3
Pop. 49,267. Halifax 12, London 199, Bradford 10, Skipton 9½, Todmorden 14 **EC** Tue **MD** Wed, Fri, Sat **see** Cliffe Castle Museum and Art Gallery, Keighley-Worth Valley Rly

★★ Dalesgate
406 Skipton Road, Utley, Keighley BD20 6HP
☎ 01535-664930 **Fax** 01535-611253
20 bedrs, all ensuite, ✝ **P** 30 ♨ Rest Resid **CC** MC Visa Amex DC ♿
See advert on next page

DALESGATE HOTEL

Charming stone-built Victorian house, once a manse, with a modern extension. On the edge of the Dales and Bronte country.

406 SKIPTON ROAD, UTLEY, KEIGHLEY BD20 6HP
Tel: 01535-664930 Fax: 01535-611253
www.dalesgate.co.uk

KENDAL Cumbria 10B2
Pop. 21,596. London 257, M6 (jn 37) 5½, Ambleside 13, Brough 28, Kirkby Lonsdale 12, Penrith 25, Ulverston 24 **MD** Sat **see** 13th cent Parish Church, Castle ruins, Abbot Hall Art Gallery and Museum, Sandes Hospital ℹ Town Hall, Highgate 01539-725758

★★★ ✤ Stonecross Manor
Milnthorpe Road, Kendal LA9 5HP
📞 01539-733559 **Fax** 01539-736386
30 bedrs, all ensuite, 🄰 ☎ ⠿ 130 ⊕ **℃** MC Visa Amex JCB 🔳 🖾 ⟊

★★ Heaves
Levens, Kendal LA8 8EF
📞 015395-60396 **Fax** 015395-60269
Closed 24-29 Dec
15 bedrs, 11 ensuite, 🛏 ⠿ 60 **P** 24 ⊕ Rest Resid **℃** MC Visa Amex DC JCB 🔳

★ County
Station Road, Kendal LA9 6BT
📞 01539-722461 **Fax** 01539-732644
37 bedrs, all ensuite, 🛏 ☎ ⠿ 60 ⊕ **SB** £28-£37 **DB** £56-£74 **HB** £200-£285 **L** ⬤ **D** £9.95 **D** ⬤ ✕ **LD** 20:00 **℃** MC Visa

---

Jolly Anglers Inn Awaiting Inspection
Burneside, Kendal LA9 5QS
📞 01539-732552
6 bedrs, 1 ensuite, 2 🎮 🛏 ⊕ ⟊

Roadchef Lodge Lodge
Killington Lake Motorway Service Area, M6 Southbound, Nr Kendal LA8 0NW
📞 01539-621666 **Fax** 01539-621660
Closed 24 Dec-2 Jan
36 bedrs, all ensuite, ⠿ 5 **P** 150 **Room** £47.95 **℃** MC Visa Amex DC ⟊

KENILWORTH Warwickshire 7F3
Pop. 21,400. Warwick 4½, London 96, Birmingham 19, Coventry 6, Tamworth 23 **℃** Mon, Thur **see** Castle ruins, Parish Church of St Nicholas ℹ Library, 11 Smalley Place 01926-852595

★★★ Chesford Grange
Chesford Bridge, Kenilworth CV8 2LD
📞 01926-859331 **Fax** 01926-859075
154 bedrs, all ensuite, 🛏 ☎ ⠿ 860 **P** 550 ⊕ **SB** £105-£110 **DB** £115-£120 **L** £12.95 **L** ⬤ **D** £16.50 **D** ⬤ ✕ **LD** 22:00 Restaurant closed L Sat **℃** MC Visa Amex DC 🔳 🖾 🖾 ⟊

PRINCIPAL HOTELS

★★★ Peacock
149 Warwick Road, Kenilworth CU8 1HY
📞 01926-851156 **Fax** 01926-864644
15 bedrs, all ensuite, 🄰 ⠿ 50 ⊕ **SB** £20-£35 **DB** £50-£75 **HB** £260-£365 **L** ⬤ **D** £10 **D** ⬤ ✕ **LD** 22:30 **℃** MC Visa Amex
See advert on opposite page

★★ ✤ Clarendon House
Old High Street, Kenilworth CV8 1LZ
📞 01926-857668 **Fax** 01926-850669
31 bedrs, all ensuite, ⠿ 120 **P** 31 ⊕ **℃** MC Visa

KESWICK Cumbria 10B2
See also BORROWDALE and THORNTHWAITE
Pop. 5,600. Ambleside 16, London 285, Carlisle 31, Cockermouth 11, Egremont 25, Penrith 16 **℃** Wed **MD** Sat **see** Derwentwater, Friar's Crag, School of Industrial Arts, Castlerigg prehistoric stone circle ℹ Moot Hall, Market Square 017687- 72645

★★★★ Keswick Country House

Station Road, Keswick CA12 4NQ
PRINCIPAL HOTELS
☎ 017687-72020 Fax 017687-71300
74 bedrs, all ensuite, ④ ★ ✦ ♨ 100 P 150
♨ SB £80 DB £115 L £8 L ● D £16.95 ✕
LD 22:00 ㏄ MC Visa Amex DC ▣

★★★ Borrowdale Gates Country House ♨ ♨

Grange-In-Borrowdale, Keswick CA12 5UQ
☎ 017687-77204 Fax 017687-77254
Closed Jan

A delightful and charming Lakeland house, nestling peacefully in wooded gardens with breathtaking views of Borrowdale. Relaxing and comfortable with an 'away from it all' atmosphere.
29 bedrs, all ensuite, P 40 ♨ Rest Resid SB £42.50-£67.50 DB £80-£120 HB £375-£487.50 L £8 D £27 ✕
LD 20:45 ㏄ MC Visa Amex ♿

★★★ Dale Head Hall Lakeside ♨

Lake Thirlmere, Keswick CA12 4TN
☎ 017687-72478 Fax 017687-71070
E-mail enquiry@dale_head_hall.co.uk
9 bedrs, all ensuite, ④ P 20 ♨ Rest Resid
SB £57.50-£72.50 DB £65-£95 HB £357-£413 L ●
D £27.50 ✕ LD 20:00 ㏄ MC Visa Amex ▣

★★★ Derwentwater ♨

Portinscale, Keswick CA12 5RE
☎ 017687-72538 Fax 017687-71002
E-mail derwentwater.hotel@dial.pipex.com

A traditional Lakeland building, furnished and decorated in a Victorian style. Set in sixteen acres on the shores of Lake Derwentwater. Panoramic lake views from many bedrooms.
47 bedrs, all ensuite, ④ ★ ✦ ♨ 20 P 120 ♨ SB £75-£85 DB £130-£160 HB £350-£420 L ● D £24.95 ✕
LD 21:30 ㏄ MC Visa Amex DC JCB ▣ ♿
See advert on opposite page

★★★ Queen's

Main Street, Keswick CA12 5JF
☎ 017687-73333 Fax 017687-71144

Situated in the geographical centre of Cumbria, the Queen's offers friendly, efficient service, a popular restaurant, fully decked out bar with log stove and conservatory style roof.
37 bedrs, all ensuite, ④ ⚲ ✦ ♨ 60 P 8 ♨ SB £25-£40 DB £50-£79.50 HB £299 L £6.50 D £15.95 ✕
LD 21:30 Restaurant closed 24/25 DEC ㏄ MC Visa Amex DC JCB

★★ Applethwaite Country House

Applethwaite, Keswick CA12 4PL
☎ 017687-72413 Fax 017687-75706
E-mail ryan@applethwaite.freeserve.co.uk
Closed Nov-Feb

Victorian Lakeland stone residence in idyllic location off the beaten track, just 1½ miles from Keswick with stunning panoramic views. Friendly relaxed atmosphere. Fresh home cooking, good value wines. Vegetarians welcomed.
12 bedrs, all ensuite, ④ P 10 No children under 5 ♨ Rest Resid SB £30-£37.50 DB £60-£75 HB £285-£325
D £17.50 ✕ LD 19:00 ㏄ MC Visa ▣

★★ Chaucer House
Derwentwater Place, Keswick CA12 4DR
☎ 017687-72318 **Fax** 017687-75551
Closed Dec-Jan

At Chaucer House you can be sure of comfort, willing service and home cooked food in plenty. Friendly relaxing atmosphere. A family run and managed hotel. Car park. Lift to all floors. Free midweek golf.
34 bedrs, 31 ensuite, ④ ➤ ⊡ **P** 25 ⊕ Rest Resid ⓒ MC Visa Amex JCB ♿

★★ Crow Park
The Heads, Keswick CA12 5ER
☎ 017687-72208 **Fax** 017687-74776
27 bedrs, all ensuite, ④ ⚲ ➤ ⋕ 20 **P** 27 No children under 2 ⊕ **SB** £21.50-£28.50 **DB** £43-£57 **HB** £195-£279 **D** £11 ✕ **LD** 20:00 ⓒ MC Visa ♿

★★ Daleview
Lake Road, Keswick CA12 5DQ
☎ 017687-72666 **Fax** 017687-74879
Closed Dec
14 bedrs, all ensuite, **P** 17 ⊕ Rest Resid **SB** £28-£32 **DB** £54-£64 **HB** £245-£265 L ➍ **D** £13.50 ✕ **LD** 20:30 ⓒ MC Visa

★★ Highfield
The Heads, Keswick CA12 5ER
☎ 017687-72508
Closed Dec-Jan
18 bedrs, all ensuite, ④ **P** 19 No children under 8 ⊕ Rest Resid **SB** £30-£35 **DB** £50-£70 **HB** £270-£350 L ➍ **D** £15.50 ✕ **LD** 20:00 ⓒ MC Visa

★★ Lairbeck ⌂
Vicarage Hill, Keswick CA12 5QB
☎ 017687-73373 **Fax** 017687-73144
E-mail rogerc@lairbeck.demon.co.uk
Closed Jan-Feb
14 bedrs, all ensuite, **P** 16 No children under 5 ⊕ Rest Resid **SB** £29-£36 **DB** £58-£72 **HB** £287-£330 **D** £16 ✕ **LD** 19:30 ⓒ MC Visa ♿

⌂ ★★ ✦ Lyzzick Hall
Underskiddaw, Keswick CA12 4PY
☎ 017687-72277 **Fax** 017687-72278
Closed Jan-Feb

In a stunning location north of Keswick, a family run Victorian manor house with highly acclaimed cuisine, rambling gardens and a superb indoor swimming pool, sauna and jacuzzi.
29 bedrs, all ensuite, **P** 40 ⊕ **SB** £39-£45 **DB** £78-£90 **HB** £330-£350 L £11 L ➍ **D** £20 ✕ **LD** 21:30 ⓒ MC Visa Amex ▣ ▨

★★ Thwaite Howe ⌂
Thornthwaite, Keswick CA12 5SA
☎ 01768-778281 **Fax** 01768-778529
Closed Nov-Feb
8 bedrs, all ensuite, ➤ **P** 12 No children under 12 ⊕ Rest Resid **DB** £64 **HB** £308-£322 **D** £17.50 ✕ **LD** 19:00 ⓒ MC Visa

★ ✦ Linnett Hill
4 Penrith Road, Keswick CA12 4HF
☎ 017687-73109
10 bedrs, all ensuite, ⊠ **P** 12 No children under 5 ⊕ Rest Resid ⓒ MC Visa JCB ♿

★ Swinside Lodge ⌂ ⌂ ⌂
Blue Ribbon Hotel
Grange Road, Newlands, Keswick CA12 5UE
☎ 017687-72948 **Fax** 017687-72948
Closed Dec-Jan

Quietly situated informal country hotel offering the highest standards of comfort, service and hospitality. Noted for superb food. A warm welcome awaits you.
7 bedrs, all ensuite, ☒ **P** 12 No children under 10 **SB** £52–£65 **DB** £86–£120 **D** £25 ✕ **LD** 20:00 **CC** MC Visa

---

KETTERING Northamptonshire 8C3
Pop. 43,800. Bedford 25, London 75, Huntingdon 26, Market Harborough 11, Northampton 14, Peterborough 28½ **EC** Thu **MD** Wed, Fri, Sat **see** Church with 177ft spire, art gallery and museum. The Mission House ⓘ Coach House, Sheep Street 01536-410266

★★★★ Kettering Park 🛏 🛏 🛏

Kettering Parkway, Kettering NN15 6XT
☎ 01536-416666 **Fax** 01536-416171
E-mail kpark@shireinns.co.uk
119 bedrs, all ensuite, ☒ ♪ ⊢ ▣ ⚌ 260 **P** 200 ⊞ **SB** £120–£140 **DB** £140–£160 **L** £13 **D** £22 ✕ **LD** 21:45 Restaurant closed L Sat, Sun **CC** MC Visa Amex DC 🗺 🕱 🕮 🕱 🕱 ☖

KEYNSHAM Somerset 3E1
Bath 7, London 111, Bristol 5½, Radstock 12, Shepton Mallet 16, Tetbury 20, Wells 17 **EC** Wed **see** Museum, Roman Villa, St John's Church

★★ Grange
42 Bath Road, Keynsham BS18 1SN
☎ 0117-986 9181 **Fax** 0117-986 6373

Privately owned, beautifully decorated bedrooms hotel, ideally situated between Bath (8 miles) and Bristol city centre (5 miles). The main farmhouse now extends into the peaceful surroundings of the former orchard.
30 bedrs, all ensuite, ☒ ⚌ 30 **P** 25 ⊞ **SB** £48–£73 **DB** £65–£85 **L** £5.50 **L** 👎 **D** £9.95 **D** 👎 ✕ **LD** 20:45 **CC** MC Visa Amex 🕱 ☖

KIDDERMINSTER Worcestershire 7E3
See also STONE
Pop. 53,600. Bromsgrove 9, London 122, Birmingham 17, Bridgnorth 13, Leominster 25, Wolverhampton 15, Worcester 14 **EC** Wed **MD** Tue, Thur, Fri, Sat **see** St Mary's Church, Statue of Sir Rowland Hill, Caldwell Tower ⓘ Severn Valley Railway Station, Comberton Hill 01562-829400

★★★ ✧ Brockencote Hall
Chaddesley Corbett, Kidderminster DY10 4PY
☎ 01562-777876 **Fax** 01562-777872
17 bedrs, all ensuite, ☒ ▣ ⚌ 25 **P** 45 ⊞ **SB** £97–£112 **DB** £125–£150 **L** £19.50 **D** £24.50 ✕ **LD** 21:30 Restaurant closed L Sat **CC** MC Visa Amex DC ☖

★★ Cedars
Mason Road, Kidderminster DY11 6AL
☎ 01562-515595 **Fax** 01562-751103
Closed 22 Dec-2 Jan

Pleasant conversion of a Georgian building with a most charming quiet garden at the rear. Ideally situated for exploring the Severn Valley.
21 bedrs, all ensuite, ♀ ♪ ⊢ ⚌ 25 **P** 22 ⊞ Resid **SB** £41–£58 **DB** £56–£72 **D** £15 **D** 👎 ✕ **LD** 20:30 **CC** MC Visa Amex DC ☖

KING'S LYNN Norfolk 9D3
Pop. 42,300. Ely 29, London 99, Fakenham 22, Spalding 28, Swaffham 15, Thetford 27, Wisbech 13 **EC** Wed **MD** Tue, Fri, Sat **see** Guildhall of St George, Old Guildhall, Custom House, Hampton Court, Thoresby College, St Nicholas' Chapel, Red Mount Chapel, Museum and Art Gallery ⓘ Old Gaol House, Saturday Market 01553-763044

★★★ Butterfly
Beveridge Way, Hardwick Narrows Estate,
King's Lynn PE30 4NB
☎ 01553-771707 **Fax** 01553-768027
E-mail kingsbutterfly@line.net

This purpose built hotel provides polite and friendly service in an informal atmosphere. The pine furnished Walts restaurant and bar offers a la carte and daily specials. Bedrooms are light and well laid out with fitted furniture.
50 bedrs, all ensuite, ♀ ★ ⅲ 50 **P** 85 ⊕ **SB** £57-£72 **DB** £64.50-£79.50 **L** £11.50 **L** ⬤ **D** £15 **D** ⬤ ✕ **LD** 22:00 《 MC Visa Amex DC JCB ⅙

★★★ Congham Hall ♗ ♗ ♗ ♗
Gold Ribbon Hotel
Grimston, King's Lynn PE32 1AH
☎ 01485-600250 **Fax** 01485-601191
14 bedrs, all ensuite, ⚘ ⅲ 12 **P** 50 No children under 12 ⊕ Rest Resid **SB** £95-£140 **DB** £125-£220 **L** £9.50 **L** ⬤ **D** £27.50 **D** ⬤ ✕ **LD** 21:30 《 MC Visa Amex DC JCB ⅜ ▨

★★★ Knights Hill Village
South Wootton, King's Lynn PE30 3HQ
☎ 01553-675566 **Fax** 01553-675568

A sympathetically restored farm complex set in 11 acres of ground. Well appointed accommodation, choice of restaurant style and an extensive health and leisure club.

57 bedrs, all ensuite, ◧ ★ ⅲ 300 **P** 350 ⊕ **SB** £88.25 **DB** £116.50 **L** £10 **D** £16.95 ✕ **LD** 22:00 《 MC Visa Amex DC ▣ ▤ ▨ ▨

★★ ✣ Grange
Willow Park, Off South Wootton Lane,
King's Lynn PE30 3BP
☎ 01553-673777 **Fax** 01553-673777
9 bedrs, all ensuite, ★ ⅲ 15 **P** 16 ⊕ Rest Resid **SB** £40-£45 **DB** £50-£55 **HB** £385-£420 **L** £6 **D** £14.50 **D** ⬤ ✕ **LD** 20:30 《 MC Visa Amex

★★ Tudor Rose
St Nicholas Street, Tuesday Market Place,
King's Lynn PE30 1LR
☎ 01553-762824 **Fax** 01553-764894

At the only owner run, fully licensed hotel in town, enjoy the friendly attention, comfortable rooms, homemade food and a choice of four traditional ales.
13 bedrs, 11 ensuite, ★ ⊕ 《 MC Visa Amex DC ⅙

KINGHAM Oxfordshire   4A1
Pop. 650. Oxford 23, London 79, Burford 9,
Chipping Norton 4½, Moreton-in-Marsh 7½, Stow-on-the-Wold 5½

★★★ Mill House ♗
Kingham OX7 6UH
☎ 01608-658188 **Fax** 01608-658492
E-mail stay@millhouse-hotel.co.uk

Superbly converted Cotswold-stone mill house set in nine tranquil acres with its own trout stream. 23 luxury ensuite bedrooms. Exceptional award winning cuisine, and outstanding choice of over 120 wines. Idyllic surroundings for complete relaxation.
23 bedrs, all ensuite, ④ ♪ ► ⅲ 70 **P** 60 ⊞ **SB** £80-£90 **DB** £110-£130 **HB** £402-£560 **L** £13.95 **L** ◖ **D** £22.75 **D** ◖ ✕ **LD** 21:30 **CC** MC Visa Amex DC ◪ &

KINGSBRIDGE Devon   3D4
Pop. 4,200. Totnes 12, London 203, Plymouth 20
EC Thu **MD** Wed, Fri ▨ The Quay 01548-853195

⚘ ★★★ ✤ Buckland Tout Saints
Goveton, Kingsbridge TQ7 2DS
▣ 01548-853055 **Fax** 01548-856261
13 bedrs, all ensuite, ► ⅲ 30 **P** 16 ⊞ Rest Resid
CC MC Visa Amex DC JCB

Crabshell Lodge **Lodge**
Embankment Road, Kingsbridge TQ7 1JZ
▣ 01548-853301 **Fax** 01548 856283
24 bedrs, all ensuite, ► ⅲ 15 **P** 40 ⊞ **SB** £35-£39 **DB** £52-£58 **HB** £221-£265 **L** ◖ **D** ◖ ✕ **LD** 21:00
CC MC Visa Amex DC

KINGSTON UPON THAMES Surrey   4C2
Pop. 140,210. London 10, Croydon 11, Epsom 6½, Leatherhead 8½, Staines 9½, Uxbridge 15, Woking 14 **EC** Wed **MD** Daily **see** Saxon Coronation Stone

---

★★★ Kingston Lodge   **Heritage** HOTELS
Kingston Hill,
Kingston upon Thames KT2 7NP
▣ 0181-541 4481 **Fax** 0181-547 1013
62 bedrs, all ensuite, ④ ► ⅲ 60 **P** 74 ⊞ **CC** MC Visa Amex DC JCB &

★★ Hotel Antoinette
26 Beaufort Road, Kingston upon Thames KT1 2TQ
▣ 0181-546 1044 **Fax** 0181-547 2595
E-mail hotelantoinette@btinternet.com

Late 19th century houses converted into a hotel, divided into two buildings and separated by gardens. In a quiet residential area.
100 bedrs, all ensuite, ▣ ⅲ 120 **P** 100 ⊞ Rest Resid **SB** £48 **DB** £58-£64 ✕ **LD** 21:15 **CC** MC Visa Amex ▨

KINGTON Herefordshire   7D3
Pop. 2,000. Hereford 19, London 151, Brecon 28, Builth Wells 20, Knighton 13, Leominster 13 **EC** Wed **MD** Tue **see** Parish Church, 15th cent Farm house, Offa's Dyke gardens

---

★★ ✤ Burton
Mill Street, Kington HR5 3BQ
▣ 01544-230323 **Fax** 01544-230323
Closed 1st week Jan

Attractively modernised coaching inn situated in a small market town near the Welsh Border. Ideal location for exploring Mappa Mundi in Hereford, the castles of Brecon and Ludlow, Offa's Dyke footpath, painting and golfing. Excellent food and service.
15 bedrs, all ensuite, ④ ► ⅲ 150 **P** 40 ⊞ **SB** £40 **DB** £55-£58 **L** £15 **L** ◖ **D** £15 **D** ◖ ✕ **LD** 21:30 **CC** MC Visa Amex DC

KNUTSFORD Cheshire   7E1
Pop. 14,200. Newcastle-under-Lyme 24, London 173, M6 (jn 19) 3, Altrincham 7½, Congleton 14, Northwich 7, Warrington 11, Stockport 14, Macclesfield 11 **EC** Wed **MD** Fri, Sat **see** 17th cent Unitarian Chapel (grave of Mrs Gaskell), Gaskell Memorial Tower, The Sessions House, Georgian Church (1744) ▨ Council Offices, Toft Road 01565-632611

★★★★ Cottons ⌂ ⌂
Manchester Road, Knutsford WA16 0SU
☎ 01565-650333 **Fax** 01565-755351
E-mail cottons@shireinns.co.uk
99 bedrs, all ensuite, ▦ ⌀ ⊣ 🖬 ⁝⁝⁝ 200 **P** 180 ⊞
SB £115–£139 **DB** £135–£159 **L** £12 **D** £20 ✕ **LD** 21:45
Restaurant closed L Sat, Sun **((** MC Visa Amex DC
▣ ▣ ▣ ▣ ▣ &

★★ Longview ⌂ ⌂ ⌂
Manchester Road, Knutsford WA16 0LX
☎ 01565-632119 **Fax** 01565-652402
E-mail longview_hotel@compuserve.com
Closed Christmas & New Year
23 bedrs, all ensuite, ⊣ **P** 26 ⊞ Rest Resid **SB** £45–
£75 **DB** £65–£90 **L** ● **D** £17 **D** ● ✕ **LD** 21:00
Restaurant closed D Sun **((** MC Visa Amex DC
See advert on this page

Mere Court Hotel Awaiting Inspection
Warrington Road, Knutsford WA16 0RW
☎ 01565-831000 **Fax** 01565-831001
E-mail sales@merecourt.co.uk
35 bedrs, all ensuite, ▦ ♀ ⌀ ⊣ 🖬 ⁝⁝⁝ 110 **P** 150 ⊞
L £10 **L** ● **D** £15 **D** ● ✕ **LD** 22:00 **((** MC Visa Amex
DC JCB &

LAKENHEATH Suffolk 9D3
Mildenhall 7, London 78, Bury St Edmunds 16,
King's Lynn 28, Newmarket 16, Thetford 12.

★★ ✤ Lakenheath
124 High Street, Lakenheath IP27 9EN
☎ 01842-860691 **Fax** 01842-860691
E-mail lakenhotel@aol.com
10 bedrs, all ensuite, ▦ ⌀ ⊣ **P** 20 ⊞ Rest Resid
SB £49.50 **DB** £59.50 **L** £10 **L** ● **D** £11.95 **D** ● ✕
LD 21:30 Restaurant closed D Sun **((** MC Visa Amex
JCB

LANCASTER Lancashire 10B3
Pop. 45,100. M6 (jn 34) 4½, London 238, Blackpool
24, Kendal 22, Kirkby Lonsdale 16, Preston 22,
Settle 25 **EC** Wed **MD** Daily **see** Castle, RC Cathedral,
John of Gaunt's Gateway, Royal Grammar School,
St Mary's Church, Town Hall Gardens, old Town
Hall (now museum), Custom House ℹ 29 Castle
Hill 01524-32878

★★★★ Lancaster House ⌂
Green Lane, Ellel, Lancaster LA1 4GJ
☎ 01524-844822 **Fax** 01524-844766
E-mail lochouse@elh.co.uk

A genuine northern welcome awaits you.
Renowned as Lancaster's premier hotel. 80
luxurious bedrooms (50% non-smoking),
complemented by unrivalled levels of hospitality
and extensive leisure facilities.
80 bedrs, all ensuite, ♀ ⌀ ⊣ ⁝⁝⁝ 150 **P** 120 ⊞
Room £72–£94 **HB** £346.50–£451.50 **L** £11 **L** ● **D** £18.50
D ● ✕ **LD** 21:30 **((** MC Visa Amex DC JCB ▣ ▣ ▣
&

★★★ Posthouse   **Posthouse**
Caton Road, Waterside Park,
Lancaster LA1 3RA
☎ 01524-65999 **Fax** 01524-841265
157 bedrs, all ensuite, ▦ ⊣ ▣ ⁝⁝⁝ 120 **P** 200 ⊞
((MC Visa Amex DC ▣ ▣ ▣ &

★★ Hampson House
Hampson Green, Lancaster LA2 0JB
☎ 01524-751158 **Fax** 01524-751779
14 bedrs, all ensuite, ⊞ ⊶ ⠿ 100 **P** 50 ⊞ **SB** £40
DB £50 **HB** £280 **L** £7 **L** ☛ **D** £10 **D** ☛ ✗ **LD** 21:30
₵₵ MC Visa Amex ⬥

LASTINGHAM North Yorkshire   11E2
Pop. 112. Pickering 9, London 233, Helmsley 11,
Scarborough 25

★★★ Lastingham Grange
Lastingham YO62 6TH
☎ 01751-417345 **Fax** 01751-417358
Closed Dec-Feb

Peacefully located, family run country house hotel
set in ten acres of own grounds, on the edge of the
moors.
12 bedrs, all ensuite, ⊶ **P** 30 ⊞ Rest Resid **SB** £79-
£82 **DB** £149-£155 **HB** £665-£686 **L** £16.75 **D** £30.75
✗ **LD** 20:30

LAVENHAM Suffolk   5E1
Pop. 1,700. Sudbury 6½, London 65, Aldeburgh 41,
Bury St Edmunds 11, Clacton 33, Harwich 31,
Haverhill 10, Ipswich 19, Saxmundham 37,
Stowmarket 15 **see** 16th cent half-timbered Guildhall
(with Museum), mainly Perp Church, Market Cross
🅸 Lady Street 01787-248207

★★★ Swan ⊠   **Heritage**
High Street, Lavenham CO10 9QA   HOTELS
☎ 01787-247477 **Fax** 01787-248286
46 bedrs, all ensuite, ⊞ ⊶ ⠿ 40 **P** 60 ⊞ **SB** £84.95
DB £139.90 **HB** £448-£595 **L** £9.95 **D** £24.95 ✗
LD 21:30 ₵₵ MC Visa Amex DC

LEAMINGTON SPA Warwickshire   8A4
Pop. 54,700. Banbury 20, London 93, Coventry 8½,
Daventry 18, Rugby 14, Tamworth 28, Warwick 2
MD Wed, Fri **see** Royal Pump Room, Jephson

Gardens, All Saint's Church, Museum and Art
Gallery 🅸 Jephson Lodge, The Parade 01926-
311470

★★★ Angel
Regent Street, Leamington Spa CV32 4NZ
☎ 01926-881296 **Fax** 01926-881296
48 bedrs, all ensuite, ⊞ ⊶ 🗉 ⠿ 40 **P** 28 ⊞ ⊞ Resid
SB £35-£55 **DB** £50-£65 **L** £9.50 **L** ☛ **D** £14.50 **D** ☛ ✗
LD 21:30 Restaurant closed **D** Sun ₵₵ MC Visa Amex
DC ⬥

★★★ Falstaff
16-20 Warwick New Road,
Leamington Spa CV32 5JQ
☎ 01926-312044 **Fax** 01926-450574
63 bedrs, all ensuite, ⊶ ⠿ 80 **P** 70 ⊞ ₵₵ MC Visa
Amex DC
See advert on this page

★★★ Leamington Hotel & Bistro ⊠
64 Upper Holly Walk, Leamington Spa CV32 4JL
☎ 01926-883777 **Fax** 01926-330467
30 bedrs, all ensuite, ⠿ 48 **P** 22 ⊞ ₵₵ MC Visa
Amex JCB

FALSTAFF HOTEL
rac
★★★

- **Magnificent fully refurbished Victorian property in a
  tranquil location within walking distance of the town
  centre.**
- **63 luxurious en suite bedrooms with satellite channels
  and all modern amenities.**
- **Weddings, Conferences & Special Occasion Dining
  successfully catered for.**
- **Licensed to perform Registry Marriages.**
- **Ideally located for Stratford Upon Avon, Warwick Castle
  and the historic town centre making the Falstaff a perfect
  choice for a leisure break.**
- **Within close proximity of M40 (J13), M5 & M42 and
  Birmingham NEC.**
- **Free on site parking.**

**16-20 Warwick New Road, Leamington Spa,
Warwickshire CV32 5JQ
Tel: 01926 312 044   Fax: 01926 450 574**

★★ Abbacourt 🛏 🛏
40 Kenilworth Road, Leamington Spa CV32 6JF
📞 01926-451755 **Fax** 01926-886339
E-mail abbacourthotel@maganto.freeserve.co.uk
24 bedrs, all ensuite, ♀ ⊁ ∰ 40 **P** 35 ⊕ **SB** £50
DB £70 **HB** £80 **L** £10 **D** £13 **D** 🍵 ✕ **LD** 21:30 **CC** MC
Visa Amex DC

★ Lansdowne 🛏 🛏 🛏
Blue Ribbon Hotel
Clarendon Street, Leamington Spa CV32 4PF
📞 01926-450505 **Fax** 01926-421313
14 bedrs, all ensuite, ⊘ **P** 11 No children under 5 ⊕
Rest Resid **SB** £49.95-£56.95 **DB** £65-£69.90
HB £304.50 **D** £15.95 ✕ **LD** 21:30 **CC** MC Visa &

LEATHERHEAD Surrey   4C3
Pop. 40,400. Epsom 4, London 18, M25 (jn 9) ½,
Dorking 5, Guildford 12, Reigate 8½

★★ Bookham Grange
Little Bookham Common,
Bookham, Leatherhead KT23 3HS
📞 01372-452742 **Fax** 01372-450080
E-mail bookhamgrange@easynet.co.uk

This Victorian country house hotel, set in two and a
half acres of landscaped gardens, blends the best
of tradition with modern facilities. Leatherhead,
Epsom, Guildford and London are all within easy
reach by train or car.
21 bedrs, all ensuite, ⊘ ⊁ ∰ 100 **P** 80 ⊕ **SB** £60-
£66 **DB** £80 **L** £13.50 **D** £13.50 ✕ **LD** 21:30 **CC** MC
Visa Amex DC

LEEDS West Yorkshire   11D3
Pop. 454,700. Pontefract 13, London 191, M1 (jn
46) 1½, Bradford 9, Halifax 15, Harrogate 15,
Huddersfield 15, York 24 **MD** Daily **see** TownHall, Art
Gallery, Museum, Churches, Kirkstall Abbey, Armley
Mills 🅩 The Arcade, City Station 0113-242-5242

★★★★★ 42 The Calls Town House 🛏 🛏 🛏 🛏
42 The Calls, Leeds LS2 7EW
📞 0113-244 0099 **Fax** 013-234 4100
E-mail admin@42thecalls.co.uk
Closed Christmas
41 bedrs, all ensuite, ♀ ⊘ ⊁ ☎ ∰ 70 **P** 25 ⊕ Resid
SB £106 **DB** £145 ✕ **LD** 22:00 **CC** MC Visa Amex DC &

★★★★ Hotel Metropole
King Street, Leeds LS1 2HQ
📞 0113-245 0841 **Fax** 0113-242 5156
118 bedrs, all ensuite, ⊘ ⊁ ☎ ∰ 200 **P** 40 ⊕
SB £110.95-£130 **DB** £132.90-£152.90 **L** £12 **D** £16.95
✕ **LD** 21:30 Restaurant closed L Sat & Sun **CC** MC
Visa Amex DC &

PRINCIPAL HOTELS

★★★★ Le Meridien Queens
City Square, Leeds LS1 1PL
📞 0113-243 1323 **Fax** 0113-242-5154
199 bedrs, all ensuite, ⊘ ⊁ ☎ ∰ 600 **P** 100 ⊕
SB £99 **DB** £99 **HB** £117 **L** £12.95 **L** 🍵
D £17.50 **D** 🍵 ✕ **LD** 22:00
CC MC Visa Amex DC &

Le MERIDIEN

★★★ Golden Lion
Briggate, Leeds LS1 4AE
📞 0113-243 6454 **Fax** 0113-242 9327
89 bedrs, all ensuite, ⊁ ☎ ∰ 120 **P** 30 ⊕ **SB** £85-
£95 **DB** £90-£100 **L** £9 **D** £14 ✕ **LD** 21:45 Restaurant
closed L Sun **CC** MC Visa Amex DC JCB

★★★ Merrion
Merrion Centre, Leeds LS2 8NH
📞 0113-243 9191 **Fax** 0113-242 3527
109 bedrs, all ensuite, ⊁ ☎ ∰ 80 ⊕ **SB** £98.75
DB £118.50 **L** £15 **D** £15 ✕ **LD** 22:30 **CC** MC Visa
Amex DC JCB

★★★ Milford Lodge
A1 Great North Road, Peckfield, Leeds LS25 5LQ
📞 01977-681800 **Fax** 01977-681245
E-mail enquiries@mlh.co.uk

Easily accessible and offering modern spacious
accommodation. The Watermill Restaurant and Bar

ENGLAND

features a working waterwheel and offers an extensive menu of both modern and traditional dishes.
46 bedrs, all ensuite, ♪ ↑ ⅲ 70 **P** 80 ⊞ **SB** £59 **DB** £59 **L** ➋ **D** £14 **D** ➋ ✕ **LD** 22:00 **C** MC Visa Amex DC &

★★★ Posthouse Leeds/Bradford **Posthouse**
Otley Road, Bramhope,
Leeds LS16 9JJ
📞 0113-284 2911 **Fax** 0113-284 3451
124 bedrs, all ensuite, ↑ ⅰ ⅲ 180
P 240 ⊞ **C** MC Visa Amex DC JCB
🔳🔳🔳 &

★★★ Wentbridge House ⅱ ⅱ
Wentbridge, Nr Pontefract WF8 3JJ
📞 01977-620444 **Fax** 01977-620148

Fine Georgian manor house dating from 1700. Set in 20 acres of the beautiful Went Valley, four miles south of the A1/M62 junction. Award winning cuisine and an excellent wine cellar.
19 bedrs, all ensuite, ④ ⅲ 130 **P** 100 ⊞ **SB** £60-£95 **DB** £70-£105 **L** £12.50 **L** ➋ **D** £21 ✕ **LD** 21:30 **C** MC Visa Amex DC &
See advert on this page

LEEMING BAR North Yorkshire 11D2
Pop. 1,500. Boroughbridge 16, London 224, Scotch Corner 11, Leyburn 13, Ripon 14 **EC** Thu

★★ Motel Leeming
Leeming Bay, Bedale, Leeming Bar DL8 1DT
📞 01677-422122 **Fax** 01677-424507
40 bedrs, all ensuite, ④ ↑ ⅲ 100 **P** 100 ⊞ **C** MC Visa Amex DC &

★★ White Rose
Leeming Bar, Northallerton DL7 9AY
📞 01677-422707 **Fax** 01677-425123
E-mail royston@whiterosehotel.co.uk
18 bedrs, all ensuite, ♀ ♪ ↑ **P** 50 ⊞ **SB** £38 **DB** £48 **L** £5.75 **L** ➋ **D** £10.50 **D** ➋ ✕ **LD** 21:30 **C** MC Visa Amex DC

LEICESTER Leicestershire 8B3
Pop. 280,000. London 97, M1(jn 21) 4, Ashby-de-la-Zouch 17, Coventry 25, Hinckley 13, Loughborough 11, Market Harborough 15, Melton Mowbray 15, Nottingham 26, Rugby 20, Stamford 32. **MD** Daily **see** Cathedral, St Mary de Castro Church, St Nicholas' and other churches, Jewry Wall Museum, Leicester Castle remains, Guildhall, Newarke Gateway (with Museum) **ℹ** 7-9 Every Street, Town Hall Square 0116-265 0555

★★★ Leicester Stage
Leicester Road, Wigston Fields,
Leicester LE18 1JW
📞 0116-288 6161 **Fax** 0116-281 1874
75 bedrs, all ensuite, ④ ♀ ⅲ 350 **P** 200 ⊞ **SB** £48-£85 **DB** £52-£99 **L** £5.95 **D** £17.50 **D** ➋ ✕ **LD** 22:00 **C** MC Visa Amex DC 🔳🔳🔳 &

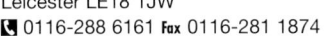

★★★ Posthouse **Posthouse**
Braunstone Lane East,
Leicester LE3 2FW
📞 0116-263 0500 **Fax** 0116-282 3623
172 bedrs, all ensuite, ↑ ⅰ ⅲ 90 **P** 250 ⊞ **C** MC Visa Amex DC JCB &

★★★ ❖ Regency
360 London Road, Stoneygate, Leicester LE2 2PL
📞 0116-270 9634 **Fax** 0116-270 1375

An exquisitely restored Victorian town house hotel, formerly a convent, with many interesting historical features, is the ideal venue for all your hospitality needs. Satellite TV in all rooms.
32 bedrs, all ensuite, ⚎ 90 **P** 50 ⊟ **SB** £35-£46 **DB** £54-£62 **L** £7 **D** £13 ✕ **LD** 22:00 Restaurant closed L Sat **cc** MC Visa Amex

★★ Red Cow ⍭ ⍭ ⍭
Hinckley Road, Leicester Forest East, Leicester LE3 3PG
📞 0116-238 7878 **Fax** 0116-238 6539

Historic thatched pub with attractive modern hotel annexe adjacent.
31 bedrs, all ensuite, ♀ ⊁ **P** 64 ⊟ ⊟ Rest **SB** £32.45-£43.45 **DB** £36.40-£49.40 **L** ⍟ **D** £7.50 **D** ⍟ ✕ **LD** 22:00 **cc** MC Visa Amex ♿
See advert on this page

LEISTON Suffolk   9F4

★ White Horse ⍭
Station Road, Leiston IP16 4HD
📞 01728-830694 **Fax** 01728-833105
E-mail whihorse@global.co.uk
13 bedrs, 11 ensuite, ⊁ **P** 14 ⊟ **cc** MC Visa Amex DC ♿

LEOMINSTER Herefordshire   7E3
Pop. 10,000. Bromyard 9½, London 148, Hereford 12, Knighton 18, Ludlow 11 **EC** Thu **MD** Fri ▧ 1 Corn Square 01568-616460

★★★ Talbot
West Street, Leominster HR6 8EP
📞 01568-616347 **Fax** 01568-614880

Town centre hotel, originally a 15th century coaching house, beams and open fire. Ideal touring location for Mid-Wales and Herefordshire. All bedrooms ensuite with modern day facilities.
20 bedrs, all ensuite, ⊁ ⚎ 130 **P** 20 ⊟ **SB** £47-£52 **DB** £68-£74 **HB** £343 **L** £10.50 **L** ⍟ **D** £17 **D** ⍟ ✕ **LD** 21:30 **cc** MC Visa Amex DC JCB
See advert on opposite page

ENGLAND

Talbot Hotel

A former Coaching Inn originating from the 15th Century, steeped in character with oak beams, period furniture and log fire during winter months. All bedrooms are en-suite with shower/bath, direct dial telephones, colour television, tea/coffee making facilities and hair dryer, a number of rooms also have trouser presses. The Talbot Hotel Restaurant offers an fine selection of food which includes table d'hôte lunch and dinner menus. Bar meals, sandwiches and snacks are available every day. Local sporting facilities include golfing, fishing, horse riding, gliding, paragliding, light aircraft and helicopter tuition.

Leominster is a small, ancient market town recognised as 'The Gateway to Mid Wales' also an ideal location for touring Herefordshire and Shropshire. Group rates are available for parties of 20 plus.

Leominster, Herefordshire HR6 8EP
Telephone (01568) 616347   Fax (01568) 614880

★★ ✦ Royal Oak
South Street, Leominster HR6 8JA
☎ 01568-612610 **Fax** 01568-612710
18 bedrs, all ensuite, 4 ⊁ ⊞ 200 P 25 ⊕ SB £35
DB £48 HB £216-£285 L £7.50 L ⬤ D £10.25 ✕
LD 21:00 ℂℂ MC Visa Amex DC

LEWES East Sussex   5D4
Pop. 15,000. East Grinstead 21, London 51, Brighton 8½, Eastbourne 16, Hastings 29, Haywards Heath 13, Uckfield 8 **EC** Wed **MD** Mon **see** Castle and Museum ⓘ 187 High Street 01273-483448

★★★ ✦ Shelleys
High Street, Lewes BN7 1XS
☎ 01273-472361 **Fax** 01273-483152
19 bedrs, all ensuite, ⊞ 50 P 25 ⊕ SB £95-£101
DB £129-£142 HB £455-£490 L £12.50 D £24 ✕
LD 21:15 ℂℂ MC Visa Amex DC JCB

★★★ ✦ White Hart
High Street, Lewes BN7 1XE
☎ 01273-476694 **Fax** 01273-476695
54 bedrs, all ensuite, 4 ⚹ ⊁ ⊞ 400 P 40 ⊕ SB £54
DB £76 HB £291 L £10.50 L ⬤ D £11.50 D ⬤ ✕
LD 22:15 ℂℂ MC Visa Amex DC ▢ ▢ ▢ ⅋
See advert on this page

LEYBURN North Yorkshire   10C2
Harrogate 31, London 235, Boroughbridge 26, Darlington 24, Hawes 16, Northallerton 18, Skipton 34, Thirsk 24 ⓘ Thornborough Hall 01969-623069

★ Golden Lion
Market Square, Leyburn DL8 5AS
☎ 01969-622161 **Fax** 01969-623836
Closed 25-26 Dec

Traditional Yorkshire stone, market square hotel, set in the heart of town.
16 bedrs, all ensuite, ⚹ ⊞ ⊞ 20 P 130 ⊕ SB £22-£32 DB £44-£64 HB £184-£251 L £9 L ⬤ D £15 D ⬤ ✕
LD 21:00 ℂℂ MC Visa Amex ⅋

LICHFIELD Staffordshire   7F2
Pop. 28,300. Coventry 25, London 116, Ashbourne 26, Burton-on-Trent 13, Stafford 16, Stoke 29, Stone 21, Sutton Coldfield 8, Tamworth 7, Uttoxeter 17, Walsall 9½, Wolverhampton 14 **EC** Wed **MD** Mon, Fri, Sat **see** Cathedral, Birthplace of Dr Samuel Johnson (Statue adjacent), Museum, St John's Hospital (Almshouses) ⓘ Donegal House, Bore Street 01543-252109

★★★ ✦ Little Barrow
Beacon Street, Lichfield WS13 7AR
☎ 01543-414500 **Fax** 01543-415734

Privately owned hotel, close to the cathedral and town centre with modern ensuite bedrooms, including two family rooms. Lounge bar, attractive

air-conditioned restaurant, function room, conferences.
24 bedrs, all ensuite, ⚲ ⅲ 80 **P** 70 ⅇ **SB** £52.50-£62.50 **DB** £70-£80 **L** £11 **L** ⬤ **D** £16.50 **D** ⬤ ✕ **LD** 21:30 Restaurant closed L Bank Holidays ⲥⲥ MC Visa Amex DC JCB

★★ ✦ Angel Croft
Beacon Street, Lichfield WS13 7AA
☎ 01543-258737 **Fax** 01543-415605
17 bedrs, all ensuite, ④ ⅲ 20 **P** 60 ⅇ **SB** £49.50-£60 **DB** £60-£72.75 **L** £9 **D** £11 **D** ⬤ ✕ **LD** 20:45 Restaurant closed D Sun ⲥⲥ MC Visa DC

LIFTON Devon 2C3
Pop. 930. Okehampton 14, London 206, Holsworthy 13, Launceston 3½, Tavistock 9½

★★★ Arundell Arms ⌇ ⌇ ⌇
Lifton PL16 0AA
☎ 01566-784666 **Fax** 01566-784494
E-mail arundellarms@btinternet.com
Closed Christmas
28 bedrs, all ensuite, ⚤ ⅲ 100 **P** 80 ⅇ **SB** £44-£72 **DB** £88-£110 **HB** £434-£504 **L** £15.50 **L** ⬤ **D** £28.50 **D** ⬤ ✕ **LD** 21:30 ⲥⲥ MC Visa Amex DC ☑

BRANSTON HALL
HOTEL

Branston Hall Hotel is a beautiful country house hotel of great architectural merit and distinction. The elegant Hall is surrounded by 88 acres of wooded parkland and lakes yet is only 5 minutes from the heart of historic Lincoln. Branston Hall is also home to the delightful Lakeside Restaurant which all year round offers fine food and an extensive wine list.

BRANSTON PARK, BRANSTON, LINCOLN LN4 1PD
Tel: 01522-793305
Fax: 01522-790549

★★ Thatched Cottage ⌇ ⌇
Sprytown, Lifton PL16 0AY
☎ 01566-784224 **Fax** 01566-784334
E-mail victoria@thatchedcott.v-net.com
5 bedrs, all ensuite, ⚤ ⅲ 12 **P** 14 No children under 12 ⅇ Rest Resid **SB** £42.50 **DB** £85 **HB** £418 **L** £14.95 **L** ⬤ ✕ **LD** 21:30 ⲥⲥ MC Visa Amex DC JCB &

LINCOLN Lincolnshire 8C1
Pop. 84,400. Sleaford 17, London 133, Gainsborough 18, Grantham 25, Horncastle 21, Louth 26, Market Rasen 15, Newark 17 **EC** Wed **MD** Daily **see** Cathedral, Castle (1069) and Court House, Jew's House, the Stonebow (15th-16th cent) with Guildhall above ⅰ 9 Castle Hill 01522-529828

★★★ Bentley
Newark Road, South Hykeham, Lincoln LN6 9NH
☎ 01522-878000 **Fax** 01522-878001

Welcome to Lincoln's newest and only hotel sporting a smart leisure club, indoor pool and large conference facilities. Popular with both corporate and leisure markets.
54 bedrs, all ensuite, ④ ♀ ⚲ 🖂 ⅲ 300 **P** 140 ⅇ **SB** £60-£76 **DB** £75-£85 **HB** £343-£378 **L** £9.95 **L** ⬤ **D** £15 **D** ⬤ ✕ **LD** 21:45 ⲥⲥ MC Visa Amex DC ☒ ☒ ☒ &

★★★ Branston Hall
Branston Park, Branston, Lincoln LN4 1PD
☎ 01522-793305 **Fax** 01522-790549
E-mail brahal@enterprise.net
43 bedrs, all ensuite, ④ ⚲ 🖂 ⅲ 200 **P** 70 ⅇ **SB** £59.50 **DB** £82.50-£100 **L** £12.50 **D** £22.50 ✕ **LD** 21:30 ⲥⲥ MC Visa Amex DC JCB ☒ &
See advert on this page

ENGLAND

★★★ Grand
St Mary's Street, Lincoln LN5 7EP
☎ 01522-524211 Fax 01522-537661

Family owned for over 60 years and renowned throughout the county for its excellent cuisine. Situated in the heart of the city.
46 bedrs, all ensuite, 🛁 🛏 ⚌ 80 P 30 ⊞ SB £50-£65 DB £65-£75 HB £305-£340 L £10 L 🍽 D £14 D 🍽 ✕ LD 22:00 ⓒ MC Visa Amex DC

★★★ Moor Lodge
Branston, Lincoln LN4 1HU
☎ 01522-791366 Fax 01522-794389
24 bedrs, all ensuite, 🛏 ⚌ 200 P 150 ⊞ ⓒ MC Visa Amex DC ♿

★★★ Posthouse
Eastgate, Lincoln LN2 1PN

Posthouse

☎ 01522-520341 Fax 01522-510780
70 bedrs, all ensuite, 🛏 ☎ ⚌ 90 P 110 ⊞
SB £269 ✕ LD 22:30
ⓒ MC Visa Amex DC JCB

★★★ White Hart
Bailgate, Lincoln LN1 3AR

Heritage
HOTELS

☎ 01522-526222 Fax 01522-531798
48 bedrs, all ensuite, 🛁 🔌 🛏 ☎ ⚌ 90
P 60 ⊞ SB £99.50 DB £108 HB £370 L 🍽
D 🍽 ✕ LD 21:30
ⓒ MC Visa Amex DC JCB

★★ Castle
Westgate, Lincoln LN1 3AS
☎ 01522-538801 Fax 01522-575457
E-mail castlehotel@ukcomplete.co.uk
19 bedrs, all ensuite, 🛁 🔌 🛏 ⚌ 40 P 20 No children under 10 ⊞ SB £60 DB £74 HB £276.50 L 🍽 D 🍽 ✕ LD 21:30 ⓒ MC Visa DC JCB ♿

★★ Hillcrest
15 Lindum Terrace, Lincoln LN2 5RT
☎ 01522-510182 Fax 01522-510182
E-mail jennifer@hillcresthotel.freeserve.co.uk
Closed Christmas-New Year

Hillcrest, good old fashioned hospitality, warm welcome and a smile. Privately owned Victorian rectory. Peaceful location. Seven minute walk to the Cathedral and city. Parking with CCTV.
16 bedrs, all ensuite, 🛁 🛏 ⚌ 20 P 10 ⊞ Rest Resid
SB £50 DB £72 L £7 D £14 ✕ LD 20:45 Restaurant closed L & D Sun ⓒ MC Visa Amex JCB

LISKEARD Cornwall   2B3
Pop. 7,400. Tavistock 18, London 214, Bodmin 13, Fowey 17, Launceston 14, Looe 7½, St Austell 18, Saltash 13

♙ Pencubitt Awaiting Inspection
Lemellion Hill, Liskeard PL14 4EB
☎ 01579-342694
Closed Nov
10 bedrs, all ensuite, 🛏 ⚌ 40 P 40 ⊞ Rest Resid
ⓒ MC Visa Amex ♋

LIVERPOOL Merseyside   10B4
Pop. 457,500. London 198, M62 (jn 4) 3½, Birkenhead 1, Ormskirk 13, St Helens 11, Southport 18, Warrington 17 EC Wed MD Daily see Anglican Cathedral, Metropolitan Cathedral, Walker Art Gallery, City Museum, St George's Hall, University, Town Hall, Philharmonic Hall, Buil and Design 🛈 Claydon Square Shopping Centre 0151-709 3631

★★★★ Swallow
One Queen Square,
Liverpool L1 1RH

☎ 01604-768700 Fax 01604-702487
E-mail info@swallowhotels.com

This new 4 star luxury hotel is well placed in the centre of cosmopolitan Liverpool, with excellent leisure and conference facilities with air conditioning throughout.
146 bedrs, all ensuite, ⬛ ⦂⦂⦂ 250 **P** 150 ⊕ **SB** £105 **DB** £120 **L** £20 **D** £20 **℅** MC Visa Amex DC 🔲 🔳 🔲 ⛹

★★★ Gladstone
Lord Nelson Street, Liverpool L3 5QB
📞 0151-709 7050 **Fax** 0151-709 2193
154 bedrs, all ensuite, ⭺ ⬛ ⦂⦂⦂ 600 **P** 200 ⊕ **SB** £45 **DB** £50 **HB** £55 **L** £8.95 **L** ⬤ **D** £16.50 **D** ⬤ ✕ **LD** 22.30 **℅** MC Visa Amex DC JCB 🔳 ⛹

★★★ Royal
Marine Terrace, Liverpool L22 5PR
📞 0151-928 2332 **Fax** 0151-949 0320
E-mail royalhotel@compuserve.com
25 bedrs, all ensuite, ⬜ ♀ ⚲ ⦂⦂⦂ 100 **P** 25 ⊕ **SB** £45 **DB** £65 **D** £9.95 **D** ⬤ ✕ **LD** 21:30 **℅** MC Visa Amex DC JCB

Campanile Liverpool **Lodge**
Chaloner Street, Queens Dock,
Liverpool L3 4AJ
📞 0151-709 8104 **Fax** 0151-709 8725

Campanile hotels offer comfortable and convenient budget accommodation and a traditional French style Bistro providing freshly cooked food for breakfast, lunch and dinner. All rooms ensuite with tea/coffee making facilities, DDT and TV with Sky channels.

103 bedrs, all ensuite, ⭺ ⦂⦂⦂ 20 **P** 103 ⊕ Rest Resid **SB** £42.50 **DB** £47 **L** £5.75 **D** £10.55 ✕ **LD** 22:00 **℅** MC Visa Amex DC ⛹

Park
Netherton, Liverpool L30 3SU
📞 0151-525 7555 **Fax** 0151-525 2481

Friendly service in homely surrounding with a professional attitude, which is the hallmark of this winning team. Situated near Aintree race course, minutes from city centre, home of the Beatles, Albert Dock and two famous cathedrals. 30 mins from Chester.
62 bedrs, all ensuite, ⬛ ⦂⦂⦂ 500 **P** 250 **SB** £48 **DB** £51 **L** £6.95 **D** £10.95 **℅** MC Visa Amex DC

LIVERSEDGE West Yorkshire   11D4
Wakefield 10, London 192, Bradford 7,
Huddersfield 7½, Leeds 10

★★ Healds Hall ₪
Leeds Road, Liversedge WF15 6JA
📞 01924-409112 **Fax** 01924-401895
Closed 1 Jan

Family run hotel and award winning restaurant with large gardens. On A62, near M1 and M62. Ideal for dales with special weekend breaks available.
25 bedrs, all ensuite, ♀ ⭺ ⦂⦂⦂ 120 **P** 80 ⊕ **SB** £55 **DB** £75 **HB** £350 **L** £9.50 **L** ⬤ **D** £18.50 **D** ⬤ ✕ **LD** 21:00 Restaurant closed L Sat, D Sun **℅** MC Visa Amex DC ⛹

LIZARD Cornwall 2A4
Pop. 880. Helston 11, London 282, Falmouth 19

★★★ Housel Bay 🏊
Housel Cove, Lizard TR12 7PG
📞 01326-290417 **Fax** 01326-290359
21 bedrs, all ensuite, 🔲 📺 ⊞ 20 **P** 30 🅿 **SB** £30-£68
DB £60-£99 **HB** £360.50-£452 **L** £9.50 **D** £19.50 ✕
LD 21:00 **CC** MC Visa Amex

LONG EATON Derbyshire 8B2
Pop. 42,500. M1 (jn 25) 5, London 121, Ashby-de-la-Zouch 15, Derby 9½, Nottingham 7 **EC** Thu
MD Wed, Fri, Sat **see** Church, Trent Lock

★★ Europa
20 Derby Road, Long Eaton,
Nottingham NG10 1LW
📞 0115-972 8481 **Fax** 0115-946 0229
15 bedrs, all ensuite, 🕊 ⊞ 40 **P** 27 🅿 **SB** £36.95-£39.95 **DB** £42.95-£46.95 **HB** £300-£315 **L** £7.50
D £10 ✕ **LD** 20:30 Restaurant closed D Sun **CC** MC Visa JCB

LOOE Cornwall 2B4
Pop. 5,000. Saltash 15, London 227, Bodmin 13, Fowey 19, (fy 10), Liskeard 7½, Plymouth (fy) 18, **EC** Thu 🛈 The Guildhall, Fore Street 01503-262072

★★★ Talland Bay
Talland Bay, Looe PL13 2JB
📞 01503-272667 **Fax** 01503-272940
Closed Jan-late Feb
19 bedrs, all ensuite, 🔲 🕊 ⊞ 30 **P** 20 🅿 Resid
SB £47-£76 **DB** £94-£152 **HB** £390.60-£604.80 **L** £11
D £22 ✕ **LD** 21:00 **CC** MC Visa Amex DC 🐾 🖼

★★ Fieldhead
Portuan Road, Hannafore, Looe PL13 2DR
📞 01503-262689 **Fax** 01503-264114
E-mail field.head@virgin.net
14 bedrs, all ensuite, 🕊 ⊞ 20 **P** 14 🅿 Rest Resid
SB £34-£53.50 **DB** £52-£84 **HB** £285-£365 **L** £8.50
D £21 ✕ **LD** 20:45 Restaurant closed L Mon-Sat
CC MC Visa Amex 🐾

★★ Klymiarven
Barbican Hill, Looe PL13 1BH
📞 01503-262333 **Fax** 01503-262333
Closed Jan
14 bedrs, all ensuite, ♀ 🐾 🕊 **P** 14 🅿 Rest Resid
SB £44-£54 **DB** £78-£98 **HB** £299-£364 **L** £9.95 **L** 🕊
D £14.95 **D** 🕊 ✕ **LD** 21:30 **CC** MC Visa Amex JCB 🐾
See advert on opposite page

LOSTWITHIEL Cornwall 2B3
Pop. 2,400. Liskeard 11, London 232, Bodmin 5½, Fowey 7, St Austell 8½ **EC** Wed

★★★ Lostwithiel Hotel Golf & Country Club
Lower Polscue, Lostwithiel PL22 0HQ
📞 01208-873550 **Fax** 01208-873479
E-mail reception@golf-hotel.co.uk
18 bedrs, all ensuite, 🕊 ⊞ 150 **P** 120 🅿 **SB** £40-£46
DB £80-£92 **HB** £266-£336 **L** 🕊 **D** £16.95 **D** 🕊 ✕
LD 21:00 **CC** MC Visa Amex DC 🔲 🖼 🖻 🖼 🖾 🖼 ⚘

Royal Oak Awaiting Inspection
Duke Street, Lostwithiel PL22 1AH
📞 01208-872552
6 bedrs, 5 ensuite, 🕊 ⊞ 16 **P** 14 🅿 **SB** £35 **DB** £58
L £8 **L** 🕊 **D** £10 **D** 🕊 ✕ **LD** 21:30 **CC** MC Visa Amex DC JCB

LOUGHBOROUGH Leicestershire 8B3
Pop. 51,900. Leicester 11, London 109, M1 (jn 23) 3, Ashby-de-la-Zouch 12, Derby 16, Melton Mowbray 15, Nottingham 15 **EC** Wed **MD** Thu **see** War Memorial with Carillon Tower (47 bells), restored remains of 13th cent Rectory, University of Technology, Parish Church, Great Central Railway (steam trains) 🛈 John Storer House, Wards End 01509-218113

★★★ Quality
New Ashby Road,
Loughborough LE11 0EX
📞 01509-211800 **Fax** 01509-211868
E-mail admin@gb613.u-net.com

A modern hotel, close to the town centre and ideal for many attractions - Donnington race track, Sherwood Forest and Belvoir Castle. Alton Towers is only 25 miles away.
94 bedrs, all ensuite, 🕊 ⊞ 225 **P** 125 🅿 **SB** £91
DB £124 **L** £9.50 **D** £14.50 ✕ **LD** 21:45 Restaurant closed L Sat **CC** MC Visa Amex DC JCB 🔲 🖼 🖾 ⚘

KLYMIARVEN HOTEL

Tel/Fax 01503 262333 Barbican Hill, East Looe, Cornwall PL13 1BH

The Klymiarven Hotel and the "New Freddies Restaurant" is set in East Looe, high up overlooking the harbour and town. Just 5 minutes walk to the town centre, beach and quay. The Hotel has been completely refurbished and offers a quality holiday in an informal and relaxed manner - the perfect place to relax.

ENGLAND

Our 70 seat "Freddies Restaurant" provides

★ Fresh produce cooked to order
★ A La Carte and Table D'Hote Menus
★ Extensive wine list
★ Superb views

❍ All our rooms are en suite many with balconies
❍ Most rooms have harbour views
❍ Private car park
❍ Outdoor heated swimming pool - open from May
❍ Short breaks available - early and late season

★★ Cedars ▯

Cedar Road, Loughborough LE11 2AB
📞 01509-214459 **Fax** 01509-233573

A well established hotel situated on the outskirts of Loughborough in a quiet and secluded area. Extensive private car parking.
36 bedrs, all ensuite, ⟵ ⠿ 30 **P** 50 ⊟ **SB** £55 **DB** £68 **L** £14.95 **L** 🍷 **D** £14.95 **D** 🍷 ✕ **LD** 21:15 Restaurant closed D Sun ⊄ MC Visa Amex DC ⌂ 🖼

★★ Great Central

Gt Central Road, Loughborough LE11 RW
📞 01509-263405 **Fax** 01509-264130
E-mail grtcenho@globalnet.co.uk
22 bedrs, all ensuite, ⌀ ⟵ ⠿ 100 **P** 30 ⊟ **SB** £32 **DB** £48 **L** £12 **L** 🍷 **D** £7 **D** 🍷 ✕ **LD** 21:30 Restaurant closed D Sun ⊄ MC Visa ⌂

LOUTH Lincolnshire 11F4
Pop. 14,700. Horncastle 13, London 148, Boston 30, Hull (fy) 32, Lincoln 26, Grimsby 16, Market Rasen 14, Skegness 23 **EC** Thu **MD** Wed, Fri, Sat
▯ New Market Hall, off Cornmarket 01507-609289

★★★ Beaumont

Victoria Road, Louth LN11 0BX
📞 01507-605005 **Fax** 01507-607768

Privately owned luxury hotel with a warm and cosy atmosphere situated on the outskirts of Louth. Its English charm is enhanced by the Italian touch of the owners. Outstanding cuisine.
17 bedrs, all ensuite, ♀ ⟵ 🖽 ⠿ 112 **P** 65 ⊟ **SB** £40-£50 **DB** £60-£75 **L** £6 **L** 🍷 **D** £8 **D** 🍷 ✕ **LD** 21:30 Restaurant closed Sun ⊄ MC Visa Amex DC ⌂

Kenwick Park Hotel and Leisure Club
Kenwick Park, Louth LN11 8NR
☎ 01507-608806 **Fax** 01507-608027
E-mail kenwick-park@lincsonline.com
24 bedrs, all ensuite, ⊱ ⊞ 100 **P** 60 ⊕ ⟨⟨ MC Visa
Amex DC ⬚ ⬚ ⬚ ⬚ ⬚ ⬚ ⬚ ⬚
See advert on this page

LOWER BEEDING West Sussex   4C3
M23 5, London 38, Brighton 19, Crawley 7,
Haywards Heath 10, Horsham 5

★★★★ South Lodge ♙ ♙ ♙
Blue Ribbon Hotel
Brighton Road, Lower Beeding RH13 6PS
☎ 01403-891711 **Fax** 01403-891766
E-mail inquiries@southlodgehotel.dial.iql.co.uk
39 bedrs, all ensuite, ⬚ ⊞ 85 **P** 100 ⊕ ⟨⟨ MC Visa
Amex DC JCB ⬚ ⬚ ⬚ &
See advert on this page

LOWER SLAUGHTER Gloucestershire   4A1
Pop. 200. Stow-on-the-Wold 3, London 87, Burford
11, Cheltenham 15, Cirencester 17, Evesham 18 **see**
Brick Mill, Cotswold stone cottages

★★★ Lower Slaughter Manor ♙ ♙ ♙
Gold Ribbon Hotel
Lower Slaughter GL54 2HP
☎ 01451-820456 **Fax** 01451-822150
E-mail lowsmanor@aol.com
Closed Jan
16 bedrs, all ensuite, ⬚ ♪ ⊞ 20 **P** 30 No children
under 10 ⊕ **SB** £125-£300 **DB** £150-£350 **L** £19.95
L ⬤ **D** £42.50 ✕ **LD** 21:30 ⟨⟨ MC Visa Amex DC ⬚ ⬚

LOWESTOFT Suffolk   9F3
Pop. 58,000. Saxmundham 23, London 117,
Aldeburgh 27, Great Yarmouth 10, Norwich 27,
Scole 29, Stowmarket 45 **EC** Thu **MD** Fri, Sat, Sun **see**
St Margaret's Church, Sparrow's Nest, Lighthouse,
Somerleyton Hall ⓘ East Point Pavilion, Royal Plain
01502-523000

★★★ Hotel Hatfield
The Esplanade, Lowestoft NR33 0QP
☎ 01502-565337 **Fax** 01502-511885
33 bedrs, all ensuite, ⬚ ⬚ ⊞ 100 **P** 26 ⊕ ⟨⟨ MC
Visa Amex DC JCB

LOWESWATER Cumbria 10A2
Pop. 230. Keswick 11, London 296, Cockermouth 11, Workington 10 **EC** Mon **see** Loweswater, Crummock Water, Scale Force -120ft waterfall

★ Grange Country House
Loweswater CA13 0SU
☎ 01946-861211
11 bedrs, 10 ensuite, ④ ★ ⅲ 25 **P** 20 ⊕ Rest Resid
SB £30-£32 **DB** £60-£64 **HB** £290-£305 **L** £10.50 **D** £14
D ● ✕ **LD** 20:00 ⑆

LUDLOW Shropshire 7E3
Pop. 9,000. Worcester 29, London 143, Bridgnorth 19, Kidderminster 25, Knighton15, Leominster 11, Shrewsbury 27 **EC** Thu **MD** Mon, Fri, Sat **see** Castle ruins, remains of Norman circular chapel, St Laurence's Church, Old Inns, Reader's House, Butter Cross, Broad Gate, Museum, Craft Centre *i* Castle Street 01584-875053

★★★ Dinham Hall ⬧ ⬧
By the Castle, Ludlow SY8 1EJ
☎ 01584-876464 **Fax** 01584-876019
15 bedrs, all ensuite, ④ ♫ ★ ⅲ 24 **P** 16 ⊕ **SB** £65
DB £100 **HB** £560 **L** £22 **L** ● **D** £22 ✕ **LD** 21:00 ⑆ MC
Visa Amex DC JCB ▣ ▣

★★★ Overton Grange ⬧ ⬧ ⬧
Ludlow SY8 4AD
☎ 01584-873500 **Fax** 01584-873524
16 bedrs, all ensuite, ★ ⅲ 175 **P** 80 ⊕ ⑆ MC Visa Amex DC

LUTON Bedfordshire 4C1
Pop. 169,000. St Albans 10, London 31, M1 (jn 10) 1½, Baldock 13, Bedford 19, Biggleswade 19, Dunstable 5, Hatfield 13 **MD** Daily **see** Church of St Mary, Museum (Wardown Park), Luton Hoo (Faberge collection) *i* 65-67 Bute Street 01582-401579

★★★ ✤ Gateway
Dunstable Road, Luton LU4 8RQ
☎ 01582-575955 **Fax** 01582-490065
109 bedrs, all ensuite, ★ ▣ ⅲ 80 **P** 117 ⊕ ⑆ MC Visa Amex DC ▣ ⑆

LYDFORD Devon 2C3
Pop. 1,400. Okehampton 8½, London 200, Launceston 12, Tavistock 8½ **see** Gorge, St Petroc's Church, Lydford Gorge (& waterfall), Castle ruins

★★ Lydford House ⬧
Lydford EX20 4AU
☎ 01822-820347 **Fax** 01822-820442
E-mail relax@lyndfordhouse.co.uk
Closed Christmas
12 bedrs, all ensuite, ④ ★ ⅲ 20 **P** 30 No children under 5 ⊕ **SB** £37 **DB** £74 **L** £8.50 **D** £15.50 ✕
LD 20:00 Restaurant closed L Mon-Sat ⑆ MC Visa ▣

LYME REGIS Dorset 3E3
Pop. 3,500. Dorchester 26, London 147, Axminster 5, Crewkerne 15, Exeter 28 **EC** Thu **see** Parish Church, The Cobb (Harbour) Museum, 250-year-old Umbrella Cottage, Charton Bay *i* Guildhall Cottage, Church Street 01297-442138

★★★ Alexandra
Pound Street, Lyme Regis DT7 3HZ
☎ 01297-442010 **Fax** 01297-443229
E-mail alexandra@lymeregis.co.uk.
Closed Christmas-New Year
27 bedrs, 24 ensuite, ★ ⅲ 60 **P** 20 ⊕ **SB** £45-£50
DB £75-£122 **HB** £342-£456 **L** £12.95 **L** ● **D** £22.50
D ● ✕ **LD** 21:00 ⑆ MC Visa Amex DC
See advert on this page

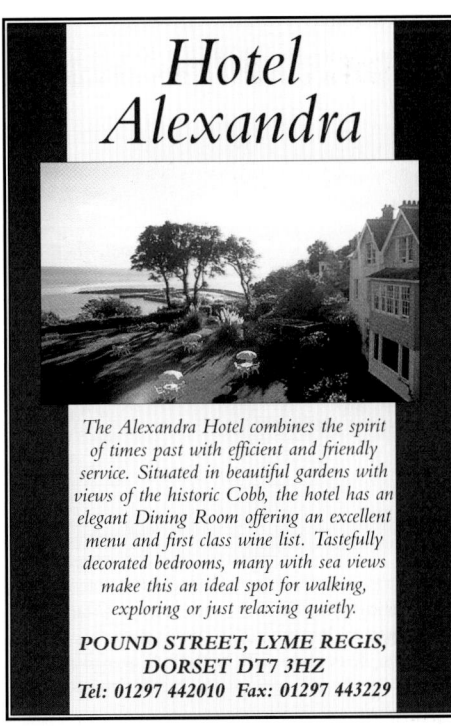

ENGLAND

★★★ Dower House
Rousdon, Lyme Regis DT7 3RB
☎ 01297-21047 **Fax** 01297-24748
Closed Jan

Nestling in magnificent country with the main south front facing out to sea over views of fields and woodlands. Relax in the grounds, the sauna or in the new indoor heated swimming pool.
9 bedrs, all ensuite, 4 ✦ P 30 ⊕ SB £38-£48 DB £60-£80 HB £305-£375 L £18.95 L ☕ D £18.95 D ☕ ✕
LD 21:00 ℂℂ MC Visa Amex

★★★ Fairwater Head
Hawkchurch, Axminster EX13 5TX
☎ 01297-678349 **Fax** 01297-678459
E-mail reception@fairwater.demon.co.uk
Closed Jan-Feb
20 bedrs, all ensuite, ♀ ✦ ⚌ 15 P 30 ⊕ SB £73-£76
DB £126-£132 HB £483-£504 L £12 D £22 ✕ LD 20:30
ℂℂ MC Visa Amex DC

Bay
Marine Parade, Lyme Regis DT7 3JQ
☎ 01297-442059

Only yards from the sea, with no traffic noise, this year-round hotel is a short stroll from the harbour and famed for its views and seafood.
23 bedrs, 20 ensuite, 3 ✦ P 18 ⊕ SB £28-£38
DB £56-£70 HB £260-£290 D £13 ✕ LD 20:00 ℂℂ MC Visa

Pop. 15,000. Lyndhurst 8, London 92, Bournemouth 16, Ringwood 13 **EC** Wed **MD** Sat **see** 13th cent Beaulieu Abbey, Palace House & National Motor Museum 5½m NE �**i** St Barb Museum, New Street 01590-672422

★★★ Passford House
Mount Pleasant, Lymington S04 8LS
☎ 01590-682398 **Fax** 01590-683494
55 bedrs, all ensuite, 4 ♀ ✦ ⚌ 50 P 100 ⊕ SB £65-£85 DB £90-£150 L £14 L ☕ D £25.50 D ☕ ✕
LD 21:30 ℂℂ MC Visa Amex DC JCB

★★★ Stanwell House
14-15 High Street, Lymington SO4 9AA
☎ 01590-677123 **Fax** 01590-677756

A charming 18th century hotel with well-furnished bedrooms and walled gardens. Close to the quay and yacht marina and near the New Forest.
31 bedrs, all ensuite, 4 ✦ ⚌ 60 ⊕ SB £50 DB £95
L £6.50 L ☕ D £20 D ☕ ✕ LD 21:30 ℂℂ MC Visa
Amex DC
See advert on opposite page

Pop. 700. M5 (jn 22) 4, Axbridge 7, London 139, Bridgwater 13, Wells 18, Weston-super-Mare 6 **see** Perp Church

Short Breaks
Many hotels provide special rates for weekend and mid-week breaks – sometimes these are quoted in the hotel's entry, otherwise ring direct for the latest offers.

The Stanwell House Hotel is a superb example of Georgian architecture, sympathetically restored to combine luxury, style and informal comfort.

The dining facilities are excellent. The Bistro and Bar are a group of rooms, truly Georgian, stunningly simple

The Stanwell House Hotel is ideally located for the New Forest and Lymington Marinas

Stanwell House Hotel
15 High Street, Lymington,
Hampshire SO41 9AA
Tel: 01590 677123

★★ Batch Country
Batch Lane, Lympsham BS24 0EX
☎ 01934-750371 **Fax** 01934-750501
Closed Christmas

Rural, peaceful and secluded, standing in its own grounds with panoramic views from all rooms. A short distance from the M5.
10 bedrs, all ensuite, ▥ ♀ ♪ ▦ 100 **P** 80 ⊞ Rest
Resid **SB** £42-£46 **DB** £32-£35 **HB** £275-£295 **L** £5.50
L ♥ **D** £14 **D** ♥ ✕ **LD** 20:30 **CC** MC Visa Amex DC
See advert under Weston-super-Mare

ENGLAND

LYNDHURST Hampshire   4A4
Pop. 3,000. London 84, M27 (jn 1) 3, Bournemouth 19, Lymington 8, Ringwood 14, Salisbury 19,
EC Wed **see** Church, 14th cent Queen's House
▨ New Forest Visitor Centre 01703-282269

★★★ ✦ Forest Lodge
Pikes Hill, Lyndhurst SO43 7AS
☎ 01703-283677 **Fax** 01703-283719
E-mail information@carehotels.co.uk
28 bedrs, all ensuite, ▥ ⚲ ▦ 100 **P** 50 ⊞ **SB** £65-£70 **DB** £110-£125 **HB** £345 **D** £21.50 ✕ **LD** 20:45
CC MC Visa Amex DC ▣ &
See advert on this page

★★★ Parkhill Country House ▦ ▦
Beaulieu Road, Lyndhurst SO43 7FZ
☎ 01703-282944 **Fax** 01703-283268
19 bedrs, all ensuite, ▥ ♪ ⚲ ▦ 65 **P** 73 ⊞ **DB** £110-£156 **HB** £385-£609 **L** £16 **D** £27 ✕ **LD** 21:00 **CC** MC
Visa Amex DC JCB ⊰ ▣

LYNMOUTH Devon   3O2
Minehead 16, London 184, Barnstaple 17, Ilfracombe 17, South Molton 20 **see** Valley of Rocks, Watersmeet, Glen Lyn, Doone Valley and Oare Church, Shelley's Cottage, Countisbury Church (16th cent), Exmoor, 16th cent Culbone Church - reputed smallest in England

★★★ Tors
Lynmouth EX35 6NA
📞 01598-753236 **Fax** 01598-752544
Closed Jan-Feb
35 bedrs, 33 ensuite, ⊬ 🖪 ⋕ 90 **P** 40 ⊞ ℂℂ MC Visa
Amex DC ⇃

★★ Bath
Sea Front, Lynmouth EX35 6EL
📞 01598-752238 **Fax** 01598-752544
Closed Nov-Feb
24 bedrs, all ensuite, ⊬ **P** 13 ⊞ **SB** £28.50-£38.50
DB £57-£77 **HB** £212-£280 **L** £8 **D** £16 ✕ **LD** 20:30
ℂℂ MC Visa Amex DC

LYNTON Devon   2C2
Lynmouth ½, London 185, Barnstaple 16,
Ilfracombe 16 **EC** Sat (win) 🖪 Town Hall, Lee Road
01598-752225

★★ Exmoor Sandpiper
Countisbury, Lynton EX35 6NE
📞 01598-741263 **Fax** 01598-741358
E-mail exmoorsandpiper@demon.co.uk
16 bedrs, all ensuite, 🗹 ⊬ **P** 70 ⊞ **SB** £46.10
DB £92.20 **HB** £290-£330 **L** £7.20 **L** 🍷 **D** £26.90 **D** 🍷
✕ **LD** 21:00 Restaurant closed L Mon-Sat ℂℂ MC
Visa

★★ Sandrock 🖥
Longmead, Lynton EX35 6DH
📞 01598-753307 **Fax** 01598-752665

Inviting hospitable hotel in sunny position
surrounded by Exmoor's stunning coastal scenery
and beauty spots. Ensuite rooms with modern
comforts. Own car park.
9 bedrs, 7 ensuite, ⊬ **P** 9 ⊞ **SB** £21.50-£24.50
DB £43-£49 **HB** £227.90-£264 **D** £14.50 **D** 🍷 ✕
LD 19:30 ℂℂ MC Visa Amex

★ Seawood 🖥
North Walk, Lynton EX35 6HJ
📞 01598-752272 **Fax** 01598-752272
Closed Nov-Mar

Elegant Victorian building nestling on wooded cliffs
overlooking the sea.
12 bedrs, all ensuite, 🗹 ⊬ **P** 12 No children under
12 ⊞ Rest Resid **SB** £27-£30 **DB** £54-£60 **HB** £250-
£290 **D** £13 ✕ **LD** 19:00

LYTHAM ST ANNES Lancashire   10B4
Pop. 40,100. Preston 14, London 224, Blackpool
4½ **EC** Wed **see** Parish Church, St Annes Pier,
Lifeboat Memorial, Motive Power Museum 🖪 290
Clifton Drive South 01253-725610

★★★★ Clifton Arms 🖥
West Beach, Lytham St Annes FY8 5QJ
📞 01253-739898 **Fax** 01253-730657
E-mail info@cliftonarms.demon.co.uk

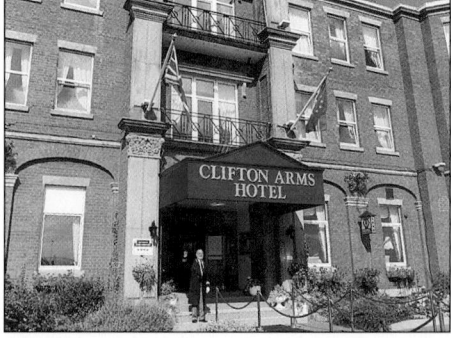

The historic Clifton Arms Hotel is situated
overlooking Lytham Green. The elegant decor and
surroundings create a stylish hotel whilst retaining
its reputation for friendly hospitality.
44 bedrs, all ensuite, 🗹 🖪 ⋕ 200 **P** 70 ⊞ **SB** £87.50-
£97.50 **DB** £108-£118 **L** £16.50 **L** 🍷 **D** £25 **D** 🍷 ✕
LD 22:00 ℂℂ MC Visa Amex DC ♿

★★★ Bedford
307-311 Clifton Drive South,
Lytham St Annes FY8 1HN
☎ 01253-724636 Fax 01253-729244
E-mail bedford@cyberscape.co.uk
36 bedrs, all ensuite, ▦ ✿ ⌗ ▣ ⁑ 150 **P** 25 ⊕
SB £39-£45 **DB** £65-£75 **HB** £245-£262.50 **L** £8 **L** ☛
D £15 **D** ☛ ✗ **LD** 20:30 **C** MC Visa Amex DC JCB ▥
▨ ㅤ
See advert on this page

★★★ Chadwick
South Promenade, Lytham St Annes FY8 1NP
☎ 01253-720061 Fax 01253-714455
E-mail chadwick-hotel.co.uk

The Chadwick is a family run award winning hotel
situated on the seafront. It is renowned for good
food, service and comfort. North West Tourist
Board, Silver "Best Small Hotel of the Year Award
1999."
75 bedrs, all ensuite, ▦ ♀ ✿ ▣ ⁑ 70 **P** 40 ⊕ Rest
Resid **SB** £40-£46 **DB** £60-£66 **HB** £278-£314 **L** £7.80
L ☛ **D** £16 **D** ☛ ✗ **LD** 20:30 **C** MC Visa Amex DC
JCB ▥ ▥ ▨ ㅤ

★★★ Fernlea
11-17 South Promenade,
Lytham St Annes FY8 1LU
☎ 01253-726726 Fax 01253-721561
100 bedrs, all ensuite, ▦ ▣ ⁑ 250 **P** 85 ⊕ Resid
SB £36-£39 **DB** £72-£78 **L** £11 **D** £15 ✗ **LD** 20:30
C MC Visa Amex ▥ ▥ ▥ ▥ ㅤ
See advert on this page

Facilities for the disabled

Hotels do their best to cater for disabled
visitors. However, it is advisable to contact
the hotel direct to ensure it can provide
particular requirement.

ENGLAND

★★ Lindum
63-67 South Promenade, Lytham St Annes FY8 1LZ
☎ 01253-721534 Fax 01253-721364

Seafront family run hotel situated on the main promenade, opposite all amenities and close to fine shops and golf courses. Renowned for its excellent food and friendly welcome.
78 bedrs, all ensuite, ⚲ ⊁ 🖃 ⠿ 70 **P** 20 ⊞ Rest Resid **SB** £28-£40 **DB** £50-£60 **HB** £250-£260 **L** £9 **D** £13.50 **D** ⬤ ✕ **LD** 19:00 Restaurant closed L Mon-Sat ⸨ MC Visa Amex DC JCB 🖼 🖾

MACCLESFIELD Cheshire 7E1
Pop. 48,200. Leek 12, London 167, Altrincham 14, Buxton 11, Congleton 8, Knutsford 11, Stockport 11 **EC** Wed **MD** Daily **see** Museum (silk industry), Glacial Stone, Market Stone, St Michael's Church, Unitarian Chapel 🛈 Town Hall, Market Place 01625-504114

★★★★ ✤ Shrigley Hall
Shrigley Park, Pott Shrigley,
Macclesfield SK10 5SB
☎ 01625-575757 Fax 01625-573323

PARAMOUNT
HOTEL·GROUP

A Regency country house hotel, restored to its former elegance, set in 262 acres of parkland.
150 bedrs, all ensuite, 🎿 ♀ ⚲ ⊁ 🖃 ⠿ 350 **P** 300 ⊞ **SB** £115 **DB** £145 **D** ⬤ ✕ **LD** 21:30 Restaurant closed L Sat and Sun ⸨ MC Visa Amex DC 🖾🖾🖼🖻🖾🖾🖾 ♿

MADELEY Staffordshire 7E1
Pop. 3,500. Newcastle-under-Lyme 5, London 154, Market Drayton 11, Nantwich 11, Whitchurch 16

★★ Wheatsheaf Inn at Onneley
Barhill Road, Madeley CW3 9QF
☎ 01782-751581 Fax 01782-751499
5 bedrs, all ensuite, ⊁ ⠿ 60 **P** 150 ⊞ ⸨ MC Visa Amex DC

MAIDENHEAD Berkshire 4C2
Pop. 60,500. Slough 6, London 26, A308(M) 1½, Henley-on-Thames 8½, High Wycombe 9½, Reading 12, Windsor 6½ **EC** Thu **MD** Fri, Sat **see** Brunel's viaduct, Oldfield House 🛈 Library, St Ives Road 01628-781110

★★★★ Fredrick's ♖ ♖ ♖
Blue Ribbon Hotel
Shoppenhangers Road, SL6 2PZ
☎ 01628-581000 Fax 01628-771054
E-mail reservations@fredericks-hotel.co.uk
Closed 24-31 Dec

The Lösel family continues to maintain the smooth operation of this excellent hotel and its renowned restaurant, combining a guaranteed warm, friendly hospitality and personal service with the highest standards of professionalism.
37 bedrs, all ensuite, ⚲ ⠿ 120 **P** 90 ⊞ **SB** £168 **DB** £210 **L** £25.50 **L** ⬤ **D** £35.50 ✕ **LD** 21:45 Restaurant closed L Sat ⸨ MC Visa Amex DC JCB ♿

★★★★ Monkey Island ♖ ♖
Bray-on-Thames, Maidenhead SL6 2EE
☎ 01628-623400 Fax 01628-784732
E-mail monkeyisland@btconnect.com
Closed 26 Dec-15 Jan
26 bedrs, all ensuite, ⠿ 150 **P** 100 ⊞ **SB** £109-£112 **DB** £159-£174 **L** £21 **D** £28 **D** ⬤ ✕ **LD** 21:30 Restaurant closed L Sat ⸨ MC Visa Amex DC 🖾 🖾
See advert on opposite page

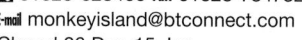

★★★ ✦ Thames
Ray Mead Road, Maidenhead SL8 8NR
☎ 01628-628721 **Fax** 01628-773921
Closed 23 Dec-2 Jan

Recently refurbished 3 star riverside hotel with terrace bar overlooking the river. Offering a superb choice of bar food and a carvery restaurant. Wedding and conference facilities. Special weekend rates.
33 bedrs, all ensuite, ➤ ⠿ 65 **P** 45 ⊞ **SB** £60-£92.50 **DB** £75-£110 **L** ⬤ **D** £18 **D** ⬤ ✕ **LD** 21:30 Restaurant closed L Mon-Sat & D Sun ⲥ MC Visa Amex DC

MAIDSTONE Kent   5E3
Pop. 137,600. M20 (jn 6) 2, London 36, Ashford 18, Canterbury 27, Tenterden 18, Tonbridge 13 **EC** Wed **MD** Mon, Tue **see** Archbishop Palace 🖪 The Gatehouse, Old Palace Gardens 01622-673581

★★★ Russell
136 Boxley Road, Maidstone ME14 2AE
☎ 01622-692221 **Fax** 01622-762084
42 bedrs, all ensuite, 🛿 ⠿ 300 **P** 100 ⊞ ⲥ MC Visa Amex DC ♿

★★ Grangemoor
St Michaels Road, Maidstone ME16 8BS
☎ 01622-677623 **Fax** 01622-678246
Closed 25-30 Dec
51 bedrs, all ensuite, 🛿 ➤ ⠿ 150 **P** 70 ⊞ **SB** £40-£48 **DB** £50-£52 **L** £10 **D** £14.50 **D** ⬤ ✕ **LD** 21:30 ⲥ MC Visa

Roadchef Lodge Lodge
Maidstone Motorway Service Area, Junction 8 M20, Hollingbourne ME17 1SS
☎ 01622-631100 **Fax** 01622-739535
Closed 25 Dec, 1 Jan
58 bedrs, all ensuite, ⠿ 20 **P** 100 **Room** £49.95 ⲥ MC Visa Amex DC ♿

ENGLAND

MALMESBURY Wiltshire 3F1
Pop. 4,150. Swindon 15, London 92, M4 (jn 17) 5½, Bath 24, Bristol 26, Chippenham 9, Cirencester 11, Tetbury 4½ **EC** Thu see Abbey, Market Cross, St John's Almshouses, Old Bell Museum, Athelston Museum (local history) **i** Town Hall, Market Lane 01666-823748

★★★ Knoll House 🛏 🛏
Swindon Road, Malmesbury SN16 9LU
📞 01666-823114 **Fax** 01666-823897

12 miles from Swindon and ideally located for Bath, Cheltenham, the Cotswolds, Westonbirt Arboretum, Castle Combe. Two acres of attractive gardens, outdoor heated pool, croquet lawn, log fires, excellent cuisine.
22 bedrs, all ensuite, ♀ ♬ ✝ ⅲ 50 **P** 40 ⊕ **SB** £60 **DB** £82.50 **L** ● **D** £20 ✕ **LD** 21:30 ℂℂ MC Visa Amex ⊰ ♿

★★★ Old Bell
Abbey Row, Malmesbury SN16 0AG
📞 01666-822344 **Fax** 01666-825145
31 bedrs, all ensuite, ✝ ⅲ 45 **P** 30 ⊕ ℂℂ MC Visa Amex DC JCB ♿

★★★ Whatley Manor 🛏
Easton Grey, Malmesbury SN16 0RB
📞 01666-822888 **Fax** 01666-826120

Between Bath and the Cotswolds, convenient to M4 and M5, Whatley Manor is set in the heart of

unspoilt countryside in traditional surroundings. Fine food, unobtrusive service and relaxed atmosphere.
29 bedrs, all ensuite, ᙡ ♬ ✝ ⅲ 30 **P** 60 ⊕ Rest Resid **SB** £82-£92 **DB** £96-£132 **L** £16 **L** ● **D** £29 **D** ● ✕ **LD** 21:00 ℂℂ MC Visa Amex DC ⊰ 🖼🖼🖼🖼

★★ Mayfield House 🛏
Crudwell, Malmesbury SN16 9EW
📞 01666-577409 **Fax** 01666-577977
23 bedrs, all ensuite, ✝ ⅲ 30 **P** 40 ⊕ Rest Resid **SB** £46-£48 **DB** £69-£72 **HB** £222 **L** £5.95 **L** ● **D** £16 **D** ● ✕ **LD** 21:00 ℂℂ MC Visa Amex DC JCB

MALTON North Yorkshire 11E3
Pop. 4,500. Beverley 26, London 205, Bridlington 28, Helmsley 16, Pickering 8, Scarborough 24, Thirsk 25, York 17 **EC** Thu **MD** Tue, Fri, Sat see Relic of Gilbertine Priory, Town Hall, 17th cent Malton Lodge, St Michael's Church, Roman Museum, Old Malton Priory, Flamingo Land Zoo **i** 58 Market Place 01653-600048

★★★ Burythorpe House 🛏 🛏
Burythorpe, Malton YO17 9LB
📞 01653-658200 **Fax** 01653-658204
16 bedrs, all ensuite, ᙡ ✝ ⅲ 18 **P** 50 ⊕ ⊕ Resid **SB** £45 **DB** £58-£96 **L** £11.95 **L** ● **D** £18 **D** ● ✕ **LD** 21:30 ℂℂ MC Visa 🖼🖼🖼🖼🖼 ♿

★★★ Green Man
15 Market Street, Malton YO17 0LY
📞 01653-600370 **Fax** 01653-696006

A classic coaching inn with an excellent reputation for comfort and hospitality. Situated in the heart of a bustling market town, the Green Man offers traditional Yorkshire food and fine ales.
24 bedrs, all ensuite, ✝ ⅲ 100 **P** 40 ⊕ **SB** £35-£55 **DB** £70-£99 **HB** £300 **L** £10.50 **D** £17.50 ✕ **LD** 21:15 ℂℂ MC Visa Amex DC

★★ Talbot

Yorkersgate, Malton YO17 0AA
☎ 01653-694031 **Fax** 01653-693355

Recently totally refurbished elegant Georgian coaching inn with 31 pretty ensuite bedrooms. Excellent food and friendly service. Near to York, Castle Howard, Flamingo Land and the North York Moors National Park. Ample parking.
31 bedrs, all ensuite, ⁴ ✝ ⋕ 70 **P** 30 ⊞ **SB** £42.50-£52.50 **DB** £85-£105 **HB** £200-£250 **L** £9.95 **D** £17.50 ✕ **LD** 21:00 **CC** MC Visa Amex DC

★ Wentworth Arms

Town Street, Malton YO17 0HD
☎ 01653-692618
Closed Christmas
5 bedrs, 4 ensuite, ⁴ **P** 30 No children ⊞ **SB** £23 **DB** £46 **L** £6 **D** £8 ✕ **LD** 21:00 **CC** MC Visa Amex JCB

MALVERN Worcestershire	7E4

Pop. 30,200. Tewkesbury 13, London 118, Hereford 19, Ledbury 7, Worcester 8 **EC** Wed **MD** Fri *see* College, Priory Church and Gateway, St Anne's Well, Priory remains and St Wulstan's Church, Little Malvern (Priory and grave of Sir Edward Elgar), Malvern Hills (views) 🖪 Winter Gardens, Grange Road 01684-892289

★★★ Colwall Park

Colwall, Great Malvern WR13 6QG
☎ 01684-540206 **Fax** 01684-540847
E-mail colwallparkhotel@hotmail.com
24 bedrs, all ensuite, ♀ ♪ ✝ ⋕ 180 **P** 40 ⊞
SB £59.50-£75 **DB** £90-£115 **HB** £416.50-£556.50
L £12 **D** £22.50 ✕ **LD** 21:00 **CC** MC Visa Amex DC JCB

★★ Great Malvern

Graham Road, Great Malvern WR14 2HN
☎ 01684-563411 **Fax** 01684-560514
Closed Christmas
14 bedrs, 13 ensuite, ♪ ☰ ⋕ 60 **P** 9 ⊞ **SB** £55
DB £80 **L** £6 **L** ● **D** £11.50 **D** ● ✕ **LD** 21:00
Restaurant closed L & D Sun **CC** MC Visa Amex DC ঙ

★★ Holdfast Cottage 🎴 🎴

Little Malvern, Malvern WR13 6NA
☎ 01684-310288 **Fax** 01684-311117
E-mail holdcothot@aol.com
Closed Christmas

Pretty, wisteria-covered, oak-beamed country house hotel set in gardens and private woodland. Highly acclaimed restaurant with menu that changes nightly. Personal service and peace assured.
8 bedrs, all ensuite, ✝ ⋕ 12 **P** 16 ⊞ Rest Resid
SB £45-£48 **DB** £82-£90 **HB** £336-£360 **D** £22 ✕
LD 20:45 Restaurant closed D Sun **CC** MC Visa

★★ Malvern Hills

Wynds Point, Malvern WR13 6DW
☎ 01684-540690 **Fax** 01684-540327
E-mail malhilhotl@aol.com

A character bedroomed country house hotel set amidst the tranquillity of the Malvern Hills, with direct access for walking. Excellent cuisine and real ales. Pets welcome.
15 bedrs, all ensuite, ⁴ ♪ ✝ ⋕ 50 **P** 40 ⊞ **SB** £34-£40 **DB** £64-£75 **HB** £295-£325 **L** £12.50 **L** ●
D £19.50 **D** ● ✕ **LD** 21:00 **CC** MC Visa Amex DC

★★ ✤ Mount Pleasant
Belle Vue Terrace, Great Malvern WR14 4PZ
☎ 01684-561837 **Fax** 01684-569968
Closed 25-26 Dec

Elegant Georgian building (c.1730) with terraced gardens. Ideally located near shops and theatre, yet with direct footpath to hills. Stunning views. Emphasis on good food and comfort.
15 bedrs, 14 ensuite, ⊞ 80 **P** 20 ⊕ **SB** £52-£56 **DB** £74-£85 **HB** £265-£325 **L** £10.50 **L** ✈ **D** £16.75 **D** ✈ ✕ **LD** 21:30 **CC** MC Visa Amex DC

★★ ✤ Thornbury House
Avenue Road, Great Malvern WR14 3AR
☎ 01684-572278 **Fax** 01684-577042

Situated in a peaceful tree lined avenue close to the town centre, Winter Gardens and railway station, the hotel's aim is to accommodate its guests in a relaxed and friendly atmosphere with comfortable rooms and fine dining.
17 bedrs, 14 ensuite, ④ ✈ **P** 10 ⊕ Rest Resid **SB** £45 **DB** £65 **HB** £246 **D** £18 **D** ✈ ✕ **LD** 21:00 **CC** MC Visa Amex DC JCB

MALVERN WELLS Worcestershire   7E4

★★★ Cottage in the Wood
Holywell Road, Malvern Wells WR14 4LG
☎ 01684-575859 **Fax** 01684-560662
20 bedrs, all ensuite, ④ ✈ ⊞ 14 **P** 45 ⊕ Rest Resid **SB** £72-£82 **DB** £89.50-£139 **HB** £348-£552 **L** £13.95 **D** £27 ✕ **LD** 21:00 **CC** MC Visa Amex

MANCHESTER Greater Manchester   10C4
See also ALTRINCHAM, ASHTON-UNDER-LYNE and STOCKPORT
Pop. 450,100. Stockport 6, London 184, M602 6, Altrincham 8, Bolton 11, Bury 8, Oldham 7, Rochdale 10, Walkden 7, Warrington 16 **see** Cathedral, John Ryland's Library, City Art Gallery, Museum, Heaton Hall, Platt Hall Gallery of English Costume, Museum of Science and Technology
☑ Town Hall, Lloyd Street. 0161-234 3157

★★★★ Copthorne
Clippers Quay, Salford Quays, Manchester M5 2XP
☎ 0161-873 7321 **Fax** 0161-873 7318
E-mail manchester@mill-cop.com
166 bedrs, all ensuite, ♀ ☱ ⊞ 150 **P** 120 ⊕
Room £145-£170 **L** £13 **L** ✈ **D** £32.50 **D** ✈ ✕ **LD** 22:15 **CC** MC Visa Amex DC ⊠ ⊞ ⊞ ⅙

★★★★ Le Meridien Victoria & Albert ⊞ ⊞
Water Street, Manchester M3 4JQ
☎ 0161-832 1188 **Fax** 0161-834 2484
E-mail vameridien@aol.com

Le **MERIDIEN**

Built as a warehouse in 1843 and lovingly restored as a luxurious hotel, Le Meridien Victoria and Albert stands on the banks of the Irwell. The warmth of your welcome makes this beautiful hotel a relaxing home from home.
156 bedrs, all ensuite, ☱ ⊞ 350 **P** 100 ⊕ **SB** £90-£169 **DB** £99-£175 **D** £34 ✕ **LD** 22:00 **CC** MC Visa Amex DC ⊞ ⊞ ⅙
See advert on opposite page

★★★★ Palace
Oxford Street, Manchester M60 7HA
☎ 0161-288 1111 **Fax** 0161-288 2222
E-mail palace.prinpalhotels.co.uk
250 bedrs, all ensuite, ♀ ⌀ ☱ ⊞ 850
⊕ **Room** £129 **L** ✈ **D** ✈ Restaurant
closed L Sat, Sun
CC MC Visa Amex DC ⅙

PH
PRINCIPAL
H O T E L S

★★★ ✤ Novotel Manchester
Worsley Brow, Manchester M28 4YA
☎ 0161-799 3535 **Fax** 0161-703 8207
E-mail h0807@accor-hotels.com
119 bedrs, all ensuite, ♪ ⅋ 🖭 ⠿ 240 **P** 135 ⊞
DB £55-£84 **L** £13.50 **L** 🍴 **D** £16 **D** 🍴 ✗ **LD** 0:00
CC MC Visa Amex DC JCB ⅂ 🖼 ⅋

★★★ Posthouse   **Posthouse**
Palatine Road, Northenden, M22 4FH
☎ 0161-998 7090 **Fax** 0161-946 0139
Closed 22 Dec-4 Jan
190 bedrs, all ensuite, ⅋ 🖭 ⠿ 150 **P** 200 ⊞ **SB** £67-
£99 **DB** £77-£109 **L** £12.50 **D** £18 ✗ **LD** 22:30
Restaurant closed L Sat **CC** MC Visa Amex DC JCB

★★★ Stanneylands ⅂ ⅂ ⅂
Stanneylands Road, Wilmslow SK9 4EY
☎ 01625-525225 **Fax** 01625-537282
E-mail gordon.beech@the-stanneylands-hotel.co.uk

The Stanneylands Hotel is a strikingly handsome
house set in beautiful gardens, the oak-panelled
dining room serving outstanding cuisine and fine
wines.
31 bedrs, all ensuite, ④ ⠿ 100 **P** 80 ⊞ **SB** £54.50-
£97 **DB** £85.50-£115 **L** £13.50 **D** £28 ✗ **LD** 22:00
Restaurant closed D Sun (cold buffet) **CC** MC Visa
Amex DC ⅋

★★★ ✤ Trafford Hall
23 Talbot Road, Old Trafford, Manchester M16 0PE
☎ 0161-848 7791 **Fax** 0161-848 0219
34 bedrs, all ensuite, ④ ⅋ ⠿ 40 **P** 65 ⊞ **SB** £39.50-
£44.50 **DB** £49.50-£66.50 **L** 🍴 **D** £12.50 **D** 🍴 ✗
LD 21:30 Restaurant closed D Fri, Sat **CC** MC Visa
Amex DC

★★★ ✤ Waterside Hotel & Leisure Club
Wilmslow Road, Didsbury, Manchester M20 0PW
☎ 0161-445 0225 **Fax** 0161-446 2090
E-mail office@watersidehotel.co.uk
46 bedrs, all ensuite, ♀ ♪ ⠿ 300 **P** 200 ⊞ **SB** £75-
£80 **DB** £89-£94 **L** £10.95 **L** 🍴 **D** £18 **D** 🍴 ✗ **LD** 21:30
Restaurant closed D Sun **CC** MC Visa Amex DC 🖭 🖼
🖭 🖾

★★★ Willow Bank
340/342 Wilmslow Road, Fallowfield,
Manchester M14 6AF
☎ 0161-224 0461 **Fax** 0161-257 2561

A former Edwardian private house with modern extensions.
116 bedrs, all ensuite, ♪ ⫶ 50 **P** 118 ⊞ Rest Resid
SB £52 **DB** £62 **L** £7 **L** ♥ **D** £11 **D** ♥ ✕ **LD** 22:00 《 MC Visa Amex DC
See advert on previous page

★★ Albany ⫸
21 Albany Road, Chorlton, Manchester M21 0AY
☎ 0161-881 6774 **Fax** 0161-862 9405

Refered to as 'the hidden gem' of Manchester hotels. Conveniently situated only 10 minutes from the centre and airport and offering individually styled fully-fitted quality accommodation to chose from.
15 bedrs, all ensuite, ⫶ ⫶ 30 **P** 6 ⊞ Rest Resid
SB £49.50-£79.50 **DB** £59.50-£89.50 **HB** £399.75 **L** £10
L ♥ **D** £13.95 **D** ♥ ✕ **LD** 21:30 Restaurant closed L Sun 《 MC Visa DC

★★ Comfort Inn
Hyde Road, Birch Street, M12 5NT
☎ 0161-220 8700 **Fax** 0161-220 8848
E-mail admin@gb615.u-net.com

Purpose built hotel with all rooms ensuite and well equipped and competitive room rates. Large car park. Facilities for meetings and conferences.
90 bedrs, all ensuite, ♀ ⫶ ⫶ 100 **P** 100 ⊞
SB £53.50-£61 **DB** £60-£68 **L** £9.75 **L** ♥ **D** £9.75 **D** ♥
✕ **LD** 21:30 Restaurant closed L Sun 《 MC Visa Amex DC ⊞ ৬

★★ ✦ Crescent Gate
Park Crescent, Victoria Park, Manchester M14 5RE
☎ 0161-224 0672 **Fax** 0161-257 2822
E-mail cgh@dial.pipex.com
Closed Christmas
24 bedrs, 20 ensuite, ⫶ **P** 14 ⊞ Rest Resid 《 MC Visa Amex DC JCB

★★ Elm Grange ⫸
561 Wilmslow Road, Withington, Manchester
☎ 0161-445 3336 **Fax** 0161-445 3336

Situated in the pleasant suburban area of Didsbury, South Manchester, only minutes away from the motorway junctions of M56 and M63. Ideal for visitors to the university, various polytechnic colleges, hospitals, shopping centres, restaurants and theatres.
27 bedrs, 18 ensuite, **P** 30 ⊞ Rest Resid **SB** £42.50-£45 **DB** £58-£64 **HB** £315-£330 **L** ♥ **D** £13 ✕ **LD** 21:00 Restaurant closed D Sun 《 MC Visa Amex ৬

ENGLAND

★ ✤ Baron
116 Palatine Road, West Didsbury, M20 9ZA
☎ 0161-434 3688 **Fax** 01203-520680
16 bedrs, all ensuite, ⊞ 20 **P** 16 No children under
8 ⊞ Rest Resid ℂℂ MC Visa

Jurys Manchester Awaiting Inspection
56 Great Bridgewater Street, Manchester
☎ 0161-953 8888
E-mail bookings@jurys.com
Closed Dec 24-26th
265 bedrs, all ensuite, ♀ ♪ ⊠ 🖃 ⊞ 50 ⊞ **SB** £62-
£67 **DB** £69-£75 **L** 🍵 **D** £15.50 **D** 🍷 ✗ **LD** 21.30
ℂℂ MC Visa Amex DC ♿

Swallow Four Seasons
Awaiting Inspection
Hale Road, Hale Barns,
Altrincham WA15 8XW
☎ 0161-904 0301 **Fax** 0161-980 1787
E-mail reservations@fourseasonshotels.co.uk

SWALLOW
HOTELS

A modern hotel, excellently situated close to
junction 6 of the M56. The hotel has a restaurant,
Irish bar, cocktail bar, lounge with a new leisure
club opening in October 1999.
147 bedrs, all ensuite, ④ ♪ 🖃 ⊞ 180 **P** 360 ⊞
SB £54.50-£109.50 **DB** £69.50-£119.50 **L** £18.95
L 🍷 **D** £20.95 **D** 🍷 ✗ **LD** 22:30 Restaurant
closed L Sat ℂℂ MC Visa Amex DC 🖃 🖾 🖾

Campanile Manchester Lodge
55 Ordsall Lane, Regent Road, M5 4RS
☎ 0161-833 1845 **Fax** 0161-833 1847

hotel
grill
Campanile

Campanile hotels offer comfortable and convenient
budget accommodation and a traditional French
style Bistro providing freshly cooked food for
breakfast, lunch and dinner. All rooms ensuite with
tea/coffee making facilities, DDT and TV with Sky
channels.
105 bedrs, all ensuite, 🛏 ⊞ 30 **P** 105 ⊞ Rest Resid
ℂℂ MC Visa Amex DC ♿

MANCHESTER AIRPORT Gtr Manchester   10C4
See also WILMSLOW
Congleton 16, London 177, M56 (jn 5) ½,
Altrincham 5, Macclesfield 12, Manchester 9½,
Stockport 6½ 🅸 Arrivals Hall 0161-436 3344

★★★★ Belfry 🍴 🍴
Stanley Road, Handforth SK9 3LD
☎ 0161-437 0511 **Fax** 0161-499 0597
E-mail andrew.beech@thebelfryhotel.co.uk
Closed 26-27 Dec
80 bedrs, all ensuite, 🖃 ⊞ 180 **P** 150 ⊞ ℂℂ MC Visa
Amex DC ♿

★★★ Posthouse   **Posthouse**
Ringway Road, Wythenshawe,
Manchester Airport M90 3NS
☎ 0161-437 5811 **Fax** 0161-436 2340
290 bedrs, all ensuite, ♪ 🛏 🖃 ⊞ 80 **P** 300 ⊞
SB £79-£125 **DB** £93-£135 **L** £12.95 **L** 🍷 **D** £17.95
D 🍷 ✗ **LD** 22:00 Restaurant closed L Sat ℂℂ MC Visa
Amex DC JCB 🖃 🖾 🖾 ♿

MARCH Cambridgeshire   9D3
Pop. 15,400. Cambridge 30, London 85, Ely 18,
Huntingdon 23, Peterborough 16, Wisbech 11
EC Tue **MD** Wed, Sat

★★ Olde Griffin Inn
High Street, March PE15 9JS
☎ 01354-652517 **Fax** 01354-650086
20 bedrs, 19 ensuite, ④ ⊞ 100 **P** 30 ⊞ **SB** £38.50-
£42.50 **DB** £55-£60 **L** £7.50 **L** 🍷 **D** £9.50 **D** 🍷 ✗
LD 21:30 Restaurant closed D Mon-Tue ℂℂ MC Visa
Amex DC ♿

MARKET DRAYTON Shropshire   7E2
Pop. 9,500. Newport 11, London 153, Nantwich 14,
Newcastle-under-Lyme 13, Shrewsbury 19,
Whitchurch 13 **EC** Thu **MD** Wed **see** Parish Church
(Norman west door), Grammar School (assoc
Robert Clive) 🅸 49 Cheshire Street 01630-652139

★★★ Goldstone Hall
Goldstone, Market Drayton TF9 2NA
☎ 01630-661202 **Fax** 01630-661585

Seventeenth century manor where even 'The Times' thinks the food is sublime and Derek Cooper enthused "the feast which was turning into a banquet went on ....."
8 bedrs, all ensuite, 4 ♀ ⅲ 60 **P** 60 ⊟ Resid **SB** £65 **DB** £87.50 **L** £20 **D** £30 ✕ **LD** 22:30 **CC** MC Visa Amex DC JCB ▦

MARKET HARBOROUGH Leicestershire   8B3
Pop. 16,300. Northampton 17, London 82, Coventry 28, Kettering 11, Leicester 15, Melton Mowbray 22 **EC** Wed **MD** Tue, Sat **i** Library, Adam and Eve Street 01858-468106

★★ Sun Inn ⌾
Main Street, Marston Trussell LE16 9TY
☎ 01858-465531 **Fax** 01858-433155

Fully refurbished 17th century inn set in delightful countryside on the Leicestershire/Northamptonshire border. 20 ensuite rooms. Conference and function facilities with private bar. Excellent cuisine.
20 bedrs, all ensuite, 4 ↑ ⅲ 60 **P** 50 ⊟ **SB** £47.50 **DB** £60 **L** £15 **D** £15 ✕ **LD** 21:30 **CC** MC Visa Amex ▧ ☖

MARLBOROUGH Wiltshire   4A2
Pop. 7,000. Newbury 19, London 72, M4 (jn 15) 8, Andover 21, Chippenham 18, Devizes 14, Farringdon 21, Swindon 11 **EC** Wed **MD** Wed, Sat **i** Car Park, George Lane 01672-513989

★★★ Castle & Ball   Heritage HOTELS
High Street, Marlborough SN8 1LZ
☎ 01672-515201 **Fax** 01672-515895
34 bedrs, all ensuite, 4 ↑ ⅲ 45 **P** 48 ⊟ **CC** MC Visa Amex DC

★★★ ✦ Ivy House
Marlborough SN8 1HJ
☎ 01672-515333 **Fax** 01672-515338

Overlooking Marlborough's famous High Street, this hotel combines the luxuries of 3 star accommodation, first class food and friendly, efficient service with the character of a Listed Georgian building.
30 bedrs, all ensuite, ⅲ 100 **P** 45 ⊟ **SB** £65-£75 **DB** £79-£99 **L** £9.50 **D** £19 ✕ **LD** 21:30 **CC** MC Visa Amex

---

MARLOW Buckinghamshire   4C2
Pop. 15,000. Slough 11, London 31, M40 (jn 4) 3, Henley-on-Thames 7½, High Wycombe 4½, Oxford 27, Reading 13 **EC** Wed **i** Court Garden, Pound Lane 01628-483597

★★★★ Compleat Angler ⌾ ⌾   Heritage HOTELS
Marlow Bridge, Marlow SL7 1RG
☎ 01628-484444 **Fax** 01628-486388
65 bedrs, all ensuite, 4 ↑ ☰ ⅲ 100 **P** 100 ⊟ **SB** £148 **DB** £187 **L** £19 **D** £34.50 ✕ **LD** 22:00 **CC** MC Visa Amex DC JCB ▧ ▨ ☖

★★★★ Danesfield House
Henley Road, Marlow SL7 2EY
☎ 01628-891010 **Fax** 01628-890408

ENGLAND

Built at the turn of the century, the hotel stands in 65 acres of grounds overlooking the River Thames, with spectacular views.
87 bedrs, all ensuite, ▦ ✗ ▣ ⁝⁝⁝ 100 **P** 90 ⌁ **SB** £145 **DB** £175 **L** £24.50 **D** £35.50 ✗ **LD** 22:00 **CC** MC Visa Amex DC JCB ⋩ ▨ ▨ ৬

In the picturesque village of Mawdesley, yet within easy reach of M6 motorway (jn 27). Its peaceful setting will be appreciated by business people and pleasure travellers alike.
56 bedrs, all ensuite, ▦ ♀ ✗ ⁝⁝⁝ 50 **P** 150 ⌁ **SB** £45-£50 **DB** £55-£60 **L** £10.50 **L** ▰ **D** £10.50 **D** ▰ ✗ **LD** 22:00 **CC** MC Visa Amex DC ▣ ▨ ▨ ৬

MATLOCK Derbyshire   7F1
Pop. 19,600. Derby 18, London 144, Ashbourne 13, Buxton 20, Chesterfield 10 **EC** Thu **MD** Tue, Fri **see** High Tor (673ft), Hall Leys Park, Riber Castle, Fauna Reserve, Artists Corner

★★★ New Bath   𝓗𝓮𝓻𝓲𝓽𝓪𝓰𝓮
                                                   HOTELS
New Bath Road,
Matlock Bath DE4 3PX
☎ 01629-583275 **Fax** 01629-580268
55 bedrs, all ensuite, ▦ ⊷ ⁝⁝⁝ 180 **P** 200 ⌁ **SB** £80 **DB** £100 **L** £10.95 **L** ▰ **D** £19.95 **D** ▰ ✗ **LD** 21:30 Restaurant closed L Sat **CC** MC Visa Amex DC JCB ▨ ⋩ ▨ ▨

★★★ Riber Hall
Matlock DE4 5JU
☎ 01629-582795 **Fax** 01629-580475
E-mail info@riber-hall.co.uk
14 bedrs, all ensuite, ▦ ♀ ✗ ⊷ ⁝⁝⁝ 20 **P** 50 No children under 10 ⌁ Resid **SB** £92.50-£107 **DB** £118.50-£162 **L** £13 **L** ▰ **D** £27 **D** ▰ ✗ **LD** 21:30 **CC** MC Visa Amex DC JCB ▨

MAWDESLEY Lancashire   10B4
Ormskirk 7, London 210, M6 (jn 27) 6, Chorley 8, Preston 12, Southport 11 **see** Rufford Old Hall

★★★ Mawdesley
Hall Lane, Mawdesley, Ormskirk L40 2QZ
☎ 01704-822552 **Fax** 01704-822096
E-mail mawdesleyh@aol.com
Closed 25-26 Dec

MELKSHAM Wiltshire   3F1
Pop. 10,000. Marlborough 20, London 93, Bath 12, Chippenham 7, Devizes 7½, Frome 14, Radstock 17, Warminster 13 **EC** Wed **MD** Sat **see** Parish Church, Georgian houses, Lacock Abbey 3m N (NT)
🄸 Round House, Church Street 01225-707424

★★ Conigre Farm
Semington Road, Melksham SN12 6BZ
☎ 01225-702229 **Fax** 01225 707392
8 bedrs, all ensuite, ▦ ♀ ⊷ ⁝⁝⁝ 30 **P** 14 ⌁ Rest Resid **SB** £43 **DB** £62 **HB** £277 **L** ▰ **D** £14 **D** ▰ ✗ **LD** 21:45 Restaurant closed L Mon-Tue **CC** MC Visa ৬

★★ Shaw Country
Bath Road, Shaw, Melksham SN12 8EF
☎ 01225-702836 **Fax** 01225-790275
E-mail shawcountryhotel@ukbusiness.com
Closed 26-28 Dec
13 bedrs, all ensuite, ▦ ⊷ ⁝⁝⁝ 30 **P** 40 ⌁ **SB** £44 **DB** £65 **L** £12.50 **L** ▰ **D** £12.50 ✗ **LD** 21:00 **CC** MC Visa Amex DC JCB

MELTON MOWBRAY Leicestershire   8B3
Pop. 23,600. Kettering 29, London 104, Grantham 16, Leicester 15, Loughborough 15, Nottingham 18, Stamford 20 **EC** Thu **MD** Tue, Sat **see** Church (13th cent enlarged 1550), 17th cent Bede House, Anne of Cleves House 🄸 Carnegie Museum, Thorpe End 01664-480992

★★★★ Stapleford Park ⌂ ⌂ ⌂
Blue Ribbon Hotel
Stapleford, Melton Mowbray LE14 2EF
☎ 01572-787522 **Fax** 01572-787651
E-mail amt@stapleford.co.uk

Neither words nor pictures can adequately describe this most imposing of Grade I Listed 15th-18th century stately home, set in 500 acres of parkland with a lake.
51 bedrs, all ensuite, ▥ ♥ ☎ ☷ 200 **P** 100 ⊕
SB £193.87 **DB** £193.87 **L** £12.50 **L** ♥ **D** £39.50 **D** ♥
✕ **LD** 21:45 **CC** MC Visa Amex DC ▣ ▣ ▣ ▣ ▣ ▣ ▣ ▣ ▣ ⟪

★★★ Sysonby Knoll
Asfordby Road, Melton Mowbray LE13 0HP
☎ 01664-563563 **Fax** 01664-410364
E-mail sysonbyknoll@btinternet.com
Closed Christmas-New Year

Privately owned hotel in grounds of 4 acres with river frontage. Our lively restaurant is locally popular and our reputation for good food and exceptional hospitality has given us a loyal following of regular guests.
24 bedrs, all ensuite, ▥ ♪ ♥ ☷ 24 **P** 50 ⊕ Rest
Resid **SB** £42.50-£59 **DB** £59-£75 **L** £7 ♥ **D** £13.25
✕ **LD** 21:00 Restaurant closed L Sat **CC** MC Visa
Amex DC JCB ⌕ ▣ ⟪

★★ Quorn Lodge
46 Asfordby Road, Melton Mowbray LE13 0HR
☎ 01664-566660 **Fax** 01664-480660

An original hunting lodge with luxury ensuite bedrooms. Excellent food and a good wine list are offered in the delightful restaurant overlooking the garden. A warm welcome assured.
19 bedrs, all ensuite, ▥ ☷ 85 **P** 33 ⊕ Rest Resid
SB £39.50-£49.50 **DB** £55-£75 **L** £9 **D** £15.75 ✕
LD 21:00 Restaurant closed D Sun, L Mon **CC** MC
Visa Amex JCB ⟪

MIDDLE WALLOP Hampshire　　　　　4A3
Andover 7, London 72, Amesbury 10, Salisbury 12, Stockbridge 5½

★★★ Fifehead Manor
Middle Wallop, Salisbury SO20 8EG
☎ 01264-781565 **Fax** 01264-781400
17 bedrs, all ensuite, ♥ ☷ 30 **P** 30 ⊕ **SB** £75-£90
DB £110-£140 **L** £17.50 **L** ♥ **D** £25 **D** ♥ ✕ **LD** 21:30
CC MC Visa Amex ⟪
See advert on opposite page

MIDDLESBROUGH Cleveland　　　　11D2
See also CRATHORNE
Pop. 143,000. Stockton 4, London 247, Helmsley 28, Pickering 38, Sunderland 27, Whitby 30
MD Daily **see** Municipal Art Gallery, Dorman Museum, Parks, Bridges, RC Cathedral, Ormesby Hall 3m SE, Newham Grange (farm museum), Captain Cook's Birthplace Museum, Preston Hall Museum and Stockton Transport Museum (4m W) ▣ 51 Corporation Road 01642-243425

★★★ Posthouse　　　　　**Posthouse**
Low Lane, Stainton Village,
Middlesbrough TS17 9LW
☎ 01642-591213 **Fax** 01642-594989
135 bedrs, all ensuite, ♥ ☷ 120 **P** 210 ⊕ **CC** MC
Visa Amex DC ⟪

ENGLAND

FIFEHEAD MANOR

Lovely historic manor house surrounded by peaceful gardens. Wonderfully atmospheric candlelit medieval dining hall, serving outstanding cuisine created by Chef de Cuisine Frederick Roy. Ideal for conferences or special occasions.

A truly memorable experience.

Middle Wallop, Stockbridge, Hampshire SO20 8EG
Tel: 01264 781565
Fax: 01264 781400

MIDSOMER NORTON Somerset   3E1
Frome 7, London 112, Bath 9, Bristol 12, Glastonbury 16

★★★ Centurion
Charlton Lane, Midsomer Norton BA3 4BD
☎ 01761-417711 **Fax** 01761-418357
Closed 25-26 Dec
44 bedrs, all ensuite, ⚲ ⠿ 160 **P** 100 ⊞ **SB** £62-£65
DB £72-£75 **HB** £308-£378 **L** ⬤ **D** £16.50 **D** ⬤ ✕
LD 21:30 **CC** MC Visa Amex DC JCB ▣ ▣ ▣ ▣ &

MILDENHALL Suffolk   9D3
Pop. 12,800. Newmarket 9, London 71, Bury St Edmunds 12, Ely 15, King's Lynn 35, Thetford 11
EC Thu **MD** Fri **see** St. Mary's Church, 15th cent Market Cross

★★★ Riverside
Mill Street, Mildenhall IP28 7DP
☎ 01638-717274 **Fax** 01638-715997
21 bedrs, all ensuite, ⠿ ▣ ⠿ 60 **P** 50 ⊞ **CC** MC Visa Amex DC JCB ▣

★★★ Smoke House
Beck Row, Mildenhall IP28 8DH
☎ 01638-713223 **Fax** 01638-712202

Oak beams, log fires and a warm welcome await you at the Smoke House. Facilities include modern bedrooms, two bars, two lounges and a restaurant.
94 bedrs, all ensuite, ▣ ⠿ 120 **P** 200 ⊞ **SB** £75
DB £90 **HB** £350-£560 **L** £22.50 **D** £22.50 **D** ⬤ ✕
LD 21:45 **CC** MC Visa Amex DC ▣ ▣ &

MILFORD-ON-SEA Hampshire
Pop. 4,750. Lymington 4, London 96, Bournemouth 14 **see** Norman Parish Church, Hurst Castle 3m SE

★★★ ❖ Westover Hall
Park Lane, Milford-on-Sea SO4 0PT
☎ 01590-643044 **Fax** 01590-644490

Privately owned historic country house hotel. Magnificent stained glass windows, minstrel's gallery and tastefully furnished bedrooms. Italian cuisine, stunning sea views and 200 yards from the beach.
13 bedrs, all ensuite, ▣ ♀ ⠿ ⠿ 50 **P** 50 ⊞ **SB** £50-£65 **DB** £110-£130 **L** £19.50 **D** £25 ✕ **LD** 21:00 **CC** MC Visa Amex DC
See advert on next page

WESTOVER HALL

This Victorian mansion was built in 1897 for the German industrialist Alexander Siemens without regard to cost and was acknowledged to be the most luxurious residence along the south coast of England.

Today, Westover Hall is owned and run by a family who recognise its heritage and take great pride in its appearance and the style of personal service afforded to all who visit.

The wealth of antique furniture, art, glass and books add to the stylish atmosphere which runs throughout to the tastefully furnished bedrooms, many of which have direct sea views.

Resident guests enjoy a full choice of dishes from our award-winning candlelit restaurant.

Westover Hall is superbly placed for enjoying the New Forest and the coast, with uninterrupted views of Christchurch Bay and

the Needles rocks on the Isle of Wight. The charming Saxon village of Milford-on-Sea is a few minutes' walk away, and the peaceful beach a mere 200 yards. Three miles away is Lymington with its yacht marina and ferries to the Isle of Wight. Wilton House, Exbury Gardens, Henry VIII's Hurst Castle, the National Motor Museum and Nelson's boat yard at Bucklers Hard are all within a half an hour drive.

We look forward to welcoming you.
Stewart Mechem and Nicola Musetti
Resident Proprietors.

WESTOVER HALL, PARK LANE, MILFORD-ON-SEA, LYMINGTON, HANTS. SO41 0PT
Tel: 01590 643044 Fax: 01590 644490
email: westoverhallhotel@barclays.net

MILTON COMMON Oxfordshire	4B2

London 46, M40 (jn 7) ½, Aylesbury 13, High Wycombe 16, Oxford 10, Wallingford 18

★★★ Oxford Belfry
Brimpton Grange, Milton Common OX9 2JW
☎ 01844-279381 **Fax** 01844-279624
97 bedrs, all ensuite, ⚹ ⚙ 250 **P** 180 ⊟ ℂ MC Visa Amex DC 🔲 🔲 🔲 🔲 ⅙

MILTON KEYNES Buckinghamshire	4C1

Pop. 184,630. London 56, M1 (jn 14) 1, Bedford 13, Bletchley 5½, Buckingham 13, Newport Pagnell 4, Towcester 13 **MD** Tue, Sat **see** Modern town centre, Broughton Church, Bradwell Abbey, Stacey Hill Collection 🗓 411 Secklow Gate East 01908-232525

★★★ Posthouse   **Posthouse**
500 Saxon Gate West,
Milton Keynes MK9 2HQ
☎ 01908-667722 **Fax** 01908-674714
153 bedrs, all ensuite, ⚹ ⚙ ⅰ 150 **P** 85 ⊟ **SB** £120 **DB** £131 **L** £6 **D** £8 ✕ **LD** 22:30 ℂ MC Visa Amex DC 🔲 🔲 🔲 ⅙

★★★ Quality
Monks Way, Two Mile Ash,
Milton Keynes MK8 8LY
☎ 01908-561666 **Fax** 01908-568303
E-mail admin@gb616.u-net.com

The Quality Hotel is in an ideal location for shopping in central Milton Keynes, taking a trip to Whipsnade Zoo or Woburn Abbey, or enjoying the thrills of Silverstone.
88 bedrs, all ensuite, ⚹ ⅰ 150 **P** 150 ⊟ **SB** £91 **DB** £124 **L** £9.95 **D** £14.50 ✕ **LD** 22:00 Restaurant closed L Sat ℂ MC Visa Amex DC JCB 🔲 🔲 🔲 ▶ ⅙

★★ Swan Revived 🍴 🍴
High Street, Newport Pagnell MK16 8AR
☎ 01908-610565 **Fax** 01908-210995
E-mail swanrevived@btinternet.com

Traditional coaching inn, recently refurbished. Theme pub, wood panelled restaurant, good food and wine, home hospitality, fully equipped bedrooms. Discover Milton Keynes, Woburn, Silverstone and Towcester.
40 bedrs, all ensuite, ④ ⚹ ⚙ ⅰ 70 **P** 18 ⊟ **SB** £42.50-£75 **DB** £60-£79.50 **HB** £500 **L** £15 **L** ⚐ **D** £15 ✕ **LD** 22:00 Restaurant closed L Sat ℂ MC Visa Amex DC

Campanile Milton Keynes **Lodge**
40 Penn Road (off Watling Street),
Fenny Stratford, Bletchley MK2 2AU
☎ 01908-649819 **Fax** 01908-649818

Campanile hotels offer comfortable and convenient budget accommodation and a traditional French style Bistro providing freshly cooked food for breakfast, lunch and dinner. All rooms ensuite with tea/coffee making facilities, DDT and TV with Sky channels.
80 bedrs, all ensuite, ⅰ ⊟ ℂ MC Visa Amex DC

MINEHEAD Somerset	3D2

Pop. 11,200. Taunton 24, London 167, Bridgwater 26, Dunster 2, Lynmouth 16 **EC** Wed **see** 14th cent Parish church, 17th cent Quirke's Almshouses, 14th cent Fishermen's Chapel, West Somerset Rly 🗓 17 Friday Street 01643-702624

★★★ Benares
Northfield Road, Minehead TA24 5PT
☎ 01643-704911 **Fax** 01643-706373
Closed 9 Nov-25 Mar
19 bedrs, all ensuite, ⚲ P 22 ⊞ Rest Resid **SB** £50
DB £90 **HB** £350-£378 **L** £7 **D** £20.50 **D** ♥ ✕ **LD** 20:30
《 MC Visa Amex DC

★★ Beaconwood
Church Road, North Hill, Minehead TA24 5SB
☎ 01643-702032 **Fax** 01643-702032
13 bedrs, all ensuite, ⚲ P 20 ⊞ Rest Restricted
《 MC Visa ⤳ ▣ ▣

★★ Rectory House ▯
Northfield Road, Minehead TA24 5QH
☎ 01643-702611
Closed Jan
7 bedrs, all ensuite, ⚲ P 9 ⊞ Rest Resid **SB** £25
DB £50 **HB** £273 **D** £19.50 ✕ **LD** 20:00 《 MC Visa

MONK FRYSTON North Yorkshire 11D4
Pop. 770. Doncaster 20, London 184, Castleford 7,
Selby 7, Tadcaster 9, Leeds 14

★★★ Monk Fryston Hall

Monk Fryston LS25 5DU
☎ 01977-682369 **Fax** 01977-683544
E-mail monkfryston.hall@virgin.net
30 bedrs, all ensuite, ▣ ♀ ⌁ ⚲ ⋕ 100 P 100 ⊞
SB £76.50-£84 **DB** £99-£150 **L** £15.80 **D** £22.50 **D** ♥
✕ **LD** 21:30 《 MC Visa Amex DC ▣ ⅙
See advert on this page

MORECAMBE Lancashire 10B3
Pop. 36,700. Lancaster 3½, London 242,
Ambleside 33, Broughton-in-Furness 42, Kendal
22, Kirkby Lonsdale 17 **EC** Wed **MD** Tue, Sat
🛈 Station Buildings, Central Promenade 01524-582808

★★★ Elms

Bare, Morecambe LA4 6DD
☎ 01524-411501 **Fax** 01524-831979

Situated in its own landscaped gardens, the newly
refurbished Elms Hotel is perfect for pleasure,
business and conferences. Licensed restaurant
with excellent cuisine.
40 bedrs, all ensuite, ▣ ⚲ ▣ ⋕ 200 P 80 ⊞ **SB** £40-
£61 **DB** £73-£90 **L** £10.25 **L** ♥ **D** £16.95 **D** ♥ ✕
LD 21:30 Restaurant closed L Sat 《 MC Visa Amex
DC ⅙

★★★ Headway
East Promenade, Morecambe LA4 5AN
☎ 01524-412525 **Fax** 01524-832630
E-mail admin@headway.net1.co.uk
54 bedrs, all ensuite, ▣ ⚲ ▣ ⋕ 200 P 20 ⊞ Rest
Resid **SB** £30-£35 **DB** £60-£70 **HB** £270-£279 **L** £7.95
L ♥ **D** £10.95 **D** ♥ ✕ **LD** 20:30 《 MC Visa Amex DC
⅙

★★ Clarendon
Marine Road West, Morecambe LA4 4EP
☎ 01524-410180 **Fax** 01524-421616
Well appointed hotel, near to all local attractions
and featuring ensuite rooms, lift to all floors and a
first class restaurant. Two bars with snacks served

daily. Illustrated brochure on request. Special
weekly rates.
31 bedrs, 29 ensuite, 2 ⋒ ⊁ ⊡ ⠿ 100 **P** 21 ⊈
SB £36-£40 **DB** £48-£52 **HB** £220-£300 **L** £7.50
D £12.50 ✕ **LD** 21:00 Restaurant closed L Mon-Sat
⊄ MC Visa Amex DC ♿

★ Channings
455 Marine Road East, Bare, Morecambe LA4 6AD
☎ 01524-417925 **Fax** 01524-417819
20 bedrs, 18 ensuite, ⊁ ⠿ 30 ⊈ Rest Resid ⊄ MC
Visa Amex DC

Strathmore
Marine Road East, Morecambe LA4 5AP
☎ 01524-421234 **Fax** 01524-414242

Walk this way and experience Lancastrian
hospitality at its best. Whether on business or
pleasure, our commitment is to you - our guest.
51 bedrs, all ensuite, ④ ⊡ ⠿ 200 **P** 24 ⊈ ⊄ MC
Visa Amex DC

MORETON Merseyside   7D1
Pop. 15,000. Birkenhead 4, London 201, Chester
18, Queensferry 17 ⦗⦘ Wed

Leasowe Castle
Leasowe, Moreton L46 3RF
☎ 0151-606 9191 **Fax** 0151-678 5551

Historic building circa 1595 converted to an hotel.
Minutes from M53. Ideal stopover for Wales and

Lakes. Beautiful restaurant, full a la carte and table
d'hote menu. Personal and friendly service.
50 bedrs, all ensuite, ⊡ ⠿ 250 **P** 200 ⊈ ⊄ MC Visa
Amex DC JCB ⊞ ▦

MORETON-IN-MARSH Gloucestershire   4A1
Pop. 2,900. Chipping Norton 8½, London 83,
Banbury 19, Evesham 14, Stow-on-the-Wold 4½,
Stratford-upon-Avon 16 ⦗⦘ Wed

★★★ Manor House ♟ ♟
High Street, Moreton-in-Marsh GL56 0LJ
☎ 01608-650501 **Fax** 01608-651481
E-mail themanor2@aol.com
39 bedrs, all ensuite, ④ ⊡ ⠿ 75 **P** 25 ⊈ **SB** £65
DB £90 **L** £14.95 **L** ⚑ **D** £25.50 ✕ **LD** 21:30 ⊄ MC
Visa Amex DC ⊞ ▦

MORETONHAMPSTEAD Devon   3D3
Pop. 1,400. Exeter 13, London 182, Ashburton 13,
Crediton 11, Okehampton 13, Plymouth 29,
Tavistock 21 ⦗⦘ Thu

★★★★ Manor House Hotel
& Golf Course ♟ ♟
Moretonhampstead TQ13 8RE
☎ 01647-440355 **Fax** 01647-440961
90 bedrs, all ensuite, ④ ⌀ ⊁ ⊡ ⠿ 100 **P** 70 ⊈
SB £75 **DB** £110-£140 **L** £12.95 **D** £19 ✕
LD 21:30 Restaurant closed L Mon-Sat
⊄ MC Visa Amex DC ⊞ ▦ ▦ ⊞ ♿

PRINCIPAL
H O T E L S

MORPETH Northumberland   13F3
⦁ The Chantry, Bridge Street 01670-511323

★★★★ Linden Hall ♟ ♟
Longhorsley, Morpeth NE65 8XF
☎ 01670-516611 **Fax** 01670-788544
50 bedrs, all ensuite, ④ ⊁ ⊡ ⠿ 300 **P** 350 ⊈
SB £97.50 **DB** £125-£195 **L** £17.95 **L** ⚑ ✕ **LD** 21:45
⊄ MC Visa Amex DC ⊞ ⊞ ▦ ⊞ ▦ ▦ ♿

MOULSFORD-ON-THAMES Oxfordshire   4B2
Pop. 400. Reading 11, London 49, Henley-on-
Thames 12, Newbury 14, Wallingford 4, Wantage 15

★★ Beetle & Wedge ♟ ♟
Ferry Lane, Moulsford-on-Thames OX10 9JF
☎ 01491-651381 **Fax** 01491-651376
10 bedrs, all ensuite, ④ ⊁ ⠿ 50 **P** 35 ⊈ **SB** £90
DB £120-£150 **L** £18 **D** £35 ✕ **LD** 22:00 ⊄ MC Visa
Amex DC JCB ♿

ENGLAND

MUCH WENLOCK Shropshire   7E2
Bridgnorth 9, London 146, Craven Arms 16,
Shrewsbury 12, Telford 11 ℹ Museum, High Street
01952-727679

★★★ Raven ☗ ☗
Much Wenlock TF13 6EN
☎ 01952-727251 **Fax** 01952-728416
15 bedrs, all ensuite, ④ ⌀ P 30 ⏦ SB £65 DB £95
L £15 L ☞ ✕ LD 21:15 ⸨ MC Visa Amex DC

MUDEFORD Dorset   3F3
Pop. 3,846. Lyndhurst 13, London 97,
Bournemouth 7, Christchurch 2, Lymington 10,
Ringwood 9½ ⸨ Wed

★★★ Avonmouth   **Heritage**
                                   HOTELS
Christchurch, Mudeford BH23 3NT
☎ 01202-483434 **Fax** 01202-479004
40 bedrs, all ensuite, ♀ ⌀ ☇ ⫼ 50 P 75 ⏦ SB £55-
£79 DB £70-£118 HB £350-£450 L £13.50 L ☞
D £20 D ☞ ✕ LD 21 Restaurant closed
L Mon-Sat ⸨ MC Visa Amex DC JCB ⤲

MUNGRISDALE Cumbria   10B1
M6 (jn 40) 12, Windermere 24, London 288, Kendal
38, Keswick 9½, Penrith 13

★ Mill ☗ ☗
Mungrisdale CA11 0XR
☎ 01768-779659 **Fax** 01768-779155
Closed Nov-Feb
7 bedrs, 4 ensuite, ♀ ☇ P 15 ⏦ SB £35-£40 DB £60-
£70 D £26.50 D ☞ ✕ LD 20:00 ▣ ♿

NANTWICH Cheshire   7E1
Pop. 11,700. London 162, Chester 18, Middlewich
9½, Newcastle-under-Lyme 13, Sandbach 9½,
Whitchurch 10, Wrexham 18 ⸨ Wed **MD** Thu, Sat **see**
Churche's Mansion, Sweet Briar Hall ℹ Church
House, Church Walk 01270-610983

★★★ Rookery Hall ☗ ☗ ☗
Gold Ribbon Hotel
Worleston, Nantwich CW5 6DQ
☎ 01270-610016 **Fax** 01270-626027

Award winning country house hotel set in 38 acres
of peaceful countryside, offering 45 luxuriously
appointed bedrooms, several elegant lounges and
a fine dining restaurant.
45 bedrs, all ensuite, ☇ ▣ ⫼ 100 P 150 ⏦ SB £120
DB £165 L £17 D £35 ✕ LD 21:45 ⸨ MC Visa Amex
DC ▨ ▣ ♿

Malbank Awaiting Inspection
14 Beam Street, Nantwich CW5 5LL
☎ 01270-626011 **Fax** 01270-624435
11 bedrs, all ensuite, ⏦ ⸨ MC Visa Amex DC ♿

NEW ALRESFORD Hampshire   4B3
Alton 8, London 56, Winchester 5.

★★ Swan
11 West Street, New Alresford SO24 9AD
☎ 01962-732302 **Fax** 01962-735274
E-mail swanhotel@btinternet.com

In the 18th century, the Swan was a staging post on the London-Southampton run. The original 17th century gabled building has been well matched by a new bedroom wing.
23 bedrs, all ensuite, ▥ ≣ 120 **P** 90 ⊞ **CC** MC Visa ⅙
See advert on opposite page

NEW MILTON Hampshire	4A4
Pop. 21,300. Lyndhurst 10, London 94, **EC** Wed

★★★★★ Chewton Glen ⫯ ⫯ ⫯
Gold Ribbon Hotel
Christchurch Road, New Milton BH25 6QS
☎ 01425-275341 **Fax** 01425-272310
E-mail reservations@chewtonglen.com

A luxurious Georgian country house hotel set in 70 acres of parkland. Impeccable decor makes an exquisite background to a life of luxury, with cuisine of the highest standard, outstanding service and excellent sporting facilities. Situated near the coast.
54 bedrs, all ensuite, ➷ ≣ 80 **P** 100 No children under 7 ⊞ **SB** £236-£516 **DB** £252-£532 **HB** £1,085 **L** £13.50 **D** £45 ✕ **LD** 21:30 **CC** MC Visa Amex DC ▤
⅓ ☒ ▣ ▸ ▨ ▨ ⅙
See advert on this page

ENGLAND

NEWBURY Berkshire   4B3

Pop. 31,200. Reading 15, London 54, M4 (jn 13)
3½, Andover 16, Basingstoke 16, Marlborough 19,
Oxford 26, Winchester 24 **EC** Wed **MD** Thu, Sat
i The Wharf 01635-30267

★★★★ Donnington Valley Hotel & Golf Course ⌂ ⌂

Blue Ribbon Hotel
Old Oxford Road, Newbury RG14 3AG
☎ 01635-551199 **Fax** 01635-551123
E-mail 106543.3217@compuserve.com

Donnington Valley blends charm and luxury, with a
high standard of cuisine. Surrounded by a fabulous
re-designed 18 hole golf course (6500 yards) with
new clubhouse.
58 bedrs, all ensuite, ⊁ ▣ ⋕ 140 **P** 160 ⊞
SB £131.50 **DB** £143 **L** £15 **L** ⚕ **D** £23.50 **D** ⚕ ✕
LD 22:00 **CC** MC Visa Amex DC ▣ ⌖

★★★★ Regency Park ⌂

Bowling Green Road, Thatcham, RS18 3RP
☎ 01635-871555 **Fax** 01635-871571

Formerly a family home, the original house stands
in five acres of beautiful grounds and is flanked by
attractive modern extensions. Interiors are light and
spacious with comfortable furnishings and tasteful
decor throughout.
46 bedrs, all ensuite, ⊁ ▣ ⋕ 140 **P** 120 ⊞ **SB** £95
DB £115 **L** £14.95 **L** ⚕ **D** £22 **D** ⚕ ✕ **LD** 22:30 **CC** MC
Visa Amex DC ▨ ⌖

★★★★ Vineyard at Stockcross ⌂ ⌂ ⌂ ⌂

Gold Ribbon Hotel
Stockcross, Newbury RG20 8JU
☎ 01635-528770 **Fax** 01635-528398
E-mail general@the-vineyard.co.uk
Closed 27-30 Dec

This former Victorian hunting lodge set in the heart
of Berkshire, close to the M4, is a 'restaurant with
suites' and a showcase for the finest Californian
wines. The Vineyards Spa is an oasis of tranquillity
for relaxation and indulgence.
33 bedrs, all ensuite, ▣ ✐ ⊁ ▣ ⋕ 20 **P** 45 ⊞
SB £158 **DB** £188-£511 **L** £20 **L** ⚕ **D** £39 **D** ⚕ ✕
LD 22:00 **CC** MC Visa Amex DC ▣ ▨ ▦ ⌖

★★★ Hollington House ⌂ ⌂ ⌂

Blue Ribbon Hotel
Woolton Hill, Newbury RG20 9XA
☎ 01635-255100 **Fax** 01635-255075
E-mail hollington.house@newbury.net

Hollington House has 15 acres of beautifully
maintained gardens and woodland. The bedrooms
are huge and luxurious with enormous bathrooms,
and many have double jacuzzi baths.
20 bedrs, all ensuite, ▣ ⋕ 30 **P** 50 ⊞ Resid
SB £105-£175 **DB** £145-£295 **L** £12 **D** £32.50 ✕
LD 21:30 **CC** MC Visa Amex DC ▣ ⌁ ▨ ▦ ⌖

ENGLAND

NEWBY BRIDGE Cumbria 10B2
M6 16, London 262, Ambleside 12, Kendal 15,

★★★ Whitewater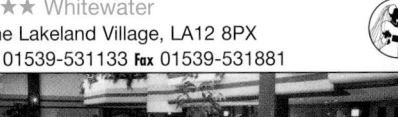
The Lakeland Village, LA12 8PX
📞 01539-531133 **Fax** 01539-531881

Imaginatively converted from a centuries old mill,
nestling in a valley on the banks of the River Leven,
only five minutes from Lake Windermere. 35
bedrooms with ensuite facilities, on site health and
fitness club.
35 bedrs, all ensuite, ④ 🖭 ⊞ 70 **P** 50 ⊞ **SB** £70
DB £100 **HB** £342 **L** £12.50 **L** 🍷 **D** £19 **D** 🍷 ✕
LD 21:15 Restaurant closed L Mon-Sat **cc** MC Visa
Amex DC 🖵 🖾 🖾 🖾 🖾
See advert on this page

NEWCASTLE UPON TYNE Tyne & Wear 11D1
See also GATESHEAD
Pop. 203,600. London 273 **EC** Wed **MD** Tue, Thur,
Sat, Sun 🚹 Library, Princess Square 0191-261 0610

★★★★ Copthorne Newcastle 🏮 🏮
The Close, Quayside, NE1 3RT
📞 0191-222 0333 **Fax** 0191-230 1111

A stylish, modern hotel situated on the historic
quayside making the most of its location. All
bedrooms, bars, restaurants and leisure club
overlook the River Tyne and its famous bridges.
156 bedrs, all ensuite, 🏊 🛬 🖭 ⊞ 250 **P** 180 ⊞
Room £135-£220 **L** £12 **L** 🍷 **D** £17.50 **D** 🍷 ✕ **LD** 22:15
Restaurant closed L Sat **cc** MC Visa Amex DC JCB
🖵 🖾 🖾 ♿

★★★★ Swallow Gosforth Park 🛏 🛏
High Gosforth Park, Gosforth,
Newcastle upon Tyne NE3 5HN
📞 0191-236 4111 **Fax** 0191-236 8192
E-mail info@swallowhotels.com

Set in over 12 acres of woodlands, close to the racecourse and the A1. The hotel has an award winning restaurant plus a choice of bars and a luxurious leisure club.
178 bedrs, all ensuite, 🛗 🛏 🖵 ⚟ 600 **P** 300 🔌
SB £105-£110 **DB** £125 **L** £18.50 **D** £24.50 ✕ **LD** 23:00
CC MC Visa Amex DC JCB 🏧 🏧 🏧 🏧 🏧 🛗

★★★★ Vermont 🛏 🛏 🛏
Blue Ribbon Hotel
Castle Garth, Newcastle upon Tyne NE1 1RQ
📞 0191-233 1010 **Fax** 0191-233 1234
E-mail info@vermont-hotel.co.uk
101 bedrs, all ensuite, 🛗 〽 🖵 ⚟ 400 **P** 60 🔌
SB £85-£145 **DB** £105-£165 **L** £13.50 **D** £15.50 ✕
LD 22:30 **CC** MC Visa Amex DC JCB 🏧 🛗

★★★ Caledonian
Osborne Road, Newcastle upon Tyne NE2 2AT
📞 0191-281 7881 **Fax** 0191-281 6241
89 bedrs, all ensuite, 🛏 🖵 ⚟ 100 **P** 42 🔌 **SB** £77
DB £87 **D** £12.50 ✕ **LD** 22:30 **CC** MC Visa Amex DC
JCB 🏧

★★★ Novotel Newcastle
Ponteland Road, Newcastle upon Tyne NE3 3HZ
📞 0191-214 0303 **Fax** 0191-214 0633
E-mail h118@accor-hotels.com
126 bedrs, all ensuite, 〽 🛏 🖵 ⚟ 220 **P** 260 🔌
SB £78 **DB** £89 **L** £12 **L** 🍷 **D** £15 **D** 🍷 ✕ **LD** 0:00 **CC** MC
Visa Amex DC 🏧 🏧 🏧 🏧 🛗

★★★ Posthouse
Posthouse
New Bridge Street, NE1 8BS
📞 0191-232 6191 **Fax** 0191-261 8529
166 bedrs, all ensuite, 🛏 🖵 ⚟ 600 **P** 180 🔌
SB £64.95-£98.95 **DB** £74.90-£108.90 **L** £10 **L** 🍷
D £20 **D** 🍷 ✕ **LD** 22:30 **CC** MC Visa Amex DC 🏧 🏧
🛗

★★★ Quality
Newgate Arcade, NE1 5SX
📞 0191-232 5025 **Fax** 0191-232 8428
93 bedrs, all ensuite, ♀ 🛏 🖵 ⚟ 100 **P** 120
🔌 **SB** £75-£95 **DB** £80-£105 ✕ **LD** 21:30 **CC** MC Visa
Amex DC 🛗

★★★ Swallow Imperial Hotel
Jesmond Road, Jesmond,
Newcastle upon Tyne NE2 1PR
📞 0191-281 5511 **Fax** 0191-281 8472
E-mail info@swallowhotels.com

Conveniently located on the outskirts of Newcastle city centre, a recent extensive refurbishment has added style and elegance to this friendly hotel, which also has leisure facilities.
122 bedrs, all ensuite, 🛏 🖵 ⚟ 150 **P** 110 🔌 **SB** £75-£95 **DB** £95-£105 **L** £9.50 **D** £18 ✕ **LD** 21:45 **CC** MC
Visa Amex DC 🏧 🏧 🏧

★★ Cairn
97-103 Osborne Road,
Newcastle upon Tyne NE2 2TA
📞 0191-281 1358 **Fax** 0191-281 9031

ENGLAND

Superbly situated ½ mile from the city centre, in the selected area of Jesmond, minutes from a metro station. Restaurant and Oswald's Bar open every night.
50 bedrs, all ensuite, 4 ⌁ ⋮⋮⋮ 120 **P** 18 ⊞ **SB** £55 **DB** £68 **D** £9 ✗ **LD** 21:15 **CC** MC Visa Amex DC

NEWCASTLE UNDER LYME Staffordshire 7E1
Pop. 73,500. Stone 8½, London 149, M6 (jn 15) 2½, Congleton 12, Leek 11, Nantwich 13, Stoke 2 **EC** Thu **MD** Mon, Fri, Sat **see** Museum, Guildhall, Castle Mound *i* Library, Ironmarket 01782-711964

★★ Borough Arms
King Street, Newcastle-under-Lyme ST5 1HX
☎ 01782-629421 **Fax** 01782-712388
45 bedrs, all ensuite, ⋮⋮⋮ 90 **P** 45 ⊞ **CC** MC Visa Amex DC

★★ Comfort Inn
Liverpool Road, ST5 9DX
☎ 01782-717000 **Fax** 01782-713669
E-mail admin@gb617.u-net.com

A great location from which to enjoy the thrills of Alton Towers or to explore the famous Staffordshire Potteries such as Wedgewood or Royal Doulton.
75 bedrs, all ensuite, ⌁ ⋮⋮⋮ 150 **P** 126 ⊞ Rest Resid **SB** £53.50-£61.25 **DB** £60.25-£68 **L** £7.50 **L** ☛ **D** £10.75 **D** ☛ ✗ **LD** 21:30 **CC** MC Visa Amex DC JCB ⊞ ♿

NEWMARKET Suffolk 9D4
Pop. 16,900. Bishop's Stortford 32, London 63, Bury St Edmunds 14, Cambridge 13, Ely 13, Thetford 18 **EC** Wed **MD** Tue, Sat **see** Devil's Dyke' (prehistoric earthworks), Cooper Memorial, Nell Gwynne's House, race courses *i* 63 The Rookery 01638-667200

♕ ★★★ Bedford Lodge,
Bury Road, Newmarket CB8 7BX
☎ 01638-663175 **Fax** 01638-667391

Situated among trees in private grounds, one mile north of the town. A warm and friendly welcome assured. Excellent dinners or bar meals served nightly.
56 bedrs, all ensuite, ⌁ ⊡ ⋮⋮⋮ 200 **P** 100 ⊞ **CC** MC Visa Amex DC JCB ⊡ ⊞ ▥ ♿

★★★ ✣ Rutland Arms
High Street, Newmarket CB8 8NB
☎ 01638-664251 **Fax** 01638-666298
46 bedrs, all ensuite, ⌁ ⋮⋮⋮ 80 **P** 40 ⊞ **SB** £72.25 **DB** £89.50 **L** £15.50 **L** ☛ **D** £15.50 **D** ☛ ✗ **LD** 22:00 **CC** MC Visa Amex DC

★★★ ✤ Swynford Paddocks
Six Mile Bottom, Newmarket CB8 0UE
☎ 01638-570234 Fax 01638-570283
Closed 27-30 Dec

An elegant 18th century country house hotel nestling in idyllic countryside with racehorses grazing its pastures. Conveniently situated for both Newmarket and Cambridge, the hotel offers delightful accommodation and a first-class restaurant.
15 bedrs, all ensuite, ▨ ⛺ ♨ 30 P 120 ⊕ ℂℂ MC Visa Amex DC ▨
See advert on previous page

NEWQUAY Cornwall   2B3
Pop. 16,900. Bodmin 18, London 252, Redruth 15, St Austell 14, Truro 18, Wadebridge 14 **EC** Wed (win)
▨ Municipal Offices, Marcus Hill 01637-871345

★★★ Barrowfield
Hilgrove Road, Newquay TR7 2QY
☎ 01637-878878 Fax 01637-879490
E-mail booking@barrowfield.prestel.co.uk
83 bedrs, all ensuite, ▨ ⛺ ▣ ♨ 150 P 60 ⊕ SB £25-£42 DB £50-£84 HB £183-£348 L ☕ D £16 D ☕ ✕ LD 21:00 ℂℂ MC Visa Amex ▨ ⤴ ▨ ▨ ▨
See advert on opposite page

Short Breaks

Many hotels provide special rates for weekend and mid-week breaks – sometimes these are quoted in the hotel's entry, otherwise ring direct for the latest offers.

★★★ Hotel Bristol
Narrowcliff, Newquay TR7 2PQ
☎ 01637-875181 Fax 01637-879347
E-mail hotelbristol.nqy@btinternet.com

Enjoy traditional hospitality and fine cuisine at one of Newquay's leading hotels. Owned and managed since 1927 by four generations of the Young family.
74 bedrs, all ensuite, ⛺ ▣ ♨ 250 P 100 ⊕ SB £55-£60 DB £90-£100 HB £294-£369 L £11 L ☕ D £18.50 D ☕ ✕ LD 20:45 ℂℂ MC Visa Amex DC JCB ▨ ▨ ▨
See advert on opposite page

★★★ Kilbirnie
Narrowcliff, Newquay TR7 2RS
☎ 01637-875155 Fax 01637-850769

Centrally situated to town and beaches. Excellent accommodation, cuisine and service. Heated swimming pools, sauna, solarium, spa bath. Snooker room. Lift to all floors.
68 bedrs, all ensuite, ▣ ♨ 150 P 50 ⊕ DB £56-£72 HB £200-£275 D £12.50 ✕ LD 20:30 ℂℂ MC Visa Amex DC JCB ▨ ⤴ ▨ ▨ ▨ ♿
See advert on opposite page

ENGLAND

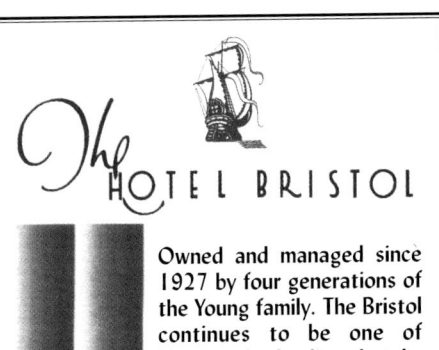

★★★ Riviera

Lusty Glaze Road, Newquay TR7 3AA

☎ 01637-874251 **Fax** 01637-850823
48 bedrs, all ensuite, ▦ ✎ ⊡ ⊞ 200 **P** 70 ⊕ **SB** £25-
£35 **DB** £50-£70 **HB** £196-£315 **L** £9.95 **L** ☕ **D** £14.95
D ☕ ✕ **LD** 20:45 Restaurant closed L Mon-Sat
ⓒ MC Visa Amex ✺ ▦ ▣ ▣
See advert on opposite page

★★★ Trebarwith

Trebarwith Crescent, Newquay TR7 1BZ
☎ 01637-872288 **Fax** 01637-875431
Closed Nov-Mar

A Victorian hotel in a fine cliff top location with
unrestricted views of the sea. Terraced sub-tropical
garden with direct access to the beach. The
restaurant overlooks the sea.
41 bedrs, all ensuite, ▦ **P** 31 ⊕ Rest Resid **SB** £21-
£43 **DB** £32-£68 **HB** £121-£270 **L** £6 **D** £14 ✕ **LD** 20:30
ⓒ MC Visa Amex JCB ▣ ▣ ▣ ▣
See advert on opposite page

★★ ✤ Beachcroft

Cliff Road, Newquay TR7 1SW
☎ 01637-873022 **Fax** 01637-873022
Closed Oct-Apr
68 bedrs, all ensuite, ☼ ⊡ **P** 50 ⊕ **SB** £21-£27
DB £42-£54 **HB** £149-£228 **L** ☕ **D** £8 ✕ **LD** 20:00
ⓒ MC Visa DC JCB ▣ ✺ ▣ ▣ ▣ ♿

★★ Great Western

Cliff Road, Newquay TR7 2PT
☎ 01637-872010 **Fax** 01637-874435
72 bedrs, 70 ensuite, ☼ ⊡ ⊞ 120 **P** 45 ⊕ **SB** £28-
£38 **DB** £50-£70 **HB** £142-£249 **D** £12 ✕ **LD** 19:45
ⓒ MC Visa Amex DC ▣ ♿

NEWTON ABBOT Devon 3D3

Pop. 22,300. Ashburton 7½, London 183, Exeter
15, Torquay 6, Totnes 8 **EC** Thu **MD** Wed, Sat ⑂ 6
Bridge House, Courtenay Street 01626-67494

★★★ Passage House

Hackney Lane, Kingsteignton,
Newton Abbot TQ12 3QH
☎ 01626 355515 **Fax** 01626-363336

A modern purpose-built hotel with a Swiss chalet
appearance, standing on the beautiful Teign
Estuary.
38 bedrs, all ensuite, ☼ ⊡ ⊞ 120 **P** 150 ⊕ Rest
Resid **SB** £65-£75 **DB** £75-£85 **L** £9.95 **D** £18.95 ✕
LD 21:30 ⓒ MC Visa Amex DC ▣ ▣ ▣

NORTH STOKE Oxfordshire 4B2

Henley-on-Thames 13, London 48, Newbury 19,
Oxford 16, Reading 14

★★★ Springs

Wallingford Road, OX10 6BE

☎ 01491-836687 **Fax** 01491-836877
E-mail springsuk@ad.com

The Springs is an idyllic country hideaway, with an
18 hole golf course, offering excellent
accommodation, award winning food, excellent
corporate facilities and unobtrusive service.
30 bedrs, all ensuite, ⊞ 50 **P** 120 ⊕ **SB** £94.50-£110
DB £131-£184 **L** £15 **D** £27 **D** ☕ ✕ **LD** 21:50 ⓒ MC
Visa Amex DC JCB ✺ ▣ ▣ ▣

NORTHAMPTON Northamptonshire 4B1
Pop. 186,000. M1 (jn 15) 4, London 66, Bedford 22, Buckingham 21, Daventry 12, Kettering 14, Market Harborough 17, Rugby 20, Towcester 8½ **EC** Thu **MD** Wed, Fri, Sat **see** Abington Park Museum, Church of Holy Sepulchre (12th cent interior, rare round church), St John's Church (former medieval Hospital), Museum and Art Gallery, County Hall, Guildhall, Queen Eleanor Cross 2m S, Althorp House 5m *i* Mr Grant's House, St Giles Square 01604-22677

★★★★ Swallow
Eagle Drive, Northampton NN4 7HW
☎ 01604-768700 **Fax** 01604-769011
E-mail info@swallowhotels.com

This contemporary hotel is set in landscaped grounds overlooking Delapre Lake and Golf Course. It is just five minutes from the M1 and has leisure facilities and awards for fine food.
120 bedrs, all ensuite, ⚲ ⊞ 180 **P** 200 ⊞ **SB** £50-£105 **DB** £80-£115 **D** £11.50 ✗ **LD** 22:30 **CC** MC Visa Amex DC 🗷 🗷 🗷 ⅙

★★★ Grand
15 Gold Street, Northampton NN1 1RE
☎ 01604-250511 **Fax** 01604-234534
E-mail grand@msihotels.co.uk
56 bedrs, all ensuite, ⌀ ⚲ ⊞ ⊞ 130 **P** 72 ⊞ **SB** £45-£90 **DB** £70-£99 **L** £10 **D** £20 ✗ **LD** 21:30 Restaurant closed L Sat & Sun, D Sun **CC** MC Visa Amex DC

★★★ ❖ Lime Trees
8 Langham Place, Barrack Road, Northampton NN2 6AA
☎ 01604-632188 **Fax** 01604-233012
E-mail info@limetreeshotel.co.uk
Closed Christmas
27 bedrs, all ensuite, ④ ⌀ ⊞ 50 **P** 25 ⊞ **SB** £47-£69 **DB** £65-£85 **L** £12 **L** ⬤ **D** £18.50 **D** ⬤ ✗ **LD** 21:00 Restaurant closed L Sun **CC** MC Visa Amex DC ⅙

★★★ Quality
Ashley Way, Weston Favell, Northampton NN3 3EA
☎ 01604-739955 **Fax** 01604-415023
66 bedrs, all ensuite, ♀ ⌀ ⚲ ⊞ ⊞ 180 **P** 100 ⊞
SB £39.50-£91.50 **DB** £64-£134 **L** £5.25 **L** ⬤
D £10.95 **D** ⬤ ✗ **LD** 21:45 Restaurant closed L Sat **CC** MC Visa Amex DC

★★ ❖ Aviator
Sywell Airport, Sywell, Northampton NN6 0BT
☎ 01604-642111 **Fax** 01604-790701
51 bedrs, all ensuite, ♀ ⚲ ⊞ 100 **P** 100 ⊞ **SB** £45 **DB** £52.50 **L** ⬤ **D** £10 ✗ **LD** 21:30 Restaurant closed D Sun **CC** MC Visa Amex DC ⅙

NORTHWICH Cheshire 7E1
Pop. 18,000. Middlewich 6, London 173, M6 (jn 19) 6, Altrincham 13, Chester 18, Knutsford 7, Warrington 11, Whitchurch 24 **EC** Wed **MD** Tue, Fri, Sat **see** Parish Church, Memorial Hall, Anderton Lift (connecting R Weaver to the Trent and Mersey Canal) 2½ m

★★★ Quality Northwich
London Road, Northwich CW9 5HD
☎ 01606-44443 **Fax** 01606-42596

A charming two storied hotel which actually floats on water.
60 bedrs, all ensuite, ⚲ ⊞ ⊞ 80 **P** 70 ⊞ **CC** MC Visa Amex DC JCB 🗷 🗷 ⅙

NORWICH Norfolk 9F3
Pop. 173,300. Scole 19, London 111, Cromer 23, East Dereham 16, Great Yarmouth 18, Lowestoft 27, Thetford 28 **EC** Thu **MD** Daily **see** Cathedral (mainly Norman, entire length 461 ft with many notable items), 40 City Churches, King Edward VI School, Erpingham Gate with archway built 1420, remains of city wall *i* Guildhall, Gaol Hill 01603-666071

★★★★ Dunston Hall ⬚ ⬚
Ipswich Road, Norwich NR14 8PQ
☎ 01508-470444 **Fax** 01508-471499
72 bedrs, all ensuite, ⬚ ⬚ ⬚ ⬚ 300 **P** 500 ⬚ ℂℂ MC
Visa Amex DC ⬚ ⬚ ⬚ ⬚ ⬚ ⬚ ⬚

★★★★ Swallow
Sprowston Manor
Wroxham Road, Norwich NR7 8RP
☎ 01603-410871 **Fax** 01603-423911
E-mail info@swallowhotels.com

A Victorian manor house set in 10 acres of
parkland, by the 18 hole Sprowston Park Golf
Course. The hotel has awards for fine food and a
luxurious healh spa.
94 bedrs, all ensuite, ⬚ ⬚ 150 **P** 100 ⬚ **SB** £97
DB £113 **HB** £487 **L** £19.95 **D** £19.95 ✗ **LD** 22:00
ℂℂ MC Visa Amex DC ⬚ ⬚ ⬚ ⬚ ⬚

★★★ Barnham Broom
Hotel, Golf & Leisure ⬚
Honingham Road, Barnham Broom,
Norwich NR9 4DD
☎ 01603-759393 **Fax** 01603-758224

Set in 250 acres of countryside only 10 miles west
of Norwich. Two 18 hole golf courses, an extensive
leisure complex and a conference centre.
53 bedrs, all ensuite, ⬚ 200 **P** 200 ⬚ **SB** £68-£72
DB £92-£98 **HB** £313-£346 **L** £9.95 **L** ⬚ **D** £17.50 **D** ⬚
✗ **LD** 21:30 ℂℂ MC Visa Amex DC JCB ⬚ ⬚ ⬚ ⬚ ⬚
⬚ ⬚

★★★ George
10 Arlington Lane, Newmarket Road,
Norwich NR2 2DA
☎ 01603-617841 **Fax** 01603-663708
E-mail reservations@georgehotel.co.uk
39 bedrs, all ensuite, ⬚ ⬚ ⬚ ⬚ 60 **P** 40 ⬚ **SB** £46-
£61.50 **DB** £72-£100 **L** £8.95 **L** ⬚ **D** £15.50 ✗
LD 22:00 Restaurant closed L Sun ℂℂ MC Visa Amex
⬚ ⬚
See advert on this page

★★★ Oaklands
89 Yarmouth Road, Norwich NR7 0HH
☎ 01603-434471 **Fax** 01603-700318
38 bedrs, all ensuite, ⬚ 180 **P** 90 ⬚ ℂℂ MC Visa
Amex

★★★ Posthouse   **Posthouse**
Ipswich Road, Norwich NR4 6EP
☎ 01603-456431 **Fax** 01603-506400
120 bedrs, all ensuite, ⬚ ⬚ ⬚ ⬚ 120 **P** 180 ⬚
SB £79 **DB** £89 **L** ⬚ **D** ⬚ ✗ **LD** 22:30 ℂℂ MC Visa
Amex DC JCB ⬚ ⬚ ⬚

★★★ Quality
2 Barnard Road, Bowthorpe,
Norwich NR5 9JB
☎ 01603-741161 **Fax** 01603-741500
E-mail admin@gb619.u-net.com

This comfortable, modern hotel is situated on the A1047, close to the centre of Norwich and offers a superb carvery, comfortable bar and leisure centre with indoor pool.
80 bedrs, all ensuite, ♀ ⅲ 200 **P** 100 ❹ **SB** £91.25 **DB** £124 **L** £8.95 **D** £14.50 ✕ **LD** 21:45 **CC** MC Visa Amex DC JCB ▣ ▣ ▦ ⅖

★★★ ❖ Swallow Nelson
Prince Of Wales Road,
Norwich NR1 1DX
☎ 01603-760260 **Fax** 01603-620008
E-mail info@swallowhotels.com

Situated by the River Wensum in the heart of Norwich with a private riverside garden. The hotel has two restaurants, bar, lounge and a leisure club.
132 bedrs, all ensuite, ▣ ✎ ♀ ▣ ⅲ 70 **P** 160 ❹ **SB** £92 **DB** £105 **L** £9.95 **L** ♥ **D** £16.50 **D** ♥ ✕ **LD** 21:45 **CC** MC Visa Amex DC ▣ ▣ ▦ ⅖

★★ Annesley House 🄬 🄬
6 Newmarket Road, Norwich NR2 2LA
☎ 01603-624553 **Fax** 01603-621577
Closed Christmas-New Year

Three listed Georgian buildings, restored and refurbished to a high standard. Set in beautifully landscaped grounds in a conservation area, yet just a short stroll to the city centre.
26 bedrs, all ensuite, **P** 25 ❹ Rest Resid **SB** £66-£77.50 **DB** £77.50-£90 **HB** £240-£330 **L** £9 **L** ♥ **D** £18.50 **D** ♥ ✕ **LD** 21:00 **CC** MC Visa Amex DC JCB

NOTTINGHAM Nottinghamshire   8B2
Pop. 279,700. Leicester 26, London 123, M1 (jn 26) 5, Ashby-de-la-Zouch 21, Derby 15, Grantham 24, Mansfield 14, Melton Mowbray 18, Newark 19
EC Mon **see** Parish Church (15th cent), Castle (now art gallery and museum), Statue of Robin Hood
🄻 1-4 Smithy Row 0115 947-0661

ENGLAND

WESTMINSTER
H O T E L

Conveniently located for Nottingham's Tourist attractions, its celebrated shopping centres and wealth of sporting venues our family owned and run hotel is decorated and equipped to the highest standards. Included in our 72 rooms are 2 Four Poster bedded rooms and also 19 Superior rooms which are air conditioned and offer the additional attraction of king-size beds, dedicated PC/Fax connection points and in the bathroom, the luxury of a shower unit which also provides a relaxing steam shower. Dinner in the informal atmosphere of our highly acclaimed restaurant where excellent food and good wines are sensibly priced will simply add to the enjoyment of your stay. The hotel also has 5 meeting rooms including a function suite for up to 60, all of which are air conditioned.

312 Mansfield Road, Nottingham NG5 2EF
Tel: 0115 955 5000 Fax: 0115 955 5005
E-mail: mail@westminster-hotel.co.uk
Web site: www.westminster-hotel.co.uk

INVESTOR IN PEOPLE

VAT Reg. No: 520 6115 93
The Westminster Hotel Ltd. Registered Office: 312 Mansfield Road, Nottingham NG5 2EF. Registered in England No. 2311762

★★★ Bestwood Lodge
Bestwood Country Park, Arnold,
Nottingham NG5 8NE
☎ 0115-920 3011 **Fax** 0115-967 0409
Closed 25 Dec

A former Victorian hunting lodge set in beautiful
parkland and within easy reach of Robin Hood
country and Nottingham city centre. Offers
comfortable rooms, and good cuisine accompanied
with a friendly atmosphere and excellent service.
40 bedrs, all ensuite, 🛗 ♪ ↑ ♨ 200 **P** 120 🍴
SB £65-£79.50 **DB** £79.50-£120 **HB** £585 **L** £9.95 **L** 🍷
D £18.50 **D** 🍷 ✕ **LD** 21:00 **CC** MC Visa Amex DC 📺 🖼
See advert on previous page

★★★ ✦ Novotel Nottingham/Derby
Bostock Lane, Long Eaton, Nottingham NG10 4EP
☎ 0115-946 5111 **Fax** 0115-946 5900
E-mail h0507@accor-hotels.com
108 bedrs, all ensuite, ♀ ♪ ↑ ♨ 220 **P** 150 🍴
SB £66 **DB** £74.50 **L** £13 **D** £15 ✕ **LD** 0:00 **CC** MC Visa
Amex DC 🛝 ♿

★★★ Posthouse   **Posthouse**
N**o**ttingham City
St James's Street, Nottingham NG1 6BN
☎ 0115-947 0131 **Fax** 0115-948 4366
130 bedrs, all ensuite, ↑ ♨ 600 🍴 **CC** MC Visa
Amex DC

★★★ Posthouse Notts/Derby   **Posthouse**
Bostocks Lane, Sandiacre,
Nottingham NG10 5NJ
☎ 0115-939 7800 **Fax** 0115-949 0469
93 bedrs, all ensuite, ↑ ♨ 60 **P** 250 🍴 **SB** £94
DB £104 **L** £5.95 **L** 🍷 **D** £17 ✕ **LD** 22:30 **CC** MC Visa
Amex DC 🖼

★★★ Strathdon 🛏
Derby Road, Nottingham NG1 5FT
☎ 0115-941 8501 **Fax** 0115-948 3725
68 bedrs, all ensuite, ↑ ♨ 150 **P** 10 🍴 **SB** £73
DB £107-£127 **L** £15.30 **D** £17.10 ✕ **LD** 22:00
Restaurant closed L Sat **CC** MC Visa Amex DC ♿

★★★ Westminster 🛏 🛏
312 Mansfield Road, Nottingham NG5 2EF
☎ 0115-955 5000 **Fax** 0115-955 5005
E-mail mail@westminster-hotel.co.uk
Closed Christmas
72 bedrs, all ensuite, 🛗 ♪ 📺 ♨ 60 **P** 64 🍴 Rest
Resid **SB** £80-£90 **DB** £104-£114 **L** 🍷 **D** £16 ✕
LD 21:15 Restaurant closed L Sat-Sun, D Sun **CC** MC
Visa Amex DC ♿
See advert on previous page

★★ Haven
Grantham Road (A52), Whatton NG13 9EU
☎ 01949-850800 **Fax** 01949-851454
33 bedrs, all ensuite, 🛗 ↑ ♨ 100 **P** 72 🍴 **SB** £37.50
DB £49.50 **L** 🍷 **D** £5.50 **D** 🍷 ✕ **LD** 21:45 **CC** MC Visa
Amex DC JCB ♿

★★ ✦ Nottingham Stage
Gregory Boulevard, Nottingham NG7 6LB
☎ 0115-960 3261 **Fax** 0115-969 1040
58 bedrs, all ensuite, ♀ ♨ 100 **P** 70 🍴 **SB** £35-
£44.50 **DB** £50-£54.50 **L** 🍷 **D** £8.50 **D** 🍷 ✕ **LD** 21:30
CC MC Visa Amex DC

★★ Rufford
Melton Road, West Bridgford,
Nottingham NG2 7NE
☎ 0115-981 4202 **Fax** 0115-945 5801
Closed Christmas & New Year
34 bedrs, all ensuite, ♨ 30 **P** 34 🍴 Resid **SB** £39.95-
£42.50 **DB** £47-£52.50 **L** 🍷 **D** 🍷 ✕ **LD** 20:30
Restaurant closed Fri-Sun **CC** MC Visa Amex DC
JCB

Welbeck Awaiting Inspection
Talbot Street, Nottingham NG1 5GS
☎ 0115-841 1001
96 bedrs, all ensuite

Quality
George Street, Nottingham NG1 3BP
☎ 0115-947 5641 **Fax** 0115-948 3292

An 18th century coaching inn in the centre of Nottingham, the Quality Hotel has undergone restoration to offer all modern comforts and is well positioned for shopping and nightlife.
70 bedrs, all ensuite, ✦ 🖭 ⁙ 180
P 70 🄳 ℂℂ MC Visa Amex DC JCB 🖾 ⅊

OAKHAM Rutland   8C3

Pop. 10,000. Kettering 20, London 95, Grantham 20, Leicester 19, Melton Mowbray 9, Stamford 10 ℇℂ Thu **MD** Wed, Sat **see** Castle remains with fine Norman Great Hall, unique collection of horseshoes; Rutland County Museum, in 1794 riding school 🛈 Library, Catmos Street 01572-724329

★★★ Boultons ⋷

4 Catmose Street, Oakham LE15 6HW
☎ 01572-722844 **Fax** 01572-724473
E-mail bhotbedd@sprynet.co.uk
25 bedrs, all ensuite, ✦ ⁙ 60 P 15 🄳 ℂℂ MC Visa Amex DC ⅊

OKEHAMPTON Devon   2C3

Pop. 4,800. Exeter 22, London 192, Ashburton 27, Bideford 26, Crediton 17, Launceston 19, Tavistock 16 ℇℂ Wed **MD** Sat **see** Castle ruins. 17th cent Town Hall, All Saints Parish Church, Fitz Well, St James's Church (14th cent tower) 🛈 3 West Street 01837-53020

★★ Oxenham Arms

South Zeal, Okehampton EX20 2JT
☎ 01837-840244 **Fax** 01837-840791
E-mail jhenry1928@aol.com
8 bedrs, all ensuite, ▦ ✦ P 8 🄳 **SB** £40-£45 **DB** £50-£60 **HB** £280 **L** £10 **L** ⅊ **D** £15 **D** ⅊ ✕ **LD** 21:00 ℂℂ MC Visa Amex DC JCB

OLDHAM Lancashire   10C4

Pop. 93,500. Glossop 12, London 186, A627(M) ½, Barnsley 29, Bury 10, Manchester 7, Rochdale 5½ ℇℂ Tue **MD** Mon, Fri, Sat **see** Art Gallery, Parish Church (crypt), Town Hall, Bluecoat School 🛈 11 Albion Street 0161-627 1024

★★★ Hotel Smokies Park

Ashton Road, Bardsley, Oldham OL8 3HX
☎ 0161-624 3405 **Fax** 0161-626 5267
73 bedrs, all ensuite, ♀ ⁂ 🖭 ⁙ 150 P 110 🄳 🄳 Rest Club **SB** £35-£70 **DB** £50-£80 **L** ⅊ **D** £6.75 **D** ⅊ ✕ **LD** 22.30 Restaurant closed L Sat ℂℂ MC Visa Amex 🖾 🖾

★★ High Point

Napier Street, Oldham OL8 1TR
☎ 0161-624 4130 **Fax** 0161-627 2757
19 bedrs, all ensuite, ▦ ⁑ ⁙ 30 P 30 🄳 **SB** £35-£40 **DB** £45-£50 **L** £10.95 **L** ⅊ **D** £11.95 ✕ **LD** 21:30
Restaurant closed L Sat ℂℂ MC Visa Amex

OTTERBURN Northumberland   13E3

Pop. 300. Corbridge 22, London 299, Alnwick 27, Bellingham 8½, Hexham 23, Jedburgh 27, Newcastle 32. **see** Otterburn Tower

★★ Percy Arms

Otterburn NE19 1NR
☎ 01830-520261 **Fax** 01830-520567
28 bedrs, all ensuite, ▦ ✦ ⁙ 30 P 70 🄳 **SB** £50-£64 **DB** £60-£90 **L** ⅊ **D** £12.50 **D** ⅊ ✕ **LD** 21:10
Restaurant closed L Mon-Sat ℂℂ MC Visa Amex DC
🗹

OTTERY ST MARY Devon   3D3

Pop. 7,400. Honiton 5½, London 158, Exeter 12, Lyme Regis 18, Tiverton 19 ℇℂ Wed, Sat **see** St Mary's Church (14th cent clock), Cadhay (16th cent manor house) 1m NW, Circular Tumbling Weir 🛈 10b Broad Street 01404-813964

★★ Tumbling Weir ⋷ ⋷

Ottery St Mary EX11 1AQ
☎ 01404-812752 **Fax** 01404-812752
E-mail b.p.young@compuserve.com

A beautifully thatched 17th century cottage hotel standing in a parkland setting, between the River Otter and its millstream, complete with a very fine restaurant.
11 bedrs, all ensuite, ✦ ⁙ 100 P 11 🄳 Rest Resid
SB £42.50 **DB** £64 **HB** £315 **D** £19.95 ✕ **LD** 20:30
Restaurant closed L Mon ℂℂ MC Visa JCB

OXFORD Oxfordshire   4B2
Pop. 115,800. High Wycombe 26, London 56, M40 (jn 7) 8½, Aylesbury 22, Banbury 23, Bicester 12, Burford 20, Chipping Norton 20, Faringdon 17 MD Wed see Colleges, Cathedral, Bodleian Library, Sheldonian Theatre, Ashmolean, History of Science and University Museums, Botanic Garden, many churches, Martyrs Memorial, Carfax Tower ⓘ The Old School, Gloucester Green 01865-726871

★★★★ Randolph ♟ ♟   **Heritage** HOTELS
Beaumont Street, Oxford OX1 2LN
☎ 01865-247481 **Fax** 01865-791678
E-mail heritagehotels_oxford.randolph@forte-hotels.com
119 bedrs, all ensuite, 🅰 �🏇 🖃 ⚌ 300 P 55 ⚐
Room £125-£155 L £12 D £20 ✕ LD 21:45 ⓒ MC Visa Amex DC JCB ♿

★★★ Cotswold Lodge
66a Banbury Road, Oxford OX2 6JP
☎ 01865-512121 **Fax** 01865-512490

Beautiful Victorian building, half a mile from the city centre in a conservation area. Providing the business person or tourist with an ideal location. Award winning restaurant.
50 bedrs, all ensuite, ⚌ 150 P 60 ⚐ SB £95 DB £115 L £10 L ⚊ D £18 D ⚊ ✕ LD 22:00 ⓒ MC Visa Amex DC JCB ♿

★★★ ❖ Eastgate   **Heritage** HOTELS
Merton Street, Oxford OX1 4BE
☎ 0870 400821 **Fax** 01865-791681
64 bedrs, all ensuite, 🅰 ⌀ �🏇 🖃 P 25 ⚐ SB £85-£105 DB £110-£140 L ⚊ D ⚊ ✕ LD 01:00 ⓒ MC Visa Amex DC JCB

★★★ Studley Priory ♟ ♟ ♟
Horton-cum-Studley, Oxford OX33 1AZ
☎ 01865-351203 **Fax** 01865-351613
E-mail res@studley-priory.u.net.com
18 bedrs, all ensuite, 🅰 ⚌ 40 P 100 ⚐ SB £105-£115 DB £120-£250 L £25 L ⚊ D £25 ✕ LD 21:30 ⓒ MC Visa Amex DC JCB 🔲 🔲

★★ Balkan Lodge
315 Iffley Road, Oxford OX4 4AG
☎ 01865-244524 **Fax** 01865-251090
13 bedrs, all ensuite, 🅰 P 13 No children ⚐ Rest Resid SB £55.50-£58.50 DB £58.50-£68.50 D £15.50 ⓒ MC Visa

★★ Foxcombe Lodge
Fox Lane, Boars Hill, Oxford OX1 5DP
E-mail jill@foxcombe.demon.co.uk
☎ 01865-326326 **Fax** 01865-730628
20 bedrs, all ensuite, �🏇 ⚌ 90 P 38 ⚐ ⓒ MC Visa Amex DC JCB 🔲 ♿

★★ Palace
250 Iffley Road, Oxford OX4 1SE
☎ 01865-727627 **Fax** 01865-200478
8 bedrs, all ensuite, ☒ P 8 ⚐ SB £45-£55 DB £60-£67 D £8.50 ✕ LD 20:30 Restaurant closed D Sun ⓒ MC Visa

★★ Victoria
180 Abingdon Road, Oxford OX1 4RA
☎ 01865-724536 **Fax** 01865-794909
20 bedrs, all ensuite, 🅰 �🏇 ⚌ 20 P 20 ⚐ Rest Resid SB £50.50-£57.50 DB £72.50-£78.50 L £10.50 L ⚊ D £15.50 ✕ LD 21:00 ⓒ MC Visa

PADSTOW Cornwall   2B3
Pop. 2,500. Wadebridge 7½, London 246, Newquay 14, St Austell 18, Truro 23 EC Wed MD Thu see 13th-15th cent St Petroc's Church, Tropical Bird and Butterfly Garden, Trevose Head ⓘ Red Brick Building, North Quay 01841-533449

★★★ Metropole   **Heritage** HOTELS
Station Road, Padstow PL28 8DB
☎ 01841-532486 **Fax** 01841-532867
50 bedrs, all ensuite, 🅰 ⏇ 🖃 ⚌ 15 P 38 ⚐ SB £55-£100 DB £80-£120 HB £275-£485 L ⚊ D ⚊ ✕ LD 21:00 ⓒ MC Visa Amex DC ⚲

★★★ Old Custom House Inn
South Quay, Padstow PL28 8BY
☎ 01841-532359 **Fax** 01841-533372
26 bedrs, all ensuite, 🅰 P 9 ⚐ SB £50.50-£72.50 DB £63-£99 HB £289.50-£415.50 ✕ LD 21:30 ⓒ MC Visa Amex DC

PAIGNTON Devon   3D3
Pop. 40,500. Torquay 3, London 191, Dartmouth (fy) 7½, Totnes 6 EC Wed ⓘ Esplanade 01803-558383

ENGLAND

★★★ Redcliffe
4 Marine Drive, Paignton TQ3 2NL
☎ 01803-526397 **Fax** 01803-528030
E-mail redclfe@aol.com
63 bedrs, all ensuite, ▣ ⅲ 150 **P** 100 ⊕ ℂℂ MC Visa
Amex ▣ ⊰ ⊠ ▦

★★ Dainton
95 Dartmouth Road, Three Beaches Goodrington,
Paignton TQ4 6NA
☎ 01803-550067 **Fax** 01803-666339
E-mail jamr@dainton-hotel.co.uk
11 bedrs, all ensuite, ④ ☒ ♁ **P** 20 ⊕ Rest Resid
ℂℂ MC Visa Amex JCB ♿

★★ Preston Sands
Marine Parade, Sea Front,
Paignton TQ3 2NU
☎ 01803-558718 **Fax** 01803-522875
31 bedrs, all ensuite, ♁ ⅲ 40 **P** 24 No children
under 10 ⊕ Rest Resid ℂℂ MC Visa Amex

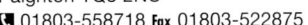

★★ Torbay Holiday Motel
Totnes Road, Paignton TQ4 7PP
☎ 01803-558226 **Fax** 01803-663375
E-mail enquiries@thm.co.uk
66 bedrs, all ensuite, ♀ ⌀ ♁ ⅲ 80 **P** 100 ⊕ **SB** £32-
£35 **DB** £50-£56 **HB** £273-£294 **L** 🍴 **D** £7 **D** 🍴 ✕
LD 21:00 ℂℂ MC Visa ▣ ⊰ ⊠ ▦ ♿
See advert on this page

PAINSWICK Gloucestershire   **7E4**
Pop. 3,000. Stroud 3½, London 103, Cheltenham
10, Gloucester 6 **EC** Wed **MD** Fri **see** 14th cent Church,
Painswick House

★★★ Painswick ☐ ☐ ☐
Kemps Lane, Stroud, Painswick GL6 6YB
☎ 01452-812160 **Fax** 01452-814059
19 bedrs, all ensuite, ④ ♁ ⅲ 45 **P** 25 ⊕ **SB** £75-£85
DB £110-£175 **L** £16 **D** £26 ✕ **LD** 21:30 ℂℂ MC Visa
Amex JCB

PANGBOURNE Berkshire   **4B2**
Pop. 2,500. Reading 6, London 45, M4 (jn 12) 5,
Basingstoke 18, Newbury 13, Wallingford 10,
Wantage 18

★★★ ✦ Copper Inn
Church Road, Pangbourne RG8 7AR
☎ 0118-984 2244 **Fax** 0118-984 5542
22 bedrs, all ensuite, ④ ⌀ ♁ ⅲ 60 **P** 20 ⊕
SB £89.50-£109.50 **DB** £134-£153 **L** £16.95 **L** 🍴
D £21.95 ✕ **LD** 21:30 ℂℂ MC Visa Amex DC ♿

★★★ ✦ George
The Square, Pangbourne RG8 7AJ
☎ 01189-842237 **Fax** 01189-844354
24 bedrs, all ensuite, ④ ♁ ⅲ 80 **P** 30 ⊕ **SB** £75-£85
DB £85-£100 **L** £11.95 **D** £14 **D** 🍴 ✕ **LD** 22 ℂℂ MC
Visa Amex DC

PAPWORTH EVERARD Cambridgeshire   **9D4**
Cambridge 8, M11 (jn 13) 6½, London 60,
Huntingdon 7, Royston 13, St Neots 9

Papworth
Ermine Street South, Papworth Everard CB3 8PB
☎ 01954-718851 **Fax** 01954-718069
Closed 25-26 Dec
A pleasant hotel situated in a peaceful countryside
with 20 ensuite bedrooms, restaurant and relaxing
lounge all on ground floor. Homelike with friendly
hospitality.
20 bedrs, all ensuite, ⅲ 45 **P** 50 ⊕ ℂℂ MC Visa
Amex DC

PARBOLD Lancashire   **10B4**
Pop. 2,700. M6 (jn 27) 3, London 199, Ormskirk
6½, Preston 15, Skelmersdale 4½, Southport 13,
Wigan 8

★★ Lindley
912 Lancaster Lane, Parbold, Wigan WN8 7AB
☎ 01257-462804 **Fax** 01257-464628

Beautiful well appointed restaurant and hotel. 8 letting bedrooms, all ensuite. Delightful bar and restaurant with picture window views. A la carte and table d'hote menus. Ample car parking. 5 minutes from junction 27, M6.
8 bedrs, all ensuite, **P** 50 ⌒ Rest Resid **SB** £38 **DB** £50 **L** £9.45 **D** £12.50 ✕ **LD** 21:30 Restaurant closed L Sat ⪢ MC Visa Amex

---

PARKHAM Devon   2C2
Bideford 6, London 208, Bude 17, Holsworthy 13, Great Torrington 8

★★★ Penhaven Country House ⚲ ⚲
Bideford, Parkham EX39 5PL
☎ 01237-451711 **Fax** 01237-451878
E-mail penhaven@sosi.net
12 bedrs, all ensuite, ④ ↑ **P** 50 No children under 10 ⌒ Rest Resid **SB** £60-£65 **DB** £120-£130 **HB** £419-£445 **L** £11 **D** £16 ✕ **LD** 21:00 ⪢ MC Visa Amex DC

PATTERDALE Cumbria   10B2
Pop. 600. M6 (jn 36) 28, London 276, Ambleside 8, Kendal 20, Penrith 14 **see** Quaint Church, old Spinning Gallery, Aira Force, Ullswater, Helvellyn 3,118ft

★★ Patterdale
Patterdale CA11 0NN
☎ 01768-482231 **Fax** 01768-482440
Closed Jan & Feb
63 bedrs, all ensuite, ↑ ⊡ ⣿ 90 **P** 40 ⌒ **SB** £25-£30 **DB** £50-£60 **HB** £300 **L** £8 **L** ⬤ **D** £16 ✕ **LD** 20:00 Restaurant closed L Mon-Sat ⪢ MC Visa ▣ ▣ ⓺

PENDOGGETT Cornwall   2B3
Camelford 6½, London 234, Bodmin 10, Wadebridge 6½ **EC** Thu

★★ Cornish Arms
St Kew, Pendoggett PL30 3HH
☎ 01208-880263 **Fax** 01208-880335
E-mail cornisharm@aol.com
7 bedrs, 5 ensuite, ↑ ⣿ 15 **P** 55 ⌒ **SB** £39 **DB** £59 **HB** £265.65 **L** ⬤ **D** £15.50 **D** ⬤ ✕ **LD** 21:30 ⪢ MC Visa Amex DC JCB

PENRITH Cumbria   10B1
Pop. 12,200. Kendal 25, London 276, M6 (jn 40) ½, Alston 19, Ambleside 22, Brough 21, Carlisle 18, Keswick 16 **EC** Wed **MD** Tue ⓲ Robinson's School, Middlegate 01768-867466

★★★★ North Lakes ⚲
Ullswater Road, Penrith CA11 8QT
☎ 01768-868111 **Fax** 01768-868291
E-mail nlakes@shireinns.co.uk
84 bedrs, all ensuite, ④ ⏛ ↑ ⊡ ⣿ 200 **P** 150 ⌒ **SB** £102-£137 **DB** £125-£160 **L** £12 **D** £20 ✕ **LD** 21:30 Restaurant closed L Sat, Sun ⪢ MC Visa Amex DC ▣ ▣ ▣ ▣ ⓺

★★★ George
23 Devonshire Street, Penrith CA11 7SU
☎ 01768-862696 **Fax** 01768-868223
34 bedrs, all ensuite, ↑ ⣿ 140 **P** 32 ⌒ ⪢ MC Visa
See advert on opposite page

★★★ Westmorland
Orton, Penrith CA10 3SB
☎ 015396-24351 **Fax** 015396-24354
53 bedrs, all ensuite, ↑ ⊡ ⣿ 150 **P** 100 ⌒ Rest Resid ⪢ MC Visa Amex DC ⓺

★★ Brantwood Country
Stainton, Penrith CA11 0AP
☎ 01768-862748 **Fax** 01768-890164

Early 18th century building with oak beams and log fires (in winter) - very rural with large secure car park in over three acres of private gardens.
11 bedrs, all ensuite, ⣿ 50 **P** 36 ⌒ ⪢ MC Visa Amex

ENGLAND

THE GEORGE HOTEL

A truly and charming coaching inn dating back more than 300 years situated in the attractive market town of Penrith. The ideal base from which to explore the Lake District with only 4 miles to Lake Ullswater. 34 en suite bedrooms with trouser press, hairdrier, tea maker, telephone and SKY channels. Restaurant with superb home cooking and carvery. Two bars and bar meals served lunch and evening. Private car park.

Devonshire Street, Penrith, Cumbria CA11 7SU.
Tel: 01768 862696 • Fax: 01768 868223

The Queens Hotel
Penzance
RAC ★★★

Elegant Victorian Hotel enjoying pride of place on the sea front promenade of Penzance with majestic views which sweep across Mounts Bay to St. Michael's Mount and Lizard Peninsular. Excellent restaurant with local seafood. Lands End, Minack Theatre, Tate Gallery within a short drive.

The Promenade, Penzance TR18 4HG
Tel: 01736 362371
Fax: 01736 350033
EMail: enquiries@Queens_Hotel.com

PENZANCE Cornwall 2A4
Pop. 19,500. Redruth 17, London 281, Helston 13, St Ives 8 **EC** Wed **MD** Tue, Thur, Sat **see** Penlee Memorial Park, with Museum, Market Cross, Nautical Museum, Geological Museum, Gulval Church, Madron Church ℹ Station Road 01736-62207

★★★ Mount Prospect
Britons Hill, Penzance TR18 3AE
📞 01736-363117 **Fax** 01736-350970
E-mail mtpross2000@aol.com
Closed Christmas & New Year
21 bedrs, all ensuite, ♫ ⊦ ⠇ 100 **P** 14 ⊞ Resid
SB £39-£49 **DB** £65-£80 **HB** £308-£330 **L** ♥ **D** £13 **D** ♥
✕ **LD** 20:30 **CC** MC Visa Amex JCB ⫞ ▣

★★★ Queens ⓡ
Promenade, Penzance TR18 4HG
📞 01736-362371 **Fax** 01736-350033

An elegant Victorian hotel enjoying pride of place on seafront promenade of Penzance with majestic views of the sweep across Mount's Bay from St Michael's Mount to the Lizard peninsula.
70 bedrs, all ensuite, ▤ ⊦ ▣ ⠇ 150 **P** 45 ⊞ **SB** £40-£53 **DB** £76-£110 **HB** £316-£435 **L** ♥ **D** £15.95 **D** ♥ ✕
LD 20:45 **CC** MC Visa Amex DC ▣ ▣ ♿
See advert on this page

★★ Tarbert Hotel & Restaurant
11 Clarence Street, Penzance TR18 2NU
📞 01736-363758 **Fax** 01736-331336
Closed Christmas-New Year
12 bedrs, all ensuite, **P** 5 No children under 4 ⊞
Rest Resid **SB** £33-£36 **DB** £56-£76 **HB** £257-£330 **L** ♥
D £18.50 ✕ **LD** 20:30 **CC** MC Visa Amex

PETERBOROUGH Cambridgeshire 8C3
Pop. 136,000. Alconbury 13, London 83, Kettering 28, Leicester 42, Spalding 17, Stamford 14, Wisbech 20 **EC** Thu **MD** Wed, Fri, Sat **see** Cathedral, Bishop's Palace, Museum, Old Guildhall, 15th cent St John's Church ℹ 45 Bridge Street 01733-317336

★★★★ Swallow ⚞
Peterborough Business Park,
Lynchwood, Peterborough PE2 6GB
☎ 01733-371111 **Fax** 01733-236725
E-mail info@swallowhotels.com

This stylish, modern hotel with leisure facilities is set in 11 acres of landscaped grounds and is well placed for touring the countryside of Cambridgeshire.
163 bedrs, all ensuite, ▥ ✝ ⚌ 300 **P** 200 ⊞
SB £105-£115 **DB** £115-£135 **L** £15.50 **D** £17.50 ✕
LD 22:00 《 MC Visa Amex DC ▣ ▦ ▦ ⅋

★★★ Bull
Westgate, Peterborough PE1 1RB
☎ 01733-561364 **Fax** 01733-557304
103 bedrs, all ensuite, ⌀ ✝ ⚌ 200 **P** 120 ⊞
SB £74.75 **DB** £86.50 **L** £15.50 **D** £15.50 ✕ **LD** 22:00
《 MC Visa Amex DC

★★★ Butterfly
Thorpe Meadows, Off Longthorpe Parkway,
Peterborough PE3 6GA
☎ 01733-64240 **Fax** 01733-65538
E-mail peterborough@lineone.net

The hotel sits at the waters edge, overlooking Peterborough's international rowing course at lovely Thorpe Meadows. The pine furnished Walts Restaurant and bar offers a la carte, daily specials and a buffet style self service. Bedrooms are well laid out.

70 bedrs, all ensuite, ♀ ✝ ⚌ 80 **P** 85 ⊞ **SB** £77
DB £84.50 **L** £15 **L** ♥ **D** £15 **D** ♥ ✕ **LD** 22:00 《 MC
Visa Amex DC ⅋

★★★ Orton Hall
The Village, Orton Longueville,
Peterborough PE2 7DN
☎ 01733-391111 **Fax** 01733-231912
65 bedrs, all ensuite, ▥ ✝ ⚌ 120 **P** 200 ⊞
SB £93.50 **DB** £116.50 **D** £19.50 ✕ **LD** 21:30 《 MC
Visa Amex DC ▦

★★★ Posthouse   **Posthouse**
Norman Cross, Peterborough PE7 3TB
☎ 01733-240209 **Fax** 01733-244455
93 bedrs, all ensuite, ⌀ ✝ ⚌ 50 **P** 150 ⊞ **SB** £88.95
DB £98.90 **L** £10 **L** ♥ **D** £15 **D** ♥ ✕ **LD** 22:30 《 MC
Visa Amex DC ▣ ▦ ▦ ⅋

PETERLEE Co. Durham   11D1
Pop. 22,000. Stockton 17, London 260, Darlington 23, Durham 11, Newcastle 20, Sunderland 11
EC Wed ℹ 20 The Upper Chare 0191-586 4450

★★ Hardwicke Hall Manor
Heslenden Road, Blackhall,
Peterlee TS27 4PA
☎ 01429-836326 **Fax** 01429-837676
15 bedrs, all ensuite, ▥ ♀ ⌀ ✝ ⚌ 60 **P** 103 ⊞
SB £49.50-£59.50 **DB** £59.50-£69.50 **D** £15.95 ✕
LD 21:30 《 MC Visa Amex DC

PEVENSEY East Sussex   5D4
Pop. 2,500. Uckfield 19, London 65, Eastbourne 4, Hastings 12, Lewes 17 **EC** Thu **see** Castle ruins, Martello Towers ℹ Pevensey Castle, High Street 01323-761444

★★ ✣ Priory Court
Pevensey Castle, Pevensey BN24 5LG
☎ 01323-763150 **Fax** 01323-768558
E-mail prioryct@easynet.co.uk
9 bedrs, 7 ensuite, ▥ ✝ ⚌ 20 **P** 50 ⊞ **SB** £22-£29
DB £44-£75 **HB** £238-£295 **L** £9.95 **L** ♥ **D** £11.95 ✕
LD 21:30 《 MC Visa ⅋
See advert on opposite page

PICKERING North Yorkshire   11E2
Pop. 6,000. Malton 8, London 213, Bridington 31, Helmsley 13, Scarborough 16, Whitby 20 **EC** Wed **MD** Mon **see** Castle ruins, Church (15th cent mural paintings), Steam Railway ℹ Eastgate Car Park 01751-473791

🕯 ★★★ Blacksmith's Country House ꭚ ꭚ
Hartoft End, Rosedale Abbey, Pickering YO18 8EN
📞 01751-417331 **Fax** 01751-417167

Lovely 16th century hostelry, fully refurbished.
Retaining all the ambiance of years past. Cosy
lounges, superb food and wine in wonderful
surroundings. Quality ensuites, panoramic views.
Ideal walking base.
14 bedrs, all ensuite, ⊁ **P** 75 ⊕ **SB** £45 **DB** £70
HB £235-£266 **D** £15 ✗ **LD** 21:00 ⟨⟨ MC Visa Amex DC

★★ White Swan at Pickering ꭚ ꭚ
The Market Place, Pickering YO18 7AA
📞 01751-472288 **Fax** 01751-475554
12 bedrs, all ensuite, ⊁ ⠸ 20 **P** 35 ⊕ ⟨⟨ MC Visa
Amex

PLYMOUTH Devon   2C4
See also IVYBRIDGE
Pop. 242,500. Ashburton 24, London 211,
Kingsbridge 20, Saltash 4, Tavistock 14, Totnes 22
see Citadel, The Hoe (Drake's Statue), Elizabethan
House, Museum and Art Gallery, Smeaton's Tower
(Aquarium), RC Cathedral. Brunel's Rly Bridge.
Tarmar Road Bridge, Barbican (curio shops).
🛈 Island House, 9 The Barbican 01752-264849

★★★★ Copthorne Plymouth
Armada Way, Plymouth PL1 1AR
📞 01752-224161 **Fax** 01752-670688
135 bedrs, all ensuite, ♀ ⊁ 🖪 ⠸ 140 **P** 53 ⊕
SB £65-£120 **DB** £79-£149 **L** £10 **L** 🖤 **D** £14 **D** 🖤 ✗
LD 22:30 ⟨⟨ MC Visa Amex DC JCB 🖫 🔀 ᓬ

★★★ Boringdon Hall
Colebrook, Plympton, Plymouth PL7 4DP
📞 01752-344455 **Fax** 01752-346578
40 bedrs, all ensuite, 🄴 ⊁ ⠸ 120 **P** 200 ⊕ **SB** £80
DB £90-£100 **HB** £378 **L** £15 **D** £18.95 ✗ **LD** 21:30
Restaurant closed L Sat ⟨⟨ MC Visa Amex 🖫 🔀 🖾
🖸 🔀

ENGLAND

★★★ Elfordleigh
Colebrook, Plympton, Plymouth PL7 5EB
📞 01752-336428 **Fax** 01752-344581
18 bedrs, all ensuite, ④ ⅓ ⅲ 300 **P** 250 ⊞
SB £52.50 **DB** £62.50 **L** ● **D** £15.95 ✕ **LD** 21:00
Restaurant closed L Mon-Sat ⅏ MC Visa Amex ▣
⅔ ▣ ▦ ▣ ▣ ▣ ▣

★★★ New Continental
Mill Bay Road, Plymouth PL1 3LD
📞 01752-220782 **Fax** 01752-227013
E-mail www.newconti@aol.com
Closed Christmas-New Year
99 bedrs, all ensuite, ④ ⅓ ▣ ⅲ 400 **P** 100 ⊞
SB £58-£80 **DB** £73-£160 **HB** £300 **L** £10.95 **D** £17.25
✕ **LD** 22:00 Restaurant closed L Sat-Thu ⅏ MC Visa
Amex ▣ ▣ ▦ ⅋
See advert on previous page

★★★ Novotel Plymouth
Marsh Mills Roundabout, 270 Plymouth Road,
Plymouth PL6 8NH
📞 01752-221422 **Fax** 01752-223922
E-mail h0508@accor-hotels.com
100 bedrs, all ensuite, ⌀ ⅓ ▣ ⅲ 200 **P** 150 ⊞
SB £67.50-£71.50 **DB** £76-£80 **L** £11 **L** ● **D** £14 **D** ●
✕ **LD** 23:45 ⅏ MC Visa Amex DC ⅔ ⅋

★★★ Posthouse   **Posthouse**
The Hoe, Plymouth PL1 3DL
📞 01752-662828 **Fax** 01752-660974
106 bedrs, all ensuite, ⅓ ▣ ⅲ 80 **P** 157 ⊞ ⅏ MC
Visa Amex DC JCB ⅔

★★★ Strathmore
Elliot Street, The Hoe, Plymouth PL1 2PR
📞 01752-662101 **Fax** 01752-223690
54 bedrs, all ensuite, ⅓ ▣ ⅲ 90 ⊞ **SB** £35-£40
DB £47-£52 **D** £13 **D** ● ✕ **LD** 21:00 ⅏ MC Visa Amex
JCB

★★ Camelot
5 Elliot Street, Plymouth PL1 2PP
📞 01752-221255 **Fax** 01752-603660
17 bedrs, all ensuite, ⅲ 60 ⊞ Resid **SB** £39 **DB** £50
L £13 **D** £13 ✕ **LD** 20:30 ⅏ MC Visa Amex DC JCB

★★ Invicta
11 Osborne Place, Lockyer Street, The Hoe,
Plymouth PL1 2PU
📞 01752-664997 **Fax** 01752-664994
Closed 24 Dec-4 Jan

Friendly, family hotel opposite the famous Plymouth
Hoe, very close to the city centre, historic Barbican
and Brittany Ferries. 23 well appointed bedrooms.
23 bedrs, 21 ensuite, ⅲ 60 **P** 10 ⊞ Rest Resid
SB £44-£48 **DB** £54-£58 **HB** £255.50-£259 **D** £10.50
D ● ✕ **LD** 21:00 Restaurant closed Sun ⅏ MC Visa
Amex

★★ Langdon Court ▣
Down Thomas, Wembury,
Plymouth PL9 0DY
📞 01752-862358 **Fax** 01752-863428
E-mail langdon@eurobell.co.uk

Charming Tudor manor, with rare 17th century
walled garden, standing amid glorious South Hams
countryside. 6 miles to Plymouth city centre and
one mile to Wembury beach. Civil wedding licence.
19 bedrs, all ensuite, ④ ⌀ ⅓ ⅲ 60 **P** 50 ⊞
SB £39.50-£56 **DB** £68-£78 **L** £6 **L** ● **D** £21 **D** ● ✕
LD 21:30 ⅏ MC Visa Amex DC JCB

★ Drake
1 Windsor Villas, Lockyer Street The Hoe,
Plymouth PL1 2QD
📞 01752-229730 **Fax** 01752-255092
Closed Christmas
35 bedrs, 30 ensuite, 5 ⌂ ♀ ⅲ 20 **P** 25 ⊞ Rest
Resid **SB** £42 **DB** £52 **HB** £245 **L** ● **D** £12 ✕ **LD** 20:00
⅏ MC Visa Amex DC JCB

ENGLAND

★ Imperial
Lockyer Street, The Hoe, Plymouth PL1 2QD
☎ 01752-227311 Fax 01752-674986
22 bedrs, 17 ensuite, ♀ ⅲ 16 P 14 ⊞ Rest Resid
SB £35-£45 DB £45-£58 HB £250-£320 L ♥ D £13 ✗
LD 20:15 cc MC Visa Amex DC JCB

★ Victoria Court
64 North Road East, Plymouth PL4 6AL
☎ 01752-668133 Fax 01752-668133
E-mail victoria.court@btinternet.com
Closed 21 Dec-2 Jan
13 bedrs, all ensuite, ♪ ⅲ 10 P 6 ⊞ Rest Resid
SB £39-£42 DB £49-£52 HB £259-£346.50 D £14.50 ✗
LD 20:00 cc MC Visa Amex DC

POLPERRO Cornwall   2B4
Pop. 1,700. Looe 4, London 231, Fowey (fy) 9 EC Sat

★ ✦ Claremont
The Coombes, Polperro PL13 2RG
☎ 01503-272241 Fax 01503-272152
E-mail wmsmith1@aol.com
12 bedrs, all ensuite, ↖ P 16 ⊞ Rest Resid
SB £21.95-£25.95 DB £43.90-£47.90 D £12 ✗
LD 20:30 cc MC Visa Amex

POOLE Dorset   4A4
Pop. 135,000. Ringwood 12, London 106,
Blandford Forum 13, Bournemouth 4, Dorchester
23, Sandbanks 4½, Wareham 9 EC Wed MD Tue, Sat
see Old Town House (orig Guildhall), Pottery, 14th
cent Gateway and walls, Guildhall (1761) ⊠ The
Quay 01202-673322

★★★★ Haven ⚮ ⚮
Banks Road, Sandbanks,
Poole BH13 7QL
☎ 01202-707333 Fax 01202-708796
E-mail reservations@fjbhotels.co.uk
Closed 30 Dec-04 Jan

An exclusive hotel located on the tip of Sandbanks
Peninsula. The Haven offers splendid sea views,
award winning cuisine, first class accommodation
and leisure facilities.
94 bedrs, all ensuite, ♪ ▣ ⅲ 160 P 150 ⊞ SB £70-
£125 DB £140-£250 HB £480-£840 L £15 D £22.50 ✗
LD 21:30 Restaurant closed L Sat cc MC Visa Amex
DC ▣ ✈ ⊞ ⊞ ⊞ ⊞

★★★ ✦ Harbour Heights
73 Haven Road, Poole BH13 7LW
☎ 01202-707272 Fax 01202-708594
49 bedrs, all ensuite, ↖ ▣ ⅲ 20 P 80 ⊞ SB £48
DB £8 HB £350 L £11.50 L ♥ D £17 ✗ LD 21:30 cc MC
Visa Amex DC JCB &

★★★ ✦ Salterns
38 Salterns Way, Lilliput, Poole BH14 8JR
☎ 01202-707321 Fax 01202-707488
20 bedrs, all ensuite, ↖ ⅲ 120 P 300 ⊞ cc MC Visa
Amex DC JCB ▣
See advert on this page

★★★ Sandbanks
Banks Road, Poole BH13 7PS
☎ 01202-707377 **Fax** 01202-708885
E-mail reservations@sandbankshotel.co.uk
Closed 30 Dec-4 Jan

Located on a long stretch of sandy beach (Blue flag award), the Sandbanks hotel is perfect for families. Award winning cuisine and special children's facilities.
113 bedrs, all ensuite, 170 **P** 200 **SB** £55-£85 **DB** £110-£170 **HB** £420-£630 **L** £14.50 **L** **D** £18.50 ✕ **LD** 21:00 Restaurant closed L Sat **℃** MC Visa Amex DC

★★ Norfolk Lodge
1 Flaghead Road, Canford Cliffs, Poole BH13 7JL
☎ 01202-708614 **Fax** 01202-708661
19 bedrs, 17 ensuite, **P** 17 Rest Resid **SB** £42 **DB** £58 **HB** £205-£235 **L** £8.50 **D** £11 ✕ **LD** 20:00 Restaurant closed L Mon-Sat **℃** MC Visa Amex DC JCB

★★ Quarterdeck
2 Sandbanks Road, Poole BH14 8AQ
☎ 01202-740066 **Fax** 01202-736780
15 bedrs, all ensuite, **P** 32 Rest Resid **SB** £46-£48 **DB** £60-£68 **L** £9.95 **L** **D** £15.95 **D** ✕ **LD** 21:00 Restaurant closed L Mon-Sat, D Sun **℃** MC Visa Amex

PORLOCK Somerset 3D2
Pop. 1,400. Minehead 5½, London 173, Lynmouth 11 **EC** Wed

★★ Oaks
Blue Ribbon Hotel
Porlock TA24 8ES
☎ 01643-862265 **Fax** 01643-863131
9 bedrs, all ensuite, **P** 12 No children under 8 Rest Resid **SB** £55 **DB** £95 **HB** £420 **D** £27 ✕ **LD** 20:30 **℃** MC Visa Amex

★ Ship Inn
High Street, Porlock TA24 8QD
☎ 01643-862507 **Fax** 01643-863224
11 bedrs, all ensuite, **P** 20 **SB** £27.50 **DB** £50 **L** **D** £15 **D** ✕ **LD** 21:30 **℃** MC Visa

PORLOCK WEIR Somerset 3D2
Pop. 1,400. Minehead 7½, London 175, Lynmouth 13

★★★ Anchor & Ship
Porlock Weir TA24 8PB
☎ 01643-862753 **Fax** 01643-862843
Closed Jan
20 bedrs, all ensuite, 40 **P** 20 **℃** MC Visa Amex
See advert on opposite page

PORTSCATHO Cornwall 2B4
Pop. 500. St Austell 15, London 255, Falmouth (fy) 14, Newquay 25, Truro (fy) 10 **see** Quay

★★★ Rosevine
Blue Ribbon Hotel
Porthcurnick Beach, Portscatho TR2 5EW
☎ 01872-580206 **Fax** 01872-580230
E-mail info@makepeacehotels.co.uk
Closed Nov-Jan

Cornwall's newest luxury hotel with award winning cuisine. Overlooking sub-tropical gardens with glorious sea views. Deluxe bedrooms with many thoughtful extras and a heated indoor swimming pool are to be enjoyed.
17 bedrs, all ensuite, **P** 40 **℃** MC Visa
See advert on opposite page

EXMOOR NATIONAL PARK
PORTLOCK HARBOUR

Quiet comfortable hotel at water's edge of small picturesque harbour amidst Exmoor's magnificent scenery and spectacular coastline near North Devon border.

Superb food and attentive service.

ANCHOR HOTEL
Tel: 01643 862753
Fax: 01643 862843

PORTSMOUTH & SOUTHSEA Hampshire　4B4
Pop. 181,000. Cosham 4, London 71, M275 1½
MD Thu, Sat *see* Cathedral, Dicken's Birthplace and Museum, Dockyard (Nelson's flagship Victory and Museum), HMS Mary Rose. Southsea; D-Day Memorial, Castle ℹ Clarence Esplanade, Southsea 01705-832464 and The Hard 01705-826722

ENGLAND

National Code & Number Change
Telephone codes and numbers in Portsmouth change in April 2000.
01705-XXXXXX becomes 023-92XX XXXX
eg 01705-926222 becomes 023-9292 6222

★★★ ✧ Innlodge
Burrfields Road, Portsmouth PO3 5HH
☎ 01705-650510 **Fax** 01705-693458
73 bedrs, all ensuite, ⁴ ⚌ 150 **P** 400 ⊞ ⟪ MC Visa Amex DC ▣ ▨ ⟨

★★★ Posthouse　　　　　**Posthouse**
Pembroke Road, Portsmouth PO1 2TA
☎ 01705-827651 **Fax** 01705-756715
167 bedrs, all ensuite, ✗ ⊁ ▣ ⚌ 220 **P** 80 ⊞
SB £69.95-£99.95 **DB** £79.95-£109.95 **D** ☛ ✕ **LD** 22:00
Restaurant closed (L) Saturday ⟪ MC Visa Amex DC ▣ ▨ ▨ ▨ ⟨

★★★ Queen's
Clarence Parade, Southsea PO5 3LJ
☎ 01705-822466 **Fax** 01705-821901

Splendid Edwardian style with panoramic views of the Solent, offering a selection of bars and an award winning restaurant. Easily accessible from M275 and continental ferry port. Ample, secure, free parking.
73 bedrs, all ensuite, ▣ ⚌ 150 **P** 100 ⊞ ⟪ MC Visa Amex DC JCB ⚘

★★★ ✧ Royal Beach
South Parade, Portsmouth PO4 0RN
☎ 01705-731281 **Fax** 01705-817572
115 bedrs, all ensuite, ⊁ ▣ ⚌ 250 **P** 50 ⊞ **SB** £75
DB £85 **D** £15.50 ✕ **LD** 21:45 ⟪ MC Visa Amex DC JCB

★★ ✦ Beaufort
71 Festing Road, Portsmouth PO4 0NQ
☎ 01705-823707 **Fax** 01705-870270
20 bedrs, all ensuite, ④ ♀ ♬ **P** 10 No children under
10 ⊟ Rest **SB** £40-£55 **DB** £48-£78 **HB** £240-£290 **L** ♥
✕ **LD** 20:00 **CC** MC Visa Amex DC

★★ ✦ Sandringham
Osborne Road, Clarence Parade,
Portsmouth PO5 3LR
☎ 01705-826969 **Fax** 01705-822330
44 bedrs, all ensuite, ④ ☰ ⌗ 120 ⊟ Resid **SB** £35-
£45 **DB** £50-£56 **HB** £200-£225 **D** £11.50 ✕ **LD** 20:30
CC MC Visa Amex ⊞

★★ ✦ Seacrest
12 South Parade, Portsmouth PO5 2JB
☎ 01705-875666 **Fax** 01705-832523
28 bedrs, all ensuite, ④ ⊁ ☰ **P** 10 ⊟ Resid **CC** MC Visa

Solent Awaiting Inspection
14-17 South Parade, Southsea PO5 2JB
☎ 01705-875566 **Fax** 01705-872023
50 bedrs, all ensuite, ♬ ☰ ⌗ 45 **P** 4 ⊟ Resid
SB £45-£55 **DB** £52.50-£67.50 **HB** £247.50-£315 **L** ♥
D ♥ ✕ **LD** 20:45 Restaurant closed L Sun **CC** MC
Visa Amex DC JCB ⊞ ⅙

PRESTBURY Cheshire   7E1

★★★ ✦ Bridge
Prestbury SK10 4DQ
☎ 01625-829326 **Fax** 01625-827557

Situated in the pretty village of Prestbury and
originally dating from 1626, the Bridge Hotel
combines old world character and charm with all
the comfort and facilities of a modern hotel.
23 bedrs, all ensuite, ♬ ⌗ 100 **P** 52 ⊟ **SB** £51.50-
£93.50 **DB** £103-£107 **L** ♥ **D** £10.95 ✕ **LD** 21:45 Rest
closed D Sun **CC** MC Visa Amex DC JCB ⅙

PRESTON Lancashire   10B4
ℹ Guildhall, Lancaster Road 01772-253731

★★★ Novotel Preston
Reedfield Place, Walton Summit, Preston PR5 8AA
☎ 01772-313331 **Fax** 01772-627868
E-mail h0838@accor-hotels.com
98 bedrs, all ensuite, ♬ ⊁ ☰ ⌗ 180 **P** 120 ⊟
SB £50-£63.50 **DB** £50-£72 **L** £6.95 **D** £13.50 ✕
LD 00:00 **CC** MC Visa Amex DC ⅔ ⊞ ⅙

★★★ Posthouse   **Posthouse**
The Ringway, Preston PR1 3AU
☎ 01772-259411 **Fax** 01722-201923
119 bedrs, all ensuite, ⊁ ☰ ⌗ 120 **P** 25 ⊟ **SB** £58.95-
£88.95 **DB** £58.95-£88.95 **HB** £32-£35 **L** £5.95 **L** ♥
D £10 **D** ♥ ✕ **LD** 22:30 **CC** MC Visa Amex DC ⅙

★★★ Swallow ⅋
Preston New Road, Samlesbury,
Preston PR5 0UL
☎ 01772-877351 **Fax** 01772-877424
E-mail info@swallowhotels.com

Extensively refurbished, this friendly hotel is well
placed for the best of the North West, including
Blackpool and the Lake District. It also has leisure
facilities.
78 bedrs, all ensuite, ⊁ ☰ ⌗ 250 **P** 300 ⊟ **SB** £80
DB £110 **L** £8.95 **D** £17.75 ✕ **LD** 21:30 Restaurant
closed L Sat **CC** MC Visa Amex DC ⊡ ⊞ 🖭 ⊞ ⅙

★★ Claremont
516 Blackpool Road, Ashton, Preston PR2 1HY
☎ 01772-729738 **Fax** 01772-726274
14 bedrs, all ensuite, ④ ♬ ⌗ 75 **P** 25 ⊟ **SB** £38.50
DB £55 **D** £11.95 ✕ **LD** 20:30 **CC** MC Visa Amex DC

PRINCES RISBOROUGH Buckinghamshire   4C2

★★ Rose & Crown
Wycombe Road, Saunderton, HP27 9NP
☎ 01844-345299 **Fax** 01844-343140
Closed Christmas
15 bedrs, all ensuite, ⌗ 30 **P** 40 ⊟ **SB** £65-£68.25
DB £77-£80.95 **D** ♥ ✕ **LD** 22:00 Restaurant closed D
Sun **CC** MC Visa Amex DC

PULBOROUGH West Sussex   4C4

★★ ✤ Chequers
Church Place, Pulborough RH20 1AD
☎ 01798-872486 **Fax** 01798-872715
11 bedrs, 10 ensuite, ④ ⊩ ⠿ 19 **P** 16 ⊞ ⲥ MC Visa Amex DC

QUORN Leicestershire   8B3

★★★★ Quorn Country ♖ ♖ ♖
Charnwood House, 66 Leicester Road, Quorn LE12 8BB
☎ 01509-415050 **Fax** 01509-415557

You'll find the comfortable atmosphere of this four star award winning hotel is 'designed to impress

but not overwhelm'.
23 bedrs, all ensuite, ④ ⠿ 100 **P** 100 ⊞ **SB** £97-£101.95 **DB** £116-£133.90 **L** £15 **D** £20 ✕ **LD** 21:45 Restaurant closed L Sat ⲥ MC Visa Amex DC ▣ �

---

RAMSBOTTOM Lancashire   10C4

★★★ Old Mill
Springwood Street, Ramsbottom BL0 9DS
☎ 01706-822991 **Fax** 01706-822291

Friendly hotel with superb leisure club offering sauna, solarium and pool. The Garden restaurant offers wonderful views and highly acclaimed French/English cuisine.
36 bedrs, all ensuite, ④ ⠿ 35 **P** 100 ⊞ ⲥ MC Visa Amex DC ③ ⊞

RANGEWORTHY Gloucestershire   3E1

★★ Rangeworthy Court ♖
Church Lane, Rangeworthy BS17 5ND
☎ 01454-228347 **Fax** 01454-228945
E-mail hotel@rangeworthy.demon.co.uk

Friendly, comfortable 17th century country manor house with log fires, excellent gardens and good parking. High quality food. Easily reached off the M4 and M5.
13 bedrs, all ensuite, ④ ♀ ♪ ⊩ ⠿ 16 **P** 30 ⊞
SB £62-£75 **DB** £70-£85 **L** ♥ **D** £18.50 **D** ♥ ✕
LD 21:00 ⲥ MC Visa Amex DC ⌁

ENGLAND

RAVENSTONEDALE Cumbria 10B2
Kirkby Lonsdale 21, London 267, Brough 9, Hawes
21, Kendal 18, Penrith 28 **see** Parish Church,
Scandal Beck Valley

Black Swan
Kirkby Stephen, Ravenstonedale CA17 4NG
☎ 01539-623204 **Fax** 01539-623604

Superb cuisine, fine wines, real ales. Ideal for
touring Lakes and Dales, fishing and walking. 10
minutes - jn 38 M6.
17 bedrs, all ensuite, ⚲ ⚏ 20 **P** 40 ⏣ ⓒ MC Visa
Amex DC JCB 🔲 ◪ &

UPCROSS
HOTEL & RESTAURANT
RAC
★★★ *Reading*

- House of character and warmth.
- One of the best restaurants in Berkshire.
- Daily and à la carte menu.
- Conferences, weddings and private parties.

Featured on BBC television.

Easy access from junctions 11 and 12 of the M4

BERKELEY AVENUE, READING RG1 6HY
Tel: 0118 9590796 Fax: 0118 9576517

READING Berkshire 4B2
Pop. 131,000. Slough 18, London 38, A329 (M) 1½,
Bagshot 16, Basingstoke 16, Farnham 25, Henley-
on-Thames 8, Newbury 15, Staines 22, Wallingford
14 **MD** Mon, Wed, Fri, Sat **see** Art Gallery and
Museum (Roman collection from Silchester), Town
Hall, remains of Norman Abbey, Churches - St
Laurence's, St Mary's, St Matthew's, St Giles,
Greyfriars 🛈 Town Hall, Blagrave Street 0118-956
6226

★★★ Hanover International, Reading

Pingewood, Reading RG33 3UN
☎ 0118-950 0885 **Fax** 0118-939 1996

Stunning modern hotel in a spectacular lakeside
setting, convenient for London, Windsor Castle,
Legoland, M4 Heathrow and Gatwick. Extensive
indoor and outdoor leisure facilities, including
watersports.
81 bedrs, all ensuite, ♀ ⊡ ⚏ 110 **P** 225 ⏣ **SB** £42-
£125 **DB** £84-£147 **L** £14.50 **D** £18.25 ✕ **LD** 21:30
Restaurant closed L Sat ⓒ MC Visa Amex DC ③ ☒
🔲 🔳 ☒ ◪ ☒ &

★★★ Posthouse   **Posthouse**
Basingstoke Road, Reading RG2 0SL
☎ 0118-987 5485 **Fax** 0118-931 1958
202 bedrs, all ensuite, ⋗ ⚲ ⚏ 100 **P** 450 ⏣ **SB** £69-
£129 **DB** £79-£139 **L** £7.95 **L** ⚌ **D** £15 **D** ⚌ ✕
LD 22:30 Restaurant closed (L) saturday ⓒ MC Visa
Amex DC ③ ☒ 🔲 &

★★ Mill House
Old Basingstoke Road, Swallowfield,
Reading RG7 1PY
☎ 0118-988 3124 **Fax** 0118-988 5550
Closed 24 Dec-3 Jan
10 bedrs, all ensuite, ④ ⋗ ⚲ ⚏ 100 **P** 60 ⏣ **SB** £65-
£70 **DB** £80-£100 **L** £15 **L** ⚌ **D** £20 **D** ⚌ ✕ **LD** 21:30
Restaurant closed L Sat & Mon, D Sun ⓒ MC Visa
Amex ◪
See advert on opposite page

Mill House Hotel

Charming family run Georgian House set in beautiful gardens beside the River Loddon. Ten individually decorated bedrooms offering en suite facilities and views over the gardens and River. All rooms offer Satellite Television, direct dial telephone, Tea & coffee making facilities, trouser press, room service.
Our elegant restaurant offer Table d'hote, a la carte and bar menu to suit all diners. Full conference facilities and celebrations catered for.

Old Basingstoke Road, Swallowfield, Reading RG7 1PY
Tel: 0118 988 3124 Fax: 0118 988 5550

★★ ❖ Rainbow Corner
132 Caversham Road, Reading RG1 8AY
📞 0118-958 8140 **Fax** 0118-958-6500
E-mail marcladi@aol.com
24 bedrs, all ensuite, ⚊ ⚌ 30 **P** 21 ⊞ Resid **℃** MC Visa Amex DC

★★ Upcross ⛲
68 Berkeley Avenue, Reading RG1 6HY
📞 0118 959 0796 **Fax** 0118 957 6517
26 bedrs, all ensuite, ♀ ⌀ ⚊ ⚌ 60 **P** 60 ⊞ Rest
Resid **SB** £32.50-£72.50 **DB** £51-£82.50 **L** £15 **L** ☞
D £17.50 **D** ☞ ✕ **LD** 22:00 Restaurant closed L Sat
℃ MC Visa Amex DC JCB ♿
See advert on opposite page

REDCAR Cleveland   11D2
Pop. 36,400. London 254, Middlesbrough 8½,
Northallerton 31, Pickering 36, Whitby 22 **EC** Wed

★★ ❖ Hotel Royal York
27 Coatham Road, Redcar TS10 1RP
📞 01642-486221 **Fax** 01642-486221
50 bedrs, all ensuite, ☎ ⚌ 200 **P** 300 ⊞ **℃** MC Visa
Amex DC ▨ ♿

REDDITCH Worcestershire   7F3
Pop. 79,700. Stratford-upon-Avon 15, London 108,
Evesham 16 **EC** Wed **MD** Tue, Wed, Thur, Fri, Sat
ℹ Civic Square, Alcester Street 01527-60806

★★★ Quality
Pool Bank, Mount Pleasant, B97 4JS
📞 01527-541511 **Fax** 01527-402600
E-mail admin@gb646.u-net.com

Approximately a half hours drive from the National Exhibition Centre, Warwick, Stratford, Worcester, and the Cotswolds. Fifty eight ensuite bedrooms, set in seven acres of gardens and woods.
58 bedrs, all ensuite, ⚊ ⚌ 160 **P** 100 ⊞ **SB** £82.75-£91.25 **DB** £107.25-£124.50 **L** £11.50 **D** £14.50 ✕
LD 21:15 **℃** MC Visa Amex DC JCB ♿

Campanile Redditch Lodge
Far Moor Lane, Winyates Green,
Redditch B98 0SD
☎ 01527-510710 **Fax** 01527-517269

Campanile hotels offer comfortable and convenient budget accommodation and a traditional French style Bistro providing freshly cooked food for breakfast, lunch and dinner. All rooms ensuite with tea/coffee making facilities, DDT and TV with Sky channels.
50 bedrs, all ensuite, ⚲ ⠿ 20 **P** 50 No children under 18 ⊞ Rest Resid **SB** £41.95 **DB** £46.90 **L** £5.95 **D** £10.95 ✕ **LD** 22:00 **CC** MC Visa Amex DC ⅋

REDRUTH Cornwall   2A4
Pop. 10,200. Bodmin 30, London 263, Falmouth 10, Helston 10, Newquay 15, Penzance 17, St Ives 14, Truro 9 **EC** Thu **MD** Fri

★★ Aviary Court ⌑
Mary's Well, Illogan, Redruth TR16 4QZ
☎ 01209-842256 **Fax** 01209-843744
E-mail aviarycourt@connexions.co.uk.
6 bedrs, all ensuite, **P** 25 No children under 3 ⊞ Rest Resid **SB** £44 **DB** £60 **HB** £258 **L** £9 **D** £13 ✕ **LD** 20:45 Restaurant closed L Mon-Sat **CC** MC Visa Amex

---

REIGATE Surrey   5D3
Pop. 21,800. Purley 8½, London 21, M25 (jn 8) 2, Crawley 10, Dorking 6, East Grinstead 14, Epsom 9, Haywards Heath 18, Leatherhead 8½, Mitcham 12, Redhill 1½ **EC** Wed **see** Castle grounds and Baron's Cave, St Mary's Church

★★★ ✤ Bridge House
Reigate Hill, Reigate RH2 9RP
☎ 01737-246801 **Fax** 01737-223756
39 bedrs, all ensuite, ⠿ 100 **P** 110 ⊞ **CC** MC Visa Amex DC

★★★ Reigate Manor
Reigate Hill, Reigate RH2 9PF
☎ 01737-240125 **Fax** 01737-223883
E-mail hotel@reigatemanor.btinternet.com
50 bedrs, all ensuite, ④ ⠿ 200 **P** 130 ⊞ **SB** £90-£120 **DB** £100-£140 **L** £11.50 **L** ● **D** £14.50 **D** ● ✕ **LD** 22:00 Restaurant closed L Sat **CC** MC Visa Amex DC ⌧ ▦

RENISHAW Derbyshire   8B1
Pop. 1,800. Mansfield 13, London 151, M1 (jn 30) 2, Chesterfield 7, Doncaster 22, Sheffield 9, Worksop 9

Sitwell Arms
Station Road, Renishaw S21 3WF
☎ 01246-435226 **Fax** 01246-433915

Easy access to Sheffield and Chesterfield. Fourposter suites, delightful restaurant, bar and banqueting suite with reasonably priced menus. Friendly hotel, meetings, conferences and weddings from 6-200 catered for.
30 bedrs, all ensuite, ④ ⠿ 150 **P** 100 ⊞ **SB** £22.50-£47.95 **DB** £55.50-£67.50 **D** £9.95 ✕ **LD** 21:30 **CC** MC Visa Amex

---

RICHMOND North Yorkshire   10C2
Pop. 7,300. Boroughbridge 25, London 233, Brough 32, Darlington 12, Leyburn 10, Middleton-in-Teesdale 28, Northallerton 14 **EC** Wed **MD** Sat **see** Holy Trinity Church, St Mary's Church, Green Howards' Museum, Castle ruins ⅋ Friary Garden, Victoria Road 01748-850252

★★ Frenchgate ⌑
59/61 Frenchgate, Richmond DL10 7AE
☎ 01748-822087 **Fax** 01748-823596
11 bedrs, all ensuite, ♀ ⌀ ⚲ ⠿ 26 **P** 9 ⊞ **SB** £37 **DB** £60 **HB** £344 **L** ● **D** ● ✕ **LD** 21:45 **CC** MC Visa Amex DC JCB

★★ King's Head ⓡ
Market Place, Richmond DL10 4HS
☎ 01748-850220 **Fax** 01748-850635
E-mail res@khead.demon.co.uk
30 bedrs, all ensuite, ▦ ⋔ ⫴ 200 **P** 25 ⊟ **SB** £55-£63 **DB** £86-£96 **HB** £333-£417 **L** £10 **L** ⦿ **D** £17.95
D ⦿ ✕ **LD** 21:15 Restaurant closed L Mon-Sat
㏄ MC Visa Amex DC JCB

RICHMOND-UPON-THAMES Surrey   4C2
Pop. 41,000. London 8½, Kingston upon Thames 3½, Mitcham 9, Slough 13, Staines 16, Weybridge 10 **EC** Wed **see** Remains of Palace on the Green, Maids of Honour Row, Almshouses ⓘ Old Town Hall, Whittaker Avenue 0181-940 9125

★★★★ ✦ Richmond Gate
Richmond Hill, Richmond-upon-Thames TW10 6RP
☎ 0181-940 0061 **Fax** 0181-332 0354
66 bedrs, all ensuite, ▦ ⫴ 70 **P** 50 ⊟ ㏄ MC Visa Amex DC JCB 🔲 🔳 🔲

Petersham
Nightingale Lane,
Richmond-upon-Thames TW10 6UZ
☎ 0181-940 7471 **Fax** 0181-939 1098

With breathtaking views of the Thames, the Petersham, just eight miles from Heathrow and Central London, is ideal for receptions, meetings and weekend breaks. Excellent and busy restaurant overlooking the River Thames.
60 bedrs, all ensuite, 🔲 ⫴ 28 **P** 50 ⊟ ㏄ MC Visa Amex DC

RINGWOOD Hampshire   4A4
Romsey 17, London 93, Bournemouth 12, Dorchester 32, Lymington 13, Salisbury 16, Southampton 18 **EC** Thu **MD** Wed ⓘ The Furlong 01425-470896

Struan Country Inn
Horton Road, Ashley Heath, Ringwood BH24 2EG
☎ 01425-473553 **Fax** 01425-480529

Superb country inn, with restaurant, bar and 10 ensuite bedrooms. Situated on the edge of the New Forest, easy access for Bournemouth, Poole, Christchurch, Salisbury. Golfing, walking, fishing and riding available.
10 bedrs, all ensuite, ▦ ⋔ **P** 72 ⊟ **SB** £40-£50 **DB** £50-£70 **HB** £245-£280 **L** £8 **D** £13 ✕ **LD** 21:45
㏄ MC Visa Amex ♿

RIPON North Yorkshire   11D3
Pop. 14,600. Harrogate 11, London 216, Boroughbridge 6, Darlington 35, Leyburn 20, Northallerton 18, Skipton 29, Thirsk 11 **EC** Wed **MD** Thu **see** Cathedral, St Wilfrid's Church, Wakeman's House (13th cent), Wakeman's Horn blown nightly at 9 pm, Fountains Abbey 3m SW, Newby Hall, 3½m SE ⓘ Minster Road 01765-604625

★★ Unicorn
Market Place, Ripon HG4 1BP
☎ 01765-602202 **Fax** 01765-690734
E-mail unicornhotel@bronco.co.uk
Closed Christmas
33 bedrs, all ensuite, ⋔ ⫴ 60 **P** 19 ⊟ **SB** £47 **DB** £67 **HB** £252 **L** £8.95 **L** ⦿ **D** £14.95 **D** ⦿ ✕ **LD** 21:00
Restaurant closed L Mon-Fri ㏄ MC Visa Amex DC JCB

ROCHESTER Kent   5E2
Pop. 144,700. London 30, Canterbury 26, Maidstone 8, Tonbridge 19 **EC** Wed **MD** Fri **see** Castle (open to public), Cathedral, 17th cent Guildhall, Corn Exchange ⓘ Eastgate Cottage, High Street 01634-843666

★★★★ Bridgewood Manor 🛏 🛏 🛏
Bridgewood Roundabout,
Maidstone Road, Rochester ME5 9AX
📞 01634-201333 **Fax** 01634-201330
E-mail bridgewoodmanor@marstonhotels.co.uk
100 bedrs, all ensuite, 🍴 ▣ ⠿ 200 **P** 175 ⊟ **SB** £104
DB £130 **HB** £408 **L** £18 **D** £26 ✕ **LD** 22:00 **CC** MC Visa
Amex DC 🗗 🖼 🖼 🖼 🖼 🖟

★★★ Posthouse   **Posthouse**
Maidstone Road, Chatham,
Rochester ME5 9SF
📞 01634-687111 **Fax** 01634-684512
145 bedrs, all ensuite, 🖉 🍴 ▣ ⠿ 110
P 250 ⊟ **DB** £60-£72 **HB** £59-£99 **L** £8.95
L 🍷 **D** £16 **D** 🍷 ✕ **LD** 22:00
CC MC Visa Amex DC 🗗 🖼 🖼 🖼 🖟

★ Royal Victoria & Bull
16-18 High Street, Rochester ME1 1PX
📞 01634-846266 **Fax** 01634-832312

Historic hotel in the centre of Rochester with
Dickens connections. Our Giannino's Restaurant
offers an extensive range of Italian dishes at
excellent value for money and is open all year
round.
28 bedrs, 21 ensuite, 1 🐾 🔟 🍴 ⠿ 120 **P** 25 ⊟
SB £45-£57.50 **DB** £57-£72.50 **L** £10 **L** 🍷 **D** £10 ✕
LD 22:30 **CC** MC Visa Amex DC

ROCHFORD Essex   5E2
Pop. 13,900. Romford 26, London 42, Brentwood
21, Chelmsford 18, Colchester 36, Dartford
Crossing 26, Southend-on-Sea 3. **MD** Tue

★★★ Renouf
Bradley Way, Rochford SS4 1BU
📞 01702-541334 **Fax** 01702-549563
23 bedrs, all ensuite, 🍴 ⠿ **P** 30 ⊟ **SB** £49.50-£59.50
DB £69.50-£79.50 **L** £30 **D** £30 ✕ **LD** 21:45
Restaurant closed **L** Sat **CC** MC Visa Amex DC 🖟
See advert on this page

ENGLAND

ROCK Cornwall   2B3
Pop. 1,000. Camelford 14, London 241, Wadebridge 6½ **EC** Wed

★★ Mariners
Slipway, Rock, Nr Wadebridge PL27 6LD
☎ 01208-862312 **Fax** 01208-863827
E-mail amiller767@aol.com
Closed Nov-Mar
22 bedrs, all ensuite, **↠ ⋕** 35 **P** 22 **⊞ SB** £35-£40 **DB** £55-£60 **HB** £296-£322 **L ♥ D** £16 **D ♥ ✕ LD** 21:00
CC MC Visa Amex JCB
See advert on opposite page

ROMALDKIRK Co. Durham   10C2
Pop. 160. Boroughbridge 47, London 254, Brough 16, Darlington 21, Durham 26, Middleton-in-Teesdale 4, West Auckland 14 **see** Bowes Museum, 12th-14th cent Cathedral of the Dales, Market Cross, Barnard Castle

★★ Rose & Crown ⿴ ⿴
Barnard Castle, Romaldkirk DL12 9EB
☎ 01833-650213 **Fax** 01833-650828
E-mail hotel@rose-and-crown.co.uk
Closed 25-26 Dec

An 18th century stone-built traditional coaching inn set on the middle green in one of Teesdale's loveliest locations.
12 bedrs, all ensuite, **④ ↠ P** 40 **⊞ SB** £62 **DB** £84 **HB** £415 **L** £13.50 **L ♥ D** £24 **D ♥ ✕ LD** 21:00
Restaurant closed L Mon-Sat, D Sun **CC** MC Visa ◔

ROMSEY Hampshire   4B3
Pop. 14,700. Winchester 10, London 75, M27 (jn 2) 3, Andover 17, Lyndhurst 9½, Ringwood 17, Salisbury 15, Southampton 8 **EC** Wed **see** Abbey Church, Palmerston's Statue, King John's House (13th cent) **ℹ** 1 Latimer Street 01794-512987

★★★ White Horse
Market Place, Romsey SO5 8NA
☎ 01794-512431 **Fax** 01794-517485
33 bedrs, all ensuite, **↠ ⋕** 40 **P** 50 **⊞ SB** £60-£95 **DB** £92-£106 **HB** £325-£375 **L** £5.95 **L ♥ D** £9.95 **D ♥ ✕ LD** 21:00 **CC** MC Visa Amex DC JCB ◔

Heritage HOTELS

ROSS-ON-WYE Herefordshire   7E4
Pop. 8,500. Gloucester 16, London 121, M50 (jn 4) 1½, Chepstow 24, Hereford 14, Ledbury 12, Monmouth 10, Tewkesbury 24 **EC** Wed **MD** Thu, Sat **ℹ** Swan House, Edde Cross Street 01989-562768

★★★ Chase ⿴
Gloucester Road,
Ross-on-Wye HR9 5LH
☎ 01989-763161 **Fax** 01989-768330
38 bedrs, all ensuite, **④ ⋕** 300 **P** 150 No children **⊞ SB** £60 **DB** £75 **L** £12.50 **L ♥ D** £17 **D ♥ ✕ LD** 21:45
CC MC Visa Amex DC
See advert on this page

BRIDGE HOUSE HOTEL

Quiet riverside hotel, yet only ten minutes easy walk along the river into Ross-on-Wye. Hospitality, service and quality restaurant meals are our speciality.

**WILTON, ROSS-ON-WYE, HEREFORDSHIRE HR9 6AA
Tel: 01989 562655**

★★★ Pencraig Court Country House ♮ ♮
Pencraig, Ross-on-Wye HR9 6HR
☎ 01989-770306 **Fax** 01989-770040
E-mail mike@pencraig-court.co.uk

A Georgian country hotel and restaurant in pleasant 4 acre grounds with country views of the Wye Valley.
11 bedrs, all ensuite, 🅿 ♪ ⊁ ∷ 25 **P** 25 ♨ Rest
Resid **SB** £45-£50 **DB** £67.50-£72.50 **HB** £316.75-£334.25 **D** £23 ✕ **LD** 21:00 **CC** MC Visa Amex ⊠

★★★ Pengethley Manor ♮ ♮
Ross-on-Wye HR9 6LL
☎ 01989-730211 **Fax** 01989-730238
E-mail reservations@penethleymanor.co.uk
25 bedrs, all ensuite, 🅿 ⊁ ∷ 25 **P** 70 ♨ **SB** £75
DB £120 **HB** £450 **L** £10 **L** ▪ **D** £25 **D** ▪ ✕ **LD** 21:30
CC MC Visa Amex DC JCB ⫶ ▣ ▨ ▦ ♿

★★★ Royal
Palace Pound,
Ross-on-Wye HR9 5HZ
☎ 01989-565105 **Fax** 01989-768058
40 bedrs, all ensuite, ⊁ ∷ 40 **P** 40 ♨
SB £45-£55 **DB** £90-£110 **HB** £570-£650
L £11.95 **D** £19.95 ✕ **LD** 21:15
CC MC Visa Amex DC

★★ ❖ Bridge House
Wilton, Ross-on-Wye HR9 6AA
☎ 01989-562655 **Fax** 01989-567652
9 bedrs, 8 ensuite, ⊁ **P** 15 ♨ Resid **SB** £33.50-£34
DB £52 **HB** £230 **D** £15.50 ✕ **LD** 20:00 **CC** MC Visa
See advert on this page

★★ ❖ Castle Lodge
Wilton, Ross-on-Wye HR9 6AD
☎ 01989-562234 **Fax** 01989-768322
10 bedrs, all ensuite, ⊁ ∷ 20 **P** 30 ♨ **CC** MC Visa
Amex

★★ ❖ Chasedale
Walford Road, Ross-on-Wye HR9 5PQ
☎ 01989-562423 **Fax** 01989-567900
10 bedrs, all ensuite, ⊁ ∷ 40 **P** 14 ♨ **SB** £29.50-£33
DB £59-£66 **HB** £260-£275 **L** £10.80 **D** £13.75 ✕
LD 21:00 Restaurant closed L Mon-Sat **CC** MC Visa
DC JCB

★★ Orles Barn
Wilton, Ross-on-Wye HR9 6AE
☎ 01989-562155 **Fax** 01989-768470
Closed Nov

This privately owned and personally run 17th century converted farmhouse on one and a half acres, with a heated swimming pool offers an excellent menu in a relaxing atmosphere.
9 bedrs, all ensuite, ♀ ♪ ⊁ ∷ 12 **P** 20 ♨ Rest
Resid **SB** £45-£48 **DB** £58-£68 **HB** £225-£295 **L** £11.50
D £16.50 **D** ▪ ✕ **LD** 21:15 Restaurant closed L Mon-Sat **CC** MC Visa Amex JCB ⫶ ♿
See advert on opposite page

ENGLAND

Orles Barn Hotel

This 17th Century converted Barn was recently taken over by Rob & Samantha Luscombe from South Africa. Their warm & friendly style, together with the excellent food, outdoor BBQs around the heated pool, and comfortable en suite rooms, makes this the ideal spot from which to explore the Wye Valley. Special Golfers breaks are arranged by Rob, himself a single figure player.

**Orles Barn Hotel, Wilton, Ross-on-Wye, Herefordshire HR9 6AE
Tel: 01989 562155   Fax: 01989 768470**

★ Rosswyn
High Street, Ross-on-Wye HR9 5BZ
☎ 01989-562733 **Fax** 01989-562733
8 bedrs, 7 ensuite, 🗻 ♬ ✝ ### 12 **P** 8 ⊞ **SB** £30-£40
DB £60-£80 **L** ● **D** £12.95 **D** ● ✕ **LD** 21:30
Restaurant closed D Sun ⓒ MC Visa Amex

ROTHERHAM South Yorkshire   11D4
Pop. 80,200. Mansfield 23, London 161, M1 (jn 34)
2½, Barnsley 11, Chesterfield 16, Sheffield 5½,
EC Thu **MD** Mon, Fri, Sat **see** Ancient Bridge with
Chapel, All Saints' Church, Museum and Art Gallery
🛈 Library, Walker Place 01709-823611

★★★★ Hellaby Hall 🛱
Old Hellaby Lane, Hellaby, S66 8SN
☎ 01709-702701 **Fax** 01709-700979
E-mail hhh@scottishhighlandhotels.co.uk
52 bedrs, all ensuite, 🗻 ♬ ✝ 🖃 ### 140 **P** 235 ⊞
SB £45-£94 **DB** £79-£110 **L** £10.50 **D** £20 **D** ● ✕
LD 22:00 ⓒ MC Visa Amex DC 🖃 ☒ ⅙

★★★ Consort
Brampton Road, Thurcroft, Rotherham S66 9JA
☎ 01709-530022 **Fax** 01709-531529
18 bedrs, all ensuite, ### 300 **P** 90 ⊞ ⓒ MC Visa
Amex DC ⅙

★★★ Elton
Main Street, Bramley, Rotherham S66 0SF
☎ 01709-545681 **Fax** 01709-549100
29 bedrs, all ensuite, ♀ ✝ ### 40 **P** 44 ⊞ **SB** £61.95-
£76.95 **DB** £67.90-£93.90 **L** £12.50 **L** ● **D** £20 **D** ● ✕
LD 21:30 ⓒ MC Visa Amex DC JCB ⅙

★★★ Swallow 🛱
West Bawtry Road, S60 4NA
☎ 01709-830630 **Fax** 01709-830549
E-mail info@swallowhotels.com

SWALLOW
HOTELS

A modern hotel, conveniently located for the M1
motorway. The hotel has an award winning
restaurant, bar and a leisure club.
100 bedrs, all ensuite, ✝ 🖃 ### 300 **P** 262 ⊞ **SB** £60-
£85 **DB** £74-£99 **D** £17 ✕ **LD** 21:30 ⓒ MC Visa Amex
DC 🖃 ☒ 🖭 ⅙

★★ Brecon

Moorgate Road, Rotherham S60 2AY
☎ 01709-828811 **Fax** 01709-513030

A family run hotel where you will find true Yorkshire hospitality. Excellent restaurant, good standard of accommodation. Ideal location for the M1 and Meadowhall Shopping Centre.
27 bedrs, 22 ensuite, 5 🐾 🛏 ♨ 40 **P** 40 ⊞ Rest
CC MC Visa Amex DC

★★ Brentwood

Moorgate Road, Rotherham S60 2TY
☎ 01709-382772 **Fax** 01709-820289
30 bedrs, 25 ensuite, ④ 🛏 ♨ 24 **P** 86 ⊞ **SB** £35-£49
DB £49-£56 **HB** £300 **L** £11 **L** 🍷 **D** £15 ✕ **LD** 21:00
CC MC Visa Amex DC JCB

Campanile Rotherham **Lodge**

Lowton Way, off Denby Way,
Hellaby Industrial Estate,
Rotherham S66 8RY
☎ 01709-700255 **Fax** 01709-545169

Campanile hotels offer comfortable and convenient budget accommodation and a traditional French style Bistro providing freshly cooked food for breakfast, lunch and dinner. All rooms ensuite with tea/coffee making facilities, DDT and TV with Sky channels.
50 bedrs, all ensuite, 🛏 ♨ 25 **P** 50 ⊞ Rest Resid
SB £41.95 **DB** £46.90 **L** £5.75 **L** 🍷 **D** £10.85 **D** 🍷 ✕
LD 22:00 **CC** MC Visa Amex DC ♿

ROTHERWICK Hampshire   4B3
Pop. 500. Camberley 13, London 43, Basingstoke 7, Farnham 13, Reading 12

★★★★ Tylney Hall 冊 冊 冊
Gold Ribbon Hotel
Rotherwick, Hook RG27 9AZ
☎ 01256-764881 Fax 01256-768141
E-mail sales@tylneyhall.com
110 bedrs, all ensuite, ④ ♪ ⅲ 100 P 120 ⊞ SB £115 DB £145 L £23 D £33 ✕ LD 21:30 ℂℂ MC Visa Amex DC JCB 国 ⊀ 困 圖 ▶ 風 困
See advert on opposite page

Campanile hotels offer comfortable and convenient budget accommodation and a traditional French style Bistro providing freshly cooked food for breakfast, lunch and dinner. All rooms ensuite with tea/coffee making facilities, DDT and TV with Sky channels.
53 bedrs, all ensuite, ♀ ⼻ ⅲ 35 P 53 ⊞ Rest Resid SB £41.95 DB £46.90 HB £329 L £5.75 L ♥ D £10.85 D ♥ ✕ LD 22:00 ℂℂ MC Visa Amex DC &

RUGBY Warwickshire   8B3
Pop. 59,700. London 81, M1 (jn 18) 2½, Banbury 25, Coventry 12, Daventry 10, Leicester 20, Nuneaton 16, Warwick 14 MD Mon, Fri, Sat see Rugby School, Art Gallery, Percival Guildhouse, Town Hall 🅸 Library, St Matthews Street 01788-535348

★★★ Posthouse   **Posthouse**
Crick, Rugby NN6 7XR
☎ 01788-822101 Fax 01788-823955
88 bedrs, all ensuite, ⼻ ⅲ 200 P 250 ⊞ L £7 D £8 ✕ LD 22:30 ℂℂ MC Visa Amex DC JCB 国 困 圖

RUNCORN Cheshire   7E1
Northwich 11, London 184, M56 (jn 12) 5, Chester 14, Liverpool 13, Nantwich 23, St Helens 8½, Warrington 8½, Whitchurch 27 EC Wed MD Tue, Thur, Sat see Rebuilt All Saints' Church, Castle Inn, Runcorn-Widnes High Level Road Bridge, Norton Priory & Museum open to public (excavation)

★★★ Posthouse   **Posthouse**
Wood Lane, Beechwood,
Runcorn WA7 3HA
☎ 01928-714000 Fax 01928-714611
135 bedrs, all ensuite, ⼻ ▣ ⅲ 500
P 250 ⊞ SB £94.95 DB £104.90 D £7
D ♥ ✕ LD 22:00
ℂℂ MC Visa Amex DC JCB 国 困 圖 &

Campanile Runcorn Lodge
Lowlands Road, Runcorn WA7 5TP
☎ 01928-581771 Fax 01928-581730

RUSHDEN Northamptonshire   8C4
Pop. 24,600. Bedford 14, London 64, Huntingdon 23, Kettering 11, Northampton 15, Peterborough 28, Stamford 29 EC Thu MD Sat

Rilton
High Street, Rushden NN10 9BT
☎ 01933-312189 Fax 01933-358593

This impressive Victorian building has been totally refurbished. Dedicated to offering a friendly atmosphere and service, the staff will endevour to make your stay enjoyable, for business or pleasure.
25 bedrs, all ensuite, ④ ♀ ⼻ ⅲ 100 P 60 ⊞
SB £32.50-£35 DB £37.50-£45 HB £245-£287 L ♥
D £10 D ♥ ✕ LD 21:00 ℂℂ MC Visa JCB

RUSHYFORD Co. Durham   11D1
Pop. 250. Darlington 9, London 253, A1(M) 2, Alston 41, Durham 8½, Middleton-in-Teesdale 14, West Auckland 7½ see Auckland Castle and Deer House (4½m W)

ENGLAND

★★★ Swallow Eden Arms
Rushyford DL17 0LL
☎ 01388-720541 **Fax** 01388-721871
E-mail info@swallowhotels.com

A former 17th century coaching inn with newly refurbished bedrooms and leisure club. The hotel's restaurant has awards for its fine food.
45 bedrs, all ensuite, 4 ⊷ ⋕ 100 **P** 100 ⊕ **SB** £88-£105 **DB** £125-£140 **L** £11.50 **D** £21.50 ✕ **LD** 22:00
Restaurant closed L Sat **CC** MC Visa Amex DC JCB
▣ 🖾 📶 🖾

RYE East Sussex   5E3
Pop. 4,800. Hawkhurst 13, London 63, Folkestone 25, Hastings 11, Tenterden 10 **EC** Tue **MD** Thu **see** Cinque Port, 12th cent Ypres Tower (museum), Flushing Inn (15th cent), Mermaid Inn (15th cent)
🔢 The Heritage Centre, Strand Quay 01797-226696

★★★ ❖ Flackley Ash
Peasmarsh, Rye TN31 6YH
☎ 01797-230651 **Fax** 01797-230510
E-mail flackleyash@marstonhotels.co.uk

A Georgian hotel set in five acres of beautiful grounds in a quiet village, three and a half miles north west of Rye.
42 bedrs, all ensuite, 4 ⊷ ⋕ 100 **P** 70 ⊕ **SB** £75-£95 **DB** £115-£145 **HB** £432 **L** £14 **L** ● **D** £22.50 **D** ●
✕ **LD** 21:30 **CC** MC Visa Amex DC JCB ▣ 🖾 📶
See advert on this page

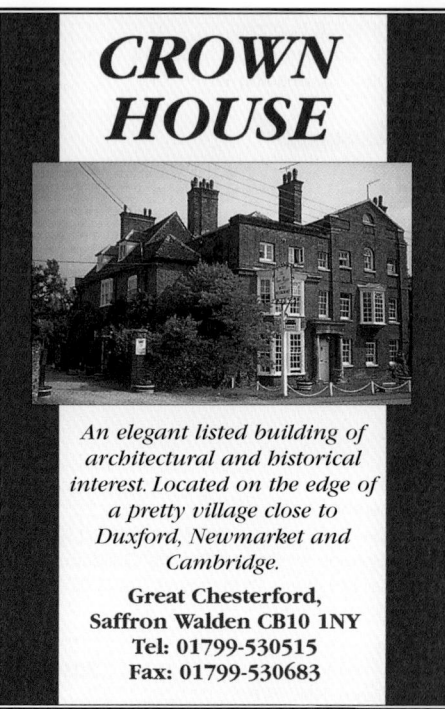

★★★ Mermaid
Mermaid Street, Rye TN31 7EY
☎ 01797-223065 **Fax** 01797-225069
31 bedrs, all ensuite, ⊞ ⚌ 60 **P** 26 ⊞ **SB** £68-£72
DB £136-£154 **HB** £620-£655 **L** £16 **L** ● **D** £29 **D** ● ✕
LD 21.15 **CC** MC Visa Amex DC JCB

SAFFRON WALDEN Essex   **5D1**
Pop. 14,000. Bishop's Stortford 11, London 43,
M11 (jn 9) 4½, Braintree 19, Dunmow 13, Haverhill
12, Royston 13 **EC** Thu **MD** Tue, Sat **see** Audley End
Mansion 🛈 Market Square 01799-510444

★★ Crown House
Great Chesterford, Saffron Walden CB10 1NY
☎ 01799-530515 **Fax** 01799-530683
18 bedrs, all ensuite, ⊞ ♪ ★ ⚌ 30 **P** 30 ⊞ **SB** £48-
£80 **DB** £68-£95 **L** ● **D** £14.95 **D** ● ✕ **LD** 21:30
CC MC Visa Amex �
See advert on opposite page

ST AGNES Cornwall   **2A4**
Pop. 2,500. Bodmin 26, London 269, Newquay 11,
Redruth 7½, Truro 8 **EC** Wed **see** Church, Ancient
Cross, St Agnes Head, Beacon

★★★ Rose-in-Vale Country House ⍨
Mithian, St Agnes TR5 0QD
☎ 01872-552202 **Fax** 01872-552700
E-mail reception@rose-in-vale-hotel.co.uk
Closed Jan-Feb
18 bedrs, all ensuite, ⊞ ♪ ★ ⚌ 50 **P** 40 ⊞ Rest
Resid **SB** £48 **DB** £86 **HB** £336-£359 **L** £10.50 **L** ●
D £21.95 **D** ● ✕ **LD** 20:30 **CC** MC Visa ⍨ ▦ ⊠ �

★★ ✛ Rosemundy House
8 Rosemundy, St Agnes TR5 0UF
☎ 01872-552101 **Fax** 01872-554000
Closed Jan
44 bedrs, all ensuite, ★ **P** 36 No children under 4 ⊞
Rest Resid **SB** £26-£42 **DB** £52-£84 **HB** £175-£310 **L** ●
✕ **LD** 20:00 **CC** MC Visa ⍨ ⊠

ST ALBANS Hertfordshire   **4C2**
Pop. 77,200. London 19, M10 (jn 1) 1½, Aylesbury
23, Barnet 9½, Dunstable 13, Hatfield 6, Luton 10,
Watford 7 **EC** Thu **MD** Wed, Sat **see** 11th cent
Cathedral, Abbey Gateway, St Michael's Church
(effigy of Sir Francis Bacon), 'Fighting Cocks' Inn,
'Verulanium' - Roman excavations, Museum,
Hypocaust (in Verulanium Park) 🛈 Town Hall,
Market Place 01727-864511

★★★★ Sopwell House
Cottonmill Lane, St Albans AL1 2HQ
☎ 01727-864477 **Fax** 01727-844741

Owner-managed, beautifully maintained, elegant
country residence, set in parkland. Facilities for
conferences, banquets and exhibitions.
126 bedrs, all ensuite, ⊞ ♪ ★ ☎ ⚌ 400 **P** 350 ⊞
SB £89.25-£126.25 **DB** £128.75-£167.75 **L** £16.95 **L** ●
D £24.50 **D** ● ✕ **LD** 21:45 Restaurant closed L Sat,
D Sun **CC** MC Visa Amex DC ▦ ⊠ ▦ ⊠
See advert on this page

ENGLAND

★★★ St Michaels Manor ⌂ ⌂
Fishpool Street, St Albans AL3 4RY
📞 01727-864444 **Fax** 01727-848909
E-mail smmanor@globalnet.co.uk
23 bedrs, all ensuite, 🖵 ♀ ⚏ 30 **P** 70 ⊟ **SB** £105-£195 **DB** £135-£275 **L** £15.75 **L** ☞ **D** £29.50 **D** ☞ ✕ **LD** 21:30 **CC** MC Visa Amex
See advert on this page

★★ Lake ⌂
234 London Road, St Albans AL1 1JQ
📞 01727-840904 **Fax** 01727-862750

Modern hotel on main road into St. Albans with car parking to the front and rear.
43 bedrs, all ensuite, 🖵 ⚏ 200 **P** 75 ⊟ **SB** £34.50-£75 **DB** £64.50-£86 **L** £11 **D** £15 **D** ☞ ✕ **LD** 21:30 **CC** MC Visa Amex DC

★ Avalon ⌂
260 London Road, St Albans AL1 1TJ
📞 01727-856757 **Fax** 01727-856750
15 bedrs, all ensuite, ♀ ✎ ⚏ 30 **P** 14 No children under 3 ⊟ Rest Resid **SB** £50-£55 **DB** £65-£70 **D** £11 ✕ **LD** 19:00 **CC** MC Visa Amex JCB

ST AUSTELL Cornwall	2B4

Pop. 19,000. Liskeard 18, London 232, Bodmin 11, Fowey 7½, Newquay 14, Truro 14 **EC** Thu **see** Church (12th-15th cent), China Clay quarries (tours), Market House (1791), Mengu Stone

★★★★ Carlyon Bay
Sea Road, Carlyon Bay,
St Austell PL25 3RD
📞 01726-812304 **Fax** 01726-814938
E-mail info@carlyonbay.co.uk

A large holiday hotel in a cliff top location offering spectacular views. The hotel's 18 hole golf course runs along the cliff top adjacent to the hotel.
73 bedrs, all ensuite, ♀ ✎ 🖥 ⚏ 100 **P** 100 ⊟ **SB** £76-£93 **DB** £146-£220 **HB** £350-£819 **L** £13.95 **L** ☞ **D** £24 **D** ☞ ✕ **LD** 21:00 **CC** MC Visa Amex DC 🖅 ⛲ 🎱 ▣ 🎾 🐎 ⛳
See advert on opposite page

★★★ Cliff Head ⌂
Sea Road, Carlyon Bay, St Austell PL25 3RB
📞 01726-812345 **Fax** 01726-815511
48 bedrs, 46 ensuite, 🖵 ⚏ 230 **P** 60 ⊟ ⊟ Rest Resid **SB** £42-£52 **DB** £72-£82 **L** £7.95 **L** ☞ **D** £9.95 **D** ☞ ✕ **LD** 21:30 **CC** MC Visa Amex DC 🖅 🎾 🎱 🐎

★★ Boscundle Manor ⌂ ⌂
Tregrehan, St Austell PL25 3RL
📞 01726-813557 **Fax** 01726-814997
Closed Nov-Mar
12 bedrs, all ensuite, ⊢ **P** 15 ⊟ Rest Resid **SB** £65-£75 **DB** £110-£130 **HB** £455-£595 **D** £20 ✕ **LD** 20:00 **CC** MC Visa Amex JCB 🖅 ⛲ 🎾 ▣ 🐎

ENGLAND

Facilities for the disabled

Hotels do their best to cater for disabled visitors. However, it is advisable to contact the hotel direct to ensure it can provide particular requirement.

★★ White Hart
Church Street, St Austell PL25 4AT
☎ 01726-72100 Fax 01726-74705
Closed 25-26 Dec
18 bedrs, all ensuite, ⋕ 50 ⊕ SB £44 DB £69.50
HB £280 L £7.75 D £12.50 ✕ LD 21:00 ⊂⊂ MC Visa Amex DC

ST IVES Cambridgeshire	9D4

Pop. 14,800. Royston 20, London 61, Biggleswade 19, Cambridge 13, Ely 18, Huntingdon 5½, Peterborough 23 **MD** Mon, Fri **see** All Saint's Church, Stone Bridge (with Chapel), Norris Museum and Library

★★★ Dolphin
Bridge Foot, London Road,
St Ives PE17 4EP
☎ 01480-466966 Fax 01480-495597
Closed 24-30 Dec & 1-2 Jan

Delightfully situated on the banks of the River Ouse, close to the centre of historic St Ives, with unrivalled views over the river and surrounding meadowland. Table d'hote and speciality meals. Real ales. Function suite.
67 bedrs, all ensuite, ④ ✗ ⋕ 150 **P** 400 ⊕ SB £68-£78 DB £90-£100 L £5.50 D £17.50 D ✿ ✕ LD 21:30 ⊂⊂ MC Visa Amex DC ⊠ ⅃

★★★ Olivers Lodge ⌇
Needingworth Road, St Ives PE17 4JP
☎ 01480-463252 Fax 01480-461150

Privately owned hotel in an attractive garden, close to the centre and river of historic St Ives, and only 20 minutes from Cambridge. Real ale bar, great food and numerous daily specials. New conservatory restaurant.
16 bedrs, all ensuite, ⊦ ⋕ 70 **P** 30 ⊕ SB £58-£68 DB £70-£85 L £12 D £16 ✕ LD 21:30 ⊂⊂ MC Visa Amex JCB ⅃

★★★ Slepe Hall
Ramsey Road, St Ives PE17 4RB
☎ 01480-463122 Fax 01480-300706
E-mail mail@slepehall.co.uk
Closed 25-29 Dec
16 bedrs, all ensuite, ④ ⊦ ⋕ 200 **P** 70 ⊕ SB £55-£70 DB £70-£90 L £13.95 L ✿ D £14.95 D ✿ ✕ LD 21:30 ⊂⊂ MC Visa Amex DC

ST IVES Cornwall 2A4
Pop. 11,000. Redruth 14, London 277, Helston 15, Penzance 8 **EC** Thu *i* Guildhall, Street-an-Pol 01736-796297

★★★ Porthminster
The Terrace, St Ives TR26 2BN
☎ 01736-795221 **Fax** 01736-797043
44 bedrs, all ensuite, ♈ 🖥 **###** 60 **P** 40 ⊞ **SB** £52-£63 **DB** £104-£126 **L** £7.50 **D** £19.50 ✕ **LD** 20:30 **CC** MC Visa Amex DC ▣ ⚲ ⚹ 📶

★★ Chy-an-dour
Trelyon Avenue, St Ives TR26 2AD
☎ 01736-796436 **Fax** 01736-795772
Closed Jan

This 19th century former sea captain's house has been extended to form a most attractive two star hotel with panoramic views of St Ives Bay, beach and harbour. All rooms ensuite, chef proprietor.
23 bedrs, all ensuite, 🖥 **P** 23 No children under 5 ⊞ Rest Resid **SB** £46-£53 **DB** £62-£88 **HB** £280-£371 **L** ⬤ **D** £17 **D** ⬤ ✕ **LD** 20:00 **CC** MC Visa JCB ⚹

ST MAWES Cornwall 2B4
Pop. 1,100. St Austell 18, London 251, Falmouth (fy) 15, Truro 18 (fy 9½)

★★★ Idle Rocks ⛊
Harbourside, St Mawes TR2 5AN
☎ 01326-270771 **Fax** 01326-270062

A warm welcome is guaranteed at this charming waterside hotel with its fine furnishings, highly rated restaurant and tranquil setting. Something for every season, from log fires to sunny luncheons on the hotel's private terrace.
24 bedrs, all ensuite, 🞄 ♈ **###** 20 **P** 5 ⊞ **CC** MC Visa Amex
See advert on this page

SALCOMBE Devon 2C4
Pop. 2,451. Kingsbridge 6½, London 211, Plymouth 22 **EC** Wed *i* Council Hall, Market St. 01548-843927

★★★ Bolt Head ⛊
Cliff Road, Salcombe TQ8 8LL
☎ 01548-843751 **Fax** 01548-843061
E-mail info@bolthead-salcombe.co.uk
Closed Nov-Mar
28 bedrs, all ensuite, ♈ **P** 30 ⊞ **SB** £56-£89 **DB** £112-£204 **HB** £462-£714 **L** £18.50 **L** ⬤ **D** £25 ✕ **LD** 20:45 **CC** MC Visa Amex DC ⚹

★★★ Heron House
Thurlestone Sands, Salcombe TQ7 3JY
☎ 01548-561308 **Fax** 01548-560180

Set in an area of outstanding natural beauty, adjacent to coastal path, bird reserve, golf course and sandy beach. Furnished to high standard with award winning restaurant. Ample parking.
16 bedrs, all ensuite, ♀ ✗ ⊁ **P** 50 ⊕ **SB** £40-£62 **DB** £80-£145 **HB** £275-£510 **L** ❢ **D** £23.95 ✗ **LD** 20:30 **CC** MC Visa ⊰

★★★ Soar Mill Cove ☼ ☼ ☼
Blue Ribbon Hotel
Soar Mill Cove, Malborough, Salcombe TQ7 3DS
☎ 01548-561566 **Fax** 01548-561223
E-mail info@makepeacehotels.co.uk

Dramatically situated luxury hotel with award winning cuisine. Completely within National Trust coastline, overlooking a glorious sandy beach. Delexe bedrooms with many thoughtful extras and heated indoor swimming pool are to be enjoyed.
21 bedrs, all ensuite, ④ ⊁ **P** 50 ⊕ Rest Resid **SB** £72-£150 **DB** £130-£200 **HB** £480-£690 **L** £13 **L** ❢ **D** £34 ✗ **LD** 21:00 **CC** MC Visa Amex JCB ⊡ ⊰ ▧ ▨ ⊞
See advert on this page

★★★ ❖ Tides Reach
South Sands, Salcombe TQ8 8LJ
☎ 01548-843466 **Fax** 01548-843954
E-mail enquire@tidesreach.com
Closed Dec-Feb
38 bedrs, all ensuite, ⊁ ⊡ **P** 50 No children under 8 ⊕ **SB** £62-£90 **DB** £106-£192 **HB** £455-£690 **L** ❢ **D** £26.75 ✗ **LD** 21:00 **CC** MC Visa Amex DC JCB ⊡ ⊞ ▣ ▧ ⊞

★★ Grafton Towers ☼
Moult Road, Salcombe TQ8 8LG
☎ 01548-842882 **Fax** 01548-842857
Closed Nov-Feb
13 bedrs, all ensuite, ⊁ **P** 14 No children under 14 ⊕ Rest Resid **SB** £35.50-£38 **DB** £65-£70 **HB** £305-£335 **D** £17.50 ✗ **LD** 20:00 **CC** MC Visa

---

SALE Cheshire   10C4
Altrincham 3, London 183, Macclesfield 17, Manchester 5, Stockport 8.

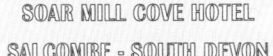

★★★ Amblehurst
44 Washway Road, Sale M33 1QZ
📞 0161-973 8800 **Fax** 0161-905 1697
E-mail amblehurst@aol.com
65 bedrs, all ensuite, ▣ ✗ ♨ 70 **P** 52 ⊞ **SB** £65-£75
DB £75-£85 **L** £12 **L** ♥ **D** £14 **D** ♥ ✗ **LD** 22:00
Restaurant closed L Sat, D Sun **((** MC Visa Amex
DC ▣ ⅙

SALISBURY Wiltshire   4A3
Pop. 37,000. Basingstoke 36, London 83,
Amesbury 8, Andover 18, Blandford Forum 23,
Ringwood 16, Shaftesbury 20, Southampton 22,
Winchester 23 **EC** Wed **MD** Tue, Sat **see** Cathedral (404
ft spire), the North Canonry, Bishop's Palace (now
Choir School), Mompesson House (NT), Old Sarum
2m N 🛈 Fish Row 01722-334956

★★★ Red Lion
Milford Street, Salisbury SP1 2AN
📞 01722-323334 **Fax** 01722-325756
E-mail reception@the-redlion.co.uk

Traditional 13th century coaching inn, famous for
its creeper-clad courtyard, charm and antique filled
rooms. An ideal touring base for a wealth of nearby
attractions.
54 bedrs, all ensuite, ▣ ✗ ▣ ♨ 100 **P** 10 ⊞
SB £88.50 **DB** £117.50 **L** £5.75 **D** £16.50 ✗ **LD** 21:00
((MC Visa Amex DC ⅙

★★★ White Hart   *Heritage* <small>HOTELS</small>
St John Street,
Salisbury SP1 2SD
📞 01722-327476 **Fax** 01722-412761
68 bedrs, all ensuite, ▣ ✈ ♨ 80 **P** 96 ⊞ **SB** £90.50
DB £131 **HB** £392-£490 **L** £7.95 **L** ♥
D £18.50 **D** ♥ ✗ **LD** 21:30 Restaurant
closed L Sat **((** MC Visa Amex DC JCB

★★ Pembroke Arms
Minster Street, Wilton,
Salisbury SP2 0BH
📞 01722-743328 **Fax** 01722-744886
8 bedrs, all ensuite, ▣ ♨ 100 **P** 70 ⊞ **SB** £40-£50
DB £60-£70 **L** ♥ **D** ♥ ✗ **LD** 21:30 **((** MC Visa Amex
DC

SALTBURN-BY-THE-SEA Cleveland   11E2
Pop. 6,100. Guisborough 6, London 252, Darlington
29, Middlesbrough 12, Scarborough 35 **EC** Wed **see**
Guisborough Priory, Chapel Beck Gallery
Guisborough 🛈 Station Square 01287-622422

★★★ Grinkle Park ♞
Grinkle Lane, Easington,
Saltburn-by-the-Sea TS13 4UB
📞 01287-640515 **Fax** 01287-641278
E-mail grinkle.parkhotel@bass.com

Stone-built manorial style building in tranquil
parkland, with extensive gardens.
20 bedrs, all ensuite, ▣ ✈ ♨ 60 **P** 150 ⊞ **SB** £77.65
DB £95.55 **HB** £72 **L** £13.25 **L** ♥ **D** £19.95 **D** ♥ ✗
LD 21:00 **((** MC Visa Amex DC ▣ ▣

SANDBACH Cheshire   7E1
Pop. 17,100. London 161, M6 (jn 17) 1, Congleton
7, Knutsford 12, Middlewich 5, Nantwich 9½,
Newcastle-under-Lyme 11 **EC** Tue **MD** Thu **see**
Remarkable sculptured Saxon Crosses in Market
Sq, 17th cent Old Hall, now hotel, Church

★★ Grove House ♞ ♞ ♞
Mill Lane, Wheelock, Sandbach CW11 4RD
📞 01270-762582 **Fax** 01270-759465
Closed 27-30 Dec

Restaurant with rooms, family owned and run. Relaxing ambience, individually styled rooms. Excellent restaurant offering ambitious modern cooking by chef-proprietor. Two miles from jn 17 on M6.

8 bedrs, all ensuite, ⊩ ⠇⠇⠇ 15 **P** 40 ⊕ Rest Resid ℂℂ MC Visa Amex

---

SANDWICH Kent   5F3

Pop. 4,650. Canterbury 12, London 70, Dover 10, Folkestone 15, Margate 8½ **EC** Wed **MD** Thu see Cinque Port, The Barbican (Tudor) Guildhall, Fisher Gate, old Town Walls, Richborough Castle & Roman fort 1½ m NW

★★★ Bell ⟨ℝ⟩

The Quay, Sandwich CT13 9EF

☎ 01304-613388 **Fax** 01304-615308

E-mail hotel@princes-leisure.co.uk

Famed for its excellent cuisine, the Bell offers individually furnished bedrooms, with views over the ancient town or the River Stour. Relax in traditional comfort.

33 bedrs, all ensuite, ⊩ ⠇⠇⠇ 100 **P** 8 ⊕ **SB** £75 **DB** £100 **HB** £355-£410 **L** £10.95 **D** £10.95 **D** ☛ ✕ **LD** 21:30 ℂℂ MC Visa Amex DC

See advert on this page

SAUNTON Devon   2C2

Barnstaple 7, London 200, Dunster 39

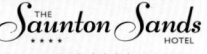

★★★★ Saunton Sands

Saunton EX33 1LQ
☎ 01271-890212 Fax 01271-890145
E-mail info@sauntonsands.co.uk

The Saunton Sands provides a wealth of facilities including a luxuriously refurbished terrace lounge, large outdoor pool and indoor heated pool, spa bath, sauna, solarium, snooker, etc.
92 bedrs, all ensuite, ♀ ⌀ ☲ ⚌ 150 P 140 ⊞
SB £68-£98 DB £132-£210 HB £340-£819 L £11 L 🍷
D £23 D 🍷 ✕ LD 21:00 CC MC Visa Amex DC 🖃 ⅃ 🖾
🖾 🖾 🖾 🖾 ⅃
See advert on previous page

SAWREY Cumbria   10B2
Ambleside 6, M6 (jn 36) 29, London 269, Coniston 5½, Windermere 10 (Fy 3) see Hill Top

★★ Sawrey

Far Sawrey, Ambleside LA22 0LQ
☎ 015394-43425 Fax 015394-43425
Closed Christmas

An attractive two storey, 18th century inn built in traditional Lake District style. Former stables converted into a bar.
18 bedrs, all ensuite, ☚ ⚌ 35 P 30 ⊞ SB £29-£32
DB £58-£64 HB £199-£252 L £9 L 🍷 D £12.50 D 🍷 ✕
LD 20:45 CC MC Visa JCB ⅃

SCARBOROUGH North Yorkshire   11E2
Pop. 53,000. Driffield 21, London 213, Beverley 33, Bridlington 17, Malton 24, Pickering 16, Whitby 24 EC Wed MD Thu see Spa, Castle ruins, St Mary's Church (Anne Bronte's grave) 🗓 Pavilion House, Valley Bridge Road 01723-373333

★★★ Ambassador

Centre of the Esplanade, Scarborough YO11 2AY
☎ 01723-362841 Fax 01723-362841
59 bedrs, all ensuite, ☷ ♀ ⌀ ☚ ☲ ⚌ 140 ⊞ SB £28-£30 DB £56-£60 HB £196-£210 L £9.95 D £14.95 D 🍷
✕ LD 20:30 Restaurant closed L Mon-Sat CC MC Visa Amex 🖃 🖾 ⅃
See advert on this page

ENGLAND

★★★ Clifton
Queens Parade, Scarborough YO12 7HX
☎ 01723-375691 **Fax** 01723-364203

Friendly resort hotel overlooking the beautiful North Bay, castle and headland. A reputation for good food and service, all rooms ensuite with satellite TV, direct dial telephones, tea/coffee facilities. Large free car park.
71 bedrs, all ensuite, ④ ⊡ ⠿ 180 **P** 40 ⊕ **SB** £30-£49.50 **DB** £60-£99 **HB** £200-£240 **L** £9.95 **L** ⬤
D £17.50 ✕ **LD** 21:15 ⓒ MC Visa Amex DC ▦ ♿

★★★ East Ayton Lodge
Moor Lane, East Ayton, Scarborough YO13 9EW
☎ 01723-864227 **Fax** 01723-862680
31 bedrs, all ensuite, ⸚ ⠿ 80 **P** 50 ⊕ ⓒ MC Visa Amex JCB ♿

★★★ Esplanade
Belmont Road, Scarborough YO11 2AA
☎ 01723-360382 **Fax** 01723-376137

A four storey white Georgian building, with a feature window to the restaurant giving views over Scarborough's South Bay.
73 bedrs, all ensuite, ⸚ ⊡ ⠿ 140 **P** 14 ⊕ **SB** £32-£45 **DB** £64-£84 **HB** £252-£322 **D** £16.25 ✕ **LD** 20:30 ⓒ MC Visa Amex DC JCB

★★★ Hackness Grange Country
North York Moors National Park, Hackness, Scarborough YO13 0JW
☎ 01723-882345 **Fax** 01723-882391

Elegant, Georgian country house hotel, overlooking a lake brimming with wildlife, set in the heart of the North York Moors National Park. Leisure facilities include pool, tennis and golf.
28 bedrs, all ensuite, ④ ⠿ 20 **P** 50 ⊕ **SB** £67.50 **DB** £90-£120 **HB** £275-£395 **L** £12.50 **D** £25 ✕ **LD** 21:15 ⓒ MC Visa Amex DC ▣ ▣ ▣ ♿

★★★ Hotel St Nicholas
St Nicholas Cliff, Scarborough YO11 2EU
☎ 01723-364101 **Fax** 01723-500538

An ideal location for business or leisure. RAC 3 star hotel, which offers a range of superb conference rooms, leisure club with indoor swimming pool, security car parking and a choice of excellent cuisine complemented by the finest wines.
144 bedrs, all ensuite, ④ ⸚ ⊡ ⠿ 600 **P** 20 ⊕ **SB** £57-£77 **DB** £75-£102 **HB** £294-£340 **L** £8 **D** £13.95 ✕ **LD** 21:15 ⓒ MC Visa Amex DC ▣ ▣ ▦ ▣

★★★ Palm Court
St Nicholas Cliff, Scarborough YO11 2ES
☎ 01723-368161 **Fax** 01723-371547
47 bedrs, all ensuite, ⊡ ⠿ 150 **P** 106 ⊕ Rest Resid ⓒ MC Visa Amex DC ▣ ▦

★★★ Wrea Head Country ♔

Barmoor Lane, Scalby, YO13 0PB
☎ 01723-378211 **Fax** 01723-371780

Stylish country house hotel, with elegant accommodation and award winning cuisine, set in landscaped gardens and woodland on the outskirts of North York Moors National Park.
20 bedrs, all ensuite, ④ ♯♯ 30 **P** 50 ⊞ Rest Resid
SB £57.50-£67.50 **DB** £99-£135 **HB** £275-£350
L £12.50 **L** ☞ **D** £25 ✕ **LD** 21:30 **CC** MC Visa Amex DC

★★ ♣ Beidebecke's
1-3 The Crescent, Scarborough YO11 2PW
☎ 01723-365766
30 bedrs, all ensuite, ⚹ ☰ ♯♯ 25 **P** 15 ⊞ **CC** MC Visa ♿
See advert on this page

★★ Bradley Court
7-9 Filey Road, Scarborough YO11 2SE
☎ 01723-360476 **Fax** 01723-376661

Friendly staff and comfortably appointed, this 40 bedroom hotel offers quality service and fine English food. Close to beach and town centre. Private floodlit car park.
40 bedrs, all ensuite, ⚹ ☰ ♯♯ 200 **P** 40 ⊞ **CC** MC Visa Amex DC

★★ Brooklands
Esplanade Gardens, South Cliff, YO11 2AW
☎ 01723-376576 **Fax** 01723-376576

The Brooklands Hotel is situated on the South Cliff, less than one minute's walk on level ground to the Esplanade, Spa and Cliff tramway.
63 bedrs, 62 ensuite, ☰ ♯♯ 120 ⊞ Rest Resid
SB £20-£30 **DB** £40-£60 **HB** £175-£297 **L** £6 **D** £9 ✕
LD 19:30 **CC** MC Visa ▣ ▣

★★ Gridleys Crescent ♔ ♔
1-2 Belvoir Terrace, Scarborough YO11 2PP
☎ 01723-360929 **Fax** 01723-354126
E-mail reception@crescent-hotel.co.uk
20 bedrs, all ensuite, ④ ☰ ♯♯ 30 No children under 6 ⊞ **SB** £45 **DB** £75 **L** £9.95 **L** ☞ **D** £16 **D** ☞ ✕
LD 21:30 Restaurant closed L:m,t,w,t,f,sat **CC** MC Visa Amex

★★ La Baia
24 Blenheim Terrace, Scarborough YO12 7HD
☎ 01723-370780
Closed Nov-Feb
12 bedrs, all ensuite, ⊞ Rest Resid SB £30 DB £44
HB £196 D £9 ✕ LD 19:00 ℂℂ MC Visa JCB

★★ Lynton
104 Columbus Ravine, Scarborough YO12 7QZ
☎ 01723-374240
8 bedrs, all ensuite, ♀ ♫ ⠿ 12 P 8 No children
under 3 ⊞ Rest Resid SB £22-£23 DB £44-£46 D £10
✕ LD 20:00 ℂℂ MC Visa

★★ Red Lea
Prince Of Wales Terrace, South Cliff,
Scarborough YO11 2AJ
☎ 01723-362431 Fax 01723-371230
E-mail redlea@globalnet.co.uk
67 bedrs, all ensuite, ▣ ⠿ 40 ⊞ Rest Resid SB £34-
£35 DB £66-£68 HB £285-£295 L £9 L ▼ D £12 ✕
LD 20:30 Restaurant closed L Mon-Sat ℂℂ MC Visa
Amex ▣ ⊞ ▦

★★ Ryndle Court
47 Northstead Manor Drive,
Scarborough YO12 6AF
☎ 01723-375188 Fax 01723-375188
Closed Nov-Jan excl Christmas
14 bedrs, all ensuite, ⠿ 16 P 10 ⊞ Rest Resid
SB £28-£36 DB £56-£58 HB £190-£210 L £8 L ▼ D £9
D ▼ ✕ LD 17:00 Restaurant closed L Mon-Sat
ℂℂ MC Visa DC JCB
See advert on this page

★★ Southlands
15 West Street, Scarborough YO11 2QW
☎ 01723-361461 Fax 01723-376035

On beautiful South Cliff, close to seafront and town
centre with a large private car park. Excellent five
course menu and in house entertainment.
58 bedrs, all ensuite, ☇ ⛶ ⠿ P 35 ⊞ Rest Resid
SB £25-£36 DB £50-£72 HB £210-£270 L ▼ D £12 ✕
LD 20:30 ℂℂ MC Visa

ENGLAND

★★ Sunningdale
105 Peasholm Drive, Scarborough YO12 7NB
☎ 01723-372041 **Fax** 01723-354691
11 bedrs, all ensuite, 🍴 Rest Resid **SB** £22-£25
DB £44-£50 **HB** £190-£210 **D** £8 ✕ **LD** 19:00 **CC** MC
Visa Amex JCB
See advert on previous page

SCOTCH CORNER North Yorkshire   11D2
Boroughbridge 28, London 236, A1(M) 1½, Brough
24, Darlington 7½, Leyburn 15, Middleton-in-
Teesdale 21 **EC** Wed 🛈 Motorway Service Area A1
01325-377677

★★★ Quality Scotch Corner
Scotch Corner, Darlington DL10 6NR
☎ 01748-850900 **Fax** 01748-825417
E-mail admin@gb609.u-net.com

The hotel's superb leisure facilities include an
indoor pool, spa, sauna, professional gym, aerobics
studio and beauticians. Ideally located for exploring
the best of North Yorkshire.
90 bedrs, all ensuite, 🛉 🖺 ⠿ 280 **P** 200 🍴
SB £79.50-£91 **DB** £100.50-£112.75 **L** £6.95 **D** £14.50
✕ **LD** 21:45 **CC** MC Visa Amex DC JCB 🖻 🖾 🖳 ⚓

SCUNTHORPE Lincolnshire   11E4
Pop. 59,000. Lincoln 28, London 161, M181 2,
Doncaster 22, Gainsborough 16, Goole 21,
Grimsby 30, Hull 26 **MD** Fri, Sat **see** Church of St
Laurence, Normandy Hall

★★★ Wortley House
Rowland Road, Scunthorpe DN16 1SU
☎ 01724-842223 **Fax** 01724-280646
E-mail wortley.hotel@virgin.net
38 bedrs, all ensuite, ♀ 🛉 ⠿ 300 **P** 100 🍴 **SB** £55-
£70.50 **DB** £60-£77 **D** £14.50 **D** ✕ **LD** 21:30 **CC** MC
Visa Amex DC JCB

SEAHOUSES Northumberland   13F3
Pop. 1,800. Alnwick 14, London 321, Berwick-
upon-Tweed 22, Coldstream 29 **EC** Wed **see**
Bamburgh Castle, Sand Dunes, Farne Islands - Bird
Sanctuary and Seal Colony 🛈 Seafield Road
01665-720884

★★ Bamburgh Castle
Seahouses NE68 7SQ
☎ 01665-720283 **Fax** 01665-720848

Enjoying probably the finest location on the
Northumberland coast with commanding sea views
from the restaurant. Log fires in the lounges.
Secure car park and garden.
20 bedrs, all ensuite, 🗔 🛉 ⠿ 20 **P** 25 🍴 **SB** £35.95-
£42.95 **DB** £67.90-£75.90 **HB** £280-£315 **L** 🍷 **D** £19
D 🍷 ✕ **LD** 20:30 🖾

★★ Beach House
Seafront, Seahouses NE68 7SR
☎ 01665-720337 **Fax** 01665-720921
Closed Nov-Mar
14 bedrs, all ensuite, 🛉 **P** 26 🍴 Rest Resid **CC** MC
Visa Amex JCB

★★ Olde Ship 🍴
9 Main Street, Seahouses NE68 7RD
☎ 01665-720200 **Fax** 01665-721383
Closed Dec-Jan

Built originally as a farmhouse about 1745 and later
to become licensed in 1812, the inn is small, but

ENGLAND

most comfortable in a traditional old fashioned style.
16 bedrs, all ensuite, ⚃ **P** 14 No children under 10 ⊟ **SB** £32-£38.50 **DB** £64-£77 **HB** £280-£340 **L** £8 **D** £14.50 ✕ **LD** 20:15 **CC** MC Visa JCB

St Aidans
Sea Front, Seahouses NE68 7SR
☎ 01665-720355 **Fax** 01665-721989
E-mail staiden@globalnet.co.uk
Closed mid Nov-mid Feb

Our friendly, family run hotel has probably the finest location on the Northumberland coast, with outstanding sea views from every room. Quietly situated, minutes stroll from the village centre.
8 bedrs, all ensuite, ☒ ➤ **P** 16 ⊟ Rest Resid **SB** £30-£39.50 **DB** £50-£75 **D** £13 ✕ **LD** 20:30 **CC** MC Visa ♿

SEDGEFIELD Cleveland 11D1
Pop. 5,300. Stockton 8, London 252, A1(M) 2½, Durham 9, Darlington 13 **EC** Wed **MD** Tue

★★★ Hardwick Hall
Sedgefield TS21 2EH
☎ 01740-620253 **Fax** 01740-622771

A splendid country house-style hotel set in the peaceful seclusion of parkland. The bedrooms are thoughtfully furnished and equipped and a strong feature of the hotel.

---

17 bedrs, all ensuite, ⚃ ➤ ∷ 100 **P** 300 ⊟ **SB** £60-£68 **DB** £70-£78 **L** £7.50 **L** ♥ **D** £7.50 **D** ♥ ✕ **LD** 21:45 **CC** MC Visa Amex DC

SEDLESCOMBE East Sussex 5E3
Pop. 1,500. Hurst Green 6½, London 56, Eastbourne 15, Hastings 7, Hawkhurst 7½, Lewes 21, Rye 10 **EC** Wed

★★★ ✦ Brickwall
The Green, Sedlescombe TN33 0QA
☎ 01424-870253 **Fax** 01424-870785
26 bedrs, all ensuite, ⚃ ➤ **P** 35 ⊟ Resid **SB** £50-£55 **DB** £78-£84 **HB** £340-£390 **L** £15 **D** £21.50 **D** ♥ ✕ **LD** 21:00 **CC** MC Visa Amex DC JCB ⚡ ♿

SENNEN Cornwall 2A4
Pop. 770. Penzance 9½, London 291 **see** Cove

★★ Old Success
Sennen Cove TR19 7DG
☎ 01736-871232 **Fax** 01736-871457
12 bedrs, 10 ensuite, ⚃ ➤ ∷ 36 **P** 15 ⊟ **CC** MC Visa Amex

---

SETTLE North Yorkshire 10C3
Pop. 2,400. Burnley 23, London 229, Hawes 22, Kirkby Lonsdale 16, Skipton 16 **EC** Wed **MD** Tue
🛈 Town Hall, Cheapside 01729-825192

★★★ Falcon Manor
Skipton Road, Settle BD24 9BD
☎ 01729-823814 **Fax** 01729-822087
E-mail falconm@netcomuk.co.uk

A Grade II Listed building, built in 1841, retaining many period features. Renowned for its excellent cuisine, beautiful views and friendly atmosphere. Non residents welcome.
19 bedrs, all ensuite, ⚃ ➤ ∷ 90 **P** 80 ⊟ **SB** £57.50-£70 **DB** £85-£110 **HB** £434-£521.50 **L** £11.95 **L** ♥ **D** £24.50 **D** ♥ ✕ **LD** 21:30 **CC** MC Visa Amex ♿

SHAFTESBURY Dorset   3F2

Pop. 6,500. Salisbury 20, London 103, Blandford Forum 11, Sherborne 16, Warminster 15, Wincanton 11 **EC** Wed **MD** Thu **see** Abbey ruins, Castle Hill, Gold Hill **i** Bell Street 01747-853514

Royal Chase

Royal Chase Roundabout, Shaftesbury SP7 8DB
C 01747-853355 **Fax** 01747-851969
E-mail royalchasehotel@btinternet.com

A family owned, country house hotel situated in the heart of Thomas Hardy country. The perfect setting for a weekend break or business meeting.
35 bedrs, all ensuite, **↑ ⊞** 150 **P** 100 **⊕ CC** MC Visa Amex DC ▣

SHAP Cumbria   10B2

Pop. 1,300. Kendal 16, London 273, M6 (jn 39) 3, Penrith 9

★★★ Shap Wells

Shap CA10 3QU
C 01931-716628 **Fax** 01931-716377
E-mail manager@shapwells.com
Closed 2 Jan-10 Feb

Nestling in a secluded valley, high in the fells, Shap Wells is the ideal place from which to explore the Lakes, Dales and Border Country.
96 bedrs, all ensuite, **↑ ⊡ ⊞** 400 **P** 200 **⊕ SB** £50-£55 **DB** £75-£80 **L** £8 **L ♥ D** £15 **D ♥ ✗ LD** 20:30 **CC** MC Visa Amex DC JCB ▨ ▧ &

SHEFFIELD South Yorkshire   11D4

Pop. 528,000. Mansfield 22, London 154, M1 30, Barnsley 14, Buxton 25, Chesterfield 12, Glossop 24, Huddersfield 26, Rotherham 5½, Worksop 18 **MD** Daily **see** Cathedral, University, City Museum and Mappin Art Gallery, Graves Art Gallery, Cutlers Hall **i** Peace Gardens 0114-273 4671

★★★★ Swallow ⍟

Kenwood Road, Sheffield S7 1NQ
C 0114-258 3811 **Fax** 0114-250 0138
E-mail info@swallowhotels.com

SWALLOW HOTELS

A luxury hotel set in its own landscaped grounds with an ornamental lake. The hotel has a restaurant and a cocktail bar as well as a Swallow Leisure Club.
116 bedrs, all ensuite, **④ ↑ ⊡ ⊞** 200 **P** 200 **⊕ SB** £95-£105 **DB** £120-£150 **L** £13.95 **D** £19.95 **✗ LD** 21:45 **CC** MC Visa Amex DC ▣ ▧ ▨ ▨ &

★★★ Charnwood

10 Sharrow Lane, Sheffield S11 8AA
C 0114-258 9411 **Fax** 0114-255 5107
Closed 25 Dec- 3 Jan

This charming Georgian residence has elegant public areas amd conference facilities, charming bedrooms, and two excellent restaurants. Situated 1.5 miles south west of the city centre, only 10 mins by car from Derbyshire's Peak District National Park.
22 bedrs, all ensuite, **⌁ ⊞** 100 **P** 22 **⊕ SB** £80 **DB** £95 **D** £14.50 **✗ LD** 22:30 Restaurant closed D Sun **CC** MC Visa Amex DC &

ENGLAND

★★★ Novotel Sheffield
Arundel Gate, Sheffield S1 2PR
☎ 0114-278 1781 Fax 0114-278 7744
E-mail h1348@accor-hotels.com
144 bedrs, all ensuite, ⌀ ⸆ ☐ ⫶ 200 P 40 ⊕ ⊕
Rest Resid SB £85 DB £94 L £10.50 L ♥ D £15 D ♥
✕ LD 23:59 ⦅ MC Visa Amex DC ▣ &

★★★ Posthouse **Posthouse**
Manchester Road, Sheffield S10 5DX
☎ 0114-267 0067 Fax 0114-268 2620
136 bedrs, all ensuite, ⸆ ☐ ⫶ 300 P 150 ⊕ ⦅ MC
Visa Amex DC JCB ▣ ▤ ▨

SHEPPERTON Middlesex 4C3
Richmond upon Thames 9, London 17, Chertsey 4,
Esher 5, Kingston upon Thames 8, Staines 4

★★★ Warren Lodge
Church Square, Shepperton TW17 9JZ
☎ 01932-242972 Fax 01932-253883
E-mail 106345.3471@compuserve.com

Convenient for London, Legoland, Windsor, Hampton
Court and many other local attractions. Ideal riverside
location for the business traveller, conference
delegate or a visiting tourist. Ideal for leisure break.
48 bedrs, all ensuite, ⫶ 100 P 16 ⊕ Rest Resid
SB £84-£88 DB £91-£95 L £11.95 L ♥ D £14.95 D ♥
✕ LD 21:45 ⦅ MC Visa Amex DC &

SHERBORNE Dorset 3E2
Pop. 7,600. Shaftesbury 16, London 120, Blandford
Forum 20, Crewkerne 14 EC Wed MD Thu, Sat ⓘ 3
Tilton Court, Digby Road 01935-815341

★★★ Eastbury
Long Street, Sherborne DT9 3BY
☎ 01935-813131 Fax 01935-817296
15 bedrs, all ensuite, ④ ⫶ 40 P 50 ⊕ SB £49.50
DB £79 HB £444.50 L £12.95 L ♥ D £16.95 D ♥ ✕
LD 21:30 ⦅ MC Visa Amex
See advert on next page

★★★ Sherborne **Heritage** HOTELS
Horsecastles Lane,
Sherborne DT9 6BB
☎ 01935-813191 Fax 01935-816493
59 bedrs, all ensuite, ⸆ ⫶ 75 P 100 ⊕ ⦅ MC Visa
Amex DC JCB

SHIPHAM Somerset 3E1
Pop. 1,150. M5 (jn 22) 7, Axbridge 3, London 135,
Bath 24, Bristol 15, Bridgwater 18, Wells 11,
Weston-super-Mare 9

★★★ Daneswood House
Cuck Hill, Shipham BS25 1RD
☎ 01934-843145 Fax 01934-843824
E-mail daneswoodhousehotel@compuserve.com
12 bedrs, all ensuite, ④ ⌀ ⫶ 30 P 35 ⊕ SB £65
DB £79.50 L £15.95 D £29.95 ✕ LD 21:30 ⦅ MC Visa
Amex DC

SHREWSBURY Shropshire 7D2
Pop. 87,300. Wellington 11, London 154,
Bridgnorth 21, Ludlow 27, Newport 18, Welshpool
18, Whitchurch 18, Wrexham 29 EC Thu MD Tue,
Wed, Fri, Sat see Castle (regimental museum),
Council House, Abbey Church, Old Market Hall,
Statue of Charles Darwin, Owens Mansions,
Butcher Row ⓘ Music Hall, The Square 01743-
350761

★★★ Albright Hussey ♜ ♜ ♜
Ellesmere Road, Shrewsbury SY4 3AF
☎ 01939-290571 Fax 01939-291143
E-mail abhhotel@aol.com

Charming 16th century moated manor house, only
two miles from Shrewsbury town, where tranquillity,
superb food, fine wines and impeccable service
combine in an atmosphere of quiet elegance.
14 bedrs, all ensuite, ④ ♀ ⌀ ⸆ ⫶ 250 P 100 No
children under 3 ⊕ Rest Resid SB £73-£85 DB £95-
£135 HB £493.50-£626.50 L £5.60 D £24.50 D ♥ ✕
LD 22:00 ⦅ MC Visa Amex DC &

★★★ Prince Rupert
Butcher Row, Shrewsbury SY1 1UQ
☎ 01743-499955 **Fax** 01743-357306
69 bedrs, all ensuite, ⊞ ⌀ ⊁ ⊡ ⠿ 120 **P** 70 ⊕
SB £75-£85 **DB** £85-£160 **HB** £530-£900 **L** £9.50 **L** ♥
D £18.50 **D** ♥ ✕ **LD** 21:45 **CC** MC Visa Amex DC ⊞
⊞ ⊞

★★ Nesscliffe
Nesscliffe, Shrewsbury SY4 1DB
☎ 01743-741430 **Fax** 01743-741104
E-mail sales@nesscliffe.enta.net

Grade II Listed building dates back to the 19th century and provides exceptional levels of comfort and hospitality. All 8 bedrooms individually furnished on a traditional theme with up to date modern facilities. Restaurant and bar open all day.
8 bedrs, all ensuite, ⊞ ⠿ 20 **P** 60 ⊕ **SB** £45 **DB** £55
L £6.50 **L** ♥ **D** £9.95 **D** ♥ ✕ **LD** 21:30 **CC** MC Visa Amex

★★ Shelton Hall
Shelton, Shrewsbury SY3 8BH
☎ 01743-343982 **Fax** 01743-241515
Closed 26-27 Dec
9 bedrs, all ensuite, ⠿ 50 **P** 50 ⊕ **SB** £45-£50
DB £62-£68 **HB** £260-£280 **L** £11 **D** £17 ✕ **LD** 20:30
CC MC Visa Amex JCB

Short Breaks

Many hotels provide special rates for
weekend and mid-week breaks –
sometimes these are quoted in
the hotel's entry, otherwise ring
direct for the latest offers.

SIDMOUTH Devon 3D3
Pop. 12,700. Honiton 9½, London 162, Axminster
14, Exeter 16, Lyme Regis 16 **EC** Thu ⑦ Ham Lane
01395-516441

★★★★ Belmont
The Esplanade, Sidmouth EX10 8RX
☎ 01395-512555 **Fax** 01395-579101
E-mail info@belmont-hotel.co.uk

Located on Sidmouth's beautiful esplanade, the
elegant facilities make this one of England's finest
hotels.
54 bedrs, all ensuite, ♀ ⌀ ⊡ ⠿ 50 **P** 50 ⊕ **SB** £57-
£102 **DB** £98-£204 **HB** £343-£714 **L** £14 **L** ♥ **D** £24
D ♥ ✕ **LD** 21:00 **CC** MC Visa Amex DC ⅗
See advert on next page

★★★★ Riviera
The Esplanade, Sidmouth EX10 8AY
☎ 01395-515201 **Fax** 01395-577775
E-mail enquiries@hotelriviera.co.uk

A majestic Regency hotel, situated on the
Esplanade with panoramic sea views and a
splendid terrace overlooking Lyme Bay.
27 bedrs, all ensuite, ⊁ ⊡ ⠿ 85 **P** 27 ⊕ **SB** £74-£84
DB £128-£148 **HB** £525-£630 **L** £16 **L** ♥ **D** £26 ✕
LD 21:00 **CC** MC Visa Amex DC ⅗
See advert on next page

ENGLAND

★★★★ Victoria ⌇
Esplanade, Sidmouth EX10 8RY
☎ 01395-512651 **Fax** 01395-579154
E-mail info@victoriahotel.co.uk

Magnificent rooms, renowned cuisine and superb
leisure facilities make the Victoria one of England's
finest hotels.
61 bedrs, all ensuite, ♀ ✗ ☰ ⠿ 100 **P** 100 ⊕
SB £60-£104 **DB** £114-£226 **HB** £350-£791 **L** £15 **L** ●
D £25 **D** ● ✗ **LD** 21:00 ⟨⟨ MC Visa Amex DC ☒ ⋨ ▨
▨ ▨ ᕒ
See advert on opposite page

★★★ ✦ Royal Glen
Glen Road, Sidmouth EX10 8RW
☎ 01395-513221 **Fax** 01395-514922
E-mail sidmouthroyalglen.hotel@virgin.net
Closed 2-31 Jan

In a secluded position close to the seafront, this
one time Royal residence will appeal to those
seeking old world charm, comfort, good catering
and personal service.
32 bedrs, all ensuite, ⌇ **P** 14 ⊕ Rest Resid **SB** £30-
£43 **DB** £56-£74 **HB** £215-£366 **L** £8 **L** ● **D** £15 ✗
LD 20:30 ⟨⟨ MC Visa ☒

★★★ Salcombe Hill House
Beatlands Road, Sidmouth EX10 8JQ
☎ 01395-514697 **Fax** 01395-578310
Closed end Oct-1 Mar

28 bedrs, all ensuite, ⌇ ☰ **P** 40 ⊕ **SB** £27.50-£47
DB £55-£94 **HB** £230-£390 **L** £9.95 **D** £15.50 ✗
LD 20:30 Restaurant closed L Mon-Sat ⟨⟨ MC Visa
JCB ⋨ ▨

★★★ Westcliff
Manor Road, Sidmouth EX10 8RU
☎ 01395-513252 **Fax** 01395-578203
Closed Nov-Mar

A spaceous, brick built hotel in the Dutch style,
now tastefully modernised and family run, set in
two acres of superb gardens overlooking the
Esplanade and Lyme Bay
40 bedrs, all ensuite, ☰ **P** 40 ⊕ **SB** £47-£68 **DB** £88-
£128 **HB** £348-£455 **L** £12.50 **D** £22 ✗ **LD** 20:45
Restaurant closed L Mon-Sat ⟨⟨ MC Visa ⋨ ▨ ▨

★★ ❖ Abbeydale
Manor Road, Sidmouth EX10 8RP
☎ 01395-512060 Fax 01395-515566
Closed 24 Oct-1 Mar
17 bedrs, all ensuite, 🖵 P 24 No children under 4 ⊞
Rest Resid SB £31-£49 DB £62-£100 HB £280-£406
L £9 L ● D £14 ✕ LD 20:00 ₵ MC Visa 🅰

★★ Brownlands 🚲
Sid Road, Sidmouth EX10 9AG
☎ 01395-513053 Fax 01395-513053
E-mail brownlands.hotel@virgin.net
Closed Nov-mid Mar
14 bedrs, all ensuite, 🛬 P 25 No children under 8 ⊞
SB £45-£48 DB £75-£96 HB £328-£402 L £12.50 L ●
D £19.95 ✕ LD 20:00 Restaurant closed L Mon-Sat
🅰

★★ Byes
Sid Road, Sidmouth EX10 9AA
☎ 01395-513129 Fax 01395-513311

Brick-built hotel set in own grounds. A few minutes walk from amenities.
14 bedrs, all ensuite, 🖵 ♀ 🛬 ⁂ 60 P 22 ⊞ Rest
Resid SB £26-£34 DB £52-£68 HB £217-£301 L ●
D £12.75 D ● ✕ LD 19:30 ₵ MC Visa Amex DC JCB
🅰
See advert on previous page

★★ Royal York & Faulkner
Esplanade, Sidmouth EX10 8AZ
☎ 0800-220714 Fax 01395-577472
E-mail yorkhotel@eclipse.co.uk
Closed Jan
68 bedrs, all ensuite, 🛬 🖵 P 20 ⊞ SB £28.50-£46.50
DB £57-£93 HB £228-£360 L £8 L ● D £13.50 ✕
LD 20:30 ₵ MC Visa JCB 🅰 🅰 🅰

★★ Westbourne
Manor Road, Sidmouth EX10 8RR
☎ 01395-513774 Fax 01395-512231
Closed Nov-Feb
12 bedrs, 11 ensuite, 1 ℞ 🛬 P 14 ⊞ Resid ♿

★★ Woodlands
Cotmaton Cross, Sidmouth EX10 8HG
☎ 01395-513120 Fax 01395-513348
E-mail info@woodlands-hotel.com
20 bedrs, all ensuite, ♀ 🛬 ⁂ P 20 ⊞ Resid
SB £18.50-£46 DB £37-£90 HB £168-£330 L £6.99 L ●
D £9.99 D ● ✕ LD 20:00 ₵ MC Visa ♿

SITTINGBOURNE Kent	5E3

Pop. 37,950. Rochester 11, London 42, M2 (jn 5) 3½, Ashford 20, Canterbury 17, Maidstone 13, Margate 31 EC Wed MD Fri see St Michael's Church (Easter Sepulchre), Dolphin Sailing Barge Museum, 15th cent Old Court Hall (Milton)

★★★ Coniston
London Road, Sittingbourne ME10 1NT
☎ 01795-472131 Fax 01795-428056

Family run hotel, 1 mile from Sittingbourne station and town centre with excellent a la carte restaurant for lunch and dinner parties, 7 days a week. 2 bars and banqueting facilities for 200. Licensed for weddings in the gardens or indoors.
62 bedrs, all ensuite, 🛬 ⁂ 150 P 150 ⊞ ₵ MC Visa Amex DC ♿
See advert on opposite page

SKEGNESS Lincolnshire	9D2

Pop. 15,500. Boston 21, London 139, Horncastle 21, Louth 23, Sleaford 38 EC Thu (win) MD Daily (sum) see St Clement's Church, Natureland (Aquarium and Marine Zoo) 🛈 Embassy Centre, Grand Parade 01754-764821

★★★ Crown
Drummond Road, Skegness PE25 3AB
☎ 0500-007274 (free) Fax 01754-610847
27 bedrs, all ensuite, 🖵 ⁂ 150 P 85 ⊞ SB £45
DB £65 HB £295 L £13 D £13 ✕ LD 21:00 ₵ MC Visa
Amex DC JCB 🅰 ♿
See advert on opposite page

CONISTON HOTEL

Family run hotel, 1 mile from Sittingbourne station and town centre. 62 en-suite rooms, television, tea/coffee making. Direct dial telephones. Excellent a la carte restaurant for luncheon and dinner parties. 7 days a week. 2 bars and banqueting facilities for 200. Licensed for civil wedding services in the large gardens or indoor wedding room. Parking for 100 cars. The hotel is open all year.

LONDON ROAD, SITTINGBOURNE, KENT ME10 1NT
Tel: (01795) 472131/472907
Fax: (01795) 428056

CROWN HOTEL

The Crown Hotel situated just 1½ miles from the Town Centre, near the Seacroft Golf Course and Bird Sanctuary offers 27 ensuite bedrooms with tea and coffee making facilities, direct telephone, Colour Satellite TV, indoor heated Swimming Pool and fine A La Carte Restaurant.

DRUMMOND ROAD, SKEGNESS LINCS. PE25 3AB
Tel: "Free" 0500 007274
Fax: (01754) 610847

★★ Vine
Vine Road, Skegness PE25 3DB
☎ 01754-763018 **Fax** 01754-769845

A 17th century vine-covered building with a bowling green and Victorian-style garden in the grounds.
20 bedrs, all ensuite, ⅘ ↖ ♨ 120 **P** 80 ⊟ **SB** £45
DB £65 **L** £9.50 **D** £16.50 ✕ **LD** 21:00 **CC** MC Visa Amex DC JCB

★ ✦ Crawford
South Parade, Skegness PE25 3HR
☎ 01754-764215
20 bedrs, all ensuite, ▣ ⊟ **SB** £28.79 **DB** £47 **HB** £170
L ☛ **D** £9 ✕ **LD** 18:00 **CC** MC Visa ▣ ▣ ▣

SKIPTON North Yorkshire   10C3
Pop. 13,500. Halifax 17, London 204, Bradford 19, Burnley 18, Harrogate 22, Leeds 26, Leyburn 34
ℹ Old Town Hall, 9 Sheep Street 01756-792809

★★★ Hanover International, Skipton
Keighley Road, Skipton BD23 2TA
☎ 01756-700100 **Fax** 01756-700107

Offers stunning views of the Yorkshire Dales, a state registered nursery and extensive leisure club. The Waterside Restaurant has an enviable reputation for mouth-watering cuisine.
75 bedrs, all ensuite, ⅘ ♀ ✗ ↖ ▣ ♨ 400 **P** 120 ⊟
SB £78-£80 **DB** £88-£90 **HB** £300-£348 **L** ☛ **D** £17 **D** ☛
✕ **LD** 22:00 **CC** MC Visa Amex DC ▣ ▣ ▣ ▣ ♿

★★ Red Lion
Burnsall, Skipton BD23 6BT
☎ 01756-720204 **Fax** 01756-720292
E-mail redlion@daelnet.co.uk
11 bedrs, all ensuite, 🄰 ⚲ ⵘ 30 **P** 70 ⊞ **L** £14.95
L ● **D** £23.95 **D** ● ✕ **LD** 21:30 ⟨⟨ MC Visa Amex DC

SLEAFORD Lincolnshire   8C2
Pop. 10,000. London 116 **EC** Thu **MD** Mon, Fri, Sat
🛈 Money's Yard, Carre Street 01529-414294

★★★ ✦ Lincolnshire Oak
East Road, Sleaford NG34 7EH
☎ 01529-413807 **Fax** 01529-413710
E-mail lincs.oak@pipemedia.co.uk

A mid-19th century hotel in well established
grounds, just outside the town centre on the A153
Sleaford/Horncastle road.
17 bedrs, all ensuite, ⵘ 140 **P** 60 ⊞ ⟨⟨ MC Visa
Amex 🔳

★★ Carre Arms
1 Mareham Lane, Sleaford NG34 7JP
☎ 01529-303156 **Fax** 01529-303139

Busy family run hotel with 13 ensuite bedrooms.
The restaurant/brasserie serves only fresh,
homemade foods. Enjoy real ales in spacious bars
and glass covered courtyard. Within easy reach of
RAF Cranwell and RAF Digby.
13 bedrs, all ensuite, ♀ ⚲ **P** 80 ⊞ **SB** £50 **DB** £70
L £10 **D** ● ✕ **LD** 21:45 ⟨⟨ MC Visa JCB

SLOUGH Berkshire   4C2
Pop. 100,200. London 20, M4 (jn 5) 2½, Henley-on-
Thames 14, High Wycombe 13, Reading 18 **EC** Wed
MD Daily **see** 12th cent Church of St Laurence

★★★★ Copthorne
Cippenham Lane, Slough SL1 2YE
☎ 01753-516222 **Fax** 01753-516237
219 bedrs, all ensuite, ⚲ 🖭 ⵘ 250 **P** 300 ⊞ **SB** £55-
£151.50 **DB** £80-£189 **L** £19.50 **D** £19.50 **D** ● ✕
LD 22:00 Restaurant closed L Sat-Sun ⟨⟨ MC Visa
Amex DC JCB 🔳 🔳 🔳 ᵫ

SOLIHULL West Midlands   7F3
Pop. 94,000. Warwick 13, London 105, Birmingham
7½, Bromsgrove 18, Coventry 12, Evesham 27,
Stratford-upon-Avon 19 **EC** Wed **see** Church,
timbered houses 🛈 Library, Homer Road 0121-704
6130

★★★ ✦ Arden
Coventry Road, Bickenhill, Solihull B92 0EH
☎ 01675-443221 **Fax** 01675-443221
146 bedrs, 124 ensuite, 22 🕭 ⛏ 🖭 ⵘ 180 **P** 250 ⊞
SB £65-£104 **DB** £75-£123 **L** £14.10 **L** ● **D** £14.40 ✕
LD 22:00 Restaurant closed L Sat ⟨⟨ MC Visa Amex
DC 🔳 🔳 🔳 🔳 ᵫ

★★★ ✦ Swallow St John's
651 Warwick Road, Solihull B91 1AT
☎ 0121-711 3000 **Fax** 0121-705 6629
E-mail info@swallowhotels.com

SWALLOW
HOTELS

Set in leafy suburbs, the hotel is handy for the
NEC, Stratford and Warwick. It has a bar plus a
choice of two restaurants and a leisure club.
177 bedrs, all ensuite, ⛏ 🖭 ⵘ 800 **P** 450 ⊞ **SB** £55-
£135 **DB** £70-£145 **D** £20.50 ✕ **LD** 21:45 Restaurant
closed L Sat ⟨⟨ MC Visa Amex DC 🔳 🔳 🔳 ᵫ

★ ✤ Flemings
141 Warwick Road, Olton, B92 7HW
☎ 0121-706 0371 **Fax** 0121-706 4494
78 bedrs, all ensuite, ⚲ ₩ 22 **P** 70 ⊞ Rest Resid
SB £32-£45 **DB** £45-£56 **D** £5.95 **D** ➽ ✕ **LD** 21:30
Restaurant closed L Sat, Sun ⟨⟨ MC Visa Amex DC
JCB ⊞

SONNING Berkshire   4B2

★★★★ French Horn
Sonning RG4 6TN
☎ 01189-692204 **Fax** 01189-442210
E-mail thefrenchhorn@compuserve.com
Closed 26 Dec, Good Friday
20 bedrs, all ensuite, ₩ 20 **P** 40 ⊞ ⟨⟨ MC Visa
Amex DC

SOUTH MILFORD North Yorkshire   11D3
Pop. 1,600. Doncaster 20, London 184, Leeds 13,
York 17 **see** Steeton Gateway

★★★ Posthouse   **Posthouse**
Junction A1/A63, LS25 5LF
☎ 01977-682711 **Fax** 01977-685462
97 bedrs, all ensuite, ♀ ⚲ ₩ 160 **P** 200 ⊞ **SB** £49-
£75 **DB** £49-£75 **L** ➽ **D** ➽ ✕ **LD** 22:30 ⟨⟨ MC Visa
Amex DC JCB ⊞ 📺 📟 ⊠ ⟨⟨

SOUTH MIMMS Hertfordshire   4C2
Barnet 3½, London 15, A1(M) & M25 1, Ealing 15,
Enfield 8, Harrow 11, Hatfield 7, Hoddesdon 14, St
Albans 6½ **EC** Thu 🛈 M25 Service Area 01707-643233

★★★ Posthouse   **Posthouse**
Jn 23 M25/A1(M),
South Mimms EN6 3NH
☎ 01707 643311 **Fax** 01703-646728
143 bedrs, all ensuite, ⚲ ₩ 180 **P** 200 ⊞ ⟨⟨ MC
Visa Amex DC ⊞ ⊞ 📺 ⊠ ⟨⟨

SOUTH MOLTON Devon   2C2
Pop. 3,900. Tiverton 17, London 180, Barnstaple
11, Crediton 26, Great Torrington 15, Okehampton
29 **EC** Wed **MD** Thu 🛈 1 East St 01769-574122

★★ Heasley House
Heasley Mill, South Molton EX36 3LE
☎ 01598-740213 **Fax** 01598-740677
E-mail heasleyhouse@enterprise.net
Closed Feb
8 bedrs, 5 ensuite, ⚲ **P** 11 ⊞

SOUTH NORMANTON Derbyshire   8B2
Pop. 7,600. M1 (jn 28) 1, London 140, Ashbourne
19, Chesterfield 12, Derby 16, Mansfield 7, Matlock
12, Nottingham 14 **EC** Wed

★★★★ Swallow 🍴
Junction 28 M1, Carter Lane East,
South Normanton DE55 2EH
☎ 01773-812000 **Fax** 01773-580032
E-mail info@swallowhotels.com

SWALLOW
HOTELS

A modern, four star, hotel excellently situated for
exploring Robin Hood country. Award winning
restaurant and luxurious leisure club.
160 bedrs, all ensuite, ⚲ ₩ 220 **P** 220 ⊞ **SB** £55-
£105 **DB** £75-£115 **L** £11.95 **D** £16.50 ✕ **LD** 22:00
Restaurant closed L Sat ⟨⟨ MC Visa Amex DC ⊞ ⊞
📺 ⟨⟨

SOUTH SHIELDS Tyne & Wear   11D1
Pop. 87,200. Sunderland 7, London 277, Durham
19, Newcastle 9½ **EC** Wed **MD** Mon, Sat **see** Roman
Fort and Museum 🛈 Museum Ocean Road 0191-
454 6612

★★★ Sea
Sea Road, South Shields NE33 2LD
☎ 0191-427 0999 **Fax** 0191-454 0500
33 bedrs, all ensuite, ⚃ ⚲ ₩ 200 **P** 70 ⊞ ⟨⟨ MC
Visa Amex DC

SOUTHAMPTON Hampshire   4B4
Pop. 196,500. Winchester 12, London 77, M271 (jn
4) 3, Fareham 12, Lyndhurst 9½, Ringwood 18,
Romsey 8, Salisbury 22 **MD** Thu, Fri, Sat **see** Old
Gates Towers and Town Walls, Docks, Museums:
Tudor House, Bargate, Pilgrim Fathers' Memorial
🛈 9 Civic Centre Road 01703-221106

National Code & Number Change

Telephone codes and numbers in Southampton change in April 2000.
01703-XXXXXX becomes 023-80XX XXXX
eg 01703-806222 becomes 023-8080 6222

★★★ Botley Park Hotel, Golf and Country Club

Winchester Road, Boorley Green, Botley SO32 2UA
☎ 01489-780888 **Fax** 01489-789242
E-mail info@botleypark.macdonald-hotel.co.uk
100 bedrs, all ensuite, ♀ ♪ ★ ▦ 200 **P** 250 ⊕
SB £60-£110 DB £70-£120 L £13.25 L ♥ D £24.50
D ♥ ✕ LD 22:00 Restaurant closed L Sat ⊂⊂ MC Visa
Amex DC ▣ ▦ ▣ ▣ ▣ ▣ ▣ ⅄

★★★ County

Highfield Lane, Portswood, SO17 1AQ
☎ 01703-359955 **Fax** 01703-583910
E-mail countysoton@msjhotels.co.uk

Within easy reach of the M3 and M27, the perfect venue for business or leisure. 66 ensuite bedrooms, many recently refurbished and superb conference rooms catering for 2-200 delegates.
66 bedrs, all ensuite, ★ ▦ 160 **P** 70 No children ⊕
SB £79 DB £92.50 L ♥ D £13.95 D ♥ ✕ LD 21:30
⊂⊂ MC Visa Amex DC ▦

★★★ Novotel Southampton

1 West Quay Road, Southampton SO15 1RA
☎ 01703-330550 **Fax** 01703-222158
E-mail h1073@accor-hotels.com
121 bedrs, all ensuite, ♪ ★ ▣ ▦ 500 **P** 300 ⊕
SB £60-£80 DB £60-£90 L ♥ D £10 D ♥ ✕ LD 0:00
⊂⊂ MC Visa Amex DC ▣ ▦ ▣ ⅄

★★★ Posthouse Eastleigh   **Posthouse**

Leigh Road, Eastleigh, SO5 5PG
☎ 01703-619700 **Fax** 01703-643945
117 bedrs, all ensuite, ♪ ★ ▣ ▦ 240 **P** 150 ⊕
SB £69.95-£99.95 DB £80.90-£110.95 ✕ LD 22:00
Restaurant closed (L) Saturday ⊂⊂ MC Visa Amex
DC ▣ ▦ ▣ ▣ ⅄

★★★ Posthouse   **Posthouse**
Southampton Waterfront

Herbert Walker Avenue, Southampton SO1 0HJ
☎ 01703-330777 **Fax** 01703-332510
128 bedrs, all ensuite, ★ ▣ ▦ 200 **P** 250 ⊕ ⊂⊂ MC
Visa Amex DC ▣ ▦ ▣ ⅄

★★ Elizabeth House

43-44 The Avenue, Southampton SO17 1XP
☎ 01703-224327 **Fax** 01703-224327
E-mail elizabeth.house.hotel@cwcom.net
Closed Christmas & New Year

Elegant Victorian residence with pleasant gardens, on the main access route to and from the North. Convenient for city centre, airport, docks, university and motorways.
21 bedrs, all ensuite, ★ 40 **P** 23 ⊕ Rest Resid
SB £45 DB £55 L ♥ D £8 D ♥ ✕ LD 21:00 Restaurant
closed L Sat-Sun ⊂⊂ MC Visa JCB

★★ Star Hotel & Restaurant

26 High Street, Southampton SO14 2NA
☎ 01703-339939 **Fax** 01703-335291
Closed 22 Dec-03 Jan
44 bedrs, 37 ensuite, ♪ ★ ▣ ▦ 70 **P** 30 ⊕ SB £40-
£50 DB £55-£65 L £7 D £14 ✕ LD 21:30 Restaurant
closed L Sat ⊂⊂ MC Visa Amex DC JCB

Roadchef Lodge **Lodge**

M27 Westbound, Rownhams, SO16 8AP
☎ 01703-741144 **Fax** 01703-740204
Closed 24-27 Dec
39 bedrs, all ensuite, ▦ 15 **P** 120 **Room** £47.95 ⊂⊂ MC
Visa Amex DC ⅄

SOUTHEND-ON-SEA Essex   5E2
See also WESTCLIFF-ON-SEA
Pop. 165,400. Romford 25, London 42, Brentwood
21, Chelmsford 19, Colchester 37, Dartford
Crossing 21, Rainham 26 **MD** Thu, Fri, Sat **see** Pier -
over 1½ miles long, Civic House (formerly 16th cent
Manor House), 13th cent Southchurch Hall ▨ 19
High Street 01702-215120

★ Tower
146 Alexandra Road, Southend-on-Sea SS1 1HE
📞 01702-348635 **Fax** 01702-433044
32 bedrs, 31 ensuite, 🛏 ⅲ 40 **P** 3 ⊕ Rest Resid
《 MC Visa Amex DC ♿
See advert on this page

SOUTHPORT Lancashire   10B4
Pop. 93,500. Ormskirk 8, London 211, Chorley 19,
Liverpool 18, Preston 17 **see** St Cuthburt's Church,
Atkinson Art Gallery, Floral Hall 🖊 112 Lord St.
01704-533333

★★★★ Prince of Wales
Lord Street, Southport PR8 1JS
📞 01704-536688 **Fax** 01704-543932
E-mail princeofwales@paramount-hotels.co.uk

PARAMOUNT
HOTEL·GROUP

Am elegant Victorian hotel located in the heart of
the coastal resort and golfing haven of Southport.
Four star standard with excellent car parking,
Colonial Restaurant and Carvery, two bars and
complimentary entry to the Victoria Sports and
Leisure Club.
103 bedrs, all ensuite, 🗗 🛏 ▣ ⅲ 500
P 98 ⊕ **SB** £90 **DB** £105 **HB** £308 **L** £9.95
L ♥ **D** £17 **D** ♥ ✕ **LD** 21:30
《 MC Visa Amex DC

★★★ Scarisbrick 🖥
239 Lord Street, Southport PR8 1NZ
📞 01704-543000 **Fax** 01704-533335
77 bedrs, all ensuite, 🗗 🛏 ▣ ⅲ 180 **P** 60 ⊕ 《 MC
Visa Amex DC ♿

★★★ Stutelea Hotel & Leisure Club
Alexandra Road, Southport PR9 0NB
📞 01704-544220 **Fax** 01704-500232
E-mail info@stutelea.co.uk
20 bedrs, all ensuite, 🗗 ♀ ♪ ▣ ⅲ 30 **P** 18 ⊕ **SB** £65
DB £90-£95 **L** £7 **D** £18 ✕ **LD** 21:00 《 MC Visa Amex
DC JCB 🖫 🗒 🖾

★★★ Tree Tops Country House 🖥 🖥
Southport Old Road, Formby,
Southport L37 0AB
📞 01704-879651 **Fax** 01704-879651

Ideal for business or pleasure, situated just off the
beaten track, in quiet and tranquil surroundings,
offering top class dining in our country house
restaurant.
11 bedrs, all ensuite, ⅲ 200 **P** 150 No children
under 5 ⊕ **SB** £48-£60 **DB** £85-£95 **L** £8.50 **L** ♥ **D** £20
✕ **LD** 21:30 《 MC Visa Amex DC ⅔ ♿

★★ Balmoral Lodge
41 Queens Road, Southport PR9 9EX
☎ 01704-544298 **Fax** 01704-501224
E-mail balmorallg@aol.com

Family run hotel, with a reputation for excellent food and hospitality, designed to cater for both business and leisure guests. Garden rooms with balconies, free sauna.
15 bedrs, all ensuite, 4 ⅲ 40 **P** 10 ⊕ Rest ⅽⅽ MC Visa Amex DC JCB 📟 ⅃

★★ Metropole
Portland Street, Southport PR8 1LL
☎ 01704-536836 **Fax** 01704-549041

One of Southport's finest family run hotels offering traditional standards of comfort and courtesy. Central location ideal for business or leisure breaks. Golf holidays arranged.
23 bedrs, all ensuite, ⊬ **P** 12 ⊕ ⅽⅽ MC Visa Amex JCB 🖼

SOUTHWOLD Suffolk   9F3
Pop. 4,000. Saxmundham 14, London 109, Aldeburgh 17, Lowestoft 11, Norwich 29 **EC** Wed **MD** Mon, Thur ⅈ Town Hall, Market Place 01502-724729

Pier Avenue
Station Road, Southwold IP18 6AY
☎ 01502-722632 **Fax** 01502-722632

Family run Edwardian hotel within walking distance of the beach and town centre. The vibrantly decorated Seafood Restaurant offers some of the most imaginative fish dishes in the region.
13 bedrs, all ensuite, 4 ⊬ ⅲ 40 **P** 8 ⊕ ⅽⅽ MC Visa Amex DC

SPALDING Lincolnshire   8C2
Pop. 19,000. Peterborough 17, London 101, Boston 16, Grantham 30, King's Lynn 28, Sleaford 19, Stamford 19, Wisbech 20 **EC** Thu **MD** Tue **see** Church (13th cent), Ayscoughfee Hall
ⅈ Ayscoughfee Hall, Churchgate 01775-725468

★★ Cley Hall
22 High Street, Spalding PE11 1TX
☎ 01775-725157 **Fax** 01775-710785
E-mail cleyhall@enterprise.net
12 bedrs, all ensuite, 4 ♀ ⊬ ⅲ 40 **P** 15 ⊕ **SB** £30-£55 **DB** £55-£70 **L** 📞 **D** £11.95 **D** 📞 ✕ **LD** 21:30 Restaurant closed D Sun ⅽⅽ MC Visa Amex DC JCB ⅃

★★ ✦ Woodlands
80 Pinchbeck Road, Spalding PE11 1QF
☎ 01775-769933 **Fax** 01775-711369

A family run hotel within easy walking distance of Spalding town centre. The Woodlands Hotel offers you a blend of relaxation and quality of service second to none. An ideal base for exploring the historic Fenlands, or just taking that well earned break.
17 bedrs, all ensuite, ⊬ ⅲ 60 **P** 40 ⊕ ⅽⅽ MC Visa Amex DC ⅃

ENGLAND

STAFFORD Staffordshire 7E2

Pop. 62,680. Lichfield 16, London 132, M6 (jn 14) 2 EC Wed MD Tue, Fri, Sat Ancient High House, Greengate Street 01785-240204

★★★ Quality Stafford

Pinford Lane, Penkridge, Stafford ST19 5QP
01785-712459 Fax 01785-715532
47 bedrs, all ensuite, 300 P 160 SB £40-£115 DB £50-£125 L D LD 21:30 Restaurant closed L Sat CC MC Visa Amex DC

★★ Abbey

65-68 Lichfield Road, Stafford ST14 4LW
01785-258531 Fax 01785-246875
17 bedrs, all ensuite, P 21 Rest Resid SB £32-£35 DB £46-£50 L £8 D £8 LD 20:30 Restaurant closed Sun CC MC Visa Amex JCB

★ Albridge

Wolverhampton Road, Stafford ST17 4AW
01785-54100
Closed 25-26 Dec
10 bedrs, 8 ensuite, P 20 SB £22-£27 DB £33-£38 LD 21:30 Restaurant closed D Sun CC MC Visa Amex DC

STAINES Surrey 4C2

Pop. 19,000. London 17, M25 (jn 13) 1, Bagshot 10, Kingston upon Thames 9½, Reading 22, Uxbridge 11, Woking 9 EC Thu MD Wed, Sat

★★★ Thames Lodge

Thames Street, Staines TW18 4SF
01784-464433 Fax 01784-454858
79 bedrs, all ensuite, 50 P 33 SB £124.75-£145.50 DB £154.50-£166 L £10 L D £14.95 D LD 21:30 CC MC Visa Amex DC JCB

STALHAM Norfolk 9F2

Norwich 14, London 125, Great Yarmouth 17

★★ Kingfisher

High Street, Stalham NR12 9AN
01692-581974 Fax 01692-582544
18 bedrs, all ensuite, 100 P 40 CC MC Visa

STAMFORD Lincolnshire 8C3

Pop. 17,700. London 91, Grantham 21, Kettering 23, Leicester 32, Melton Mowbray 20, Spalding 19 Arts Centre, 27 Street Mary's St 01780-55611

★★★ Garden House

St Martin's, Stamford PE9 2LP
01780-763359 Fax 01780-763339

An 18th century family run hotel close to Stamford's centre. Twenty ensuite rooms, all individually furnished. Restaurant, bar, Victorian conservatory and beautiful gardens. Free parking. Personal service assured.
20 bedrs, all ensuite, 4 20 P 30 SB £50-£65 DB £70-£85 L £10 D £15 LD 21:30 CC MC Visa Amex

★★★ George of Stamford

Blue Ribbon Hotel
St Martins, Stamford PE9 2LB
01780-750750 Fax 01780-750701
E-mail georgehotelofstamford@btinternet.com
47 bedrs, all ensuite, 4 50 P 120 SB £78 DB £105 L £14 L LD 22:30 CC MC Visa Amex DC

★★ Crown

All Saints Place, Stamford PE9 2AG
01780-763136 Fax 01780-756111
E-mail thecrownhotel@excite.com
Closed Christmas

This friendly hotel is situated in the heart of the picturesque market town. The restaurant offers wholesome food and the bar has a selection of well kept ales.
17 bedrs, all ensuite, 4 40 P 40 SB £42 DB £55 L £8 D £11 LD 21:30 CC MC Visa Amex DC

Bredbury Hall
Hotel and Country Club Ltd.

Bredbury Hall Hotel is a family run independent hotel, set in the beautiful Goyt Valley, yet located less than one mile off M60 motorway and seven miles from Manchester international airport.

The hotel offers all the services and standards of a luxury hotel. The 135 bedrooms are tastefully decorated and have en-suite corner bath and shower, hair dryers, satellite TV and direct dial telephones, and a modern conference centre for up to 150 people.

We have an exclusive country club open Monday, Wednesday, Friday and Saturday evenings.

Leisure facilities are planned for early 2000.

**Dark Lane, Goyt Valley, Bredbury, Stockport, Cheshire, SK6 2DH
Tel: 0161 430 7421 Fax: 0161 430 5079**

★★ Lady Anne's
37-38 High Street, Saint Martins, PE9 2LJ
☎ 01780-481184 Fax 01780-765422
Closed 26-30 Dec
29 bedrs, all ensuite, 🗔 ♪ ⊁ ⠿ 130 P 100 ⊕
SB £52-£56 DB £68-£90 L £11.95 L ● D £19.50 D ●
✕ LD 21:30 CC MC Visa Amex DC ⊠ ᵭ

STEVENAGE Hertfordshire   4C1
Pop. 77,400. Hatfield 10, London 31, A1(M) (jn 7)
1½, Baldock 6, Bedford 20, Bishop's Stortford 21,
Luton 12 MD Thu, Fri, Sat see Knebworth House 3m S

★★★ Novotel Stevenage
Knebworth Park, Stevenage SG1 2AX
☎ 01438-742299 Fax 01438-723872
E-mail h0992@accor-hotels.com
100 bedrs, all ensuite, ♪ ⊁ 🖃 ⠿ 140 P 100 ⊕
SB £92-£95 DB £102-£105 L £13.50 L ● D £16 D ● ✕
LD 0:00 CC MC Visa Amex DC ⊰ ᵭ

★★★ Posthouse   **Posthouse**
Old London Road, Broadwater,
Stevenage SG2 8DS
☎ 01438-365444 Fax 01438-741308
54 bedrs, all ensuite, ⊁ ⠿ 60 P 60 ⊕ CC MC Visa
Amex DC JCB

STEYNING West Sussex   4C4
Pop. 4,400. Crawley 20, London 50, Brighton 11,
Haywards Heath 18, Horsham 16, Pulborough 11,
Worthing 7 EC Thu

★★★ Old Tollgate
The Street, Bramber, Steyning BN44 3WE
☎ 01903-879494 Fax 01903-813399
E-mail otr@fastnet.co.uk

An old toll house with a modern extension housing luxuriously appointed bedrooms. Masses of olde worlde charm, popular restaurant.
31 bedrs, all ensuite, 🗔 ♀ ♪ 🖃 ⠿ 50 P 60 ⊕
SB £71.95 DB £78.90 L £13.95 D £19.95 ✕ LD 21:45
CC MC Visa Amex DC ᵭ

STILTON Cambridgeshire 8C3
Huntingdon 15, London 77, Oundle 12,
Peterborough 6, Ramsay 11

★★★ Bell Inn ⌇ ⌇
Great North Road, Stilton, Peterborough PE7 3RA
☎ 01733-241066 **Fax** 01733-245173
Closed Christmas
19 bedrs, all ensuite, 🖫 ⌗ 90 **P** 30 ⊕ **CC** MC Visa
Amex DC JCB

STOCKPORT Cheshire 10C4
Pop. 289,000. Buxton 18, London 179, M63 ½,
Altrincham 8½, Glossop 11, Huddersfield 27,
Knutsford 14, Macclesfield 12, Manchester 6,
Oldham 11 **EC** Thu **MD** Tue, Fri, Sat **see** Art Gallery
Museum, Bramall Hall, Bramhall 2½ m S
🛈 Graylaw House, Chestergate 0161-474 3320

★★★ Bredbury Hall
Hotel & Country Club

Goyt Valley, Bredbury, Stockport SK6 2DU
☎ 0161-430 7421 **Fax** 0161-430 5079
120 bedrs, all ensuite, ⌗ 200 **P** 300 ⊕ **SB** £57
DB £74 **D** £15 ✕ **LD** 23:30 Restaurant closed Sun
CC MC Visa Amex DC ☑ ▧
See advert on opposite page

STOCKTON-ON-TEES Cleveland 11D2
Pop. 86,800. Thirsk 22, London 243, Darlington 11,
Durham 19, Middlesbrough 4, Northallerton 19,
Sunderland 26 **EC** Thu **MD** Wed, Fri, Sat **see** 18th cent
Town Hall, Preston Hall, Darlington and Stockton
Railway Museum 🛈 Theatre Yard, off High Street
01642-615080

★★★★ Swallow ⌇ ⌇
10 John Walker Square,
Stockton-on-Tees TS18 1AQ
☎ 01642-679721 **Fax** 01642-601714
E-mail info@swallowhotels.com

SWALLOW
HOTELS

This modern hotel, within easy reach of the North
York Moors, has an excellent range of facilities
including a choice of restaurants, cocktail bar,
spacious lounge and Swallow Leisure Club.
125 bedrs, all ensuite, ⌁ ▤ ⌗ 300 **P** 600 ⊕ **SB** £85-
£110 **DB** £99-£130 **D** £12 ✕ **LD** 22:00 **CC** MC Visa
Amex DC ▣ ▨ ▧

STOKE GABRIEL Devon 3D4
Pop. 1,200. Torquay 6, London 221, Dartmouth 7,
Totnes 4

★★★ Gabriel Court
Stoke Hill, Stoke Gabriel TQ9 6SF
☎ 01803-782206 **Fax** 01803-782333
19 bedrs, all ensuite, ⌁ ⌗ 20 **P** 21 ⊕ Rest Resid
CC MC Visa Amex DC ⌇ ▧

STOKE-ON-TRENT Staffordshire 7E1
See also NEWCASTLE-UNDER-LYME
Pop. 250,000. Lichfield 29, London 152, M6 (jn 5)
3, Ashbourne 22, Congleton 13, Leek 11,
Newcastle-under-Lyme 2, Newport 21, Sandbach
13, Stone 8, Uttoxeter 15 **EC** Thu **MD** Wed, Fri, Sat **see**
Josiah Wedgwood monument, Town Hall, Royal
Doulton works 🛈 Potteries Shopping Centre,
Quadrant Road 01782-284600

★★★ George ⌇ ⌇
Swan Square, Burslem, Stoke-on-Trent ST6 2AE
☎ 01782-577544 **Fax** 01782-837496
E-mail georgestoke@btinternet.com
Closed 24-26 Dec

Situated centrally for all local businesses, pottery
factories and tours. Alton Towers just 30 minutes
drive. Award winning restaurant, friendly and
comfortable surroundings.
39 bedrs, all ensuite, ♀ ⌀ ▤ ⌗ 180 **P** 15 ⊕ **SB** £40-
£70 **DB** £60-£90 **L** £10.95 **L** ▣ **D** £15.95 **D** ▣ ✕
LD 21:15 **CC** MC Visa Amex DC ▧

★★★ North Stafford
Station Road,
Stoke-on-Trent ST4 2AE
☎ 01782-744477 **Fax** 01782-744580
80 bedrs, all ensuite, ♀ ♪ ✝ ▣ ⠿ 450 **P** 120 ⏣
SB £105-£109 **DB** £125-£130 **HB** £350-£406
L £9.50 **L** ● **D** £17.95 ✕ **LD** 21:30
Restaurant closed L Sat
《 MC Visa Amex DC 戋

PRINCIPAL HOTELS

★★★ ❖ Posthouse
Clayton Road,
Newcastle-under-Lyme ST5 4DL
☎ 01782-717171 **Fax** 01782-717138
119 bedrs, all ensuite, ✝ ⠿ 70 **P** 400 ⏣ **SB** £88.95
DB £98.90 **L** £7.95 **D** £11.95 ✕ **LD** 22:30 Restaurant
closed L Sat 《 MC Visa Amex DC ▣ ▣ ▣

Posthouse

Pop. 600. Bromsgrove 7, London 120,
Kidderminster 2½, Stourbridge 8 **see** Church

★★★★ Stone Manor
Stone, Nr Kidderminster DY10 4PJ
☎ 01562-777555 **Fax** 01562-777834
E-mail bev@stonemanor.freeserve.co.uk

Set in 25 acres of landscaped gardens, the 4 star
Stone Manor is the perfect hotel for a quality,
peaceful and relaxing stay. Sumptuous lounges,
tennis court, croquet lawn, putting green, pool, a la
carte restaurant and 52 wonderfully appointed
bedrooms.
52 bedrs, all ensuite, ▣ ✝ ⠿ 150 **P** 400 ⏣
SB £78.25-£128.25 **DB** £86.50-£136.50 **L** £12.95 **L** ●
D £17.50 **D** ● ✕ **LD** 22:00 《 MC Visa Amex DC ▣ ▣

Pop. 2,100. Chipping Norton 9, London 84, Burford
10, Cheltenham 18, Circencester 19, Evesham 16,
Moreton-in-Marsh 4½ **EC** Wed **see** Town Hall, St
Edward's Church, St Edward's Hall ℹ Hollis House,
The Square 01451-831082

★★★★ Wyck Hill House 徻 徻 徻
Burford Road, GL54 1HY
☎ 01451-831936 **Fax** 01451-832243
E-mail wyck@wrensgroup.com
32 bedrs, 31 ensuite, 1 徻 ▣ ♀ ♪ ✝ ▣ ⠿ 24 **P** 80 ⏣
SB £105 **DB** £150-£250 **L** £17.50 **L** ● **D** £36.50 ✕
LD 21:30 《 MC Visa Amex DC

★★★ Fosse Manor 徻 徻
Fosseway, Stow-on-the-Wold GL54 1JX
☎ 01451-830354 **Fax** 01451-832486
Closed 22-29 Dec

Rurally located Cotswold manor house in
landscaped gardens.
17 bedrs, 9 ensuite, ▣ ♀ ♪ ✝ ⠿ 40 **P** 60 ⏣ **SB** £55
DB £118 **HB** £425 **L** £15 **D** £25 **D** ● ✕ **LD** 21.30 《 MC
Visa Amex DC JCB

★★★ Grapevine
Sheep Street, Stow-on-the-Wold GL54 1AU
☎ 01451-830344 **Fax** 01451-832278
E-mail enquiries@vines.co.uk
22 bedrs, all ensuite, ▣ ⠿ 20 **P** 23 ⏣ 《 MC Visa
Amex DC JCB

★★★ Stow Lodge
The Square, Stow-on-the-Wold GL54 1AB
☎ 01451-830485 **Fax** 01451-831671
E-mail enquiries@stowlodge.com
Closed Christmas & Jan

Cotswold stone hotel set back in its own grounds,
overlooking the market square.

21 bedrs, all ensuite, ▣ **P** 30 No children under 5 ⊕
SB £50-£100 **DB** £70-£120 **HB** £250-£400 **D** £17.50
D 🍴 ✕ **LD** 21:00 ⊄ MC Visa DC JCB

STRATFORD-UPON-AVON Warwickshire   4A1
Pop. 20,900. Oxford 39, London 93, Banbury 20,
Birmingham 23, Chipping Norton 21, Evesham 14,
Moreton-in-Marsh 16, Warwick 8, Worcester 27
EC Thu **MD** Tue, Fri **see** Shakespeare's birthplace
(Henley St), (tomb in Holy Trinity Church), Royal
Shakespeare Theatre and Museum, New Place,
Nash's House, New Place Museum, adj), Hall's
Croft, Elizabethan Garrick Inn and other old inns
ℹ Bridgefoot 01789-293127

★★★★ Alveston Manor   *Heritage* HOTELS
Clopton Bridge,
Stratford-upon-Avon CV37 7HP
📞 01789-204581 **Fax** 01789-414095
E-mail heritagehotels-stratford-upon-avon.alveston
manor@fortehotels.com
114 bedrs, all ensuite, ▣ ⊀ ⁝⁝ 140 **P** 200 ⊕
SB £105.50 **DB** £151.50 **HB** £553 **L** £15
D £25 ✕ **LD** 21:30
⊄ MC Visa Amex DC JCB

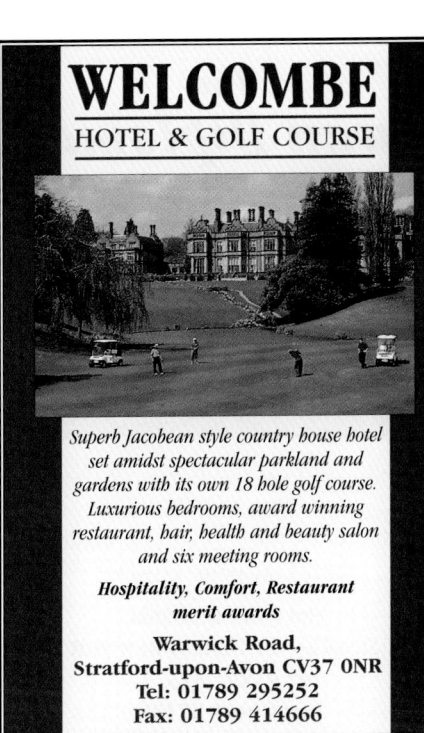

★★★★ ❖ Billesley Manor
Billesley, Stratford-upon-Avon B49 6NF
📞 01789-279955 **Fax** 01789-764145
41 bedrs, all ensuite, ▣ ⁝⁝ 100 **P** 100 ⊕ ⊄ MC Visa
Amex DC ▣ ▨

★★★★ Shakespeare ⏚   *Heritage* HOTELS
Chapel Street,
Stratford-upon-Avon CV37 6ER
📞 01789-294771 **Fax** 01789-415411
74 bedrs, all ensuite, ▣ ⊀ ▣ ⁝⁝ 100
P 45 ⊕ **SB** £105.50 **DB** £156 **HB** £623
L £8 **D** £21 ✕ **LD** 21:30
⊄ MC Visa Amex DC JCB

★★★★ Stratford Manor ⏚
Warwick Road,
Stratford-upon-Avon CV37 0PY
📞 01789-731173 **Fax** 01789-731131
E-mail stratfordmanor@marstonhotels.co.uk
103 bedrs, all ensuite, ▣ ⊀ ▣ ⁝⁝ 360 **P** 220 ⊕
SB £104-£124 **DB** £130-£150 **HB** £455 **L** £15.50 **D** £25
D 🍴 ✕ **LD** 22:00 Restaurant closed Sat ⊄ MC Visa
Amex DC ▣ ▨ ▨ ▨ ⅊

★★★★ Welcombe
Hotel and Golf Course ⏚ ⏚ ⏚
Warwick Road,
Stratford-upon-Avon CV37 0NR
📞 01789-295252 **Fax** 01789-414666
67 bedrs, all ensuite, ⁝⁝ 120 **P** 100 ⊕ ⊄ MC Visa
Amex DC ⅌ ▨ ▨ ▨ ⅊
See advert on this page

★★★ Grosvenor
Warwick Road, Stratford-upon-Avon CV37 6YT
📞 01789-269213 **Fax** 01789-266087
67 bedrs, all ensuite, ⊀ ⁝⁝ 100 **P** 50 ⊕ **SB** £82.25
DB £99.50 **L** £15.50 🍴 **D** £15.50 **D** 🍴 ✕ **LD** 21.30
⊄ MC Visa Amex DC ⅊

★★★ Swan's Nest   *Heritage* HOTELS
Bridgefoot,
Stratford-upon-Avon CV37 7LT
📞 01789-266761 **Fax** 01789-414547
E-mail heritagehotels_stratford-upon-
avon.swansnest@forte-hotels.com
68 bedrs, all ensuite, ✐ ⊀ ⁝⁝ 120 **P** 100
⊕ **SB** £99 **DB** £110 **L** £7.95 🍴 **D** £9.95
D 🍴 ✕ **LD** 22:30
⊄ MC Visa Amex DC JCB ⅊

★★ Stratford Court
Avenue Road, Stratford-upon-Avon CV37 6UX
☎ 01789-297799 Fax 01789-262449

Beautiful Edwardian residence in an acre of walled gardens. Only 10 minutes walk from town centre. A peaceful setting where guests can be served with care and courtesy.
11 bedrs, all ensuite, 🔟 ⌁ P 20 No children under 12 ⊖ Resid **SB** £55 **DB** £95-£150 **D** £16.50 ✗ **LD** 20:30 ℂℂ MC Visa

---

Pop. 1,000. Reading 9½, London 48, Basingstoke 21, Newbury 12, Wallingford 6, Wantage 14

★★★★ Swan Diplomat
Streatley-on-Thames RG8 9HR
☎ 01491-878800 Fax 01491-872554
E-mail sales@swan-diplomat.co.uk
46 bedrs, all ensuite, 🔟 ♀ ⌁ ⋕ 90 P 135 ⊖ **SB** £72-£114 **DB** £110-£161.70 **L** £22.50 **L** ⍾ **D** £32 **D** ⍾ ✗ **LD** 22:00 Restaurant closed L Mon-Sat ℂℂ MC Visa Amex DC ③ 🔀 🖳 ⅛
See advert on this page

Pop. 9,600. Glastonbury 2, London 128, Bridgewater 13, Crewkerne 23, Ilminster 21, Taunton 20, Wincanton 23 **EC** Wed

★★★ Wessex
High Street, Street BA16 0EF
☎ 01458-443383 Fax 01458-446589
E-mail wessex@hotel-street.freeserve.co.uk
50 bedrs, all ensuite, ♀ ⌁ ▣ ⋕ 250 P 92 ⊖ **SB** £45.95-£55.95 **DB** £61.90-£71.90 **HB** £286.25-£397.50 **L** £7 **L** ⍾ **D** £15 **D** ⍾ ✗ **LD** 21:30 ℂℂ MC Visa Amex DC ⅛

Stamford 8, London 99, Bourne 15½, Grantham 11½, Oakham 7

★★ Ram Jam Inn
Great North Road, Stretton, Oakham LE15 7QX
☎ 01780-410776 Fax 01780-410361
Closed Christmas

The hotel offers a cafe, bar, bistro, real garden and orchard. Influences are continental and English country house, with polished pine terracotta floors and marble tops and an open fire.
7 bedrs, all ensuite, ♪ ⌁ ⋕ 90 P 64 ⊖ **SB** £51.05 **DB** £67.10 **L** ⍾ **D** £10 **D** ⍾ ✗ **LD** 21:30 ℂℂ MC Visa Amex

ENGLAND

STROUD Gloucestershire 7E4

Pop. 38,200. Cirencester 12, London 100, M5 (jn 13) 5, Bath 27, Bristol 30, Tetbury 8½ **EC** Thu **MD** Sat
ⓘ Subscription Rooms, George Street 01453-765768

★★ ✣ **Bell**
Wallbridge, Stroud GL5 3JA
☎ 01453-763556 **Fax** 01453-758611

Extensively renovated and extended to its present size. The sympathy with which the new wing was blended with the original Victorian building won a number of prestigious awards. Beautifully situated on the banks of the Stroudwater Canal.
12 bedrs, 10 ensuite, 🅰 ♀ 🔗 ➤ ⠿ 30 **P** 30 🍴 **SB** £35
DB £45 **HB** £275 **L** £7.95 **L** ➤ **D** £11.95 **D** ➤ ✕
LD 21:30 **CC** MC Visa Amex DC ♿

STUDLAND Dorset 3F3

Pop. 500. Wareham 9½, London 126 (fy 111)

★★★ ✣ Knoll House
Ferry Road, Studland BH19 3AH
☎ 01929-450450 **Fax** 01929-450423
E-mail enquiries@knollhouse.co.uk
Closed Nov-Mar

A country house style building set in gardens and pine trees above Studland Bay. Good food and leisure facilities with many amenities for families.
79 bedrs, 57 ensuite, ➤ **P** 100 🍴 Rest Resid **SB** £80
DB £160 **HB** £630 **L** £17 **D** £17 ✕ **LD** 20:15 **CC** MC Visa
🔲 🔗 🎾 📺 ▶ 🔲 ♿
See advert on this page

The Pullman Lodge Hotel

Privately owned and personally run modern hotel, situated on coast. Families welcome, large play area, meals served from 12 noon until 10pm. Also on offer a complete wedding package, extensive conference and private function facilities.

	MIN.	MAX.
Single	£35.00	£45.00
Double	£45.00	£55.00
Family Room	£50.00	£60.00

WHITBURN ROAD, SEABURN SR6 8AA
Tel: (0191) 5292020
Fax: (0191) 5292077

SUDBURY Suffolk · 5E1
Pop. 10,067. Braintree 14, London 60, Bury St. Edmunds 16, Colchester 14, Harwich 30, Haverhill 16, Ipswich 21 **EC** Wed **MD** Thu, Sat **ℹ** Town Hall, Market Hill 01787-881320

★★★ Mill
Walnut Tree Lane, Sudbury CO10 6BD
☎ 01787-375544 **Fax** 01787-373027
56 bedrs, all ensuite, ▣ ✝ ‖ 70 **P** 60 ⟐ **SB** £67.95 **DB** £87 **L** £14.50 **L** ⬥ ✕ **LD** 21:30 **CC** MC Visa Amex DC 🔟

SUNDERLAND Tyne & Wear · 11D1
Pop. 190,000. Stockton 26, London 269, Durham 13, Middlesbrough 27, Newcastle 12 **see** St Peter's Church **ℹ** Crowtree Leisure Centre 0191-565 0960

★★★★ Swallow
Queens Parade, Seaburn,
Sunderland SR6 8DB
☎ 0191-529 2041 **Fax** 0191-529 4227
E-mail info@swallowhotels.com

SWALLOW
HOTELS

In a prime seafront position overlooking Whitburn Sands, this hotel has excellent leisure facilities and awards for fine food. An ideal base for exploring Catherine Cookson country.
98 bedrs, all ensuite, ✝ ▣ ‖ 250 **P** 125 ⟐ **SB** £90 **DB** £110 **L** £10.95 **D** £21.95 ✕ **LD** 21:45 **CC** MC Visa Amex DC 🔟 🔟 🔟 ♿

★★★ Pullman Lodge
Ocean Park, Whitburn Road, Seaburn,
Sunderland SR6 8AA
☎ 0191-529 2020 **Fax** 0191-529 2077
16 bedrs, all ensuite, ✝ ‖ 180 **P** 94 ⟐ **CC** MC Visa Amex DC
See advert on this page

★★★ Quality
Witney Way, Boldon, NE35 9PE
☎ 0191-519 1999 **Fax** 0191-519 0655
E-mail admin@gb621.u-net.com

Quality Hotel

Ideally located for Newcastle or Sunderland, and at the gateway to one of the finest touring areas in Britain at the junction of the A19 and A184. Full leisure centre, free parking.
82 bedrs, all ensuite, ✝ ‖ 230 **P** 150 ⟐ **SB** £91 **DB** £124 **L** £6.50 **D** £14.50 ✕ **LD** 21:45 **CC** MC Visa Amex DC JCB 🔟 🔟 🔟 ♿

SUTTON Surrey · 5D3
Pop. 167,000. Mitcham 3½, London 11, Croydon 4, Epsom 4½, Kingston upon Thames 6½, Purley 5, Reigate 9½ **EC** Wed

ENGLAND

★★ Thatched House ⬚
135 Cheam Road, Sutton SM1 2BN
📞 0181-642 3131 **Fax** 0181-770 0684
32 bedrs, 28 ensuite, 1 ⬚ ⬚ ➤ ⬚ 50 **P** 20 ⬚ Rest
Resid ⬚ MC Visa DC JCB

SUTTON COLDFIELD Warwickshire   **7F2**

Pop. 103,000. Coventry 19, London 113, M6 (jn 6)
4, Birmingham 7, Lichfield 8½, Newport 31

★★★★ New Hall ⬚ ⬚ ⬚
Gold Ribbon Hotel
Walmley Road, Sutton Coldfield B76 1QX
📞 0121-378 2442 **Fax** 0121-378 4637

This Thistle country house hotel is the oldest
inhabited moated manor house in England. Set in a
country park, New Hall is ideal as a touring base
for visiting Warwick Castle, the Cotswolds and all
that Birmingham has to offer.
60 bedrs, all ensuite, ⬚ 50 **P** 80 ⬚ ⬚ MC Visa
Amex DC JCB ⬚ ⬚ ⬚ ⬚

★★★ Moor Hall ⬚
Moor Hall Drive, Sutton Coldfield B75 6LN
📞 0121-308 3751 **Fax** 0121-308 8974
E-mail mail@moorhallhotel.co.uk

Delightful country house hotel set in parkland yet
within easy reach of Birmingham city centre.
Executive rooms overlooking the sunken garden.
RAC commended restaurant. Traditional personal
service a speciality.

75 bedrs, all ensuite, ⬚ ♀ ⬚ ➤ ⬚ ⬚ 200 **P** 164 ⬚
SB £99-£109 **DB** £112-£122 **L** £10.95 **L** ⬚ **D** £19.50 ✕
LD 22:30 ⬚ MC Visa Amex DC ⬚ ⬚ ⬚ ⬚

SUTTON IN THE ELMS Leicestershire   **8B3**

M1 (jn 20) 6, London 95, Coventry 15, Leicester 9

★★ Mill On The Soar
B4114 Coventry Road, Sutton in the Elms LE9 6QD
📞 01455-282419 **Fax** 01455-285937

Nicely converted old mill building which retains
many original features, including a working wheel,
in the heart of the Leicestershire countryside.
20 bedrs, all ensuite, ⬚ 180 **P** 200 ⬚ ⬚ MC Visa ⬚
See advert on this page

The Pines Hotel

Burlington Rd
Swanage
Dorset
BH19 1LT

★ ★ ★

Tel: 01929 425211
Fax: 01929 422075

This 50 bedroomed family run Hotel occupies the most envied position in Swanage, situated at the secluded end of the bay.
Every bedroom is equipped with en-suite bathroom, colour TV, radio, telephone and tea making facilities.
Ease of access is assured by a lift to all floors.
Children of all ages are welcome and specially catered for.
Our reputation is founded on cuisine and service.

SUTTON-ON-SEA Lincolnshire 9D1
Skegness 15, London 154, Boston 32, Grimsby 30, Horncastle 22, Louth 16

★★★ Grange & Links ⚑
Sea Lane, Sandilands, LN12 2RA
☎ 01507-441334 **Fax** 01507-443033
24 bedrs, all ensuite, 🄳 ⵑ ⵯ 300 **P** 60 ⊞ **SB** £59.50
DB £71.50 **HB** £300 **L** £8 **D** £20 ✕ **LD** 20:30 **CC** MC Visa Amex DC ⊞ ⊡ ▨ ⊞

SWAFFHAM Norfolk 9E3
Pop. 5,600. Newmarket 33, London 96, East Dereham 12, Ely 26, Fakenham 16, King's Lynn 15, Thetford 18, Wisbech 26

★★ Lydney House
Norwich Road, Swaffham PE37 7QS
☎ 01760-723355 **Fax** 01760-721410
12 bedrs, all ensuite, 🄳 ⵯ 120 **P** 80 ⊞ **CC** MC Visa Amex

---

SWANAGE Dorset 4A4
Pop. 9,650. Wareham 9½, London 126 (fy 115)
ℹ White House, Shore Road 01929-422885

★★★ Pines ⚑
Burlington Road, Swanage BH19 1LT
☎ 01929-425211 **Fax** 01929-422075

Family-run, large modern hotel in secluded position. Fine sea views. Children of all ages are welcome and specially catered for.
48 bedrs, all ensuite, ⵁ ⵑ ▣ ⵯ 60 **P** 60 ⊞
SB £42.50-£53 **DB** £85-£106 **HB** £378-£427.50
L £12.50 **L** ⵯ **D** £19 **D** ⵯ ✕ **LD** 20:30 **CC** MC Visa ⵒ
See advert on this page

★★ Havenhurst
3 Cranborne Road, Swanage BH19 1EA
☎ 01929-424224 **Fax** 01929-424224

The Havenhurst is a comfortable hotel of charm and character situated just a short stroll from the shops and sandy beach. Excellent home cooked cuisine, all 17 rooms ensuite, fully licensed bar lounge, attractive patio and garden and free car parking.
17 bedrs, all ensuite, ⵯ 40 **P** 20 ⊞ **SB** £18-£29
DB £36-£58 **HB** £195-£260 **L** £6 **D** £14 ✕ **LD** 20:00
CC MC Visa

SWINDON Wiltshire 4A2
Pop. 173,000. Wantage 17, London 77, M4 (jn 15) 4½, Burford 19, Cirencester 15, Devizes 15, Faringdon 12, Malborough 11, Oxford 29, Tetbury 19 **MD** Mon, Wed, Sat **see** Railway Works, Railway Museum ℹ 37 Regent Street 01793-530328

★★★★ Blunsdon House

Blunsdon, Swindon SN2 4AD

☎ 01793-721701 **Fax** 01793-721056
E-mail pdodds@bhhotel.demon.co.uk

Set in 30 acres of beautiful Wiltshire countryside with splendid views, in a location that provides an ideal base for touring the nearby Cotswolds. A hotel that offers 3 bars and 2 restaurants. Extensive leisure facilities and a 9 hole par 3 golf course.
135 bedrs, all ensuite, 🖳 ♀ ⌀ 🖬 ⁑ 300 **P** 300 ⊕
SB £94-£124 **DB** £122-£225 **L** £10.75 **L** 🍽 **D** £15 ✕
LD 22:00 **CC** MC Visa Amex DC JCB 🖪 🖾 🖾 🖭 🖾 🖾
♿

★★★ Chiseldon House

New Road, Chiseldon, Swindon SN4 0NE
☎ 01793-741010 **Fax** 01793-741059
21 bedrs, all ensuite, 🖳 🐂 ⁑ 65 **P** 50 ⊕ **CC** MC Visa Amex DC ⌁

★★★ Marsh Farm ⌂

Coped Hall, Wootton Bassett SN4 8ER

☎ 01793-848044 **Fax** 01793-851528

A Victorian farmhouse with modern additions, set in delightful grounds in the countryside two miles from Swindon and close to junction 16 of the M4.
38 bedrs, all ensuite, ♀ ⌀ ⁑ 150 **P** 150 ⊕ **SB** £25-£85 **DB** £50-£99 **L** £12 **L** 🍽 **D** £21 ✕ **LD** 21:00 **CC** MC Visa Amex DC ♿
See advert on this page

★★★ Pear Tree at Purton ⌂ ⌂ ⌂

Blue Ribbon Hotel
Church End, Purton, Swindon SN5 9ED

☎ 01793-772100 **Fax** 01793-772369
E-mail peartreepurton@msn.com
Closed 26-30 Dec

Cotswold-stone former vicarage, three miles west of Swindon, tastefully extended and set in more than seven acres of attractive lawned gardens.
18 bedrs, all ensuite, 🖳 ♀ ⌀ 🐂 ⁑ 60 **P** 70 ⊕ Rest Resid **SB** £90-£95 **DB** £90-£95 **HB** £650-£765 **L** £18 **D** £30 **D** 🍽 ✕ **LD** 21:15 Restaurant closed L Sat **CC** MC Visa Amex DC JCB ♿

Stanton House Hotel

A Cotswold stone country house hotel set in the tranquil surroundings of beautiful Wiltshire countryside, yet also on the edge of the Cotswolds. This typically English hotel has the unusual factor of having a Japanese restaurant and a Japanese food shop.

The ideal venue for a business meeting, conference or simply just to get away from it all for a weekend break with a difference.

THE AVENUE, STANTON FITZWARREN, SWINDON, WILTSHIRE SN6 7SD
Tel: (01793) 861777 Fax: (01793) 861857

Villiers Inn

★★★

Villiers Inn is a warm-hearted, full-service hotel with personality!

A farmhouse in the 1800's – now converted to include 33 first class en-suite bedrooms.

Offering a choice of restaurants – The informal and popular "Pig on the Wall" or the "Conservatory" for a slightly more formal ambience.

A purpose built conference centre for up to 90 guests.

MOORMEAD ROAD, WROUGHTON, SWINDON SN4 9BY
Tel: 01793-814744 Fax: 01793-814119

★★★ ✦ Posthouse   **Posthouse**
Marlborough Road, Coate,
Swindon SN3 6AQ
📞 01793-524601 **Fax** 01793-512887
98 bedrs, all ensuite, ✝ ⅲ 80 **P** 200 ⊞ **SB** £99-£109
DB £110-£130 **L** £7.95 **L** ● **D** £10 **D** ● ✕ **LD** 22:30
㏄ MC Visa Amex DC ▣ ▣ ▣ ▣

★★★ Stanton House ⌇
The Avenue, Stanton Fitzwarren, Swindon SN6 7SD
📞 01793-861777 **Fax** 01793-861857
86 bedrs, all ensuite, ▣ ⅲ 110 **P** 110 ⊞ **SB** £65
DB £75-£115 **L** £15 ✕ **LD** 22:00 ㏄ MC Visa Amex DC
JCB ▣ ♿
See advert on this page

★★★ Villiers Inn
Moormead Road, Wroughton,
Swindon SN4 9BY
📞 01793-814744 **Fax** 01793-814119
E-mail villiers.inn@villiers-hotels.demon.co.uk

Villiers Inn aims to provide exceptional value for money whilst avoiding the dreary monotony that is so typical of the economy genre.
33 bedrs, all ensuite, ▣ ♀ ♪ ✝ ⅲ 120 **P** 60 ⊞
SB £49-£69 **DB** £69-£89 **L** ● **D** £10 **D** ● ✕ **LD** 21:30
㏄ MC Visa Amex DC ♿
See advert on this page

SYMONDS YAT Herefordshire	7E4

Pop. 500. Gloucester 20, London 125, Chepstow 17, Hereford 17, Monmouth 7, Ross-on-Wye 6½

★★ ✦ Old Court
Symonds Yat West HR9 6DA
📞 01600-890367 **Fax** 01600-890964
E-mail oldcourt@aol.com
18 bedrs, 15 ensuite, ▣ ♪ ✝ ⅲ 60 **P** 50 No children under 12 ⊞ **SB** £49 **DB** £78 **L** ● **D** £21 **D** ●
✕ **LD** 21:30 ㏄ MC Visa Amex DC ⌇

TAPLOW Buckinghamshire   4C2

Pop. 2,200. M4 (jn 7) 3, London 24, Bagshot 17, Henley-on-Thames 10, High Wycombe 9, Reading 14, Slough 4½ **EC** Wed

★★★★★ Cliveden ♖ ♖ ♖ ♖

Gold Ribbon Hotel

Taplow SL6 0JF

☎ 01628-668561 **Fax** 01628-661837

Historic house, successively the home of a Prince of Wales, three dukes and the Astor family, now the ultimate in luxurious hotels. Set in 376 acres of superb National Trust garden and parkland beside the River Thames.

39 bedrs, all ensuite, ▨ ♬ ⊁ ☐ ⁑ 42 ⊞ **DB** £290-£410 **L** £26 **L** ⬤ **D** £39 **D** ⬤ ✕ **LD** 21:30 **CC** MC Visa Amex DC ▣ ⋠ ⊞ ⊞ ⊡ ⊞ ⊞ ⊞ ⊞ ⅋

TARPORLEY Cheshire   7E1

Pop. 2,000. Nantwich 10, London 172, Chester 11, Middlewich 13, Northwich 11, Warrington 19, Whitchurch 14 **EC** Wed **see** Medieval Church, Castle ruins

★★★ ✤ Willington Hall

Willington, Tarporley CW6 0NB

☎ 01829-752321 **Fax** 01829-752596

Closed 25 Dec

10 bedrs, all ensuite, ⊁ ⁑ 12 **P** 60 ⊞ **SB** £49-£61 **DB** £83-£87 **L** £14 **D** £18.50 **D** ⬤ ✕ **LD** 21:30 Restaurant closed D Sun **CC** MC Visa Amex DC ▣

TAUNTON Somerset   3E2

Pop. 55,300. London 143, M5 (jn 25) 1½, Bridgwater 10, Dunster 22, Exeter 33, Glastonbury 22, Honiton 18, Ilminster 12 **see** Castle, St Mary Magdalene Church, St James's Church, Priory Gatehouse, West Somerset Rly **ℹ** Paul Street 01823-336344

★★★ Castle ♖ ♖ ♖ ♖

Gold Ribbon Hotel

Castle Green, Taunton TA1 1NF

☎ 01823-272671 **Fax** 01823-336066

E-mail reception@the-castle-hotel.com

The Castle is one of England's most historic hotels. Renowned for fine food and the warmth of its hospitality, it is the ideal centre for discovering the West Country.

44 bedrs, all ensuite, ▨ ♬ ⊁ ☐ ⁑ 100 **P** 40 ⊞ **SB** £88 **DB** £132 **L** £15 **L** ⬤ **D** £25 **D** ⬤ ✕ **LD** 21:00 **CC** MC Visa Amex DC ⅋

★★★ Posthouse   **Posthouse**

Deane Gate Avenue, Taunton TA1 2UA

☎ 01823-332222 **Fax** 01823-332266

99 bedrs, all ensuite, ♀ ♬ ⊁ ☐ ⁑ 300 **P** 300 ⊞ **SB** £99.95 **DB** £108.90 **L** £8 **D** £10 ✕ **LD** 22:30 **CC** MC Visa Amex DC ⅋

★★ Falcon

Taunton TA3 5DM

☎ 01823-442502 **Fax** 01823-442670

Comfortable country house hotel standing in own grounds, only one mile from M25 (jn 25) and two miles from town centre. Spacious conference facilities and a la carte restaurant.

11 bedrs, all ensuite, ▨ ⊁ ⁑ 50 **P** 30 ⊞ Rest Resid **SB** £45-£55 **DB** £55-£65 **L** £7 **D** £16.50 ✕ **LD** 20:30 **CC** MC Visa Amex DC

Roadchef Lodge Lodge
Taunton Deane Motorway Service Area, M5
Southbound, Trull TA3 7PF
☎ 01823-332228 Fax 01823-338131
Closed 24 Dec-2 Jan
39 bedrs, all ensuite, ⚌ 12 P 150 Room £47.95 CC MC
Visa Amex DC ♿

TELFORD Shropshire   7E2
Pop. 119,000. Wolverhampton 17, London 167,
M54 (jn 6) 1, Wellington 3, Bridgnorth 12,
Shrewsbury 14 see Ironbridge Gorge 🆚 Telford
Shopping Centre 01952-291370

⊕ ★★★ Clarion Madeley Court ⍼ ⍼

Telford TF7 5DW
☎ 01952-680068 Fax 01952-684275
E-mail admin@gb068.u-net.com
47 bedrs, all ensuite, ⚌ ♀ ⌀ ✈ ⚌ 175 P 120 ⊞
Rest Resid SB £98 DB £110 L ⬤ D £6.95 D ⬤ ✕
LD 21:45 CC MC Visa Amex DC

★★ Hundred House Hotel, Restaurant & Inn
Bridgenorth Road (A442), Norton, Telford TF11 9EE
☎ 01952-730353 Fax 01952-730355
E-mail hphundredhouse@compuserve.com

A stylishly refurbished 18th century inn set in lovely
gardens with Tudor out-buildings forming a rear
courtyard. On the main A442, five miles south east
of Telford.
10 bedrs, all ensuite, ✈ ⚌ 20 P 30 ⊞ SB £69-£85
DB £95-£110 HB £390 L £10 L ⬤ D £20 D ⬤ ✕
LD 22:00 CC MC Visa Amex

★★ White House ⍼
Wellington Road, Muxton, Telford TF2 8NG
☎ 01952-604276 Fax 01952-670336
30 bedrs, all ensuite, ✈ P 100 ⊞ CC MC Visa Amex
JCB ♿

TENTERDEN Kent   5E3
Pop. 6,900. Maidstone 18, London 54, Ashford 12,
Folkestone 23, Hastings 20, Hawkhurst 10, Rye 10,
Tonbridge 24 EC Wed MD Fri 🆚 Town Hall, High
Street 01580-763572

★★ Little Silver ⍼ ⍼
St Michaels, Tenterden TN30 6SP
☎ 01233-850321 Fax 01233-850647

Personally owned, landscaped gardens. Intimate
restaurant, beamed sitting room with log fire,
Victorian style conservatory overlooking waterfall
rockery. Luxury bedrooms, fourposters and jacuzzi
baths. Facilities for disabled.
10 bedrs, all ensuite, ⚌ ♀ ⌀ ⚌ 140 P 50 ⊞ ⊞
Resid SB £65-£85 DB £90-£115 HB £800-£940 L £15
D £25 ✕ LD 20:30 CC MC Visa Amex JCB ♿

TETBURY Gloucestershire   3F1
Pop. 4,700. Swindon 19, London 96, Bath 23,
Bristol 26, Cheltenham 24, Chippenham 14,
Cirencester 10, Gloucester 19 EC Thu see 'Chipping
Steps', Market Hall, St Mary's Church, Jacobean
and Georgian Houses in Long St, Police bygones
Museum, Westonbirt Arboretum 3½ m SW 🆚 Old
Court House, Long Street 01666-503552

★★★ Calcot Manor ⍼ ⍼ ⍼
Blue Ribbon Hotel

Tetbury GL8 8YJ
☎ 01666-890391 Fax 01666-890394
E-mail reception@calcotmanor.com

Charming Cotswold stone manor house originally dating back to the 15th century.
27 bedrs, all ensuite, ⑦ ⅲ 60 **P** 100 ⊞ **SB** £115 **DB** £125-£175 **L** £17 **L** ♥ **D** £22 **D** ♥ ✕ **LD** 21:30 ℂℂ MC Visa Amex DC ⅔ ⊠ ⅄

★★★ Snooty Fox ⓡ

Market Place, Tetbury GL8 8DD
☎ 01666-502436 **Fax** 01666-503479
E-mail res@snooty-fox.co.uk

A former 16th century coaching inn, the Snooty Fox is famed for its warmth of hospitality, celebrated for its cuisine and renowned for its attention to detail. Perfect base for exploring the Cotswolds. Website: www.hatton-hotels.co.uk
12 bedrs, all ensuite, ⅲ 15 ⊞ ℂℂ MC Visa Amex DC

TEWKESBURY Gloucestershire   7E4
Pop. 9,200. Stow-on-the-Wold 20, London 104, M5 (jn 9) 1½, Cheltenham 9, Evesham 13, Gloucester 10, Ledbury 14, Ross-on-Wye 24, Worcester 15 **EC** Thu **MD** Wed, Sat **see** Fine Norman Abbey ⓘ Museum, 64 Barton Street 01684-295027

★★★ ✤ Bell

54 Church Street, Tewkesbury GL20 5SA
☎ 01684-293293 **Fax** 01684-295938
25 bedrs, all ensuite, ⏰ ⅲ 50 **P** 40 ⊞ ℂℂ MC Visa Amex DC

THAME Oxfordshire   4B2
Pop. 10,800. High Wycombe 15, London 45, M40 (jn 7) 4, Aylesbury 9, Bicester 13, Oxford 13, Reading 23, Wallingford 17 **EC** Wed **MD** Tue ⓘ Market House, North Street, 01844-212834

★★★ Spread Eagle ⓡ ⓡ

16 Cornmarket, Thame OX9 2BR
☎ 01844-213661 **Fax** 01844-261380
Closed 28-30 Dec

ENGLAND

Caringly modernised coaching inn, set in the country market town of Thame. Extensive conference/banqueting facilities, civil licence for marriages. Large car park.
33 bedrs, all ensuite, ⑦ ♪ ⅲ 250 **P** 80 ⊞ **SB** £89.95-£104.95 **DB** £124.85-£142.85 **HB** £370-£450 **L** £18 **D** £22 ✕ **LD** 22:00 ℂℂ MC Visa Amex DC JCB

THETFORD Norfolk   9E3
Pop. 20,000. Newmarket 18, London 81, Bury St Edmunds 12, King's Lynn 27, Norwich 28, Scole 18, Stowmarket 21, Swaffham 18 **EC** Wed **MD** Tue, Sat

★★ Comfort Inn

Thetford Road, Northwold, IP26 5LQ
☎ 01366-728888 **Fax** 01366-727121
E-mail admin@gb632.u-net.com

A peaceful and spacious modern hotel set in landscaped grounds, which include a picturesque waterfall and pond, close to beautiful Elveden Forest.
34 bedrs, all ensuite, ⏰ ⅲ 150 **P** 250 ⊞ **SB** £53-£61 **DB** £60-£68 **D** £10.75 ✕ **LD** 21:45 ℂℂ MC Visa Amex DC ⊠ ⅄

THIRSK North Yorkshire 11D2
Pop. 7,400. Boroughbridge 12, London 220,
Helmsley 14, Leyburn 24, Malton 25, Northallerton
8½, Stockton 22, York 23 **EC** Wed **MD** Mon, Thur, Sat
🛈 14 Kirkgate 01845-522755

★★ Angel Inn

Long Street, Topcliffe, Thirsk YO7 3RW
📞 01845-577237 **Fax** 01845-578000
15 bedrs, all ensuite, ⚑ 150 **P** 150 ⊞ **SB** £42.50-£45
DB £59-£63 **L** £12 **D** £15 ✕ **LD** 21:30 **CC** MC Visa ▣

★★ Sheppard's ⊟
Church Farm, Front Street, Sowerby,
Thirsk YO7 1JF
📞 01845-523655 **Fax** 01845-524720
Closed 1st week Jan
8 bedrs, all ensuite, ▣ ⚑ 50 **P** 30 No children under
10 ⊞ **SB** £62 **DB** £84 **L** £18.50 **L** 🍽 **D** £18.50 ✕
LD 21:30 **CC** MC Visa

THORNBURY Gloucestershire 3E1
Pop. 14,800. Chippenham 25, London 117, Bath
23, Bristol 12, Chepstow 10, Gloucester 23, Tetbury
20 **EC** Thu **MD** Thu, Sat **see** Castle (begun 1511, never
completed), Church

★★★ Thornbury Castle ⊟ ⊟ ⊟
Gold Ribbon Hotel

Thornbury BS35 1HH
📞 01454-281182 **Fax** 01454-416188
E-mail thornburycastle@compuserve.com
Closed 3 days in Jan

A genuine Tudor castle (once owned by Henry VIII),
set in 15 acres of regal splendour including a Tudor
garden. Fourposters, tapestries, mullioned
windows, oak panelling, huge fireplaces - it's all
here!
19 bedrs, all ensuite, ▣ ⚑ 28 **P** 50 ⊞ **SB** £85-£105
DB £125-£155 **L** £16.50 **D** £39.50 ✕ **LD** 21:30 **CC** MC
Visa Amex DC

THORNTHWAITE Cumbria 10A2
Pop. 150. Keswick 3½, London 289, Carlisle 27,
Cockermouth 8

★★ Ladstock Country House
Thornthwaite CA12 5RZ
📞 01768-778210 **Fax** 01768-778088

Ladstock is a fine, grand, rambling house, set in
beautiful landscaped gardens overlooking Skiddaw
3200ft and related Fells, also Bassenthwaite Lake.
A perfect centre for walking, or enjoying all outdoor
activities on a short or long break.
22 bedrs, 18 ensuite, ⚑ 200 **P** 100 ⊞ **SB** £50
DB £70-£85 **L** 🍽 **D** £16 **D** 🍽 ✕ **LD** 20:30 **CC** MC Visa
JCB

ENGLAND

THORNTON HOUGH Merseyside   7D1

Pop. 800. M53 (jn 4) 2, Chester 16, London 199, Birkenhead 8, Ellesmere Port 8 **EC** Thu

★★★ ✣ Thornton Hall

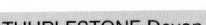

Neston Road, Thornton Hough CH63 1JF
☎ 0151-336 3938 **Fax** 0151-336 7864
E-mail thorntonhallhotel@btinternet.com
63 bedrs, all ensuite, **ℝ ⅲ** 250 **P** 160 ⊞ **SB** £85
DB £104 **L** £11.50 **D** £22 ✕ **LD** 21:00 Restaurant
closed L Sat **CC** MC Visa Amex DC JCB 🔲 🔲 🔲 ♿

THURLESTONE Devon   2C4

Pop. 930. Kingsbridge 3½, London 207, Plymouth 20 **see** Perp Church

★★★★ Thurlestone

Thurlestone TQ7 3NN
☎ 01548-560382 **Fax** 01548-561069
E-mail enquiries@thurlestone.co.uk
65 bedrs, all ensuite, **ℝ 🔲 ⅲ** 100 **P** 120 ⊞ **CC** MC
Visa Amex 🔲 🔲 🔲 🔲 🔲 🔲 🔲 🔲 🔲 ♿

TINTAGEL Cornwall   2B3

Pop. 1,800. Launceston 19, London 230, Bude 17, Camelford 5 **EC** Wed **MD** Thu **see** 'King Arthur's Castle', 'King Arthur's Hall', Saxon Church

★★ Bossiney House

Bossiney, Tintagel PL34 0AX
☎ 01840-770240 **Fax** 01840-770501
E-mail bossineyhh@eclipse.co.uk
Closed Dec-Jan
20 bedrs, 18 ensuite, **ℝ P** 30 ⊞ Rest Resid **SB** £22-
£33 **DB** £44-£66 **HB** £252-£296 **D** £14 ✕ **LD** 21:00
CC MC Visa Amex DC JCB 🔲 🔲

★★ ✣ Port William Inn

Trebarwith Strand, Tintagel PL34 0HB
☎ 01840-770230 **Fax** 01840-770936
E-mail william@eurobell.co.uk

Probably the best location in Cornwall, romantically situated 50 yards from the sea, beach and cliffs at Trebarwith Strand.
6 bedrs, all ensuite, **ℝ P** 50 ⊞ **SB** £40-£51.50
DB £50-£73 **D** 🔲 ✕ **LD** 21:30 **CC** MC Visa Amex
See advert on opposite page

TIVETSHALL ST MARY Norfolk   9E3

Diss 7, London 104, Bungay 12, Bury St Edmunds 26, Ipswich 27, Norwich 15, Thetford 20

★★ Old Ram Coaching Inn

Ipswich Road, Tivetshall St Mary NR15 2DE
☎ 01379-676794 **Fax** 01379-608399
E-mail theoldram@btinternet.com
Closed 25-26 Dec

A 17th century, Grade II Listed coaching inn, well known for its quality food and superb accommodation. Log fires in winter, al fresco dining in summer.
11 bedrs, all ensuite, 🔲 **ⅲ** 20 **P** 120 ⊞ **SB** £49
DB £68 **HB** £370 **L** £8 **D** £8 ✕ **LD** 22:00 **CC** MC Visa

---

TONBRIDGE Kent   5D3

Pop. 30,400. Sevenoaks 7, London 32, Maidstone 13, Rochester 19, Tenterden 24, Tunbridge Wells 4, Westerham 14 **EC** Wed **MD** Sat **see** 16th cent Chequers Inn, Port Reeve's House, remains of 12th cent castle 🅸 Castle, Castle Street 01732-770929

★★★ Langley

18-20 London Road, Tonbridge TN10 3DA
☎ 01732-353311 **Fax** 01732-771471
34 bedrs, all ensuite, **ℝ 🔲 ⅲ** 25 **P** 47 ⊞ **CC** MC Visa
Amex DC JCB

TORMARTON Gloucestershire   3F1

M4 (jn 18) 1½, London 102, Bath 11, Bristol 15, Chippenham 11, Stroud 20

The Compass Inn

The Compass Inn is a traditional country inn with 25 recently built en-suite rooms. There are 2 restaurants, one of which is open all day as are the bars. Adjacent to junction 18 on the M4, the Compass is close to both Bristol and bath and is on the edge of the Cotswolds.

Tormarton, Nr. Badminton, South Gloucestershire GL9 1JB
Telephone:
Badminton (01454) 218242/218577
Fax: (01454) 218741

★★ ✤ Compass Inn
Badminton, Tormarton GL9 1JB
☎ 01454-218242 **Fax** 01454-218741
E-mail info@compass-inn.co.uk
Closed 25-26 Dec
26 bedrs, all ensuite, ♪ ➤ ⋕ 60 **P** 160 ⊞ **SB** £69-£85.50 **DB** £79.95-£99.95 **L** ⬤ **D** £15 **D** ⬤ ✕ **LD** 21:15 ⊄ MC Visa Amex DC JCB ♿
See advert on this page

TORPOINT Cornwall   2C4
Pop. 9,500. Saltash 13½, London 243 (fy 215), Liskeard 15, Looe 15½, Plymouth (fy) 4 **EC** Wed **see** Anthony House (NT)

★★ Whitsand Bay
Portwinkle, Crafthole, Torpoint PL11 3BU
☎ 01503-230276 **Fax** 01503-230329
36 bedrs, all ensuite, ➤ ⋕ 150 **P** 50 ⊞ **SB** £23-£45 **DB** £46-£72 **HB** £220-£333 **D** £18.50 ✕ **LD** 20:30 ⊄ MC Visa ▣ ▣ ▣ ▣

TORQUAY Devon   3D3
Pop. 120,000. Newton Abbot 6, London 189, Dartmouth (fy) 10, Totnes 8 **EC** Wed, Sat ▮ Vaughan Parade 01803-297428

★★★★★ ✤ Imperial
Parkhill Road, Torquay TQ1 2DG
☎ 01803-294301 **Fax** 01803-298293

PARAMOUNT
HOTEL·GROUP

The Imperial has recently benefitted from a major refurbishment and is now fully restored to its 1920s glory. With its unique cliff top location there are magnificent views over Torbay.
154 bedrs, all ensuite, ♪ ➤ ☎ ⋕ 250 **P** 120 ⊞ **SB** £70-£95 **DB** £140-£190 **HB** £65-£90 **L** £10 **D** £21 **D** ⬤ ✕ **LD** 21:30 ⊄ MC Visa Amex DC JCB ▣ ▣ ▣ ▣ ▣ ▣ ▣

★★★★ Grand
Seafront, Torquay TQ2 6NT
☎ 01803-296677 **Fax** 01803-213462
E-mail grandhotel@netsite.co.uk

Set in its own grounds with panoramic views over Torbay. Award winning cuisine, sumptuous surroundings, indoor and outdoor swimming pools, and friendly, attentive staff.
110 bedrs, all ensuite, ♀ ♪ ➤ ☎ ⋕ 300 **P** 70 ⊞ **SB** £67-£82 **DB** £110-£155 **HB** £330-£465 **L** £15.50 **L** ⬤ **D** £24 ✕ **LD** 21:30 ⊄ MC Visa Amex DC JCB ▣ ▣ ▣ ▣ ▣ ▣

★★★★ Palace
Babbacombe Road, Torquay TQ1 3TG
☎ 01803-200200 **Fax** 01803-299899
E-mail mail9@palacetorquay.co.uk
141 bedrs, all ensuite, ☎ ⋕ 1,100 **P** 150 ⊞ **SB** £70 **DB** £140 **HB** £795 **L** £15 **D** £23 ✕ **LD** 21:15 ⊄ MC Visa Amex DC ▣ ▣ ▣ ▣ ▣ ▣ ▣
See advert on opposite page

★★★ Belgrave
Sea Front, Torquay TQ2 5HE
☎ 01803-296666 Fax 01803-211308
70 bedrs, all ensuite, ✦ ▣ ☷ 150 P 80 ⊕ SB £38.50-
£52 DB £77-£104 HB £277-£371 D £12.95 ✕ LD 20:30
《 MC Visa Amex DC ⊰

★★★ Corbyn Head ☵
Sea Front, Torbay Road, Torquay TQ2 6RH
☎ 01803-213611 Fax 01803-296152
51 bedrs, all ensuite, ☷ 60 P 50 ⊕ 《 MC Visa
Amex DC ⊰ ⅋
See advert on this page

⌘ ★★★ ✢ Homer's
Warren Road, Torquay TQ2 5TN
☎ 01803-213456 Fax 01803-213458

★★★ Livermead Cliff
Sea Front, Torquay TQ2 6RQ
☎ 01803-299666 Fax 01803-294496
E-mail livermeadcliffhotel@btinternet.com
64 bedrs, all ensuite, ⌀ ✦ ▣ ☷ 80 P 72 ⊕ SB £38-
£56 DB £70-£110 HB £280 L £9.95 L ● D £17.95 D ●
✕ LD 20:30 《 MC Visa Amex DC JCB ⊰ ▣ ⅋

★★★ Livermead House
Sea Front, Torquay TQ2 6QJ
☎ 01803-294361 **Fax** 01803-200758
E-mail rewhotels@aol.com
68 bedrs, all ensuite, ↟ ⊞ ⚏ 300 **P** 120 ⊕ ((MC
Visa Amex DC ⸙ ⊠ ▦ ⊠ ▦ &
See advert on previous page

★★★ Osborne ☃ ☃
Hesketh Crescent, Meadfoot, Torquay TQ1 2LL
☎ 01803-213311 **Fax** 01803-296788
29 bedrs, all ensuite, ⊞ ⚏ 80 **P** 81 ⊕ **SB** £45-£68
DB £90-£136 **HB** £406-£574 **L** ☞ **D** £17.95 **D** ☞ ✕
LD 21:30 ((MC Visa Amex ⊠ ⸙ ⊠ ▦ ⊠ ▦ &

★★★ ✤ Toorak
Chestnut Avenue, Torquay TQ2 5JS
☎ 01803-291444 **Fax** 01803-291666
92 bedrs, all ensuite, ↟ ⊞ ⚏ 200 **P** 75 ⊕ ((MC
Visa Amex ⊠ ⸙ ▦ ⊠ ▦

★★ Abbey Court
Falkland Road, Torquay TQ2 5JR
☎ 01803-297316 **Fax** 01803-297316
25 bedrs, 22 ensuite, **P** 16 ⊕ ((MC Visa ⸙

★★ Ansteys Lea
Babbacombe Road, Torquay TQ1 2QJ
☎ 01803-294843 **Fax** 01803-214333
Closed Jan-Feb

Elegant Victorian hotel set in own landscaped
gardens.
24 bedrs, all ensuite, ♀ ✿ ↟ ⚏ **P** 20 ⊕ Rest Resid
SB £23-£29 **DB** £46-£58 **HB** £172-£220 **L** ☞ **D** £10.25
D ☞ ✕ **LD** 19:30 ((MC Visa DC JCB ⸙ ⊠ ▦ ▦

★★ Apsley
Torwood Gardens Road, Torquay TQ1 1EG
☎ 01803-292058 **Fax** 01803-215105
33 bedrs, 32 ensuite, 1 ♖ ↟ ⚏ 50 **P** 20 ⊕ Rest
Resid **SB** £23-£30 **DB** £46-£60 **HB** £187-£230 **D** £7.50
✕ **LD** 20:00 ((MC Visa Amex

★★ Barn Hayes Country
Brim Hill, Maidencombe, Torquay TQ1 4TR
☎ 01803-327980 **Fax** 01803-327980
Closed Jan

Friendly and comfortable hotel with lovely gardens,
in an area of outstanding natural beauty
overlooking countryside and sea. Prestigious award
from the RAC for 1997.
10 bedrs, all ensuite, ↟ **P** 14 ⊕ Rest Resid **SB** £29-
£31 **DB** £58-£62 **HB** £259-£273 **L** ☞ **D** £15 ✕ **LD** 19:00
((MC Visa ⸙

★★ Burlington
462-466 Babbacombe Road, Torquay TQ1 1HN
☎ 01803-294374 **Fax** 01803-200189

ENGLAND

E-mail burlington.hotel@virgin.net
55 bedrs, all ensuite, ▨ ⊁ **P** 20 ⊕ Rest Resid
SB £30-£35 **DB** £50-£60 **HB** £175-£220 **L** £6.50 **L** ☞
D £10 **D** ☞ ✕ **LD** 20:00 ℂℂ MC Visa ▣ ▤ ▥

★★ Bute Court
Belgrave Road, Torquay TQ2 5HQ
☎ 01803-293771 **Fax** 01803-213429
45 bedrs, all ensuite, ⊁ ▣ ⁂ 35 **P** 37 ⊕ **SB** £19-£32
DB £38-£63 **HB** £145-£265 **L** ☞ **D** £9 ✕ **LD** 20:00
ℂℂ MC Visa Amex DC ⤳ ▥
See advert on opposite page

★★ Cavendish
Belgrave Road, Torquay TQ2 5HN
☎ 01803-293682 **Fax** 01803-292802
63 bedrs, all ensuite, ▣ ⁂ 50 **P** 40 ⊕ ℂℂ MC Visa
DC ▣ ⤳ ▥ ▤ ▥

★★ Coppice
Barrington Road, Torquay TQ1 2QJ
☎ 01803-297786 **Fax** 01803-211085
Closed Dec-Jan
39 bedrs, all ensuite, ⊁ **P** 32 ⊕ ▣ ⤳ ▥ ▤ ▥

★★ Gresham Court
Babbacombe Road, Torquay TQ1 1HG
☎ 01803-293007 **Fax** 01803-215951
E-mail gresham@swingler.globalnet.co.uk
Closed Dec-Mar

Centrally situated, a perfect venue for holiday/mini-
break. Family owned and managed, established 40
years with a well deserved reputation for quality and
service. Bay Award for 'Hygiene & Healthy Eating'.
30 bedrs, all ensuite, ⊁ ▣ **P** 14 ⊕ Resid **SB** £22-£29
DB £44-£58 **HB** £180-£220 **L** ☞ **D** £9 ✕ **LD** 20:00
ℂℂ MC Visa Amex JCB

★★ ❖ Howden Court
23 Croft Road, Torquay TQ2 5UD
☎ 01803-294844 **Fax** 01803-211350
Closed Nov-Mar
35 bedrs, all ensuite, ⊁ **P** 35 ⊕ Rest ℂℂ MC Visa ♿

★★ Meadfoot Bay
Meadfoot Sea Road, Torquay TQ1 2LQ
☎ 01803-294722 **Fax** 01803-214473
E-mail meadfoot@which.net
Closed Jan-Feb
22 bedrs, all ensuite, ⊁ ⁂ 42 **P** 20 No children
under 2 ⊕ Rest Resid **SB** £18-£33 **DB** £36-£66
HB £179-£220 **D** £11.95 ✕ **LD** 19:30 ℂℂ MC Visa

★★ Norcliffe
Babbacombe Downs Road, Torquay TQ1 3LF
☎ 01803-328456 **Fax** 01803-328023
27 bedrs, all ensuite, ▨ ♀ ⊁ ▣ ⁂ 80 **P** 20 ⊕
SB £16-£25 **DB** £32-£50 **HB** £190-£240 **L** ☞ **D** £11 ✕
LD 19:15 ℂℂ MC Visa ▣ ▥ ▤ ▥

★★ Roseland
Warren Road, Torquay TQ2 5TT
☎ 01803-213829 **Fax** 01803-291266
E-mail burlington.hotel@virgin.net
40 bedrs, all ensuite, ▨ ♀ ⊁ ▣ ⁂ 60 ⊕ Resid
SB £25-£30 **DB** £50-£60 **HB** £195-£240 **L** ☞ **D** £8 **D** ☞
✕ **LD** 20:15 ℂℂ MC Visa ▣ ▤ ▥

★★ Shedden Hall
Shedden Hill, Torquay TQ2 5TX
☎ 01803-292964 **Fax** 01803-295306
E-mail sheddenhtl@aol.com
Closed Jan
25 bedrs, all ensuite, ▨ **P** 30 No children under 4 ⊕
Rest Resid **SB** £26-£33.50 **DB** £52-£67 **HB** £207-£259
L ☞ **D** £11 ✕ **LD** 20:00 ℂℂ MC Visa Amex DC JCB ⤳

★★ Sydore
Meadfoot Road, Torquay TQ1 2JP
☎ 01803-294758 **Fax** 01803-294489
E-mail hotel,sydore@virgen.net

Elegant early Victorian villa, set in its own grounds
with award winning gardens, croquet lawn and sun
terrace. Close to harbour.
13 bedrs, all ensuite, ▨ ♀ ⊁ ⁂ 12 **P** 17 ⊕ Rest
Resid **DB** £36-£72 **HB** £169-£250 **L** ☞ **D** £10 **D** ☞ ✕
LD 20:30 ℂℂ MC Visa Amex JCB ▥

★ ✤ Fairmount House
Herbert Road, Chelston, Torquay TQ2 6RW
☎ 01803-605446 **Fax** 01803-605446
Closed Nov-Feb
8 bedrs, all ensuite, ↑ **P** 9 ⊞ Resid **cc** MC Visa
Amex ⅋

★ Sunleigh
Livermead Hill, Torquay TQ2 6QY
☎ 01803-607137
Closed Nov-Mar exc Christmas-New Year
20 bedrs, all ensuite, ↑ **P** 17 No children under 2 ⊞
Rest Resid **SB** £20-£27 **DB** £40-£54 **HB** £175-£224
D £10.95 ✕ **LD** 19:00 **cc** MC Visa Amex DC

TOTNES Devon	3D3

Pop. 6,200. Newton Abbot 8, London 191,
Ashburton 8, Dartmouth 13 (fy 11), Kingsbridge 12,
Plymouth 22, Torquay 8 **EC** Thu **MD** Tue, Fri **see**
Church (15th cent), Castle ruins, Butterwalk,
Guildhall (16th cent) and Museum, Totnes Museum,
East Gate **i** The Plains 01803-863168

★★ Old Church House Inn
Torbryan, Ipplepen, Totnes TQ12 5UR
☎ 01803-812372 **Fax** 01803-812180
11 bedrs, all ensuite, ⊞ 30 **P** 30 ⊞ **cc** MC Visa ⅋

★★ Royal Seven Stars
The Plains, Totnes TQ9 5DD
☎ 01803-862125 **Fax** 01803-867925

Charming 1660 former coaching inn. Well equipped
bedrooms with direct telephone, colour TV,
beverage tray, hair dryers. Restaurant service for
breakfast and evening dinner; bar meals available.
Easy drive to coastal resorts and Dartmoor National
Park.
16 bedrs, 14 ensuite, ⊞ ↑ ⊞ 60 **P** 20 ⊞ **SB** £46-£55
DB £58-£66 **HB** £245-£395 **L** £10.50 **L** ⬤ **D** £17 **D** ⬤ ✕
LD 21:15 Restaurant closed L Mon-Sat **cc** MC Visa
Amex DC

★ Sea Trout Inn ⬚ ⬚
Staverton, Totnes TQ9 6PA
☎ 01803-762274 **Fax** 01803-762506

Attractive beamed country inn situated in the
peaceful village of Staverton by the River Dart.
Pleasant cottage style rooms with good food and
service. Choice of restaurant, two bars and patio
gardens.
11 bedrs, all ensuite, ⊞ ♀ ⌇ ↑ ⊞ 16 **P** 50 ⊞
SB £36-£42.50 **DB** £28-£35 **HB** £275-£295 **L** £10 **L** ⬤
D £19 **D** ⬤ ✕ **LD** 21:45 **cc** MC Visa Amex ⊡ ⊞

TRING Hertfordshire	4C2

Pop. 12,000. Watford 16, London 32, Aylesbury 7,
Dunstable 10, High Wycombe 16, Rickmansworth
15, St Albans 15 **EC** Wed **MD** Mon, Fri

★★★★ Pendley Manor ⬚
Cow Lane, Tring HP23 5QY
☎ 01442-891891 **Fax** 01442-890687

Grade II Listed luxury country house hotel, 71
bedrooms, many with fourposter beds. Excellent
conference facilities, all meeting rooms have natural
light. Award winning restaurant, leisure facilities.
71 bedrs, all ensuite, ⊞ ↑ ⊡ ⊞ 220 **P** 200 ⊞ **cc** MC
Visa Amex DC ⊞ ⊞ ⊞ ⅋

TROWBRIDGE Wiltshire	3F1

Pop. 30,600. Devizes 7, London 93, Bath 11,
Chippenham 12, Frome 8, Warminster 9 **EC** Wed

MD Tue, Fri, Sat **see** Parish Church, Town Hall, 18th cent Lock-up (Blind House), The Courts, Holt 3m N
i St Stephen's Place 01225-777054

★★ Hilbury Court
Hilperton Road, Trowbridge BA14 7JW
i 01225-752949 **Fax** 01225-777990
Closed Xmas-New Year
10 bedrs, all ensuite, 4 ♀ **P** 25 ⊕ ⊕ Rest **SB** £45-£55 **DB** £58-£68 **D** ♥ ✕ **LD** 21:00 Restaurant closed Sun **CC** MC Visa JCB ▣

TRURO Cornwall   2B4
Pop. 16,000. St Austell 14, London 246, Bodmin 24, Falmouth 11, Helston 16, Newquay 18, Redruth 8 **EC** Wed **see** Cathedral, County Museum and Art Gallery, Trelissick Gdns 4m S **i** Municipal Buildings, Boscawen Street 01872-74555

★★★ Alverton Manor 🎔
Tregolls Road, Truro TR1 1ZQ
i 01872-276633 **Fax** 01872-222989
34 bedrs, all ensuite, ⚘ ▣ ⠿ 200 **P** 120 ⊕ **SB** £67 **DB** £99 **HB** £312 **L** £10 **D** £21.50 **D** ♥ ✕ **LD** 21:30
CC MC Visa Amex DC JCB ▣ ▣ �
See advert on this page

★★ Carlton
Falmouth Road, Truro TR1 2HL
i 01872-272450 **Fax** 01872-223938
Closed 24 Dec-5 Jan

An established, family run hotel with a friendly atmosphere. Large restaurant with varied choice of menus. Sauna, spa and solarium available.
28 bedrs, all ensuite, ⚘ ⠿ 80 **P** 31 ⊕ Rest Resid **SB** £33.95-£38.95 **DB** £46.95 **HB** £190-£256 **D** £9 **D** ♥ ✕ **LD** 20:00 **CC** MC Visa Amex DC ▣

🌠 ★★ ✦ Polsue Manor
Ruan High Lanes, Truro TR2 5LU
i 01872-501270 **Fax** 01872-501270
Closed 31 Oct-mid Mar
12 bedrs, 10 ensuite, ⚘ ⠿ 20 **P** 20 ⊕ Rest Resid **CC** MC Visa JCB

TUNBRIDGE WELLS Kent   5D3
Pop. 45,300. Tonbridge 4, London 36, Eastbourne 29, East Grinstead 13, Maidstone 16, Uckfield 16 **EC** Wed **MD** Wed **see** The Pantiles, 17th cent King Charles the Martyr Church, Holy Trinity Church **i** Old Fish Market, The Pantiles 01892-515675

Short Breaks

Many hotels provide special rates for weekend and mid-week breaks – sometimes these are quoted in the hotel's entry, otherwise ring direct for the latest offers.

ENGLAND

★★★★ Spa
Langton Road, Mount Ephraim,
Tunbridge Wells TN4 8XJ
☎ 01892-520331 **Fax** 01892-510575
E-mail info@spahotel.co.uk

Family owned, traditional hotel renowned for its hospitality. Set in beautiful gardens overlooking the town. The hotel has individually designed bedrooms, award winning restaurant and extensive leisure facilities.
70 bedrs, all ensuite, ▣ ♫ ⊟ ⠿ 300 P 150 ⊞
SB £88.50-£98.50 DB £113-£169 L £15 L ● D £19
D ● ✕ LD 21:30 Restaurant closed L Sat ⓒ MC Visa Amex DC ▣ ▣ ▣ ▣ ▣ ▣ ▣ ⓔ

★★★ ❖ Royal Wells Inn
Mount Ephraim,
Tunbridge Wells TN4 8BE
☎ 01892-511188 **Fax** 01892-511908
Closed Christmas
18 bedrs, all ensuite, ▣ ♣ ⊟ ⠿ 100 P 25 ⊞ SB £55-£85 DB £85-£110 L £10.50 L ● D £26.50 D ● ✕
LD 22:00 Restaurant closed L & D Sun-Mon ⓒ MC Visa Amex DC
See advert on this page

★★ Russell
80 London Road, Tunbridge Wells TN1 1DZ
☎ 01892-544833 **Fax** 01892-515846
E-mail rushotel@globalnet.co.uk
26 bedrs, all ensuite, ♣ ⠿ 40 P 20 ⊞ SB £48-£68
DB £58-£82 L £11.50 D £14.95 D ● ✕ LD 22:00
ⓒ MC Visa Amex DC JCB ⓔ

TUTBURY Staffordshire 7F2
Pop. 3,200. Burton-on-Trent 4, London 125, Ashbourne 15, Derby 11, Uttoxeter 10 **EC** Wed **see** 15th cent Castle, Norman Church, N. Staffs Traction Engines

ENGLAND

★★★ Ye Olde Dog & Partridge ⌐
High Street, Tutbury DE13 9LS
☎ 01283-813030 **Fax** 01283-813178
Closed 25 Dec

The hotel has 20 ensuite bedrooms - all individually designed and furnished to the highest standards. Short breaks available all year.
20 bedrs, all ensuite, 🅃 🏃 ✦ **P** 150 ⊕ **SB** £55-£75 **DB** £55-£99 **L** £5.75 **D** £5.75 ✕ **LD** 21:45 **CC** MC Visa Amex
See advert on opposite page

TWO BRIDGES Devon   2C3
Exeter 24, London 193, Ashburton 11, Tavistock 9

★★ Two Bridges ⌐ ⌐
Two Bridges, Nr Yelverton, Dartmoor PL20 6SW
☎ 01822-890581 **Fax** 01822-890575

Historic 18th century hotel with a beautiful riverside location at the heart of Dartmoor. Award winning restaurant, cosy bars and comfortable lounges. Warmest welcome guaranteed.
29 bedrs, all ensuite, 🅃 ✦ ⦂ 150 **P** 150 ⊕ **SB** £35-£45 **DB** £70 **HB** £350 **L** £11.95 **L** 🍵 **D** £19.50 **D** 🍵 ✕ **LD** 21:30 **CC** MC Visa Amex DC ▱

TYNEMOUTH Tyne & Wear   11D1
Pop. 50,000. Tyne Tunnel 2½, London 280, Alnwick 36, Coldstream 54, Newcastle 8, Sunderland 11
EC Wed

★★★ Grand
Grand Parade, Tynemouth NE30 4ER
☎ 0191-293 6666 **Fax** 0191-293 6665
E-mail info@grand-hotel.demon.co.uk
45 bedrs, all ensuite, 🅃 🏃 ⊡ ⦂ 100 **P** 24 ⊕ **SB** £45-£85 **DB** £50-£90 **L** £11.75 **L** 🍵 **D** £14.75 **D** 🍵 ✕ **LD** 22:00 **CC** MC Visa Amex DC

★★★ Park
Grand Parade, Tynemouth NE30 4JQ
☎ 0191-257 1406 **Fax** 0191-257 1716
E-mail parkhotel@aol.com
50 bedrs, all ensuite, 🅃 ✦ ⦂ 350 **P** 400 ⊕ **SB** £39-£49 **DB** £50-£69 **HB** £350-£420 **L** 🍵 **D** £6.95 **D** 🍵 ✕ **LD** 21:30 Restaurant closed D Sun **CC** MC Visa Amex DC ⊞ ▦ ♿

UCKFIELD East Sussex   5D3
Pop. 18,800. East Grinstead 13, London 43, Eastbourne 19, Haywards Heath 12, Lewes 8, Tunbridge Wells 16 **EC** Wed

★★★★ Buxted Park Country House ⌐
Buxted, Uckfield TN22 4AY
☎ 01825-732711 **Fax** 01825-732770
E-mail buxtedpark@cix.compulink.co.uk
44 bedrs, all ensuite, ♀ 🏃 ⦂ 150 **P** 150 ⊕ **SB** £95-£100 **DB** £130-£200 **L** £14.95 **L** 🍵 **D** £25 **D** 🍵 ✕ **LD** 22:00 Restaurant closed L Sat **CC** MC Visa Amex DC JCB ⅀ ⊞ ▦ ⊞

UMBERLEIGH Devon   2C2

★★ Rising Sun Inn ⌐ ⌐
Umberleigh EX37 9DU
☎ 01769-560447 **Fax** 01769-560764
E-mail risingsuninn@btinternet.com

Ideal for touring, 8 miles from busy Barnstaple, this quiet 13th century inn overlooks the Taw. Chas and Heather offer warm hospitality, comfortable accommodation, excellent food/wine.
9 bedrs, all ensuite, ⦂ 70 **P** 30 ⊕ **CC** MC Visa ▱

UPHOLLAND Lancashire 10B4
Pop. 7,800. M6 (jn 26) 1½, London 193, Ormskirk 7½, St Helens 7, Wigan 4½ **see** Church, Beacon Park

★★★ ❖ Holland Hall
Lafford Lane, Upholland WN8 0QZ
☎ 01695-624426 **Fax** 01695-622433

An attractive country hotel situated in the heart of Lancashire overlooking Dean Wood and adjoining golf course, yet only 3 minutes from the M6. A perfect location for tourists, businessmen or those wanting to get away from the pace of the cities.
32 bedrs, all ensuite, 4 ⚙ 150 **P** 150 ⊟ **SB** £45-£59 **DB** £60-£78 **L** ● **D** £10 **D** ● ✕ **LD** 22:30 Restaurant closed D Sun ⟨⟨ MC Visa Amex DC

Lords of the Manor

Situated in the village of Upper Slaughter, Lords of the Manor stands within eight acres of gardens and park land. Delicious food and fine wine are at the heart of this recently refurbished country house hotel. The Lord's is ideally located for exploring the nearby Cotswold villages.

**Upper Slaughter,
Bourton-On-The-Water,
Gloucs. GL54 2JD**
Tel: 01451 820243 Fax: 01451 820696
Email: lordsofthemanor@btinternet.com

UPPER SLAUGHTER Gloucestershire 7F4
Pop. 188. Stow-on-the-Wold 3, London 87, Burford 11, Cheltenham 15, Cirencester 17, Evesham 18 **see** Church, Bridge, Well nearby

★★★ Lords Of The Manor ░ ░ ░
Blue Ribbon Hotel
Upper Slaughter GL54 2JD
☎ 01451-820243 **Fax** 01451-820696
E-mail lordsofthemanor@btinternet.com

A 17th century former rectory set amidst eight acres of gardens. Comfortable surroundings and fine cuisine make it an ideal base to explore the Cotswolds.
27 bedrs, all ensuite, 4 ⚙ 20 **P** 40 No children under 12 ⊟ **SB** £98 **DB** £138-£295 **L** £16 **L** ● ✕ **LD** 21:30 ⟨⟨ MC Visa Amex DC JCB ▣
See advert on this page

UPPINGHAM Rutland 8C3
Pop. 4,000. Kettering 14, London 89, Leicester 18, Market Harborough 12, Melton Mowbray 15, Peterborough 21 **EC** Thu **MD** Fri **see** Uppingham School (apply to Porter), Church

★★ Lake Isle ░
High Street East, Uppingham LE15 9PZ
☎ 01572-822951 **Fax** 01572-822951
12 bedrs, all ensuite, ✝ ⚙ 10 **P** 6 ⊟ **SB** £45-£59 **DB** £65-£79 **L** £10.50 **D** £23.50 ✕ **LD** 21:30 Restaurant closed L Mon ⟨⟨ MC Visa Amex DC

Marquess of Exeter Awaiting Inspection
52 Main Street, Lyddington, Uppingham LE15 9LT
☎ 01572-822477 **Fax** 01572-821343
16 bedrs, all ensuite, ⚙ 30 **P** 30 ⊟ ⟨⟨ MC Visa Amex DC ♿

ENGLAND

UPTON-UPON-SEVERN Worcestershire 7E4
Pop. 1,600. Tewkesbury 6, London 111, M50 4,
Bromyard 17, Evesham 13, Ledbury 10, Worcester
10 **EC** Thu **see** Church, Bridge, old houses ⓘ 4 High
Street 01684-594200

★★★ ✤ White Lion
High Street, Upton-upon-Severn WR8 0HJ
☎ 01684-592551 **Fax** 01684-593333
Closed Christmas
10 bedrs, all ensuite, ♀ ⊁ ☷ 26 **P** 19 ⊕ **SB** £53
DB £77 **L** £12.50 **L** ● **D** £17.75 **D** ✕ **LD** 21:15
CC MC Visa Amex JCB

VERYAN Cornwall 2B4
Pop. 800. St Austell 12, London 245, Falmouth (fy)
16, Newquay 20, Truro 20 (fy 11) **see** 15th cent
Church, Carne Beacon (Ancient Burial Place)

★★★★ Nare ⓡ ⓡ
Carne Beach, Veryan, Truro TR2 5PF
☎ 01872-501279 **Fax** 01872-501856
E-mail hotel@veryan.avel.co.uk
Closed 3 Jan-1 Feb
38 bedrs, all ensuite, ④ ⊁ ☲ **P** 80 ⊕ **SB** £65-£141
DB £130-£272 **HB** £525-£1,834 **L** £13.50 ● **D** £31
D ● ✕ **LD** 21:30 **CC** MC Visa ▣ 🏊 ⊞ ▣ ▣ ▣ ⅙

WAKEFIELD West Yorkshire 11D4
Pop. 75,800. Barnsley 9½, London 182, M1 2½,
Bradford 14, Doncaster 19, Huddersfield 13, Leeds
9, Pontefract 9 **EC** Wed **MD** Mon, Tue, Thur, Fri, Sat
see Cathedral, Ancient Bridge with Chantry Chapel,
Museum, City Art Gallery, St Helen's Church
ⓘ Town Hall, Wood Street 01924-305000

★★★★ ✤ Cedar Court
Denby Dale Road, Wakefield WF4 3QZ
☎ 01924-276310 **Fax** 01924-280221

Yorkshires largest privately owned and operated
conference hotel, located at junction 39 of M1, 151
luxury bedrooms, 17 conference rooms, monitored
car parking for 350 cars.
151 bedrs, all ensuite, ⊁ ☲ ☷ 400 **P** 350 ⊕ **SB** £58-
£99 **DB** £67.50-£108.50 **L** £10.95 **D** £19 ✕ **LD** 22:00
Restaurant closed **L** Sat **CC** MC Visa Amex DC ⊞ ⅙

★★★ Hotel St Pierre ⓡ
Barnsley Road, Newmillerdam,
Wakefield WF2 6QG
☎ 01924-255596 **Fax** 01924-252746
54 bedrs, all ensuite, ④ ♬ ⊁ ☲ ☷ 120 **P** 65 ⊕
SB £47-£72.50 **DB** £54.50-£80 **L** £9.95 **L** ● **D** £14.95
D ● ✕ **LD** 22:00 Restaurant closed **L** Sat **CC** MC Visa
Amex DC ⊞ ⅙

★★★ Posthouse **Posthouse**
Queens Drive, Ossett,
Wakefield WF5 9BE
☎ 01924-276388 **Fax** 01924-276437
99 bedrs, all ensuite, ♬ ⊁ ☲ ☷ 150 **P** 160
⊕ **SB** £29-£99 **DB** £49-£99 **L** £7.95 **L** ●
D £9.95 **D** ● ✕ **LD** 22:30
CC MC Visa Amex DC JCB

Campanile Wakefield **Lodge**
Monkton Road, Wakefield WF2 7AL
☎ 01924-201054 **Fax** 01924-201055

Campanile hotels offer comfortable and convenient
budget accommodation and a traditional French style
Bistro providing freshly cooked food for breakfast,
lunch and dinner. All rooms ensuite with tea/coffee
making facilities, DDT and TV with Sky channels.
77 bedrs, all ensuite, ♬ ⊁ ☷ 20 **P** 77 ⊕ **Room** £29.95-
£37 **L** £5.75 **D** £10.85 ✕ **LD** 21:45 **CC** MC Visa Amex
DC ⅙

WALLASEY Merseyside 10B4
Pop. 62,500. Birkenhead 3, London 201 **MD** Daily
exc Wed

★★ Grove House 🛏 🛏
Grove Road, Wallasey L45 3HF
📞 0151-639 3947 **Fax** 0151-639 0028

Twin gabled Victorian building with modern
extentions, set in wooded gardens.
14 bedrs, all ensuite, 🔲 🛏 ⅲ 80 **P** 40 🍴 **SB** £51-£60
DB £57-£66 **L** £12.95 **L** 🍷 **D** £16.95 ✕ **LD** 21:30
Restaurant closed L Sat **CC** MC Visa Amex DC

WALLINGFORD Oxfordshire   4B2
See also NORTH STOKE
Pop. 6,500. Henley-on-Thames 11, London 46,
Aylesbury 25, Basingstoke 28, High Wycombe 21,
Newbury 18, Oxford 12, Reading 14, Wantage 14
EC Wed **MD** Fri 🔲 Town Hall, Market Place 01491-
826972

★★★ George
High Street, Wallingford OX10 0BS
📞 01491-836665 **Fax** 01491-825359
39 bedrs, all ensuite, 🛏 ⅲ 120 **P** 40 🍴 **SB** £95.50
DB £120 **L** £12.50 **L** 🍷 **D** £14.50 ✕ **LD** 22:00 **CC** MC
Visa Amex DC

WALSALL West Midlands   7F2
Pop. 265,900. Birmingham 8½, London 120, M6 (jn
9) 1, Lichfield 9½, Stafford 17, Sutton Coldfield 9,
Wolverhampton 6½ **EC** Thu **MD** Mon, Tue, Fri, Sat **see**
St Matthew's Parish Church, Art Gallery and
Museum, Arboretum

★★★ Boundary
Birmingham Road, Walsall WS5 3AB
📞 01922-633555 **Fax** 01922-612034
94 bedrs, all ensuite, 🛏 📺 ⅲ 65 **P** 250 🍴 **CC** MC
Visa Amex DC JCB 🔲 🔲

★★★ Quality
20 Wolverhampton Road West,
Bentley, Walsall WS2 0BS
📞 01922-724444 **Fax** 01922-723148
E-mail admin@gb622.u-net.com

The Quality Hotel is an attractive, modern hotel
offering a sumptuous carvery, spacious rooms plus
a relaxing leisure centre. The hotel has excellent
access from J10 of the M6.
155 bedrs, all ensuite, 🛏 ⅲ 180 **P** 160 🍴 **SB** £91
DB £124.50 **L** £9.75 **D** £14.50 ✕ **LD** 21:45 **CC** MC Visa
Amex DC JCB 🔲 🔲 🔲 ♿

★★ Abberley
29 Bescot Road, Walsall WS2 9AD
📞 01922-627413 **Fax** 01922-720933
E-mail abberley.hotel@virgin.net
28 bedrs, all ensuite, ♀ 🏊 ⅲ 80 **P** 30 🍴 Resid
SB £41.95-£44.95 **DB** £45-£54.95 **L** 🍷 **D** £12 **D** 🍷 ✕
LD 21:00 Restaurant closed D Sun **CC** MC Visa Amex
DC JCB ♿

★★ ✤ Royal
Ablewell Street, Walsall WS1 2EL
📞 01922-624555 **Fax** 01922-30028
28 bedrs, all ensuite, 🛏 📺 ⅲ 200 **P** 40 🍴 **SB** £25-
£33 **DB** £39-£49 **HB** £267 **D** £6 ✕ **LD** 21:00 Restaurant
closed Sun **CC** MC Visa Amex DC

Facilities for the disabled

Hotels do their best to cater for disabled
visitors. However, it is advisable to contact
the hotel direct to ensure it can provide
particular requirement.

ENGLAND

WALTHAM ABBEY Essex   **5D2**
London 14, M25 (jn 26) 1½, Cheshunt 3, Epping 6,
Hertford 10, Potters Bar 11 ⓘ 54 Sun Street
01992-652295

★★★★ Swallow

Old Shire Lane,
Waltham Abbey EN9 3LX
☎ 01992-717170 **Fax** 01992-711841
E-mail info@swallowhotels.com

This attractive, modern hotel is situated on the
edge of rural Essex, handy for London. It has full
leisure facilities and two restaurants.
163 bedrs, all ensuite, ⓣ ⁂ 220 **P** 250 ⓔ **SB** £105
DB £130 **L** £16.50 **D** £19.50 ✕ **LD** 22:45 **CC** MC Visa
Amex DC ❸ ⊞ ▦ ♿

WARE Hertfordshire   **5D1**
Pop. 16,700. Hoddesdon 4, London 24, Baldock
16, Bishop's Stortford 10, Hatfield 8½, Royston 17
EC Thu **MD** Tue **see** Parish Church

★★★ County Ware
Baldock Street, Ware SG12 9DR
☎ 01920-409955 **Fax** 01920-468016
E-mail countyware@msihotels.co.uk
50 bedrs, all ensuite, ⓣ ▣ ⁂ 200 **P** 64 ⓔ **SB** £37.50-
£91.50 **DB** £75-£111 **L** ♥ **D** £13.50 **D** ✕ **LD** 21:30
Restaurant closed **L** Sat **CC** MC Visa Amex DC ♿

★★★ Vintage Court

Puckeridge, Ware SG11 1SA
☎ 01920-822722 **Fax** 01920-822877
Closed 25th DEC-3rd JAN
30 bedrs, all ensuite, ⓣ ⁂ 90 **P** 80 ⓔ **SB** £68.55-
£85.50 **DB** £77.50-£94.45 **L** £12 **L** ♥ **D** £18.85 **D** ♥ ✕
LD 21:15 Restaurant closed **L** Sat **CC** MC Visa Amex
DC ⊞
See advert on this page

VINTAGE COURT HOTEL

*Family owned hotel set in peaceful Hertfordshire
with spacious, tastefully furnished ensuite
bedrooms. Self-contained banqueting suite for up
to 140 guests. Conference facilities include three
large lecture rooms.*

**VINTAGE CORNER, PUCKERIDGE,
NR WARE, HERTS. SG11 1SA
AT THE JUNCTION OF A10 & A120
Tel: (01920) 822722 Fax: (01920) 822877**

WAREHAM Dorset   **3F3**
Pop. 6,300. Bournemouth 13, London 117,
Blandford Forum 14, Dorchester 16, Ringwood 21,
Weymouth 17 **EC** Wed (win) **MD** Thu **see** Parish
Church, St Martin's Church (Lawrence of Arabia)
ⓘ Trinity Church, South Street 01929-552740

★★★ Priory ⓡ ⓡ ⓡ
Blue Ribbon Hotel
Church Green, Wareham BH20 4ND
☎ 01929-551666 **Fax** 01929-554519
E-mail reception@theprioryhotel.co.uk
19 bedrs, all ensuite, ④ ♪ No children under 8 ⓔ
Resid SB £80 **DB** £100-£240 **L** ♥ **D** £26.50 ✕ **LD** 22:00
CC MC Visa Amex DC ⊡

★★★ Springfield Country
Hotel & Leisure Club ⓡ
Grange Road, Stoborough, Wareham BH20 5AL
☎ 01929-552177 **Fax** 01929-551862
48 bedrs, all ensuite, ⓣ ▣ ⁂ 200 **P** 200 ⓔ **SB** £63-
£83 **DB** £100-£130 **HB** £350-£455 **L** £12 **L** ♥ **D** £19.50
D ♥ ✕ **LD** 21:00 **CC** MC Visa Amex DC JCB ❸ ⋺ ⊞
▦ ◪ ⊞ ⊞ ♿

★★ Cromwell House
Lulworth Cove, Wareham BH20 5RJ
01929-400253 Fax 01929-400566
E-mail alistair@lds.co.uk
Closed Christmas

Set in secluded gardens, just 200 yards from Lulworth Cove, with spectacular sea views. All bedrooms ensuite, secluded gardens and swimming pool (May-October). Fish specialities. Bar/wine list. Groups welcome.
17 bedrs, all ensuite, 1 25 P 17 Rest Resid SB £26-£38.50 DB £54-£70 HB £234-£304 L D £13 LD 20:30 CC MC Visa Amex DC JCB

★★ Worgret Manor
Worgret, Wareham BH20 6AB
01929-552957 Fax 01929-554804
E-mail worgretmanor@freeserve.co.uk
Closed 1-14 Jan

A pretty, privately owned Georgian manor house converted into an attractive hotel.
13 bedrs, 11 ensuite, 100 P 50 SB £50-£55 DB £50-£80 HB £280-£350 L £14 L D £14 D LD 22:00 CC MC Visa Amex DC

★ Black Bear
14 South Street, Wareham BH20 4LT
01929-553339 Fax 01929-552846
15 bedrs, all ensuite, 40 CC MC Visa

WARKWORTH Northumberland 13F3
Morpeth 18, London 298, Alnwick 9, Newcastle 32, Rothbury 21

★★ Warkworth House
16 Bridge Street, Warkworth NE65 0XB
01665-711276 Fax 01665-713323
E-mail wecp,e@warkworthhousehotel.co.uk
14 bedrs, all ensuite, P 14 No children
SB £49 DB £85 HB £295 L £8 D £16 LD 20:30 CC MC Visa Amex DC

WARMINSTER Wiltshire 3F2
Central Car Park 01985-218548

★★★★ Bishopstrow House
Warminster BA12 9HH
01985-212312 Fax 01985-216769
30 bedrs, all ensuite, 60 P 60 CC MC Visa Amex DC JCB

★★ Old Bell
Market Place, Warminster BA12 9AN
01985-216611 Fax 01985-217111
20 bedrs, 14 ensuite, 100 P 20 CC MC Visa Amex

WARRINGTON Cheshire 10B4
Pop. 190,000. M6 (jn 21) 4, London 183, M62 2½, Chester 20, Liverpool 17, Manchester 16, Northwich 11, Wigan 12 EC Thu MD Daily exc Thur see Parish Church, Holy Trinity Church, Museum and Library 21 Rylands Street 01925-442180

★★★★ Park Royal International
Stretton Road, Stretton, Warrington WA4 4NS
01925-730706 Fax 01925-730740
140 bedrs, all ensuite, 400 P 400
SB £89.25-£110.75 DB £108.50-£129 L £13.25 L D £18.45 D LD 22:00 CC MC Visa Amex DC JCB
See advert on opposite page

★★ Paddington House
514 Manchester Road, Warrington WA1 3TZ
01925-816767 Fax 01925-816651

ENGLAND

Situated in its own tree-lined gardens, Paddington House provides an ideal setting for conferences, functions or wedding receptions. Conveniently located just off the M6, M56 and M62.
37 bedrs, all ensuite, ⚃ ♪ ✝ ⊡ ⠿ 180 **P** 50 ⊕
SB £55–£62.50 DB £67.50–£75 L £6 L ♥ D £12.95 D ♥ ✕ LD 21:30 ⸤ MC Visa Amex DC &

WARWICK Warwickshire　　　　　　　　8A4
See also LEAMINGTON SPA
Banbury 20, London 92, Birmingham 21, Coventry 10, Rugby 14, Stratford-upon-Avon 8 **EC** Thu **MD** Sat **see** Castle, St Mary's Church, St Nicholas' Church, St John's House (Museum), Lord Leycester Hospital
ℹ Court House, 2 Jury Street 01926-492212

★★★ ❖ Glebe
Church Street, Barford, Warwick CV35 8BS
📞 01926-624218 **Fax** 01926-624625
41 bedrs, all ensuite, ⊡ ⠿ 130 **P** 80 ⊕ ⸤ MC Visa Amex DC JCB ▣ ▣ ▣

★★★ Warwick Arms
17 High Street, Warwick CV34 4AT
📞 01926-492759 **Fax** 01926-410587
34 bedrs, all ensuite, ✝ ⠿ 80 **P** 18 ⊕ SB £40–£55 DB £50–£59 L £9.50 L ♥ D £13.95 D ♥ ✕ LD 21:30 Restaurant closed L Mon-Sat, D Sun ⸤ MC Visa Amex

---

WASHINGTON Tyne & Wear　　　　　　11D1
Pop. 60,500. Durham 11, London 271, Newcastle 6, Sunderland 6½ **see** Washington Old Hall, Holy Trinity Church, Waterfowl Park

★★★ Posthouse　　　　　　**Posthouse**
Emerson District 5, SO15 1HJ
📞 0191-416 2264 **Fax** 0191-415 3371
138 bedrs, all ensuite, ✝ ⊡ ⠿ 200 **P** 250 ⊕
SB £84.95 DB £94.90 L £12 L ♥ D £17 D ♥ ✕ LD 22:15 Restaurant closed (L) SATURDAY ⸤ MC Visa Amex DC JCB &

Campanile Washington Lodge
Emerson Road, Washington NE37 1LE
☎ 0191-416 5010 Fax 0191-416 5023

Campanile hotels offer comfortable and convenient budget accommodation and a traditional French style Bistro providing freshly cooked food for breakfast, lunch and dinner. All rooms ensuite with tea/coffee making facilities, DDT and TV with Sky channels.

77 bedrs, all ensuite, ✝ ⵌ 20 **P** 77 ⵌ Rest Resid
SB £44.45 **DB** £49.40 **L** £5.95 **D** £10.85 ✕ **LD** 22:00
CC MC Visa Amex DC ⵌ

WATERMILLOCK Cumbria   10B2
Pop. 460. M6 (jn 40) 6, London 281, Ambleside 15, Kendal 26, Keswick 17, Penrith 7

★★★ Leeming House ⵌ ⵌ   **Heritage**
Blue Ribbon Hotel   HOTELS
Watermillock, Ullswater CA11 0JJ
☎ 01768-486622 Fax 01768-486443
40 bedrs, all ensuite, ✝ ⵌ 20 **P** 50 ⵌ
SB £40-£85 **DB** £80-£170 **HB** £395-£432.50
L £13.95 **L** ⵌ **D** £23.50 ✕ **LD** 21:00
CC MC Visa Amex DC JCB 🖪

WATFORD Hertfordshire   4C2
Pop. 76,000. Aylesbury 23, London 16, M1 (jn 5) 3, Barnet 10, Dunstable 18, Harrow 7, Rickmansworth 3, St Albans 7 **MD** Tue, Fri, Sat **see** St Mary's Church, Bedford Almshouses, Cassiobury Park

★★★ White House
Upton Road, Watford WD1 2EL
☎ 01923-237316 Fax 01923-233109
87 bedrs, 81 ensuite, 6 ⵌ ⵌ ⵌ ✝ ⵌ ⵌ 200 **P** 45 ⵌ
SB £82.50-£97.50 **DB** £106-£146 **L** £12.95 **L** ⵌ
D £18.95 ✕ **LD** 21:45 **CC** MC Visa Amex DC ⵌ
See advert on opposite page

WEEDON BEC Northamptonshire   4B1
Pop. 2,450. Towcester 8½, London 69, M1 (jn 16) 3, Daventry 4, Hinckley 26, Leicester 30, Northampton 8½, Nuneaton 29, Rugby 13 **see** Parish Church

★★ Globe
High Street, Weedon Bec NN7 4QD
☎ 01327-340336 Fax 01327-349058
E-mail gfu20@ dial.pipex.co.uk

A part two and part three storey property of rendered elevations under a pitched slate roof. Originally built in the 18th century as a posting house, it has been successfully modernised to retain its period charm.
18 bedrs, all ensuite, ⵌ ✝ ⵌ 30 **P** 40 ⵌ **SB** £32-£50
DB £45-£60 **L** £14 **D** £14 ✕ **LD** 22:00 Restaurant closed D Sun **CC** MC Visa Amex ⵌ

WELLS Somerset   3E2
Pop. 9,400. Shepton Mallet 5½, London 122, Bath 19, Bristol 21, Glastonbury 5½, Radstock 12, Weston-super-Mare 19 **EC** Wed **MD** Wed, Sat **see** Cathedral, Bishop's Palace, Browne's Gate, Old Deanery, Almshouse, Town Hall, medieval Tithe Barn, Museum, St Cuthbert's Church, Vicar's Close 🛈 Town Hall, Market Place 01749-672552

★★★ Swan
Sadler Street, Wells BA5 2RX
☎ 01749-678877 Fax 01749-677647
E-mail swan@heritagehotels.co.uk
38 bedrs, all ensuite, ⵌ ⵌ ✝ ⵌ 100 **P** 35 ⵌ **SB** £74-£77.50 **DB** £92.50-£102.50 **L** £13.95 **D** £18.50 ✕
LD 21:30 **CC** MC Visa Amex DC ⵌ
See advert on opposite page

★★ White Hart ⵌ
Sadler Street, Wells BA5 2RR
☎ 01749-672056 Fax 01749-672056
E-mail whitehart@wells.demon.co.uk
13 bedrs, all ensuite, ✝ ⵌ 80 **P** 15 ⵌ **SB** £50-£55
DB £65-£70 **L** ⵌ **D** £15 **D** ⵌ ✕ **LD** 21:30 **CC** MC Visa Amex
See advert on opposite page

WELWYN Hertfordshire 4C2
Pop. 40,700. Welwyn Garden City 3, London 26, A1(M) (jn 6) 1, Baldock 11, Hertford 6, Luton 11, Stevenage 6 **see** Knebworth House

★★★ ✤ Quality
Welwyn AL6 9XA
☎ 01438-716911 **Fax** 01438-714065
E-mail admin@gb623.u-net.com

The hotel is situated just off the A1(M) at Welwyn, with easy access to Hertfordshire, St Albans and Hatfield. The hotel offers a restaurant, cocktail bar and mini gym.
96 bedrs, all ensuite, ⊹ ∰ 200 **P** 150 ⊞ **SB** £82.75-£91 **DB** £107-£124 **L** £8.25 **D** £14.50 ✕ **LD** 21:45 Restaurant closed L Sat ((MC Visa Amex DC JCB 🅿 ⅏

WEST WITTON North Yorkshire 10C2
Harrogate 35, London 239, Darlington 28, Hawes 12, Leyburn 4, Northallerton 22, Skipton 30, Thirsk 28

★★ Wensleydale Heifer ⅏ ⅏ ⅏
Wensleydale, West Witton DL8 4LS
☎ 01969-622322 **Fax** 01969-624183
E-mail heifer@daelnet.co.uk
15 bedrs, 14 ensuite, 1 ⌂ ④ ⊹ ∰ 14 **P** 50 ⊞ **SB** £60 **DB** £72-£98 **L** £14.50 **L** ⍨ **D** £19.50 **D** ⍨ ✕ **LD** 21:30 ((MC Visa Amex DC JCB

WESTCLIFF-ON-SEA Essex 5E2
Romford 24, London 41, Brentwood 20, Chelmsford 20, Dartford Crossing 20, Rainham 25, Southend 1 **EC** Wed **see** Beecroft Art Galleries

★★★ Westcliff
Westcliff Parade, SS0 7QW
☎ 01702-345247 **Fax** 01702-431814
E-mail westcliff@msihotels.co.uk
55 bedrs, all ensuite, ④ ✒ ▣ ∰ 200 ⊞ **SB** £65 **DB** £79.50 **L** £9.95 **L** ⍨ **D** £15.95 **D** ⍨ ✕ **LD** 21:30 Restaurant closed L Sat ((MC Visa Amex DC

★★ Balmoral
34-36 Valkyrie Road, Westcliff-on-Sea SS0 8BU
☎ 01702-342947 **Fax** 01702-337828

First class accommodation totally refurbished with designer furnishings, Sky TV, luxury suites, superb bar and restaurant. Enclosed off street parking with night porter security.
29 bedrs, all ensuite, ⊹ ∰ 15 **P** 20 ⊞ Resid **SB** £41 **DB** £65 **HB** £252 **D** £10 ✕ **LD** 19:30 Restaurant closed D Sun ((MC Visa Amex ⅏

WESTERHAM Kent 5D3
Pop. 3,400. Bromley 11, London 23, M25 (jn 5) 4½, Croydon 12, East Grinstead 13, Godstone 6½, Sevenoaks 6 **EC** Wed **see** General Wolfe's birthplace 1727, Quebec House, Wolfe's Statue, Statue of Sir Winston Churchill, Chartwell 1½ m SE

★★★ King's Arms ⅏
Market Square, Westerham TN16 1AN
☎ 01959-562990 **Fax** 01959-561240
17 bedrs, all ensuite, ④ ⊹ ∰ 30 **P** 100 ⊞ **SB** £83.75 **DB** £103.50-£112.50 **L** ⍨ **D** ⍨ ✕ **LD** 22:00 Restaurant closed D Sun ((MC Visa Amex

Roadchef Lodge Clacket Lane Lodge
M25 Westbound, Westerham TN16 2ER
☎ 01959-565577 **Fax** 01959-561311
Closed 24-27 Dec
58 bedrs, all ensuite, ∰ 24 **P** 100 **Room** £49.95 ((MC Visa Amex DC ⅏

WESTON-SUPER-MARE Somerset 3E1
Pop. 59,600. Bath 31, London 136, M5 (jn 21) 4, Bridgwater 18, Bristol 20, Glastonbury 24, Radstock 26, Wells 19 **EC** Thu **MD** Sun **see** Floral Clock, Winter Gardens, Museum, Seaworld, Tropicana, Steepholm and Flatholm Islands
i Beach Lawns 01934-626838

ENGLAND

RAC ★★ **BATCH** COUNTRY HOTEL

Lympsham, Nr Weston-Super-Mare, Somerset
Tel: 01934 750371 Fax: 01934 750501
Proprietors: Mr & Mrs D. J. Brown

A family run hotel with a long reputation for its friendly atmosphere and traditional á la carte cuisine. Delightfully situated in its own grounds with panoramic views of the beautiful Somerset countryside from all rooms. The hotel lies within easy reach of the area's many historical attractions. Five golf courses lie nearby. The rooms are all ensuite and individually styled to a high standard. Easy to reach from motorway (M5). Egon Ronay/Ashley Courtenay Recommended. Unlimited free parking. Short Breaks available.

★★★ Beachlands
17 Uphill Road North,
Weston-super-Mare BS23 4NG
☎ 01934-621401 Fax 01934-621966
E-mail beachlands@wsmare.freeserve.co.uk
Closed 24 Dec-5 Jan
24 bedrs, all ensuite, ♪ ⚏ 60 P 26 ⊕ SB £39.50-£44.50 DB £79-£89 HB £294 L 🍷 D £15.50 D 🍷 ✕ LD 20:30 Restaurant closed L Mon-Sat ℂℂ MC Visa Amex JCB ▣ ▥ ⅏

★★★ ✤ Commodore
Beach Road, Sand Bay, Kewstoke,
Weston-super-Mare B22 9UZ
☎ 01934-415778 Fax 01934-636483
19 bedrs, all ensuite, ⚏ 120 P 80 ⊕ ℂℂ MC Visa ▥ ⅏

★★★ ✤ Royal Pier
Birnbeck Road, Weston-super-Mare BS23 2EJ
☎ 01934-626644 Fax 01934-624169
40 bedrs, all ensuite, ▣ ⚏ 60 P 70 ⊕ SB £45-£55 DB £70-£78 HB £245 L £8.75 L 🍷 D £14.95 D 🍷 ✕ LD 21:00 ℂℂ MC Visa Amex DC

★★ Arosfa
Lower Church Road, Weston-super-Mare BS23 2AG
☎ 01934-419523 Fax 01934-636084
46 bedrs, all ensuite, ♪ ⚏ 100 P 16 ⊕ ℂℂ MC Visa Amex DC ⅏

★★ Bay
60 Knightstone Road, Seafront,
Weston-super-Mare BS23 2BE
☎ 01934-624137 Fax 01934-626969
11 bedrs, all ensuite, ♪ P 8 ⊕ SB £32.50-£40 DB £55 HB £249-£324 D £12 ✕ LD 19:30 ℂℂ MC Visa Amex DC

★★ Dauncey's
Claremont Crescent, Weston-super-Mare BS23 2EE
☎ 01934-621144 Fax 01934-620281

Family run terraced Victorian hotel with pleasant gardens and good sea views from bar, patio and garden across Weston Bay.
80 bedrs, 74 ensuite, ♪ ⚏ 50 ⊕ SB £28.50-£31 DB £57-£62 HB £248.50-£267.75 L £8.50 D £11 D 🍷 ✕ LD 19:00 ℂℂ MC Visa JCB

★★ Dorville
Madeira Road, Weston-super-Mare BS23 2EX
☎ 01934-621522 Fax 01934-645585
Closed Dec-Feb
41 bedrs, 27 ensuite, ▣ ⚏ 50 P 10 No children under 5 ⊕ SB £25-£33 DB £48-£60 HB £137-£210 L £6 D £9 ✕ LD 19:30 ▥ ⅏

★★ Queenswood
Victoria Park, Weston-super-Mare BS23 2HZ
☎ 01934-416141 Fax 01934-621759
E-mail queenswood.hotel@btinternet.com
17 bedrs, all ensuite, ♪ ♪ ⚏ 30 P 6 ⊕ Resid SB £40-£45 DB £65-£70 HB £266-£280 L £10 L 🍷 D £16.50 D 🍷 ✕ LD 20:30 ℂℂ MC Visa Amex DC JCB

WESTONBIRT Gloucestershire   3F1
Swindon 20, London 97, Bath 19, Bristol 22, Tetbury 3 **see** Arboretum (150 acres of forest trees and shrubs)

★★★ Hare & Hounds
Tetbury, Westonbirt GL8 8QL
☎ 01666-880233 **Fax** 01666-880241
31 bedrs, all ensuite, ⬜ ✎ ✝ ⦂⦂⦂ 150 **P** 80 ⊞ **SB** £73-£118 **DB** £91-£136 **HB** £354 **L** £12.75 **L** ● **D** £19.50
D ● ✕ **LD** 21:00 **CC** MC Visa Amex DC JCB ▦ ▣ ▦
♿
See advert on this page

★★★ Crown ⌂
Wetheral, Carlisle CA4 8ES
☎ 01228-561888 **Fax** 01228-561637
E-mail crown@shireinns.co.uk
51 bedrs, all ensuite, ⬜ ✎ ✝ ⦂⦂⦂ 175 **P** 80 ⊞
SB £102-£122 **DB** £126-£140 **L** £10 **D** £20 ✕ **LD** 21:30
Restaurant closed L Sat, Sun **CC** MC Visa Amex DC
▣ ▦ ▨ ▦

Kingston upon Thames 8, London 18, Bagshot 11, Ealing 14, Epsom 12, Leatherhead 9½, Woking 7
EC Wed **see** St James's Church (Chantrey Monument), Museum

★★★★ Oatlands Park ⌂ ⌂
Oatlands Drive, Weybridge KT13 9HB
☎ 01932-847242 **Fax** 01932-842252

A country house hotel set in 10 acres of parkland overlooking the Broadwater Lake. Easy access to the Surrey countryside making this an ideal base for touring. Extensive conference and banqueting facilities.
136 bedrs, all ensuite, ⬜ ✎ ✝ ☰ ⦂⦂⦂ 200 **P** 100 ⊞
SB £117.50-£142 **DB** £165-£185 **L** £20 **L** ● **D** £26 **D** ●
✕ **LD** 22:00 **CC** MC Visa Amex DC ▦ ▣ ▨ ▨ ♿

★★★ Ship ⌂
Monument Green, Weybridge KT13 8BQ
☎ 01932-848364 **Fax** 01932-857153

ENGLAND

39 bedrs, all ensuite, ⊞ 130 **P** 55 🛗 **SB** £109.50
DB £134 **L** £14 **D** £16 ✕ **LD** 21:45 Restaurant closed
L Sat **CC** MC Visa Amex DC JCB

WEYMOUTH Dorset	373

Dorchester 8, London 130, Axminster 30, Lyme
Regis 28, Wareham 17 **EC** Wed **MD** Thu **see** St Mary's
Church, King George III Statue, Guildhall 🔢 The
King's Statue, Esplanade 01305-785747

★★★ Hotel Rex 🔝
29 The Esplanade, Weymouth DT4 8DN
📞 01305-760400 **Fax** 01305-760500

A Georgian town house, once the Duke of
Clarence's summer residence, situated on the
Esplanade, close to shops, beach and harbour.
31 bedrs, all ensuite, 4️⃣ 🐾 🔳 ⊞ 60 **P** 8 🛗 **SB** £42-
£52 **DB** £68-£95 **HB** £236-£300 **D** £12 ✕ **LD** 22:00
CC MC Visa Amex DC

★★★ Portland Heights
Yeates Corner, Portland DT5 2EN
📞 01305-821361 **Fax** 01305-860081
E-mail reception@phh.wdi.co.uk
65 bedrs, all ensuite, ♀ 🏊 🐾 ⊞ 200 **P** 250 🛗
SB £50-£64 **DB** £60-£74 **HB** £282-£320 **L** £10 **L** 📶
D £17.50 **D** 📶 ✕ **LD** 21:00 **CC** MC Visa Amex DC 📥 🔳
🔳 🔳

★★ Central
15 Maiden Street, Weymouth DT4 8BB
📞 01305-760700 **Fax** 01305-760300
Closed Dec-Feb
28 bedrs, all ensuite, 🔳 **P** 10 🛗 Resid **SB** £30-£38
DB £58-£70 **HB** £147-£214 **L** £6.50 **D** £8 ✕ **LD** 20:00
CC MC Visa Amex ♿

★★ Crown
51/52 St Thomas Street, Weymouth DT4 8EQ
📞 01305-760800 **Fax** 01305-760300
86 bedrs, all ensuite, 🔳 ⊞ 120 **P** 12 🛗 **SB** £33-£35
DB £58-£64 **HB** £160-£229 **L** £6 **D** £10 ✕ **LD** 20:00
CC MC Visa DC ♿

★★ ✤ Fairhaven
37 The Esplanade, Weymouth DT4 8DH
📞 01305-760200 **Fax** 01305-760300
Closed Nov-Feb
76 bedrs, all ensuite, 🔳 **P** 14 🛗 Resid **SB** £30-£38
DB £58-£70 **HB** £151-£230 **L** £6.50 **D** £8 ✕ **LD** 20:00
CC MC Visa Amex 🔳

★★ ✤ Glenburn
42 Preston Road, Weymouth DT3 6PZ
📞 01305-832353 **Fax** 01305-835610
13 bedrs, all ensuite, ⊞ 70 **P** 30 No children under
3 🛗 Rest Resid **CC** MC Visa

★★ ✤ Moonfleet Manor
Moonfleet, Weymouth DT3 4ED
📞 01305-786948 **Fax** 01305-774395
38 bedrs, all ensuite, 🔳 ⊞ 50 **P** 100 🛗 **CC** MC Visa
Amex 🔳 🔳 🔳 🔳 🔳 🔳 🔳 ♿

★★ Prince Regent
139 The Esplanade, Weymouth DT4 7NR
📞 01305-771313 **Fax** 01305-778100
E-mail hprwey@aol.co.uk

An elegant Victorian hotel situated on Weymouth's
seafront, enjoying magnificent views across
Weymouth Bay
50 bedrs, all ensuite, ♀ 🏊 🔳 ⊞ 200 **P** 18 🛗 **SB** £55-
£75 **DB** £65-£85 **HB** £297-£367 **L** £6 **L** 📶 **D** £12.25
D 📶 ✕ **LD** 20:30 Restaurant closed **L** Mon-Fri **CC** MC
Visa Amex DC 🔳

WHITBY North Yorkshire	11E2

See also GOATHLAND
Pop. 14,300. Scarborough 19, London 232,
Middlesbrough 30, Pickering 20 **EC** Wed **MD** Sat **see**
Abbey ruins, St Mary's Church, Pannett Park, Town
Hall, Capt Cook's house 🔢 Langborne Road
01947-602674

★★ Old West Cliff
42 Crescent Avenue, Whitby YO21 3EQ
☎ 01947-603292 **Fax** 01947-821716

Family run hotel situated in the most prominent position in Whitby. Two minutes walk from the cliff top, cliff lift, crazy golf, paddling pool, tennis courts, swimming pool and town centre.
12 bedrs, all ensuite, ⅲ 25 ⊞ SB £30 DB £49 D £11 ✕ LD 20:00 ℂℂ MC Visa Amex DC

★★ Saxonville 🛱
Ladysmith Avenue, Whitby YO21 3HX
☎ 01947-602631 **Fax** 01947-820523
E-mail saxonville@onyxnet.co.uk
Closed 31 Oct-31 Mar
22 bedrs, all ensuite, ⅲ 100 P 20 ⊞ SB £35 DB £70 HB £300 D £18.50 ✕ LD 20.30 ℂℂ MC Visa JCB

★★ White House
Upgang Lane, Whitby YO21 3JJ
☎ 01947-600469 **Fax** 01947-821600
E-mail 101745.1440@compuserve.com
11 bedrs, 9 ensuite, ⊹ ⅲ 30 P 30 ⊞ SB £26.50-£30.50 DB £53-£61 HB £250-£295 L £8 D £11 ✕ LD 21:30 ℂℂ MC Visa JCB

WHITCHURCH Hampshire 4B3
Pop. 4,200. Basingstoke 12, London 59 **MD** Fri

★★ ✤ White Hart
Newbury Street, Whitchurch RG28 7DN
☎ 01256-892900 **Fax** 01256-896628
20 bedrs, 10 ensuite, 4 ℞ ④ ♀ ⊹ ⅲ 40 P 20 ⊞ SB £20-£46 DB £30-£56 HB £350 L ♥ D £11.95 D ♥ ✕ LD 21:30 ℂℂ MC Visa Amex 🈲

WHITEHAVEN Cumbria 10A2
Pop. 26,700. Cockermouth 13, London 311, Egremont 5, Workington 7½ **EC** Wed **MD** Thu, Sat **see** St Nicholas Church tower and remains, Pottery Craft Centre, Museum in 19th cent Market Hall, St Bees Head 🖊 Market Hall, Market Place 01946-695678

★★ Chase
Corkickle, Whitehaven CA28 8AA
☎ 01946-693656 **Fax** 01946-590807
11 bedrs, all ensuite, ④ ⊹ ⅲ 60 P 50 ⊞ SB £39 DB £54 L £8 D £12 D ♥ ✕ LD 21:00 Restaurant closed L Sat, D Sun ℂℂ MC Visa ♿

WHITLEY BAY Tyne & Wear 11D1
Pop. 38,000. Tyne Tunnel 5, London 282, Alnwick 34, Sunderland 14 **MD** Daily 🖊 Park Road 0191-200 8535

★★★ Windsor
South Parade, Whitley Bay NE26 2RF
☎ 0191-251 8888 **Fax** 0191-297 0272

Modern family run hotel close to seafront and town centre. Continental style lounge bar and a la carte restaurant. An ideal base for exploring Northumbria.
62 bedrs, all ensuite, ⌕ ⊹ ▣ ⅲ 100 P 20 ⊞ SB £40-£59 DB £50-£60 D ♥ ✕ LD 21:45 ℂℂ MC Visa Amex

★★ Seacrest
North Parade, Whitley Bay NE26 1PA
☎ 0191-253 0140 **Fax** 0191-253 0140

A relaxed and friendly atmosphere awaits you in our family run 2 star hotel. Ideally situated in a central part of Whitley Bay adjoining the Promenade and close to the bus and Metro station.
22 bedrs, all ensuite, ♀ ⌕ ⅲ 50 P 4 ⊞ Rest Resid SB £30-£46 DB £50-£60 HB £220-£350 L ♥ D £8 D ♥ ✕ LD 20:30 Restaurant closed D Fri-Sun ℂℂ MC Visa Amex DC JCB 🈲

ENGLAND

WHITTINGTON Shropshire   7D2
Pop. 2,300. Shrewsbury 18, London 172, Llangollen
12, Oswestry 3, Whitchurch 17, Wrexham 16 **EC** Thu

★ ✦ Ye Olde Boot
Castle Street, Whittington SY11 4DF
📞 01691-662250
6 bedrs, all ensuite, 🛌 **P** 100 ⊞ **SB** £23 **DB** £38 ✕
LD 21:30 **CC** MC Visa

WICKFORD Essex   5E2
Basildon 4, London 33, Brentwood 11, Chelmsford
12, Southend 13

★★★ Chichester
Old London Road, Wickford SS11 8UE
📞 01268-560555 **Fax** 01268-560580
34 bedrs, all ensuite, ⠿ 100 **P** 150 No children ⊞
SB £63-£75 **DB** £82.50 **L** £11.50 **D** £15 ✕ **LD** 21:15
CC MC Visa Amex DC

WIGAN Lancashire   10B4
Pop. 88,700. London 195, M6 (jn 26) 3, Bolton 10,
Chorley 8, Manchester 19, Ormskirk 11, Preston
17, St Helens 8, Walkden 10, Warrington 12
MD Daily Wed **i** Trencherfield Mill, Wallgate 01942-
825677

★★★★ Kilhey Court ⌾
Chorley Road, Standish, Wigan WN1 2XN
📞 01257-472100 **Fax** 01257-422401
E-mail reservations@kilhey.co.uk

Set in Lancashire countryside with restful views of
lakes, well tended gardens and unspoilt woodland,
this impressive Victorian hotel offers a high
standard of four star accommodation, excellent
banqueting facilities and many opportunities for
leisure.
62 bedrs, all ensuite, 🛌 ▣ ⠿ 400 **P** 450 ⊞ **CC** MC
Visa Amex DC ▣ ▣ ▣ ▣ ▣ &

★★★ Quality Hotel Wigan
River Way, Wigan WN1 3SS
📞 01942-826888 **Fax** 01942-825800
E-mail admin@gbo58u-net.com
88 bedrs, all ensuite, ♀ ⚲ 🛌 ▣ ⠿ 200
P 100 ⊞ **SB** £45-£84.50 **DB** £60-£104
L £8.95 **L** 🍽 **D** £15.95 **D** 🍽 ✕ **LD** 21:45
CC MC Visa Amex DC JCB &

★★★ Quality Skelmersdale
Prescott Road, Upholland,
Wigan WN8 9PU
📞 01695-720401 **Fax** 01695-509953
E-mail admin@gb656.u-net.com

Ideal base for the local attractions, including steam
railways, zoos, castles and stately homes. Built in
Elizabethan times, the hotel has air-conditioning
and ample free parking.
55 bedrs, all ensuite, ⠿ 200 ⊞ **SB** £84.50-£104
DB £104 **D** £14.50 ✕ **LD** 22:00 **CC** MC Visa Amex DC

★★ Bel Air
236 Wigan Lane, Wigan WN1 2NU
📞 01942-241410 **Fax** 01942-243967
E-mail bel-air@netpages.u-net.com

A 2 star RAC award winning hotel. Eleven ensuite
rooms with all facilities. Cosy lounge bar with a
French style restaurant. Close to the town centre
and M6 junction 27.
11 bedrs, all ensuite, ▣ ♀ ⠿ 30 **P** 10 ⊞ Rest Resid
SB £39.50 **DB** £49.50 **L** £6.95 **L** 🍽 **D** £5.95 **D** 🍽 ✕
LD 21:00 **CC** MC Visa

WIGGLESWORTH North Yorkshire 10C3
Skipton 13, London 223, Clitheroe 15, Settle 6½, Slaidburn 7½

★★ Plough Inn
Wigglesworth BD23 4RJ
☎ 01729-840243 Fax 01729-840243
12 bedrs, all ensuite, ⊞ ⌗ 100 P 50 ⊞ SB £35-£38
DB £55-£60 HB £224.25-£287 L £5.50 L ♥ D £16.50
D ♥ ✕ LD 21:00 ₡ MC Visa Amex DC ৬

WIGTON Cumbria 10A1
Pop. 5,200. Penrith 22, London 298, Carlisle 11, Cockermouth 15, Keswick 20. MD Tue

★★★ Wheyrigg Hall
Wigton CA7 0DH
☎ 01697-361242 Fax 01697-361020

Friendly family run hotel and restaurant. Situated 7 miles from the sea and coastline, the Hall was developed by converting an old farmhouse. This has been extended in to one of Cumbria's best and most comfortable rural eating places.
13 bedrs, all ensuite, ⌗ 140 ⊞ ₡ MC Visa Amex DC 🖼 ৬

WILLITON Somerset 3D2
Pop. 2,200. Taunton 14, London 157, Bridgwater 16, Dunster 6, Tiverton 24 EC Sat

★★ White House
Long Street, Williton TA4 4QW
☎ 01984-632306
Closed early Nov-mid May
12 bedrs, 9 ensuite, ♠ P 15 ⊞ Rest Resid ৬

WIMBORNE MINSTER Dorset 4A4
Ringwood 10, London 103, Blandford Forum 9, Bournemouth 9, Dorchester 22, Salisbury 26, Wareham 12 MD Fri see Minster (11th cent astronomical clock and chained Library), St Margaret's Chapel and Hospital, Priest's House Museum, Julians' Bridge, Model of town (off West Row), Badbury Rings 3m NW ℹ 29 High Street 01202-886116

★★ Beechleas ⌑
Blue Ribbon Hotel
17 Poole Road, Wimborne Minster BH21 1QA
☎ 01202-841684 Fax 01202-849344
Closed 24 Dec-11 Jan

A beautifully restored, Grade II Listed, Georgian town house with delightful walled garden, award winning restaurant, log fires in winter, sunny conservatory in summer and a lovely ambiance.
9 bedrs, all ensuite, ♠ ⌗ 12 P 11 ⊞ Rest Resid
SB £69-£89 DB £89-£99 D £21.75 ✕ LD 21:30 ₡ MC Visa Amex

WINCHESTER Hampshire 4B3
Pop. 35,600. Basingstoke 18, London 65, Alton 17, Andover 14, Fareham 19, Newbury 24, Petersfield 19, Romsey 10, Salisbury 23, Southampton 12 MD Mon, Wed, Fri, Sat see Cathedral, Guildhall (with Art Gallery), Winchester College (apply porter), St Cross Hospital and Church (Wayfarer's Dole), Great Hall of Winchester Castle (legendary Round Table of King Arthur and his Knights) West Gate (Museum) ℹ Guildhall 01962-840500

★★★★ Lainston House 🛏 🛏 🛏
Blue Ribbon Hotel
Sparsholt, Winchester SO21 2LT
📞 01962-863588 **Fax** 01962-776248
E-mail enquiries@lainstonhouse.com

An elegant William and Mary house with breathtaking views over tranquil parkland and only two and a half miles from the city of Winchester and the Royal Winchester Golf Club. The popular restaurant offers gourmet food and superb service.
37 bedrs, all ensuite, 🔲 ♀ 🎣 🐾 ⊞ 80 **P** 100 🍴
SB £106 **DB** £167 **L** £15.50 **L** 🍴 **D** £35 **D** 🍴 ✕
LD 22:00 **CC** MC Visa Amex DC JCB 🔲🔲🔲🔲 ♿

★★★★ Wessex
Paternoster Row,
Winchester SO23 9LQ
📞 01962-841503 **Fax** 01962-841503
94 bedrs, all ensuite, 🔲 🎣 🐾 🔲 ⊞ 100
P 65 🍴 **SB** £96 **DB** £110-£119 **HB** £330-£386
L £7.95 **L** 🍴 **D** £16 **D** 🍴 ✕ **LD** 22:00
CC MC Visa Amex DC JCB

Heritage HOTELS

Hotel du Vin
14 Southgate Street, Winchester SO23 9EF
📞 01962-841414 **Fax** 01962-842458
E-mail admin@winchester.hotelduvin.co.uk

Stylish town house hotel and bistro situated in central Winchester offering quality accommodation together with modern bistro cooking and good value wines.
23 bedrs, all ensuite, 🔲 ⊞ 48 **P** 40 🍴 **CC** MC Visa Amex DC

WINDERMERE Cumbria 10B2
Pop. 8,000. M6 (jn 36) 16, London 246, Ambleside 5, Kendal 8, Lancaster 28, Penrith 26, Ulverston 17 **EC** Thu **see** Lake, Steamboat Museum, Aquarium, Belle Isle, Orrest Head (extensive views), St Martins Church Tower (Troutbeck) 2m N 🛈 Victoria Street 015394-46499

★★★★ Lakeside Hotel on Windermere 🛏
Newby Bridge LA12 8AT
📞 01539-531207 **Fax** 01539-531699
E-mail lshotel@aol.com

This classic hotel, with superb lakeside conservatory, award-winning restaurant & John Ruskin's Brasserie, enjoys a peaceful setting with breathtaking views of Lake Windermere. Great value breaks all year. Free use of Leisure Club at Newby Bridge.
80 bedrs, all ensuite, 🔲 🐾 🔲 ⊞ 100 **P** 200 🍴 🍴
Resid **CC** MC Visa Amex DC 🔲🔲🔲🔲🔲🔲 ♿

★★★ Beech Hill 🛏 🛏
Newby Bridge Road, Windermere LA23 3LR
📞 015394-42137 **Fax** 015394-43745
57 bedrs, all ensuite, 🔲 🐾 ⊞ 80 **P** 60 🍴 **CC** MC Visa Amex DC 🔲🔲 ♿

★★★ ✦ Craig Manor
Lake Road, Windermere LA23 2JF
📞 015394-88877 **Fax** 015394-88878
16 bedrs, all ensuite, 🐾 **P** 50 🍴 Rest Resid **CC** MC Visa Amex

ENGLAND

★★★ Gilpin Lodge 🛏 🛏 🛏
Blue Ribbon Hotel
Crook Road, Windermere LA23 3NE
📞 015394-88818 **Fax** 015394-88058
E-mail hotel@gilpin-lodge.co.uk

Friendly, relaxing, elegant hotel in 20 acres of country gardens, moors and woodland, two miles from Lake Windermere. Sumptuous bedrooms. Exquisite food.
14 bedrs, all ensuite, 🆔 🎯 25 **P** 40 No children under 7 ⊞ Rest Resid **SB** £60-£110 **DB** £80-£180 **HB** £340-£635 **L** £20 **L** 🍽 **D** £29.50 ✕ **LD** 21:00 **CC** MC Visa Amex DC JCB ⅊

★★★ Hillthwaite House 🛏
Thornbarrow Road, Windermere LA23 2DF
📞 01539-443636 **Fax** 01539-488660
30 bedrs, all ensuite, 🐦 **P** 30 ⊞ **CC** MC Visa Amex DC 🔲 ⅊

★★★ Holbeck Ghyll Country House 🛏 🛏 🛏

Blue Ribbon Hotel
Holbeck Lane, Windermere LA23 1LU
📞 015394-32375 **Fax** 015394-34743
E-mail accommodation@holbeck-ghyll.co.uk
20 bedrs, all ensuite, 🆔 ♀ 🐦 🎯 20 **P** 20 ⊞ Rest Resid **SB** £80-£135 **DB** £130-£250 **HB** £525-£1,050 **L** £17.95 **D** £37.50 ✕ **LD** 21:00 **CC** MC Visa Amex DC JCB 🔲 🖼 🔳 ⅊

★★★ Langdale Chase
Windermere LA23 1LW
📞 015394-32201 **Fax** 015394-32604
29 bedrs, all ensuite, 🆔 🐦 🎯 20 **P** 50 ⊞ **SB** £50-£80 **DB** £90-£150 **L** £12 **L** 🍽 **D** £25 **D** 🍽 ✕ **LD** 21:00 **CC** MC Visa Amex DC JCB 🔲 🔲
See advert on this page

★★★ Lindeth Howe Country House 🛏 🛏
Longtail Hill, Windermere LA23 3JF
📞 015394-45759 **Fax** 015394-46368
E-mail lindeth.howe@kencomp.net
37 bedrs, all ensuite, 🆔 🎯 15 **P** 40 ⊞ Rest Resid **SB** £52.50-£67.50 **DB** £85-£135 **HB** £325-£602 **L** £11.95 **L** 🍽 **D** £22.50 ✕ **LD** 20:30 Restaurant closed L Mon-Sat **CC** MC Visa JCB 🔲 🖼 ⅊
See advert on opposite page

★★★ Linthwaite House 🛏 🛏 🛏
Crook Road, Windermere LA23 3JA
📞 015394-88600 **Fax** 015394-88601
E-mail admin@linthwaite.com
18 bedrs, all ensuite, 🎯 40 **P** 40 ⊞ Rest Resid **CC** MC Visa Amex JCB 🔲 ⅊

★★★ Low Wood
Windermere LA23 1LP
📞 015394-33338 **Fax** 015394-34072
E-mail lowwood@elh.co.uk
117 bedrs, all ensuite, 🆔 ♪ 🐦 🔲 🎯 340 **P** 200 ⊞ **SB** £60-£62.50 **DB** £120-£125 **HB** £360-£375 **L** £10 **L** 🍽 **D** £21 **D** 🍽 ✕ **LD** 21:15 **CC** MC Visa Amex DC JCB 🔲 🖼 🔲 🖼 🔳 ⅊
See advert on opposite page

ENGLAND

★★★ Old England

Heritage
HOTELS

Church Street,
Bowness-on-Windermere,
Windermere LA23 3DF
☎ 015394-42444 **Fax** 015394-43432
E-mail heritagehotels_windermere.old.england@forte-hotels.com
76 bedrs, all ensuite, 4 ➤ 🖭 ⅲ 120 **P** 90
🐕 **SB** £39-£70 **DB** £78-£140 **HB** £384-£480
L 🍷 **D** £18 **D** 🍷 ✕ **LD** 21:30 Restaurant
closed L Mon-Sat
《 MC Visa Amex DC JCB 🐾 🖾

★★★ Wild Boar 🍴

Crook, Windermere LA23 3NF
☎ 015394-45225 **Fax** 015394-42498
E-mail wildboar@elh.co.uk

Discover our unique character and atmosphere, find us friendly but not too formal, attentive but not intrusive, traditional but never old fashioned.
36 bedrs, all ensuite, 4 ➤ ⅲ 40 **P** 80 🐕 **SB** £58
DB £103-£120 **HB** £378-£420 **L** £11 **D** £20 ✕ **LD** 21:15
《 MC Visa Amex DC JCB

★★ Broadoaks Country House 🍴🍴🍴

Blue Ribbon Hotel
Bridge Lane, Troutbeck,
Windermere LA23 1LA
☎ 015394-45566 **Fax** 015394-88766
E-mail broadoaks.com@virgin.net
14 bedrs, all ensuite, 4 ➤ ⅲ 45 **P** 30 No children
under 5 🐕 Rest Resid **SB** £67.50-£112.50 **DB** £90-£195 **L** £14.95 **D** £35 **D** 🍷 ✕ **LD** 20:00 《 MC Visa
See advert on next page

★★ Cedar Manor 🍴🍴

Ambleside Road, Windermere LA23 1AX
☎ 015394-43192 **Fax** 015394-45970
12 bedrs, all ensuite, 4 🖉 ➤ ⅲ 20 **P** 16 🐕 Rest
Resid **SB** £32-£49 **DB** £64-£75 **HB** £220-£319 **D** £19 ✕
LD 20:30 《 MC Visa

Broadoaks

COUNTRY HOUSE

RAC Small Hotel of the Year (Northern Region)

A luxury Victorian Country House, set in seven acres in the peaceful Troutbeck Valley.

We offer a warm friendly welcome. Quality, luxury and personal service are assured. Situated approximately two miles from Windermere or Ambleside with superb views of lake and fells. All bedrooms are individually designed, a choice of 4 posters Victorian with Jacuzzi, Whirlpool spa or power showers ensuite. As well as the usual tea, coffee, hair dryers, colour TV, we include Sky along with added luxuries to create an atmosphere to relax in away from the strains of modern day life. Exquisite foods and fine wines with a breakfast menu second to none are served in our restaurant.

The beautiful gardens play host to a bowling green and putting course. All types of activities arranged. Free use of corporate leisure centre. Licensed to carry out civil marriages. The relaxing atmosphere is a haven of peace where treasured memories are made on that special holiday. Explicit colour brochure. It's simply somewhere special.

Broadoaks, Bridge Lane, Troutbeck, Windermere LA21 1LA
Telephone: 01539-445566 Fax: 01539-488766
Email: broadoaks.com@virgin.net Website: www.travel.to/broadoaks

ENGLAND

★★ Glenburn
New Road, Windermere LA23 2EE
📞 015394-42649 **Fax** 015394-88998
16 bedrs, all ensuite, ☒ **P** 17 No children under 5 ⊕
DB £50-£90 **HB** £259-£389 **D** £16 ✕ **LD** 20:00 ℂℂ MC
Visa Amex DC JCB

★★ Hideaway ⌂
Phoenix Way, Windermere LA23 1DB
📞 015394-43070 **Fax** 015394-43070
Closed Jan
15 bedrs, all ensuite, ✈ **P** 16 ⊕ Rest Resid **SB** £30-
£45 **DB** £60-£100 **HB** £210-£365 **D** £17.50 ✕ **LD** 20:00
ℂℂ MC Visa Amex JCB
See advert on this page

★★ ❖ Lindeth Fell
Windermere LA23 3JP
📞 015394-43286 **Fax** 015394-47455

One of the most beautifully situated hotels in
lakeland, Lindeth Fell offers a warm and friendly
atmosphere, superior accommodation and superb
modern English cooking, at outstanding value.
15 bedrs, all ensuite, ④ ⦂⦂⦂ 12 **P** 20 ⊕ Rest Resid
SB £50-£77.50 **DB** £100-£130 **HB** £410-£500 **L** £8 **L** ●
D £19 ✕ **LD** 20:30 ℂℂ MC Visa ☒ ♿

★★ Quarry Garth
Country House ⌂ ⌂ ⌂

Troutbeck Bridge, Windermere LA23 1LF
📞 015394-88282 **Fax** 015394-46584
13 bedrs, all ensuite, ④ ✈ ⦂⦂⦂ 30 **P** 30 ⊕ **SB** £29-£69
DB £58-£138 **HB** £346.50-£556.50 **L** ● **D** £25.95 ✕
LD 20:45 Restaurant closed L Mon-Sat ℂℂ MC Visa
Amex ▦

★★ Woodlands
New Road, Windermere LA23 2EE
📞 015394-43915 **Fax** 015394-48558
Closed Christmas
14 bedrs, all ensuite, ④ **P** 14 No children under 5 ⊕
Resid ℂℂ MC Visa JCB

★★★ Castle
High Street, Windsor SL4 1LJ
📞 01753-851011 **Fax** 01753-830244
111 bedrs, all ensuite, ④ ✎ ✈ ▣ ⦂⦂⦂ 400 **P** 100 ⊕
SB £55-£90 **DB** £110-£190 **L** £14 **D** £23.50 **D** ● ✕
LD 21:45 ℂℂ MC Visa Amex DC JCB

Heritage HOTELS

★★ ❖ Aurora Garden
Bolton Avenue, Windsor SL4 3JF
📞 01753-868686 **Fax** 01753-831394
E-mail aurora@auroragarden.co.uk
19 bedrs, all ensuite, ④ ✈ ⦂⦂⦂ 90 **P** 22 ⊕ **SB** £75-£85
DB £95-£105 **L** £8.95 **L** ● **D** £12.95 **D** ● ✕ **LD** 21:30
ℂℂ MC Visa Amex DC

WINSFORD Somerset 7E1
Pop. 340. Taunton 29, London 172, Dunster 9, Lynmouth 19, South Molton 20, Tiverton 18, **see** Devil's Punch Bowl

★★★ Royal Oak ⌂
Exmoor National Park, Winsford TA24 7JE
☎ 01643-851455 **Fax** 01643-851009
E-mail royaloak.winsfordsomerset@virgin.net
14 bedrs, all ensuite, ④ ♠ ♦ P 18 ⊕ SB £65-£85
DB £85-£120 L £15 D £25 ✕ LD 21:00 Restaurant closed L Mon-Sat ⛦ MC Visa Amex DC ▣
See advert on this page

WISBECH Cambridgeshire 9D3
Pop. 23,200. Ely 23, London 94, Boston 29, Huntingdon 33, King's Lynn 13, Peterborough 20, Spalding 20, Swaffham 26 **MD** Thu, Sat **see** Church Peckover House ▯ Library, Ely Place 01945-583263

★★ Crown Lodge ⌂
Downham Road, Outwell, Wisbech PE14 8SE
☎ 01945-773391 **Fax** 01945-772668

For business or pleasure, a warm and attentive atmosphere with a high level of personal service, excellent accommodation and supported by delightful, imaginative home-made food.
10 bedrs, all ensuite, ♦ ♠ ♦ 50 P 45 ⊕ SB £45.95-£48.25 DB £61-£65 L £8 D £15.95 ✕ LD 22:00 ⛦ MC Visa Amex DC JCB ▦ ▦ ♿

★★ ❖ Rose & Crown
Market Place, Wisbech PE13 1DG
☎ 01945-589800 **Fax** 01945-474610
20 bedrs, all ensuite, ④ ♠ ♦ 180 P 20 ⊕ SB £40
DB £60 L ♦ D ♦ ✕ LD 21:30 ⛦ MC Visa Amex DC

WITNEY Oxfordshire 4B2
Pop. 19,000. Oxford 11, London 69, Bicester 18, Burford 7½, Chipping Norton 13, Faringdon 12, Wantage 17 **MD** Thu, Sat **see** Early 18th cent Blanker Hall with one-hand clock, 17th cent Butter Cross Church ▯ Town Hall, Market Square 01993-775802

★★ ❖ Marlborough
28 Market Square, Witney OX8 7BB
☎ 01993-776353 **Fax** 01993-702152
22 bedrs, all ensuite, ♠ ♦ 100 P 20 ⊕ ⛦ MC Visa Amex DC JCB

WOBURN Bedfordshire 4C1
Dunstable 9, London 43, M1 (jn 13) 4, Aylesbury 16, Baldock 22, Bedford 13, Bletchley 5, Northampton 22 **see** St Michael's Church, Woburn Abbey, Park and Wild Animal Kingdom.

★★★★ Bedford Arms
George Street, Woburn MK17 9PX
☎ 01525-290441 **Fax** 01525-290432
53 bedrs, all ensuite, ④ ♠ ♦ 60 P 80 ⊕ SB £100-£105 DB £120-£125 HB £395 L £16.95 L ♦ D £20 D ♦ ✕ LD 22:00 Restaurant closed L Sat ⛦ MC Visa Amex DC ♿

WOLVERHAMPTON West Midlands   7E2

Pop. 247,200. Birmingham 13, London 124, M6 (jn 10) 5, Bridgnorth 14, Kidderminster 15, Lichfield 14, Stafford 15, Walsall 6½ **MD** Mon, Fri, Sat **see** St Peter's Colliegiate Church, Museum and Art Gallery, St John's Church, Bantock House, Moseley Old Hall *i* 18 Queen Square 01902-312051

★★★ Connaught
Tettenhall Road, WV1 4SW
☎ 01902-424433 **Fax** 01902-710353
E-mail conhotel@wolverhampton.co.uk
81 bedrs, 80 ensuite, ⊞ ★ ⊡ ⚌ 250 **P** 100 ⊕
SB £51-£56 **DB** £60-£76.50 **HB** £245-£294 **L** £10.50
L ● **D** £12.50 **D** ● ✕ **LD** 22:30 Restaurant closed D Sun **CC** MC Visa Amex DC JCB ▨ &

★★★ ❖ Novotel Wolverhampton
Union Street, Wolverhampton WV1 3JN
☎ 01902-871100 **Fax** 01902-870054
E-mail h1188@accor-hotels.com
132 bedrs, all ensuite, ⌀ ★ ⊡ ⚌ 150 **P** 107 ⊕
SB £80 **DB** £90 **L** £10 **L** ● **D** £15 **D** ● ✕ **LD** 0:00 **CC** MC Visa Amex DC JCB ⊰ &

★★★ Quality ♜
Penn Road, Wolverhampton WV3 0ER
☎ 01902-429216 **Fax** 01902-710419
E-mail admin@gb069.u-net.com
92 bedrs, all ensuite, ⊞ ♀ ⌀ ★ ⚌ 140 **P** 120 ⊕ **SB** £79 **DB** £85-£105 **L** £11.95
L ● **D** £16.95 **D** ● ✕ **LD** 21:30
CC MC Visa ▨ ▨ ▨

WOODBRIDGE Suffolk   5F1

Pop. 7,700. Ipswich 7½, London 81, Aldeburgh 17, Saxmundham 13, Scole 23, Stowmarket 18 **MD** Thu

★★★ Seckford Hall ♜ ♜
Great Bealings, Woodbridge IP13 6NU
☎ 01394-385678 **Fax** 01394-380610
Closed 25 Dec
32 bedrs, all ensuite, ⊞ ⌀ ★ ⚌ 100 **P** 100 ⊕
SB £79-£99 **DB** £110-£165 **L** £13.50 **D** £26.50 **D** ● ✕
LD 21:30 **CC** MC Visa Amex DC JCB ▨ ▨ ▨

★★★ Ufford Park ♜
Yarmouth Road, Ufford,
Woodbridge IP12 1QW
☎ 01394-383555 **Fax** 01394-383582
E-mail uffordparkltd@btinternet.com
44 bedrs, all ensuite, ⊞ ⌀ ⚌ 200 **P** 150 ⊕
SB £78.50-£83.50 **DB** £107-£112 **HB** £365-£490 **L** £12
L ● **D** £16 ✕ **LD** 21:30 Restaurant closed L Mon-Sat
CC MC Visa Amex DC ▨ ▨ ▨ ▨ ▨ &

WOODHALL SPA Lincolnshire   8C2

Spalding 30, London 129, Boston 14, Horncastle 6, Lincoln 18, Sleaford 17. **EC** Wed **see** Springs and Mineral Baths, Wellington Monument, Tower on the moor, Tattershall Castle 3m SE *i* Museum Iddesleigh Road 01526-353775

★★★ Golf
The Broadway, LN10 6SG   PRINCIPAL HOTELS
☎ 01526-353535 **Fax** 01526-353096
50 bedrs, all ensuite, ★ ⚌ 180 **P** 100 ⊕ **SB** £50-£65
DB £60-£85 **L** £9 **D** £15.95 ✕ **LD** 21:30 Restaurant closed L Mon- Sat **CC** MC Visa Amex DC ▨ &

★★★ Petwood ♜
Stixwould Road, Woodhall Spa LN10 6QF
☎ 01526-352411 **Fax** 01526-353473

Set in 30 acres, this Edwardian hotel of historical interest offers many original features, luxury ensuite accommodation with excellent cuisine and fine wine.
47 bedrs, all ensuite, ⊞ ★ ⊡ ⚌ 150 **P** 120 ⊕ **SB** £70
DB £100 **L** £11 **L** ● **D** £17 **D** ● ✕ **LD** 21:00 Restaurant closed L Mon-Sat **CC** MC Visa Amex DC ▨ &

WOODSTOCK Oxfordshire   4B2

Pop. 2,800. Oxford 8, London 64, Banbury 15, Bicester 11, Burford 15, Chipping Norton 12.
EC Wed **see** Blenheim Place and Garden centre, Grave of Sir Winston Churchill (Bladon Church) *i* Hensington Road 01993-811038

★★★ Bear   Heritage HOTELS
Park Street, Woodstock OX20 1SZ
☎ 01993-811511 **Fax** 01993-813380
44 bedrs, all ensuite, 17. ⊞ ♀ ⌀ ★ ⚌ 40 **P** 30 ⊕
Room £120-£135 **L** £16.50 **L** ● **D** £25 **D** ● ✕ **LD** 21:45
CC MC Visa Amex DC &

WOOLACOMBE Devon   2C2

Pop. 1,200. Dunster 38, London 203, Barnstaple 13, Ilfracombe 5½, Lynmouth 20 **EC** Wed *i* Red Barn Cafe Car Park, Barton Road 01271-870553

★★★ Watersmeet ♙ ♙
Mortehoe, Woolacombe EX34 7EB
☎ 01271-870333 **Fax** 01271-870890
E-mail watersmeethotel@compuserve.com
Closed Dec-mid Feb

Commanding dramatic sea views, Watersmeet offers the comfort and luxury of a country house by the sea, award winning food and is one of the highest rated three star hotels in the south west. 24 bedrs, all ensuite, ▣ ⠿ 40 **P** 17 ⊞ **SB** £35.50-£60.50 **DB** £63-£113 **HB** £329-£553 **L** £12 **D** £16.50 ✕ **LD** 20:30 **CC** MC Visa Amex DC ▣ ⠿ ▣ ▣ ⅋

★★★ Woolacombe Bay
Woolacombe EX34 7BN
☎ 01271-870388 **Fax** 01271-870613
Closed Jan-Feb
65 bedrs, all ensuite, ▣ ▣ ⠿ 200 **P** 200 ⊞ **CC** MC Visa Amex DC JCB ▣ ⠿ ▣ ▣ ▣ ▣ ▣ ▣

★★ Headlands
Beach Road, Woolacombe EX34 7BT
☎ 01271-870320 **Fax** 01271-870320
E-mail headhotel@lineone.net
Closed Nov-Feb
14 bedrs, 10 ensuite, **P** 16 No children under 4 ⊞ **CC** MC Visa ▣

★ Crossways
The Esplanade, Woolacombe EX34 7DJ
☎ 01271-870395 **Fax** 01271-870395
Closed Nov-Feb
9 bedrs, 7 ensuite, ➤ **P** 9 ⊞ Resid **SB** £22-£29 **DB** £44-£58 **HB** £179-£225 **L** ➤ ✕ **LD** 18:30
Restaurant closed L Sat

★ Lundy House
Chapel Hill, Mortehoe, Woolacombe EX34 7RZ
☎ 01271-870372 **Fax** 01271-871001
E-mail libido.london@virgin.net
Closed Jan
8 bedrs, all ensuite, ➤ **P** 8 No children under 6 ⊞ **SB** £20-£30 **DB** £40-£54 **HB** £189-£235 **L** ➤ **D** £9.95 **D** ➤ ✕ **LD** 19:30 **CC** MC Visa

WOOLER Northumberland 13E3
Pop. 2,000. Newcastle upon Tyne 47, London 321, Alnwick 16, Berwick-upon-Tweed 17, Coldstream 13, Corbridge 38, Hexham 37. **MD** Mon, Wed, Sat *see* Ancient British Camps *i* Bus Station Car Park, High Street 01668-281602

★★ Tankerville Arms
Cottage Road, Wooler NE71 6AD
☎ 01668-281581 **Fax** 01668-281387
E-mail enquiries@tankervillehotel.co.uk
16 bedrs, all ensuite, ➤ ▣ 80 **P** 100 ⊞ **SB** £48 **DB** £80 **HB** £350 **L** £9 **D** £17 ✕ **LD** 21:00 **CC** MC Visa

WORCESTER Worcestershire 7E3
Pop. 80,000. Evesham 16, London 114, M5 (jn 7) 2½, Bromyard 14, Droitwich 6½, Hereford 25, Kidderminster 14, Ledbury 16 **MD** Wed, Fri, Sat *see* Cathedral, Greyfriars, Worcester Royal Porcelain Works *i* Guildhall, High Street 01905-726311

★★★ Giffard
Heritage HOTELS
High Street, Worcester WR1 2QR
☎ 01905-726262 **Fax** 01905-723458
102 bedrs, all ensuite, ➤ ▣ ⠿ 150 ⊞ **SB** £35-£40 **DB** £70-£80 **HB** £329-£364 **L** £6.50 **L** ➤ **D** £18.95 ✕ **LD** 21:30 **CC** MC Visa Amex DC JCB

★ ✤ Maximillian
Shrub Hill Road, Worcester WR4 9EF
☎ 0500-829145 **Fax** 01905-724935
17 bedrs, 13 ensuite, ♀ ✎ ⠿ 40 **P** 20 ⊞ **SB** £39 **DB** £52 **HB** £253.75 **D** £15 ✕ **LD** 21:00 Restaurant closed Sun **CC** MC Visa Amex DC ▣

WORKSOP Nottinghamshire 8B1
Pop. 38,000. Newark 25, London 151, Chesterfield 14, Doncaster 16, Lincoln 28, Mansfield 13, Sheffield 18 **MD** Wed, Fri, Sat *see* Priory Church, 13th cent Lady Chapel, 14th cent Gatehouse, ancient Market Cross *i* Library, Memorial Avenue 01909-501148

★★★ Charnwood ♙
Sheffield Road, Blyth, Worksop S81 8HF
☎ 01909-591610 **Fax** 01909-591429
E-mail charnwood@charnwood.com.uk
34 bedrs, all ensuite, ⠿ 150 **P** 80 ⊞ **SB** £55-£70 **DB** £60-£90 **L** £11 **L** ➤ **D** £18 **D** ➤ ✕ **LD** 21:45 **CC** MC Visa Amex DC JCB ▣ ⅋
See advert on opposite page

★★ Lion
112 Bridge Street, Worksop S80 1HT
☎ 01909-477925 Fax 01909-479038
32 bedrs, all ensuite, ⊁ ⊞ 60 P 45 ⊕ SB £55 DB £65 HB £427 L £12.75 L ☞ D £12.75 D ☞ ✕ LD 21:30
《 MC Visa Amex ⊠ 圖 ⊛

WORTHING West Sussex   4C4
Pop. 99,970. Horsham 20, London 56, Arundel 10, Brighton 11, Littlehampton 8½, Pulborough 14
MD Sat see Museum & Art Gallery, Salvington Mill, Cissbury Ring, Sompting Church (Saxon) 1½m
🛈 Chapel Road 01903-210022

★★★ Beach 🍴
Marine Parade, Worthing BN11 3QJ
☎ 01903-234001 Fax 01903-234567

Full length ground floor terrace adjacent to restaurant, foyer, lounge and terrace bar.
85 bedrs, all ensuite, 🖵 ⊞ 200 P 55 ⊕ 《 MC Visa Amex DC ⊠ ⊛
See advert on this page

★★★ ✦ Berkeley
86-95 Marine Parade, Worthing BN11 3QD
☎ 01903-820000 Fax 01903-821333
E-mail berkeley@wakefordhotels.co.uk
84 bedrs, all ensuite, ⊞ ♀ ⊘ 🖵 ⊞ 140 P 25 ⊕
SB £66.50-£70.50 DB £91-£96 HB £350 L £11.95 L ☞ D £14.95 D ☞ ✕ LD 21:15 Restaurant closed L Mon-Sat 《 MC Visa Amex DC ⊛

★★★ Chatsworth
Steyne, Worthing BN11 3DU
☎ 01903-236103 Fax 01903-823726
E-mail chatsbn@aol.com
107 bedrs, all ensuite, ⊁ 🖵 ⊞ 150 P 150 ⊕ SB £55-£65 DB £84-£92 HB £315 L £9.95 L ☞ D £15.95 ✕ LD 21:00 《 MC Visa Amex DC ⊠ ⊛

★★★ ❖ Kingsway
Marine Parade, Worthing BN11 3QQ
☎ 01903-237542 **Fax** 01903-204173
28 bedrs, all ensuite, ✝ 🖭 ✦ 40 **P** 12 ⊞ ⦅ MC Visa Amex DC ⦆

★★★ ❖ Windsor House
14/20 Windsor Road,
Worthing BN11 2LX
☎ 01903-239655 **Fax** 01903-210763
E-mail thewindsorhotel@compuserve.com
30 bedrs, all ensuite, 🄴 ✦ 150 **P** 18 ⊞ **SB** £55–£80
DB £75–£110 **HB** £260–£290 **L** £5.50 **D** £17 **D** 🍴 ✕
LD 21:30 ⦅ MC Visa Amex DC JCB ⊠ ⦆

★★ ❖ Cavendish
115-116 Marine Parade, Worthing BN11 3QG
☎ 01903-236767 **Fax** 01903-823840
15 bedrs, all ensuite, ✝ ✦ 30 **P** 6 ⊞ **SB** £45 **DB** £60–
£75 **HB** £260–£290 **L** £13 **L** 🍴 **D** £13 **D** 🍴 ✕ **LD** 21:30
⦅ MC Visa Amex DC

WROTHAM Kent   5D3
Swanley 11, London 29, M26 (jn 2), Maidstone 8,
Sevenoaks 9.

★★★ Posthouse   **Posthouse**
London Road, Wrotham,
Sevenoaks TN15 7RS
☎ 01732-883311 **Fax** 01732-885850
106 bedrs, all ensuite, ✝ ✦ 60 **P** 100 ⊞ **SB** £29–£36
Room £69–£95 **L** £14 **D** £19.50 **D** 🍴 ✕ **LD** 22:30 ⦅ MC
Visa Amex DC ⊠ ⊠ ⊠ ⦆

WROXHAM Norfolk   9F3
Pop. 1,400. Norwich 7, London 118, Cromer 18,
Fakenham 29, Great Yarmouth 19 **E** Wed

★★ Hotel Wroxham ⮞
Broads Centre, Wroxham NR12 8AJ
☎ 01603-782061 **Fax** 01603-784279

Beside the River Bure, only seven miles from
Norwich on A1151, the Hotel Wroxham is a
riverside oasis catering for the leisure and business
visitor. Its unique bar and restaurant offers a la
carte and bar snacks. Excellent wedding &
conference facilities.
18 bedrs, all ensuite, ✝ ✦ 200 **P** 60 ⊞ **SB** £35–£45
DB £60–£80 **L** £5.45 **D** £5.95 **D** 🍴 ✕ **LD** 21:00 ⦅ MC
Visa Amex JCB ☑ ⦆
See advert on this page

WYMONDHAM Norfolk   9E3
Pop. 9,100. Thetford 19, London 101, East
Dereham 11, Lowestoft 31, Norwich 9, Scole 18
MD Fri **see** Abbey Church, Market Cross.

★★ Wymondham Consort ⮞
28 Market Street, Wymondham NR18 OBB
☎ 01953-606721 **Fax** 01953-601361
E-mail reservations@wymondamconsort.freeserve.co.uk

ENGLAND

Award winning hotel and restaurant ideally situated in the centre of an historic market town. Excellent touring base for Norfolk Broads, the Norfolk coast, countryside and Norwich City.
20 bedrs, all ensuite, ④ ♪ ♔ **P** 14 No children under 8 ⊞ Rest Resid **SB** £55-£60 **DB** £68-£75
HB £255-£270 **L** £10.95 **L** ♥ **D** £16.95 **D** ♥ ✗
LD 21:30 ℂℂ MC Visa Amex DC JCB 🖾 ᴗ

YATTENDON Berkshire   4B2
Pop. 240. Reading 11, London 49, M4 (jn 13) 5½, Newbury 8

THE
ROYAL OAK

A traditional, brick-built, 16th century inn set in the heart of the attractive village of Yattendon.

THE SQUARE,
YATTENDON RG18 0UG
Tel: 01635-201325
Fax: 01635-201926

★★ Royal Oak 🏾 🏾
The Square, Yattendon RG18 OUG
☎ 01635-201325 **Fax** 01635-201926

An elegant and intimate 16th century coaching inn with a delightful summer walled garden and winter log fires! An individual hotel renowned for its creative cooking, imaginative wine list and seven enchanting bedrooms. An ideal hideaway.
7 bedrs, all ensuite, ♔ ⠇ 30 ⊞ ℂℂ MC Visa Amex DC
See advert on this page

YEOVIL Somerset   3E2
Pop. 37,900. Sherborne 5, London 125, Crewkeme 8, Dorchester 18, Glastonbury 17, Ilminster 13, Wincanton 14 **MD** Mon, Fri **see** Church, Wymondham (Hendford Manor Hall), Montacute House 4m W
ℹ Petter's House, Petter's Way 01935-71279

★★★ ✤ Manor
28 Hendford, Yeovil BA20 1TG
☎ 01935-23116 **Fax** 01935-706607
41 bedrs, all ensuite, ④ ♔ ⠇ 60 **P** 41 ⊞ ℂℂ MC Visa Amex DC

★★★ Yeovil Court 🏾 🏾
West Coker Road, Yeovil BA20 2NE
☎ 01935-863746 **Fax** 01935-863990
26 bedrs, all ensuite, ♪ ♔ ⠇ 50 **P** 46 ⊞ Rest Resid
SB £55-£65 **DB** £65-£75 **D** £19 **D** ♥ ✗ **LD** 21:45
Restaurant closed L Sat, D Sun ℂℂ MC Visa Amex DC

YORK North Yorkshire   11D3
Pop. 99,000. Selby 13, London 193, Boroughbridge 17, Harrogate 22, Helmsley 24, Leeds 24, Malton 17, Market Weighton 19, Pontefract 25, Thirsk 23
MD Daily **see** Minster, Wall and Gates, St Mary's Abbey ruins, Clifford's Tower, All Saints' Church (North St), Holy Trinity Church, Guildhall, Mansion Ho (by appt), The Shambles, City of York Art Gallery, Railway Musm, Viking Centre. ℹ Travel Office, 6 Rougier Street 01904-620557

★★★★ Royal York
Station Road, York YO24 1AA
📞 01904-653681 **Fax** 01904-623503

Set in 3 acres of private landscaped gsardens, the recently refurbished Royal York Hotel enjoys spectacular views over the city and York Minster. Large private car park and adjacent to mainline railway.
158 bedrs, all ensuite, ⌀ 🔲 ⊞ 280 **P** 120 ⊕
SB £119.50 **DB** £156 **HB** £414 **L** £11.95
L 🍷 **D** £18.50 ✕ **LD** 21:45
CC MC Visa Amex DC ⊞ 🔲 🔲 ⅄

★★★★ Swallow 🍴
Tadcaster Road, Dringhouses,
York YO2 2QQ
📞 01904-701000 **Fax** 01904-702308
E-mail info@swallowhotels.com

Standing in its own grounds, just over a mile from the city centre, this fine hotel with leisure facilities, has good views over the racecourse and the Knavesmire parkland.
112 bedrs, all ensuite, ⊞ ⊀ 🔲 ⊞ 170 **P** 200 ⊕
SB £99-£125 **DB** £115-£140 **L** £14.50 **D** £20.45 ✕
LD 22:00 **CC** MC Visa Amex DC ⊞ ⊞ 🔲 ⅄

★★★ Ambassador
123-125 The Mount, York YO2 2DA
📞 01904-641316 **Fax** 01904-640259
E-mail stay@ambassadorhotel.co.uk

Beautiful bedrooms and award winning Grays Restaurant, where the food is simple and delicious. Easy walk to the city centre or racecourse. Ample car parking.
25 bedrs, all ensuite, ⌀ 🔲 ⊞ 50 **P** 30 ⊕ Resid
SB £89-£99 **DB** £105-£115 **D** £19.50 ✕ **LD** 21:30
Restaurant closed L Mon-Sat **CC** MC Visa Amex

★★★ Dean Court
Duncombe Place, York YO1 2EF
📞 01904-625082 **Fax** 01904-620305
E-mail deancourt@btconnect.com

An unrivalled position in the heart of this historic city and in the very shadow of majestic York Minster. The imposing Grade II Listed building was originally built in 1850 to provide housing for the clergy.
39 bedrs, all ensuite, ⊞ 🔲 ⊞ 32 **P** 30 ⊕ **SB** £72-£80
DB £90-£160 **L** £9.75 **D** £23.50 ✕ **LD** 21:30 **CC** MC
Visa Amex DC JCB

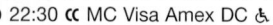

★★★ Grange 🍴 🍴 🍴
Blue Ribbon Hotel
Clifton, York YO3 6AA
📞 01904-644744 **Fax** 01904-612453
E-mail info@grangrhotel.co.uk
30 bedrs, all ensuite, ⊞ ⌀ ⊀ ⊞ 50 **P** 26 ⊕ **SB** £99-
£160 **DB** £110-£210 **L** £9.50 **L** 🍷 **D** £25 **D** 🍷 ✕
LD 22:30 **CC** MC Visa Amex DC ⅄

ENGLAND

★★★ Hudsons
60 Bootham, York YO3 7BZ
☎ 01904-621267 **Fax** 01904-654719
31 bedrs, all ensuite, 4 ♀ 🖃 ⚏ 85 **P** 34 ⊕ **SB** £60-£75 **DB** £90-£115 **L** ➤ **D** £17 **D** ➤ ✕ **LD** 21:00
Restaurant closed L Sun **CC** MC Visa Amex DC JCB
See advert on this page

★★★ Judges Lodging
9 Lendal, York YO1 2AQ
☎ 01904-638733 **Fax** 01904-679947
E-mail j.lodging@aol.com

Set in the very heart of York, the Judges Lodging hotel is a privately owned Grade I Listed building, offering impressive Minster views, spa baths and fourposter beds. With secure on site parking, leave your car and explore the history of York on foot.
14 bedrs, all ensuite, 4 **P** 16 No children under 10 ⊕ **SB** £75-£85 **DB** £95-£140 **L** ➤ **D** £14.95 **D** ➤ ✕ **LD** 21:30 **CC** MC Visa Amex DC

♤ ★★★ Middlethorpe Hall
Gold Ribbon Hotel
Bishopthorpe Road, York YO23 2GB
☎ 01904-641241 **Fax** 01904-620176
30 bedrs, all ensuite, 4 🖃 ⚏ 56 **P** 70 No children under 8 ⊕ **CC** MC Visa 🗄

★★★ Monk Bar
St Maurice's Road, York YO3 7JA
☎ 01904-638086 **Fax** 01904-629195
48 bedrs, all ensuite, 4 🐾 🖃 ⚏ 70 **P** 70 ⊕ **SB** £75 **DB** £125 **HB** £585 **L** £9.95 **D** £16.95 **D** ➤ ✕ **LD** 22:00
CC MC Visa Amex DC ♿
See advert on this page

★★★ Mount Royale ⌂ ⌂

The Mount, York YO24 1GU
☎ 01904-628856 **Fax** 01904-611171
E-mail mountroyale@mountroyale.co.uk
23 bedrs, all ensuite, ☒ ↟ ⚌ 16 P 24 ⊕ Rest Resid
SB £72.50-£100 **DB** £85-£130 **L** ● **D** £18.50 ✕
LD 21:30 **CC** MC Visa Amex DC JCB ⚏ ▣ ▨
See advert on this page

★★★ Novotel York

Fishergate, York YO1 4AD
☎ 01904-611660 **Fax** 01904-610925
E-mail h0949-gm@accor-hotels.com
124 bedrs, all ensuite, ✐ ↟ ▣ ⚌ 210 P 160 ⊕
SB £69.50-£89.50 **DB** £79.50-£99 **L** £13 **D** £13 ✕
LD 0:00 **CC** MC Visa Amex DC ▣ ⅋

★★★ Parsonage Country House ⌂ ⌂ ⌂

Main Street, Escrick, York Y04 6LF
☎ 01904-728111 **Fax** 01904-728151
21 bedrs, all ensuite, ☒ ⚌ 160 P 120 ⊕ **SB** £95
DB £120-£130 **L** £12 **L** ● **D** £19.75 ✕ **LD** 21.30 **CC** MC
Visa Amex DC
See advert on this page

★★★ Posthouse

Posthouse

Tadcaster Road, York YO24 2QF
☎ 01904-707921 **Fax** 01904-702804
143 bedrs, all ensuite, ↟ ▣ ⚌ 100 P 137 ⊕ **CC** MC
Visa Amex DC

★★ Abbots Mews

Marygate Lane, Bootham, York YO3 7DE
☎ 01904-634866 **Fax** 01904-612848
Closed Dec 31st
50 bedrs, all ensuite, ⚌ 50 P 30 ⊕ Rest Resid
SB £30-£50 **DB** £51 **L** £8.95 **D** £14.50 **D** ● ✕ **LD** 21:30
Restaurant closed L Mon-Sat, D Sun **CC** MC Visa
Amex DC ♿

ENGLAND

★★ Alhambra Court
31 St Marys, Bootham, York YO3 7DD
☎ 01904-628474 **Fax** 01904-610690

Ideal location, a quiet cul de sac five minutes walk to the city centre. Offers well appointed bedrooms, comfortable lounges, a bar and a non smoking restaurant. Private car park. Lift.
24 bedrs, all ensuite, ▣ ⊁ ⊡ **P** 20 ⊕ Rest Resid
SB £31.50-£47.50 **DB** £45-£75 **D** £13.50 ✕ **LD** 21:00
⊄ MC Visa

★★ Ashcroft
294 Bishopthorpe Road, York YO2 1LH
☎ 01904-659286 **Fax** 01904-640107
Closed Christmas
15 bedrs, all ensuite, ⊁ **P** 40 No children under 5 ⊕
SB £42-£48 **DB** £50-£80 **L** £8 **D** £14.50 ✕ **LD** 20:30
Restaurant closed Sat-Sun ⊄ MC Visa Amex DC
JCB ⅙

★★ Beechwood Close
19 Shipton Road, York YO30 5RE
☎ 01904-658378 **Fax** 01904-647124
E-mail bch@dial.pipex.com
Closed 25 Dec

Former house standing in its own grounds. Just within York city boundaries.
14 bedrs, all ensuite, ⚌ 40 **P** 36 ⊕ Rest Resid
SB £44-£46 **DB** £65-£75 **HB** £296-£359 **L** £8 **D** £14 **D** ✇
✕ **LD** 21:00 ⊄ MC Visa Amex DC JCB

★★ Cottage
3 Clifton Green, York YO3 6LH
☎ 01904-643711 **Fax** 01904-611230
Closed Christmas

Two connected stone-built Victorian houses overlooking the village green, 15 minutes from city centre.
20 bedrs, all ensuite, ▣ ⊁ **P** 12 ⊕ Resid **SB** £30-£45
DB £45-£70 **L** £13 **D** £26 ✕ **LD** 20:30 ⊄ MC Visa
Amex DC

★★ ❖ Elmbank
The Mount, York YO2 2DD
☎ 01904-610653 **Fax** 01904-627139
48 bedrs, all ensuite, ⊁ ⚌ 100 **P** 20 ⊕ ⊄ MC Visa
Amex DC 🖼

★★ Heworth Court

76-78 Heworth Green, York YO3 7TQ
☎ 01904-425156 **Fax** 01904-415290
E-mail hotel@heworth.co.uk

This family-run hotel is a brick built, two storey building with an attractive courtyard and well-maintained gardens. Situated close to the city centre. www.heworth.co.uk
25 bedrs, all ensuite, 📺 ♀ 🖊 ⅲ 18 **P** 25 ⅏ Rest Resid **SB** £45-£57.50 **DB** £45-£85 **HB** £174-£252 **L** £10.95 **D** £16.95 ✕ **LD** 21:30 **CC** MC Visa Amex DC &
See advert on previous page

★★ Kilima

129 Holgate Road, York YO24 4AZ
☎ 01904-625787 **Fax** 01904-612083
15 bedrs, all ensuite, 📺 ♪ 🖊 ⅲ 24 **P** 20 ⅏ **SB** £55 **DB** £82-£94 **HB** £354 **L** £13.50 **D** £18.95 ✕ **LD** 21:30 **CC** MC Visa Amex DC &

★★ Knavesmire Manor

302 Tadcaster Road, York YO2 2HE
☎ 01904-702941 **Fax** 01904-709274

Once a Rowntree family home (c.1833), this Georgian hotel close to the city centre overlooks York racecourse. Walled gardens and car park. Tropical indoor pool and spa.
21 bedrs, all ensuite, 📺 🖊 🔳 ⅲ 26 **P** 26 ⅏ Rest Resid **SB** £40-£59 **DB** £55-£79 **HB** £210-£280 **L** £9.95 **D** £13.50 ✕ **LD** 21:15 Restaurant closed L Mon-Sat **CC** MC Visa Amex DC JCB 🔳 🌣 📺

★★ Newington

147 Mount Vale, York YO2 2DJ
☎ 01904-625173 **Fax** 01904-679937
42 bedrs, all ensuite, 📺 🔳 **P** 35 ⅏ Rest Resid **SB** £42-£44 **DB** £58-£68 **HB** £287 **D** £14 ✕ **LD** 20:30 **CC** MC Visa Amex 🔳 📺

★★ Savages

St Peters Grove, Clifton, York YO3 6AQ
☎ 01904-610818 **Fax** 01904-627729
Closed 25-26 Dec
20 bedrs, all ensuite, 📺 **P** 15 ⅏ Resid **SB** £28-£38 **DB** £50-£68 **L** 📞 **D** £12 **D** 📞 ✕ **LD** 21:00 **CC** MC Visa Amex DC &
See advert on this page

SPENCER'S

The British Golf Directory

Courses where you can turn up and play

This new Spencer's guide provides full details of golf courses the length and breadth of Britain. All are courses where you can turn up and play, from municipal courses to some of the grandest in the land. You don't need to be members or pay membership fees. Just the rate for the round.

Whether you are an old hand or one of the new wave of golf enthusiasts you will find Spencer's Directory an invaluable companion - for your home, for your car or for your holidays.

With full-colour throughout it's easy-to-use, highly practical and perfect for browsing.

Each entry has a full quarter-page, with a description of the course, and information on yardage, par, standard scratch score, directions and green fees. There's also a full-colour route-planning and map section - a feature of all Spencer's titles.

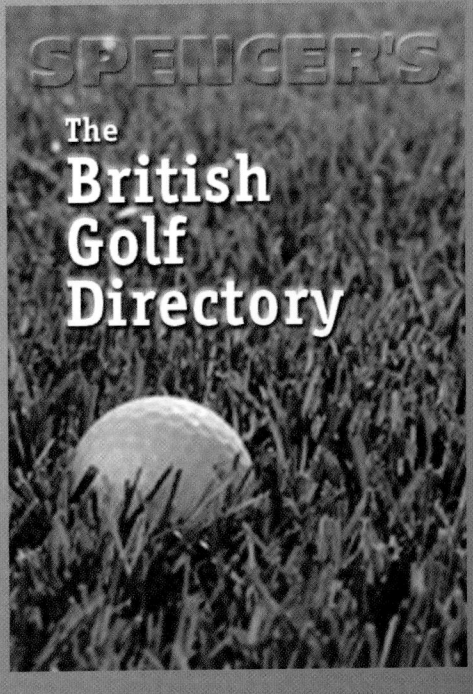

Format:	210x148mm
No. of pages:	112pp
ISBN:	1 900327 51 1
Price:	£4.99
Publication date:	April 2000

West One Publishing
Kestrel House, Duke's PLace
Marlow, Bucks SL7 2QH

tel: 01628 487722

www.WestOneWeb.com

Scotland

ABERDEEN Aberdeenshire 15F3

Pop. 214,100. Stonehaven 14, London 491, Banff 46, Braemar 58, Edinburgh 117, Glasgow 136, Huntly 38, Petershead 32 **MD** Fri **see** Cathedral of Machar, St Andrew's Episcopal Cathedral, St. Mary's RC Cathedral, University (Marischal and King's Colleges), 17th cent Mercat Cross, Art Gallery and Regional Museum **i** St Nicholas House, Broad Street 01224-632727

★★★★ Copthorne

122 Huntly Street, Aberdeen AB10 1SU
☎ 01224-630404 **Fax** 01224-640573
89 bedrs, all ensuite, **↑** **▣** **⫶** 200 **P** 20 **⊞** **SB** £50-£147 **DB** £72-£162 **L** £9.95 **D** £18.50 **✕** **LD** 22:00 **cc** MC Visa Amex DC

★★★ Posthouse   **Posthouse**

Claymore Drive, Bridge of Don,
Aberdeen AB23 8BL
☎ 01224-706707 **Fax** 01224-823923
123 bedrs, all ensuite, **↑** **▣** **P** 300 **⊞** **cc** MC Visa Amex DC JCB **&**

★★★ Westhill

Westhill, Aberdeen AB32 6TT
☎ 01224-740388 **Fax** 01224-744354
48 bedrs, all ensuite, **✐** **↑** **▣** **⫶** 300 **P** 300 **⊞**
SB £42-£65 **DB** £54-£84 **L** £7 **L** **♥** **D** £16 **D** **♥** **✕**
LD 21:30 Restaurant closed Sun **cc** MC Visa Amex DC **▦** **▦** **&**

Ardoe House

Blairs, South Deeside Road, Aberdeen AB1 5YP
☎ 01224-867355 **Fax** 01224-861283

Built in Scottish baronial style, this country house hotel is set in 20 acres of magnificent parkland. Traditional decor, enormous fireplaces and individually styled bedrooms. Award winning cuisine.
71 bedrs, all ensuite, **▣** **↑** **▣** **⫶** 200 **P** 150 **⊞** **cc** MC Visa Amex DC **&**

ABERDOUR Fife 13D2

Pop. 1,200. London 392, Edinburgh 17, Kincardine 17, Kinross 13, Kirkcaldy 8 **EC** Wed

★★★ Woodside **♟**

High Street, Aberdour KY3 0SW
☎ 01383-860328 **Fax** 01383-860920
E-mail austen_peter@compuserve.com

A traditional building with a pleasing red sandstone facade which contrasts with the white paintwork. In an attractive village, convenient for Edinburgh. Website: www.woodside-hotel.demon.co.uk.
20 bedrs, all ensuite, **▣** **↑** **⫶** 50 **P** 40 **⊞** **SB** £55-£65 **DB** £70-£80 **L** **♥** **D** £19 **D** **♥** **✕** **LD** 21:30 **cc** MC Visa Amex JCB
See advert on this page

ABERFELDY Perthshire 12C1

Pop. 1,500. Crief 22, London 438, Blairgowrie 29, Crainlarich 37, Edinburgh 68, Perth 31, Pitlochry 14 **EC** Wed **see** Blackwatch Monument, General Wade's Bridge ℹ The Square 01887-820276

★★★ ❖ Moness House

Crieff Road, Aberfeldy PH15 2DY
☎ 01887-820446 **Fax** 01887-820062
E-mail moness@btinternet.com

Historic house renowned for its fine food, friendly atmosphere and extensive leisure facilities. Located near the famous 'Berks of Aberfeldy', makes the ideal touring base.

12 bedrs, all ensuite, ♀ ⋕ 120 **P** 60 ⊕ **SB** £25-£50 **DB** £50-£75 **HB** £250-£325 **L** £7.50 **L** ● **D** £17.95 **D** ● ✕ **LD** 21:00 **CC** MC Visa Amex DC ▣ ▦ ▨ ▧

★★ Weem

Weem, Aberfeldy PH15 2LD
☎ 01887-820381 **Fax** 01887-829720
E-mail weem@compuserve.com

An elaboration of the original 17th century 'Inn of Weem', one mile from the literal centre of Scotland, this beautiful Listed building must be custodian to many interesting secrets.

12 bedrs, all ensuite, ✝ ⋕ 25 **P** 20 ⊕ **CC** MC Visa

ABERLADY East Lothian 13E2

Pop. 1,200. Haddington 5, London 374, Edinburgh 15, Glasgow 60, Peebles 32 **see** Parish Church, Mercat Cross, Nature Reserve

★★ Kilspindie House

Main Street, Aberlady EH32 0RE
☎ 01875-870682 **Fax** 01875-870504
E-mail khh@stones.com

26 bedrs, all ensuite, ▨ ✝ ⋕ 60 **P** 30 ⊕ **SB** £40-£49 **DB** £60-£74 **L** ● **D** £15 **D** ● ✕ **LD** 21:30 **CC** MC Visa DC JCB ♿

ABINGTON Lanarkshire 13D3

Pop. 200. Biggar 11, Edinburgh 30, Glasgow 36, London 351, Ayr 45, Peebles 30 **EC** Wed **see** Iron Age Fort ℹ Services, Jn 13 M74 01864-502436

★★ Abington

Carlisle Road, Abington ML12 6SD
☎ 01864-502467 **Fax** 01864-502223
E-mail enquiry@abington-hotel.nd.ree.co.uk

Easily found (M74, junction 13/14), this family run hotel stands in the heart of a tranquil village. The centres of Glasgow, Edinburgh, Ayrshire and Loch Lomond are all an hour or less away. Parking is easy and free.

28 bedrs, all ensuite, ⋕ 60 **P** 30 ⊕ **SB** £45 **DB** £60-£65 **HB** £245-£300 **D** £11.95 ✕ **LD** 20:30 **CC** MC Visa Amex DC

AIRDRIE Lanarkshire 12C2

Pop. 37,500. M8 (jn 8) 3½, Lanark 17, London 385, Edinburgh 33, Glasgow 11, Kincardine 21, Peebles 40, Stirling 19 **MD** Tue, Fri

★★★ Tudor

39 Alexandra Street, Airdrie ML6 0BA
☎ 01236-764144 **Fax** 01236-747589
20 bedrs, 18 ensuite, ⋕ 250 **P** 150 ⊕ **CC** MC Visa Amex ♿
See advert on next page

TUDOR
HOTEL

*One of Lanarkshire's oldest family
hotels. Completely refurbished
and offering a choice of three different
restaurants and various function suites.
All bedrooms equipped with cable TV.*

**39 ALEXANDRA STREET,
AIRDRIE,
LANARKSHIRE ML6 0BA
Tel: 01236-764144
Fax: 01236-747589**

ANSTRUTHER Fife   13E2
Pop. 3,300. Largs 10, London 422, Edinburgh 48,
Kircaldy 22, Perth 38, St Andrews 9, **EC** Wed
Scottish Fisheries Museum 01333-311073

★★ Craw's Nest
Bankwell Road, Anstruther KY10 3DA
01333-310691 **Fax** 01333-312216
E-mail crawsnest@compuserve.com
50 bedrs, all ensuite, 4 ‼ 250 **P** 57 ⊞ **SB** £40-£65
DB £70-£130 **L** £12.95 **L** ♥ **D** £20.50 **D** ♥ ✕ **LD** 20:30
CC MC Visa Amex DC

★★ Smugglers Inn
High Street East, Anstruther KY10 3DQ
01333-310506 **Fax** 01333-312706
E-mail smugglers@norscot.ldps.co.uk
9 bedrs, all ensuite, ↑ ‼ **P** 16 No children under 5
⊞ **SB** £27.50-£31 **DB** £55-£62 **HB** £240-£270 **L** ♥
D £6.50 **D** ♥ ✕ **LD** 14:00 **CC** MC Visa

ARBROATH Angus   13E1
Pop. 24,000. Dundee 16, London 445, Brechin 12,
Edinburgh 71, Forfar 15, Glasgow 95, Montrose 13
EC Wed **see** Abbey Ruins, St Vigean's Church and
Museum Market Place 01241-872609

★★ Hotel Seaforth
Dundee Road, Arbroath DD11 1QF
01241-872232 **Fax** 01241-877473

19 ensuite bedrooms, most overlooking the sea.
Full leisure centre. Bar, restaurant, two function
rooms. Ideal location for golf, sea angling and
shooting. Resident proprietors Bill and Sandra
Rennie.
19 bedrs, all ensuite, ♪ ↑ ‼ 120 **P** 100 ⊞ **SB** £45
DB £58 **L** £8.50 **L** ♥ **D** £10.95 **D** ♥ ✕ **LD** 20:45 **CC** MC
Visa Amex 🔲 🔲 🔲 🔲

ARISAIG Inverness-shire   14B4
Fort William 35, London 525, Edinburgh 167,
Glasgow 134, Mallaig 8

★★ Arisaig
Arisaig PH39 4NH
01687-450210 **Fax** 01687-450310
E-mail arisaighotel@dial.pipex.com
Closed 24-26 Dec

Tastefully furnished with 13 bedrooms, all ensuite.
Close to superb sandy beaches, trips to islands
during summer. Bar meals and restaurant open
daily. Children welcome.
13 bedrs, all ensuite, ↑ ‼ 20 **P** 30 ⊞ **SB** £25-£36
DB £50-£72 **L** ♥ **D** £17 **D** ♥ ✕ **LD** 20:30 **CC** MC Visa

AUCHENCAIRN Kirkcudbrightshire   12C4

Pop. 170. Dalbeattie 7, London 348, Edinburgh 91, Dumfries 21, Gatehouse of Fleet 19, Glasgow 90, New Galloway 22 **EC** Wed

★★★ Balcary Bay ⎇ ⎇
Auchencairn DG7 1QZ
☎ 01556-640217 **Fax** 01556-640272
Closed Dec-Feb

Beautiful and secluded situation ideally located for outdoor pursuits and exploring the south-west. Personal supervision ensures a warm welcome, good food and fine wines.
17 bedrs, all ensuite, ⊢ **P** 50 ⊕ **SB** £59 **DB** £104-£118 **HB** £301-£455 **L** £10.75 **L** ⊌ **D** £24.75 ✕ **LD** 20:30 **CC** MC Visa Amex

AUCHTERARDER Perthshire   13D1

Dunfermline 23, London 414, Crieff 9, Edinburgh 39, Glasgow 45, Kincardine 24, Kinross 19, Perth 14, Stirling 20 ⓘ 90 High Street 01764-663450

★★ ❖ Cairn Lodge
Orchil Road, Auchterarder PH3 1LX
☎ 01764-662634 **Fax** 01764-664866
7 bedrs, all ensuite, ⫚ 45 **P** 40 ⊕ **CC** MC Visa Amex
&

AULTBEA Ross-shire   14C2

Pop. 500. Dundonnell 20, London 602, Beauly 68, Edinburgh 238, Ullapool 50 **EC** Wed **see** Inverewe Gardens

Aultbea
Aultbea IV22 2HX
☎ 01445-731201 **Fax** 01445-731214
E-mail aultbea.hotel@btinternet.com

A traditional stone-built, 18th century hotel on the shores of Loch Ewe. Spectacular views. All day dining - fully licensed.
11 bedrs, all ensuite, ⊢ ⫚ 18 **P** 30 ⊕ **SB** £38 **DB** £76 **HB** £330-£350 **L** £6 **D** £21 ✕ **LD** 21:00 **CC** MC Visa Amex JCB

AYR Ayrshire   12C3

Pop. 49,500. Dalmellington 14, London 381, Girvan 21, Glasgow 33, Kilmarnock 12 **MD** Mon,Tue **see** Burn's Cottage, Monument, Statue, House and Gardens (Alloway), The Twa Brigs, Tam O'Shanter Inn. ⓘ Burns House, Burns Statue Square 01292-288688

★★★ Belleisle House ⚑
Doonfoot, Ayr KA7 4DU
📞 01292-442331 **Fax** 01292-445325
14 bedrs, all ensuite, ④ ⊬ ⚌ 380 **P** 50 ⊕ **SB** £50
DB £75 **L** £10 **D** £17 ✕ **LD** 21:30 **CC** MC Visa Amex ▣

★★★ ✤ Kylestrome
Miller Road, Ayr KA7 2AX
📞 01292-262474 **Fax** 01292-260863
Closed 26 Dec, 1 Jan
12 bedrs, all ensuite, ♨ ⚌ 60 **P** 40 ⊕ **SB** £50-£55
DB £75-£80 **L** £9.95 **L** ♥ **D** £17.95 **D** ♥ ✕ **LD** 22:00
CC MC Visa Amex DC ♿

★★★ Quality
Burns Statue Square, Ayr KA7 3AT
📞 01292-263268 **Fax** 01292-262293
E-mail admin@gb624.u-net.com

Magnificent Victorian building overlooking Burns
Statue Square in this lovely seaside town, the heart
of poet's country. Bedrooms ensuite with all
facilities. Including indoor leisure centre.
70 bedrs, all ensuite, ⊬ ▣ ⚌ 250 **P** 74 ⊕ **SB** £79.50-
£91 **DB** £100.50-£112.75 **D** £14.50 ✕ **LD** 21:45 **CC** MC
Visa Amex DC ▨ ▣ ♿

★★★ Savoy Park ⚑
16 Racecourse Road, Ayr KA7 2UT
📞 01292-266112 **Fax** 01292-611488
E-mail mail@savoypark.com
15 bedrs, all ensuite, ♨ ⊬ ⚌ 100 **P** 80 ⊕ **DB** £75-
£100 **L** £6 **L** ♥ **D** £16.50 **D** ♥ ✕ **LD** 21:00 **CC** MC
Visa Amex JCB
See advert on previous page

Facilities for the disabled
Hotels do their best to cater for disabled
visitors. However, it is advisable to contact
the hotel direct to ensure it can provide a
particular requirement.

BALLATER Aberdeenshire   15E4
Pop. 1,200. Braemar 16, London 479, Aberdeen 41,
Edinburgh 104, Grantown-on-Spey 37, Huntly 40,
EC Thu **see** Falls of Muick, Lochnagar 3,786 ft, Loch
Kinord 4m NE, Balmoral Castle grounds and
Craithie Church 8m W, Highland Games in Aug
🅘 Station Square 013397-55306

★★★ Darroch Learg ⚑ ⚑ ⚑
Blue Ribbon Hotel
Braemar Road, Ballater AB35 5UX
📞 013397-55443 **Fax** 013397-55252
E-mail darroch.learg@exodus.uk.com
Closed Jan
18 bedrs, all ensuite, ④ ⊬ ⚌ 20 **P** 25 ⊕ Restricted
Resid **SB** £55-£70 **DB** £80-£140 **HB** £515-£630
L £17.50 **L** ♥ **D** £31.50 ✕ **LD** 21:00 **CC** MC Visa Amex
DC JCB

★★ ✤ Monaltrie
5 Bridge Square, Ballater AB35 5QJ
📞 013397-55417 **Fax** 013397-55180
24 bedrs, all ensuite, ⊬ ⚌ 80 **P** 40 ⊕ **CC** MC Visa
Amex DC

BALLOCH Dunbartonshire   12C2
Pop. 1,700. Glasgow 18, London 406, Arrochar 18,
Crianlarich 33, Dumbarton 5, Edinburgh 60,
Lochearnhead 41, Stirling 29 **EC** Wed **see** Loch
Lomond, Cameron Estate Gardens, Wildlife &
Leisure Park 🅘 Balloch Road 01389-753533

★★ Balloch
Balloch G83 8LQ
📞 01389-752579 **Fax** 01389-755604
14 bedrs, all ensuite, ⊬ **P** 30 ⊕ **CC** MC Visa Amex
DC

BANCHORY Kincardineshire   15F4
Pop. 5,300. Fettercain 17, London 480, Aberdeen
18, Braemar 40, Edinburgh 105, Huntly 42,
Stonehaven 16 **EC** Thu **see** Bridge of Feugh, Crathes
Castle 2m E 🅘 Bridge Street 01330-822000

★★★ Banchory Lodge ⚑ ⚑ ⚑
Blue Ribbon Hotel
Dee Street, Banchory AB31 5HS
📞 01330-822625 **Fax** 01330-825019

Situated five minutes from Banchory town centre, a Georgian country house hotel in a picturesque and tranquil riverside setting beside the River Dee.
22 bedrs, all ensuite, ⁜ ⊩ ⠿ 30 **P** 50 ⊕ ⠉ MC Visa Amex DC

★★★ Raemoir House ♙ ♙ ♙
Raemoir, Banchory AB31 4ED
☎ 01330-824884 **Fax** 01330-822171
E-mail raemoirhse@aol.com

Raemoir House is a splendid country mansion set in an idyllic 3,500 acre estate, and situated on beautiful Royal Deeside.
20 bedrs, all ensuite, ⁜ ⊩ ⠿ 50 **P** 100 ⊕ **SB** £50-£70 **DB** £80-£110 **L** £14.50 **L** ⬤ **D** £26.50 **D** ⬤ ✕ **LD** 21:00 ⠉ MC Visa Amex DC ⊞ ▦ ▸ ▨ &

★★ ✤ Burnett Arms
25 High Street, Banchory AB31 5TD
☎ 01330-824944 **Fax** 01330-825553

An 18th century coaching inn, fully modernised and yet retaining the character and atmosphere of olden times. Situated in the town centre.
16 bedrs, all ensuite, ⁜ ⠿ 100 **P** 40 ⊕ ⠉ MC Visa Amex DC

BEAULY Inverness-shire   **15D3**
Pop. 3,600. Inverness 11, London 539, Achnasheen 31, Dingwall 8½, Edinburgh 164, Glasgow 162, Invermoriston 26, Ullapool 48 **EC** Thu

★★★ Lovat Arms
Main Street, Beauly IV4 7BS
☎ 01463-782313 **Fax** 01463-782862
E-mail lovat.arms@cali.co.uk
22 bedrs, all ensuite, ⁜ ⠿ 60 **P** 20 ⊕ **SB** £35-£42 **DB** £60-£100 **HB** £280-£340 **L** £8.50 **L** ⬤ **D** £22 **D** ⬤ ✕ **LD** 20:45 ⠉ MC Visa JCB ▨ ▦
See advert on this page

SCOTLAND

★★★ Priory
The Square, Beauly IV4 7BX
☎ 01463-782309 **Fax** 01463-782531

A busy family run hotel situated in the pretty village square of Beauly. Excellent accommodation, good food and friendly, efficient service are the hotel's hallmark. 12 miles from Inverness, this is an excellent base for touring North & West Highlands.
36 bedrs, all ensuite, ♀ ♪ ⊁ 🖃 ⋕ 60 **P** 20 ⊕
SB £39.50-£47.50 **DB** £59-£90 **HB** £275-£375 **L** ●
D £14.50 **D** ● ✕ **LD** 22:30 **CC** MC Visa Amex DC JCB
🐾 ⚤

BIGGAR Lanarkshire   13D3
Pop. 1,900. Abington 12, London 363, Edinburgh 28, Glasgow 36, Lanark 13, Peebles 17 **MD** Sat **see** Boghall Castle ruins, Old Church (1545), Cadger's Bridge, Gladstone Court Museum, 12th cent Biggar Motte ⓘ 155 High Street 01899-22106

★★★ Shieldhill 🍴 🍴 🍴
Quothquan, Biggar ML12 6NA
☎ 01899-220035 **Fax** 01899-221092
E-mail enquiries@shieldhill.co.uk

Sheildhill Castle (1199), 6 acres of wooded parkland; doubles, singles, jacuzzis and fourposters; oak-panelled reception rooms; open log-fires; elegant frame marquee, thermostatically heated and beautifully lit. Restaurants offer finest wines and cuisine.
16 bedrs, all ensuite, ▦ ♀ ⊁ ⋕ 30 **P** 40 ⊕ **SB** £90
DB £134 **L** £17.50 **D** £30 ✕ **LD** 21:00 **CC** MC Visa

BLAIRGOWRIE Perthshire   13D1
Pop. 5,800. Perth 15, London 431, Aberfeldy 29, Braemar 45, Brechin 29, Dundee 18, Edinburgh 56, Forfar 20, Pitlochry 23 **EC** Thu **see** Ardblair Castle, Newton Castle, Craighall Mansion ⓘ 26 Wellmeadow 01250-872960

★★ Angus
Blairgowrie PH10 6NQ
☎ 01250-872455 **Fax** 01250-875615

The Angus Hotel is one of Perthshire's most renowned hotels, offering comfort, service and a friendly atmosphere. Close to many tourist attractions.
81 bedrs, all ensuite, ⊁ 🖃 ⋕ 200 **P** 60 ⊕ **CC** MC Visa Amex DC 🐾 ⚤

BOTHWELL Lanarkshire   12C2
Pop. 5,700. M74 ½, Hamilton 2, London 380, East
Kilbride 6½, Glasgow 10 **MD** Thu **see** 14th cent
Church and Castle

★★★ Bothwell Bridge
89 Main Street, Bothwell G71 8EU
☎ 01698-852246 **Fax** 01698-854686
90 bedrs, all ensuite, ▦ ⚲ ⏏ ⁘ 400 **P** 150 ⊕
SB £40-£58 **DB** £50-£68 **L** £9 **L** ⚑ **D** £12.50 **D** ⚑ ✕
LD 22:30 **CC** MC Visa Amex DC &
See advert on opposite page

BRAEMAR Aberdeenshire   15E4
Pop. 400. Perth 47, London 463, Aberdeen 58,
Blairgowrie 45, Edinburgh 88, Glasgow 104,
Grantown-on-Spey 46, Huntly 57 **EC** Thu **see**
Balmoral Castle grounds 7m NE, Crathie Church
7m ENE, Braemar Castle ⓘ The Mews, Mar Road
013397-41600

★★★ Invercauld Arms
Braemar AB35 5YR
☎ 013397-41605 **Fax** 013397-41428
68 bedrs, all ensuite, ⚲ ⏏ ⁘ 100 **P** 100 ⊕ **CC** MC
Visa Amex DC JCB &

BRIDGE OF ALLAN Stirlingshire   12C2
Pop. 4,300. M9 (jn 11) 2, Stirling 3, London 398,
Crieff 19, Dumfermline 21, Edinburgh 37, Glasgow
29, Lochearnhead 26, Perth 31 **EC** Wed **see** Wallace
Monument

★★★ Royal ⓡ
Henderson Street, Bridge of Allan FK9 4HG
☎ 01786-832284 **Fax** 01786-834377

The Royal Hotel is situated in the Victorian Spa
town of Bridge of Allen. Refurbishment over the
past 18 months has only enhanced the ambience
and relaxing atmosphere. Additional features

include satellite TV, chocolates and mineral water in
the rooms.
32 bedrs, all ensuite, ⚲ ⏏ ⁘ 150 **P** 60 ⊕ ✕
LD 21:30 **CC** MC Visa Amex DC

CALLANDER Perthshire   12C1
Pop. 1,800. M9 (jn 11) 10, Doune 7½, London 413,
Arrochar 46, Dumbarton 32, Dumfermline 34,
Edinburgh 50, Glasgow 33, Lochearnhead 13,
Perth 34, Stirling 16 **EC** Wed **see** The Trossachs, Falls
of Bracklinn ⓘ Visitor Centre, Ancaster Square
01877-330342

★★★ Roman Camp
Country House ⓡ ⓡ ⓡ ⓡ
Main Street, Callander FK17 8BG
☎ 01877-330003 **Fax** 01877-331533
E-mail mail@roman-camp-hotel.co.uk
14 bedrs, all ensuite, ▦ ⚲ ⁘ 100 **P** 80 ⊕ **SB** £70-
£95 **DB** £110-£165 **L** £18 **D** £34 ✕ **LD** 21:00 **CC** MC
Visa Amex DC ☑ &

CAMPBELTOWN Argyll   12B3
Pop. 5,500. Tarbert 26, London 517, Edinburgh
171, Glasgow 130, Lochgilphead 51 **MD** Mon
ⓘ Mackinnon House, The Pier 01586-552056

★★ Seafield
Kilkerran Road, Campbeltown PA28 6JL
☎ 01586-554385 **Fax** 01586-522741
9 bedrs, all ensuite, ⚲ **P** 12 No children under 14 ⊕
SB £40-£50 **DB** £60-£65 **L** £11 **D** £20 ✕ **LD** 20:30
CC MC Visa Amex

CARNOUSTIE Angus   13E1
Pop. 9,217. Dundee 11, London 439, Brechin 20,
Edinburgh 65, Forfar 14, Montrose 21 **EC** Tue ⓘ 24
High Street 01241-8522258

★★★★ Letham Grange Resort ⓡ ⓡ
Colliston DD11 4RL
☎ 01241-890373 **Fax** 01241-890725
E-mail lethamgrange@sol.co.uk
40 bedrs, all ensuite, ⁘ 500 **P** 150 ⊕ **SB** £70-£100
DB £95-£135 **L** £9.25 **L** ⚑ **D** £22.50 **D** ⚑ ✕ **LD** 21:30
CC MC Visa Amex DC JCB ⊞
See advert on next page

CASTLE DOUGLAS Kirkcudbrightshire   12C4
i Markethill Car Park 01556-502611

★★ Douglas Arms 🛏
King Street, Castle Douglas DG7 1DB
☎ 01556-502231 **Fax** 01556-504000
20 bedrs, 15 ensuite, ⊢ ⅲ 150 ⊕ ℂℂ MC Visa ▣ ⌧

★★ King's Arms
St Andrews Street, DG7 1EL
☎ 01556-502626 **Fax** 01556-502097
Closed Christmas-New Year
10 bedrs, 9 ensuite, ④ ⊢ ⅲ 40 **P** 20 ⊕ **SB** £32-£35
DB £52-£56 **HB** £230 L £8 **D** £13 **D** ⬤ ✕ **LD** 20:45
ℂℂ MC Visa ⌧

CLARENCEFIELD Dumfriesshire   13D4

★★★ Comlongon Castle
Clarencefield DG1 4NA
☎ 01387-870283 **Fax** 01387-870266
Closed Christmas-New Year
12 bedrs, all ensuite, ④ ⅲ 80 **P** 40 ⊕ Resid **DB** £100
L £7.50 **L** ⬤ **D** £28 **D** ⬤ ✕ **LD** 20:00 ℂℂ MC Visa
Amex ▣ ⌧
See advert on this page

CLYDEBANK Dunbartonshire   12C2
Glasgow 5, London 393, Dumbarton 8, Edinburgh 50, Paisley 8

★★★ ✤ Patio
1 South Avenue, Clydebank Business Park, Clydebank G81 2RW
☎ 0141-951 1133 **Fax** 0141-952 3713

This modern hotel's location caters for business travellers and is a popular venue for conferences and functions. Contemporary, partial open plan public areas include a bar, restaurant and small lounge.
80 bedrs, all ensuite, ↟ ☲ ⠿ 150 P 120 ⏣ SB £68-£90 DB £88-£100 L £13 L ⭒ D £16 D ⭒ ✕ LD 22:00 Restaurant closed L Sat-Sun ₡ MC Visa Amex DC ⅙

COMRIE Perthshire   12C1

★★★ Royal ⬛
Melville Square, Comrie PH6 2DN
☎ 01764-679200 **Fax** 01764-679219
E-mail reception@royalhotel.co.uk
11 bedrs, all ensuite, ▨ ♪ ⠿ 40 P 15 ⏣ SB £40-£65 DB £80-£130 L £7.95 L ⭒ ✕ LD 21.45 ₡ MC Visa Amex JCB ▣
See advert on opposite page

CRAIL Fife   13E1
Pop. 1,200. Largo 14, London 426, Edinburgh 51, Glasgow 78, Kinross 36, Kircaldy 26, Perth 39, St Andrews 10 **EC** Wed ▮ Museum, Marketgate 01333-450869

★ ✤ Croma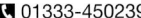
33/35 Nethergate Road, Crail KY10 3TU
☎ 01333-450239
6 bedrs, all ensuite, ↟ ⏣ SB £30-£35 DB £40-£60 D £11 ✕ LD 22:00

CRIEFF Perthshire   12C1
Pop. 5,100. Dunblane 15, London 416, Aberfeldy 23, Dunfermline 30, Edinburgh 47, Glasgow 47, Kinross 26, Kincardine 30, Lochearnhead 19, Perth 18, Pitlochry 35, Stirling 21 **EC** Wed **see** 10th cent Market Cross, Old Stocks, 17th cent Drummond Cross, Glass Works, Pottery ▮ Town Hall, High Street 01764-652578

★★ Locke's Acre
Comrie Road, Crieff PH7 4BP
☎ 01764-652526 **Fax** 01764-652526
7 bedrs, 4 ensuite, P 30 ⏣ SB £25-£28 DB £50-£54 HB £252-£280 L £9 D £14 ✕ LD 20:45 ₡ MC Visa ⅙

CUMBERNAULD Dunbartonshire   12C2
Pop. 50,000. Lanark 23, London 392, Dumbarton 26, Edinburgh 35, Glasgow 13, Kincardine 15, Stirling 13 **EC** Wed **see** Country Park

Westerwood
St Andrews Drive, Cumbernauld G38 0EW
☎ 01236-457171 **Fax** 01236-738478
49 bedrs, all ensuite, ↟ ☲ ⠿ 280 P 150 ⏣ ₡ MC Visa Amex DC ▣ ▣ ▣ ▣ ▣ ⅙
See advert on this page

SCOTLAND

CUMNOCK Ayrshire   12C3

Pop. 9,600. New Cumnock 6, London 370, Ayr 15, Dalmellington 13, Edinburgh 59, Glasgow 13, Kilmarnock 15, Lanark 31 **MD** Fri **see** Mercat Cross (1703), Peden Monument, Home of Kier Hardie

★★ Royal

1 Glaisnock Street, Cumnock KA18 1BP
📞 01290-420822 **Fax** 01290-425988
11 bedrs, 5 ensuite, ⚲ ☷ 120 **P** 6 ⊟ **CC** MC Visa DC

DALBEATTIE Kirkcudbrightshire   12C4

see 16th cent church ℹ Town Hall 01556-610117

★★★ Clonyard House

Colvend, Dalbeattie DG5 4QW
📞 01556-630372 **Fax** 01556-630422
15 bedrs, all ensuite, ⚲ ☷ 30 **P** 40 ⊟ **SB** £30-£38 **DB** £55-£65 **L** £7 **D** £15 **D** ♥ ✕ **LD** 21:00 **CC** MC Visa Amex JCB &

DINGWALL Ross-shire   15D3

London 540, Achnasheen 30, Edinburgh 167, Glasgow 178, Inverness 18

National Awaiting Inspection
High Street, Dingwall IV15 9HA
📞 01349-862166 **Fax** 01349-865178
51 bedrs, all ensuite, ⚲ ☷ 200 **P** 30 ⊟ ✕ **LD** 21:00 **CC** MC Visa Amex DC 🔲 &

DORNOCH Sutherland   15D2

Pop. 1,100. Bonar Bridge 13, London 576, Edinburgh 204, Glasgow 211, Helmsdale 28, Lairg 21 **EC** Thu ℹ The Square 01862-810400

★★ Dornoch Castle

Castle Street, Dornoch IV25 3SD
📞 01862-810216 **Fax** 01862-810981
Closed Nov-Mar
17 bedrs, all ensuite, ⚲ ▣ **P** 16 ⊟ **SB** £40.50 **DB** £72 ✕ **LD** 21:00 **CC** MC Visa Amex

---

DRYMEN Stirlingshire   12C2

Pop. 659. Bearsden 12, London 410, Crianlarich 44, Dumbarton 12, Edinburgh 54, Glasgow 17, Lochearnhead 32, Stirling 22 **EC** Wed

★★★ Buchanan Arms

Main Street, Drymen G63 0BQ
📞 01360-660588 **Fax** 01360-660943
E-mail bah@scottishhighlandhotels.co.uk

52 bedrs, all ensuite, ▣ ⚲ ☷ 150 **P** 100 ⊟ **SB** £83 **DB** £122 **L** £8.50 **L** ♥ **D** £20.50 ✕ **LD** 21:30 **CC** MC Visa Amex DC JCB 🔲 🔲 🔲 🔲 &

★★★ Winnock

The Square, Drymen G63 0BL
📞 01360-660245 **Fax** 01360-660267

The Winnock Hotel surrounds the picturesque village green in the centre of Drymen. A warm friendly welcome, comfortable rooms, good food, ales and whiskies await you.
49 bedrs, all ensuite, ☷ 120 **P** 40 ⊟ **CC** MC Visa Amex DC

DUMFRIES Dumfriesshire   10A1

Pop. 31,000. Annan 16, Carlisle 33, London 327, Beattock 19, Edinburgh 71, Glasgow 73, Langholm 28, New Galloway 23, Thornhill 14 **MD** Wed **see** Burns House, Burns Mausoleum, Burns Statue, Burgh Museum, The Auld Bridge, Greyfriars Church, St. Michael's Church, Globe Inn, Lincluden Abbey 2m NW, Sweetheart Abbey 6m S. ℹ Whitesands 01387-253862

★★★ Cairndale

English Street, Dumfries DG1 2DF
📞 01387-254111 **Fax** 01387 250555

Traditional family owned hotel with modern facilities, including excellent leisure club with heated indoor pool and spa. Close to town centre. 92 bedrs, all ensuite, ⬜ ⟟ ▣ ⦂⦂⦂ 300 **P** 60 ⧖ **SB** £65-£85 **DB** £85-£105 **HB** £245-£350 **L** £5.50 **L** ⬤ **D** £15 **D** ⬤ ✕ **LD** 21:30 ⦅ MC Visa Amex DC ▣ ⊞ ▦ ⅃
See advert on this page

★★★ Hetland Hall
Carrutherstown, Dumfries DG1 4JX
☎ 01387-840201 **Fax** 01387-840211
26 bedrs, all ensuite, ⬜ ⬀ ⟟ ⦂⦂⦂ 300 **P** 60 ⧖ **SB** £62-£75 **DB** £85-£98 **HB** £342-£372 **L** £10 **L** ⬤ **D** £18 **D** ⬤ ✕ **LD** 21:30 ⦅ MC Visa Amex DC JCB ▣ ⊞ ▦ ⊞ ⅃
See advert on this page

★★ Hill Hotel & Restaurant
18 St. Marys Street, Dumfries DG1 1LZ
☎ 01387-254893 **Fax** 01387-262553
E-mail acame45046@aol.com
8 bedrs, all ensuite, ⦂⦂⦂ 30 **P** 50 ⧖ ⦅ MC Visa Amex DC

DUNBAR East Lothian	13E2

Pop. 5,600. Cockburnspath 8½, London 365, Berwick-upon-Tweed 29, Coldstream 32, Edinburgh 29, Haddington 11, Lauder 32 **EC** Wed **see** Castle ruins, 17th cent town house, 16th cent dovecote, Parish Church ⅃ 143 High Street 01368-863353

★★ Bayswell
Bayswell Park, Dunbar EH42 1AE
☎ 01368-862225 **Fax** 01368-862225

Set by the sea on a cliff top, this fine hotel commands a spectacular view overlooking the Firth of Forth, Bass Rock, May Island and the Fife Coast and Dunbar Castle.
13 bedrs, all ensuite, ⬀ ⦂⦂⦂ 70 **P** 20 ⧖ **SB** £39-£49 **DB** £69 **L** £8 **D** £13 ✕ **LD** 21:00 ⦅ MC Visa Amex DC

SCOTLAND

DUNDEE Angus 13D1

Pop. 180,000. Glenrothes 24, London 429, Blairgowrie 18, Edinburgh 55, Forfar 14, Glasgow 78, Kinross 30, Montrose 30, Perth 21, St Andrews 12 **MD** Tue *see* Tay Bridge Road, Museum and Art Gallery, St. Andrew's Church (1772), Discovery Point with R.S.S. Discovery, Claypotts Castle, Broughty Castle ℹ️ 4 City Square 01382-434664

★★★★ Swallow 🍴

Kingsway West, Invergowrie, Dundee DD2 5JT
📞 01382-641122 **Fax** 01382-568340
E-mail info@swallowhotels.com

This redeveloped Victorian mansion is set in its own grounds just two miles from Dundee. Tastefully extended, the hotel cleverly blends old and new and has leisure facilities.
107 bedrs, all ensuite, 🔥 ⊞ 80 **P** 140 ⊞ **SB** £90 **DB** £115 **D** £20.50 ✕ **LD** 21:45 ⓒ MC Visa Amex DC 🔲 🔲 🔲 ⅃

DUNDONNELL Ross-shire 14C2

Pop. 70. Garve 31, London 583, Edinburgh 308, Gairloch 33, Glasgow 212, Ullapool 24,

★★★ Dundonnell 🍴

Little Loch Broom, by Garve, Dundonnell IV23 2QS
📞 01854-633204 **Fax** 01854-633366
E-mail selbie@dundonellhotel.co.uk.
Closed Jan
28 bedrs, all ensuite, 🔥 ⊞ 60 **P** 60 ⊞ ⓒ MC Visa Amex

DUNFERMLINE Fife 13D2

Pop. 53,000. South Queensferry 7½, London 391, A823(M) 2½, Crieff 30, Edinburgh 16, Glasgow 38, Kincardine 10, Kinross 12, Kirkcaldy 12, St Andrews 39, Stirling 22 **EC** Wed *see* Royal Palace ruins, Abbey Church (Bruce's Tomb, St. Margaret's Shrine), Andrew Carnegie Birthplace Memorial (Moodie St) ℹ️ 13-15 Maygate 01383-720999

★★★ Elgin

Charlestown, Dunfermline KY11 3EE
📞 01383-872257 **Fax** 01383-873044
12 bedrs, all ensuite, ⊞ 150 **P** 80 ⊞ ⓒ MC Visa Amex DC JCB

★★★ King Malcolm

Queensferry Road, Dunfermline KY11 5DS
📞 01383-722611 **Fax** 01383-730865
48 bedrs, all ensuite, 🔥 ⊞ 150 **P** 60 ⊞ ⓒ MC Visa Amex DC JCB

★★★ Pitbauchlie House

47 Aberdour Road, Dunfermline KY11 4PB
📞 01383-722282 **Fax** 01383-620738
E-mail info@pitbauchlie.com

Situated in landscaped gardens, minutes from M90. Conference, banqueting, bars and restaurant facilities. Excellent food with the chef taking advantage of Scotland's natural larder.
50 bedrs, all ensuite, ④ ♪ 🔥 ⊞ 150 **P** 80 ⊞ **SB** £65 **DB** £81 **L** £10 **L** 💧 **D** £20 **D** 💧 ✕ **LD** 21:00 ⓒ MC Visa Amex DC 🔲 ⅃

★★★ Pitfirrane Arms

Main Street, Crossford, Dunfermline KY12 8NJ
📞 01383-736132 **Fax** 01383-621760
38 bedrs, all ensuite, 🔥 ⊞ 100 **P** 72 ⊞ ⓒ MC Visa Amex ⅃

Halfway House

Main Street, Kingseat, Dunfermline KY12 0TJ
📞 01383-731661 **Fax** 01383-621274

Thirty minutes from Princes Street, within easy reach of Perth, Stirling, Glasgow and St Andrews. Enjoy the relaxing atmosphere of the bars and restaurants. Nearest motorway junction: exit 3 on the M90.
12 bedrs, all ensuite, ⊁ ⠿ 150 **P** 100 ⠀ **(C** MC Visa Amex ⠀

DUNKELD Perthshire   13D1

Pop. 600. Bankfoot 6, London 432, Blairgowrie 11, Dundee 28, Edinburgh 57, Glasgow 69, Perth 15, Pitlochry 13 **EC** Thu ⠀ The Cross 01350-727688

★★★ Kinnaird ⠀ ⠀ ⠀ ⠀
Gold Ribbon Hotel

Kinnaird Estate, Dunkeld PH8 0LB
📞 01796-482440 **Fax** 01796-482289
Closed Mon-Wed Jan & Feb

An imposing three storey, old granite country mansion close to the River Tay. The hotel is set back from a quiet road in its own garden, but enjoys the 9,000 acres of the mainly wooded Kinnaird estate.
9 bedrs, all ensuite, ⊁ ⠿ ⠿ 25 **P** 20 No children under 12 ⠀ Resid **SB** £165-£255 **DB** £165-£255 **L** £20 **D** £45 ✗ **LD** 21:30 **(C** MC Visa Amex ⠀ ⠀ ⠀

★★ Atholl Arms

Bridge Street, Dunkeld PH8 0AQ
📞 01350-727219 **Fax** 01350-727219
14 bedrs, 11 ensuite, ⊁ ⠿ 30 **P** 20 No children under 8 ⠀ **SB** £35-£45 **DB** £55-£65 **L** £10 **L** ⠀ **D** £15 **D** ⠀ ✗ **LD** 20:45 **(C** MC Visa Amex ⠀

DUNOON Argyll   12B2

Pop. 8,800. Arrochar 39, London 466 (Fy 412), Edinburgh 118 (Fy 69), Glasgow 76 (Fy 24), Inveraray 39. **EC** Wed ⠀ 7 Alexandra Parade 01369-703785

★★ Argyll

Argyll Street, Dunoon PA23 7NE
📞 01369-702059 **Fax** 01369-704483
E-mail info@argyll-hotel.co.uk
33 bedrs, all ensuite, ⊁ ⠿ ⠿ 60 ⠀ **SB** £30-£50 **DB** £50-£70 **L** ⠀ **D** £8.50 **D** ⠀ ✗ **LD** 20:00 **(C** MC Visa

★★ Esplanade

West Bay, Dunoon PA23 7HU
📞 01369-704070 **Fax** 01369-702129
E-mail mail@ehd.co.uk
Closed Nov-Apr

Dunoon's premier family owned and run hotel, in a beautiful setting overlooking the River Clyde, offering quality breaks and appetising meals. Entertainment most evenings. 4 nights **DB** £158, 7 nights **DB** £225. www.ehd.co.uk
51 bedrs, all ensuite, ⠿ ⠿ ⊁ ⠿ ⠿ 80 **P** 20 ⠀ **SB** £30-£40 **DB** £60-£80 **HB** £220-£250 **L** £5.95 **L** ⠀ **D** £13.50 ✗ **LD** 20:00 **(C** MC Visa Amex

---

EAST KILBRIDE Lanarkshire   12C2

Pop. 76,000. Hamilton 6½, London 383, Edinburgh 41, Glasgow 8, Kilmarnock 18, Kincardine 33, Lanark 20, Largs 33, Paisley 12, Peebles 46, Stirling 31 **EC** Wed **see** Church with crown tower, Mains Castle, Museum

★★★ Bruce
35 Cornwall Street, East Kilbride G74 1AF
☎ 01355-229771 **Fax** 01355-242216
E-mail enquiries@maksu-group.co.uk

Adjoining the main shopping centre, this luxuriously refurbished hotel with stunning public areas offers ensuite rooms, nightclub, award winning restaurant and a cocktail bar. Free parking.
65 bedrs, all ensuite, 4 ♀ ♪ ➤ ▤ ⦙⦙ 300 **P** 35 ⬡
SB £95-£105 **DB** £125-£145 **L** £9.50 **L** ♥ **D** £16.50 ✕
LD 21:45 Restaurant closed L Sat-Sun **CC** MC Visa
Amex DC ⅃

★★★ Stuart
Cornwall Way, East Kilbride G74 1JR
☎ 013552-21161 **Fax** 013552-64410
38 bedrs, all ensuite, 4 ♀ ♪ ▤ ⦙⦙ 200 ⬡ **SB** £68-£72
DB £80-£100 **L** £7 **L** ♥ **D** £14 **D** ♥ ✕ **LD** 22:00 **CC** MC
Visa Amex DC

EDINBURGH   13D2
See also UPHALL
Pop. 444,700. Dalkeith 7, London 375, Dunfermline 16, Galashiels 32, Glasgow 45, Haddington 15, Kinross 26, Kirkcaldy 25, Peebles 23, Stirling 36 **see** Castle and War Memorial, Palace of Holyrood, St Giles' Cathedral, National Museum, 17th cent White Horse Close, Outlook Tower, Parliament House ⅈ 3 Princes Street 0131-557 1700

★★★★★ Balmoral ⅊ ⅊ ⅊
1 Princes Street, Edinburgh EH2 2EQ
☎ 0131-556 2414 **Fax** 0131-557 3747
186 bedrs, all ensuite, ➤ ▤ ⦙⦙ 350 ⬡ **CC** MC Visa
Amex DC JCB ▣ ✕ ▨ ⅃

★★★★ Carlton Highland ⅊ ⅊
North Bridge, Edinburgh EH1 1SD
☎ 0131-472 3000 **Fax** 0131-556 2691
E-mail chh@scottishhighlandhotels.co.uk
197 bedrs, all ensuite, ➤ ▤ ⦙⦙ 300 ⬡ **SB** £125
DB £193 **L** £9.50 **D** £16.50 ✕ **LD** 22:30 **CC** MC
Visa Amex DC ▣ ✕ ▨ ✕ ⅃

★★★★ Royal Terrace
18 Royal Terrace, Princes Street,
Edinburgh EH7 5AQ
☎ 0131-557 3222 **Fax** 0131-557 5334
94 bedrs, all ensuite, 4 ▤ ⦙⦙ 100 ⬡ **CC** MC Visa
Amex DC ▣ ✕ ▨

★★★★ Swallow Royal Scot ⅊
111 Glasgow Road, EH12 8NF
☎ 0131-334 9191 **Fax** 0131-316 4507
E-mail info@swallowhotels.com

A smart, modern hotel in Edinburgh's suburbs, just 2 miles from the airport. The hotel has a restaurant, lounge, a choice of bars, leisure club and hairdressing salon.
259 bedrs, all ensuite, ➤ ▤ ⦙⦙ 300 **P** 300 ⬡
SB £110-£145 **DB** £125-£185 **L** £16 **D** £24.50 ✕
LD 22:00 **CC** MC Visa Amex DC ▣ ✕ ▨ ⅃

★★★ ✤ Barnton
562 Queensferry Road, Edinburgh EH4 6AS
☎ 0131-339 1144 **Fax** 0131-339 5521
50 bedrs, all ensuite, ➤ ▤ ⦙⦙ 150 **P** 100 ⬡ **CC** MC
Visa Amex DC ▨ ⅃

★★★ Braid Hills
134 Braid Road, Edinburgh EH10 6JD
☎ 0131-447 8888 **Fax** 0131-452 8477
E-mail bookings@braidhillshotel.co.uk

Magnificently situated only two miles from the city centre, yet a world away from the noise and congestion of the centre itself. An independently owned hotel.

68 bedrs, all ensuite, ▣ ⠿ 160 **P** 38 ⊞ **SB** £75 **DB** £125 **L** £8 **L** ⬤ **D** £17.50 **D** ⬤ ✕ **LD** 21:15 ⓒ MC Visa Amex DC JCB

★★★ Norton House ⦂ ⦂ ⦂
Blue Ribbon Hotel
Ingliston, Edinburgh EH28 8LX
☎ 0131-333 1275 **Fax** 0131-333 5305
47 bedrs, all ensuite, ♀ ⬧ ⠿ 300 **P** 150 ⊞ **SB** £120-£135 **DB** £145-£185 **L** £16 **L** ⬤ **D** £26 **D** ⬤ ✕ **LD** 22:00 Restaurant closed L Sat ⓒ MC Visa Amex DC JCB
&

★★★ Old Waverley
43 Princes Street, Edinburgh EH2 2BY
☎ 0131-556 4648 **Fax** 0131-557 6316
E-mail owh@scottishhighlandhotels.co.uk
66 bedrs, all ensuite, ♀ ⬧ ⬦ ▣ ⠿ 50 ⊞ **SB** £95-£99 **DB** £152-£158 **HB** £399-£518 **L** £7.30 **L** ⬤ **D** £17 ✕ **LD** 22:00 ⓒ MC Visa Amex DC

★★★ Posthouse ⦂   **Posthouse**
Corstorphine Road, Edinburgh EH12 6UA
☎ 0131-334 0390 **Fax** 0131-334 9237
303 bedrs, all ensuite, ⬦ ▣ ⠿ 100 **P** 300 ⊞ ⓒ MC Visa Amex DC ▦ ▦ ▦ &

★★★ Quality
Cramond Foreshore, Edinburgh EH4 5EP
☎ 0131-336 1700 **Fax** 0131-336 4934
E-mail admin@gb625.u-net.com

Situated on the Forth foreshore amidst beautiful parkland, the hotel, with its leisure facilities and restaurant specialising in Scottish fare makes a peaceful and relaxing base from which to explore Edinburgh.

86 bedrs, all ensuite, ⬦ ▣ ⠿ 200 **P** 100 ⊞ **SB** £82.75-£91 **DB** £107-£124 **L** £8.50 **D** £14.50 ✕ **LD** 21:15 ⓒ MC Visa Amex DC JCB ▦ ▦ &

★★ Allison House
15-17 Mayfield Gardens, Edinburgh EH9 2AX
☎ 0131-667 8049 **Fax** 0131-667 5001
E-mail dh007ljh@msn.com

Family run hotel, one mile from city centre. Twenty-two ensuite bedrooms, Murray's restaurant, residents bar, conference room and private parking. Warm, friendly welcome awaits. Theatre, golf and short breaks our speciality.

23 bedrs, 22 ensuite, ▣ ⬦ ⠿ 25 **P** 12 No children under 12 ⊞ Resid **SB** £25-£45 **DB** £50-£90 **D** £9 **D** ⬤ ✕ **LD** 21:00 ⓒ MC Visa Amex DC JCB

★★ Iona
17 Strathearn Place, Edinburgh EH9 2AL
☎ 0131-447 5050/6264 **Fax** 0131-452 8574
E-mail ronald.pugh@dial.pipex.com

Family-run hotel set in a quiet location close to many attractions and city centre. Rooms are ensuite with tea/coffee facilities, TV, telephone, and radio. Private parking, lounge bar, restaurant, residents' lounge. Ideal for business or pleasure.

17 bedrs, all ensuite, ⬦ ⠿ 20 **P** 16 ⊞ **SB** £25-£33 **DB** £45-£85 **L** £7 **D** £13 ✕ **LD** 21:00 ⓒ MC Visa &

★★ Murrayfield
18 Corstorphine Road, Edinburgh EH12 6HN
☎ 0131-337 1844 **Fax** 0131-346 8159
33 bedrs, all ensuite, ⬦ ⠿ 20 **P** 33 ⊞ ⓒ MC Visa Amex DC

★★ Orwell Lodge

29 Polwarth Terrace, Edinburgh EH11 1NH
☎ 0131-229 1044 Fax 0131-228 9492

Once an elegant Victorian mansion, now offering excellent accommodation. All rooms ensuite and individually decorated with TV, radio, telephone, hairdryer, tea and coffee-making facilities. All rooms are no smoking. Large car park.
10 bedrs, all ensuite, 4 ⊡ ⠿ 250 **P** 40 ⊞ **SB** £45-£49 **DB** £70-£75 **L** ⬤ **D** ⬤ ✕ **LD** 20:30 Restaurant closed D Sun **CC** MC Visa Amex

★★ Royal Ettrick

13 Ettrick Road, Edinburgh EH10 5BJ
☎ 0131-228 6413 Fax 0131-229 7330

A privately owned hotel with a relaxed, friendly atmosphere, 10 minutes from the city centre and Edinburgh Conference Centre. Beautiful conservatory restaurant serving lunches, dinners and real ale.
12 bedrs, 9 ensuite, 3 � ♦4⊟府&♦ ♀ ⫟ ⠿ 80 **P** 25 No children under 2 ⊞ **SB** £49.50-£65 **DB** £70-£95 **HB** £65 **L** £7 **D** £10 ✕ **LD** 20:15 **CC** MC Visa Amex

★★ Thrums

14 Minto Street, Edinburgh EH9 1RQ
☎ 0131-667 8545 Fax 0131-667 8707
Closed Christmas
14 bedrs, all ensuite, ⫟ **P** 10 ⊞ Restricted **SB** £35-£45 **DB** £60-£70 **D** £10.50 ✕ **LD** 20:30 **CC** MC Visa

Carlton Greens Awaiting Inspection
2 Carlton Terrace, Edinburgh EH7 5DD
☎ 0131-556 6570 Fax 0131-557 6680

Jurys Edinburgh Inn Awaiting Inspection
Jeffrey Street, Edinburgh EH1 1DG
☎ 0131-200 3300 Fax 0131-200 0400
E-mail bookings@jurys.com
Closed 24-26 Dec

Jurys Edinburgh Inn offers 3 star facilities with a prime city-centre location. Only minutes walk from all major tourist attractions and venues, it's the perfect choice for business or leisure travellers.
186 bedrs, all ensuite, ♀ ⌁ ⊡ ⠿ 40 ⊞ **SB** £68-£92 **DB** £75-£100 **L** ⬤ **D** £15.50 ✕ **LD** 21:30 **CC** MC Visa Amex DC ⅙

Pop. 750. Brechin 6, London 459, Edinburgh 85, Montrose 12, Stonehaven 22

★★★ Glenesk

High Street, Edzell DD9 7TF
☎ 01356-648319 Fax 01356-647333

Splendid family run hotel situated in its own grounds adjoining the 18 hole golf course. Recommended by both golf parties and families who enjoy the friendly atmosphere and Scottish hospitality. Includes extensive leisure facilities. Comfortable rooms.

24 bedrs, all ensuite, ✦ ♨ 200 **P** 80 ⊕ **SB** £40-£55 **DB** £60-£90 **L** ☛ **D** £17 **D** ☛ ✕ **LD** 20:45 **CC** MC Visa Amex DC 🎱 🖼 📺 🖼

FALKIRK Stirlingshire   13D2
ERSKINE Renfrewshire   12C2
Pop. 9,000. Glasgow 10, London 397, M8 ½, Dumbarton 6, Edinburgh 55, Largs 24, Paisley 6 **EC** Wed

★★★ ✤ Posthouse Glasgow   **Posthouse**
Erskine
Erskine PA8 6AN
📞 0141-812 0123 **Fax** 0141-812 7642
166 bedrs, all ensuite, ▣ ♨ 600 **P** 400 ⊕ **CC** MC Visa Amex DC JCB 🎱 🖼 📺 🖼 ♿

FALKIRK Stirlingshire   13D2
Pop. 36,700. Armadale 7½, London 394, M9 (jn 6), Dumbarton 35, Edinburgh 25, Glasgow 23, Kincardine 7, Stirling 11. **EC** Wed **see** Falkirk Town Steeple, Roman remains (Antonine Walls) ℹ 2-4 Glebe Street 01324-620244

★★ Comfort Inn
Manor Street, Falkirk FK1 1NT
📞 01324-624066 **Fax** 01324-611785
E-mail admin@gb626.u-net.com

Midway between Edinburgh and Glasgow. Ideal for both holidaymaker and businessman. Comfortable ensuite bedrooms with all the usual facilities, hospitality tray, four conference rooms and mini-gym.
33 bedrs, all ensuite, ✦ ▣ ♨ 180 **P** 17 ⊕ **SB** £53.50-£61.25 **DB** £60.25-£68 **Room** £46.75-£54.50 **D** £9.75 ✕ **LD** 21:30 **CC** MC Visa Amex DC JCB 🖼

FORRES Morayshire   15E3
Pop. 7,400. Grantown-on-Spey 21, London 527, Carrbridge 26, Edinburgh 152, Elgin 12, Glasgow 169, Inverness 27 **EC** Wed ℹ 116 High Street 01309-672938

★★★ Ramnee 👤 👤 👤
Victoria Road, Forres IV36 0BN
📞 01309-672410 **Fax** 01309-673392
Closed 1-3 Jan
20 bedrs, all ensuite, ▣ ✦ ♨ 100 **P** 50 ⊕ **CC** MC Visa Amex DC JCB

★★ Park
Victoria Road, Forres IV36 0BN
📞 01309-672611 **Fax** 01309-672328
12 bedrs, 10 ensuite, ⚲ **P** 20 ⊕ **SB** £39.50-£45 **DB** £55 **HB** £350 **L** £11 **L** ☛ **D** £16.50 ✕ **LD** 20:00 **CC** MC Visa Amex DC

FORT WILLIAM Inverness-shire   14C4
Pop. 4,300. Ballachulish 14, London 490, Crianlarich 51, Edinburgh 132, Glasgow 99, Oban 48 **EC** Wed ℹ Cameron Square 01397-703781

★★★★ Inverlochy Castle 👤 👤 👤 👤
Gold Ribbon Hotel
Torlundy, Fort William PH33 6SN
📞 01397-702177 **Fax** 01397-702953
E-mail info@inverlochy.co.uk
Closed 6 Jan-2 Feb
17 bedrs, all ensuite, ▣ ♀ ⚲ ♨ 34 **P** 17 ⊕
Restricted Resid **SB** £180-£225 **DB** £290-£450 **L** £28 **L** ☛ **D** £45 **D** ☛ ✕ **LD** 21:15 **CC** MC Visa Amex 🖼 📀 🖼

★★★ Moorings 👤 👤 👤
Banavie, Fort William PH33 7LY
📞 01397-772797 **Fax** 01397-772441
Closed Christmas

Lying alongside the Caledonian Canal at the famous Neptune's Staircase, under the shadows of Ben Nevis, Aonach Mor and surrounding mountains, the Moorings Hotel offers style and comfort coupled with the convenience of a modern hotel.
21 bedrs, all ensuite, ▣ ✦ ♨ 80 **P** 60 ⊕ **SB** £48-£62 **DB** £72-£96 **HB** £399-£497 **L** ☛ **D** £26 **D** ☛ ✕ **LD** 21:30 **CC** MC Visa Amex DC ♿

★★ Caledonian
Achintore Road, Fort William PH33 6RW
☎ 01397-703117 **Fax** 01397-700550
86 bedrs, all ensuite, 🛉 🔄 ⅲ 80 **P** 70 ⊕ ℂℂ MC Visa
Amex DC 🖼

★★ Grand 🍴🍴
Gordon Square, Fort William PH33 6DX
☎ 01397-702928 **Fax** 01397-702928
E-mail djhaines@compuserv.com
Closed Jan

Family owned and operated hotel, situated in the
town centre, offering comfortable accommodation
at affordable prices. Both the bar and restaurant
offer excellent fayre.
33 bedrs, all ensuite, 🕱 🛉 ⅲ 100 **P** 20 ⊕ **SB** £31-
£40 **DB** £26-£35 **HB** £252-£350 **L** 🍷 **D** £17 **D** 🍷 ✕
LD 20:30 Restaurant closed L Wed ℂℂ MC Visa
Amex DC JCB

FORTINGALL Perthshire	12C1

Killin 16, London 451, Edinburgh 76, Glasgow 70,
Aberfeldy 8½

★★ Fortingall
Fortingall PH15 2NQ
☎ 01887-830367 **Fax** 01887-830367
Closed Nov-Mar
10 bedrs, 9 ensuite, 1 🏠 🛉 **P** 15 ⊕ **SB** £26-£35
DB £50-£58 **HB** £270-£290 **L** £10 **L** 🍷 **D** £16 **D** 🍷 ✕
LD 21:00 ℂℂ MC Visa

GAIRLOCH Ross-shire	14B2

Pop. 1,000. Achnasheen 28, London 596,
Edinburgh 221, Glasgow 225, Ullapool 57 **EC** Wed **see**
Loch Maree, View points at Gairloch, Crask and
Red Point, Victoria Falls, Inverewe Gardens 5m
🛈 Auchtercairn 01445-712130

Creag Mor Hotel
and Restaurants

Gairloch, Ross-Shire. IV21 2AH.
Tel: 01445 712068. Fax: 01445 712044.
email106505. 1440@compuserve.com
*Situated admidst the spectacular scenery of Ross-Shire on
the north west coast of Scotland. This luxurious family
run Hotel with its warm relaxed atmosphere overlooks
Old Gairloch harbour and beyond to the Isle of Skye and
the Outer Hebrides. Golf course, fishing and the sub
tropical Inverewe Gardens all nearby. Wine and dine in
one of our superb restaurants specialising in salmon,
trout, venison, prime Highland beef and locally landed
seafoods. We have an extensive wine list and over 100
malt whiskies to choose from...Come and enjoy the best
of Highland hospitality.*

RAC★★★ STB★★★★ *Highly commended*

★★★ Creag Mor
Charleston, Gairloch IV21 2AH
☎ 01445-712068 **Fax** 01445-712044
E-mail 106505.1440@compuserve.com
Closed Nov-Feb
17 bedrs, all ensuite, 🕱 ⅲ 50 **P** 30 ⊕ **SB** £38-£45
DB £76-£90 **HB** £399-£455 **L** £12.50 **D** £26 **D** 🍷 ✕
LD 21:30 ℂℂ MC Visa Amex DC JCB
See advert on this page

★★ ✤ Old Inn
Gairloch IV21 2BD
☎ 01445-712006 **Fax** 01445-712445
14 bedrs, all ensuite, 🛉 ⅲ 60 **P** 50 ⊕ ℂℂ MC Visa
Amex

GALASHIELS Selkirkshire	13E3

Pop. 13,450. Melrose 4, London 344, Edinburgh 31,
Glasgow 67, Jedburgh 17, Kelso 18, Lauder 13,
Peebles 18 **EC** Wed 🛈 St Johns Street 01896-755551

★★★ Kingsknowes
Selkirk Road, Galashiels TD1 3HY
☎ 01896-758375 **Fax** 01896-750377
11 bedrs, all ensuite, ♀ 🕱 🛉 ⅲ 80 **P** 100 ⊕ **SB** £49
DB £68-£74 **HB** £294 **L** £9 **L** 🍷 **D** £12 **D** 🍷 ✕ **LD** 21:30
ℂℂ MC Visa Amex DC 🖼 🖼

SCOTLAND

★★ Abbotsford Arms
63 Stirling Street, Galashiels TD1 1BY
☎ 01896-752517 **Fax** 01896-750744

Family hotel tastefully decorated. Small and friendly with a reputation for good food, served all day from 12 noon. Close to town centre.
14 bedrs, 10 ensuite, ♪ ⁑ 150 **P** 10 ⊕ **SB** £38-£40 **DB** £50-£60 **L** £8 **D** £10 **D** ● ✕ **LD** 21:00 **CC** MC Visa

---

GATEHOUSE OF FLEET Kirkcudbrightshire 12C4
Pop. 900. Castle Douglas 14, London 358, Dumfries 35, Edinburgh 102, Girvan 47, Glasgow 89, New Galloway 19, Stranraer 44 **ℹ** Car Park 01557-814212

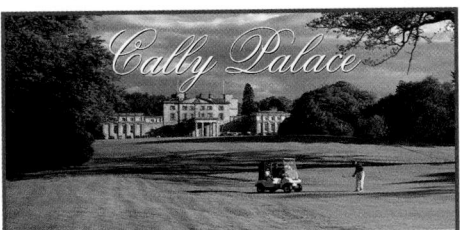

Cally Palace

Gatehouse of Fleet DG7 2DL
Tel 01557 814341 Fax 01557 814522
www.mcmillanhotels.com

The Cally Palace, dating back to 1763, is an imposing country mansion set in 150 acres of parkland and mature woodland. Surrounding the hotel is its own private 18 hole golf course, maintained to a high standard for the exclusive use of its guests. The spacious lounges have been sympathetically restored, and the addition of a large conservatory, indoor swimming pool, jacuzzi, sauna and snooker room compliment the Cally facilities. Dining in the rosetted restaurant with its resident pianist is always an enjoyable experience and spacious suites, large luxury bedrooms and family rooms with balcony give an excellent choice of accommodation.

 ★★★★ STB  AA ROSETTE FOR FOOD

★★★★ Cally Palace 🛎 🛎
Gatehouse of Fleet DG7 2DL
☎ 01557-814341 **Fax** 01557-814522
E-mail cally@cphotel.demon.co.uk
Closed Jan-Feb
56 bedrs, all ensuite, ▦ ✦ ⁑ 40 **P** 100 ⊕ **SB** £57-£63 **DB** £52-£57 **HB** £434-£462 **L** £12 **L** ● **D** £24 ✕ **LD** 21:00 **CC** MC Visa Amex ▣ ▦ ▸ ▨ ▨ ▦ ⅙
See advert on this page

★★★ Murray Arms
Main Street, Gatehouse of Fleet DG7 2HY
☎ 01557-814207 **Fax** 01557-814370
13 bedrs, all ensuite, ↰ ⁑ 100 **P** 30 ⊕ **SB** £45-£50 **DB** £80-£95 **L** ● **D** £18 **D** ● ✕ **LD** 21:45 **CC** MC Visa Amex DC

GLASGOW 12C2
See also CLYDEBANK
Pop. 753,000. Hamilton 11, London 388, M8 1, Dumbarton 15, Edinburgh 45, Gourock 25, Kilmarnock 20, Kincardine 28, Lanark 25, Paisley 6½, Stirling 26 **see** Glasgow Cathedral, University, Art Gallery and Museum (Kelvingrove Park), Old Glasgow Museum, Transport Museum, Burrell Collection, Tolbooth Steeple, Iron Steeple, St Andrew's Church **ℹ** 35 St Vincent Place 0141-204 4400

★★★★ Beardmore
Beardmore Street, Clydebank, Glasgow G81 4SA
☎ 0141-951 6000 **Fax** 0141-951 6018
E-mail beardmore.hotel@hci.co.uk
168 bedrs, all ensuite, ↰ ✦ ⁑ 170 **P** 150 ⊕ **CC** MC Visa Amex DC ▣ ▣ ▦ ⅙

★★★ Dalmeny Park Country House ♠
Lochlibo Road, Barrhead, G78 1LG
☎ 0141-881 9211 Fax 0141-881 9214
E-mail enquiries@maksu-group.co.uk

Nestling in 7 acres of beautiful gardens, 8 minutes from Glasgow city centre. 20 individual classic ensuite rooms. Conference facilities for 300. Award winning garden restaurant.
20 bedrs, all ensuite, ⁴ ♀ ♪ ♈ ⠇ 200 P 200 ⊕ SB £63-£69 DB £85-£91 L £8 L ● D £17 D ● ✕ LD 21:30 ⓒ MC Visa Amex DC

★★★ Jurys Glasgow
Great Western Road, Glasgow G12 0XP
☎ 0141-334 8161 Fax 0141-334 3846
E-mail bookings@jurys.com
137 bedrs, all ensuite, ♀ ♪ ⊡ ⠇ 140 P 250 ⊕ SB £114.50 DB £124 L £10.50 L ● D £17.50 ✕ LD 21:30 ⓒ MC Visa Amex DC ⊡ ⊞ ⊠ ⅃

★★★ Kings Park ♠ ♠ ♠
Mill Street, Rutherglen, Glasgow G73 2AR
☎ 0141-647 5491 Fax 0141-613 3022
E-mail enquiries@maksu-group.co.uk

Only 5 minutes from Glasgow city centre and East Kilbride, recently refurbished throughout offering excellent conference facilities for 350. All ensuite rooms. Beautiful terrace restaurant.
26 bedrs, all ensuite, ⁴ ♈ ⠇ 250 P 150 ⊕ SB £63-£69 DB £85-£91 L £8 L ● D £17 D ● ✕ LD 21:30 ⓒ MC Visa Amex DC ⅃

★★★ Macdonald
Mains Avenue, Eastwood Toll, Giffnock, Glasgow G46 6RA
☎ 0141-638 2225 Fax 0141-638 6231
56 bedrs, all ensuite, ♈ ⠇ 160 P 150 ⊕ ⓒ MC Visa Amex DC ⊠ ⅃

★★★ Posthouse Glasgow City
Posthouse
Bothwell Street, Glasgow G2 7EN
☎ 0141-248 2656 Fax 0141-221 8986
247 bedrs, all ensuite, ⊡ ⠇ 800 P 30 ⊕ ⓒ MC Visa Amex DC JCB

★★★ Sherbrooke Castle
11 Sherbrooke Avenue, Glasgow G41 4PG
☎ 0141-427 4227 Fax 0141-427 5685
25 bedrs, all ensuite, ⁴ ♪ ♈ ⠇ 200 P 60 ⊕ SB £50-£130 DB £55-£150 L £12.50 L ● D £18.80 D ● ✕ LD 21:45 ⓒ MC Visa Amex DC ⅃

★★★ Swallow ♠ ♠
517 Paisley Road West, Glasgow G51 1RW
☎ 0141-427 3146 Fax 0141-427 4059
E-mail info@swallowhotels.com

This popular hotel, with leisure facilities, is located just a few minutes from the city centre and is only five minutes' walk from the Burrell collection.
117 bedrs, all ensuite, ♈ ⊡ ⠇ 320 P 150 ⊕ SB £85 DB £110 L £9.50 D £17 ✕ LD 21:30 Restaurant closed L Sat ⓒ MC Visa Amex DC ⊡ ⊞ ⊠

Facilities for the disabled
Hotels do their best to cater for disabled visitors. However, it is advisable to contact the hotel direct to ensure it can provide a particular requirement.

★★ Argyll
973 Sauchiehall Street, Glasgow G3 7TQ
☎ 0141-337 3313 **Fax** 0141-337 3283
E-mail argyll_angus.hotel@virgin.net

Excellent location ½ mile west of city centre. Close to all amenities. 38 bedrooms all ensuite. Traditional restaurant/bar. Decorated to high standard. A warm welcome awaits. Free parking.
38 bedrs, all ensuite, ④ ⌀ ☐ ⅲ 30 ⊞ **SB** £44-£54 **DB** £58-£68 **L** £5.95 **D** £10 **D** ☞ ✕ **LD** 21:30
Restaurant closed L Sat-Sun **CC** MC Visa Amex

★★ Quality
Gordon Street, Glasgow G1 3SF
☎ 0141-221 9680 **Fax** 0141-226 3948
E-mail admin@gb627.u-net.com

Elegant Victorian city centre hotel with meeting rooms available, situated in the heart of Glasgow close to Transport Museum and art galleries.
222 bedrs, all ensuite, ★ ☐ ⅲ 600 **P** 500 ⊞
SB £82.75-£91 **DB** £107-£124 **L** £7.45 **D** £14.50 ✕
LD 21:30 Restaurant closed L Sun **CC** MC Visa Amex
DC JCB ▣ ▨ ▧ ⓖ

★ Dunkeld
10/12 Queen's Drive, Glasgow G42 8BS
☎ 0141-424 0160 **Fax** 0141-423 4437
E-mail dunkeldhot@aol.com

This elegant Victorian residence is located in the south side for all Glasgow's tourist and sports attractions.
19 bedrs, all ensuite, ④ ♀ ⌀ ★ ⅲ 100 **P** 8 ⊞
Restricted **SB** £27-£39.50 **DB** £40-£55 **HB** £273-£353
L £6 **D** £11 ✕ **LD** 20:30 **CC** MC Visa Amex JCB

GLASGOW AIRPORT Renfrewshire   **12C2**
🛈 0141-848 4440

★★★ ✤ Dean Park
91 Glasgow Road, Renfrew PA4 8YB
☎ 0141-304 9955 **Fax** 0141-885 0681
E-mail salesdeanpark@cosmopolitan.sol.co.uk
118 bedrs, all ensuite, ④ ★ ⅲ 300 **P** 180 ⊞ **SB** £45-£68 **DB** £50-£86 **L** £6.95 **L** ☞ **D** £10.95 **D** ☞ ✕
LD 21:45 **CC** MC Visa Amex DC ⓖ

★★★ Glynhill
169 Paisley Road, Renfrew PA4 8XB
☎ 0141-886 5555 **Fax** 0141-885 2838
E-mail glynhillleisurehotel@msn.com

Ideal, convenient base for business executives and tourists alike. Glasgow centre 7 miles via adjacent M8, airport 1 mile. Set in a quiet location with two excellent restaurants, superb leisure club, major conference centre and friendly efficient staff.
125 bedrs, all ensuite, ★ ⅲ 450 **P** 230 ⊞ **SB** £69-£94 **DB** £79-£104 **HB** £375 **L** £7 **L** ☞ **D** £15 ✕ **LD** 22:30
CC MC Visa Amex DC JCB ▣ ▨ ▧ ⓖ

★★★ ✦ Posthouse
Glasgow Airport
Posthouse

Abbotsinch, Glasgow PA3 2TR
☎ 0141-887 1212 **Fax** 0141-887 3738
297 bedrs, all ensuite, ▣ ⋕ 175 **P** 70 ⊞ ⟨⟨ MC Visa Amex DC

GLENCAPLE Dumfriesshire
13D4
Pop. 270. Cummertrees 10, London 325, Brampton 37, Carlisle 31, Dumfries 5, Edinburgh 76, Glasgow 78, Langholm 31

★★ Nith
Glencaple DG1 4RE
☎ 01387-770213 **Fax** 01387-770568
10 bedrs, 7 ensuite, ⊢ ⋕ 130 **P** 20 ⊞ ⟨⟨ MC Visa ⌧

GLENMORISTON Inverness-shire
14C3
Invergarry 22, London 539, Beauly 14, Edinburgh 173, Glasgow 148, Inverness 14

★★ Cluanie Inn ⌇
Glenmoriston, Inverness IV3 6YW
☎ 01320-340238 **Fax** 01320-340293

Lying between Loch Ness and the Isle of Skye, this newly refurbished Highland inn offers a range of facilities and services, the restaurants catering for every requirement. Children welcome. Dogs allowed.
14 bedrs, 12 ensuite, ④ ⊢ **P** 50 ⊞ **SB** £37.50 **DB** £79 **D** £18.50 ✕ **LD** 20:30 ⟨⟨ MC Visa Amex ⌧ ▦

GRANTOWN-ON-SPEY Morayshire
15E3
Pop. 1,400. Tomintoul 13, London 508, Braemar 46, Carrbridge 10, Edinburgh 131, Elgin 8, Glasgow 147, Kingussie 26 **EC** Thu **see** Parish Church ⓘ 54 High Street 01479-872773

★★ Culdearn House ⌇ ⌇ ⌇
Woodlands Terrace, Grantown-on-Spey PH26 3JU
☎ 01479-872106 **Fax** 01479-873641

Closed Nov-Feb
9 bedrs, all ensuite, **P** 10 No children under 10 ⊞ Resid **SB** £45-£65 **DB** £90-£130 (Prices include dinner) ⟨⟨ MC Visa Amex DC JCB ⅙

GRETNA Dumfriesshire
10B1
Pop. 2,200. Carlisle 9, London 303, Beattock 30, Brampton 15, Dumfries 24, Edinburgh 82, Glasgow 85, Langholm 15 **EC** Wed ⓘ Old Blacksmith's Shop 01461-337834

★★ Gretna Chase
Gretna DG16 5JB
☎ 01461-337517 **Fax** 01461-337766
9 bedrs, all ensuite, ④ ⊢ ⋕ 30 **P** 40 ⊞ ⟨⟨ MC Visa Amex

★★ Solway Lodge
Annan Road, Gretna DG16 5DN
☎ 01461-338266 **Fax** 01461-337791
10 bedrs, all ensuite, ④ ⊢ **P** 30 ⊞ **SB** £39.50 **DB** £55 ✕ **LD** 21:00 ⟨⟨ MC Visa Amex DC

★ Royal Stewart Motel
Glasgow Road, Gretna CA6 5DT
☎ 01461-338210
12 bedrs, all ensuite, ④ ⊢ ⋕ 60 **P** 24 ⊞ ⟨⟨ MC Visa Amex

HALKIRK Caithness
15E1
Thurso 6, Edinburgh 263, London 638, Inverness 116, Wick 17

★★ Ulbster Arms ⌇
Halkirk KW12 6XY
☎ 01847-831641 **Fax** 01847-831206

There is no finer background than the beauty of Caithness for what could arguably be the finest shooting and fishing holiday in Scotland. The charm of 19th century Ulbster Arms might be attraction enough, but there is a great deal more.

26 bedrs, all ensuite, ⅋ P 30 ⊕ SB £37 DB £61-£76
L ● D £21.50 D ● ✕ LD 20:45 ℂℂ MC Visa JCB ▣

HAMILTON Lanarkshire   12C2
ℹ Services, M74 Northbound 01698-285590

Roadchef Lodge **Lodge**
M74 Northbound, Hamilton ML3 6JW
☎ 01698-891904 **Fax** 01698-891682
Closed 25-27 Dec
36 bedrs, all ensuite, ⅲ 25 P 120 **Room** £47.95 ℂℂ MC
Visa Amex DC ⅊

HAWICK Roxburghshire   13E3
Pop. 16,500. Corbridge 50, London 330, Edinburgh
48, Glasgow 80, Jedburgh 15, Kelso 21, Langholm
23, Selkirk 12 ℹ Drumlanrig's Tower 01450-372547

★★ Elm House
17 North Bridge Street, Hawick TD9 9BD
☎ 01450-372866 **Fax** 01450-374175

A late Victorian house near the city centre
converted into a hotel.
15 bedrs, all ensuite, ⅋ ⅲ 40 P 11 ⊕ SB £28-£30
DB £38-£44 L £7 L ● D £11 D ● ✕ LD 21:30
Restaurant closed L Sun ℂℂ MC Visa JCB ⅊

★★ Kirklands
West Stewart Place, Hawick TD9 8BH
☎ 01450-372263 **Fax** 01450-370404
9 bedrs, all ensuite, ⅋ P 20 ⊕ SB £40-£52 DB £65-
£80 HB £250-£295 D £15 ✕ LD 21:00 ℂℂ MC Visa
Amex DC ▧

Don't forget to mention
the guide

When booking direct, please remember to
tell the hotel that you chose it from
RAC Inspected Hotels 2000

HOWWOOD Renfrewshire   12C2
Paisley 8, London 401, M8 9, Edinburgh 60,
Glasgow 15, Greenock 18, Irvine 17

★★★ Bowfield Hotel & Country Club ▥ ▥
Bowfield, Howwood PA9 1DB
☎ 01505-705225 **Fax** 01505-705230
23 bedrs, all ensuite, ⅲ 60 P 100 ⊕ ℂℂ MC Visa
Amex DC ▣▥▤▥▥ ⅊
See advert on this page

HUMBIE East Lothian   13E2
Edinburgh 18, London 358, Galashiels 22,
Haddington 10

★★★ Johnstounburn House ▥ ▥
Humbie EH35 5PL
☎ 01875-833696 **Fax** 01875-833626
20 bedrs, 18 ensuite, 1 ▨ ⅋ ⅲ 30 P 100 ⊕ ℂℂ MC
Visa Amex DC JCB ▣

HUNTLY Aberdeenshire   15E3
Pop. 4,250. Kildrummy 15, London 512, Aberdeen
38, Banff 21, Braemar 57, Edinburgh 137, Glasgow
154 ℹ 9a The Square 01466-792255

★★ Old Manse of Marnoch 🅱 🅱 🅱
Blue Ribbon Hotel
Bridge of Marnoch, By-Huntly AB54 7RS
☎ 01466-780873 **Fax** 01466-780873

A destination for the discerning traveller, this Georgian country house offers choice food, wines and luxury accommodation. Ideally situated to explore Grampian and Northeast Scotland.
5 bedrs, all ensuite, 🅰 🛏 **P** 10 No children under 12 🍴 Restricted **SB** £54–£60 **DB** £84.60–£94 **HB** £487.20 **D** £27 ✕ **LD** 20:00 **CC** MC Visa JCB

GLENGARRY CASTLE

A fine Victorian mansion standing in 60 acres of grounds overlooking Loch Oich. Family run for over 40 years the hotel offers its guests a relaxed, friendly atmosphere. Ideal situation for day trips to Isle of Skye, Loch Ness and Glencoe/Fort William area.

Please write or phone for our brochure.

**INVERGARRY,
INVERNESS-SHIRE PH35 4HW
Tel: 01809 501254 Fax: 01809 501207**

INVERARAY Argyll   12B1
Pop. 450. Arrochar 21, London 444, Crianlarich 39, Edinburgh 99, Glasgow 57, Lochgilphead 24, Oban 38 **EC** Wed **see** Inveraray Castle, Bell Tower, Crarae Gardens (9½m SW) 🛈 Front Street 01499-302063

Loch Fyne **Awaiting Inspection**
Inveraray PA32 8XT
☎ 01499-302148 **Fax** 01499-302348

INVERGARRY Inverness-shire   14C4
Pop. 150. Spean Bridge 15, London 513, Edinburgh 148, Fort William 25, Glasgow 124

★★★ Glengarry Castle 🅱 🅱
Invergarry PH35 4HW
☎ 01809-501254 **Fax** 01809-501207
E-mail castle@glengarry.net/
Closed mid Nov-late Mar

Fine Victorian mansion in extensive wooded grounds on the shores of Loch Oich. Privately owned and personally managed by the MacCallum family for over 40 years.
26 bedrs, all ensuite, 🅰 🛏 **P** 25 🍴 Restricted **SB** £49–£54 **DB** £78–£136 **HB** £364–£567 **L** 🍷 **D** £24 ✕ **LD** 20:30 Restaurant closed L Mon-Sat **CC** MC Visa 🔲 🔳
See advert on this page

INVERNESS Inverness-shire   15D3
Pop. 41,000. Carrbridge 23, London 529, Achnasheen 42, Beauly 12, Dingwall 14, Edinburgh 154, Elgin 39, Glasgow 165, Invermoriston 28, Ullapool 55 **EC** Wed **MD** Mon, Tue **see** Episcopal Cathedral, Castle, Town House, Town Steeple, Castle Stewart 🛈 Castle Wynd 01463-234353

★★★★ Swallow Kingsmills 🅱
Culcabock Road, Inverness IV2 3LP
☎ 01463-237166 **Fax** 01463-225208
E-mail info@swallowhotels.com

SWALLOW
HOTELS

The magnificent Kingsmills is one of the finest hotels in the Highlands. It has its own leisure facilities and golf on the doorstep.
82 bedrs, all ensuite, ⊨ 🖵 ⠿ 100 **P** 130 ⊕ **SB** £85-£110 **DB** £125-£155 **HB** £405-£565 **L** £10.50 **D** £23 ✕ **LD** 21:30 **CC** MC Visa Amex DC 🖩 🖻 🖾 ⅋

★★★ Loch Ness House ⍟
Glenurquhart Road, Inverness IV3 6JL
📞 01463-231248 **Fax** 01463-239327
22 bedrs, all ensuite, ④ ⊨ ⠿ 150 **P** 80 ⊕ **SB** £60-£80 **DB** £60-£98 **HB** £385-£455 **L** £9 **D** £17 ✕ **LD** 21:00 **CC** MC Visa Amex DC JCB

★★★ Lochardil House ⍟
Stratherrick Road, Inverness IV2 4LF
📞 01463-235995 **Fax** 01463-713394
12 bedrs, all ensuite, ♀ ⠿ 150 **P** 100 ⊕ **SB** £63-£70 **DB** £80-£90 **HB** £450-£475 **L** £10 **L** ⍟ **D** £15 **D** ⍟ ✕
LD 21:00 **CC** MC Visa Amex DC JCB

★★★ White Lodge
15 Bishops Road, Inverness IV3 5SB
📞 01463-230693 **Fax** 01463-230693
7 bedrs, all ensuite, ⊠ **P** 7 No children under 10

★ Station ⍟
18 Academy Street, Inverness IV1 1LG
📞 01463-231926 **Fax** 01463-710705
E-mail shi@dial.pipex.com
67 bedrs, all ensuite, ⌀ ⊨ 🖵 ⠿ 180 **P** 20 ⊕ **SB** £62-£65 **DB** £95-£99 **L** £6.50 **L** ⍟ **D** £17.95 **D** ⍟ ✕
LD 21:15 **CC** MC Visa Amex DC JCB
See advert on this page

INVERURIE Aberdeenshire	15F3

Pop. 6,150. London 500, Edinburgh 125, Glasgow 145 🅸 Town Hall, Market Place 01467-620600

★★★ Strathburn
Burghmuir Drive, Inverurie AB51 4GY
📞 01467-624422 **Fax** 01467-625133
25 bedrs, all ensuite, ⠿ 30 **P** 40 ⊕ **CC** MC Visa Amex ⅋

ISLE OF ARRAN	12B3

🅸 The Pier, Brodick 01770-302140

★★★ Kinloch
Blackwaterfoot KA27 8ET
📞 01770-860444 **Fax** 01770-860447
E-mail kinloch@cqm.co.uk.

The Kinloch has 44 bedrooms with private facilities, colour TV, coffee making facilities and hairdryer. Also has 7 fully contained suites and sports facilities.
44 bedrs, all ensuite, ④ ⊨ 🖵 ⠿ 150 **P** 50 ⊕ **CC** MC Visa Amex DC 🖩 🖻 🖾 🖻 🖻

SCOTLAND

ISLE OF BUTE — 12B2

ℹ️ 15 Victoria Street, Rothesay 01700-502151

★★ Ardmory House 🛏 🛏 🛏 🛏
Ardmory Road, Ardbeg PA20 0PG
📞 01700-502346 Fax 01700-505596
E-mail ardmory.house.hotel@dial.pipex.com

Set in its own grounds, 1 mile from Rothesay. Bedrooms and restaurant non-smoking. Lunch time snacks, evening bar meals and extensive dinner menu with cuisine described as traditional Scottish with an international flavour. Panoramic views over the Clyde.
5 bedrs, all ensuite, 🛏 ⅲ 50 P 12 ⊕ SB £45 DB £70 HB £335 L £6 L 🍴 D £17.50 D 🍴 ✕ LD 21:00 ⓒ MC Visa Amex DC JCB

ISLE OF ISLAY — 12A2

★★ Port Askaig
Port Askaig PA46 7RD
📞 01496-840245 Fax 01496-840295
10 bedrs, 6 ensuite, ♀ 🛏 P 12 No children under 5
⊕ SB £35-£39 DB £66-£72 HB £330-£375 L £10.50
L 🍴 D £18 D 🍴 ✕ LD 21:00 ♿
See advert on this page

ISLE OF MULL — 12A1

★★★ ✤ Western Isles
Tobermory PA75 6PR
📞 01688-302012 Fax 01688-302297
E-mail wihotel@aol.com.
Closed 18-28 Dec
25 bedrs, all ensuite, ④ 🛏 ⅲ 50 P 20 ⊕ ⓒ MC Visa Amex

ISLE OF SKYE — 14B3

ℹ️ Broadford 01471-822361 or Meall House, Portree 01478-612137

★★★ Cuillin Hills 🛏 🛏 🛏
Portree IV51 9LU
📞 01478-612003
E-mail office@cuillinhills.demon.co.uk
30 bedrs, all ensuite, ④ 🛏 ⅲ 120 P 60 ⊕ SB £35-£56 DB £70-£136 HB £245-£560 L 🍴 D £26 D 🍴 ✕ LD 21:00 Restaurant closed (L) m,t,w,t,f,sat ⓒ MC Visa Amex ♿
See advert on opposite page

★★ ✤ Ardvasar
Ardvarsar IV48 8RS
📞 01471-844223 Fax 01471-844495
E-mail christine@ardvasar-hotel.demon.co.uk
10 bedrs, all ensuite, ④ 🛏 ⅲ 50 P 30 ⊕ SB £45-£50 DB £80-£100 HB £385 L £10 L 🍴 D £28.50 D 🍴 ✕ LD 22:00 ⓒ MC Visa 🖼

★★ Hotel Eilean Iarmain 🛏 🛏 🛏
Sleat, Sleat IV43 8QR
📞 01471-833332 Fax 01471-833275
16 bedrs, all ensuite, ④ 🛏 ⅲ 100 P 30 ⊕ SB £63-£80 DB £100-£125 HB £563-£773 L £16.50 D £30.50 ✕ LD 20:45 ⓒ MC Visa Amex 🎵

★★ Royal
Bank Street, Portree IV51 9BU
📞 01478-612525 Fax 01478-613198
24 bedrs, all ensuite, 🛏 ⅲ 120 P 20 ⊕ ⓒ MC Visa 🖼 🖼

The Isle of Skye

Set in its own grounds overlooking Portree Bay with spectacular views of the Cuillin mountains. Enjoy the peace and tranquillity of Skye from the Cuillin Hills Hotel where high standards of comfort and service and award-winning cuisine combine with the warmth of Highland hospitality.

Cuillin Hills Hotel, Portree, Isle of Skye IV51 9LU
Tel: 01478 612003
Fax: 01478 613092

KELSO Roxburghshire   13E3
Pop. 5,200. Jedburgh 11, London 338, Coldstream 9, Edinburgh 44, Galashiels 18, Hawick 21, Lauder 18, Selkirk 19 **EC** Wed **see** 12th cent Abbey remains
ℹ Town House, The Square 01573-223464

★★★ ✦ Cross Keys
36-37 The Square, Kelso TD5 7HL
☎ 01573-223303 **Fax** 01573-225792
E-mail cross-keys-hotel@easynet.co.uk
28 bedrs, all ensuite, ♪ 🛏 ⛶ ⅲ 280 **P** 20 ⊟
SB £41.50-£49.50 **DB** £57-£85 **L** £8 **D** £16 **D** 🍷 ✕
LD 21:15 **CC** MC Visa Amex DC &

★★★ ✦ Ednam House
Bridge Street, Kelso TD5 7HT
☎ 01573-224168 **Fax** 01573-226319
Closed Christmas-New Year
32 bedrs, all ensuite, 🛏 ⅲ 250 **P** 100 ⊟ **SB** £53
DB £72-£102 **D** £11 ✕ **LD** 21:00 **CC** MC Visa

★★★ Roxburghe Hotel
& Golf Course 🎏 🎏 🎏
Kelso TD5 8JZ
☎ 01573-450331 **Fax** 01573-450611
E-mail sunlaws.roxgc@virgin.net
Closed 23-29 Dec

Baronial style house well situated in its own 200 acre sporting estate.
22 bedrs, all ensuite, ④ 🛏 ⅲ 50 **P** 100 ⊟ **SB** £95
DB £120 **L** £10.50 **L** 🍷 **D** £29.50 ✕ **LD** 21:30 **CC** MC Visa Amex DC ▣ ▶ ▨ ▨

KENMORE Perthshire   12C1
Pop. 600. Aberfeldy 5½, London 444, Crianlarich 31, Edinburgh 74, Glasgow 74 **EC** Wed

★★★ Kenmore
The Square, Kenmore PH15 2NU
☎ 01887-830205 **Fax** 01887-830262
41 bedrs, all ensuite, ♀ ♪ 🛏 ⛶ ⅲ 100 **P** 60 ⊟
SB £40-£60 **DB** £70-£100 **HB** £346-£487 **L** £10 **L** 🍷
D £25 **D** 🍷 ✕ **LD** 22:00 **CC** MC Visa Amex JCB ▶ ▨ ▨ &

SCOTLAND

KILCHRENAN Argyll 12B1
Dalmally 18, London 473, Edinburgh 115, Glasgow 85, Inveraray 32, Oban 19

★★★ Taychreggan 🍴🍴🍴🍴
Kilchrenan, Taynuilt PA35 1HQ
📞 01866-833211 **Fax** 01866-833244
E-mail taychreggan@btinternet.com
19 bedrs, all ensuite, 🔟 ✟ ⊞ 20 **P** 40 No children under 14 ⊕ **SB** £62-£67 **DB** £104-£114 **L** £17 **D** £30 ✕ **LD** 20:45 **CC** MC Visa Amex 🖼️

KINGUSSIE Inverness-shire 15D3
Pop. 1,300. Newtonmore 3, London 488, Carrbridge 19, Edinburgh 112, Fort William 47, Glasgow 124, Grantown-on-Spey 26 **EC** Wed **see** Highland Folk Museum, China Studios, Wildlife Park (5m) 🛈 King Street 01540-661297

★★ Royal
29 High Street, Kingussie PH21 1HX
📞 01540-661898 **Fax** 01540-661061
54 bedrs, all ensuite, ✟ ⊞ 100 **P** 10 ⊕ **SB** £20-£32 **DB** £32-£54 **HB** £198 **L** 💷 **D** £12 **D** ✕ **LD** 21:30 **CC** MC Visa Amex DC JCB ⅙

KINROSS Kinross-shire 13D2
Pop. 4,500. South Queensferry 17, London 401, M90 (jn 6) 1, Dundee 30, Dunfermline 12, Edinburgh 27, Glasgow 45, Kincardine 17, Kirkcaldy 16, Perth 16, St Andrews 35, Stirling 23 **EC** Thu 🛈 Service Area, M90 01577-863680

★★★ Green 🍴
2 The Muirs, Kinross KY13 8AS
📞 01577-863467 **Fax** 01577-863180
E-mail reservations@green-hotel.com

Ideally situated in central Scotland. Leisure complex with indoor pool, sauna, solarium, exercise facility and squash court. Two all weather tennis courts. Own two 18 hole golf courses. Curling rink.
47 bedrs, all ensuite, 🔟 ✟ ⊞ 100 **P** 60 ⊕ **SB** £75-£95 **DB** £130-£155 **HB** £420-£595 **L** £12 **L** 💷 **D** £23 **D** 💷 ✕ **LD** 21:30 **CC** MC Visa Amex DC 🖼🖼🖼🖼🖼 🖼🖼⅙

★★ Kirklands
20 High Street, Kinross KY13 7AN
📞 01557-863313 **Fax** 01577-863313
9 bedrs, all ensuite, **P** 12 ⊕ **SB** £39 **DB** £60-£70 **HB** £250-£300 **L** 💷 **D** £11 **D** 💷 ✕ **LD** 21:00 **CC** MC Visa Amex

KIRKCALDY Fife 13D2
Pop. 49,800. M90 9, South Queensferry 16, London 400, Dundee 29, Dunfermline 12, Edinburgh 25, Kinross 16, St Andrews 23 **EC** Wed **see** Sailor's Walk (NT Scot), Ravenscraig Castle ruins, Art Gallery and Museum, Royal Palace of Falkland 9½ m NW 🛈 19 Whytescauseway 01592-267775

★★★ ✤ Dean Park
Chapel Level, Kirkcaldy KY2 6QW
📞 01592-261635 **Fax** 01592-261371
41 bedrs, all ensuite, 🔟 ⌀ 📧 ⊞ 240 **P** 240 ⊕ **SB** £59 **DB** £89 **L** £5.50 **L** 💷 **D** £19.50 **D** 💷 ✕ **LD** 21:30 **CC** MC Visa Amex DC JCB ⅙

★★ ✤ Belvedere
Coxstool, West Wemyss KY1 4SL
📞 01592-654167 **Fax** 01592-655279

21 ensuite bedrooms, with panoramic views across the Firth of Forth and to Edinburgh beyond. Excellent restaurant, using the best products from Scotland's natural larder.
20 bedrs, all ensuite, ⌀ ✟ ⊞ 12 **P** 50 ⊕ **SB** £45-£57.50 **DB** £65-£75 **HB** £297.50 **L** £14.50 **L** 💷 **D** £17.50 **D** 💷 ✕ **LD** 21:15 **CC** MC Visa Amex

KYLE OF LOCHALSH Ross-shire   14B3

Pop. 900. Invergarry 48, London 561, Achnasheen 35, Edinburgh 196, Glasgow 174, Invermoriston 56 **EC** Thu **see** Harbour, Eilean Donan Castle, Castle Moil on Isle of Skye, Balmacara House (4m E) *i* Car Park 01599-534276

★★★ Lochalsh

Ferry Road, Kyle of Lochalsh IV40 8AF
☎ 01599-534202 **Fax** 01599-534881
E-mail md.macrae@lochalsh-hotel.demon.co.uk

A family owned hotel overlooking the Isle of Skye. An oasis of comfort and good living in the Scottish Highlands, with 38 rooms all ensuite.
38 bedrs, all ensuite, 🐾 ⬛ ⊞ 70 **P** 40 ⊕ **SB** £35-£60 **DB** £60-£120 **L** £6.50 **D** £20.50 ✕ **LD** 21:30 **CC** MC Visa Amex DC ⊠ �&

LANGBANK Renfrewshire   12C2

Pop. 800. Glasgow 14, London 402, M8 (jn 31) 1½, Dumbarton (via tollbridge) 10, Edinburgh 59, Glasgow 14, Greenock 7, Paisley 9½ **EC** Wed

★★★★ Gleddoch House 🛋 🛋

Langbank PA14 6YE
☎ 01475-540711 **Fax** 01475-540201
38 bedrs, all ensuite, ④ 🐾 ⊞ 100 **P** 150 ⊕ **SB** £90-£95 **DB** £130-£140 **L** £15 **D** £34 **D** 🍽 ✕ **LD** 21:00 **CC** MC Visa Amex DC �ⓟ ⊠ ⊠ ⊠
See advert on this page

LARGS Ayrshire   12B2

Pop. 10,000. Irvine 17, London 408, Ayr 31, Edinburgh 74, Glasgow 29, Gourock 14, Kilmarnock 26, Paisley 23 **EC** Wed *i* Promenade 01475-673765

★★★ Brisbane House 🛋 🛋

Greenock Road, Esplanade,
Largs KA30 8NF
☎ 01475-687200 **Fax** 01475-676295
E-mail enquiries@maksu-group.co.uk

A central promenade setting, minutes from town centre offering stunning views of the Islands. Superb cuisine in luxurious surroundings. Beautiful gardens. All rooms ensuite.
23 bedrs, all ensuite, ④ ♀ ✗ ⊞ 150 **P** 60 ⊕ **SB** £60-£80 **DB** £80-£120 **L** £12 **L** 🍽 **D** £21.50 **D** 🍽 ✕ **LD** 21:30 **CC** MC Visa Amex DC &

SCOTLAND

★★★ Priory House

John Street, Broomfield, Largs KA30 8DR
☎ 01475-686460 **Fax** 01475-689070
E-mail enquiries@maksu-group.co.uk

Situated on an elevated promenade site with stunning views of the islands, this luxurious and friendly hotel offers the highest standards of cuisine and comfort.
21 bedrs, all ensuite, 📺 ♀ ⌀ 🛏 ⅲ 150 **P** 50 🍴
SB £60-£80 **DB** £80-£120 **L** £6 **L** 🍷 **D** £19.75 **D** 🍷 ✕
LD 21:30 **CC** MC Visa Amex DC ♿

★★ Queens
North Promenade, Largs KA30 8QW
☎ 01475-675311 **Fax** 01475-675313
16 bedrs, all ensuite, ⌀ ⅲ 40 **P** 30 🍴 **SB** £40-£45
DB £60-£80 **HB** £365-£385 **L** £10.95 **L** 🍷 **D** 🍷 ✕
LD 21:00 **CC** MC Visa

LOCHEARNHEAD Perthshire   12C1
Callander 14, London 427, Crianlarich 16, Edinburgh 64, Glasgow 47, Stirling 30 **see** Edinample falls, Rob Roy tomb

★★ Clachan Cottage
Lochearnhead FK19 8PU
☎ 01567-830247 **Fax** 01567-830300
21 bedrs, all ensuite, 🛏 ⅲ 60 **P** 50 🍴 **SB** £27 **DB** £54
HB £269 **L** £10 **D** £18 ✕ **LD** 21:00 **CC** MC Visa

LOCHINVER Sutherland   14C1
Pop. 350. Inchnadamph 13, London 620, Dingwall 74, Durness 52, Edinburgh 245, Glasgow 249, Lairg 44, Ullapool 34 **EC** Tue **MD** Fri ℹ️ Main Street 01571-844330

★★★ Inver Lodge 🛎 🛎 🛎
Lochinver IV27 4LU
☎ 01571-844496 **Fax** 01571-844395
E-mail inverlodge@compuserve.com
Closed Nov-Mar

Modern, 2-storey hotel in own grounds in an elevated situation overlooking village, harbour and Loch Inver.
20 bedrs, all ensuite, 🛏 ⅲ 30 **P** 30 No children under 7 🍴 **SB** £80 **DB** £120-£130 **HB** £539-£560 **L** 🍷 **D** £28 ✕ **LD** 21:00 **CC** MC Visa Amex DC JCB 🖥️ 📋 📺
See advert on opposite page

LOCHMADDY North Uist   14A2
Ferry to Uig (Skye) ℹ️ Pier Road 01876-500321

★★ Lochmaddy
Lochmaddy HS6 5AA
☎ 01876-500331 **Fax** 01876-500210
15 bedrs, all ensuite, 🛏 **P** 30 🍴 **SB** £32.50-£40
DB £60-£75 **HB** £294-£357 **D** £15 ✕ **LD** 20:45 **CC** MC Visa Amex 📋

LOCKERBIE Dumfriesshire   13D4
Pop. 3,000. Carlisle 24, London 318, Beattock 14, Edinburgh 66, Glasgow 69, Langholm 18 **EC** Tue **MD** Tue, Thur, Fri **see** Old Tower, Roman Camp

★★★ Dryfesdale 🛎 🛎
Lockerbie DG11 2SF
☎ 01576-202427 **Fax** 01576-204187

Carefully converted 18th century mansion with splendid views, set in 5 acres of mature gardens.
15 bedrs, all ensuite, 🛏 ⅲ 40 **P** 50 🍴 **SB** £60 **DB** £87
HB £455 **L** £11 **D** £19 ✕ **LD** 21:00 **CC** MC Visa Amex ♿
See advert on opposite page

★★★ Lockerbie Manor
Boreland Road, Lockerbie DG11 2RG
01576-202610 **Fax** 01576-203046
E-mail manorhotel@lockerbie.freeserve.co.uk
28 bedrs, all ensuite, 150 **P** 80 **SB** £48-£72 **DB** £60-£85 **HB** £275-£315 **L** £11.50 **L** **D** £16.95 **D** **LD** 21:00 **CC** MC Visa Amex DC
See advert on previous page

★★★ Queens
Annan Road, Lockerbie DG11 2RB
01576-202415 **Fax** 01576-203901

This 3 star hotel has superb facilities including full leisure complex. Only two minutes from M74 motorway at Lockerbie.
21 bedrs, all ensuite, 300 **P** 200 **SB** £25-£39 **DB** £55-£65 **D** £12.95 **LD** 21:00 **CC** MC Visa

LYBSTER Caithness 15E1
Pop. 900. Wick 15, London 625, Helmsdale 22, Thurso 27

★★★ Portland Arms
Lybster KW3 6BS
01593-721721 **Fax** 01593 721722
E-mail portland.arms@btconnect.com
22 bedrs, all ensuite, 180 **P** 20 **SB** £45 **DB** £68 **L** £5.95 **L** **D** £10 **D** **LD** 21:00 **CC** MC Visa Amex

MALLAIG Inverness-shire 14B4
Pop. 1,050. Fort William 43, London 533, Edinburgh 175, Glasgow 142 **EC** Wed 01687-462170

★★ Marine
Station Road, Mallaig PH41 4PY
01687-462217 **Fax** 01687-462821
19 bedrs, all ensuite, **P** 6 **SB** £25-£38 **DB** £52-£70 **L** £9 **D** £17 **D** **LD** 21:00 **CC** MC Visa

★★ Morar
Mallaig PH40 4PA
01687-462346 **Fax** 01687-462212
28 bedrs, all ensuite, 100 **P** 100 **CC** MC Visa

★★ West Highland
Mallaig PH41 4QZ
01687-462210 **Fax** 01687-462130
Closed Oct-Mar
34 bedrs, all ensuite, **P** 40 **CC** MC Visa

MARKINCH Fife 13D2
Kirkcaldy 10, London 410, Edinburgh 35, Freuchie 5, Kinross 15, Lundin Links 9½

★★★★ Balbirnie House
Blue Ribbon Hotel
Balbirnie Park, Markinch KY7 6NE
01592-610066 **Fax** 01592-610529
E-mail balbirnie@btinternet.com

A quite unique multi-award winning hotel combining understated luxury with superb service and outstanding value. A delightful Grade 'A' listed house, centrepiece of a beautiful 40 acre country estate.
30 bedrs, all ensuite, 150 **P** 120 **SB** £115-£120 **DB** £210-£220 **L** £16.50 **L** **D** £29.50 **D** **LD** 21:30 Restaurant closed L Sat **CC** MC Visa Amex DC

MAYBOLE Ayrshire 12C3
Dalmellington 17, London 392, Ayr 11, Edinburgh 82, Girvan 13, Glasgow 44

★★ Ladyburn ☻ ☻ ☻
Blue Ribbon Hotel
Ladyburn, Maybole KA19 7SG
☎ 01655-740585 **Fax** 01655-740580
E-mail jhdh@ladyburn.freeserve.co.uk
Closed Nov-Mar
8 bedrs, 7 ensuite, ♀ ✗ ⅲ 24 **P** 12 No children
under 16 ♿ Restricted Resid **SB** £100-£115 **DB** £145-
£170 **L** ☎ **D** £30 ✗ **LD** 20:00 **CC** MC Visa Amex

MELROSE Roxburghshire   13E3
Pop. 2,000. St Boswells 2½, London 340,
Edinburgh 35, Galashiels 4, Glasgow 71, Hawick
14, Jedburgh 12, Lauder 11, Kelso 13 **EC** Thu **see**
Abbey ruins, Abbey Museum, 17th cent Cross,
Dryburgh Abbey ⓘ Abbey House 01896-822555

★★★ Dryburgh Abbey
Dryburgh Village, St Boswells TD6 0RQ
☎ 01835-822261 **Fax** 01835-823945
E-mail enquiries@dryburgh.co..uk

Impressive red sandstone mansion stunningly set in its
own grounds beside the ruins of the Dryburgh Abbey,
on the banks of the River Tweed. Family owned and
run - renowned for our hospitality and cuisine.
38 bedrs, all ensuite, ④ ➤ ▣ ⅲ 130 **P** 100 ♿
SB £49.50-£63.50 **DB** £89-£120 **HB** £346.50-£472.50
L £8 **L** ☎ **D** £24 **D** ☎ ✗ **LD** 21:15 **CC** MC Visa Amex
JCB ▣ ▣ ♿

★★ George & Abbotsford
High Street, Melrose TD6 9PD
☎ 01896-822308 **Fax** 01896-823363
31 bedrs, all ensuite, ➤ ⅲ 150 **P** 150 ♿ **CC** MC Visa
Amex DC

MOFFAT Dumfriesshire   13D3
Pop. 2,200. Beattock 2, London 335, Edinburgh 51,
Glasgow 53, Hawick 44, Peebles 33, Selkirk 34,
Thornhill 31 **EC** Wed ⓘ Churchgate 01683-220620

★★★ Auchen Castle ☻
Beattock, Moffat DG10 9SH
☎ 01683-300407 **Fax** 01683-300667
E-mail auchencastle@vacations.scotland.co.uk
Closed Christmas-New Year

In 30 acres of magnificent gardens. Private trout
loch. Ideally based for golfing, walking, fishing.
Explore the Borders or the countryside of Burns,
Scott and Buchan.
25 bedrs, all ensuite, ④ ♀ ✗ ➤ ⅲ 70 **P** 50 ♿ **SB** £60
DB £95-£110 **L** ☎ **D** £20 ✗ **LD** 21:30 **CC** MC Visa
Amex DC JCB ▣
See advert on this page

SCOTLAND

★★★ Moffat House

High Street, Moffat DG10 9HL
☎ 01683-220039 **Fax** 01683-221288

An 18th century, list 'A' John Adam mansion house, comprising main block and two wings. Set in two and a half acres of beautiful gardens. Central to the village.
20 bedrs, all ensuite, ④ ♀ ☂ ⅲ 80 **P** 42 ⊞ **SB** £35-£57.50 **DB** £67.50-£87 **HB** £299-£375 **L** £9 **D** £21 **D** ◗ ✕ **LD** 20:45 **CC** MC Visa Amex ఈ

★★ Beechwood Country House ⛉ ⛉

Harthope Place, Moffat DG10 9RS
☎ 01683-220210 **Fax** 01683-220889
Closed Jan-14 Feb
7 bedrs, all ensuite, ☂ ⅲ 12 **P** 12 ⊞ Resid **SB** £53 **DB** £76 **HB** £365 **L** £14.50 **D** £23.50 ✕ **LD** 21:00 Restaurant closed L Mon-Wed **CC** MC Visa Amex JCB

★★ Star

44 High Street, Moffat DG10 9EF
☎ 01683-220156 **Fax** 01683-221524

Although the narrowest hotel, as seen in the Guinness book of Records, only 20ft wide, the interior and welcome are heart warming. Excellent accommodation, real ales and good homecooking restaurant.
8 bedrs, all ensuite, ⅲ 50 ⊞ **SB** £36-£40 **DB** £50-£56 **D** £6 **D** ◗ ✕ **LD** 20:45 **CC** MC Visa Amex

★ Well View ⛉ ⛉ ⛉
Blue Ribbon Hotel

Ballplay Road, Moffat DG10 9JU
☎ 01683-220184 **Fax** 01683-220088

Mid-Victorian villa set in half an acre of garden and overlooking the town, with superb views of surrounding hills.
6 bedrs, all ensuite, ④ ☂ ⅲ 10 **P** 8 ⊞ Restricted **SB** £50-£60 **DB** £68-£100 **HB** £400-£560 **L** £13 **D** £27 ✕ **LD** 20:30 Restaurant closed L Sat **CC** MC Visa Amex

---

NAIRN Nairnshire 15D3

Pop. 10,000. Grantown-on-Spey 23, London 529, Carrbridge 24, Edinburgh 154, Elgin 21, Glasgow 171, Inverness 15 **EC** Wed **ℹ** 62 King Street 01667-452753

★★ Alton Burn

Alton Burn Road, Nairn IV12 5ND
☎ 01667-452051 **Fax** 01667-456697
E-mail altonburn@tesco.net.
Closed Jan-Mar
25 bedrs, all ensuite, ♀ ☂ ⅲ 60 **P** 50 ⊞ **SB** £30-£35 **DB** £50-£55 **HB** £287 **L** £8.75 **L** ◗ **D** £16 **D** ◗ ✕ **LD** 21:00 Restaurant closed L Mon-Fri **CC** MC Visa Amex ⇗ ▣ ▨ ▨ ఈ

NETHY BRIDGE Inverness-shire 15E3

★★ Nethybridge

Nethy Bridge PH25 3DP
☎ 01479-821203 **Fax** 01479-821686
E-mail reception@nethybridgehotel.freeserve.co.uk

A Victorian hotel of character set amidst the splendour of the Cairngorms, with many full sized golf courses close at hand, plus castles and the whisky trail.

69 bedrs, all ensuite, ▦ ⅄ ▣ ⠿ 130 **P** 80 ⊞ **SB** £39-£50 **D** £15 ✕ **LD** 20:30 ⦅ MC Visa JCB ▨ ⅋

NEW GALLOWAY Kirkcudbrightshire   12C4

Pop. 300. Crocketford 13, London 349, Dalmellington 21, Dumfries 23, Edinburgh 83, Gatehouse of Fleet 19, Glasgow 69, Stranraer 44, Thornhill 22 **EC** Thu **see** Kells Church, Kenmure Castle, Loch Ken

★ Kenmure Arms
High Street, New Galloway DG7 3RL
📞 01644-420240 **Fax** 01644-420240
12 bedrs, 8 ensuite, ▨ ⅄ ⠿ 60 **P** 12 ⊞ ⦅ MC Visa ▨

NEWTON STEWART Wigtownshire   12C4

Pop. 2,000. New Galloway 17, London 367, Edinburgh 101, Gatehouse of Fleet 18, Girvan 30, Glasgow 82, Stranraer 22 **EC** Wed **MD** Thu
🛈 Dashwood Square 01671-402431

★★★ Kirroughtree House ▯ ▯
Blue Ribbon Hotel
Newton Stewart DG8 6AN
📞 01671-402141 **Fax** 01671-402425
E-mail kirroughtree@n-steward.demon.co.uk
Closed 3 Jan-17 Feb
17 bedrs, all ensuite, ▦ ⌁ ⅄ ⠿ 20 **P** 50 No children under 10 ⊞ **SB** £75-£80 **DB** £130-£180 **HB** £476-£651 **L** £13.50 **L** ▰ **D** £30 ✕ **LD** 21:00 ⦅ MC Visa ▨
See advert on this page

★★ Crown
101 Queen Street, Newton Stewart DG8 6JW
📞 01671-402727 **Fax** 01671-402727

Family run hotel. All bedrooms ensuite, extensive bar, a la carte, table d'hote menus. We cater for bus parties, functions and weddings.
11 bedrs, all ensuite, ⅄ ⠿ 100 **P** 20 ⊞ **SB** £25-£30 **DB** £50-£60 **HB** £238-£250 **L** £6 **D** £14 ✕ **LD** 21:00 ⦅ MC Visa ⅋

NEWTONMORE Inverness-shire   15D4

Blair Atholl 34, London 485, Dalwhinnie 10, Edinburgh 109, Fort William 45, Glasgow 121, Kingussie 2½ **EC** Wed

SCOTLAND

412 Newtonmore

★★ ✤ Glen
Main Street, Newtonmore PH20 1DD
☎ 01540-673203
9 bedrs, 5 ensuite, ⚡ ⌗ 50 P 15 ♿ ㏄ MC Visa
Amex DC

★★ Mains
Mains Street, Newtonmore PH20 1DE
☎ 01540-673206 Fax 01540-673881
31 bedrs, all ensuite, ⚡ P 35 ♿ SB £20-£32 DB £32-
£54 HB £198 L ⚑ D £12 D ⚑ ✕ LD 21:30 ㏄ MC Visa
Amex ⊠ ♿

NORTH BERWICK East Lothian   **13E2**
Pop. 5,200. East Linton 6, London 377, Berwick-
upon-Tweed 41, Edinburgh 22, Glasgow 67,
Haddington 11 **EC** Thu **see** Burgh Museum, 12th cent
St Andrew's Kirk **ℹ** Quality Street 01620-892197

★★★ Marine   *Heritage*
Cromwell Road, EH39 4LZ   HOTELS
☎ 01620-892406 Fax 01620-894480
83 bedrs, all ensuite, ④ ⚡ ☰ ⌗ 300 P 103 ♿
SB £55-£75 DB £60-£100 HB £310-£425
L £11.95 D £19.95 ✕ LD 21:30 ㏄ MC
Visa Amex DC ♿ ▣ ▣ ▣ ▣ ♿

OBAN Argyll   **12B1**
Pop. 7,000. Dalmally 23, London 477, Ballachulish
37, Edinburgh 121, Fort William 48, Glasgow 90,
Lochgilphead 36 **EC** Thu **see** RC Cathedral, McCraig
Tower, St John's Episcopal Cathedral, Museum
ℹ Argyll Square 01631-563122

★★★ ✤ Alexandra
Corran Esplanade, Oban PA34 5AA
☎ 01631-562381 Fax 01631-564497
Closed Jan

Seaside hotel in own grounds. Extensive private
parking. Superb open views of Oban Bay.
60 bedrs, all ensuite, ④ ⚡ ☰ ⌗ 150 P 80 ♿ ㏄ MC
Visa Amex ▣ ▣ ▣ ▣ ♿

★★★ Royal
Argyll Square, Oban PA34 4BE
☎ 01631-563021 Fax 01631-562811

The Royal Hotel, built in 1895, offers traditional
Scottish hospitality within quality modern
surrounds. In the very heart of Oban, the hotel's
Victorian facade dominates the town square.
91 bedrs, all ensuite, ⚡ ☰ ⌗ 100 P 18 ♿ SB £30-
£45 DB £60-£90 HB £300-£340 D £13.50 ✕ LD 20:30
㏄ MC Visa Amex ♿

★★ Falls Of Lora
Connel, Oban PA37 1PB
☎ 01631-710483 Fax 01631-710694
Closed Christmas-Jan

Set back from the A85, five miles from Oban and
overlooking Loch Etive, this is a fine owner-run
Victorian hotel with a modern extension. Edinburgh
and Glasgow are just a three hour drive away.
30 bedrs, all ensuite, ④ ⚡ ⌗ 50 P 40 ♿ SB £30-£53
DB £39-£111 L £8 L ⚑ D £17.50 D ⚑ ✕ LD 21:30
㏄ MC Visa Amex DC ♿
See advert on opposite page

LANCASTER —HOTEL—

Family run, seafront hotel with heated indoor pool, Spa, Sauna and Sunbeds. Fully Licensed. 25 ensuite heated rooms with tea making facilities, colour TV (Sky and Video), trouser presses and hair dryers. Ample parking, No coaches.

STB ★★   *RAC* ★★

OBAN, ARGYLL PA34 5AD
Tel and Fax: 01631 562587

★★ Foxholes
Cologin, Lerags, Oban PA34 4SE
☎ 01631-564982
Closed Nov-Mar

Situated in its own grounds, in a quiet glen three miles from Oban.
7 bedrs, all ensuite, **P** 8 Restricted Resid **SB** £35-£37 **DB** £52-£56 **HB** £277-£295 **D** £15 ✗ **LD** 20:00 **(C** MC Visa

★★ King's Knoll
Dunollie Road, Oban PA34 5JH
☎ 01631-562536 **Fax** 01631-566101
E-mail kingsknoll@aol.com
Closed 25 Dec-31 Jan

15 bedrs, 13 ensuite, 4 ♔ ⌗ 40 **P** 20 **SB** £18-£32.50 **DB** £40-£65 **HB** £215-£273 **D** £12 **D** ✗ **LD** 21:00 **(C** MC Visa &

★★ Lancaster
Corran Esplanade, Oban PA34 5AD
☎ 01631-562587 **Fax** 01631-562587
27 bedrs, 24 ensuite, ♔ ⌗ 30 **P** 20 **SB** £25-£30 **DB** £54-£58 **HB** £157-£189 **L** £7 **L** **D** £10 **D** ✗ **LD** 19:45 **(C** MC Visa
See advert on this page

ONICH Inverness-shire   12B1
Pop. 280. Ballachulish 4, London 478, Edinburgh 121, Fort William 10, Glasgow 89, Oban 48 **(C** Thu

★★★ Allt-nan-Ros
Onich PH33 6RY
☎ 01855-821210 **Fax** 01855-821462
E-mail allt-nan-ros@zetnet.co.uk

A country house style hotel, formerly a Victorian shooting lodge and summer residence. Set in 4 acres of award winning gardens, streams and wooded walks.
20 bedrs, all ensuite, 4 ♔ **P** 30 **SB** £37.50-£55 **DB** £75-£110 **HB** £325-£472.50 **D** £28.50 ✗ **LD** 21:00 **(C** MC Visa Amex DC

★★★ Onich
Onich PH33 6RY
☎ 01855-821214 **Fax** 01855-821484
Closed Christmas

Superb lochside garden location between Glencoe and Ben Nevis provides friendly base for touring highlands. Hearty bar meals all day with traditional Scottish cuisine in dining room.
25 bedrs, all ensuite, ♨ ⊞ 30 **P** 50 ⊕ **SB** £35-£47 **DB** £60-£84 **HB** £301-£406 **L** £8 **L** ● **D** £21 **D** ● ✕ **LD** 21:00 **CC** MC Visa Amex DC

★★ Loch Leven ⓡ
North Ballachulish, Onich PH33 6SA
☎ 01855-821236 **Fax** 01855-821550
10 bedrs, all ensuite, ♨ **P** 60 ⊕ **CC** MC Visa

PERTH Perthshire	13D1

Pop. 40,100. London 416, M90 (jn 10) 2, Blairgowrie 15, Dundee 21, Edinburgh 41, Glasgow 57 **EC** Wed **MD** Fri 🛈 45 High Street 01738-638353

★★★ Kinfauns Castle ⓡ ⓡ ⓡ
Kinfauns, Perth PH2 7JZ
☎ 01738-620777 **Fax** 01738-620778
E-mail email@kinfaunscastle.co.uk
Closed Jan
16 bedrs, all ensuite, 4️⃣ ⌁ ♨ ⊞ 50 **P** 40 No children under 12 ⊕ **SB** £120-£180 **DB** £170-£280 **L** £18.50 **D** £32 ✕ **LD** 21:00 **CC** MC Visa Amex DC JCB

★★★ Lovat
90-92 Glasgow Road, Perth PH2 0LT
☎ 01738-636555 **Fax** 01738-643123
E-mail email@lovat.co.uk
31 bedrs, all ensuite, ♀ ⌁ ⊞ 180 **P** 40 ⊕ **SB** £69-£75 **DB** £92-£102 **HB** £269.50-£472.50 **L** £9.95 **L** ● **D** £19.95 **D** ● ✕ **LD** 21:30 **CC** MC Visa Amex DC JCB
🉐
See advert on this page

★★★ Murrayshall House ⓡ ⓡ ⓡ
Scone, Perth PH2 7PH
☎ 01738-551171 **Fax** 01738-552595
27 bedrs, all ensuite, ♨ ⊞ 140 **P** 100 ⊕ **CC** MC Visa Amex DC 🉐 🖥 🅿 🉐 ♿

★★★ Quality
Leonard Street, Perth PH2 8HE
☎ 01738-624141 **Fax** 01738-639912
E-mail admin@gb628.u-net.com

A grand Victorian city centre hotel, providing easy access to major championship golf courses.
70 bedrs, all ensuite, ♨ 🖥 ⊞ 300 **P** 100 ⊕ **SB** £79.50-£91 **DB** £100.50-£112.75 **L** £7.50 **D** £14.50 ✕ **LD** 21:30 **CC** MC Visa Amex DC ♿

★★★ Queen's
Leonard Street, Perth PH2 8HB
☎ 01738-442222 **Fax** 01738-638496
E-mail email@queensperth.co.uk
51 bedrs, all ensuite, 4️⃣ ♀ ⌁ 🖥 ⊞ 250 **P** 60 ⊕ **SB** £75-£80 **DB** £99-£105 **HB** £315-£507.50 **L** £10 **L** ● **D** £22.50 **D** ● ✕ **LD** 21:15 **CC** MC Visa Amex DC JCB 🉐 🉐 🖥

★★ Salutation
South Street, Perth PH2 8PH
☎ 01738-630066 **Fax** 01738-633598
84 bedrs, all ensuite, 4️⃣ ⌁ ♨ ⊞ 300 ⊕ **SB** £59-£63 **DB** £74-£80 **HB** £514.50-£542.50 **L** £9 **L** ● **D** £15 **D** ● ✕ **LD** 21:30 **CC** MC Visa Amex

SCOTLAND

PITLOCHRY Perthshire   13D1
Pop. 2,500. Dunkeld 12, London 444, Aberfeldy 14,
Blairgowrie 23, Braemar 41, Dalwhinnie 31,
Edinburgh 69, Glasgow 80 **EC** Thu (win) **see** Loch
Faskally and Dam ('Fish Ladder') **i** 22 Atholl Road
01796-472215

★★★ Dundarach
Perth Road, Pitlochry PH16 5DJ
📞 01796-472862 **Fax** 01796-473024
E-mail hotelpitlochry@btinternet.com
Closed Dec-Feb
38 bedrs, all ensuite, 🗄 ⅲ 42 **P** 42 ⚓ **CC** MC Visa
Amex JCB ♿

★★★ Pine Trees 🏃 🏃
Strathview Terrace, Pitlochry PH16 5QR
📞 01796-472121 **Fax** 01796-472460
E-mail info@pinetrees-hotel.demon.co.uk
19 bedrs, all ensuite, ♀ 🐾 ⅲ 30 **P** 25 ⚓ **DB** £54-£60
D £26 ✕ **LD** 20:30 **CC** MC Visa Amex DC 🅿

★★ ✿ Acarsaid
8 Atholl Road, Pitlochry PH16 5BX
📞 01796-472389 **Fax** 01796-473952
Closed Jan-Mar
19 bedrs, all ensuite, 🗄 ⅲ 35 **P** 20 No children
under 12 ⚓ Resid **CC** MC Visa ♿

★★ Balrobin
Higher Oakfield, Pitlochry PH16 5HT
📞 01796-472901 **Fax** 01796-474200
E-mail balrobin@globalnet.co.uk
Closed Nov-Feb

Traditional Scottish house in own grounds
commanding panoramic view.
15 bedrs, 14 ensuite, ♀ 🐾 **P** 16 No children under 5
⚓ Resid **SB** £25-£35 **DB** £48-£64 **HB** £245-£301 **D** £15
✕ **LD** 20:00 **CC** MC Visa

★★ Knockendarroch House 🏃 🏃 🏃
Higher Oakfield, Pitlochry PH16 5HT
📞 01796-473473 **Fax** 01796-474068
E-mail inq@knockendarroch.co.uk
Closed mid Nov-1 Mar
12 bedrs, all ensuite, 🗄 🖂 **P** 15 No children under
12 ⚓ **DB** £56-£72 **HB** £235-£360 **D** £21 ✕ **LD** 20:30
CC MC Visa Amex
See advert on this page

PORT WILLIAM Wigtownshire   12C4
Pop. 530. Wigtown 10, London 384, Edinburgh
118, Gatehouse of Fleet 35, Girvan 47, Glasgow
98, New Galloway 35, Stranraer 23 **EC** Wed

★★★ Corsemalzie House 🏃 🏃
Port William DG8 9RL
📞 01988-860254 **Fax** 01988-860213
Closed mid Jan-end Feb
14 bedrs, all ensuite, ♀ 🥊 🐾 ⅲ 30 **P** 35 ⚓ **SB** £38-
£48 **DB** £76-£96 **HB** £336-£399 **L** £11.50 **L** 🍷
D £22.50 **D** 🍷 ✕ **LD** 20:45 **CC** MC Visa Amex 🎾

PORTPATRICK Wigtownshire   12B4
Glenluce 13, London 395, Edinburgh 126,
Gatehouse of Fleet 47, Glasgow 89½, New
Galloway 47, Stranraer 7½ **EC** Thu

★★★ Fernhill ♟ ♟
Heugh Road, Portpatrick DG9 8TD
📞 01776-810220 **Fax** 01776-810596

The hotel overlooks the picturesque harbour of
Portpatrick, with breathtaking views over the Irish
Sea. Local seasonal produce is served in the award
winning conservatory restaurant, with lobster the
house speciality.
20 bedrs, all ensuite, ⊁ ⠿ 12 **P** 40 ⊕ **CC** MC Visa
Amex DC JCB &

RHU Dunbartonshire   12B2
Pop. 1,900. Helensburgh 2, London 412, Arrochar
15, Edinburgh 67, Glasgow 24

★★ Ardencaple
Shore Road, Rhu G84 8LA
📞 01436-820200 **Fax** 01436-821099
25 bedrs, all ensuite, ⊁ **P** 50 ⊕ **CC** MC Visa Amex
DC &

ROSEBANK Lanarkshire   12C2
Pop. 100. Abington 22, London 373, M74 (jn 4) 4,
Edinburgh 36, Glasgow 17, Kilmarnock 29, Lanark
7, Stirling 31

★★★ Popinjay ♟
Rosebank ML8 5QB
📞 01555-860441 **Fax** 01555-860204
46 bedrs, all ensuite, ⊁ ⠿ 200 **P** 300 ⊕ **CC** MC Visa
Amex DC ▣ &

ROSYTH Fife   13D2
South Queensferry 4, London 384, M9 (spur) 6,
M90 (jn 1) ½, Dunfermline 3, Edinburgh 13½,
Glasgow 41

★★ ✥ Gladyer Inn
10 Heath Road/Ridley Drive,
Rosyth KY11 2BT
📞 01383-419977 **Fax** 01383-411728
E-mail gladyer@aol.com
21 bedrs, all ensuite, ⠿ 120 **P** 97 ⊕ **SB** £39.50
DB £55 **L** £10 **L** ● **D** £20 **D** ● ✕ **LD** 21:30 Restaurant
closed L & D Mon **CC** MC Visa Amex 🔲

ST ANDREWS Fife   13E1
Pop. 13,500. M90 27, Kirkcaldy 24, London 424,
Dundee 12, Edinburgh 49, Glasgow 75, Kinross 35,
Perth 32 **EC** Thu **see** Cathedral Ruins, Chapter House
and Museum 🛈 70 Street 01334-472021

★★★★ Rusacks   Heritage HOTELS
Pilmour Links, St Andrews KY16 9JQ
📞 01334-474321 **Fax** 01334-477896
E-mail heritagehotels-st.andrews.rusacks@forte-
hotel.com
48 bedrs, all ensuite, ⊁ ▣ ⠿ 80 **P** 20
⊕ **SB** £45-£116 **DB** £90-£232 **HB** £60-£286
L £5.50 **L** ● **D** £30 ✕ **LD** 22:00 **CC** MC Visa
Amex DC JCB 🔲

★★★ Scores
The Scores, St Andrews KY16 9BB
📞 01334-472451 **Fax** 01334-473947
Closed 21-26 Dec
30 bedrs, all ensuite, ▣ ⠿ 120 **P** 10 ⊕ **CC** MC Visa
Amex DC JCB

★★ Parkland ♟
Double Dykes Road, St Andrews KY16 9DS
📞 01334-473620 **Fax** 01334-473620
Closed Christmas & New Year
9 bedrs, 7 ensuite, ♀ **P** 9 ⊕ **SB** £45 **DB** £75 **L** £5.95
D £16.50 ✕ **LD** 20:30 Restaurant closed L & D Mon,
D Sun **CC** MC Visa

ST FILLANS Perthshire   12C1
Pop. 250. Comrie 5, London 423, Crieff 12,
Edinburgh 58, Glasgow 54, Lochearnhead 6½,
Stirling 27 **EC** Wed

★★★ Four Seasons ♟ ♟ ♟
St Fillans PH6 2NF
📞 01764-685333 **Fax** 01764-685444
Closed Jan-Mar
12 bedrs, all ensuite, ⊁ ⠿ 60 **P** 40 ⊕ **SB** £36-£56
DB £72-£88 **HB** £374.50-£430.50 **L** £14.95 **L** ●
D £23.95 **D** ● ✕ **LD** 21:30 Restaurant closed L Mon-
Sat **CC** MC Visa ▣

SCOTLAND

SHETLAND ISLANDS 13F1
i The Market Cross, Lerwick 01595-693434

★★★ Busta House *R*
Brae ZE2 9QN
☎ 01806-522506 **Fax** 01806-522588
E-mail busta@mes.co.uk
Closed 23 Dec-2 Jan
20 bedrs, all ensuite, ⁴ ✗ ✝ **P** 35 ⊞ **SB** £70 **DB** £91-£115 **L** £9 **L** ✿ **D** £23 ✗ **LD** 21:00 Restaurant closed L Mon-Sat **cc** MC Visa Amex DC

★★★ Shetland
Holmsgarth Road, Lerwick ZE1 0PW
☎ 01595-695515 **Fax** 01595-695828
E-mail shetland-hotels@mes.co.uk
63 bedrs, all ensuite, ⁴ ♀ ✝ ▣ ⌗ 200 **P** 100 ⊞ **SB** £76.95 **DB** £89.80 **L** £8 **L** ✿ **D** £17 ✗ **LD** 21:30 **cc** MC Visa Amex DC ﹠

SHIELDAIG Ross-shire 14B3
Locharron 14, London 586, Edinburgh 221, Glasgow 197, Kyle of Lochalsh 37 **see** Shieldaig Island

★ Tigh An Eilean *R R R*
Shieldaig IV54 8XN
☎ 01520-755251 **Fax** 01520-755321
Closed late Oct-Apr
11 bedrs, all ensuite, ✝ **P** 11 ⊞ **SB** £48.55
DB £107.40 **L** ✿ **D** £26.15 **D** ✿ ✗ **LD** 20:30 **cc** MC Visa ▣

SPEAN BRIDGE Inverness-shire 14C4
Pop. 140. Fort William 9½, London 499, Dalwhinnie 35, Edinburgh 133, Glasgow 112, Invergarry 16, Kingussie 38 **EC** Thu *i* 01397-712576

★★ Letterfinlay Lodge *R*
Loch Lochy, Spean Bridge PH34 4DZ
☎ 01397-712622
Closed Nov-Mar
13 bedrs, 9 ensuite, ✝ ⌗ 60 **P** 60 ⊞ **SB** £30-£38
DB £60-£76 **HB** £295-£380 **L** ✿ **D** £19.50 **D** ✿ ✗ **LD** 21:30 **cc** MC Visa Amex DC JCB ▣

STIRLING Stirlingshire 12C2
Pop. 29,800. Falkirk 10, London 395, M9 2½, Dumbarton 34, Edinburgh 35, Glasgow 26, Kincardine 12, Kinross 23, Lochearnhead 30, Perth 33 **EC** Wed **MD** Thu **see** Castle, Parliament Hall, Chapel Royal, S African Memorial, Museum and Art Gallery, Tolbooth (1701), Mercat Cross, Darnley's House, Argyll's Lodging, Old Bridge, Church of Holy Rude, Mar's Work, Guildhall, Bruce's Statue
i Dumbarton Road 01786-475019

★★★★ Stirling Highland *R R*
Spittal Street, Stirling FK8 1DU
☎ 01786-272727 **Fax** 01786-272829
E-mail sthh@scottishhighlandhotels.co.uk
94 bedrs, all ensuite, ✝ ▣ ⌗ 100 **P** 95 ⊞
SB £118.50-£122 **DB** £165-£172 **L** £11 **D** £19.95 ✗
LD 22:00 Restaurant closed L Sat **cc** MC Visa Amex DC JCB ▣▣▣▣▣ ﹠

★★★ Golden Lion
8-10 King Street, Stirling FK8 1BD
☎ 01786-475351 **Fax** 01786-472755
E-mail sales@miltonhotels.com
67 bedrs, all ensuite, ✗ ✝ ▣ ⌗ 300 **P** 40 ⊞ **SB** £59-£89 **DB** £79-£99 **HB** £343 **L** ✿ **D** £12 **D** ✿ ✗ **LD** 23:00 **cc** MC Visa Amex DC

STRACHUR Argyll 12B2
Pop. 750. Arrochar 21, London 444, Dunoon 19, Edinburgh 98, Glasgow 56, Inveraray 21

★★★ Creggans Inn *R R*
Strachur PA27 8BX
☎ 01369-860279 **Fax** 01369-860637

The new restaurant enhances our long-standing reputation for superb food and wine. 17 refurbished ensuite rooms. 15 bedrooms, 1 suite, 1 junior suite. Sporting activities within Strachur Park now available.
17 bedrs, all ensuite, ✝ ⌗ 70 **P** 30 ⊞ **cc** MC Visa Amex DC ▣ ﹠

STRANRAER Wigtownshire 12B4

Pop. 10,000. Glenluce 9½, London 391, Edinburgh 120, Gatehouse of Fleet 44, Girvan 30, Glasgow 82, New Galloway 44 **EC** Wed **see** Peel Tower (known as 'Stranraer Castle'), Old Town Hall, Lochinch and Castle, Kennedy Gdns 3m E, Glenluce Abbey 7½m E, Logan Botanic Garden 19m S **i** 1 Bridge Street 01776-702595

★★★★ North West Castle

Cairnryan Road, Stranraer DG9 8EH
☎ 01776-704413 **Fax** 01776-702646
E-mail mcmhotel@mcmhotel.demon.co.uk

Famed for the friendliness of its welcome, the hotel has swimming pool, games room and snooker table. There are excellent year round golf packages, and indoor curling from October to March.
73 bedrs, all ensuite, ▣ ▣ ⊞ 150 **P** 86 ⊕ **CC** MC Visa ▣ ▣ ▣ ৬

STRATHAVEN Lanarkshire 12C3

M74 (jn 8) 5, London 389, Cumnock 19, Kilmarnock 20, Glasgow 12, Edinburgh 32

★★★ Strathaven

Hamilton Road, Strathaven ML10 6SZ
☎ 01357-521778 **Fax** 01357-520789
E-mail sthotel@globalnet.co.uk
22 bedrs, all ensuite, ⊞ 180 **P** 80 ⊕ **SB** £67 **DB** £85 **L** £11.50 **D** £18.50 ✕ **LD** 21:30 **CC** MC Visa Amex DC ৬

STRONTIAN Argyll 14B4

Pop. 250. Loch Aline 20 (Fy to Oban), London 533 (fy 497) Edinburgh 176 (fy 140), Fort William 44, Glasgow 133 (fy 110), Ballachulish (fy) 20 **EC** Wed, Thur **see** Lead Mines **i** 01967-402131

★★ Strontian **R**

Strontian, Acharacle PH36 4HZ
☎ 01967-402029 **Fax** 01967-402314

A small friendly hotel lying on the shores of the lovely Loch Sunart. Fully licenced, with good food tastefully served, and well appointed bedrooms.
7 bedrs, 5 ensuite, ✈ ⊞ 100 **P** 25 ⊕ **CC** MC Visa JCB ▣ ▣

TAIN Ross-shire 15D2

Pop. 2,200. Alness 14, London 546, Bonar Bridge 14, Dingwall 25, Edinburgh 187, Glasgow 194

★★★ Mansfield House **R R R**

Scotsburn Road, Tain IV19 1PR
☎ 01862-892052 **Fax** 01862-892260
E-mail mansfield@cali.co.uk
18 bedrs, all ensuite, ▣ ⊗ ✈ ⊞ 40 **P** 70 ⊕ **SB** £65-£75 **DB** £100-£130 **HB** £525-£630 **L** £12 **L** ● **D** £25 ✕ **LD** 21:00 **CC** MC Visa Amex

★★★ Morangie House **R**

Morangie Road, Tain IV19 1PY
☎ 01862-892281 **Fax** 01862-892872

Former Victorian mansion house carefully refurbished and with an outstanding reputation for superb food and friendly but efficient service in luxurious surroundings. Ideally situated for golfing breaks with 8 superb courses within a short drive.
26 bedrs, all ensuite, ▣ ✈ ⊞ 40 **P** 40 ⊕ **SB** £50-£60 **DB** £75-£80 **L** £9 **L** ● **D** £17 **D** ● ✕ **LD** 21:45 **CC** MC Visa Amex DC ৬

★★★ Royal
High Street, Tain IV19 1AB
☎ 01862-892013 Fax 01862-893450

A family run Victorian hotel in the centre of Tain.
25 bedrs, all ensuite, ⌁ ▦ 100 P 25 ⊞ SB £40
DB £60 HB £280 L £7 L ⬤ D £7 ✕ LD 20:45 ⊄ MC
Visa Amex JCB ▦ &

TARBERT, LOCH FYNE Argyll   12B2
Pop. 230. Ardrishaig 11, London 481, Edinburgh
135, Glasgow 93, Lochgilphead 13, Whitehouse 8
ⓘ 01880-820429

★★★ Stonefield Castle
Tarbert PA29 6YJ
☎ 01880-820836 Fax 01880-820929
33 bedrs, 32 ensuite, ▦ ⌁ ⊡ ▦ 80 P 30 ⊞ ⊄ MC
Visa Amex DC ▦ ▦ ▦ &
See advert on this page

★★ ✤ Columba
East Pier Road, Tarbert, Loch Fyne PA29 6UF
☎ 01880-820808 Fax 01880-820808
E-mail columbahotel@fsbdial.co.uk
Closed 24-26 Dec
10 bedrs, all ensuite, ⌁ ▦ 30 P 10 ⊞ SB £34-£35
DB £68-£80 HB £257-£327 L ⬤ D £19 D ⬤ ✕ LD 21:00
⊄ MC Visa Amex ▦ ▦

THORNHILL Dumfriesshire   13D3
Pop. 1,500. Dumfries 14, London 341, Ayr 44,
Edinburgh 62, Glasgow 59, Moffat 31, New
Galloway 22 ⲕ Thu

★★ George
103-106 Drumlanrig Street,
Thornhill DG3 5LU
☎ 01848-330326
8 bedrs, all ensuite, ⌁ ⊞ ⊞ Rest SB £32.50 DB £50
L ⬤ D ⬤ ✕ LD 21:00 ⊄ MC Visa

★★ Trigony House ⌂ ⌂
Closeburn, Thornhill DG3 5EZ
☎ 01848-331211 Fax 01848-331303
Closed 25 Dec

Small Edwardian country house set in its own
grounds. Noted for its fine food and hospitality.
Excellent base for golfing, fishing and shooting or
just relax.
8 bedrs, all ensuite, ▦ 12 P 30 ⊞ ⊄ MC Visa

THURSO Caithness   15E1
Pop. 8,000. Helmsdale 41, London 644, Edinburgh
269, Glasgow 276, Melvich 16, Wick 20 ⲕ Thu
MD Tue ⓘ Car Park, Riverside 01847-892371

St Clair Awaiting Inspection
Sinclair Street, Thurso KW14 7AJ
📞 01847-896481 **Fax** 01847-896481
Privately owned and managed by the Hossack
family, this hotel prides itself on quality service and
personal attention. Newly refurbished throughout it
offers comfort, high standards and elegant
restaurant and bar.
36 bedrs, 29 ensuite, ✕ ⊞ 90 ⊞ ℂ MC Visa Amex
JCB 🕭

TONGUE Sutherland   15D1
Pop. 150. Lairg 36, London 613, Bettyhill 13,
Durness 37, Edinburgh 238, Glasgow 245

★★ Ben Loyal
Tongue IV27 4XE
📞 01847-611216 **Fax** 01847-611212
Closed Nov-Feb
12 bedrs, 9 ensuite, ✕ ⊞ 20 **P** 19 ⊞ ℂ MC Visa 🖫 🕭

TORRIDON Ross-shire   14C3
Achnasheen 20, London 591, Edinburgh 213,
Gairloch 30, Glasgow 227, Locharron 23 **see** Loch
Torridon, Beinn Eighe Nature Reserve

★★★ Loch Torridon 🍴 🍴 🍴
Blue Ribbon Hotel
Torridon by Achnasheen IV22 2EY
📞 01445-791242 **Fax** 01445-791296
E-mail 101453,3351@compuserve.com
20 bedrs, all ensuite, 🖫 ⊞ 20 **P** 30 ⊞ ℂ MC Visa
Amex DC 🖫 🕭

TROON Ayrshire   12C3
Pop. 14,300. Monkton 4, London 389, Ayr 7,
Edinburgh 69, Glasgow 29, Kilmarnock 9, Largs 24,
Paisley 27 **ℂ** Wed 🗓 Municipal Buildings, South
Beach 01292-317696

★★★★ Marine Highland 🍴
8 Crosbie Road, Troon KA10 6HE
📞 01292-314444 **Fax** 01292-316922
E-mail mhh@.scottishhighlandhotels.co.uk
74 bedrs, all ensuite, 🖫 🍴 ✕ 🖫 ⊞ 220 **P** 200 ⊞
SB £106.50-£118.50 **DB** £152-£177 **L** £15 **D** £24 ✕
LD 22:00 ℂ MC Visa Amex DC 🖫 🖫 🖫 🖫

★★★ South Beach 🍴
73 South Beach, Troon KA10 6EG
📞 01292-312033 **Fax** 01292-318438

A warm welcome awaits you at this privately owned
seafront hotel. Excellent base for touring and within
easy reach of Glasgow and Prestwick airports.
34 bedrs, all ensuite, ♀ 🍴 ✕ ⊞ 100 **P** 35 ⊞ **SB** £45-
£65 **DB** £65-£80 **HB** £210-£315 **L** £14.95 **D** £18.50
D 🍴 ✕ **LD** 20:45 ℂ MC Visa Amex 🖫 🕭

★★ Ardneil
51 St. Meddans Street, Troon KA10 6NU
📞 01292-311611 **Fax** 01292-318111
9 bedrs, 3 ensuite, ⊞ 100 **P** 100 ⊞ ℂ MC Visa
Amex 🖫

TURNBERRY Ayrshire   12B3
Pop. 160. Maybole 7, London 386, Ayr 15,
Dalmellington 20, Edinburgh 85, Glasgow 47

★★★★★ Turnberry 🍴 🍴 🍴 🍴
Gold Ribbon Hotel
Turnberry KA26 9LT
📞 01655-331000 **Fax** 01655-331706

Award winning Hotel, Golf Course and Spa, offering
all the charm and elegance of an Edwardian
country house, fine dining and stunning views
across the Island of Arran and Ailsa Craig.
132 bedrs, all ensuite, 🖫 🍴 ✕ 🖫 ⊞ 130 **P** 200 ⊞
SB £145-£232 **DB** £167-£270 **L** £24.50 **L** 🍴 **D** £48 ✕
LD 22:00 ℂ MC Visa Amex DC JCB 🖫 🖫 🖫 🖫 🖫 🖫
🖫 🕭

SCOTLAND

★★★ Malin Court ℝ ℝ ℝ ℝ
Turnberry KA26 9PB
📞 01655-331457 Fax 01655-331072
E-mail info@malincourt.co.uk

Malin Court overlooks Turnberry's famous 'open' championship golf course and the Firth of Clyde. Mouthwatering menus are complemented by a comprehensive wine list of both traditional and new world wines. Internet: http://www.malincourt.co.uk
18 bedrs, all ensuite, ✝ ⬚ ⊞ 200 P 100 ⬚ SB £72-£82 DB £104-£124 L £10 D £24 ✕ LD 21:00 ₡ MC Visa Amex DC ⬚ ⬚

UPHALL West Lothian　　　　　　　13D2
Edinburgh 18, London 393, M8 (jn 3) 4, Glasgow 25, Linlithgow 7, Livingstone 3

★★★★ Houstoun House ℝ
Uphall EH52 6JS
📞 01506-853831 Fax 01506-854220
E-mail info@houston.macdonald-hotels.co.uk

Dating back to 17th century, set in 20 acres of gardens and woodland, the original character remains in the furnishings of many bedrooms and public areas. Award winning cuisine.
72 bedrs, all ensuite, ⬚ 🏊 ⊞ 250 P 200 ⬚ SB £120-£140 DB £160-£180 L £16.50 D £32.50 D ➤ ✕
LD 21:30 Restaurant closed L Sat ₡ MC Visa Amex DC ⬚ ⬚ ⬚ ⬚ ⬚

WHITBURN West Lothian　　　　　　13D2
Edinburgh 23, London 393, Bathgate 4, Glasgow 22, Lanark 15

★★★ Hilcroft ℝ
East Main Street, Whitburn EH47 0JU
📞 01501-740818 Fax 01501-744013
31 bedrs, all ensuite, ⊞ 200 P 80 ⬚ ₡ MC Visa Amex DC ⬚

WHITEBRIDGE Inverness-shire　　　　15D3
Pop. 600. Fort Angustus 9, London 530, Carrbridge 41, Edinburgh 164, Glasgow 143, Invergarry 17, Invermoriston 16

★★ Whitebridge ℝ
Whitebridge IV1 2UN
📞 ff 0800-026 6277 Fax 01456-486413
E-mail whitebridgehotel@southlochness.demon.co.uk
Closed Jan-Mar

A haven of peace amid the unspoilt Highlands of south Loch Ness. Personal attention ensures comfort and satisfaction.
12 bedrs, 10 ensuite, ✝ ⊞ 30 P 32 ⬚ SB £25-£30 DB £50-£60 HB £250 D £14 ✕ LD 20:30 ₡ MC Visa Amex DC JCB ⬚

WICK Caithness　　　　　　　　　　15E1
Pop. 7,000. Helmsdale 35, London 638, Edinburgh 263, Glasgow 270, Thurso 20 EC Wed MD Thu
⬚ Whitechapel Road 01955-602596

★★ Mackay's
Union Street, Wick KW1 5ED
📞 01955-602323 Fax 01955-605930
E-mail mackays.hotel@caithness.mm.co.uk
27 bedrs, all ensuite, ⬚ ✝ ⬚ ⊞ 150 P 20 ⬚ ₡ MC Visa Amex

Maps

Beckington

A366

A361

Frome

A362 A36

A361 A362 A36

Warminster

A361

B3092

1

Leighton A359

A36

BATH

A367 A3062

Limpley Stoke

B3110

A366

A36 A361

B3098

Leisure

Travel

Shopping

www.WestOneWeb.com

West One

Wales

Feathers Royal
Alban Square, Aberaeron SA46 0AQ
📞 01545-571750 Fax 01545-571760

Centre of pretty west Wales harbour town. Listed Georgian building completely refurbished with 19 quality ensuite bedrooms and luxury apartments. Full restaurant facilities, motoring theme bar. 250 cover function/banquet suite.
19 bedrs, all ensuite, ⊁ P 20 ⊕ ♿

ABERDYFI Gwynedd   6C3
Pop. 1,500. Newtown 39, London 215, Aberystwyth 28, Bala 39, Dolgellau 24 **EC** Wed **see** Happy Valley ('Bearded Lake'), Bird Rock 9m ℹ The Wharf Gardens 01654-767321

★★★ Trefeddian
Aberdyfi LL35 0SB
📞 01654-767213 Fax 01654-767777
Closed 14 Nov-15 March
46 bedrs, all ensuite, ⊁ ▣ P 50 ⊕ SB £40-£50 DB £80-£100 HB £329-£392 L £11 L ⬤ D £17 D ⬤ ✕ LD 20:45 (C MC Visa ▣ ▣ ▣ ♿
See advert on this page

ABERGAVENNY Monmouthshire   7D4
Pop. 12,000. Ross 22, London 143, Brecon 20, Chepstow 29, Hereford 23, Monmouth 15, Newport 18, Pontypool 10, Tredegar 11 **EC** Thu **MD** Tue, Fri **see** Castle Grounds and Museum, St Mary's Church, Sugar Loaf Mountain 4m NW, Llanvihangel Court 4½m NW, White Castle 5½m E ℹ Swan Meadow, Monmouth Road 01873-857588

Ɠ ★★★ ✤ Allt-yr-Ynys
Walterstone, Abergavenny HR2 ODU
☎ 01873-890307 **Fax** 01873-890539
E-mail allthotel@compuserve.com

Exquisite 16th century manor hotel in beautiful Welsh Borders/ Black Country mountains. Deluxe bedrooms, conference facilities and a fine dining restaurant. Private clay shooting and river frontage with fishing. Access to golf, walks, cycling.
19 bedrs, all ensuite, ⬚ ♀ ♪ ⊱ ⅲ 80 **P** 50 ⊕
SB £65-£70 **DB** £85-£90 **L** £15 **D** £20 **D** ⬛ ✕ **LD** 22:00
Restaurant closed L Mon ⅭⅭ MC Visa Amex ⊡ ⊠ ▦
▣ ♿
See advert on this page

Rock & Fountain Awaiting Inspection
Main Road, Clydach, Abergavenny NP7 0LL
☎ 01873-830393
9 bedrs, all ensuite, ⅲ 70 **P** 50 ⊕ ⅭⅭ MC Visa ♿

ABERGELE Conwy   **6C1**
Pop. 12,315. Mold 24, London 215, Colwyn Bay 7, Denbigh 8, Rhyl 5, Queensferry 26 **EC** Thu **MD** Mon **see** St Michael's Church 1m W, Gwyrch Castle

★★★ Kinmel Manor
St Georges Road, Abergele LL22 9AS
☎ 01745-832014 **Fax** 01745-832014
51 bedrs, all ensuite, ⊱ ⅲ 250 **P** 100 ⊕ **SB** £50
DB £70 **HB** £340 **L** £11 **D** £15 ✕ **LD** 21:45 ⅭⅭ MC Visa Amex DC ⊡ ⊠ ▦

ABERPORTH Ceredigion   **6B3**
Pop. 800. Lampeter 27, London 230, Aberwystwyth 33, Cardigan 6½, Carmarthen 26

★★★ Penrallt ⚲
Aberporth, Cardigan SA43 2BS
☎ 01239-810227 **Fax** 01239-811375
Closed 25-31 Dec

Country house hotel set in beautiful grounds overlooking the spectacular Cardigan Bay coastline. All bedrooms ensuite, colour TV, tea maker, direct dial phones. Restaurant renowned for good food.
16 bedrs, all ensuite, ⊱ ⅲ 70 **P** 100 ⊕ **SB** £54
DB £90 **HB** £452 **L** £12.50 **D** £18 **D** ⬛ ✕ **LD** 21:00
ⅭⅭ MC Visa Amex DC ⋺ ⊠ ▦ ▧

ABERYSTWYTH Ceredigion   **6C3**
Pop. 15,300. Rhayader 34, London 211, Aberdyfi 28, Bala 47, Cardigan 38, Dolgellau 33, Lampeter 24, Newtown 43 **EC** Wed **MD** Mon **see** Castle ruins and Gorsedd Circle, National Library of Wales, Plant Breeding Station, Vale of Rheidol Narrow Gauge Railway to Devil's Bridge, Nanteds Mansion.
ℹ Terrace Road 01970-612125

WALES

★★★ Belle Vue Royal
Marine Terrace, Aberystwyth SY23 2BA
☎ 01970-617558 **Fax** 01970-612190

A combination of Victorian architecture and modern sophistication, the hotel is situated on the promenade, overlooking Cardigan Bay.
36 bedrs, all ensuite, ⦀ 60 **P** 8 ⊞ **SB** £56-£58 **DB** £84-£86 **L** £12.50 ☕ **D** £23 ✗ **LD** 21:30 **CC** MC Visa Amex DC
See advert on this page

★★★ Conrah 🏆 🏆
Chancery, Aberystwyth SY23 4DF
☎ 01970-617941 **Fax** 01970-624546
E-mail hotel@conrah.freeserve.co.uk
Closed 23-30 Dec
20 bedrs, all ensuite, ▣ ⦀ 50 **P** 50 No children under 5 ⊞ Rest Resid **CC** MC Visa Amex DC JCB ▣ 🔳

★★ Four Seasons
50-54 Portland Street, Aberystwyth SY23 2DX
☎ 01970-612120 **Fax** 01970-627458
Closed Christmas-New Year
14 bedrs, all ensuite, ✎ ⦀ 50 **P** 10 ⊞ Rest Resid **SB** £50-£55 **DB** £75-£85 **HB** £300-£350 **L** £12 **L** ☕ **D** £16 ✗ **LD** 21:00 Restaurant closed L Mon-Sat **CC** MC Visa

★★ Hafod Arms
Devils Bridge, Aberystwyth SY23 3JL
☎ 01970-890232 **Fax** 01970-890394
Closed 15 Dec-31 Jan

Standing alone at the head of the world famous Mynach Falls, overlooking the spectacular wooded gorge and adjacent to the legendary Devils Bridge. Convenient for Elan lakes and Plynlimon mountains.
16 bedrs, 15 ensuite, ▣ ⦀ 50 **P** 20 No children under 12 ⊞ **SB** £35 **DB** £60 **L** ☕ ✗ **LD** 20:00

AMLWCH Anglesey	6B1

Pop. 4,000. Bangor 19, London 256, Caernarfon 25, Holyhead 20 **EC** Wed **MD** Fri

★★ Trecastell
Bull Bay, Amlwch LL68 9SA
☎ 01407-830651 **Fax** 01407-832114
14 bedrs, 12 ensuite, 🐾 ⦀ 10 **P** 60 ⊞ **SB** £30 **DB** £45 **D** £14 ✗ **LD** 21:30 **CC** MC Visa

BALA Gwynedd   6C2

Pop. 1,850. Shrewsbury 44, London 199, Betws-y-Coed 23, Corwen 11, Dolgellau 18, Porthmadog 29, Welshpool 33 **EC** Wed **MD** Thu *i* Penllyn, Pensarn Road 01678-521021

★★ ✤ Plas Coch
High Street, Bala LL23 7AB
☎ 01678-520309 **Fax** 01678-521135
Closed 25 Dec

The hotel was originally built as a coaching inn about 1780. The rooms are therefore large and spacious. All bedrooms have private bathrooms or shower rooms.
10 bedrs, all ensuite, ⚄ 20 **P** 20 ⊞ **CC** MC Visa Amex DC JCB

BANGOR Gwynedd   6C1

Pop. 14,600. London 237, Colwyn Bay 20, Holyhead 23 **EC** Wed **MD** Fri **see** Cathedral, Art Gallery, Museum, Menai Suspension Bridge, Penrhyn Castle 1m E *i* Little Chef, A55/A5 01248-352786

★★★ ✤ Menai Court
Craig-y-Don Road, Bangor LL57 2BG
☎ 01248-354200 **Fax** 01248-354200
Closed 26 Dec-9 Jan
13 bedrs, all ensuite, ⚄ ⚄ 60 **P** 24 ⊞ Rest Resid **CC** MC Visa JCB ♿

BARMOUTH Gwynedd   6C2

Pop. 2,200. Dolgellau 10, London 216, Betws-y-Coed 35, Caernarfon 37, Portmadog 20 **EC** Wed **MD** Thu **see** St John's Church, Guild of St George Cottages, Dinas Oleu, Llanaber Church 2m, Bontddu Gold Mines *i* Old Library, Station Road 01341-280787

★★ ✤ Bae Abermaw
Panorama Road, Barmouth LL42 1DQ
☎ 01341-280550 **Fax** 01341-280346
E-mail bae.abermaw@virgin.net
18 bedrs, all ensuite, ⚄ ⚄ 75 **P** 40 ⊞ **CC** MC Visa Amex DC
See advert on this page

WALES

BARRY Vale of Glamorgan 3D1
Pop. 43,000. Cardiff 9½, London 159, Bridgend 17
📠 The Triangle, Barry Island 01446-747171

★★★ Egerton Grey
Country House 🍴🍴

Porthkerry, Barry CF62 3BZ
📞 01446-711666 **Fax** 01446-711690
E-mail info@egertongrey.co.uk

Beautiful old rectory set in a lush green valley with outstanding views to the coast. Internet:
www.egertongrey.co.uk
10 bedrs, all ensuite, 📺 ♀ 🛏 ♨ 40 **P** 40 🍴 Rest Resid
SB £65-£95 **DB** £95-£120 **HB** £350-£500 **L** £10 **L** 🍷
D £14.50 **D** 🍷 ✕ **LD** 21:30 **CC** MC Visa Amex DC JCB

BEAUMARIS Anglesey 6C1
Pop. 2,500. Bangor 7, London 244 **EC** Wed

Henllys Hall
Beaumaris LL58 8HU
📞 01248-810412 **Fax** 01248-811511
E-mail enquiries@henllys-hall.co.uk

A prestigious country house hotel and golf venue.
Set in 150 acres of parkland with panoramic views over the Menai Straits and Snowdonia.
25 bedrs, all ensuite, 📺 ♨ ♨ 120 **P** 100 🍴 **CC** MC
Visa Amex DC 🏊🎾🎱🎮🐕♿

BEDDGELERT Gwynedd 6C1
Pop. 320. Bala 30, London 230, Betws-y-Coed 17,
Caernarfon 12, Doegellau 27, Pwllheli 19 **EC** Wed

★★★ ✤ Royal Goat
Beddgelert LL55 4YE
📞 01766-890224 **Fax** 01766-890422

A traditional family owned hotel, situated in the scenic village of Beddgelert in the heart of Snowdonia National Park. "How Brave the Hound" welcome.
32 bedrs, all ensuite, 📺 🛏 🍴 ♨ 80 **P** 100 🍴 **CC** MC
Visa Amex DC 🎮♿
See advert on this page

★★ Tanronnen Inn
Beddgelert LL55 4YB
📞 01766-890347 **Fax** 01766-890606
7 bedrs, all ensuite, 🛏 ♨ 40 **P** 8 🍴 **SB** £40 **DB** £78
HB £325 **L** £9 **D** £16 ✕ **LD** 20:45 **CC** MC Visa JCB

BENLLECH BAY Anglesey   6B1

Pop. 3,500. Bangor 10, London 248, Caernarfon 16, Holyhead 20

★★ ✤ Bay Court

Beach Road, Benllech Bay LL74 8SW

📞 01248-852573 **Fax** 01248-852606

19 bedrs, 10 ensuite, ⼐ ⅲ 50 **P** 65 ⊕ **SB** £20 **DB** £40 **HB** £178 **L** £7 **L** ⬤ **D** £9.50 **D** ⬤ ✗ **LD** 21:00 **CC** MC Visa Amex DC JCB 🅰

BETWS-Y-COED Conwy   6C1

Pop. 7,000. Corwen 22, London 216, Bala 22, Bangor 20, Caernarfon 23, Doegellau 32, Llandudno 17, Porthmadog 23, Ruthin 25 **EC** Thu

ⓘ Royal Oak Stables 01690-710426

★★★ Royal Oak

Betws-y-Coed LL24 0AY

📞 01690-710219 **Fax** 01690-710603

26 bedrs, all ensuite, ⌀ ⅲ 25 **P** 100 ⊕ **SB** £38-£50 **DB** £72-£102 **HB** £336-£364 **L** £9.50 **D** £15.50 **D** ⬤ ✗ **LD** 21:00 **CC** MC Visa Amex DC JCB

See advert on this page

WALES

★★★ Waterloo
Betws-y-Coed LL24 0AR
☎ 01690-710411 **Fax** 01690-710666
E-mail reservations@waterloohotel.inbtrade.co.uk
40 bedrs, all ensuite, 🚻 ⚡ 50 P 200 ⊞ SB £53-£63
DB £86-£106 HB £371-£441 L £9.95 L ● D £16.75
D ● ✕ LD 21:30 Restaurant closed L Mon-Sat
CC MC Visa Amex DC JCB 🖳 🖾 🖩 ♿
See advert on previous page

★★ ✤ Park Hill
Llanrwst Road, Betws-y-Coed LL24 0HD
☎ 01690-710540 **Fax** 01690-710540
9 bedrs, all ensuite, 🖳 ♀ P 11 No children under 6
⊞ DB £53-£62 HB £266-£297.50 D £14.50 D ● ✕
LD 19:45 CC MC Visa DC 🖳 🖩

★★ Tan-y-Foel Country House 🐾 🐾 🐾
Blue Ribbon Hotel
Capel Garmon, Betws-y-Coed LL26 0RE
☎ 01690-710507 **Fax** 01690-710681
Closed Christmas

Luxury Welsh stone country house with unique
contemporary interior, nestling high in the hillside
with spectacular views of Snowdonia. Highly
acclaimed restaurant with outstanding cuisine.
7 bedrs, all ensuite, 🖳 ♀ 🖾 P 14 No children under
7 ⊞ Rest Resid SB £70-£90 DB £90-£150 HB £490-£700
L ● D £25 ✕ LD 19:00 CC MC Visa Amex DC JCB

BLACKWOOD Caerphilly   3D1
Pop. 7,000. Newport 13, London 150, Caerphilly 8,

★★★ Maes Manor
Blackwood NP2 0AG
☎ 01495-220011 **Fax** 01495-228217
29 bedrs, all ensuite, 🖉 🚻 ⚡ 400 P 150 ⊞
SB £57.50 DB £75 L £11 D £15 ✕ LD 21:30 CC MC Visa
Amex DC JCB ♿

BONTDDU Gwynedd   6C2
Pop. 200. Dolgellau 5, London 212, Porthmadog 25

★★★ Bontddu Hall 🐾 🐾 🐾
Bontddu LL40 2SU
☎ 01341-430661 **Fax** 01341-430284
Closed Jan-Feb
20 bedrs, all ensuite, 🖳 ♀ 🚻 P 30 No children under
3 ⊞ SB £53-£63 DB £90-£115 HB £400 L £13 L ●
D £24 D ● ✕ LD 21:30 CC MC Visa Amex DC JCB

BRECHFA Carmarthenshire   6B4

★★ Ty Mawr
Brechfa, Carmarthen SA32 7RA
☎ 01267-202332 **Fax** 01267-202437
Closed end Nov-Christmas
5 bedrs, all ensuite, ♀ 🚻 🚻 20 P 45 ⊞ SB £52
DB £84 L £6 L ● D £23 ✕ LD 21:00 CC MC Visa Amex
JCB 🖳 🖾

BRECON Powys   7D4
Pop. 7,000. Abergavenny 20, London 163, Builth
Wells 16, Hereford 36, Leominster 37, Llandovery
21, Merthyr Tydfil 18 **EC** Wed **MD** Tue, Fri 🖍 Cattle
Market Car Park 01874-622485

★★★ Nant Ddu Lodge 🐾 🐾
Cwm Taf, Brecon CF48 2HY
☎ 01685-379111 **Fax** 01685-377088
E-mail nantddulod@aol.com.
Closed 24-30 Dec
22 bedrs, all ensuite, 🖳 🖉 🚻 🚻 16 P 70 ⊞ SB £50-
£65 DB £69.50-£85 L £12 L ● D £15 D ● ✕ LD 21:30
CC MC Visa Amex

BRIDGEND Bridgend   3D1
Pop. 28,000. Cardiff 19, London 169, Hirwaun 25,
Neath 17, Pontypridd 17, Swansea 20 **EC** Wed

★★★ Coed-y-Mwstwr 🐾 🐾
Coychurch, Bridgend CF35 6AF
☎ 01656-860621 **Fax** 01656-863122
23 bedrs, all ensuite, ♀ 🖳 🚻 150 P 80 ⊞ SB £95
DB £135 L £11 L ● D £24 D ● ✕ LD 22:00 CC MC
Visa Amex DC JCB 🖳 🖻 🖾 ♿

BURTON Pembrokeshire   6A4
Pop. 191. Pembroke Dock 2½,

★★ Beggar's Reach 🐾
Milford Haven, Burton SA73 1PD
☎ 01646-600700
10 bedrs, 9 ensuite, 🚻 P 30 ⊞ SB £27.50 DB £45
HB £178.50 D £8 D ● ✕ LD 21:30 CC MC Visa

CAERNARFON Gwynedd 6B1

Pop. 9,300. Betws-y-Coed 23, London 240, Aberdaron 33, Bangor 9, Dolgellau 39, Holyhead 29, Porthmadog 19, Pwllheli 20. **EC** Thu **MD** Sat *see* Medieval Castle, Town Walls, Foundations of Segontium Roman Fort (Museum) *i* Oriel Pendeitsh, Castle Street 01286-672232

★★★ Gwesty Seiont Manor 🛏 🛏

Llanrug, Caernarfon LL55 2AQ

📞 01286-673366 **Fax** 01286-672840

28 bedrs, all ensuite, 📺 ♀ ♨ 100 **P** 80 ⊞ **SB** £90-£100 **DB** £130-£170 **HB** £525-£648 **L** £14.50 **L** 🍷 **D** £23.50 **D** 🍷 ✕ **LD** 22:00 **CC** MC Visa Amex DC 🔲 🔲 🔲 🔲

★★ Menai Bank

North Road, Caernarfon LL55 1BD

📞 01286-673297 **Fax** 01286-673297

16 bedrs, all ensuite, 🍴 **P** 10 ⊞ Rest Resid **SB** £30-£36 **DB** £46-£58 **HB** £243-£279 **L** 🍷 **D** £15 ✕ **LD** 20:30 **CC** MC Visa

CARDIFF 3D1

See also BARRY

Pop. 281,000. Newport 12, London 149, M4 4½, Bridgend 19, Caerphilly 7½, Merthyr Tydfil 23, **EC** Wed *see* Castle(Medieval, Victorian additions with lavish rooms), Cathays Park (Civic Centre), St. Fagan's Castle (Welsh Folk Museum), National Museum of Wales, City Hall, St. John's Church *i* Central Station, Central Square 01222-227281

National Code & Number Change

Telephone codes and numbers in Cardiff change in April 2000.
01222-XXXXXX becomes 029-20XX XXXX
eg 01222-206222 becomes 029-2020 6222

★★★★★ St David's
Hotel and Spa 🛏 🛏 🛏
Blue Ribbon Hotel

Havannah Street, Cardiff CF10 5SD

📞 01222-454045 **Fax** 01222-487056

E-mail sales@fifestar-g+l-wales.com

136 bedrs, all ensuite, ♪ 🔲 ♨ 200 **P** 80 ⊞ **SB** £175.50 **DB** £207 **L** 🍷 **D** 🍷 ✕ **LD** 22:30 **CC** MC Visa Amex DC JCB 🔲 🔲 🔲 ♿

★★★★ ✦ Angel

Castle Street, Cardiff CF1 2QZ

📞 01222-232633 **Fax** 01222-396212

 PARAMOUNT
HOTEL·GROUP

Elegant Victorian hotel ideally situated in the heart of the city centre, overlooking the Millennium Stadium. 102 superb ensuite bedrooms, plus leisure facilities. Free car parking (subject to availability).

102 bedrs, all ensuite, 🍴 🔲 ♨ 300 **P** 70 ⊞ **SB** £105 **DB** £130 **L** £12.95 **D** £15.95 ✕ **LD** 21:30 **CC** MC Visa Amex DC JCB 🔲

★★★★ Cardiff Bay 🛏 🛏

Schooner Way, Atlantic Wharf, CF10 4RT

📞 02920-475000 **Fax** 02920-481491

156 bedrs, all ensuite, ♪ 🍴 ♨ 250 **P** 150 ⊞ **SB** £55-£110 **DB** £70-£125 **L** £11.50 **D** £18.50 ✕ **LD** 22:00 **CC** MC Visa Amex DC JCB 🔲 🔲 🔲 🔲 ♿ See advert on this page

★★★★ Copthorne Cardiff Caerdydd ⬚
Copthorne Way, Culverhouse Cross, Cardiff CF5 6DH
📞 01222-599100 **Fax** 01222-599080
135 bedrs, all ensuite, 🛏 ▣ ⚏ 300 **P** 225 ⊕
SB £126.95 **DB** £158.90 **L** £15 **D** £18.95 ✕ **LD** 22:00
Restaurant closed L Sat ⟨⟨ MC Visa Amex DC ⧉ ⊡
⊞ ⊞ ⎃

★★★★ Jurys Cardiff
Mary Ann Street, Cardiff CF1 2EQ
📞 01222-341441 **Fax** 01222-223742
E-mail bookings@jurys.com
146 bedrs, all ensuite, ♀ ⚲ ▣ ⚏ 40 **P** 63 ⊕
SB £130.95-£150.95 **DB** £141.90-£161.90 **L** ⬤
D £16.95 ✕ **LD** 21.30 ⟨⟨ MC Visa Amex DC ⊞ ⎃

★★★★ Miskin Manor
Pendoylan Road, Groes Faen, Pontyclun CF72 8ND
📞 01443-224204 **Fax** 01443-237606

Beautiful country house situated in twenty acres of lawns and woodlands near to Cardiff. 43 spacious bedrooms, a la carte restaurant and leisure facilities.
43 bedrs, all ensuite, ⚏ 200 **P** 150 ⊕ ⟨⟨ MC Visa Amex DC ⧉ ⊞ ⊞ ⊞ ⊞

★★★ Churchills
Llandaff Place, Cardiff Road, Llandaff, Cardiff CF5 2AD
📞 01222-562372 **Fax** 01222-568347

Newly refurbished 'town-house' hotel, near to the

Cathedral village of Llandaff, within easy reach of the M4 and only minutes from the city centre.
35 bedrs, all ensuite, 🛏 ⚏ 110 **P** 70 ⊕ **SB** £40-£75
DB £60-£115 **L** £9.50 **L** ⬤ **D** £16.50 **D** ⬤ ✕ **LD** 22:00
Restaurant closed L Sat ⟨⟨ MC Visa Amex DC ⎃

★★★ Manor Parc ⬚ ⬚ ⬚
Thornhill Road, Thornhill, Cardiff CF4 5UA
📞 01222-693723 **Fax** 01222-614624
Closed 24-30 Dec
12 bedrs, all ensuite, ▣ ♀ ⚏ 100 **P** 75 ⊕ **SB** £62
DB £90 **L** £18 **L** ⬤ **D** £22.50 ✕ **LD** 21:45 Restaurant closed D Sun ⟨⟨ MC Visa Amex ⊠

★★★ Posthouse   **Posthouse**
Pentwyn Road, Pentwyn, CF2 7XA
📞 01222-731212 **Fax** 01222-549147
142 bedrs, all ensuite, 🛏 ▣ ⚏ 120 **P** 300 ⊕
SB £83.95 **DB** £92.90 **HB** £44-£74 **L** £11.50 **L** ⬤
D £11.50 **D** ⬤ ✕ **LD** 22:30 ⟨⟨ MC Visa Amex DC JCB
⧉ ⊞ ⊞ ⎃

★★★ Posthouse Cardiff City   **Posthouse**
Castle Street, Cardiff CF1 2XB
📞 01222-388681 **Fax** 01222-371495
155 bedrs, all ensuite, ⚲ 🛏 ▣ ⚏ 170 **P** 120 ⊕
Room £95 ✕ **LD** 22:00 ⟨⟨ MC Visa Amex DC JCB ⊞ ⎃

★★★ Quality
Merthyr Road (jn 32, M4),
Tongwynlais, Cardiff CF4 7LD
📞 01222-529988 **Fax** 01222-529977
E-mail admin@gb629.u-net.com

Modern, spacious hotel with excellent leisure centre including heated pool, sauna and sunbeds. Well equipped gym. Plenty of parking.
95 bedrs, all ensuite, 🛏 ▣ ⚏ 200 **P** 100 ⊕ **SB** £91
DB £124.50 **L** £9.95 **D** £14.50 ✕ **LD** 21:45 Restaurant closed L Sat ⟨⟨ MC Visa Amex DC JCB ⧉ ⊞ ⊞ ⎃

★★ ✦ Sandringham
21 St Mary Street, Cardiff CF1 2PL
☎ 01222-232161 **Fax** 01222-383998
28 bedrs, all ensuite, ⊞ 100 **P** 6 ⊕ **SB** £44-£65
DB £52-£70 **HB** £236-£300 **L** 🍷 **D** £7.50 **CC** MC Visa
Amex DC JCB

Campanile Cardiff **Lodge**
Caxton Place, Pentwynn, Cardiff CF2 7HA
☎ 01222-549044 **Fax** 01222-549900

Campanile hotels offer comfortable and convenient
budget accommodation and a traditional French
style Bistro providing freshly cooked food for
breakfast, lunch and dinner. All rooms ensuite with
tea/coffee making facilities, DDT and TV with Sky
channels.
50 bedrs, all ensuite, ✙ ⊞ 20 **P** 50 ⊕ Rest Resid
SB £34.90-£41.95 **DB** £39.85-£46.90 **HB** £343 £5.75
L 🍷 **D** £10.85 ✕ **LD** 22:00 **CC** MC Visa Amex DC &

CARDIGAN Ceredigion   6B4
Pop. 4,300. Lampeter 29, London 234, Aberystwyth
38, Carmarthen 25, Fishguard 17, Haverfordwest
26, Tenby 32. **EC** Wed. **MD** Mon, Sat **see** Castle ruins,
St. Mary's Church ℹ Theatr Mwldan, Bath House
Road 01239-613230

★★★ Penbontbren Farm
Glynarthen, Cardigan SA44 6PE
☎ 01239-810248 **Fax** 01239-811129
Closed Christmas
10 bedrs, all ensuite, ✙ ⊞ 25 **P** 50 ⊕ Rest Resid
SB £39-£46 **DB** £70-£80 **HB** £322-£357 £15 ✕
LD 20:15 **CC** MC Visa Amex DC JCB &

★★ ✦ Castell Malgwyn
Llechryd, Cardigan SA43 2QA
☎ 01239-682382 **Fax** 01239-682382

Country house hotel in 48 acres of woodlands and
grounds, with ensuite rooms. Dogs welcome.
Swimming pool. Log fires. Peace and tranquillity
with award winning service and excellent
reputation.
20 bedrs, all ensuite, ♀ 🐾 ✙ ⊞ 200 **P** 60 ⊕ **SB** £42
DB £76 **HB** £406 **L** £13.50 **L** 🍷 **D** £17.50 **D** 🍷 ✕
LD 21:30 **CC** MC Visa Amex DC JCB ⅔ 🖻

CARMARTHEN Carmarthenshire   6B4
See also BRECHFA
Pop. 12,471. Llandovery 28, London 212, Cardigan
25, Haverfordwest 30, Lampeter 23, Llanelli 16,
Swansea 27, Tenby 27 **EC** Thu **MD** Daily exc Thur,
Sun **see** St. Peter's Church, County Museum, 14th
cent Gatehouse ℹ Lammas Street 01267-231557

Falcon
Lammas Street, Carmarthen SA31 3AP
☎ 01267-234959 **Fax** 01267-221277

Two-storey long-established hotel in town centre.
14 bedrs, all ensuite, ᐧ4ᐧ 🐾 ⊞ 100 **P** 8 ⊕ Rest Resid
CC MC Visa Amex DC

CHEPSTOW Monmouthshire   3E1
Pop. 10,000. Chippenham 32, London 123, M4 2,
Abergavenny 29, Bath 25, Bristol 16, Gloucester
28, Monmouth 16, Newport 15, Pontypool 21,
Ross-on-Wye 24, Swindon 48,Tetbury 29 **EC** Wed **see**
Castle ruins, St Mary's Church ℹ Castle Car Park,
Bridge Street 01291-623772

WALES

★★ Beaufort

Beaufort Square, Chepstow NP6 5EP
📞 01291-622497 **Fax** 01291-627389
18 bedrs, all ensuite, ⚑ ⁂ 30 **P** 12 ⊞ **SB** £40.95-£45.45 **DB** £56.90-£61.40 **L** £9 **L** 💺 **D** £13.95 **D** 💺 ✕ **LD** 21:45 **CC** MC Visa Amex DC ⅙

Old Course

Newport Road, Chepstow NP6 5PR
📞 01291-626261 **Fax** 01291-626263

At the gateway to Wales, elegantly decorated giving a homely atmosphere. The ideal meeting place, free large car park. Friendly service making a relaxing stay.
31 bedrs, all ensuite, ▣ ⁂ 200 **P** 180 ⊞ **CC** MC Visa Amex DC

COLWYN BAY Conwy   6C1
Pop. 25,500. Betws-y-Coed 17, Chester 42, Denbigh 19, Llandudno 5½, Queensferry 34, Rhyl 11 **EC** Wed **see** Welsh Mountain Zoo, Harlequin Puppet Theatre, Bodnant Gardens 5m SW ℹ 40 Station Road, 01492-530478

★★★ ✦ Colwyn Bay

Penmaenhead, Colwyn Bay LL29 9LD
📞 01492-516555 **Fax** 01492-515565
43 bedrs, all ensuite, ④ ⚑ ⁂ 200 **P** 100 ⊞ **SB** £44 **DB** £59 **HB** £259-£350 **L** £9.95 **L** 💺 **D** £13.95 ✕ **LD** 21:30 Restaurant closed L Mon-Sat **CC** MC Visa Amex DC JCB
See advert on this page

★★★ Hopeside 🛎

63 Princes Drive, Colwyn Bay LL29 8PW
📞 01492-533244 **Fax** 01492-532850
E-mail hopesidecb@aol.com
18 bedrs, all ensuite, ♀ ⚑ ⚑ ⁂ 110 **P** 14 No children under 6 ⊞ **SB** £39-£49 **DB** £56-£68 **Room** £46 **L** £8 **L** 💺 **D** £16 ✕ **LD** 20:45 **CC** MC Visa Amex DC JCB ⅙

★★★ Norfolk House

Princes Drive, Colwyn Bay LL29 9PF
📞 01492-531757 **Fax** 01492-533781
Closed Christmas
23 bedrs, all ensuite, ⚑ ▣ ⁂ 20 **P** 30 ⊞ **SB** £39.50 **DB** £56 **HB** £250 **L** 💺 **D** £15.75 **D** 💺 ✕ **LD** 20:30 **CC** MC Visa Amex DC JCB

CONWY Conwy   6C1
Pop. 13,000. Colwyn Bay 5½, London 227, Bangor 16, Betws-y-Coed 14, Llandudno 4 **EC** Wed **MD** Tue, Sat **see** Castle (1284), St Mary's Church, Elizabethan Mansion (Plas Mawr), Telford's suspension bridge ℹ Castle Street 01492-592248

★★★ Groes Inn 🛎

Tyn-y-Groes, Conwy LL32 8TN
📞 01492-650545 **Fax** 01492-650855
14 bedrs, all ensuite, ♀ ⚘ ⁂ 20 **P** 100 ⊞ **SB** £63.25 **DB** £80.50 **L** £12.50 **L** 💺 **D** £25 **D** 💺 ✕ **LD** 21:00 **CC** MC Visa Amex DC JCB ⅙

WALES

★★ Deganwy Castle
Station Road, Deganwy, Conwy LL31 9DA
☎ 01492-583555 **Fax** 01492-583555
31 bedrs, all ensuite, ⊞ ♀ ★ ⦂⦂⦂ 100 **P** 70 ⊕
SB £32.50-£35 **DB** £65-£68 **L** £10 **L** ♥ **D** £6 **D** ♥ ✕
LD 21:00 **CC** MC Visa Amex DC ▣ ⊠ ▦

★★ Old Rectory ⌇ ⌇ ⌇
Gold Ribbon Hotel
Llanrwst Road, Llansanffraid Glan Conwy, Conwy
LL28 5LF
☎ 01492-580611 **Fax** 01492-584555
E-mail oldrect@aol.com
Closed 30 Nov-1 Feb

Panoramic Snowdonian vistas, relaxing country
house atmosphere, antiques and paintings abound,
glorious gardens. Gourmet cuisine from a Master
Chef of Great Britain. No smoking main house.
6 bedrs, all ensuite, ⊞ ★ ⦂⦂⦂ 12 **P** 10 No children
under 5 ⊕ Rest Resid **SB** £79-£129 **DB** £99-£149
D £29.90 ✕ **LD** 20:00 **CC** MC Visa Amex DC JCB

★★ Tir-y-Coed Country House ⌇
Rowen, Conwy LL32 8TP
☎ 01492-650219 **Fax** 01492-650219
Closed mid Nov-Feb

Relax in a picturesque Snowdonia National Park
village amidst majestic scenery. Four miles from the
historic town of Conwy, within easy reach of
mountains, coast, castles and stately homes.

8 bedrs, all ensuite, ★ **P** 8 ⊕ Rest Resid **SB** £26.50-
£30.25 **DB** £49-£56.50 **HB** £243.50-£265.50 **D** £12.75
✕ **LD** 19:30 **CC** Amex

COWBRIDGE Vale of Glamorgan 3D1

★★★ Bear ⌇
High Street, Cowbridge CF7 2AF
☎ 01446-774814 **Fax** 01446-775425
35 bedrs, all ensuite, ⊞ ★ ⦂⦂⦂ 150 **P** 60 ⊕ **CC** MC
Visa Amex
See advert on this page

CRICCIETH Gwynedd 6B2
Pop. 1,500. Porthmadog 5, London 232,
Caernarfon 17, Pwllheli 8½ **EC** Wed **see** Lloyd George
Museum, Brynawelon

Facilities for the disabled

Hotels do their best to cater for disabled
visitors. However, it is advisable to contact
the hotel direct to ensure it can provide a
particular requirement.

★★★ Bron Eifion ⬚
Criccieth LL52 0SA
☎ 01766-522385 **Fax** 01766-522003

This gracious mansion house, just a short walk from the sea, is set in 5 acres of woodland and is surrounded by the rugged mountains of Snowdon and Harlech.
19 bedrs, all ensuite, 4 ⽥ 35 **P** 80 ⊞ **SB** £59-£66 **DB** £88-£104 **L** £10.75 **L** ● **D** £19.95 ✕ **LD** 20:30 ⊂⊂ MC Visa Amex

★★ Caerwylan ⬚
Beach Bank, Criccieth LL52 0HW
☎ 01766-522547
25 bedrs, all ensuite, ⼞ ⊡ **P** 30 ⊞ Rest Resid ✕ **LD** 19:30 Restaurant closed L Mon-Sat ⊂⊂ MC Visa ▨

★★ Lion
Y Maes, Criccieth LL52 0AA
☎ 01766-522460 **Fax** 01766-523075
46 bedrs, all ensuite, ⼞ ⊡ **P** 25 ⊞ **SB** £29-£33.50 **DB** £52-£59.50 **HB** £259.50-£282.50 **L** £7.95 **L** ● **D** £16.50 **D** ● ✕ **LD** 20:30 Restaurant closed L Mon-Sat ⊂⊂ MC Visa Amex DC JCB ⋤

CRICKHOWELL Powys   7D4
Pop. 2,000. Abergavenny 6½, London 150, Brecon 14, Builth Wells 27, Tredegar 10 **EC** Wed **MD** Thu
▨ Beaufort Chambers, Beaufort Street 01873-812105

★★★ Gliffaes Country House ⬚ ⬚
Crickhowell NP8 1RH
☎ 0800-146719 **Fax** 01874-730463
E-mail calls@gliffaeshotel.com

A comfortable country house, spectacularly situated in 33 acres of magnificent grounds overlooking the River Usk. Fishing, relaxed atmosphere, imaginative menus and stunning walks.
22 bedrs, all ensuite, ⽥ 40 **P** 35 ⊞ **SB** £50.30-£115 **DB** £60.70-£125.70 **L** £18 **L** ● **D** £23.30 ✕ **LD** 21:15 Restaurant closed L Mon-Sat ⊂⊂ MC Visa Amex DC JCB ▨ ▨ ▨

★★★ ✤ Manor
Brecon Road, Crickhowell NP8 1SE
☎ 01873-810212 **Fax** 01873-811938
19 bedrs, 16 ensuite, 3 ▨ ⼞ ⽥ 300 **P** 100 ⊞ ⊂⊂ MC Visa Amex
See advert on this page

★★ ✤ Dragon House
High Street, Crickhowell NP8 1BE
☎ 01873-810362 **Fax** 01873-811868
E-mail ghhotel@provider.co.uk
15 bedrs, all ensuite, ⦀ 40 **P** 15 ⊞ **SB** £35-£45
DB £52-£59 **HB** £249-£279 **L** ⦁ **D** £16.50 **D** ⦁ ✕
LD 20:30 **CC** MC Visa Amex

CWMBRAN Torfaen   3E1
Pop. 47,000. Chepstow 19, London 141, M4 (jn 26)
4, Newport 5, Pontypool 4½ **EC** Wed **MD** Fri

★★★★ Parkway
Cwmbran Drive, Cwmbran NP44 3UW
☎ 01633-871199 **Fax** 01633-869160
Closed 27 Dec-2 Jan

Luxury 4 star hotel designed and developed on a
Mediterranean theme. The hotel boasts 70 ensuite
bedrooms and extensive leisure facilities.
70 bedrs, all ensuite, ♪ ⦁ ⦀ 500 **P** 300 ⊞ **SB** £78-
£94.55 **DB** £100-£115.40 **HB** £464.75-£547.50 **L** £8.95
L ⦁ **D** £14.95 ✕ **LD** 22:00 Restaurant closed L Sat
CC MC Visa Amex DC 🔲 🔲 🔲 ⅄
See advert on this page

DOLGELLAU Gwynedd   6C2
See also BONTDDU
Pop. 2,500. Welshpool 37, London 207, Aberdyfi
24, Aberystwyth 22, Bala 18, Betws-y-Coed 32,
Caernarfon 39 **EC** Wed **MD** Fri ⅰ Ty Meirion, Eldon
Square 01341-422888

★★ George III
Penmaenpool, Dolgellau LL40 1YD
☎ 01341-422525 **Fax** 01341-423-565
11 bedrs, all ensuite, ⦁ **P** 60 ⊞ **SB** £50 **DB** £94 **L** £12
L ⦁ **D** £20 **D** ⦁ ✕ **LD** 21:30 **CC** MC Visa JCB 🔲 ⅄

★★ ✤ Royal Ship
Queens Square, Dolgellau LL40 1AR
☎ 01341-422209 **Fax** 01341-421027

24 bedrs, 18 ensuite, ⦁ ⦀ 40 **P** 12 ⊞ **SB** £25-£35
DB £40-£60 **L** £9 **D** £14 **D** ⦁ ✕ **LD** 21:00 **CC** MC Visa
JCB

EWLOE Flintshire   7D2
Pop. 1,700. London 190, Chester 8½, Holywell 8,
Mold 4, Queensferry 3, Wrexham 12 ⅰ Services,
A55 Westbound 01244-541597

★★★★ St David's Park ⅰ ⅰ
St David's Park, Ewloe CH5 3YB
☎ 01244-520800 **Fax** 01244-520930
145 bedrs, all ensuite, ⊞ ⦁ ⅰ ⦀ 270 **P** 250 ⊞
SB £119 **DB** £130 **L** ⦁ **D** ⦁ ✕ **LD** 22:00 **CC** MC Visa
Amex DC JCB 🔲 🔲 🔲 🔲 🔲 🔲 ⅄
See advert under Chester

FISHGUARD Pembrokeshire   6A4
Lampeter 44, London 248, Cardigan 17,
Haverfordwest 15, St David's 17 **EC** Wed **MD** Thu ⅰ 4
Hamilton Street 01348-873484

WALES

★★★ Fishguard Bay

Quay Road, Goodwick, Fishguard SA64 0BT
☎ 01348-873571 **Fax** 01348-873030

Nestling in rich woodland, high above Fishguard Harbour, overlooking some of the most beautiful coastline in Wales, is the Fishguard Bay Hotel. Steeped in history, this magnificent building offers a unique and classical base to enjoy Pembrokeshire.
62 bedrs, all ensuite, ✝ 🖵 ⅲ 200 **P** 50 ⊕ ⅭⅭ MC Visa Amex DC 🖾 ₺

★★ ✤ Cartref

High Street, Fishguard SA65 9AW
☎ 01348-872430 **Fax** 01348-873664

Recently renovated friendly family run hotel with licensed restaurant and residential bar. Only 5 minutes from the ferry port. Garage available. Open 24 hours.
10 bedrs, all ensuite, ✝ **P** 3 ⊕ Rest Resid **SB** £36 **DB** £52 **HB** £240 **L** £6 ⬤ **D** £12 **D** ⬤ ✕ **LD** 21:00 ⅭⅭ MC Visa Amex

Abergwaun Awaiting Inspection

Market Square, Fishguard SA65 9HA
☎ 01348-872077 **Fax** 01348-875412

This small family run hotel in the town centre has a pleasant lounge bar and cottage restaurant with a tea room next door. Open late for ferry traffic, garage parking available. Children welcome.
11 bedrs, 7 ensuite, ④ ⅲ 40 **P** 3 ⊕ **SB** £26-£39.50 **DB** £54 **HB** £249 **L** ⬤ **D** £14.50 **D** ⬤ ✕ **LD** 21:00 ⅭⅭ MC Visa Amex DC JCB

FOUR MILE BRIDGE Anglesey   6B1

Pop. 600. Bangor 21, London 258, **EC** Thu **MD** Thu

★★★ Anchorage 🖟

Four Mile Bridge LL65 2EZ
☎ 01407-740168 **Fax** 01407-741599
26 bedrs, all ensuite, ⅲ 10 **P** 100 ⊕ **SB** £45 **DB** £70 ✕ **LD** 21:30 Restaurant closed D Sun ⅭⅭ MC Visa Amex DC JCB

HARLECH Gwynedd   6C2

Pop. 1,200. Dolgellau 20, London 226, Bala 31, Betws-y-Coed 25, Caernarfon 27, **EC** Wed
🖟 Gwyddfor House, High Street 01766-780658

★★ St David's 🖟

Harlech LL46 2PT
☎ 01766-780366 **Fax** 01766-780820
60 bedrs, all ensuite, 🖵 ⅲ 100 **P** 60 ⊕ **SB** £25-£40 **DB** £50-£80 **L** £6 **L** ⬤ **D** £14 **D** ⬤ ✕ **LD** 20.30 ⅭⅭ MC Visa Amex DC 🏊 🖾

HAVERFORDWEST Pembrokeshire   6A4

Pop. 9,200. Carmarthen 30, London 243, Cardigan 26, Fishguard 15, **EC** Thu **MD** Tue, Sat **see** Norman Castle, Priory ruins 🖟 Old Bridge 01437-763110

★★ Hotel Mariners

Mariners Square, Haverfordwest SA61 2DU
☎ 01437-763353 **Fax** 01437-764258
Closed Christmas & New Year
28 bedrs, all ensuite, ✝ ⅲ 50 **P** 50 ⊕ **SB** £51.50 **DB** £71.75 **L** ⬤ **D** £16 **D** ⬤ ✕ **LD** 21:30 Restaurant closed L Sun ⅭⅭ MC Visa Amex DC

★★ Wolfscastle Country 🐾 🐾
Haverfordwest SA62 5LZ
☎ 01437-741225 **Fax** 01437-741388
E-mail andy741225@aol.com
Closed Christmas

Small country house hotel, well known for good food. Member of Welsh Rarebits independent recommended hotels. Well situated for visiting the National Park and the coastline of Pembrokeshire. 24 bedrs, all ensuite, 📺 🐾 ♨ 160 **P** 60 ⊞ **SB** £39-£47 **DB** £73 **HB** £343 **L** £15 **D** £15 ✗ **LD** 21:15 ℂℂ MC Visa Amex JCB 🔟

HAY-ON-WYE Powys   7D4
Hereford 21, London 153, Abergavenny 26, Brecon 13, Leominster 20 **EC** Tue **MD** Mon, Thur

★★★ ✤ Swan-at-Hay
Church Street, Hay-on-Wye,
Hereford HR3 5DQ
☎ 01497-821188 **Fax** 01497-821424

Welcome to a gracious Georgian hotel and its beautiful garden. Elegant public rooms. Ideal for weddings and private parties. Conference facilities. Imaginative food freshly prepared with bar meals, vegetarian food and full a la carte menu.
19 bedrs, all ensuite, 📺 🐾 ♨ 160 **P** 18 ⊞ **SB** £40-£50 **DB** £65-£90 **HB** £336-£420 **L** £11 **D** £18.50 **D** ❤ ✗ **LD** 21:30 ℂℂ MC Visa Amex DC JCB 🔟

HOLYHEAD Anglesey   6B1
See also FOUR MILE BRIDGE & TREARDDUR BAY
Pop. 12,000. Bangor 23, London 261, Caernarfon 29 ℹ Terminal 1 01407-762622

★★ Bull
London Road, Valley LL65 3DP
☎ 01407-740351 **Fax** 01407-742328

Colour washed in cream and green, a small hotel on A5 near centre of village - three and a half miles from Irish Ferry. Bar meals lunch and evening, Les Routiers recommended.
14 bedrs, all ensuite, 🐾 **P** 100 ⊞ **SB** £33.75 **DB** £44.75 **D** £8.95 **D** ❤ ✗ **LD** 21:30 ℂℂ MC Visa Amex 🔟 ♿
See advert on this page

WALES

THE KNIGHTON HOTEL

Set in the small town of Knighton on the Shropshire, Herefordshire border, this part 17th, part 19th century hotel with a wealth of charm and character welcomes you to enjoy excellent food and individually decorated bedrooms equally suited for the business traveller or visitor.

**Broad Street, Knighton
Powys, LD7 1BL
Tel: 01547 520530
Fax: 01547 5204529**

FALCONDALE MANSION HOTEL
RAC ★★★ merit

**LAMPETER, DYFED SA48 7RX
TEL: 01570 422 910**

A Victorian country mansion set within 14 acres of mature parkland. Overlooking the university and market town of Lampeter, 9 miles from the coast. All 20 individually designed bedrooms have spa bath/shower rooms, colour TV with film system, radio, tea and coffee makers, baby listening facility, central heating, direct dial telephone and hairdryers. **Services:** 2 bars, 2 lounges, conservatory, log fires, lift. Full conference facilities with syndicate rooms. **Sports facilities:** 10 acre lake (coarse fishing by arrangement), 18 hole putting green, tennis court, golf, pony trekking.

**Please write or telephone for brochure and tariff
Fax: 01570 423 559**

KNIGHTON Powys — 7D3

Ludlow 15, London 158, Kington 13, Llandrindod Wells 18, Welshpool 34 🅘 Offa's Dyke Centre, West Street 01547-528753

★★★ Knighton

Broad Street, Knighton LD7 1BL
📞 01547-520530 **Fax** 01547-528529
15 bedrs, all ensuite, 🛏 📺 ♨ 150 **P** 15 ⊟ **L** 💬 **D** 💬
✕ **LD** 21:00 **CC** MC Visa Amex DC ⅃
See advert on this page

LAMPETER Ceredigion — 6C4

Pop. 2,700. Llandovery 19, London 203, Aberystwyth 23, Cardigan 29, Carmarthen 23, Newtown 53, Swansea 45 **EC** Wed **MD** Alt Tue

🍴 ★★★ Falcondale Mansion

Lampeter SA48 7RX
📞 01570-422910 **Fax** 01570-423559
20 bedrs, all ensuite, 4️⃣ 📺 ♨ 60 **P** 80 ⊟ **CC** MC Visa Amex 🖾 ⤢
See advert on this page

LANGLAND BAY Swansea — 2C1

Swansea 5, London 193, Llanelli 16 **EC** Wed

★★★ ✤ Osborne

Rotherslade Road, Langland Bay SA3 4QL
📞 01792-366274 **Fax** 01792-363100
36 bedrs, 34 ensuite, 🛏 📺 ♨ 50 **P** 30 ⊟ **CC** MC Visa Amex DC JCB ⅃

★★ ✤ Wittemberg

2 Rotherslade Road, Langland, Swansea SA3 4QN
📞 01792-369696 **Fax** 01792-366995
11 bedrs, all ensuite, ♀ ⌀ 🛏 **P** 10 ⊟ Rest Resid
SB £33–£44 **DB** £50–£70 **HB** £185–£280 **L** £10 **D** £15 ✕
LD 19:45 Restaurant closed L Mon-Sat **CC** MC Visa

LLANBEDR Gwynedd — 6C2

Pop. 550. Dolgellau 16, London 219, Bala 35, Betws-y-Coed 28, Caernarfon 28, Porthmadog 12

★★ Ty Mawr
Llanbedr LL45 2NH
☎ 01341-241440
Closed 24-25 Dec

Family run, fully licensed country house hotel, beautiful gardens, peaceful riverside setting. Real Ale bar, home made extensive menu. Tastefully furnished bedrooms. Close to Championship Golf Course, mountain walking, horse riding and sandy beaches.
10 bedrs, all ensuite, ♀ ⍩ P 20 ⊞ SB £25-£30 DB £50-£58 HB £210-£266 L £6 L ♥ D £13 D ♥ ✕ LD 20:45 ℂℂ MC Visa 🎿 🐕

★★ ✤ Victoria Inn
Llanbedr LL45 2LD
☎ 01341-241213 Fax 01341-241644
5 bedrs, all ensuite, ⍩ ⁞⁞⁞ 20 P 75 ⊞ SB £30 DB £58 HB £180 L £7 D £10 D ♥ ✕ LD 21:00 ℂℂ MC Visa JCB

LLANBERIS Gwynedd   6B1
Pop. 3,500. Betws-y-Coed 16, London 232, Bangor 10, Caernarfon 7, Porthmadog 23 **see** Snowdon (Rack Rly to summit), Dolbardarn Castle 🛈 41a High Street 01286-870765

★★ ✤ Lake View
Tan-y-Pant, Llanberis LL55 4EL
☎ 01286-870422 Fax 01286-872591
10 bedrs, 9 ensuite, ⍩ P 25 ⊞ Rest Resid ℂℂ MC Visa Amex DC JCB ♿

Royal Victoria Awaiting Inspection
Llanberis LL55 4TY
☎ 01286-870253

LLANDRINDOD WELLS Powys   7D3
Pop. 4,200. Hereford 41, London 171, Builth Wells 7, Knighton 18, Llandovery 27, Leominster 33, Newtown 24, Rhayader 10 **EC** Wed **MD** Fri 🛈 Old Town Hall, Memorial Gardens 01597-822600

★★ Severn Arms
Penybont, Llandrindod Wells LD1 5UA
☎ 01597-851224 Fax 01597-851693
Closed Christmas

A former coaching inn dating from 1840, with a traditional black and white facade. Conveniently situated on the A44.
10 bedrs, all ensuite, ♪ ⍩ P 60 ⊞ SB £28 DB £50 HB £198 L £7 D £14 ✕ LD 21:00 ℂℂ MC Visa Amex DC ▣

LLANDUDNO Conwy   6C1
Pop. 20,000. Colwyn Bay 4½, London 227, Bangor 19, Betws-y-Coed 19 **EC** Wed 🛈 1-2 Chapel Street 01492-876413

★★★ Bodysgallen Hall 🎗🎗🎗🎗
Gold Ribbon Hotel
Llandudno LL30 1RS
☎ 01492-584466 Fax 01492-582519
E-mail info@bodysgallen.v-net.com

Delightful 17th century house standing in 250 acres of parkland overlooking Conwy Castle and Snowdonia. Antique furniture and paintings grace the welcoming rooms.
35 bedrs, all ensuite, ▣ ♀ ♪ ⁞⁞⁞ 50 P 50 No children under 8 ⊞ SB £111.50-£117.50 DB £160-£250 Room £135-£225 HB £728-£910 L £16.50 L ♥ D £32.50 ✕ LD 21:30 ℂℂ MC Visa JCB ▣ 🐕 📺 🎿 ♿

WALES

★★★ Imperial
Vaughan Street, Llandudno LL30 1AP
☎ 01492-877466 Fax 01492-878043

Situated on the seafront, the Imperial has something for everyone, including 2 bars, a health and fitness centre with 45ʃ ozone treated swimming pool.
100 bedrs, all ensuite, ⊢ ☰ ⫶ 150 P 35 ⊕ ✕ LD 21:30 ℂℂ MC Visa Amex DC ⊡ ⊞ ▦

★★★ ✦ Risboro
Clement Avenue, Llandudno LL30 2ED
☎ 01492-876343 Fax 01492-879881
E-mail run4colin@aol.com
62 bedrs, all ensuite, ④ ⊢ ☰ ⫶ 100 P 40 ⊕ ℂℂ MC Visa Amex JCB ⊡ ⊞ ▦ ⊞

★★ Ambassador
Grand Promenade, Llandudno LL30 2NR
☎ 01492-876886 Fax 01492-876347
57 bedrs, all ensuite, ⚲ ☰ ⫶ 70 P 10 ⊕ SB £24-£38 DB £44-£76 HB £195-£270 L £6 D £12.50 ✕ LD 19:30 ℂℂ MC Visa Amex ♿

★★ Banham House Hotel & Restaurant
2 St Davids Road, Llandudno LL30 2UL
☎ 01492-875680 Fax 01492-875680

Undoubtedly one of the most delightful small, quality two star hotel and restaurants to be found in North Wales. Immaculately presented, impeccably maintained throughout. Children not accommodated.

6 bedrs, all ensuite, ♀ ⊠ P 6 No children under 12 ⊕ Rest Resid SB £30 DB £46 HB £224 L £9 D £9 ✕ LD 21:30

★★ Belle Vue
North Parade, Llandudno LL30 2LP
☎ 01492-879547 Fax 01492-870001
Closed Dec-Jan
15 bedrs, all ensuite, ⊢ ☰ P 12 ⊕ Rest Resid SB £23.50-£29.50 HB £230-£270 D £12 ✕ LD 19:00 ℂℂ MC Visa

★★ ✦ Branksome
62-64 Lloyd Street, Llandudno LL30 2YP
☎ 01492-875989 Fax 01492-875989
49 bedrs, 42 ensuite, ⊢ ⫶ 101 P 19 ⊕ Rest Resid ℂℂ MC Visa JCB

★★ Dunoon
Gloddaeth Street, Llandudno LL30 2DW
☎ 01492-860787 Fax 01492-860031
Closed mid Nov-mid Mar
55 bedrs, all ensuite, ⊢ ☰ P 24 ⊕ Rest Resid SB £37-£42 DB £52-£84 HB £210-£305 L £9 L ♥ D £14.50 ✕ LD 20:00 ℂℂ MC Visa Amex

★★ Epperstone
15 Abbey Road, Llandudno LL30 2EE
☎ 01492-878746 Fax 01492-871223
Closed Jan excl New Year

Small, select hotel, with car park, in award winning gardens. Spacious, comfortable rooms portraying Edwardian elegance. Bedrooms ensuite with excellent accessories. Convenient, level walking. All amenities.
8 bedrs, all ensuite, ⊢ P 8 ⊕ Rest Resid SB £27-£30 DB £36-£40 HB £170-£246 L £8 D £16 ✕ LD 19:30 ℂℂ MC Visa ♿

★★ Esplanade
Central Promenade, Llandudno LL30 2LL
☎ 01492-860300 Fax 01492-860418
E-mail info@esplanadehotel.co.uk
Closed 3 Jan-26 Jan

59 bedrs, all ensuite, ⊁ ▣ ⁞⁞⁞ 80 **P** 30 ⊕ **SB** £19-£46.50 **DB** £38-£78 **Room** £14-£32.50 **HB** £203-£343 **L** ●
D £10 ✕ **LD** 20:30 ₵ MC Visa Amex DC JCB ₷

★★ ❖ Headlands
Hill Terrace, Llandudno LL30 2LS
📞 01492-877485
Closed Jan-Feb
17 bedrs, 15 ensuite, ④ ⊁ **P** 10 No children under 5
⊕ Rest Resid ₵ MC Visa Amex DC

★★ Royal
Church Walks, Llandudno LL30 2HW
📞 01492-876476 **Fax** 01492-870210
E-mail royal@northwales.uk.com
38 bedrs, all ensuite, ⌀ ▣ ⁞⁞⁞ 100 **P** 30 ⊕ **SB** £23-£30 **DB** £45-£60 **HB** £195-£225 **D** £15 ✕ **LD** 20:00
₵ MC Visa Amex ₷

★★ Sandringham
West Parade, Llandudno LL30 2BD
📞 01492-876513 **Fax** 01492-872753
Closed Christmas
18 bedrs, all ensuite, ⁞⁞⁞ 70 **P** 6 ⊕ **SB** £25.50-£29
DB £51-£58 **HB** £248-£268 **L** £6.50 **L** ● **D** £14 **D** ● ✕
LD 20:30 ₵ MC Visa DC JCB ₷

ST.TUDNO HOTEL

Without doubt one of the finest seafront hotels on the coast of Britain having won a host of awards for excellence. Elegantly and lovingly furnished offering the best in service and hospitality. The Garden Room has a reputation as one of the best restaurants in Wales. Swimming pool. Lift. Car park.

**PROMENADE,
LLANDUDNO LL30 2LP
Tel: 01492 874411 / Fax: 01492 860407**

★★ ❖ Somerset
Central Promenade, Llandudno LL30 2LF
📞 01492-876540 **Fax** 01492-876540
Closed Jan-Mar
37 bedrs, all ensuite, ♀ ⊁ ▣ ⁞⁞⁞ 70 **P** 25 ⊕ Rest
Resid **SB** £29-£36 **DB** £58-£72 **L** £6.95 **L** ● **D** £15 ✕
LD 19:30 ₵ MC Visa ▨ ₷

★★ St Tudno 🕱 🕱 🕱
Gold Ribbon Hotel
Promenade, Llandudno LL30 2LP
📞 01492-874411 **Fax** 01492-860407
E-mail sttudnohotel@btinternet.com
20 bedrs, all ensuite, ④ ⌀ ⊁ ▣ ⁞⁞⁞ 40 **P** 12 ⊕ Rest
Resid **SB** £75-£90 **DB** £95-£186 **HB** £448 **L** £16.95 **L** ●
D £32 ✕ **LD** 21:30 ₵ MC Visa Amex DC JCB ▣
See advert on this page

★★ ❖ Wilton
South Parade, Llandudno LL30 2LN
📞 01492-876086 **Fax** 01492-876086
E-mail wiltonhotel@enterprise.net
Closed 15 Nov-10 Mar

Ideally situated adjacent to beach, pier and shops. All rooms are individually decorated and furnished to the highest standards. All bedrooms have bathroom ensuite, satellite TV, telephone, tea/coffee trays, and some have fourposter beds.
14 bedrs, all ensuite, ④ ⌀ ⊁ **P** 3 ⊕ Resid **SB** £24-£28 **DB** £48-£56 **Room** £21-£23 **HB** £214-£226 **D** £10 ✕
LD 19:30

★ ❖ Min-y-don
North Parade, Llandudno LL30 2LP
📞 01492-876511 **Fax** 01492-878169
28 bedrs, 19 ensuite, **P** 7 ⊕ Rest Resid **SB** £21-£23
DB £42-£46 **HB** £185 **L** ● **D** £7 **D** ● ✕ **LD** 19:30 ₵ MC
Visa Amex

★ ❖ Warwick
56 Church Walks, Llandudno LL30 2HL
☎ 01492-876823
15 bedrs, ⓒ MC Visa Amex

LLANELLI Carmarthenshire   2C1
Pop. 30,000. Neath 16, London 201, M4 5,
Carmarthen 16, Brecon 47, Llandovery 29,
Swansea 11 ⓔ Tue **MD** Thu **see** Parc Howard Mansion
ⓘ Public Library, Vaughan Street 01554-772020

★★ Miramar
158 Station Road, Llanelli SA15 1YH
☎ 01554-773607 **Fax** 01554-772454
10 bedrs, 8 ensuite, ⠿ 30 **P** 10 ⊞ **SB** £16-£24
DB £30-£40 **L** ⬤ **D** ⬤ ✕ **LD** 22:00 ⓒ MC Visa Amex
DC JCB

LLANFAIRPWLLGWYNGYLL Anglesey   6B1
Pop. 2,800. Menai Bridge 2, London 242, Bangor 4,
Caernarfon 7½, Holyhead 15 **MD** Thu ⓘ Station Site
01248-713177

★★★ Carreg Bran
Church Lane, LL61 5YH
☎ 01248-714224 **Fax** 01248-715983
29 bedrs, all ensuite, ♀ ⊘ ⠿ 100 **P** 170 ⊞
SB £50-£55 **DB** £69-£75 **L** ⬤ **D** £16.50 **D** ⬤ ✕
LD 22:00 ⓒ MC Visa Amex ▦

LLANGAMMARCH WELLS Powys   6C4
Pop. 300. Builth Wells 8, London 179, Brecon 17,
Llandovery 15, Rhayader 18 ⓔ Wed **see** Cefn Brith
Farm

★★★ Lake Country House ⌇ ⌇
Blue Ribbon Hotel
Llangammarch Wells LD4 4BS
☎ 01591-620202 **Fax** 01591-620457

A welcoming Welsh country house set in its own 50
acres, with sweeping lawns, rhododendron lined
pathways and riverside walks.
19 bedrs, all ensuite, ▦ ⠿ ⠿ 80 **P** 70 ⊞ **SB** £80-
£120 **DB** £125-£135 **HB** £504-£661 **L** £17.50 **D** £30 ✕
LD 21:45 ⓒ MC Visa Amex DC JCB ▣ ▩ ▨ ▦ ⅏

LLANGOLLEN Denbighshire   7D2
Pop. 3,100. Shrewsbury 29, London 184, Corwen
10, Mold 19, Ruthin 15, Welshpool 28, Whitchurch
23, Wrexham 11 ⓔ Thu **see** Vale of Llangollen, Parish
Church of St Collen, 14th cent bridge, Plas Newydd
(home of 'Ladies of Llangollen'), Pontcysylite
Aqueduct, Dinas Bran Castle ruins ⓘ Town Hall,
Castle Street 01978-860828

★★★ Bryn Howel Hotel
& Restaurant ⌇
Llangollen LL20 7UW
☎ 01978-860331 **Fax** 01978-860119
E-mail hotel@brynhowel.demon.co.uk
36 bedrs, all ensuite, ▦ ⊘ ⠿ ▣ ⠿ 250 **P** 200 ⊞
SB £49.50-£80.50 **DB** £99-£108 **HB** £367.50-£462
L £14.95 **L** ⬤ **D** £21 ✕ **LD** 21:00 ⓒ MC Visa Amex
JCB ▣ ▨ ⅏

★★ Hand
Bridge Street, Llangollen LL20 8PL
☎ 01978-860303 **Fax** 01978-861277
58 bedrs, all ensuite, ⠿ ⠿ 100 **P** 40 ⊞ **SB** £30-£60
DB £60-£75 **HB** £245-£315 **L** £8 **D** £14 ✕ **LD** 20:30
Restaurant closed L Mon-Sat ⓒ MC Visa Amex DC
JCB ▨

★★ ❖ Tyn-y-wern
Maes Mawr Road, Llangollen LL20 7PH
☎ 01978-860252 **Fax** 01978-860252
10 bedrs, all ensuite, ⠿ **P** 80 ⊞ **SB** £32 **DB** £48 **L** £6
D £6 ✕ **LD** 21:00 ⓒ MC Visa Amex DC JCB ▨

LLANRWST Conwy   6C1
Pop. 3,000. Corwen 23, London 218, Bala 24,
Betws-y-Coed 4, Colwyn Bay 14, Denbigh 20,
Llandudno 15, Rhyl 22, Ruthin 27 ⓔ Thu **MD** Tue

★★ Plas Maenan
Conway Valley, Llanrwst, Betws-y-Coed LL26 0YR
☎ 01492-660232 **Fax** 01492-660551
15 bedrs, all ensuite, ▦ ⠿ ⠿ 80 **P** 100 ⊞ ⓒ MC Visa

LLANTWIT MAJOR Vale of Glamorgan   3D1
Pop. 8,800. Cardiff 15, London 164, Bridgend 9½,
Caerphilly 21, Pontypridd 19

★★ West House Country
West Street, Llantwit Major CF61 1SP
☎ 01446-792406 **Fax** 01446-796147
E-mail nhoward@westhouse.u-net.com
21 bedrs, all ensuite, �4 ★ ≣ 70 **P** 50 ⊞ **SB** £49.50
DB £62.50 **HB** £275 **L** ● **D** £15.50 **D** ● ✕ **LD** 21:30
CC MC Visa Amex JCB

LLANWRTYD WELLS Powys 6C4
Pop. 500. Builth Wells 13, London 185, Brecon 24,
Llandovery 11, Knighton 36, Newtown 44,
Rhayader 21 **EC** Wed **🖈** Ty Barcud, The Square
01591-610666

★★ Lasswade House 🖫
Station Road, Llanwrtyd Wells LD5 4RW
☎ 01591-610515 **Fax** 01591-610611
8 bedrs, all ensuite, 🖉 ☒ **P** 9 No children under 14
⊞ **SB** £32.95 **DB** £65.90 **HB** £298 **D** £18.25 **D** ● ✕
LD 20:30 **CC** MC Visa JCB 🖳

★ ❖ Neuadd Arms
Llanwrtyd Wells LD5 4RB
☎ 01591-610236 **Fax** 01591-610236
20 bedrs, 15 ensuite, ★ **P** 10 ⊞ **SB** £23-£25 **DB** £46
HB £230 **D** £12 ✕ **LD** 20:30 **CC** MC Visa

LLANWYDDYN Powys 7D2
Welshpool 19, London 191, Bala 17, Machynlleth
27, Oswestry 24

★★★ Lake Vyrnwy 🖫
Llanwyddyn SY10 0LY
☎ 01691-870692 **Fax** 01691-870259
E-mail res@lakevyrnwy.com
35 bedrs, all ensuite, �4 ★ ≣ 100 **P** 70 ⊞ **SB** £75-
£139 **DB** £99-£165 **L** £15.95 **D** £25.50 ✕ **LD** 21:15
CC MC Visa Amex DC 🖳 🖳

LLYSWEN Powys 7D4
Pop. 150. Brecon 9, London 159, Abergavenny 21,
Builth Wells 12, Hereford 29, Leominster 30 **see**
Church

★★★★ Llangoed Hall 🖫 🖫 🖫
Blue Ribbon Hotel
Llyswen LD3 0YP
☎ 01874-754525 **Fax** 01874-754545
E-mail llangoed_hall_co_wales_uk@compuserve.com

Llangoed Hall is a luxurious country house set in
the breathtaking Wye Valley. The highest standards
of cuisine and service are our hallmark.
23 bedrs, all ensuite, �4 🖉 ★ ≣ 50 **P** 60 No children
under 8 ⊞ **SB** £155-£175 **DB** £185-£415 **L** £15 **L** ●
D £35 ✕ **LD** 21:30 **CC** MC Visa Amex DC JCB 🖳 🖳 🖳

MACHYNLLETH Powys 6C2
Pop. 1,904. Newtown 28, London 205, Aberdyfi 10,
Aberystwyth 17, Dolgellau 15 **EC** Thu **MD** Wed **see**
Owain Glyndwr Institute, Plas Machynlleth,
Castlereagh Memorial Clock **🖈** Canolfan Owain
Glyndwr 01654-702401

★★★ Ynyshir Hall 🖫 🖫 🖫 🖫
Gold Ribbon Hotel
Machynlleth SY20 8TA
☎ 01654-781209 **Fax** 01654-781366
E-mail info@ynyshir-hall.co.uk

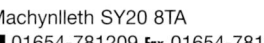

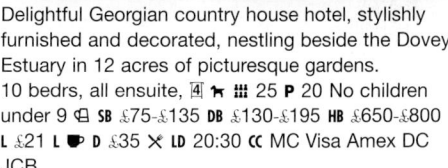

Delightful Georgian country house hotel, stylishly
furnished and decorated, nestling beside the Dovey
Estuary in 12 acres of picturesque gardens.
10 bedrs, all ensuite, �4 ★ ≣ 25 **P** 20 No children
under 9 ⊞ **SB** £75-£135 **DB** £130-£195 **HB** £650-£800
L £21 **L** ● **D** £35 ✕ **LD** 20:30 **CC** MC Visa Amex DC
JCB

WALES

★★ Wynnstay ⍭
Heol Maengwyn, Machynlleth SY20 8AE
☎ 01654-702941 **Fax** 01654-703884

Traditional former coaching hotel in a historic market town. Well appointed rooms, some fourposters, traditional Welsh and Italian food, cosy bars and lounges. Experience Wales' warmest welcome.
23 bedrs, all ensuite, ▣ ⍭ ⫽ 35 **P** 35 ⊕ **SB** £38-£45 **DB** £60-£70 **L** ⬤ **D** £12.50 **D** ⬤ ✕ **LD** 21:00 ⊂⊂ MC Visa Amex DC

MANORBIER Pembrokeshire   2B1
Pop. 350. Tenby 5, London 244, Pembroke 6 **see** 12th cent Castle, 12th cent Parish Church

★★ Castle Mead ⍭
Manorbier SA70 7TA
☎ 01834-871358 **Fax** 01834-871358
Closed Jan-Feb
8 bedrs, 8 ⍭ ⍭ **P** 15 ⊕ ⊂⊂ MC Visa JCB

MERTHYR TYDFIL Merthyr Tydfil   7D4
Pop. 42,000. Tredegar 7½, London 162, Brecon 18, Caerphilly 16, Hirwaun 6, Llandovery 31, Newport 26, Pontypridd 12 **EC** Thu **MD** Tue, Sat ℹ 14a Glebeland Street 01685-379884

★★★ ✧ Castle
Castle Street, Merthyr Tydfil CF47 8BG
☎ 01685-386868 **Fax** 01685-383898

A five storey purpose built town centre hotel, all rooms ensuite with colour TV, tea/coffee facilities, toiletries and telephones. Executive and bridal suites available.
46 bedrs, all ensuite, ▣ ⫽ 150 **P** 100 ⊕ ⊂⊂ MC Visa Amex DC ⍭ ⍭

Baverstock
Heads of the Valley Road, Merthyr Tydfil CF44 0LX
☎ 01685-386221 **Fax** 01685-723670

Located on the edge of the beautiful Brecon Beacons National Park, providing an ideal base for exploring the area. The Llewellyn Restaurant offers both a la carte and table d'hote menus.
50 bedrs, all ensuite, ⍭ ⫽ 400 **P** 300 ⊕ ⊂⊂ MC Visa Amex DC JCB ⍭ ⍭

MILFORD HAVEN Pembrokeshire   6A4
Pop. 13,750. Haverfordwest 7, London 250, Pembroke 8, Tenby 17 **EC** Thu **MD** Fri ℹ 94 Charles Street 01646-690866

★★ ✧ Lord Nelson
Hamilton Terrace, Milford Haven SA73 3AL
☎ 01646-695341 **Fax** 01646-694026
Closed Christmas Day

Overlooking the waterfront, a fine three storey Georgian hotel. Associations with Nelson.
30 bedrs, all ensuite, ⍭ ⫽ 35 **P** 26 ⊕ **SB** £25-£45 **DB** £50-£68 **L** £7 **L** ⬤ **D** £12.25 **D** ⬤ ✕ **LD** 21:30 ⊂⊂ MC Visa Amex DC

BEAUFORT PARK HOTEL

Winner of the North Wales Tourism 'Warmest Welcome Award 1996'. Surrounded by the calm beauty of the North Wales countryside and yet only ten miles from historic Chester. An independent Hotel, offering the flexibility to meet your individual needs. With 106 well appointed and tastefully decorated en suite bedrooms, extensive conference facilities and a superb restaurant providing excellent homemade cuisine. The perfect location for a relaxing and comfortable break.

MOLD, FLINTSHIRE, NORTH WALES CH7 6RQ
Tel: 01352 758646 Fax: 01352 757132

MOLD Flintshire 7D1
Pop. 8,900. Wrexham 11, London 191, Chester 11, Corwen 21, Denbigh 16, Llangollen 19, Queensferry 6½, Ruthin 10 **EC** Thu **MD** Wed, Sat 🛈 Library Museum and Gallery, Earl Road 01352-759331

★★★ Beaufort Park
Alltami Road, New Brighton, Mold CH7 6RQ
📞 01352-758646 **Fax** 01352-757132
106 bedrs, all ensuite, 🐾 ⅲ 250 **P** 200 ⊕ **CC** MC Visa Amex DC JCB 🔣 &
See advert on this page

★★ ✦ Bryn Awel
Denbigh Road, Mold CH7 1BL
📞 01352-758622 **Fax** 01352-758625
Closed Christmas
17 bedrs, 8 ensuite, 🐾 ⅲ 30 **P** 40 ⊕ **CC** MC Visa Amex DC

MORFA NEFYN Gwynedd 6B2

★★ Woodlands Hall
Edern, Morfa Nefyn LL53 6JB
📞 01758-720425 **Fax** 01758-720425

13 bedrs, 12 ensuite, 🐾 ⅲ 90 **P** 100 ⊕ ✕ **LD** 21:30 **CC** MC Visa JCB 🔣

MUMBLES Swansea 2C1
Pop. 13,700. Swansea 3½, London 193, Carmarthen 29, Llanelli 13 **EC** Wed 🛈 Oystermouth Square 01792-361302

★★★ Norton House
17 Norton Road, Mumbles SA3 5TQ
📞 01792-404891 **Fax** 01792-403210

This excellent Georgian manor house is owned and run by the Power family, with an emphasis on traditional hospitality within quality surroundings. 15 bedrs, all ensuite, 4 ⅲ 20 **P** 40 No children ⊕ **CC** MC Visa Amex DC

NEATH Neath & Port Talbot 3D1
Pop. 15,100. Hirwaun 16, London 184, M4 3, Bridgend 17, Llandovery 16, Llanelli 16, Swansea 7½ **EC** Thu **MD** Wed **see** St Thomas Church, Abbey ruins, Castle ruins, remains of Roman fort and Wildlife Park

★★ Castle
The Parade, Neath SA11 1RB
📞 01639-641119 **Fax** 01639-641624
28 bedrs, all ensuite, 4 🐾 ⅲ 120 **P** 20 ⊕ **SB** £55 **DB** £65 **L** £7 **D** £10 ✕ **LD** 22:00 **CC** MC Visa Amex DC

NEWPORT 3E1
Pop. 135,000. Chepstow 15, London 137, M4 1, Abergavenny 18, Caerphilly 11, Cardiff 12, Monmouth 22, Pontypool 9 **MD** Weekdays **see** Norman Castle Ruins (13th cent), St Woolos Cathedral, Museum and Art Gallery, Murals at Civic Centre, Transporter Bridge, Double View (Ridgeway), Roman Amphitheatre and relics in Museum at Caerleon 3m N 🛈 Museum, John Frost Square 01633-842962

★★★★ ✤ Celtic Manor Hotel, Golf & Country Club

The Coldra, Newport NP6 2YA
☎ 01633-413000 **Fax** 01633-412910

Three 18 hole golf courses and luxury clubhouse plus golf academy. 2 health and fitness clubs, with swimming pools and beauty treatments. 400 bedrooms, all ensuite, 2 restaurants, conference and meeting facilities up to 1500.

400 bedrs, all ensuite, 4 ⌀ ▣ ♨ **P** 750 ⊞ **SB** £98 **DB** £108 L £13.50 **L** ● **D** £20 **D** ● ✕ **LD** 22:30 ⟪ MC Visa Amex DC ▣ ▣ ▣ ▣ ⅙

★★★ Kings

High Street, Newport NP9 1QU
☎ 01633-842020 **Fax** 01633-244667
Closed 26 Dec-2 Jan
61 bedrs, all ensuite, ▣ ♨ 200 **P** 40 ⊞ ⟪ MC Visa Amex DC JCB
See advert on this page

★★★ St Mellons

Castleton, Newport CF3 8XR
☎ 01633-680355 **Fax** 01633-680399
41 bedrs, all ensuite, 4 ⌀ ★ ♨ 200 **P** 150 ⊞ **SB** £80-£90 **DB** £90-£100 L £16 **L** ● **D** £16 **D** ● ✕ **LD** 21:45 ⟪ MC Visa Amex ▣ ▣ ▣ ▣ ▣ ⅙

★★ Elephant & Castle

Broad Street, Newtown SY16 2BQ
☎ 01686-626271 **Fax** 01686-622123

Ideally situated near the town centre, alongside the River Severn. Popular bar and restaurant. Function rooms and fitness centre.
35 bedrs, all ensuite, ♨ 250 **P** 40 ⊞ ⟪ MC Visa Amex DC ▣

NEWTOWN Powys   7D3

Pop. 5,500. Ludlow 32, London 175, Aberystwyth 43, Builth Wells 34, Rhayader 32, Welshpool 13 **EC** Thu **MD** Tue *see* Robt Owen's grave, Owen Memorial Museum, Textile Museum ℹ Central Car Park 01686-625580

Facilities for the disabled
Hotels do their best to cater for disabled visitors. However, it is advisable to contact the hotel direct to ensure it can provide a particular requirement.

PEMBROKE Pembrokeshire   2B1

Pop. 5,500. Carmarthen 32, London 244, Cardigan 37, Haverfordwest 19 (fy 10), Tenby 10 **EC** Wed ℹ Pembroke Visitor Centre, Commons Road 01646-622388

★★★ Court
Lamphey, Pembroke SA71 5NT
☎ 01646-672273 **Fax** 01646-672480

An elegant Georgian mansion extensively refurbished with superb leisure centre. Ideally situated for local business area and exploring Pembrokeshire's coast with beautiful beaches. A Best Western hotel.
35 bedrs, all ensuite, ✝ ⅲ 90 **P** 50 ⊕ **SB** £67-£79 **DB** £80-£130 **HB** £276-£485 **L** £6.95 **L** ● **D** £18 **D** ● ✕ **LD** 21:45 **⊄** MC Visa Amex DC JCB ▣ ▣ ▣ ▣ ⅋

★★ Bethwaite's Lamphey Hall ▨ ▨ ▨
Lamphey, Pembroke SA71 5NR
☎ 01646-672394 **Fax** 01646-672369

All rooms are individually designed and decorated and equipped to the highest standards with ensuite facilities, direct dial telephone, colour TV, hairdryer and tea/coffee trays. Beds are fitted with duvets.
10 bedrs, all ensuite, ▨ ♀ ⅌ **P** 35 ⊕ **SB** £35 **DB** £50 **HB** £339.50 **L** £8.95 **L** ● **D** £18.50 **D** ● ✕ **LD** 21:30 Restaurant closed L Mon-Sat **⊄** MC Visa Amex JCB &

★★ Wheeler's Old King's Arms ▨
Main Street, Pembroke SA7 4JS
☎ 01646-683611 **Fax** 01646-682335
20 bedrs, all ensuite, ✝ **P** 20 ⊕ **⊄** MC Visa Amex JCB

PEMBROKE DOCK Pembrokeshire　　6A4
Pop. 8,200. Pembroke 2, London 246, Haverfordwest 11, Milford Haven 7, Tenby 11
▨ The Guntower, Front Street 01646-622246

★★★ Cleddau Bridge
Essex Road, Pembroke Dock SA72 6UT
☎ 01646-685961 **Fax** 01646-685746
E-mail awpl@aol.com.

Beautiful setting overlooking the river and yacht marina adjacent to Pembrokeshire National Park. Luxury rooms all ensuite with full dining facilities/bar snacks. Please ring for details of weekend breaks.
24 bedrs, all ensuite, ✝ ⅲ 250 **P** 100 ⊕ **SB** £55 **DB** £64.50 **D** £12.50 **D** ● ✕ **LD** 21:30 **⊄** MC Visa Amex DC ⊰ &

PENARTH Vale of Glamorgan　　3D1
Pop. 22,500. Cardiff 4, London 153, Bridgend 22 **EC** Wed **see** Turner House Art Gallery, St Peter's Church, Penarth Head ▨ The Esplanade, Penarth Pier 01222-708849

★★ ❖ Glendale
10 Plymouth Road, Penarth CF64 3DH
☎ 01222-706701 **Fax** 01222-709269
20 bedrs, 15 ensuite, 5 ⋒ ⅌ ⅲ 15 ⊕ **SB** £29.50 **DB** £42 **L** £5.95 **D** £12.50 ✕ **LD** 22:00 Restaurant closed L & D Sun **⊄** MC Visa Amex

PENMAEN Swansea　　2C1
M4 (jn 47) 9½, London 207, Horton 4, Swansea 7

★★ ❖ Nicholaston House
Nicholaston, Penmaen SA3 2HL
☎ 01792-371317 **Fax** 01792-371317
11 bedrs, all ensuite, ✝ ⅲ 70 **P** 35 ⊕ **⊄** MC Visa ▨

PONTYPRIDD Rhondda　　3D1
Pop. 32,000. Caerphilly 7, London 155, Bridgend 17, Cardiff 11, Merthyr Tydfil 11 **EC** Thu **MD** Wed, Sat **see** Old Bridge, St Catherine's Church ▨ Bridge Street 01443-409512

WALES

Heritage Park
Coed Cae Road, Trehafod,
Pontypridd CF37 2NP
☎ 01443-687057 Fax 01443-687060

Set in the heart of the Rhondda Valley, with 44 exquisitely decorated bedrooms, a health and leisure club, a fine restaurant and a warm Welsh welcome.
44 bedrs, all ensuite, ♫ ✝ ⁛ 240 P 150 ⊞ SB £55 DB £70 L £7.95 L ☕ D £16.95 ✕ LD 22:00 ℂℂ MC Visa Amex DC 🔲 🔲 🔲 க்

PORT TALBOT Neath & Port Talbot 2C1
Pop. 42,100. Bridgend 12, London 180, M4 2, Neath 5½, Swansea 8 ⅄ Wed MD Tue, Sat

★★★ Aberavon Beach
Port Talbot SA12 6QP
☎ 01639-884949 Fax 01639-897885

Modern seafront hotel in a residential area close to the M4 and seven miles from the centre of Swansea. Comfortable bedrooms, elegant restaurant, conference facilities, all-weather leisure centre and friendly staff.
52 bedrs, all ensuite, ✝ ▣ ⁛ 300 P 120 ⊞ SB £69-£75 DB £75-£80 HB £285 L £10 D £18.50 ✕ LD 22 ℂℂ MC Visa Amex DC 🔲 🔲 க்

PORTHCAWL Bridgend 3D1
Pop. 15,300. Bridgend 5½, London 174, Neath 16, Swansea 18 ⅄ Wed see 13th cent St John's Church (Newton) 🅸 Old Police Station, John Street 01656-786639

★★ ✤ Seaways
Mary Street, Porthcawl CF36 3YA
☎ 01656-783510
17 bedrs, 11 ensuite, ♫ ✝ P 2 ⊞ SB £20-£28 DB £34-£40 ✕ LD 21:00 ℂℂ MC Visa

---

PORTMEIRION Gwynedd 6C2
Penrhyndeudraeth 4, London 228, Betws-y-Coed 24, Caernarfon 24, Dolgellau 26

★★★ Hotel Portmeirion ⴲ
Blue Ribbon Hotel
Portmeirion LL48 6ET
☎ 01766-770000 Fax 01766-771331
E-mail hotel@portmeirion.wales.com
Closed 11 Jan-6 Feb

The Italianate village of Portmerion on its wooded peninsula overlooking Cardigan Bay has 23 cottage suites and 14 rooms in the main Hotel.
40 bedrs, all ensuite, ④ ⁛ 100 P 100 ⊞ Rest SB £95 DB £125-£180 L £14 D £26.50 ✕ LD 21:30 Restaurant closed L Mon ℂℂ MC Visa Amex DC JCB ⴲ 🔲

RUABON Wrexham 7D2
Pop. 5,500. Shrewsbury 27, London 181, Wrexham 5, Oswestry 10, Llangollen 6 ⅄ Sat

★★ Wynnstay Arms
Ruabon, Wrexham LL14 6BL
☎ 01978-822187 Fax 01978-820093
8 bedrs, 7 ensuite, ✝ ⁛ 120 P 80 ⊞ SB £32.50 DB £47.50 ✕ LD 21:00 Restaurant closed D Sun ℂℂ MC Visa Amex DC JCB

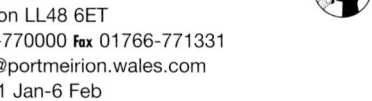

RUTHIN Denbighshire 7D1

Pop. 4,300. Wrexham 18, London 196, Betws-y-Coed 25, Corwen 12, Denbigh 7½, Llangollen 15, Mold 10 **MD** Tue, Thur, Fri **see** St Peter's Church, Castle **i** Craft Centre, Park Road 01824-703992

★★★ Ruthin Castle

Corwen Road, Ruthin LL15 2NU
☎ 01824-702664 **Fax** 01824-705978
E-mail reservations@ruthincastle.co.uk
58 bedrs, all ensuite, ④ ▣ ⊞ 150 **P** 250 ⊕ **SB** £65-£78 **DB** £85-£98 **L** £7 **D** £19.50 ✕ **LD** 21:30 **CC** MC Visa Amex DC ▣ ▨

★★ ✦ Castle

St Peters Square, Ruthin LL15 1AA
☎ 01824-702479 **Fax** 01824-703488
16 bedrs, all ensuite, ④ ⊼ ⊞ 40 **P** 16 ⊕ **CC** MC Visa Amex

Manor House Awaiting Inspection

Well Street, Ruthin LL15 1AH
☎ 01824-704830 **Fax** 01824-707333
9 bedrs, all ensuite, ✕ **LD** 21:30

ST ASAPH Denbighshire 7D1

Pop. 2,800. Mold 16, London 207, Betws-y-Coed 26, Colwyn Bay 11, Denbigh 5½, Rhyl 5½ **EC** Thu **MD** Thu

Talardy Park

The Roe, St Asaph LL17 0HY
☎ 01745-584957 **Fax** 01745-584385

Once a country manor house, the hotel retains an air of grandeur and is set in extensive grounds. High standard of decoration throughout.
18 bedrs, 8 ensuite, ⊼ ⊞ 260 **P** 200 ⊕ **CC** MC Visa ఉ

ST DAVID'S Pembrokeshire 6A4

Pop. 1,800. Haverfordwest 15, London 259, Fishguard 17 **see** Cathedral, Bishop's Palace ruins **i** City Hall 01437-720392

★★★ Warpool Court ⌖ ⌖

St David's SA62 6BN
☎ 01437-720300 **Fax** 01437-720676
E-mail warpool@enterprise.net
Closed Jan

Originally built as St David's Choir School in 1860, the hotel has panoramic views over St Bride's Bay. The building holds a celebrated collection of painted tiles many of which are hung in the bathrooms.
25 bedrs, all ensuite, ⊼ ⊞ 25 **P** 100 ⊕ **SB** £79-£90 **DB** £112-£150 **HB** £455-£623 **L** £15.50 **L** ❤ **D** £34.50 **D** ❤ ✕ **LD** 21:15 **CC** MC Visa Amex DC ▣ ▨ ▨ ▨

★★ ✦ Old Cross

Cross Square, St David's SA62 6SP
☎ 01437-720387 **Fax** 01437-720394
Closed Jan-Feb
16 bedrs, all ensuite, ⊼ **P** 18 ⊕ **SB** £28-£45 **DB** £80-£108 **HB** £250-£350 **L** ❤ **D** £17.25 ✕ **LD** 20:30 **CC** MC Visa JCB

★★ St Non's ⌖

Catherine Street, St David's SA62 6RJ
☎ 01437-720239 **Fax** 01437-721839
E-mail stnons@enterprise.net
Closed Dec
21 bedrs, all ensuite, ⊼ ⊞ 24 **P** 30 ⊕ **SB** £47-£56 **DB** £74-£82 **HB** £336-£357 **L** ❤ **D** £18.50 **D** ❤ ✕ **LD** 21:00 **CC** MC Visa

SAUNDERSFOOT Pembrokeshire 6B4

Pop. 2,500. Carmarthen 23, London 235, Cardigan 29, Fishguard 27, Haverfordwest 17, Pembroke 11, Tenby 3 **EC** Wed

★★★ St Brides

St Brides Hill, Saundersfoot SA69 9NH
☎ 01834-812304 **Fax** 01834-813303
E-mail ianbell@cipality.u-net.com
Closed 1-19 Jan
43 bedrs, all ensuite, ④ ⊼ ⊞ 150 **P** 70 ⊕ **CC** MC Visa Amex DC ▨ ఉ

WALES

★★ Merlewood
St Brides Hill, Saundersfoot SA69 9NP
☎ 01834-812421 **Fax** 01834-812421
E-mail merlewood@saundersfoot.freeserve.co.uk
Closed Nov-Mar
28 bedrs, all ensuite, ⚑ 100 **P** 20 ⊞ Resid **SB** £25-£30 **DB** £46-£56 **HB** £195-£245 **L** ⚑ **D** £12 ✕ **LD** 20:00
《 MC Visa ⚐ ▣ &

★★ Rhodewood House
St Brides Hill, Saundersfoot SA69 9NU
☎ 01834-812200 **Fax** 01834-811863
Closed Jan
44 bedrs, all ensuite, ⚐ ⚑ 150 **P** 70 ⊞ **SB** £26-£36 **DB** £42-£62 **HB** £188-£266 **D** £10.95 ✕ **LD** 20:30
《 MC Visa Amex DC ▦

SWANSEA   2C1

See also LANGLAND BAY, MUMBLES and PORT TALBOT
Pop. 173,150. Neath 7½, London 188, M4 4,
Bridgend 20, Brecon 39, Llandovery 35, Llanelli 11
EC Thu **MD** Sat **see** Civic Centre, Guildhall, Law
Courts, Brangwyn Hall (the British Empire Panels),
Glynn Vivian Art Gallery, University, St Mary's
Church ⓘ Singleton Street 01792-468321

★★★ Posthouse   **Posthouse**
39 Kingsway Circle, Swansea SA1 5LS
☎ 01792-651074 **Fax** 01792-456044
99 bedrs, all ensuite, ♀ ⚑ ⊞ ⚑ 230 **P** 44 ⊞ **SB** £55-£90 **DB** £80-£99 **L** £11.50 **L** ⚑ **D** £15.75 **D** ⚑ ✕
LD 22:30 《 MC Visa Amex DC JCB ▣ ▣ ▦

★★ ✣ Beaumont
72-73 Walter Road, Swansea SA1 4QA
☎ 01792-643956 **Fax** 01792-643044
Closed Christmas
17 bedrs, all ensuite, ⚑ **P** 14 ⊞ Rest Resid 《 MC
Visa Amex DC
See advert on this page

★★ Windsor Lodge ⚑
Mount Pleasant, Swansea SA1 6EG
☎ 01792-642158 **Fax** 01792-648996
Closed 25-26 Dec

A city centre Georgian hotel with a tranquil country house atmosphere, close to theatres, galleries and shops and convenient for beautiful Gower and Mumbles beaches.
18 bedrs, all ensuite, ⚑ ⚑ 30 **P** 20 ⊞ Rest Resid
《 MC Visa Amex DC JCB

TALSARNAU Gwynedd   6C2
Dolgellau 28, London 235, Betws-y-Coed 26,
Porthmadog 7

★★ Maes-y-Neuadd ⚑ ⚑ ⚑
Gold Ribbon Hotel

Talsarnau LL47 6YA
☎ 01766-780200 **Fax** 01766-780211
E-mail maes@neuadd.com
16 bedrs, 15 ensuite, 1 ⚑ ♦4⊞⚑⚑&♦ ⚐ ⚑ ⚑ 16
P 50 ⊞ Rest Resid **SB** £57-£143 **DB** £125-£175
HB £544.95-£702.45 **L** £13.75 **D** £26 ✕ **LD** 21:00
《 MC Visa Amex DC JCB &

TENBY Pembrokeshire   2B1
See also SAUNDERSFOOT
Pop. 4,950. Carmarthen 27, London 239,
Haverfordwest 20, Pembroke 10 **EC** Wed ⬛ The
Croft 01834-842402

★★★ Atlantic ⬛
Esplanade, Tenby SA70 7DU
☎ 01834-842881 **Fax** 01834-842881
Closed Christmas
42 bedrs, all ensuite, ⬛ ⬛ ⬛ ⬛ 10 **P** 28 ⬛ **SB** £60-
£63 **DB** £84-£126 **L** ⬛ **D** £18 ✕ **LD** 21:30 **CC** MC Visa
Amex ⬛ ⬛ &

★★★ Fourcroft
North Beach, Tenby SA70 8AP
☎ 01834-842886 **Fax** 01834-842888
E-mail tenby@walledtowns.com
46 bedrs, all ensuite, ⬛ ⬛ ⬛ 80 **P** 6 ⬛ Rest Club
Resid **CC** MC Visa Amex JCB ⬛ ⬛ ⬛

★★ ✤ Greenhills Country House
St Florence, Tenby SA70 8NB
☎ 01834-871291 **Fax** 01834-871948
Closed Nov-Apr

Family run hotel with large car park, heated
swimming pool and licensed bar. All bedrooms
ensuite with colour TVs and tea trays. Central to all
sporting facilities.
26 bedrs, all ensuite, ⬛ 50 **P** 25 ⬛ Rest Resid
SB £22-£25 **DB** £44-£50 **HB** £225 **L** £7 **D** £12 ✕
LD 20:30 ⬛ ⬛ ⬛ ⬛ &

Short Breaks

Many hotels provide special rates for
weekend and mid-week breaks –
sometimes these are quoted in
the hotel's entry, otherwise ring
direct for the latest offers.

★★ Royal Gate House
North Beach, Tenby SA70 7ET
☎ 01834-842255 **Fax** 01834-842441

Substantial five-storey hotel high above harbour
with commanding views.
59 bedrs, all ensuite, ⬛ ⬛ ⬛ ⬛ 250 **P** 35 ⬛ **SB** £42-
£44 **DB** £72-£76 **HB** £300-£320 **L** £10 **D** £17 ✕
LD 20:30 **CC** MC Visa Amex DC JCB ⬛ ⬛ ⬛ ⬛ ⬛

★★ ✤ Royal Lion
High Street, Tenby SA70 7EX
☎ 01834-842127 **Fax** 01834-842441
Closed Dec-Mar

The Royal Lion Hotel has been newly-refurbished
for 1999. Fully licensed, family run hotel, with lift,
car park and exclusive use of swimming pool and
leisure complex next door.
21 bedrs, all ensuite, ⬛ ⬛ ⬛ 70 **P** 35 ⬛ **SB** £40-£45
DB £70-£80 **HB** £292-£345 **L** £10 **L** ⬛ **D** £17 ✕
LD 20:00 Restaurant closed **D** Sun **CC** MC Visa DC

TINTERN Monmouthshire   3E1
Pop. 250. Monmouth 9½, London 138, Chepstow 6

★★ Parva Farmhouse
Tintern, Chepstow NP6 6SQ
☎ 01291-689411 **Fax** 01291-689557
9 bedrs, all ensuite, ⬛ ⬛ ⬛ 15 **P** 15 ⬛ Rest Resid
CC MC Visa Amex JCB

WALES

TREARDDUR BAY Anglesey 6B1

★★★ ✤ Beach
Lon St Ffraid, Trearddur Bay LL65 2YT
☎ 01407-860332 **Fax** 01407-861140
27 bedrs, all ensuite, ⊶ ⊞ 100 **P** 100 ⊕ ⅏ MC Visa
Amex DC ⊠ ▣ ▥

★★★ ✤ Trearddur Bay
Lon Isallt, Trearddur Bay LL65 2UN
☎ 01407-860301 **Fax** 01407-861181
43 bedrs, all ensuite, ④ ⊶ ⊞ 180 **P** 300 ⊕ ⅏ MC
Visa Amex DC JCB ▣

TYWYN Gwynedd 6C2
ℹ High Street 01654-710070

★★ Corbett Arms
Tywyn LL36 9DG
☎ 01654-710264 **Fax** 01654-710359
41 bedrs, all ensuite, ④ ⊶ ▣ ⊞ 60 **P** 40 ⊕ **SB** £20-
£38 **DB** £40-£76 **HB** £162-£258 **L** ⊮ **D** £8.95 ✕
LD 20:00 ⅏ MC Visa Amex DC ♿

★ Greenfield
High Street, Tywyn LL36 9AD
☎ 01654-710354 **Fax** 01654-710354
Closed Jan
8 bedrs, 6 ensuite, ⊕ Rest Resid **SB** £17-£19.50
DB £32-£37 **HB** £156-£166 **L** £6 **L** ⊮ **D** £7 ✕ **LD** 20:00
⅏ MC Visa JCB

USK Monmouthshire 7D4
Pop. 2,000. Chepstow 14, London 136, M4 9½,

★★★★ Cwrt Bleddyn
Llangybi, Usk NP5 1PG
☎ 01633-450521 **Fax** 01633-450220
33 bedrs, all ensuite, ♀ ⊞ 200 **P** 100 ⊕ **SB** £80-£99
DB £120-£150 **HB** £435-£465 **L** £13.95 **D** £13.95 **D** ⊮ ✕
LD 22:00 ⅏ MC Visa Amex DC JCB ▣ ⊠ ▣ ▥ ⊠ ▥

Glen-yr-Afon House
Pontypool Road, Usk NP5 1SY
☎ 01291-672302 **Fax** 01291-672597
E-mail gflodge@aol.com
26 bedrs, all ensuite, ⊶ ▣ ⊞ 120 **P** 100 ⊕ ⅏ MC
Visa Amex DC ♿
See advert on this page

WREXHAM Wrexham 7D1
Pop. 41,600. London 178, Chester 11, Llangollen
11, Mold 11 ℹ Lambpit Street 01978-292015

★★★ Llwyn Onn Hall ⌖ ⌖
Cefn Road, Wrexham LL13 0NY
☎ 01978-261225 **Fax** 01978-363233

Cream coloured Georgian building with attractive
verandah. In secluded gardens.
13 bedrs, all ensuite, ④ ♀ ⊞ 70 **P** 50 ⊕ **SB** £59
DB £79 **HB** £490 **L** £16.95 **D** £16 ✕ **LD** 21:30
Restaurant closed D Sun ⅏ MC Visa Amex DC

★★★ Wynnstay Arms
Yorke Street, Wrexham LL13 8LP
☎ 01978-291010 **Fax** 01978-362138
76 bedrs, all ensuite, ▣ ⊞ 50 **P** 50 ⊕ **SB** £41.95
DB £66.40 **L** £9 **D** £10 ✕ **LD** 21:30 ⅏ MC Visa Amex
DC ▥

SPENCER'S

The British Golf Directory

Courses where you can turn up and play

This new Spencer's guide provides full details of golf courses the length and breadth of Britain. All are courses where you can turn up and play, from municipal courses to some of the grandest in the land. You don't need to be members or pay membership fees. Just the rate for the round.

Whether you are an old hand or one of the new wave of golf enthusiasts you will find Spencer's Directory an invaluable companion - for your home, for your car or for your holidays.

With full-colour throughout it's easy-to-use, highly practical and perfect for browsing.

Each entry has a full quarter-page, with a description of the course, and information on yardage, par, standard scratch score, directions and green fees. There's also a full-colour route-planning and map section - a feature of all Spencer's titles.

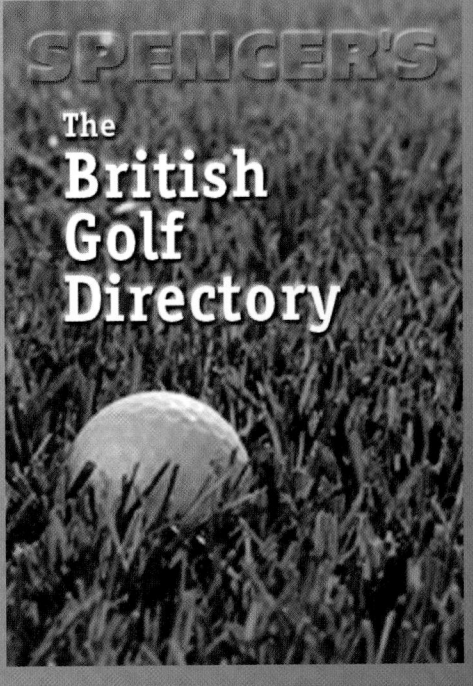

Format:	210x148mm
No. of pages:	112pp
ISBN:	1 900327 51 1
Price:	£4.99
Publication date:	April 2000

West One Publishing
Kestrel House, Duke's PLace
Marlow, Bucks SL7 2QH

West One
PUBLISHING

tel: 01628 487722

www.WestOneWeb.com

Northern Ireland & Republic of Ireland

AGHADOWEY Co. Londonderry — 17E1

★★ Brown Trout Golf and Country Inn
209 Agivey Road, Aghadowey, Near Coleraine
BT51 4AD
☎ 01265-868209 Fax 01265-868878
E-mail billohara@aol.com
17 bedrs, all ensuite, ✠ ☎ ⫶ 50 P 100 🛋 SB £50-
£60 DB £65-£85 HB £150-£175 L £10 D £17 ✕
LD 22:00 ℂℂ MC Visa Amex DC 🖾 🖾 🖾 ⅃

BALLYMENA Co. Antrim — 17E2
ℹ Council Offices, 80 Galgorm Street 01266-44111

★★★★ Galgorm Manor
136 Fenaghy Road, Ballymena BT42 1EA
☎ 01266-881001 Fax 01266-880080
E-mail galgorm.manor@galgorm.com
Closed 24-25 Dec
23 bedrs, all ensuite, ⊞ ♀ ♫ ⫶ 500 P 350 🛋 SB £99
DB £119 L £15 D £27 D ☕ ✕ LD 21:30 ℂℂ MC Visa
Amex DC 🖾 🖾 🖾 ⅃

BANGOR Co. Down — 17F2
ℹ 34 Quay Street 01247-270069

MARINE COURT HOTEL

Beautifully situated overlooking the Marina on
Bangor's Seafront, this modern hotel is an ideal
location for business or pleasure. 52 spacious
bedrooms are tastefully fitted and have en suite
facilities. Stevedore Restaurant offers both A la
Carte and Table D'hote Menus. Leisure complex
with 18m swimming pool. 12 superb golf courses
only 5 to 30 minutes drive.

THE MARINA, BANGOR, CO DOWN
Tel: 01247 451100   Fax: 01247 451200
marine.court@dial.pipex.com
www.nova.co.uk/nova/marine

★★★ Clandeboye Lodge
10 Estate Road, Clandeboye, Bangor BT19 1UR
☎ 01247-852500 Fax 01247-852772

Idyllic country setting, offering 43 luxury ensuite
rooms, equipped to international standards, with
scenic countryside views. Located 3 miles from
Bangor and Newtonards, 9 miles from city airport
and 11 miles from Belfast city centre and sea port.
43 bedrs, all ensuite, ⊞ ♫ ✠ ☎ ⫶ 250 P 250 🛋
SB £50.50-£89.50 DB £71-£105 L £5.50 D £18.50 D ☕
✕ LD 22:00 ℂℂ MC Visa Amex DC ⅃

★★★ Marine Court
The Marina, Bangor BT20 5ED
☎ 01247-451100 Fax 01247-451200
E-mail marine.court@dial.pipex.com
52 bedrs, all ensuite, ⊞ ♫ ☎ ⫶ 350 P 40 🛋 SB £80
DB £90 L ☕ D £7 D ☕ ✕ LD 21:45 ℂℂ MC Visa Amex
🖾 🖾 🖾 ⅃
See advert on this page

BELFAST — 17F2
See also NEWTOWNABBEY
Pop. 297,900. Antrim 14, Coleraine 54, Larne 19,
Londonderry 74, Newry 38 MD Mon, Tue, Fri see
University, Botanical Gardens, Museums,
Cathedrals (St Anne's Protestant, St Peter's RC).
Orneau Park, City Hall, Art Gallery. 'Titanic'
Memorial, 'Giant's Ring' - one of the largest pre-
historic earthworks in Ireland, Farrell's Fort, Belfast
ℹ St Anne's Court, 59 North Street 01232-246609

★★★ ✦ Dukes
65 University Street, Belfast BT7 1HL
☎ 01232-236666 Fax 01232-237177
21 bedrs, all ensuite, ⊞ ♀ ☎ ⫶ 120 🛋 SB £62-£95
DB £72-£110 L £9.50 L ☕ D £19 D ☕ ✕ LD 21:00
ℂℂ MC Visa Amex DC 🖾 🖾 ⅃

★★★ ✧ Jurys Belfast Inn
Fisherwick Place, Great Victoria Street, BT2 7AP
☎ 01232-533500 **Fax** 01232-533511
E-mail bookings@jurys.com
Closed 24-27 Dec
190 bedrs, all ensuite, ♀ ♬ 🖪 ⚏ 35 **P** 500 ⏻
SB £69-£73.50 **DB** £75-£80 **L** 🍽 **D** £15.50 ✕ **LD** 21:30
₡ MC Visa Amex DC 🐧

★★★ Lansdowne Court
657 Antrim Road, Belfast BT15 4EF
☎ 01232-773317

The hotel is 3 star rated with lounge bar and restaurant. It is very convenient to City Airport, ferry terminals, Central Station and Belfast Zoo.
25 bedrs, all ensuite, ₡ MC Visa Amex DC

★★★ ✧ Posthouse Belfast   **Posthouse**
Dunmurry, Belfast BT17 9ES
☎ 01232-612101 **Fax** 01232-626546
82 bedrs, all ensuite, ➤ 🖪 ⚏ 400 **P** 200 ⏻ ₡ MC Visa Amex DC 🐧

★★ ✧ Balmoral
Blacks Road, Dunmurry, Belfast BT10 0NF
☎ 01232-301234 **Fax** 01232-601455

Hotel with 44 luxury, ensuite bedrooms, situated at Dunmurry junction of the M1 motorway. Safe and secure parking for over 200 cars in enclosed compound. Eight bedrooms specially adapted for the needs of people with disabilities.
44 bedrs, all ensuite, ➤ ⚏ 300 **P** 300 ⏻ ₡ MC Visa Amex DC 🐧

McCausland **Town House Awaiting Inspection**
34-38 Victoria Street, Belfast BT1 3GH
☎ 01232-220200
Closed Dec 24-27
60 bedrs, all ensuite, ✕ **LD** 22:00

BUSHMILLS Co. Antrim	17E1

Portrush 7, Belfast 54, Ballycastle 10 **see** Giant's Causeway 🅘 44 Causeway Road 012657-31855

★★★ Bushmills Inn 🎋 🎋
9 Dunluce Road, Bushmills BT57 8QG
☎ 012657-32339 **Fax** 012657-32048
E-mail innkeepers@bushmills-inn.com
32 bedrs, all ensuite, ④ ♬ ➤ ⚏ 50 **P** 60 ⏻ **SB** £68-£98 **DB** £88-£118 **L** £9 **L** 🍽 **D** £22 **D** 🍽 ✕ **LD** 21:30
₡ MC Visa 🐧

CARRICKFERGUS Co. Antrim	17F2

Pop. 19,000. Belfast 10, Antrim 17, Ballymena 23, Larne 14 **EC** Wed **MD** Thu 🅘 Heritage Plaza, Antrim Street 01960-366455

★ Dobbins Inn
Carrickfergus BT38 7AF
☎ 01960-351905 **Fax** 01960-351905
Closed Christmas

Friendly, family owned, 16th century hotel with full bar, restaurant facilities and comfortable bedrooms, all ensuite. Fully refurbished in 1997. Regular evening entertainment and drinks promotions.
15 bedrs, all ensuite, ➤ ⏻ **SB** £44-£46 **DB** £64-£66
L 🍽 **D** £9 **D** 🍽 ✕ **LD** 21:15 ₡ MC Visa Amex DC

CRAWFORDSBURN Co. Down	17F2

Pop. 2,904. Holywood 7, Belfast 11, Bangor 2, Newtownards 6 **EC** Thu **see** Ulster Folk Museum

★★★ Old Inn 🏮
15 Main Street, Crawfordsburn BT19 1JH
📞 01247-853255 **Fax** 01247-852775
33 bedrs, all ensuite, ⊞ 120 **P** 76 ⊕ **CC** MC Visa
Amex DC ♿

DUNADRY Co. Antrim   **17F2**
Pop. 200. Belfast 12, M2 ½, Antrim 3, Ballymena
10, Larne 16 **EC** Wed

★★★★ ✤ Dunadry Inn
2 Islandreagh Drive, Dunadry BT41 2HA
📞 01849-432474 **Fax** 01849-433389
Closed 24-26 Dec
67 bedrs, all ensuite, ⊞ 350 **P** 350 ⊕ **CC** MC Visa
Amex DC 🎬 🏸 🏊 🖼

ENNISKILLEN Co. Fermanagh   **17D3**
Pop. 10,400. Dungannon 37, Belfast 74, Donegal
31, Omagh 22, Sligo 34 **EC** Wed **MD** Thu **see** Castle,
Lakes, Castle Coole (NT), Cathedral 🄸 Wellington
Road 01365-323110

★★★ Killyhevlin 🏮

Dublin Road, Enniskillen BT74 8JT
📞 01365-323481 **Fax** 01365-324726
E-mail info@killyhevlin.com

Charmingly irregular, white painted building in well-
kept grounds near A4, east of town. Fine views
over Lough Erne.
43 bedrs, all ensuite, 4 📶 ⊞ 500 **P** 450 ⊕ **SB** £55-
£65 **DB** £80-£100 **L** £13.50 **L** 📶 **D** £19.50 **D** 📶 ✕
LD 21:30 Restaurant closed L Sun **CC** MC Visa Amex
DC ♿

★ ✤ Railway

Enniskillen BT74 6AJ
📞 01365-322084 **Fax** 01365-327480
19 bedrs, 18 ensuite, ⊞ 80 ⊕ **CC** MC Visa

HILLSBOROUGH Co. Down   **17F3**
🄸 Council Offices, The Square 01846-682477

★★★ ✤ White Gables
14 Dromore Road, Hillsborough BT26 6HS
📞 01846-682755 **Fax** 01846-689532
Closed 25 Dec

Arguably the best commuter location in Northern
Ireland, the ideal base for business or relaxation.
Affordable elegance in gracious surroundings.
31 bedrs, all ensuite, ⊞ 120 **P** 100 No children
under 10 ⊕ **SB** £45-£95 **DB** £55-£115 **L** £17 **D** £24 ✕
LD 21:15 Restaurant closed L Sat-Sun, D Sun **CC** MC
Visa Amex DC ♿

HOLYWOOD Co. Down   **17F2**
Pop. 8,600. Belfast 5, Bangor 7, Newtownards 7
EC Wed **see** Holywood Priory remains, Norman motte

★★★★★ ✤ Culloden
142 Bangor Road, Craigavad, Holywood BT18 0EX
📞 01232-425223 **Fax** 01232-426777
E-mail gm.cull@hastingshotels.com
Closed 24-25 Dec

Originally built as an official palace for the Bishops
of Down, the Culloden is renowned as N.I's most
distinguished five star hotel. Surrounded by the
natural beauty of the Holywood Hills and
overlooking Belfast Lough.
79 bedrs, all ensuite, 4 🖳 ⊞ 500 **P** 500 ⊕ **SB** £140
DB £186 **L** £18.50 **L** 📶 **D** £24 **D** 📶 ✕ **LD** 21:45
Restaurant closed L Sat **CC** MC Visa Amex DC 🎬 🏸
🏊 ❄ 🏸 🎾 ♿

IRVINESTOWN Co. Fermanagh 17D2
Pop. 1,827. Dungannon 34, Belfast 71, Donegal 23, Omagh 15 **EC** Thu **MD** Wed

★★ ❖ Mahons
Enniskillen Road, Irvinestown BT74 9GS
☎ 013656-21656 **Fax** 01365-628344
E-mail mahonshotel@lakeland.net
18 bedrs, all ensuite, 🖪 ♀ ➤ ⅲ 280 **P** 50 ⊟ **SB** £30-£35 **DB** £55-£65 **HB** £295-£320 **L** £10.50 **L** ◆
D £14.50 ✕ **LD** 21:30 **CC** MC Visa Amex ▣ ▣ ⅊

LIMAVADY Co. Londonderry 17E1
🖪 Council Offices, 7 Connell Street 015047-22226

★★★★ ❖ Radisson Roe Park
Hotel & Golf Resort
Limavady BT49 9LB
☎ 015047-22222 **Fax** 015047-22313
E-mail reservation@radisson.nireland.com
64 bedrs, all ensuite, 🖪 ♪ ▣ ⅲ 440 **P** 400 ⊟ **SB** £90 **DB** £130 **L** £5.95 **L** ◆ **D** £19.50 **D** ◆ ✕ **LD** 22:00
Restaurant closed L Mon-Sat **CC** MC Visa Amex DC
▣ ▣ ▣ ▣ ▣ ⅊

NEWCASTLE Co. Down 17F3
Pop. 4,600. Belfast 26, Armagh 32, Downpatrick 11, Newry 20 **EC** Thu **MD** Tue, 🖪 Newcastle Centre, Central Promade 013967-22222

★★★★ Slieve Donard
Downs Road, Newcastle BT33 0AG
☎ 013967-23681 **Fax** 013697-24830
E-mail res.sdh@hastingshotels.com

Situated at the foot of the Mountains of Mourne, the Slieve Donard stands in six acres of private grounds, the ideal setting in which to relax in style and luxury.
130 bedrs, all ensuite, 🖪 ➤ ▣ ⅲ 1,000 **P** 500 ⊟
SB £70-£85 **DB** £100-£130 **L** £16 **D** £20 ✕ **LD** 21:30
CC MC Visa Amex DC ▣ ▣ ▣ ⅊

★★★ ❖ Burrendale Hotel
& Country Club
51 Castlewellan Road, BT33 0JY
☎ 028437-22599 **Fax** 028437-22328

Nestling between the majestic Mourne Mountains and the glimmering Irish Sea, the Burrendale Hotel and Country Club is fine example of the best in traditional hospitality.
68 bedrs, all ensuite, ➤ ▣ ⅲ 250 **P** 250 ⊟ **SB** £55-£65 **DB** £80-£100 **HB** £220-£325 **L** £6 **L** ◆ **D** £23 **D** ◆
✕ **LD** 21:30 Restaurant closed L Mon-Sat **CC** MC Visa Amex DC ▣ ▣ ▣ ⅊
See advert on this page

NORTHER IRELAND

NEWTOWNABBEY Co. Antrim 17F2

Pop. 71,900. Belfast 4, M2 2, Antrim 13,
Carrickfergus 5, Larne 15 **EC** Wed **MD** Mon

★★★ Chimney Corner

630 Antrim Road, Newtownabbey BT36 8RH
☎ 01232-844925 **Fax** 01232-844352
Closed 24-25 Dec

An attractive 'olde worlde' hotel, in a rural setting
convenient to local air and ferry ports. All 63
bedrooms offer relaxing accommodation. An on
site mini gym and sauna is provided, and guests
have free use of the adjacent 9 hole golf course.
63 bedrs, all ensuite, **☶** 250 **P** 300 ⊕ **SB** £38-£75
DB £55-£95 **L** £10.50 **L** ● **D** £16 **D** ● ✕ **LD** 21:45
CC MC Visa Amex DC ⌗ ▣ ▨ ら

PORTADOWN Co. Armagh 17E3

Pop. 24,000. Belfast 26, Armagh 10 **EC** Thu **MD** Fri,
Sat **ℹ** Cascades Leisure Complex, Thomas Street
01762-332802

Seagoe

Upper Church Lane, Portadown BT63 5JE
☎ 01762-333076 **Fax** 01762-350210

Extensively modernised hotel with lovely
landscaped garden. In rural surroundings.
40 bedrs, all ensuite, **↟** ▣ **P** 46 ⊕ **CC** MC Visa
Amex DC ら

National Code & Number Change

Telephone codes and numbers in Northern
Ireland change in April 2000. 5 and 6 digit
numbers will become 8 digit numbers.

eg Belfast
   01232-963456 becomes 028-9096 3456

Telephoning the Republic of Ireland

When telephoning the Republic of Ireland
from the United Kingdom dial 00 353 and
omit the initial 0 of the Irish code.

ADARE Co. Limerick · 18C2
Dublin 122, Cork 52, Limerick 10, Tralee 80
🅘 Heritage Centre 061-396255

★★★★★ Adare Manor Hotel & Golf Club
Adare
📞 061-396566 **Fax** 061-396124
E-mail reservations@adaremanor.com

An elaborate 19th century stone mansion, set in 20 acres of grounds beside the River Maigh. Fine furnishings and an international atmosphere.
99 bedrs, all ensuite, ⊡ ⊞ 100 **P** 70 ⊕ **SB** £135-£230 **DB** £150-£245 **L** £21.50 **D** £35 ✕ **LD** 21:00 ℂℂ MC Visa Amex DC ▣ ▣ ▣ ▣ ▣ ▣ ▣ &

★★★ Fitzgeralds Woodlands House
Knockanes, Adare
📞 061-396118 **Fax** 061-396073
57 bedrs, all ensuite, ⊕ ℂℂ MC Visa Amex DC

ATHLONE Co. Westmeath · 18D1
Dublin 77, Ballinasloe 14, Roscommon 18, Tullamore 21 🅘 Athlone Castle 0902-94630

★★★ ❖ Hodson Bay
Athlone
📞 0902-92444 **Fax** 0902-92688
E-mail info@hodsonbayhotel.com
100 bedrs, all ensuite, ⊡ ⊞ 700 **P** 200 ⊕ **SB** £90-£111 **DB** £128-£149 **L** £12 **D** £22 ✕ **LD** 21:30 ℂℂ MC Visa Amex DC ▣ ▣ ▣ ▣ &

BALLINGEARY Co. Cork · 18B3

★★ ❖ Gougane Barra
Gougane Barra, Ballingeary
📞 026-47069 **Fax** 026-47226
E-mail gouganebarrahotel@tinet.ie
Closed 15 Oct-21 Apr
27 bedrs, all ensuite, **P** 30 ⊕ **SB** £47.50-£55 **DB** £68-£80 **L** £13 **L** ☕ **D** £20 ✕ **LD** 20:15 ℂℂ Visa Amex DC

BALLYCONNELL Co. Cavan · 17D3

★★★★ Slieve Russell ⼈
Ballyconnell
📞 049-952 6444 **Fax** 049-952 6474
E-mail slieve-russell@sqgroup.com
151 bedrs, all ensuite, ⊡ ⊞ 800 **P** 500 ⊕ ℂℂ MC Visa Amex DC ▣ ▣ ▣ ▣ ▣ ▣ ▣ &

BALLYCOTTON Co. Cork · 19D4

★★★ Bayview ⼈ ⼈
Ballycotton
📞 021-646 746 **Fax** 021-464 075
E-mail bayhotel@iol.ie
Closed early Nov-Easter
35 bedrs, all ensuite, ⊡ ⊞ 35 **P** 40 ⊕ **SB** £75-£87.50 **DB** £110-£135 **L** £14.50 **L** ☕ **D** £28 **D** ☕ ✕ **LD** 21:00 Restaurant closed L Mon-Sat ℂℂ MC Visa Amex DC &

BALLYHEIGUE Co. Kerry · 18A2

★★★ White Sands
Ballyheigue
📞 066-713 3102 **Fax** 066-713 3357
Closed Oct-Mar
75 bedrs, all ensuite, ⊡ ⊞ 30 **P** 35 ⊕ **SB** £34-£41 **DB** £62-£74 **L** £10 **L** ☕ **D** £16 **D** ☕ ✕ **LD** 21:00 ℂℂ MC Visa Amex &

BALLYLICKEY Co. Cork · 18B4

⚘ ★★★ ❖ Sea View House
Ballylickey, Bantry
📞 027-50073 **Fax** 027-51555
Closed 15 Nov-15 Mar

Standing in its own grounds, a country house with magnificent views over Bantry Bay.
17 bedrs, all ensuite, ⊀ **P** 30 ⊕ **SB** £40-£52 **DB** £70-£110 **L** £13.50 **D** £26 ✕ **LD** 21:00 Restaurant closed L Mon-Sat ℂℂ MC Visa Amex DC &

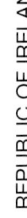

REPUBLIC OF IRELAND

Hylands
HOTEL

RAC
★★★

A traditional family owned Hotel with a reputation for good food and a warm welcoming atmosphere. Every care is taken in selecting locally grown produce offering the finest seafood selection. Situated in the picturesque village of Ballyvaughan in the heart of the unique Burren on the shores of Galway Bay. Recommended by Egon Ronay, Bridgestone, Best in Ireland and the Good Hotel Guide.
A member of the Village Inn Hotels. Tel: (01) 2958900.

BALLYVAUGHAN, CO. CLARE
Tel: (065) 77037/77015
Fax: (065) 77131

BALLYVAUGHAN Co. Clare 18B1
Dublin 148, Galway 32, Lisdoonvarna 8, Shannon 36

★★★ Gregans Castle ☐ ☐ ☐
Blue Ribbon Hotel
Ballyvaughan
☎ 065-707 7005 **Fax** 065-707 7111
E-mail res@gregans.ie
Closed Nov-Mar

The historic and mystic charm of this limestone haven is mirrored in the atmosphere of this home as you are made to feel welcome by blazing turf

fires and friendly smiles.
22 bedrs, all ensuite, ④ **P** 22 ⊞ **SB** £84-£100 **DB** £98-£130 **HB** £525-£630 **L** ● **D** £34 ✕ **LD** 20:30 ₵ MC Visa Amex ⅙

Hylands
Ballyvaughan
☎ 065-707 7037 **Fax** 065-707 7131
E-mail hylands@tynet.ie
Closed Dec-Jan
30 bedrs, all ensuite, **P** 52 ⊞ ₵ MC Visa Amex DC ⅙
See advert on this page

BALTIMORE Co. Cork 18B4

★★ Casey's of Baltimore ☐
Baltimore
☎ 028-20197 **Fax** 028-20509
E-mail caseys@tinet.ie
Closed 1-15 Nov, 22-27 Dec

Situated at the entrance to Baltimore, this superb family-run hotel is the ideal place to spend some time. Activities such as angling, golf, horse riding and sailing are available locally.
14 bedrs, all ensuite, ⌀ ⠀ 20 **P** 50 ⊞ **SB** £51.50-£90 **DB** £32.50-£90 **L** ● **D** £25 **D** ● ✕ **LD** 21:00 ₵ MC Visa Amex DC

BANTRY Co. Cork 18B4
Cork 48, Kenmare 25, Killarney 44 ▮ The Square 027-50229

★★★ Ballylickey Manor House ☐ ☐ ☐
Ballylickey, Bantry
☎ 027-50071 **Fax** 027-50124
Closed Nov-Mar
12 bedrs, all ensuite, ⼘ ⠀ 17 **P** 20 ⊞ ₵ MC Visa Amex ⅍ ▣

BLARNEY Co. Cork 18C3

Cork 6, Dublin 143, Macroom 20, Mallow 18 **see** Blarney Castle, Garrycloyne Castle and Church
ℹ 021-381624

Christy's
Blarney
📞 021-385011 **Fax** 021-385350
E-mail christys@blarney.ie
Closed 24-25 Dec

Within sight of the castle and housed under the rambling roofs of Blarney Woollen Mills, Christy's Hotel is an ideal base for a sightseeing tour of the South. Free use of adjoining sports complex.
49 bedrs, all ensuite, 🕿 ♨ 300 **P** 300 ⊕ **CC** MC Visa Amex DC JCB ⊡ 🔲 ⊡ ♿

BLESSINGTON Co. Wicklow 19F1

Naas 8, Dublin 19, Holywood 7 **see** Liffey Lake, Temple Boodinand, St Boodin's Well, 4m

★★ Downshire House 🍴
Blessington
📞 045-865199 **Fax** 045-865335
Closed 22 Dec-6 Jan
25 bedrs, all ensuite, ♨ 50 **P** 25 ⊕ **SB** £50 **DB** £88
L 💷 **D** 💷 ✕ **LD** 21:30 **CC** MC Visa 🔲

BRAY Co. Wicklow 19F1

Dublin 13, Wicklow 17

★★★ Esplanade
Strand Road, Bray
📞 01-286 2056 **Fax** 01-286-6469
E-mail espl@regencyhotels.com
Closed Dec-Jan
40 bedrs, all ensuite, 3 ♠ ♀ ♨ 120 **P** 8 ⊕ **SB** £55-£60 **DB** £90 **L** £12.95 **L** 💷 **D** £14.95 **D** 💷 ✕ **LD** 20:45 **CC** MC Visa ⊡ 🔲

★★★ Royal Hotel & Leisure Centre
Main Street, Bray
📞 01-286 2935 **Fax** 01-286 7373
E-mail royal@regencyhotels.com
91 bedrs, all ensuite, 🔳 ♀ ♨ 🕿 ♨ 250 **P** 70 ⊕
SB £68-£75 **DB** £98-£110 **HB** £149-£169 **L** £12.95 **L** 💷
D £17.95 **D** 💷 ✕ **LD** 22:30 Restaurant closed D Sun
CC MC Visa ⊡ ⊡ 🔲 ♿

BUNRATTY Co. Clare 18C2

Fitzpatrick Bunratty Shamrock
Bunratty
📞 061-361177 **Fax** 061-471252
E-mail bunratty@fitzpatricks.com
Closed 24-25 Dec
115 bedrs, all ensuite, ♨ ♨ 1,000 **P** 200 ⊕ **SB** £99
DB £143 **L** £11.50 **L** 💷 **D** £21 ✕ **LD** 22:00 **CC** MC Visa
Amex DC ⊡ ⊡ 🔲
See advert on this page

Prices are shown in Punts (£IR)

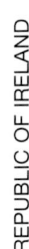

REPUBLIC OF IRELAND

CARAGH LAKE Co. Kerry 18A3
Blarney 16, Dublin 203, Tralee 20

★★ Caragh Lodge 🛏 🛏 🛏
Gold Ribbon Hotel
Caragh Lake
📞 066-976 9115 **Fax** 066-976 9316
E-mail caragh@iol.ie
Closed Oct-Easter
15 bedrs, all ensuite, **P** 20 No children under 10 ⊕
Rest **SB** £66 **DB** £99-£132 **L** ● **D** £30 ✕ **LD** 20:30
ℂℂ MC Visa Amex 🖪 🔲 🔲
See advert on this page

CASHEL Co. Galway 19D2
Galway 42, Dublin 175, Clifden 16, Maam Cross 14½

★★★ Cashel House 🛏 🛏 🛏
Gold Ribbon Hotel
Connemara, Cashel
📞 095-31001 **Fax** 095-31077
E-mail info@cashel-house-hotel.com
Closed 10 Jan-10 Feb
32 bedrs, all ensuite, 🔲 🖉 ⊁ **P** 40 No children under 5 ⊕ **SB** £61-£90 **DB** £122-£180 **HB** £540-£742.50 **L** £9 **L** ● **D** £32 ✕ **LD** 20:45 ℂℂ MC Visa Amex DC 🔲 🔲 ⴲ
See advert on this page

CASTLETOWN BERE Co. Cork 18A4

Ford Ri
Castletown Bere
📞 027-70379 **Fax** 027-70506
E-mail fordrihotel@tinet.ie

Situated in its own grounds, looking out into Bantry Bay and the fishing port of Castletown Bere. Extensive menu with seafood a speciality.
19 bedrs, all ensuite, ♀ ⊁ ⠿ 100 **P** 100 ⊞ **SB** £30-£40 **DB** £50-£60 **HB** £210-£245 **L** £10 **L** ⬤ **D** £15 **D** ⬤ ✕ **LD** 21:00 ((MC Visa ⅙

CAVAN Co. Cavan   17D3
Virginia 19, Dublin 71, Longford 35, Monaghan 29
⒤ Farnham Street 049-31942

★★★ ✧ Kilmore
Dublin Road, Cavan
⒣ 049-433 2288 **Fax** 049-433 2458
E-mail quinn-hotels@sqgroup.com
39 bedrs, all ensuite, ⠿ 500 **P** 300 ⊞ ((MC Visa Amex DC ⅙

CLIFDEN Co. Galway   16A4
Oughterard 32, Dublin 168, Ballyconeelly 5, Moyand 6 ⒤ Market Street 095-21163

★★★ ✧ Ardagh Hotel and Restaurant
Ballyconneely Road, Clifden
⒣ 095-21384 **Fax** 095-21314
E-mail ardaghhotel@tinet.ie
Closed Nov-Mar

Quiet family run hotel with spectacular views of Ardbear bay. Award winning restaurant. Individually decorated bedrooms. Attractive lounges. Golf, walking, horseriding and beaches nearby.
21 bedrs, all ensuite, **P** 40 ⊞ **SB** £60-£70 **DB** £85-£99 **HB** £400-£460 **D** £25.50 ✕ **LD** 21:30 ((MC Visa Amex DC ▣

Station House Awaiting Inspection
Clifden
⒣ 095-21699 **Fax** 095-21667
E-mail station@tinet.ie
78 bedrs, all ensuite, ♀ ⊁ ▣ ⠿ **P** 100 ⊞ **SB** £40-£100 **DB** £70-£120 **L** ⬤ **D** £21 **D** ⬤ ✕ **LD** 21:30 ((MC Visa Amex DC ▣ ▣ ▣ ⅙

CLONAKILTY Co. Cork   18B4

★★★★ Lodge & Spa
at Inchydoney Island ⒭ ⒭ ⒭
Inchydoney Island, Clonakilty
⒣ 023-33143 **Fax** 023-35229
E-mail reservations@inchydoneyisland.com

On the headland overlooking the magnificent blue flag Inchydoney beaches, this new hotel with its Thalasso spa and restaurants, pub and 67 deluxe ocean view rooms is an escape not to be missed.
67 bedrs, all ensuite, ♀ ⋏ ⊁ ▣ ⠿ 300 **P** 200 ⊞ **SB** £110-£132 **DB** £176-£220 **L** £10 **L** ⬤ **D** £28 **D** ⬤ ✕ **LD** 22:00 ((MC Visa Amex DC ▣ ▣ ▣ ▣ ⅙

Clonakilty Lodge Awaiting Inspection
Clonakilty
⒣ 023-34466 **Fax** 023-33644
E-mail clonldg@tinet.ie

Superior budget accommodation, both ensuite rooms and dormitories, within close proximity to golden beaches and town centre. Located 50 metres off the N71.
44 bedrs, all ensuite, ⠿ 60 **P** 60 **SB** £32 **DB** £54 **D** £15 ✕ **LD** 21:00 Restaurant closed L Mon-Sat ((MC Visa ⅙

CLONMEL Co. Tipperary	19D3

Dublin 107, Cahir 10½, Carrick-on-Suir 14 **see**
Museum and Art Gallery 🛈 Town Centre 052-22960

★★★ ✤ Hotel Minella

Coleville Road, Clonmel
📞 052-22388 **Fax** 052-24381

'Oh where on earth can you find a spot to compare with rare Clonmel'. The beautiful, former Quaker mansion offers 70 luxurious bedrooms, 2 banqueting suites/conference rooms, 2 restaurants, bars and the Club Minella health centre.
70 bedrs, all ensuite, 🄴 ⠿ 600 **P** 200 🅰 ℂ MC Visa Amex DC

COLLOONEY Co. Sligo	16C3

Dublin 125, Ballina 35, Boyle 18, Galway 18, Sligo 10 **see** Megalithic remains at Carroumore (8m)

♙ Markree Castle

Collooney
📞 071-67800 **Fax** 071-67840
Closed Christmas & Feb

A magnificent castle on a large estate. Spectacular plasterwork and interiors yet the atmosphere remains one of a family home. The Coopers have lived here for 350 years.
30 bedrs, all ensuite, 🐦 ⠿ 70 **P** 50 🅰 ℂ MC Visa Amex DC JCB ⊠ ⅄

CONG Co. Mayo	16B4

Dublin 143, Ballinrobe 7, Headford 10, Kilmaine 9, Maum 14 🛈 092-46542

★★★★★ Ashford Castle

Cong
📞 092-46003 **Fax** 092-46260
E-mail ashford@ashford.ie
83 bedrs, all ensuite, 🄴 ⊡ ⠿ 110 **P** 100 No children under 12 🅰 ℂ MC Visa Amex DC JCB ⊞ ⊠ ⅌ ⊠ ⊠ ⊠ ⅄
See advert on opposite page

CORK Co. Cork	18C3

Dublin 146, Macroom 23, Mallow 18, Youghal 32, 🛈 Grand Parade 021-273251

★★★★ Fitzpatrick Cork

Tivoli, Cork
📞 021-507533 **Fax** 021-507641
Closed 25 Dec
109 bedrs, all ensuite, ⊠ ⊡ ⠿ 1,200 **P** 300 🅰 ℂ MC Visa Amex DC ⊠ ⊠ ⊠ ⅌ ⊠ ⊠ ⊠ ⅄
See advert on this page

ASHFORD CASTLE

Ashford Castle incorporates the remains of a 13th century De Burgo Castle and was once the home of the Guinness family. Set on a 350 acre estate, on the shores of Lough Corrib, Ashford is a 5 star international hotel, offering 83 uniquely designed bedrooms and two restaurants, George 'V' and the Connaught Room.

Activities include a 9-hole golf course, indoor equestrian centre, lake fishing, archery, clay pigeon shooting and a health centre comprising fully equipped gymnasium, sauna, steamroom, jacuzzi (complimentary to residents in addition to golf).

Nightly entertainment is provided in our Dungeon Bar. Open year round.

**ASHFORD CASTLE HOTEL, CONG, CO. MAYO, IRELAND
Tel: 353.92.46003 Fax: 353.92.46260**
Email: ashford@ashford.ie Website: www.ashford.ie

★★★★ Hayfield Manor ⅋ ⅋ ⅋
Blue Ribbon Hotel
Perrott Avenue, College Road, Cork
☎ 021-315600 **Fax** 021-316839
E-mail reservations@hayfieldmanor.ie

Cork's newest luxury hotel, ideally located in city centre, 5km from airport. Set in three acres of mature garens, Hayfield Manor offers luxury accommodation, air conditioning throughout, excellent cuisine and leisure facilities, including an indoor pool.
87 bedrs, all ensuite, ⌀ ▣ ⫶ 120 **P** 90 ⊟ **SB** £120-£140 **DB** £180-£195 **L** £19.50 **D** £32.50 **D** ☞ ✕ **LD** 21:15 Restaurant closed L Sat **《** MC Visa Amex DC ▣ ▨ ▩ ⚅

★★★★ Jurys Cork ⅋ ⅋
Western Road, Cork
☎ 021-276622 **Fax** 021-274477
E-mail booking@jurys.com
Closed 24-27 Dec
185 bedrs, all ensuite, ▣ ⫶ 700 **P** 230 ⊟
SB £146.20 **DB** £177.65 **L** £13 **D** £16.95 ✕ **LD** 22:45
《 MC Visa Amex DC ▣ ⫶ ▨ ▩ ▨ ⚅

★★★ Jurys Cork Inn
Anderson's Quay, Cork
☎ 021-276444 **Fax** 021-276144
E-mail bookings@jurys.com
Closed 24-26 Dec
133 bedrs, all ensuite, ♀ ⌀ ▣ ⫶ 35 **P** 23 ⊟ **SB** £55-£66.50 **DB** £61-£73 **L** ☞ **D** £15.50 ✕ **LD** 21:30 **《** MC Visa Amex DC ⚅

★★ ✧ John Barleycorn Inn
Riverstown, Glanmire
☎ 021-821499 **Fax** 021-821221
Closed 25-26 Dec
17 bedrs, all ensuite, ☞ ⫶ 150 **P** 180 ⊟ **《** MC Visa Amex DC ▨ ⚅

Prices are shown in Punts (£IR)

Aaran Isle Inn **Awaiting Inspection**
14 Mardyke Parade, Cork
☎ 021-278158 **Fax** 021-278093
16 bedrs, all ensuite, ⠿ 40 **P** 20 ⊕ Resid ⓒ MC
Visa Amex DC

DELGANY Co. Wicklow 19F1

Glenview
Glen-o-the-Downs, Delgany
☎ 01-287 3399 **Fax** 01-287 7511
E-mail glenview@iol.ie
Closed 25 Dec

Only 30 minutes south of Dublin, with deluxe
bedrooms, woodland walks and terraced gardens
overlooking the famed Glen o' the Downs. State of
the art leisure club and pool. Award winning
restaurant.
75 bedrs, all ensuite, ↟ ⊡ ⠿ 200 **P** 200 ⊕ ⓒ MC
Visa Amex DC ⊡ ⊡ ⊡ ⊡ ♿

DINGLE Co. Kerry 18A3
Dublin 168, Tralee 30, Limerick 56 **see** Doon Fort,
Ballymacadole Cliffs (1½ m SE) ℹ Main Street 066-
51188

★★★ Dingle Skellig ⅋
Dingle
☎ 066-915 1144 **Fax** 066-915 1501
E-mail dsk@iol.ie
Closed Jan-Feb
115 bedrs, all ensuite, ⊡ ⠿ 250 **P** 100 ⊕ **SB** £55-
£85 **DB** £80-£140 **L** ♥ **D** £26.95 **D** ♥ ✗ **LD** 21:30
ⓒ MC Visa Amex DC ⊡ ⊡ ⊡ ⊡ ♿

DONEGAL Co. Donegal 16C2
Dublin 165, Ballybofey 17, Ballyshannon 15, Belfast
(via Derry) 112, Sligo 37 **see** Donegal Abbey ℹ The
Quay 073-21148

★★★ ✤ Harvey's Point Country
Lough Eske, Donegal
☎ 073-22208 **Fax** 073-22352
Closed Nov-Mar
20 bedrs, all ensuite, ↟ ⠿ 300 **P** 200 No children
under 10 ⊕ ⓒ MC Visa Amex DC ⊡ ⊡ ♿

DUBLIN Co. Dublin 19F1
See also HOWTH
Galway 124, Cork 146, Limerick 112, Waterford 96
see National Gallery, Trinity College & Library. St
Patrick's Cathedral, Christchurch Cathedral, City
Hall (18th cent), Theatre Royal, Phoenix Park,
Guiness Brewery, Chester Beatty Library, Leinster
House, Tailor's Hall, Georgian Square

★★★★★ Conrad International Dublin
Earlsfort Terrace, Dublin 2
☎ 01-676 5555 **Fax** 01-676 5424
E-mail reservations@conrad-international.ie
191 bedrs, all ensuite, ⊡ ⠿ 150 **P** 80 ⊕ **SB** £240
DB £282 **L** £19 **L** ♥ **D** £25 **D** ♥ ✗ **LD** 22:00 ⓒ MC
Visa Amex DC JCB ⊡ ♿

★★★★★ ✤ Doyle Berkeley Court
Lansdowne Road, Dublin 4
☎ 01-660 1711 **Fax** 01-661 7238
188 bedrs, all ensuite, ④ ⊡ ⠿ 450 **P** 230 ⊕ ⓒ MC
Visa Amex DC ⊡ ♿

★★★★★ Merrion ⅋ ⅋ ⅋
Upper Merrion Street, Dublin 2
☎ 01-603 0600 **Fax** 01-603 0700
E-mail info@merrionhotel.ie
145 bedrs, all ensuite, ♀ ⍺ ⊡ ⠿ 50 **P** 50 ⊕
SB £215-£255 **DB** £235-£280 **Room** £200-£265 **L** £13
D £23 ✗ **LD** 22:00 ⓒ MC Visa Amex DC JCB ⊡ ⊡ ⊡
♿

★★★★ Burlington Hotel
Upper Leeson Street, Dublin
☎ 01-660 5222 **Fax** 01-660 8496
530 bedrs, all ensuite, ⊡ ⠿ 1,500 **P** 420 ⊕ ⓒ MC
Visa Amex DC ⊡ ♿

★★★★ ✤ Fitzpatrick Castle
Killiney, Dun Laoghaire
☎ 01-284 0700 **Fax** 01-285 0207
E-mail dublin@fitzpatricks.com
Closed 24-25 Dec
113 bedrs, all ensuite, ④ ⍺ ⊡ ⠿ 750 **P** 200 ⊕
SB £105.50 **DB** £139 **L** £13.50 **L** ♥ **D** £22 ✗ **LD** 22:00
ⓒ MC Visa Amex DC ⊡ ⊡ ⊡

See advert on opposite page

★★★★ Gresham
O'Connell Street, Dublin
☎ 01-874 6881 **Fax** 01-878 7175
E-mail ryan@indigo.ie

Behind the elegant facade lie luxury bedrooms and spacious suites, an award winning restaurant and bars.
288 bedrs, all ensuite, ⌀ 🖸 ⊞ 300 **P** 200 ⏣
SB £120-£240 **DB** £150-£258 **L** £15 **L** ☕ **D** £22 **D** ☕ ✕
LD 21:45 **cc** MC Visa Amex DC ⌧ &

REPUBLIC OF IRELAND

★★★★ Jurys Dublin
Pembroke Road, Ballsbridge, Dublin 4
☎ 01-660 5000 **Fax** 01-660 5540
E-mail bookings@jurys.com
399 bedrs, all ensuite, ♀ ♪ 🖃 ⅲ 850 **P** 280 🗗
SB £186.50-£236 **DB** £243.50-£281.80 **L** 🍷 **D** £25 **D** 🍷
✕ **LD** 22:00 ⓒ MC Visa Amex DC 🖃 ⅈ 🖾 🖾 ⅇ

★★★ Ashling
Parkgate Street, Dublin
☎ 01-677 2324 **Fax** 01-679 3783
E-mail info@ashlinghotel.ie
Closed 24-26 Dec
150 bedrs, all ensuite, ♀ ♪ 🖾 ⅆ 🖃 ⅲ 240 **P** 150 🗗
SB £62-£78 **DB** £80-£112 **L** £11.50 **D** £18 **D** 🍷 ✕
LD 21:45 ⓒ MC Visa Amex DC ⅇ

★★★ Clarion Stephens Hall
Lower Leeson Street, The Earlsfort Centre, Dublin
☎ 01-638 1111 **Fax** 01-638 1122
E-mail stephens@premgroup.ie
Closed Christmas-New Year

Nestled in the heart of Dublin city, Stephens Hall
"All-Suite" hotel is a home away from home.
Comfortable and convenient, it offers all-suite
accommodation at affordable prices.
37 bedrs, all ensuite, ♪ 🖃 ⅲ 30 **P** 30 🗗 **SB** £130
DB £160 **L** £15 **L** 🍷 **D** £23 **D** 🍷 ✕ **LD** 21:30
Restaurant closed Sun ⓒ MC Visa Amex DC ⅇ
See advert on previous page

★★★ Deer Park Hotel & Golf Courses
Howth, Dublin
☎ 01-832 2624 **Fax** 01-839 2405
E-mail sales@deerpark.iol.ie
78 bedrs, all ensuite, ⅲ 100 **P** 200 🗗 **SB** £59-£68
DB £85-£98 **HB** £280-£299 **L** £13 **D** £24 ✕ **LD** 21:30
ⓒ MC Visa Amex DC JCB 🖃 🖾 🖻 ⅇ
See advert on previous page

Prices are shown in Punts (£IR)

★★★ Doyle Montrose
Stillorgan Road, Dublin 4
☎ 01-269 3311 **Fax** 01-269-1164
179 bedrs, all ensuite, 🖃 ⅲ 80 **P** 150 🗗 ⅇ

★★★ Doyle Tara
Merrion Road, Dublin
☎ 01-269 4666 **Fax** 01-269 1027
113 bedrs, all ensuite, ⅆ 🖃 ⅲ 180 **P** 300 🗗 ⓒ MC
Visa Amex DC ⅇ

★★★ ❖ Drury Court
28/30 Lower Stephen Street, Dublin 2
☎ 01-475 1988 **Fax** 01-478 5730
E-mail druryct@indigo.ie
32 bedrs, all ensuite, ♀ ♪ 🖃 ⅲ 50 🗗 **SB** £87
DB £139 **L** £6 **L** 🍷 **D** £15 **D** 🍷 ✕ **LD** 22 ⓒ MC Visa
Amex DC ⅇ
See advert on opposite page

🌢 ★★★ ❖ Finnstown Country House
Newcastle Road, Lucan
☎ 01-628 0644 **Fax** 01-628 1088
E-mail manager@finnstown-hotel.ie

A beautiful place in a great location. Only 8 miles
west of Dublin city centre. Awards for hospitality
and service.
51 bedrs, all ensuite, ♀ ♪ ⅆ ⅲ 100 **P** 70 🗗 **SB** £75-
£100 **DB** £110-£140 **HB** £490-£700 **L** £16.50 **L** 🍷
D £23 **D** 🍷 ✕ **LD** 21:30 Restaurant closed D Sun
ⓒ MC Visa Amex DC 🖃 🖾 🖻 🖾 🖾 ⅇ

★★★ Hibernian
Eastmoreland Place, Ballsbridge, Dublin 4
☎ 01-668 7666 **Fax** 01-660 2655
E-mail info@hibernianhotel.com
Closed Christmas
40 bedrs, all ensuite, ♪ 🖃 ⅲ 20 **P** 20 🗗 **SB** £95-
£110 **DB** £150-£185 **L** £17 **L** 🍷 **D** £35 **D** 🍷 ✕ **LD** 22:00
Restaurant closed L Sat-Sun ⓒ MC Visa Amex DC
JCB ⅇ

DRURY COURT HOTEL

Drury Court Hotel's prime position in the centre of Dublin qualifies it as an ideal base. The proximity of Drury Court to Grafton Street and St. Stephen's Green provide our guests with quick and easy access to the fashionable shopping area. It is just 5 minutes' walk from Dublin Castle and Leinster House. Also within walking distance from the hotel are many of the attractions and the traditional attractions of Dublin, Trinity College, St. Patrick's Cathedral and Christ Church Cathedral, to mention a few. For the evenings entertainment again Drury Court is in the middle of the action, with Theatres, Clubs and Venues in the immediate vicinity, whilst Dublin's Temple Bar district is just 2 minutes' walk, leaving our guests spoilt for choice.

28/30 LOWER STEPHEN STREET, DUBLIN 2
Tel: 01-475 1988

★★★ Jurys Christchurch Inn
Christchurch Place, Dublin 8
☎ 01-454 0000 **Fax** 01-454 0012
E-mail bookings@jurys.com
Closed 24-26 Dec
182 bedrs, all ensuite, ♀ ▣ **P** 30 ⊕ **SB** £68-£71.50
DB £74-£78 **L** ● **D** £15.50 ✕ **LD** 21:30 **CC** MC Visa Amex DC &

★★★ Jurys Custom House Inn
Custom House Quay, Dublin 1
☎ 01-607 5000 **Fax** 01-829 0400
E-mail bookings@jurys.com
Closed 24-27 Dec
239 bedrs, all ensuite, ♀ ▣ ⦙⦙⦙ 90 **P** 300 ⊕ **SB** £68-£71.50 **DB** £74-£78 **L** ● **D** £15.50 ✕ **LD** 21:30 **CC** MC Visa Amex DC ⊠ &

★★★ ✤ Longfields
10 Lower Fitzwilliams Street, Dublin 2
☎ 01-676 1367 **Fax** 01-676 1542
Closed 24-31 Dec

A centrally located, charming, intimate hotel with period furnishings and an excellent restaurant.
26 bedrs, all ensuite, ④ ▣ ⊕ **SB** £85-£90 **DB** £105-£129 **L** £11.95 **L** ● **D** £27.50 **D** ● ✕ **LD** 23:00
Restaurant closed L Sat, Sun **CC** MC Visa Amex DC &

★★★ Marine ⏣
Sutton Cross, Sutton, Dublin 13
☎ 01-839 0000 **Fax** 01-839 0442
Closed 25-26 Dec
50 bedrs, all ensuite, ♪ ⦙⦙⦙ 200 **P** 150 ⊕ **SB** £100-£110 **DB** £140-£180 **HB** £665-£805 **L** £14.95 **L** ● **D** £28.50 **D** ● ✕ **LD** 21:30 **CC** MC Visa Amex DC ⊡ ▦

★★★ Parnell West
38-39 Parnell Square West, Dublin 1
☎ 01-878 2694 **Fax** 01-872 5150
E-mail par.west@indigo.ie
Closed 24-27 Dec

Ideally located in the heart of Dublin City, this beautiful Georgian hotel is tastefully restored to create a warm, friendly ambiance. All bedrooms ensuite, restaurant, bar, conference facilities.
34 bedrs, all ensuite, ♀ ♪ ▣ ⦙⦙⦙ 80 ⊕ ⊕ Rest
SB £42-£45 **DB** £85-£90 **L** ● **D** ● ✕ **LD** 21:00
Restaurant closed Sun & L Mon **CC** MC Visa DC &

★★★ Posthouse
Posthouse

Dublin Airport
☎ 01-808 0500 Fax 01-844 6002
Closed 24-25 Dec
247 bedrs, all ensuite, ♪ ⠿ 150 **P** 250 ⊕ **SB** £119-£141 **DB** £130-£164 **L** £11.50 **L** ● **D** £20 **D** ● ✕
LD 22:30 Restaurant closed L Sat ℂℂ MC Visa Amex DC ও

★★★ ✤ Regency
Swords Road, Whitehall, Dublin 9
☎ 01-837 3557 Fax 01-837 9167
210 bedrs, all ensuite, ⊡ ⠿ 400 **P** 300 No children
⊕ ℂℂ MC Visa Amex ও

★★★ Royal Dublin
O'Connell Street, Dublin 1
☎ 01-873 3666 Fax 01-873 3120
E-mail enq@royaldublin.com
Closed 24-25 Dec
117 bedrs, all ensuite, ♪ ⊡ ⠿ 300 **P** 40 ⊕ **SB** £85-£102 **DB** £105-£130 **L** £12.50 **L** ● **D** £17.50 **D** ● ✕
LD 23:59 ℂℂ MC Visa Amex DC ও

★★★ Schoolhouse
2-8 Northumberland Road, Ballsbridge, Dublin 4
☎ 01-667 5014 Fax 01-667 5015
E-mail school@schoolhousehotel.iol.ie
31 bedrs, all ensuite, ♀ ♪ ⊡ ⠿ 20 **P** 16 ⊕ **SB** £109-£190 **DB** £140-£190 **L** £13 **L** ● **D** £25 **D** ● ✕ **LD** 22:30
Restaurant closed L Sat ℂℂ MC Visa Amex ও

★★★ Shelbourne Meridien
27 St Stephen's Green, Dublin 2

Le
MERIDIEN

☎ 01-676 6471 Fax 01-661 6006
E-mail rooms@shelbourne.ie
190 bedrs, all ensuite, ⌁ ⊡ ⠿ 400 **P** 40 ⊕
SB £190.32-£209.87 **DB** £232.30-£261 **L** £19.50
D £30.50 ✕ **LD** 22:30 ℂℂ MC Visa Amex DC ⊞ ⊞ ⊞

★★★ Wynns
35-39 Lower Abbey Street, Dublin 1
☎ 01-874 5131 Fax 01-874 1556
E-mail wynns@tinet.ie

Ideal city centre location close to fashionable shops, restaurants, theatres, galleries and places of interest. Conference, banqueting and wedding facilities, small or large groups. Saints and Scholars Bar and Peacock Restaurant.
70 bedrs, all ensuite, ⊡ ⠿ 200 **P** 20 ⊕ **SB** £50-£65 **DB** £75-£100 **L** £10.50 **D** £17 ✕ **LD** 21:30 ℂℂ Visa Amex DC JCB

★★ ✤ Holly Brook
Holly Brook Park, Clontarf, Dublin 3
☎ 01-833 5456 Fax 01-833 5458
22 bedrs, all ensuite, ⌁ ⠿ 340 **P** 70 ⊕ ℂℂ MC Visa Amex ও

North Star Awaiting Inspection
Amien Street, Dublin 1
☎ 01-836 3136
138 bedrs, all ensuite, ✕ **LD** 21:45

Park Lodge Awaiting Inspection
7 North Circular Road, Dublin 7
☎ 01-838 6428 Fax 01-838 0931

A hotel with the unique situation of being right next to the Phoenix Park and at the same time being just a few minutes from Dublin city centre. All rooms with TV and direct dial telephones. Lock up car park.
22 bedrs, all ensuite, **P** 20 No children under 12 ⊕
SB £34-£40 **DB** £46-£60 **L** ● **D** £16 **D** ● ✕ **LD** 20:00
Restaurant closed D Sun, Mon ℂℂ MC Visa

Red Cow Morans Awaiting Inspection
Red Cow Complex, Naas Road, Dublin 22
☎ 01-459 3650 Fax 01-459 1588
E-mail redcowhotel@morangroup.ie
123 bedrs, all ensuite, ♀ ♪ ⊡ ⠿ 720 **P** 450 ⊕
SB £95-£105 **DB** £150-£170 **L** £15.50 **L** ● **D** £23.50 ✕
LD 22:30 ℂℂ MC Visa Amex DC ও

Parliament
Lord Edward Street, Temple Bar, Dublin
☎ 01-670 8777

Located in the heart of the fashionable Temple Bar area of Dublin. Lively bar and classical restaurant 'The Senate'. All rooms ensuite with tea/coffee making facilities, trouser press, hairdryer, colour satellite TV, direct dial telephone.
63 bedrs, all ensuite, ▣ ♯♯ 30 ⊕

DUN LAOGHAIRE Co. Dublin	19F1

🄸 1 Clorinda Park North 01-280 8571

★★★ Royal Marine
Dun Laoghaire
☎ 01-280 1911 Fax 01-280 1089
E-mail ryan@indigo.ie

Victorian facade, 103-bedroom hotel set in an elegant four acres, overlooking Dublin's most prestigious site.
103 bedrs, all ensuite, ④ ▣ ♯♯ 500 **P** 450 ⊕
SB £110-£218 **DB** £140-£230 **L** £16 **L** ● **D** £19 **D** ● ✕
LD 21:45 ⸨ MC Visa Amex DC 🄰 ᴊ

★★ Kingston
Adelaide Street, Dun Laoghaire
☎ 01-280 1810 Fax 01-280 1237
E-mail info@kingstonhotel.ie
Closed 25 Dec

53 bedrs, all ensuite, ✐ ▣ ♯♯ 100 **P** 6 ⊕ **SB** £54-£59
DB £80-£85 **D** £12 **D** ● ✕ **LD** 21:45 ⸨ MC Visa Amex DC ⅋

DUNDALK Co. Louth	17E3

Drogheda 24, Dublin 59, Belfast 52, Monaghan 29
🄸 Jocelyn Street 042-35484

★★★ ❖ Ballymascanlon House
Dundalk
☎ 042-937 1124 Fax 042-937 1598
E-mail info@ballymascanlon.com
Closed 24-27 Dec
74 bedrs, all ensuite, ✐ ᕁ ▣ ♯♯ 300 **P** 300 ⊕
SB £62-£74 **DB** £85-£105 **L** £13.50 **L** ● **D** £23.50 **D** ●
✕ **LD** 21:30 ⸨ MC Visa Amex DC 🄰 🄰 🄰 🄰 🄰 ⅋

★★★ ❖ Fairways
Dublin Road, Dundalk
☎ 042-932 1500 Fax 042-932 1511
E-mail info@fairways.ie
48 bedrs, all ensuite, ♯♯ 400 **P** 400 ⊕ ⸨ MC Visa
Amex DC 🄰 🄰 🄰 🄰 🄰 🄰 ⅋

DUNFANAGHY Co. Donegal	16C1

★★★ ❖ Arnolds
Dunfanaghy
☎ 074-36208 Fax 074-36352
E-mail arnoldshotel@tinet.ie
Closed midweek Nov-Dec & Jan-Feb

Nestled in the village of Dunfanaghy, at the base of Horn Head in the dramatic reaches of North Donegal, this family run hotel is noted for its warm welcome, good food and friendly atmosphere. Horse riding from hotel stables, reduced golf and angling fees
30 bedrs, all ensuite, ♯♯ 30 **P** 50 ⊕ **SB** £52-£60
DB £66-£82 **HB** £385-£455 **L** £13 **D** £25 ✕ **LD** 21:00
⸨ MC Visa Amex DC 🄰 🄰 🄰 🄰

DUNGARVAN Co. Waterford   19D3
Dublin 126, Carrick-on-Suir 22½, Waterford 30,
Youghal 21 **see** St Augustine's Church ✚ The Square
058-41741

★★★ ✚ Lawlor's

Dungarvan
☎ 058-41056 **Fax** 058-41000
E-mail info@lawlors-hotel.ie
Closed Christmas Day
88 bedrs, all ensuite, ④ ♀ ⊁ 🖃 ⊞ 350 ⊞ **SB** £35.20-
£41.80 **DB** £60-£72.50 **L** £9.75 **L** ● **D** £16.95 **D** ● ✕
LD 21:30 **CC** MC Visa

ENNIS Co. Clare   18C2
Newmarket-on-Fergus 8½, Dublin 119, Gort 15,
Lahinch 16, Limerick 24 ✚ Clare Road 065-28366

★★★ ✚ West County
Conference & Leisure

Clare Road, Ennis
☎ 065-682 3000 **Fax** 065-682 3759
E-mail cro@lynchotels.com

Recently refurbished and 10 minutes walk from
ancient Ennis, the West County boasts a great
reputation for well furnished ensuite bedrooms and
good food. New £1m leisure club now open with 3
pools, gym, sauna. KidsPlus programme.
152 bedrs, 151 ensuite, 1 ⋒ ∅ ⊁ 🖃 ⊞ 1,650 **P** 370
⊞ **SB** £71.50 **DB** £98 **L** £9 **D** £15 **D** ● ✕ **LD** 21:30
CC MC Visa Amex DC ▣ ▣ ▣ ▣ ⅙

ENNISKERRY Co. Wicklow   19F1

★★ Enniscree Lodge ⛱ ⛱
Glencree Valley, Enniskerry
☎ 01-286 3542 **Fax** 01-286 6037
E-mail enniscre@iol.ie
Closed 25 Dec
10 bedrs, all ensuite, ⊞ 10 **P** 20 ⊞ **CC** MC Visa
Amex DC

FEAKLE Co. Clare   18C1

Smyth Village
Feakle
☎ 061-924000 **Fax** 061-924244
E-mail smythvil@iol.ie

Newly refurbished to a high standard, boasting a
truly unique country elegance with a seductive
blend of ambience, comfort and cuisine. A haven
set snugly on a hillside overlooking Ireland's most
historic village of Feakle.
36 bedrs, all ensuite, ⊁ ⊞ 120 **P** 100 ⊞ **DB** £70-£90
L £10.95 **D** £22 ✕ **LD** 21:30 **CC** MC Visa Amex ▣

GALWAY & SALTHILL Co. Galway   18C1
Dublin 124, Loughrea 23, Oughterard 16, Tuam 22
 Victoria Place, Eyre Square 091-563081

★★★★ Ardilaun House
Taylors Hill, Galway
📞 091-521433 **Fax** 091-521546
E-mail ardilaun@iol.ie
Closed 24-27 Dec

A former country mansion set in 5 acres of
beautiful grounds between Galway City and Salthill.
Well-equipped bedrooms and a restaurant with an
award winning chef. Situated two km from the
beach and Galway Golf Club. Leisure centre
opened in June 1999.
90 bedrs, all ensuite, ♀ 🖉 🛏 🖪 ⊞ 450 **P** 200 ♨
SB £66-£88 **DB** £88-£126.50 **HB** £385-£420 **L** £14
D £22.50 **D** 🍽 Restaurant closed L Sat **CC** MC Visa
Amex DC 🔀 ⅔ 🎋 🖼 🎏 &
See advert on opposite page

★★★★ Glenlo Abbey 🛏 🛏 🛏
Blue Ribbon Hotel
Bushypark (N59), Galway
📞 091-526666 **Fax** 091-527800
E-mail glenlo@iol.ie
45 bedrs, all ensuite, ④ ♀ 🖉 🖪 ⊞ 250 **P** 150 ♨
SB £146.05-£174.80 **DB** £205-£234.60 **L** £16 **L** 🍽
D £28 **D** 🍽 ✕ **LD** 21:45 **CC** MC Visa Amex DC 🖪 🎎 &
See advert on this page

REPUBLIC OF IRELAND

★★★★ Park House
Forster Street, Galway
📞 091-564924 **Fax** 091-569219
E-mail parkhousehotel@tinet.ie
Closed 24-26 Dec

Superb food and service in the Park Room restaurant, awarded 'Restaurant of the Year', and Irish Tourist Board 'Awards of Excellence'. A la carte and dinner menus.
57 bedrs, all ensuite, 🖸 ‖ 45 **P** 25 ⊞ **SB** £50-£75 **DB** £37.50-£52.50 **L** £12.95 **L** ☕ **D** £21.95 **D** ☕ ✕ **LD** 22:00 **CC** MC Visa Amex DC ♿
See advert on previous page

★★★ Flannery's
Galway City Centre, Dublin Road, Galway
📞 091-755111 **Fax** 091-753078
Closed 1 week at Christmas
140 bedrs, all ensuite, 🖸 ‖ **P** 200 ⊞ **CC** MC Visa Amex DC

★★★ Galway Ryan Hotel & Leisure Club
Dublin Road, Galway
📞 091-753181 **Fax** 091-753187
E-mail ryan@indigo.ie

A modern hotel, with well furnished rooms, situated in the suburbs of Galway City.
96 bedrs, all ensuite, 🖸 ‖ 40 **P** 100 ⊞ **SB** £65-£105 **DB** £110-£150 **L** ☕ **D** £17 **D** ☕ ✕ **LD** 21:45 **CC** MC Visa Amex DC 🔲 🔲 🔲 🔲 ♿

★★★ Jurys Galway Inn
Quay Street, Galway
📞 091-566444 **Fax** 091-568415
E-mail bookings@jurys.com
Closed 24-26 Dec
128 bedrs, all ensuite, ♀ 🖸 ‖ 30 **P** 200 ⊞ **SB** £53-£75.50 **DB** £59-£82 **D** £15.50 ✕ **LD** 21:00 **CC** MC Visa Amex DC ♿

GLANDORE Co. Cork	18B4

★★ ❖ Marine
Glandore
📞 028-33366
Closed 2 Nov-14 Mar
16 bedrs, all ensuite, **CC** MC Visa Amex

GLIN Co. Limerick	18B2

🍴 ★★★ ❖ Glin Castle
Glin
📞 068-34173 **Fax** 068-34364
E-mail knight@iol.ie
Closed Dec-Jan

The rooms have either a plush cosiness or an airy elegance, and the wonderful decor and bustling staff qualify Glin as the most comfortable of all the castles to visit.
15 bedrs, all ensuite, ④ ♪ ‖ **P** 20 No children under 10 ⊞ Resid **SB** £115-£185 **DB** £170-£270 **L** £15 **D** £27.50 ✕ **LD** 21:00 **CC** MC Visa Amex DC 🔲
See advert on opposite page

Facilities for the disabled
Hotels do their best to cater for disabled visitors. However, it is advisable to contact the hotel direct to ensure it can provide a particular requirement.

GLIN CASTLE

Glin Castle, home of the twenty-ninth Knight of Glin, has been in the FitzGerald family for seven hundred years. Neo-classical halls, elaborate plasterwork, flying staircase and mahogany library with hidden door all surveyed by ancestral portraits.

Pleasure park, walled kitched garden and spectacular spring garden with rare species. The Castle is guarded by three fort lodges, one of which is a craft shop and tea-rooms.

Glin Castle is a member of Ireland's Blue Book.

GLIN, CO LIMERICK, IRELAND
Tel: 068 34173/34112 Fax: 068 34364
Email: knight@iol.ie

Marlfield House

Set on 36 acres of magnificent gardens this family run Regency period country house is filled with numerous antiques, paintings and works of art. Marlfield's true Irish hospitality and cuisine have gained it world acclaim.

Marlfield House, Gorey, Co. Wexford, Rep. of Ireland.
Tel: 055 21124 Fax: 055 21572
E Mail: marlf@iol.ie
Website: www.marlfieldhouse.com
RAC ★★★

GOREY Co. Wexford   19F2
i Town Centre 055-21248

★★★ Marlfield House ♗ ♗ ♗
Gold Ribbon Hotel
Gorey
☎ 055-21124 **Fax** 055-21572
E-mail marlf@iol.ie
Closed Dec-Jan
20 bedrs, all ensuite, ④ ♪ ➤ ⠇ 20 **P** 40 ⊕ **SB** £85-£95 **DB** £156-£167 **HB** £699-£768 **L** £22 **L** ♥ **D** £37 ✕ **LD** 21:00 Restaurant closed L Mon-Sat **cc** MC Visa Amex DC ▨ ▨ &
See advert on this page

KENMARE Co. Kerry   18B3
Killarney 19, Dublin 200, Glengarriff 15 **see** Our Lady's Well, Cromwell's Castle (17th cent), Dunherron Castle (½m W) *i* Heritage Centre 064-41233

★★★★ Park Hotel Kenmare ♗ ♗ ♗
Gold Ribbon Hotel
Kenmare
☎ 064-41200 **Fax** 064-41402
E-mail phkenmare@iol.ie
Closed Nov-Apr

A 19th century chateau style hotel set among 11 acres of tended gardens overlooking the Kenmare Estuary.
49 bedrs, all ensuite, ④ ♀ ♪ ▣ ⠇ 60 **P** 70 ⊕ **SB** £120-£146 **DB** £220-£316 **L** £10 **L** ♥ **D** £40 ✕ **LD** 21:00 **cc** MC Visa Amex DC ▧ ▣ ▨ ▨ ▨ &

★★★★ Sheen Falls Lodge 🛏 🛏 🛏
Gold Ribbon Hotel
Kenmare
☎ 064-41600 **Fax** 064-41386
E-mail info@sheenfallslodge.ie
Closed 1 Dec-7 Feb excl Christmas
61 bedrs, all ensuite, ⚲ 🖭 ⠿ 120 **P** 75 🍴 **Room** £168-
£258 **L** 🍷 **D** £37.50 **D** 🍷 ✕ **LD** 21:30 Restaurant
closed L Mon-Sun ⸨ MC Visa Amex DC JCB ☒ ☒
▦ ▧ ▨ ▩ ▨ &

★★★ Dromquinna Manor
Blackwater Bridge, Kenmare
☎ 064-41657 **Fax** 064-41791
E-mail dromquinna@tinet.ie
46 bedrs, all ensuite, ④ ✦ ⠿ 120 **P** 60 🍴 **SB** £30-
£45 **DB** £60-£140 **HB** £400-£550 **L** £11.95 **L** 🍷 **D** £19
✕ **LD** 21:30 ⸨ MC Visa Amex DC ▣ ▨ ▨ ▨
See advert on this page

Prices are shown in Punts (£IR)

★★★ ✧ Riversdale House
Kenmare
☎ 064-41299 **Fax** 064-41075
E-mail riversdale@tinet.ie
Closed Nov-Mar

Located in seven acres of gardens on the shores of
Kenmare Bay, with breathtaking scenes of sea and
mountains. Ideal for all watersports, fishing, golf,
horse riding or just walking.
64 bedrs, all ensuite, ✦ 🖭 ⠿ 400 **P** 100 🍴 **SB** £48-
£64 **DB** £80-£90 **HB** £350-£370 **D** £16.95 ✕ **LD** 21:30
Restaurant closed L Mon-Sat ⸨ MC Visa Amex ▨
&
See advert on opposite page

Riversdale House
HOTEL

Located on the scenic shores of Kenmare Bay and backed by the Macgillycuddy Reeks and Caha Mountains, the Riversdale House Hotel is the perfect choice to tour the famous Ring of Kerry and the beautiful West Cork. Recently refurbished and extended to 64 superior rooms, the Hotel boasts 4 luxurious suites, each with private patio and panoramic views of the magnificent scenery beyond our seven acre garden. Our Waterfront Restaurant and bistro is renowned for its fine cuisine and extensive wine list, while local activities include an 18 hole golf course, deep sea angling, hill walking, cycling water-skiing and tennis.

**KENMARE, COUNTY KERRY, IRELAND
Tel: 064-41299 Fax: 064-41075**

KILKEE Co. Clare   18B2
Ennis 35, Dublin 154, Ennistimon 29 ⓘ 065-56112

Ocean Cove **Awaiting Inspection**
Kilkee
📞 065-682 3000 **Fax** 065-682 3759
E-mail cro@lynchotels.com

Overlooking Kilkee Bay, adjacent to 18 hole golf course, PADI dive centre and swimming arena. A haven for families and couples, ideal for cliffs of Mohar and North Kerry.
50 bedrs, all ensuite, 🖵 ⠿ 50 **P** 150 ⏛ **SB** £66.50-£76.50 **DB** £103-£123 **Room** £49.99 **L** 📶 **D** £10 **D** 📶 ✕ **LD** 21:30 ⓒ MC Visa 🏧 ▶ 🖭 ♿

KILKENNY Co. Kilkenny   19E2
Carlow 25, Dublin 75, Cashel 35, Port Laoise 28
ⓘ Shee Alms House, Rose Inn Street 056-51500

Hotel Kilkenny
College Road, Kilkenny
📞 056-62000 **Fax** 056-65984
E-mail kilkenny@griffingroup.ie

Hotel Kilkenny is surrounded by 5 aces of awardwinning gardens, just a few minutes walk from Kilkenny City. The hotel boasts a fabulous health & fitness club with 20m pool and excellent Broom's Bistro. Hotel Kilkenny, the resort hotel in the city.
80 bedrs, all ensuite, ⏛ ⠿ MC Visa Amex DC 🏧 🏧 🖭 ♿

KILLARNEY Co. Kerry   18B3
Castleisland 15, Dublin 187, Ballyvourney 20, Kenmare 24. ⓘ Town Hall 064-31633

★★★★★ ✦ Europe
Fuossa, Killarney
📞 064-31900 **Fax** 064-32118
Closed Nov-Feb

Killarney's most luxurious hotel, with Panorama restaurant, extensive conference facilities, a 450 seat auditorium, leisure centre, free horse riding, fishing, and indoor tennis. Superb views over the lakes of Killarney.
205 bedrs, all ensuite, 🛏 ⏛ ⠿ 500 **P** 150 ⏛ ⓒ MC Visa Amex DC 🏧 🏧 🖭 🖭 🖭 🏧 ♿
See advert on next page

★★★★ Aghadoe Heights 🛏 🛏 🛏
Blue Ribbon Hotel
Killarney
📞 064-31766 **Fax** 064-31345
E-mail aghadoehights@tinet.ie
60 bedrs, all ensuite, ♀ ♪ ⠿ 70 **P** 120 🔲 **SB** £99-
£130 **DB** £140-£205 **L** £21.50 **D** £35 ✕ **LD** 21:30
℃ MC Visa Amex DC 🔲 🔲 🔲 🔲 🔲 🔲 &
See advert on opposite page

★★★★ Dunloe Castle 🛏
Killarney
📞 064-44111 **Fax** 064-44583
Closed Oct-Apr
110 bedrs, all ensuite, ➤ 🔲 ⠿ 900 **P** 150 🔲 ℃ MC
Visa Amex DC 🔲 🔲 🔲 🔲 🔲 &

★★★★ ✤ Killarney Park
Killarney
📞 064-35555 **Fax** 064-35266
E-mail kph@iol.ie
Closed 24-26 Dec
76 bedrs, all ensuite, 🔲 🔲 ⠿ 180 **P** 80 ℃ MC
Visa Amex DC 🔲 🔲 &
See advert on this page

🐾 ★★★★ ✤ Muckross Park
Muckross Village, Killarney
📞 064-31938
E-mail muckcrossparkhotel@tinet.ie

Set in the heart of Killarney's National Park,
comprising of 27 recently refurbished superior
rooms, including suites. Our award winning
traditional Irish pub and restaurant is an experience
not to be missed.
27 bedrs, all ensuite, ⠿ 80 **P** 150 🔲 ℃ MC Visa
Amex DC

The Aghadoe Heights Hotel
Blue Ribbon Award Winner since 1995
Recently refurbished

This uniquely appointed Hotel with breathtaking panoramic views of the lakes and mountains of Killarney, provides a superb setting for South West Ireland's finest Hotel.

The elegance and style of the Hotel, recently refurbished, is evident from the moment you step through the door into the warm and welcoming reception area. All 75 rooms have direct dial telephone, satellite network, trouser press, hairdryer and minibar together with spacious bathrooms offering full facilities, toiletries, bathrobes and slippers.

No visit to Aghadoe is complete without sampling the culinary delights offered in "Fredrick's at the Heights" the hotels splendid Restaurant. Fredrick's has received recognition from all the major guides including Three Red Rosettes from the AA for seven consecutive years.

The excellent facilities include a luxurious indoor pool with special features such as a pool bar, cascading waterfall and jacuzzi, together with a sauna, plunge pool, solarium and fitness and treatment rooms.

Every day offers so much that once having experienced the unrivalled hospitality of the Aghadoe Heights you will be counting the days until you return.

Aghadoe Heights Hotel, Killarney, Co. Kerry, Ireland
Tel: 064 31766 Fax: 064 31345 E-mail: aghadoeheights@eircom.net

🛁 ★★★ ✥ Cahernane
Muckross Road, Killarney
📞 064-31895 **Fax** 064-34340
Closed 5 Nov-mid Mar
47 bedrs, all ensuite, ⛵ ⋕ 50 **P** 60 ⊕ ((MC Visa
Amex DC JCB 🔲 🔲

★★★ International Best Western
Kenmare Place, Killarney
📞 064-31816 **Fax** 064-31837
E-mail inter@iol.ie
75 bedrs, all ensuite, ⛵ 🔲 ⋕ 120 ⊕ ((MC Visa
Amex DC 🔲 ♿

★★★ ✥ Killarney Ryan
Killarney
📞 064-31555 **Fax** 064-32438
E-mail ryan@indigo.ie
Closed 5 Dec-1 Feb

A modern hotel set within extensive grounds,
featuring a leisure centre, sports hall, tennis courts,
crazy golf and play areas. An ideal location from
which to enjoy Ireland's most famed beauty spots.
164 bedrs, all ensuite, 🔲 **P** 200 ⊕ **SB** £75-£95
DB £100-£140 **L** ⬤ **D** £19 **D** ⬤ ✕ **LD** 21:45 ((MC Visa
Amex DC 🔲 🔲 🔲 ♿

★★★ White Gates

Muckross Road, Killarney
📞 064-31164 **Fax** 064-34850
Closed Christmas week
27 bedrs, all ensuite, ♀ ⋕ 30 **P** 60 ⊕ **SB** £46-£51
DB £68-£74 **L** £10 **L** ⬤ **D** £16 **D** ⬤ ✕ **LD** 21:00 ((MC
Visa Amex DC ♿

KINSALE Co. Cork   18C4
Cork 18, Dublin 164, Bandon 15 🔲 Pier Road 021-
772234

★★★ Trident

World's End, Kinsale
📞 021-772301 **Fax** 021-774173
E-mail tridentk@iol.ie

Closed 25-26 Dec
58 bedrs, all ensuite, 🔲 ⋕ 200 **P** 60 ⊕ **SB** £65-£85
DB £90-£130 **HB** £275-£395 **L** £12 **L** ⬤ **D** £21 **D** ⬤ ✕
LD 22:00 Restaurant closed L Mon-Sat ((MC Visa
Amex DC 🔲 🔲 ♿

LIMERICK Co. Limerick   18C2
Dublin 112, Adare 11½, Castleconnell 7½, Ennis 23
🔲 Arthur's Quay 061-317522

★★★★ ✥ Castletroy Park

Dublin Road, Limerick
📞 061-335566 **Fax** 061-331117
E-mail doneill@castletroy-park.ie
107 bedrs, all ensuite, ♀ ✿ 🔲 ⋕ 400 **P** 160 ⊕
SB £102 **DB** £122 **L** £15 **D** £26 ✕ **LD** 21:30 Restaurant
closed L Mon-Sat ((MC Visa Amex DC 🔲 🔲 🔲 ♿

★★★★ ✥ Jurys Limerick
Ennis Road, Limerick
📞 061-327777 **Fax** 061-326400
E-mail bookings@jurys.com
Closed 24-27 Dec
95 bedrs, all ensuite, ♀ ✿ ⋕ 200 **P** 180 ⊕
SB £124.85 **DB** £161.70 **L** £11.50 **D** £14.50 ✕
LD 22.15 ((MC Visa Amex DC 🔲 🔲 🔲 🔲 ♿

★★★★ ✥ Limerick Inn
Ennis Road, Limerick
📞 061-326666 **Fax** 061-326281
E-mail limerick-inn@limerick-inn.ie
Closed 25 Dec
153 bedrs, all ensuite, ✿ 🔲 ⋕ 800 **P** 600 ⊕
SB £104.50-£110.50 **DB** £125-£135 **L** £11.95 **L** ⬤
D £22.50 ✕ **LD** 21:45 ((MC Visa Amex DC 🔲 🔲 🔲
🔲 ♿

★★★★ Limerick Ryan
Ardhu House, Ennis Road, Limerick
📞 061-453922 **Fax** 061-326333
E-mail ryan@indigo.ie

A Georgian building dating back to 1780 which has
been recently restored to its former elegance,

giving the benefit of modern facilities. Combining the best of old and new.
181 bedrs, all ensuite, ✗ ⊡ ⦙⦙⦙ 130 **P** 200 ⊞ **SB** £75-£105 **DB** £100-£145 **L** £11 **L** ⬤ **D** £18 **D** ⬤ ✕ **LD** 21:45 ₵ MC Visa Amex DC ⊞ ⅃

★★★★ South Court ⛫ ⛫ ⛫
Raheen Roundabout, Limerick
📞 061-487487 **Fax** 061-487499
E-mail cro@lynchotels.com

Two restaurants : Boru's open for dinner daily; and Seasons a la carte, open for dinner daily (except Sun) & lunch on Saturday.
65 bedrs, all ensuite, ♀ ✗ ⊡ ⦙⦙⦙ 200 **P** 200 ⊞ **SB** £118.50 **DB** £147 **L** £10 **L** ⬤ **D** £10 **D** ⬤ ✕ **LD** 22:00 ₵ MC Visa Amex DC ⊞ ⊞ ⊠ ⅃

★★★ Jurys Limerick Inn
Lower Mallon Street, Limerick
📞 061-207000 **Fax** 061-400966
E-mail bookings@jurys.com
Closed 24-27 Dec
151 bedrs, all ensuite, ♀ ✗ ⊡ **P** 100 ⊞ **SB** £50-£59.50 **DB** £56-£66 **D** £15.50 ✕ **LD** 21:30 ₵ MC Visa Amex DC ⅃

★★ ❖ Woodfield House
Ennis Road, Limerick
📞 061-453022 **Fax** 061-326755
Closed 25 Dec
26 bedrs, all ensuite, ⊞ ♀ ✗ ⦙⦙⦙ 180 **P** 80 ⊞ **SB** £45-£50 **DB** £74-£80 **L** £9 **L** ⬤ **D** £17 **D** ⬤ ✕ **LD** 21:30 ₵ MC Visa Amex DC ⅃

MACROOM Co. Cork   18B3

★★ Castle
Macroom
📞 026-41074 **Fax** 026-41505
E-mail castlehotel@tinet.ie
Closed 24-27 Dec
42 bedrs, all ensuite, ⦙⦙⦙ 60 **P** 40 ⊞ **SB** £32-£45 **DB** £65-£90 **HB** £300-£350 **L** £10 **D** £20 ✕ **LD** 21:00 ₵ MC Visa Amex DC ⊞ ⊞ ⊠
See advert on this page

Mills Inn **Awaiting Inspection**
Ballyvourney N22, Macroom
📞 026-45237 **Fax** 026-45454
10 bedrs, all ensuite, ⛫ ⦙⦙⦙ 30 ⊞ **SB** £25-£35 **DB** £50-£60 **L** £10.50 **D** £16 ✕ **LD** 21:15 ₵ MC Visa DC ⅃

REPUBLIC OF IRELAND

MALAHIDE Co. Dublin 19F1

★★★★ Grand
Malahide
☎ 01-845 0000 **Fax** 01-845 0987
E-mail booking@thegrand.ie
Closed 25-26 Dec

The Grand Hotel is 10 minutes from Dublin Airport and 20 minutes from city centre. 150 ensuite bedrooms, many with breathtaking sea views and conference, business and leisure centre.
150 bedrs, all ensuite, ④ ♪ 🖭 ⅲ 700 **P** 300 ⊞
SB £120 **DB** £180 L £13 D £26 D ◗ ✕ **LD** 22:15 ⓒ MC Visa Amex DC 🖾 🖾 🖾 ⅙

MALLOW Co. Cork 18C3

Cashel 45, Dublin 125, Cork 20, Killarney 40, Limerick 45

★★★ Longueville House 🗎 🗎 🗎
Blue Ribbon Hotel
Mallow
☎ 022-47156 **Fax** 022-47459
E-mail info@longuevillehouse.ie
Closed 17 Dec - 11 Feb

Splendid Georgian mansion set in 500 acres overlooking the Blackwater Valley, three miles west of Mallow. Carefully preserved period ceilings and fireplaces and well chosen antique furniture.

21 bedrs, all ensuite, ♀ ♪ ⅲ 16 **P** 30 ⊞ **SB** £60-£160 **DB** £115-£170 L ◗ D £45 D ◗ ✕ **LD** 21:00 ⓒ MC Visa Amex DC 🖾 🖾

★★★ Springfort Hall
Mallow
☎ 022-21278 **Fax** 022-21557
Closed Christmas-New Year

50 bedrs, all ensuite, ⅲ 300 **P** 200 ⊞ **SB** £43-£50 **DB** £68-£80 **HB** £350-£360 L £15.50 L ◗ D £23.50 D ◗ ✕ **LD** 21:30 Restaurant closed L Sun ⓒ MC Visa Amex DC ⅙

MIDLETON Co. Cork 18C3

🖸 Jameson Centre 021-613702

★★★ ❖ Ballymaloe House
Shangarry, Midleton
☎ 021-652531 **Fax** 021-652021
E-mail bmaloe@iol.ie
Closed 24-26 Dec

A large family-run country house on a 400 acre farm, featuring home and local produce. Situated 20 miles south east of Cork, 3 miles from the coast.
32 bedrs, all ensuite, ♪ ⅲ 15 ⊞ **SB** £85-£90 **DB** £130-£140 **HB** £630-£662 L £19 L ◗ D £34.50 ✕ **LD** 21:30 ⓒ MC Visa Amex 🖾 🖾 ⅙

| MOUNTSHANNON Co. Clare | 18C1 |

★★ Mountshannon
Mountshannon
☎ 061-927162 **Fax** 061-927272
14 bedrs, all ensuite, ⓒ MC Visa Amex

| NAAS Co. Kildare | 19E1 |

★★★ ❖ Rathsallagh House
Dunlavin
☎ 045-403112 **Fax** 045-403343
E-mail info@rathsallagh.com
Closed Christmas

Grade A country house and championship golf course. Noted for warmth, friendliness and comfort. Award-winning restaurant. Close to major racecourses and Wicklow mountains.
17 bedrs, all ensuite, ▦ ♀ ⚮ ⚌ 25 **P** 80 No children under 12 ⊕ **SB** £95-£150 **DB** £110-£190 **HB** £679-£789 **L** £10 **L** ⚫ **D** £30 ✕ **LD** 20:30 ⓒ MC Visa Amex DC ▨ ▨ ▣ ▨ ▨ ⚬

★★ ❖ Harbour View
Limerick Road, Naas
☎ 045-879145 **Fax** 045-874002
Closed 25-27 Dec
10 bedrs, all ensuite, ⚌ 50 **P** 24 ⊕ **SB** £35-£40 **DB** £25-£30 **L** £7 **L** ⚫ **D** ⚫ ✕ **LD** 21:30 ⓒ MC Visa Amex DC ⚬

| NEW ROSS Co. Wexford | 19E3 |
🛈 The Quay 051-21857

★★★ Cedar Lodge ▤
Carrigbyrne, Newbawn, New Ross
☎ 051-428386 **Fax** 051-428222
Closed Jan

The Cedar Lodge is a charming country hotel and restaurant situated beneath the slopes of Carrigbyrne Forest and within easy driving of Wexford's fine beaches.
28 bedrs, all ensuite, ⚮ ⚌ 70 **P** 60 ⊕ ⓒ MC Visa

⚘ Brandon House Awaiting Inspection
New Ross
☎ 051-421703
Closed 25 Dec
36 bedrs, all ensuite, ⊕ ⓒ MC Visa Amex DC

| NEWMARKET-ON-FERGUS Co. Clare | 18C2 |
Dublin 127, Ennis 8½, Limerick 15, Shannon Airport 10

★★★★★ Dromoland Castle
Newmarket-on-Fergus
☎ 061-368144 **Fax** 061-363355
E-mail dromolan@dromoland.ie
73 bedrs, all ensuite, ⚌ 450 **P** 100 ⊕ ⓒ MC Visa Amex DC ▨ ▨ ▣ ▨ ▨ ▨ ⚬
See advert on next page

Clare Inn
Dromoland, Newmarket-on-Fergus
☎ 065-682 3000 **Fax** 061-368622
E-mail cro.lynchotels.com

A famous 16th century castle, furnished and decorated in luxurious style, only eight miles from Shannon Airport.
161 bedrs, all ensuite, ⚮ ⚌ 450 **P** 200 ⊕ ⓒ MC Visa Amex DC ▨ ▨ ▨ ▣ ▨ ▨ ▨ ⚬

REPUBLIC OF IRELAND

DROMOLAND CASTLE HOTEL

Located 13km from Shannon Airport, Dromoland Castle features among Conde Nast's Top 20 World Resorts. Stately halls, elegant public areas and beautifully furnished guest rooms are steeped in a timeless atmosphere that is unique to Dromoland. The International reputation for excellence is reflected in the award-winning cuisine of the Earl of Thomond Restaurant. Alternatively, the Fig Tree Restaurant in the newly opened Dromoland Golf & Country Club, provides a more casual atmosphere. A meticulously maintained 18-hole golf course, lake fishing, Gym, Sauna, Steam room, Health & Beauty Clinic, Tennis, Horse-riding, Clay Shooting, Boating and much more…

NEWMARKET-ON-FERGUS, CO. CLARE, IRELAND
TELEPHONE: 061-368144
FACSIMILE: 061-363355
E-mail: Dromolan@Dromoland.ie

NEWPORT Co. Mayo 16A3
Castlebar 11, Dublin 160, Bangor 32, Westport 7
📋 098-41895

★★★ Newport House
Newport
📞 098-41222 **Fax** 098-41613
Closed Oct-Mar
18 bedrs, all ensuite, P 25 ⏚ ((MC Visa Amex 🖉 🔳

ORANMORE Co. Galway 18C1
Dublin 120, Galway 5, Loughrea 17½, Tuam 21

★★★★ Galway Bay Golf & Country Club ⍟ ⍟ ⍟
Oranmore
📞 091-790500 **Fax** 091-790510
E-mail gbaygolf@iol.ie
92 bedrs, all ensuite, ⌀ ⊡ ### 200 P 300 SB £60-£75
DB £45-£60 HB £570-£675 L £12.95 L 🍷 D £25 D 🍷 ✕
LD 21:30 Restaurant closed Mon-Sat ((MC Visa
Amex DC 🄿 ⅋

OUGHTERARD Co. Galway 16B4
Dublin 145, Galway 21, Maam Cross 11 **see**
Kilcumnuin Church, St Cumnuin's Well, Aughnanure
Castle (2m S)

★★★ Ross Lake House ⍟
Rosscahill, Oughterard
📞 091-550109 **Fax** 091-550184
E-mail ireland@greenbook.ie
Closed 1 Nov-15 Mar
13 bedrs, all ensuite, ▨ ♀ 🛏 ### 30 P 50 ⏚ SB £62-
£73 DB £90-£113 L 🍷 D £24 ✕ LD 21:00 ((MC Visa
Amex DC 🄰 ⅋

Facilities for the disabled
Hotels do their best to cater for disabled visitors. However, it is advisable to contact the hotel direct to ensure it can provide a particular requirement.

PORTMAGEE Co. Kerry   18A3

Moorings **Awaiting Inspection**
Portmagee Village
📞 066-947 7108
Closed 1 Nov-1 Mar

Family owned 3 star guesthouse and restaurant
overlooking the picturesque fishing village in
Portmagee. Excellent cuisine, specialising in locally
caught seafood. Central to local amenities, including
angling, diving, watersports and 18 hole golf course.
6 bedrs, all ensuite, ℂℂ MC Visa

RATHMULLAN Co. Donegal   17D1

★★★ ✣ Rathmullan House
Letterkenny, Rathmullan
📞 074-58188 **Fax** 074-58200
E-mail rathhse@iol.ie
Closed Jan-Mar

Bow fronted country house, overlooking Lough
Swilly, set in award winning grounds which stretch
down to a sandy beach.
24 bedrs, all ensuite, 20 P 40 SB £52.50-
£57.75 DB £104.50-£115.50 HB £558.25-£596.75 L
D £30 ✕ LD 20:45 ℂℂ MC Visa Amex DC ⬚⬚⬚ ⬚

ROSCOMMON Co. Roscommon   16C4
Longford 20, Dublin 85, Athlone 18, Boyle 25,
Galway 45 Harrison Hall 0903-26342

★★★ Abbey
Roscommon
📞 0903-26240 **Fax** 0903-26021
Closed 25-26 Dec

The Abbey Hotel, set in its own private grounds, is
ideally situated for the touring holidaymaker.
Excellent restaurant and spacious comfortable
accommodation that compare favourably with the
best international standards.
25 bedrs, all ensuite, 300 P 100 SB £45-£55
DB £80-£100 L £15 L D £22.50 D ✕ LD 21:30
ℂℂ MC Visa Amex DC ⬚

ROSSLARE Co. Wexford   19F2
Wexford 10, Dublin 97, Enniscorthy 23, New Ross
34, Rosslare Harbour 8 Kilrane 053-33232

★★★★ Kelly's Resort
Rosslare
📞 053-32114 **Fax** 053-32222
E-mail kellyhot@iol.ie
Closed Dec-Feb

Since 1895 successive generations of the Kelly
family have created a truly fine resort hotel,
concentrating on year round holidays set right on a
glorious beach. The hotel has recently been
refurbished. Excellent food and wine.
99 bedrs, all ensuite, P 100 Resid ℂℂ MC Visa
Amex ⬚⬚⬚⬚⬚⬚ ⬚

ROUNDSTONE Co. Galway   16A4

★★ ❖ Eldons
Roundstone
📞 095-35933 **Fax** 095-35871
19 bedrs, all ensuite, 6 ⋒ 🖪 ⅲ 30 ⊟ ((MC Visa Amex DC ₷

★★ ❖ Roundstone House
Roundstone, Connemara
📞 095-35864 **Fax** 095-35944
13 bedrs, all ensuite, ⊟ ((MC Visa Amex
See advert on this page

Don't forget to mention the guide

When booking direct, please remember to tell the hotel that you chose it from RAC Inspected Hotels 2000

STRAFFAN Co. Kildare   19F1
Dublin 17, Naas 7

★★★★★ Kildare Hotel & Country Club 🎀 🎀 🎀
Gold Ribbon Hotel
Straffan
📞 01-601 7200 **Fax** 01 601 7299
E-mail hotel@kclub.ie

Elegant 19th century country house in a spectacular situation overlooking the River Liffey and surrounded by its own golf course. A new wing has been lovingly and sympathetically created. Superb leisure facilities.
45 bedrs, all ensuite, 🜨 🗡 🖪 ⅲ 120 **P** 500 ⊟
SB £190-£280 **DB** £280-£350 **L** £25 **D** £45 ✕ **LD** 21:45
((MC Visa Amex DC 🯄 🯄 🯄 🯄 🯄 🯄 🯄 🯄 🯄 🯄 ₷

Barberstown Castle
Straffan
📞 01-628 8157 **Fax** 01-627 7027
Closed 24-27 Dec

A country house and castle dating from the 13th century. Renowned for its restaurant awards, courtesy and care. Ideally situated only 30 mins from Dublin city centre and airport. Member of Ireland's prestigious Blue Book.
26 bedrs, all ensuite, ⅲ 100 **P** 200 No children under 12 ⊟ ((MC Visa Amex DC ₷

THOMASTOWN Co. Kilkenny   19E2
Dublin 88, Kilkenny 11, New Ross 15, Waterford 34
see Jerpoint Abbey, Water Garden

★★★★ Mount Juliet 🛏 🛏 🛏
Gold Ribbon Hotel
Thomastown
📞 056-73000 **Fax** 056-73019
E-mail info@mountjuliet.ie

A beautiful 18th century house situated in a 1,500 acre sporting estate which includes a Jack Nicklaus golf course.
59 bedrs, all ensuite, 4️⃣ 🏊 ♨ 80 **P** 100 🔌
SB £132.50-£172.50 **DB** £185-£260 **L** £16 **D** £33 ✕
LD 21:30 **CC** MC Visa Amex DC 🔲 🔲 🔲 🔲 🔲 🔲 🔲 🔲
👍

TRALEE Co. Kerry   18B3

🌙 ★★★ ✣ Ballyseede Castle
Ballyseede, Tralee
📞 066-712 5799 **Fax** 066-712 5287
12 bedrs, all ensuite, 4️⃣ ♨ 200 **P** 42 No children under 17 🔌 **SB** £65-£135 **DB** £125-£185 **L** 🍷 **D** £20
D 🍷 ✕ **LD** 21:30 **CC** MC Visa DC

Meadowlands Awaiting Inspection
Oakpark, Tralee
📞 066-718 0444 **Fax** 066-718 0964
E-mail medlands@iol.ie
Closed 24-26 Dec
27 bedrs, all ensuite, 4️⃣ ♀ 🏊 📺 ♨ 35 **P** 120 🔌
SB £60-£75 **DB** £90-£120 **HB** £434-£490 **L** £12.95 **L** 🍷
D 🍷 ✕ **LD** 21:00 Restaurant closed L Mon-Sat 👍

WATERFORD Co. Waterford   19E3
Dublin 96, Carrick on Suir 16, Kilkenny 51, New Ross 15 **see** Waterford Glass, Reginald's Tower ℹ 41
The Quay 051-875788

★★★ Dooley's
The Quay, Waterford
📞 051-73531 **Fax** 051-70262
Closed Christmas

Family run hotel situated on the quay at Waterford. High levels of comfort and personal service. Stay here in the heart of Waterford and you won't be disapppointed.
113 bedrs, all ensuite, 4️⃣ 🏊 📺 ♨ 300 🔌 **SB** £50-£60
DB £70-£100 **L** £11.95 **L** 🍷 **D** £17 **D** 🍷 ✕ **LD** 21:30
Restaurant closed L Mon-Sat **CC** MC Visa Amex DC JCB 👍

★★★ ❖ Jurys Waterford
Ferrybank, Waterford
📞 051-832111 **Fax** 051-832863
E-mail bookings@jurys.com
Closed 24-27 Dec
98 bedrs, all ensuite, 🔲 ♨ 700 **P** 200 ⊞ **SB** £103.35-
£106.15 **DB** £146.20-£149.60 **L** £13 **D** £16.50 ✕
LD 21:00 **CC** MC Visa Amex DC 🔲🔲🔲🔲 &

Granville
Waterford
📞 051-305555 **Fax** 051-305566
100 bedrs, all ensuite, 🔲 ♨ 200 **P** 300 ⊞ **CC** MC
Visa Amex DC &
See advert on previous page

Waterford Castle
The Island, Waterford
📞 051-78203 **Fax** 051-79316
19 bedrs, all ensuite, 🔲 ♨ 30 **P** 40 ⊞ **CC** MC Visa
Amex DC 🔲🔲🔲🔲
See advert on this page

WESTPORT Co. Mayo 16A4
Castlebar 11, Dublin 161, Ballina 36, Galway 51
The Mall 098-25711

★★★ ✛ Castlecourt
Castlebar Street, Westport
098-25444 **Fax** 098-28622
E-mail castlecourt@anu.ie
140 bedrs, all ensuite, 4 ⌀ ⊡ ⊞ 700 **P** 190 ⊕
SB £40-£90 **DB** £32.50-£60 **L** £10.95 **L** ● **D** £17 ✕
LD 21:00 ⊂⊂ MC Visa Amex DC ⊡ ⊠ ⊡ ⊠ ⅋
See advert on opposite page

★★★ Hotel Westport ⊠
The Demesne, Newport Road, Westport
098-25122 **Fax** 098-26739
E-mail sales@hotelwestport.ie

A uniquely comfortable, friendly hotel set in
beautiful parkland and river gardens. Extensive,
luxury swimming pool and leisure centre.
Entertainment nightly, in season. Ideal location to
enjoy lots of activities and sightseeing trips in
County Mayo.
129 bedrs, all ensuite, 4 ⊡ ⊞ 500 **P** 220 ⊕ **SB** £51-
£75 **DB** £110-£120 **L** £11 **D** £21.95 ✕ **LD** 21:30
Restaurant closed L Mon-Sat ⊂⊂ MC Visa Amex DC
⊡ ⊠ ⊡ ⅋

Clew Bay Awaiting Inspection
James Street, Westport
098-28088
E-mail clewbay@anu.ie
Closed 22-28 Dec
28 bedrs, all ensuite, ⊞ 55 ⊕ **SB** £35-£50.50 **DB** £50-
£81 **L** £9 **L** ● **D** £19 **D** ● ✕ **LD** 21:00 ⊂⊂ MC Visa

WEXFORD Co. Wexford 19F2
Dublin 87, Enniscorthy 13, New Ross 24, Waterford
38 **see** Irish National Heritage Park at Ferrycarrig
Crescent Quay 053-2311

★★★ ✛ Ferrycarrig
Ferrycarrig Bridge, P.O. Box 11, Wexford
053-20999 **Fax** 053-20982
E-mail ferrycarrig@griffingroup.ie

The hotel boasts one of the most inspiring
locations of any hotel in Ireland with sweeping
views across the River Slaney estuary. Facilities
include a fabulous health & fitness club with award
winning 20m pool, and 2 excellent waterfront
restaurants.
90 bedrs, all ensuite, ⌀ ⊡ ⊞ 400 **P** 236 ⊕ **SB** £50-
£70 **DB** £95-£140 **L** £11 **D** ● ✕ **LD** 21:30 ⊂⊂ MC Visa
Amex DC ⊡ ⊠ ⊡ ⅋

★★★ ✛ Talbot Hotel
Conf. & Leisure Centre
Trinity Street, Wexford
053-22566 **Fax** 053-23377
E-mail talbotwx@tinet.ie

A most friendly and welcoming hotel located in the
'heart of Wexford town' and overlooking Wexford
harbour.
99 bedrs, all ensuite, ⌀ ⊡ ⊞ 400 **P** 250 ⊕ **SB** £57-
£62 **DB** £89-£99 **L** £9.50 **D** £21 **D** ● ✕ **LD** 21:30
⊂⊂ MC Visa Amex DC ⊡ ⊠ ⊡ ⅋

★★★ ✤ White's Hotel & Conference Centre
George Street, Wexford
☎ 053-22311 **Fax** 053-45000
E-mail info@whiteshotel.iol.ie
82 bedrs, all ensuite, ④ 🖵 ⌗ 400 **P** 80 ⊕ **SB** £52.50-£62.50 **DB** £75-£95 **HB** £285-£335 **L** 🍽 **D** £18 **D** 🍽 ✕
LD 21:15 **CC** MC Visa Amex DC 🎦 🖼

WICKLOW Co. Wicklow   **19F1**
ℹ️ Fitzwilliam Street 0404-69117

★★★ Tinakilly Country House 🛎 🛎 🛎
Blue Ribbon Hotel
Rathnew, Wicklow
☎ 0404-69274 **Fax** 0404-67806
E-mail wpower@tinakilly.ie
53 bedrs, all ensuite, ④ 🖵 ⌗ 80 **P** 60 ⊕ **SB** £110-£117 **DB** £130-£144 **HB** £548-£590 **L** £18.50 **L** 🍽
D £35 ✕ **LD** 21:00 Restaurant closed L Mon-Sat
CC MC Visa Amex DC JCB 🎦 🖼 ♿

YOUGHAL Co. Cork   **19D3**
ℹ️ Heritage Centre 024-92390

★★ ✤ Ahernes Seafood Restaurant and Townhouse

Youghal
☎ 024-92424 **Fax** 024-93633
Closed Christmas
12 bedrs, all ensuite, ♀ ✍ ⌗ 20 **P** 12 ⊕ **SB** £75-£80
DB £80-£120 **L** £16 **L** 🍽 **D** £28.50 **D** 🍽 ✕ **LD** 21:30
CC MC Visa Amex DC ♿

★★ ✤ Devonshire Arms
Pearse Square, Youghal
☎ 024-92827 **Fax** 024-92900
10 bedrs, all ensuite, 🛏 ⌗ 150 **P** 20 ⊕ **CC** MC Visa
Amex DC ♿

Maps

Leisure

Travel

Shoppin

www.WestOneWeb.com

West One

SPENCER'S

The British Golf Directory

Courses where you can turn up and play

This new Spencer's guide provides full details of golf courses the length and breadth of Britain. All are courses where you can turn up and play, from municipal courses to some of the grandest in the land. You don't need to be members or pay membership fees. Just the rate for the round.

Whether you are an old hand or one of the new wave of golf enthusiasts you will find Spencer's Directory an invaluable companion - for your home, for your car or for your holidays.

With full-colour throughout it's easy-to-use, highly practical and perfect for browsing.

Each entry has a full quarter-page, with a description of the course, and information on yardage, par, standard scratch score, directions and green fees. There's also a full-colour route-planning and map section - a feature of all Spencer's titles.

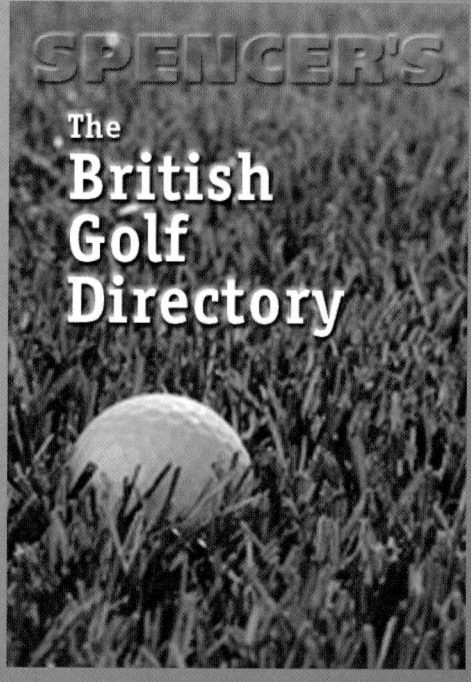

Format:	210x148mm
No. of pages:	112pp
ISBN:	1 900327 51 1
Price:	£4.99
Publication date:	April 2000

West One Publishing
Kestrel House, Duke's PLace
Marlow, Bucks SL7 2QH

tel: 01628 487722

West One
PUBLISHING

www.WestOneWeb.com

Channel Islands & Isle of Man

GUERNSEY 2A2
ℹ North Plantation, St Peter Port 01481-723552

★★★★ Old Government House
Anns Place, St Peter Port
📞 01481-724921 **Fax** 01481-724429
E-mail ogh@guernsey.net

Centrally situated in the heart of picturesque St Peter Port, the OGH hotel has just completed a £2m rebuilding and refurbishment programme making it one of the island's premier hotels. 68 ensuite bedrooms, award winning restaurant and 2 bars.
68 bedrs, all ensuite, ⚓ ▣ ⠿ 150 **P** 20 ⊕ **SB** £70 **DB** £105 **L** £14.95 **L** 🐾 **D** £18.75 **D** 🐾 ✕ **LD** 21:30 **CC** MC Visa Amex DC ⤳ ♿
See advert on this page

★★★★ St Pierre Park 🛏 🛏 🛏
St Peter Port GY1 1FD
📞 01481-728282 **Fax** 01481-712041
E-mail stppark@itt.net.

Amidst 45 acres of parkland, with a 9 hole golf course and 3 tennis courts, the St Pierre Park Hotel boasts 135 luxury ensuite bedrooms, 2 award winning restaurants and an excellent health suite with indoor heated swimming pool.
135 bedrs, all ensuite, ➹ ▣ ⠿ 200 **P** 150 ⊕ **SB** £125 **DB** £165 **L** £11.95 **L** 🐾 **D** £20 **D** 🐾 ✕ **LD** 22:30 **CC** MC Visa Amex DC ⤳ 🎿 🏊 🎾 🐕 ♿

★★★ De Havelet 🛏 🛏
Havelet, St Peter Port GY1 1BA
📞 01481-722199 **Fax** 01481-714057
34 bedrs, all ensuite, ⠿ 20 **P** 50 ⊕ **SB** £48-£60 **DB** £87-£110 **HB** £345-£450 **L** £9.50 **D** £14.50 ✕ **LD** 21:30 **CC** MC Visa Amex DC ⤳ 🎿

★★★ Green Acres 🛏
St Martins GY4 6LS
📞 01481-35711 **Fax** 01481-35978
Closed Nov-Jan
48 bedrs, all ensuite, ⠿ 30 **P** 70 ⊕ **SB** £30-£53 **DB** £60-£86 **L** 🐾 **D** £14 **D** 🐾 ✕ **LD** 20:30 **CC** MC Visa Amex ⤳

★★★ Hotel Bon Port 🛏 🛏
Moulin Huet Bay, St Martins GY4 6EW
📞 01481-39249 **Fax** 01481-39596

Situated in the midst of Guernsey's most beautiful coastal scenery, boasting spectacular views over Moulin Huet Bay, the famous Peastacks, Saints Bay and Jersey. Excellent food and views in the restaurant, health suite, Atrium and stunning grounds.

18 bedrs, all ensuite, ⚌ 40 **P** 40 No children under 2 ⊕ **SB** £45-£75 **DB** £60-£126 **HB** £315-£546 **L** £11.95 **L** ❦ **D** £17.50 ✕ **LD** 20:45 ₢ MC Visa Amex JCB ⚐ ⊡ ⊠ ▷

★★★ L'Atlantique
Perelle Bay, St Saviours GY7 9NA
☎ 01481-264056 **Fax** 01481-263800
Closed Nov-Feb
23 bedrs, all ensuite, ⚌ 20 **P** 70 ⊕ **SB** £43-£51.50 **DB** £73-£90 **HB** £343-£402.50 **L** £11.95 **L** ❦ **D** £17 **D** ❦ ✕ **LD** 21:30 Restaurant closed L Mon-Sat ₢ MC Visa Amex ⚐

★★★ La Favorita ⚐
Fermain-Bay GY4 6SD
☎ 01481-35666 **Fax** 01481-35413
E-mail info@favorita.com
Closed Jan

Set in a wooded valley, this former country house overlooks the bay and sea. St Peter Port is within easy walking distance. An indoor pool and comfortable lounges with an open fire help to make La Favorita an ideal 'Pied á Terre'.
37 bedrs, all ensuite, ♀ ⚗ ⊡ ⚌ 70 **P** 40 ⊕ **SB** £45-£53 **DB** £75-£91 **HB** £350-£406 **L** £10 **L** ❦ **D** £15 **D** ❦ ✕ **LD** 21:00 ₢ MC Visa Amex DC ⚐ ⊠ ⚐

★★★ ✦ La Trelade
Forest Road, St Martins GY4 6UB
☎ 01481-35454 **Fax** 01481-37855
E-mail latrelade@guernsey.net

Nowhere in Guernsey is more ideally situated to take advantage of the island's many natural attributes than La Trelade Hotel. Standing in its own beautiful grounds the hotel is a stroll away from rugged cliffs, quaint leafy lanes and secluded sandy bays.
45 bedrs, all ensuite, ④ ⚐ ⊡ ⚌ 200 **P** 135 ⊕ **SB** £27.50-£47 **DB** £55-£94 **HB** £276.50-£413 **L** £9 **L** ❦ **D** £14 **D** ❦ ✕ **LD** 21:00 Restaurant closed L Mon-Sat ₢ MC Visa Amex DC ⚐ ⊡

★★★ ✦ Le Chalet
Fermain-Bay GY4 6SD
☎ 01481-235716 **Fax** 01481-235718
Closed 16 Oct-12 Apr
41 bedrs, all ensuite, **P** 50 ⊕ **SB** £40-£62.50 **DB** £66-£100 **HB** £260-£400 **L** £6 **L** ❦ **D** £16 **D** ❦ ✕ **LD** 21:30 ₢ MC Visa Amex DC ⊡ ⊠

CHANNEL ISLANDS

★★★ Les Rocquettes
Les Gravees, St Peter Port GY1 1RN
📞 01481-722146 **Fax** 01481-714543

Located on the outskirts of St Peter Port, Les Roquettes offers superior bedrooms and a stylish atrium plus a new indoor pool with sauna, jacuzzi and gym.
51 bedrs, all ensuite, 🖊 📺 ☷ 50 **P** 50 ⊟ **SB** £25-£50 **DB** £50-£90 **HB** £203-£350 **L** 🍽 **D** 🍽 ✕ **LD** 21:00 ((MC Visa Amex DC 🔲 🔲 🔲 ⅋
See advert on previous page

★★★ Moore's
Pollet, St Peter Port GY1 1WH
📞 01481-235716 **Fax** 01481-235718
49 bedrs, all ensuite, 📺 ☷ 30 ⊟ **SB** £39-£75 **DB** £62-£100 **HB** £280-£420 **L** £10 **D** £16 **D** 🍽 ✕ **LD** 21:00 ((MC Visa Amex DC 🔲 🔲

★★★ Peninsula 🍴 🍴
Les Dicqs, Vale GY6 8JP
📞 01481-48400 **Fax** 01481-48706
Closed 28 Dec-5 Jan
99 bedrs, all ensuite, ♞ 📺 ☷ 200 **P** 150 ⊟ **SB** £38-£60 **DB** £58-£101 **L** £10 **D** £13 **D** 🍽 ✕ **LD** 21:30 ((MC Visa Amex DC ⅋ ⅋

★★★ ❖ Saints Bay
Icart Point, St Martins GY4 6JG
📞 01481-38888 **Fax** 01481-35558
E-mail saintsbay@aol.com
Closed Nov-Feb
36 bedrs, all ensuite, ♀ ☷ 30 **P** 24 ⊟ **DB** £56-£87 **HB** £266-£374.50 **L** 🍽 **D** £15 **D** 🍽 ✕ **LD** 21:30 ((MC Visa Amex DC ⅋ ⅋

★★★ St Margaret's Lodge 🍴 🍴
Forest Road, St Martins
📞 01481-35757 **Fax** 01481-37594
47 bedrs, all ensuite, 🖊 ♞ 📺 ☷ 140 **P** 70 ⊟ **SB** £28-£44.50 **DB** £81-£133 **HB** £283.50-£465.50 **L** £10.50 **L** 🍽 **D** £16.50 **D** 🍽 ✕ **LD** 21:30 ((MC Visa Amex DC ⅋ 🔲 ⅋

★★ Grange Lodge 🍴
The Grange, St Peter Port GY1 1RQ
📞 01481-725161 **Fax** 01481-724211
Closed 24 Dec-2 Jan
30 bedrs, all ensuite, ♞ **P** 20 ⊟ ((MC Visa ⅋ 🔲

★★ Hougue du Pommier
Castel GY5 7FQ
📞 01481-56531 **Fax** 01481-56260
43 bedrs, all ensuite, ④ ♞ **P** 70 ⊟ **SB** £30-£45 **DB** £60-£90 **HB** £297.50-£367.50 **D** £16.50 ✕ **LD** 21:30 Restaurant closed L Mon-Sat ((MC Visa Amex DC ⅋ 🔲 🔲

★★ ❖ Le Carrefour
The Grange, St Peter Port GY1 2QJ
📞 01481-713965 **Fax** 01481-714494
Closed 1 Oct-30 Apr
10 bedrs, 9 ensuite, ♀ **P** 12 ⊟ Rest Resid **SB** £37.75 **DB** £75.50 **HB** £337.75 **L** £6.50 **D** £10.50 ✕ **LD** 20:00 ((MC Visa Amex ⅋

★★ Sunnycroft 🍴
5 Constitution Steps, St Peter Port GY1 2PN
📞 01481-723008 **Fax** 01481-712225
Closed Nov-Mar

Uniquely situated, well appointed hotel with delightful terraced gardens, having wonderful views over the harbour to the neighbouring islands of Herm and Sark.
13 bedrs, all ensuite, **P** 4 No children under 14 ⊟ **SB** £27-£37 **DB** £54-£74 **HB** £231-£301 **D** £12.50 ✕ **LD** 20:00 ((MC Visa

Short Breaks
Many hotels provide special rates for weekend and mid-week breaks – sometimes these are quoted in the hotel's entry, otherwise ring direct for the latest offers.

JERSEY 2A2

Pop. 75,000. Guernsey 25, Weymouth 103 **EC** Thu
i Liberation Square, St Helier 01534-500700

★★★★ Atlantic

Le Mont de la Pulente, St Brelade JE3 8HE
☎ 01534-744101 **Fax** 01534-744102
E-mail atlantic@itl.net
Closed Jan & Feb

In private local ownership since 1970, this four star luxury hotel is the sole Channel Islands member of Small Luxury Hotels of the World.
50 bedrs, all ensuite, ▣ ⠿ 60 **P** 60 ⊟ **SB** £100-£150 **DB** £125-£225 **L** £16.50 **L** ➍ **D** £25 ✕ **LD** 21:30 **CC** MC Visa Amex DC

★★★★ Hotel La Place

Route du Coin, La Haule, St Brelade JE3 8BT
☎ 01534-744261 **Fax** 01534-745164
E-mail hotlaplace@aol.com

Situated in a peaceful, rural part of Jersey yet only half a mile from the stunning St Aubin's Bay and a mere 10 minutes drive from St Helier, the elegant Hotel La Place offers the discerning guest the highest standards of comfort, cuisine and guest care.
43 bedrs, all ensuite, ▣ ⌀ ⠿ ⠿ 100 **P** 70 ⊟ **SB** £70-£100 **DB** £100-£184 **HB** £385-£631 **L** £14 **D** £19 ✕ **LD** 21:30 Restaurant closed L Mon-Sat **CC** MC Visa Amex DC ⠿ ⠿
See advert on this page

CHANNEL ISLANDS

★★★★ Longueville Manor 🍴🍴🍴
Blue Ribbon Hotel
St Saviour's JE2 7SA
☎ 01534-725501 **Fax** 01534-731613
E-mail longman@itl.net

A 13th century Norman manor house set at the foot of a 16 acre wooded valley amidst gardens.
32 bedrs, all ensuite, 4 🐾 🖃 ⅲ 30 P 40 🍴 DB £175-£265 L £20 D £35 D 🍷 ✕ LD 21:30 cc MC Visa Amex DC 🔥 🖻

★★★★ St Brelade's Bay 🍴🍴
St Brelade's Bay JE3 8EF
☎ 01534-46141 **Fax** 01534-47278
Closed Oct-Apr
74 bedrs, all ensuite, 🖃 P 60 🍴 SB £53-£93 DB £82-£162 HB £371-£651 L £12 D £25 ✕ LD 20:50 cc MC Visa 🔥 🖬 🖻 🖾

★★★ Apollo
St Saviour's Road, St Helier JE2 4LA
☎ 01534-25441 **Fax** 01534-22120

Smart central hotel in Jersey's capital. Ideal for holiday and business. Garden, swimming pool, water chute. Indoor leisure. Bright new bedrooms. Fine food. Free parking.
85 bedrs, all ensuite, 4 🖃 ⅲ 150 P 50 🍴 SB £47-£62 DB £78-£88 L £10.50 D £13.50 ✕ LD 20:45 cc MC Visa Amex 🔥 🖻 🖬
See advert on this page

★★★ Beau Couperon
Rozel Bay, St Martin JE3 6AN
☎ 01534-865522 **Fax** 01534-865332
E-mail southern@itl.net
Closed Oct-Apr

Converted Napoleonic fortress with private access to beautiful Rozel bay and harbour; car park and heated outdoor pool. Renowned for peaceful atmosphere, friendly service and excellent restaurant with sea views.
36 bedrs, all ensuite, P 20 🍴 SB £33-£60 DB £66-£92 Room £28-£61 HB £196-£280 L 🍷 D £15.50 ✕ LD 21:30 cc MC Visa Amex DC JCB 🔥

★★★ Beaufort
Green Street, St Helier JE2 4UH
☎ 01534-32471 **Fax** 01534-20371

Luxury modern town centre hotel. New outdoor and indoor pools. Bedrooms have satellite TV, lounge armchairs, mini bar, modern points. Superb cuisine. Free car park.
54 bedrs, all ensuite, ▣ ♨ 120 **P** 40 ⌷ **SB** £56-£70 **DB** £86-£112 **L** £10 **D** £11 ✕ **LD** 20:45 **CC** MC Visa Amex DC ▣ ⅊
See advert on this page

CHANNEL ISLANDS

★★★ Beausite
Grouville Bay, Grouville JE3 9DL
📞 01534-857577 **Fax** 01534-857211
E-mail southern@itl.net
Closed end Oct
76 bedrs, all ensuite, ⊼ ⊞ Rest Resid **DB** £54.30-
£88.50 **L** ❧ **D** £10.50 **D** ❧ ✕ **LD** 20:30 **CC** MC Visa
Amex DC 🔲 🔲 🔲 🔲 ⅙
See advert on previous page

★★★ Bergerac
Portelet Bay, St Brelades JE3 8AT
📞 01534-45991 **Fax** 01534-743010
E-mail southern@itl.net
Closed Nov-March
50 bedrs, all ensuite, ⊼ **P** 100 ⊞ **SB** £31.50-£66.75
DB £63-£89 **HB** £244-£323.40 **L** ❧ **D** £10.50 ✕
LD 21:00 **CC** MC Visa Amex DC 🔲 🔲 🔲 🔲
See advert on previous page

★★★ Chateau La Chaire 🏵 🏵 🏵
Gold Ribbon Hotel
Rozel Bay JE3 6AJ
📞 01534-863354 **Fax** 01534-865137
E-mail res@chateau-la-chaire.co.uk

A charming Victorian house, beautifully decorated
and furnished. Set in terraced, wooded gardens.
14 bedrs, all ensuite, 🔲 ⚌ 20 **P** 30 No children
under 7 ⊞ **SB** £72-£97 **DB** £97-£137 **L** £13.95
D £26.50 **D** ❧ ✕ **LD** 22:00 **CC** MC Visa Amex DC

★★★ Chateau de la Valeuse 🏵 🏵 🏵
St Brelade's Bay JE3 8EE
📞 01534-46281 **Fax** 01534-47110
Closed winter

Overlooking our own award winning gardens is this
small hotel of character. Terrace and balconies
decorated with window boxes.
34 bedrs, all ensuite, ⚌ 60 **P** 30 No children under
5 ⊞ **CC** MC Visa JCB 🔲

★★★ Golden Sands 🏵
St Brelades Bay JE3 8EF
📞 01534-41241 **Fax** 01534-499366
E-mail goldensands@jerseyhols.com
62 bedrs, all ensuite, 🔲 ⊞ Rest Resid **SB** £41-£60
DB £52-£90 **D** £15 ✕ **LD** 21:00 **CC** MC Visa Amex
See advert on this page

★★★ L'Emeraude
Longueville, St Saviour's
☎ 01534-874512 **Fax** 01534-59031
Closed Oct/Nov
58 bedrs, all ensuite, ↿ ▣ **P** 40 ⊞ **SB** £40-£60
DB £60-£100 **L** ♥ **D** £10.50 ✕ **LD** 20:30 **C** MC Visa
Amex DC ⊰

★★★ Laurels
La Route du Fort, St Helier JE2 4PA
☎ 01534-36444 **Fax** 01534-59904
37 bedrs, all ensuite, ↿ **P** 16 ⊞ **SB** £40-£60 **DB** £60-
£100 **L** ♥ **D** £10.50 ✕ **LD** 20:30 **C** MC Visa Amex
DC ⊰

★★★ Les Arches
Archirondel Bay, Gorey JE3 6DR
☎ 01534-853839 **Fax** 01534-856660
E-mail casino@itl.net

Overlooking the French coast, 200 yards from the
beach, one and a half miles from Gorey Village and
the golf course.
54 bedrs, all ensuite, ↿ ⦂⦂⦂ 150 **P** 120 ⊞ **SB** £30-£43
DB £60-£86 **HB** £280-£378 **L** £12.50 **L** ♥ **D** £14.50 ✕
LD 20:45 **C** MC Visa JCB ⊰ ▨ ▣ ▨ ▨

★★★ Lobster Pot ⦚ ⦚
L'etacq, St Ouen JE3 2FB
☎ 01534-482888 **Fax** 01534-485584
12 bedrs, all ensuite, **P** 60 ⊞ **SB** £52-£70 **DB** £84-
£110 **L** £15.50 **D** £15.50 ✕ **LD** 21:00 **C** MC Visa
Amex DC

CHANNEL ISLANDS

★★★ Mermaid
St Peter's JE3 7BN
☎ 01534-41255 **Fax** 01534-45826

Ideal for business and holidaymaker, the Mermaid offers superb facilities including executive bedrooms, indoor and outdoor pools, leisure centre, tennis and fine dining.
68 bedrs, all ensuite, ### 100 **P** 150 ⊞ **SB** £46-£63 **DB** £85-£93 **L** £10 **D** £11 ✕ **LD** 21:00 **CC** MC Visa Amex DC ▣ ⚒ ▦ ▦ ▨
See advert on previous page

★★★ ✣ Old Court House
Gorey Village, Grouville JE3 9FS
☎ 01534-854444 **Fax** 01534-853587
E-mail ochhotel@itl.net
Closed Oct-Mar
58 bedrs, all ensuite, ⊬ ▣ **P** 40 ⊞ **SB** £32-£49.50 **DB** £64-£107 **HB** £273-£423.50 **L** ♥ **D** £14.50 ✕ **LD** 21:00 **CC** MC Visa Amex DC JCB ⚒ ▦ ⚃

★★★ Ommaroo
Havre des Pas, St Helier
☎ 01534-23493 **Fax** 01534-59912
85 bedrs, 84 ensuite, ⊬ ▣ ### 100 **P** 60 ⊞ **SB** £45-£65 **DB** £70-£110 **L** ♥ **D** £10.50 ✕ **LD** 20:30 **CC** MC Visa Amex DC

★★★ Pomme d'Or ⌦
Liberation Square, St Helier JE1 3UF
☎ 01534-880110 **Fax** 01534-737781
E-mail frenaie@itl.net

The Pomme d'Or Hotel is Jersey's most centrally located hotel, overlooking Liberation Square and the yacht marina. The hotel is famous for its award winning cuisine and excellent service.
141 bedrs, all ensuite, ⚲ ▣ ### 300 ⊞ **SB** £70-£75 **DB** £110-£120 **HB** £494-£529 **L** £12.50 **L** ♥ **D** £16.50 **D** ♥ ✕ **LD** 22:00 **CC** MC Visa Amex DC JCB

★★★ Revere
Kensington Place, St Helier JE2 3PA
☎ 01534-611111 **Fax** 01534-611116
E-mail revere.@itl.net

Rich in decor, ambience and character, this 17th century coach house, in the heart of town, yet only steps from the beach. Fine dining. Outdoor pool.
58 bedrs, 43 ensuite, 15 ⌂ ♦4▣⌂###&♦ ⊬ ### 15 ⊞ **SB** £40-£70 **DB** £80-£110 **HB** £357-£462 **L** ♥ **D** £12.95 ✕ **LD** 22:00 **CC** MC Visa Amex DC ⚒

★★★ Royal
David Place, St Helier JE2 4TD
☎ 01534-26521 **Fax** 01534-24035
E-mail royalhot@itl.net

A traditional town house located within the centre of St Helier, within easy walking distance of the central business district, shops and restaurants.
91 bedrs, all ensuite, ④ ▣ ### 300 **P** 20 ⊞ **SB** £51.50-£66.50 **DB** £100-£119 **HB** £359-£443 **L** £11 **D** £15.50 **D** ♥ ✕ **LD** 21:00 **CC** MC Visa Amex DC

★★★ Royal Yacht

Weighbridge, St Helier
☎ 01534-720511 **Fax** 01534-767729
E-mail casino@itl.net

Centrally situated in the island capital, St Helier, facing the marina and harbour, this long established Victorian hotel has all modern facilities including a sauna. There is a choice of restaurants and several bars.
45 bedrs, all ensuite, ⌀ ⊡ ♨ 80 ⊞ SB £42-£45
DB £84-£90 HB £381.50-£402.50 L £12.50 D £18.50
✕ LD 21:45 ₡ MC Visa Amex JCB

★★★ Shakespeare ⍭

Samares, St Clement
☎ 01534-851915 **Fax** 01534-856269
Closed Nov-Feb/Mar
32 bedrs, all ensuite, ♈ ⊡ ♨ 20 P 30 ⊞ SB £40-£60
DB £60-£100 D £10.50 ✕ LD 20:30 ₡ MC Visa Amex DC

★★★ Silver Springs

St Brelade JE3 8DB
☎ 01534-46401 **Fax** 01534-46823
E-mail silver@itl.net
Closed mid Oct-mid Apr
88 bedrs, all ensuite, P 70 ⊞ Resid ₡ MC Visa Amex ⍭ ⊠ ⅙
See advert on this page

★★★ Somerville ⍭

Mont du Boulevard, St Aubin's Bay JE3 8AD
☎ 01534-741226 **Fax** 01534-746621
E-mail somerville@jerseyhols.com
59 bedrs, all ensuite, ⊡ P 40 No children under 4 ⊞
SB £40-£55 DB £64-£94 HB £294-£399 L £7 L ♥ D £15
✕ LD 21:00 ₡ MC Visa Amex ⍭
See advert on this page

CHANNEL ISLANDS

510 Jersey

★★★ Washington
Clarendon Road, St Helier JE2 3YW
☎ 01534-37981 **Fax** 01534-89899
Closed Oct
36 bedrs, all ensuite, ✝ **P** 15 ⊞ **SB** £40-£55 **DB** £60-£100 **L** ● **D** £10.50 ✗ **LD** 20:30 **CC** MC Visa Amex DC ⊰

★★ Beau Rivage
St Brelade's Bay JE3 8EF
☎ 01534-745983 **Fax** 01534-747127
E-mail welcome@jerseyweb.demon.co.uk
Closed Nov-Mar
27 bedrs, all ensuite, ④ ⊡ **P** 12 ⊞ **DB** £45-£124
HB £200-£480 **D** £13 ✗ **LD** 19:45 **CC** MC Visa Amex JCB ♿
See advert on this page

★★ Dolphin ⌑ ⌑
Gorey Pier, Gorey
☎ 01534-853370 **Fax** 01534-855343
E-mail casino@itl.net

Overlooking the sandy beach of Grouville and the picturesque Gorey Harbour. The restaurant is renowned for its excellent cuisine. Fisherman's Bar. All rooms are ensuite with modern facilities. Open all year round. ½ mile from golf course.
16 bedrs, all ensuite, ⦀ 20 ⊞ ⊞ Rest **SB** £27-£34.50
DB £54-£69 **HB** £266-£318.50 **L** £10.50 **D** £14.50 ✗
LD 22:15 **CC** MC Visa Amex JCB

★★ Maison Gorey
Gorey Village, Gorey JE3 9EP
☎ 01534-857775 **Fax** 01534-857779
Closed Oct-Apr
30 bedrs, all ensuite, ✝ **P** 4 ⊞ **SB** £40-£55 **DB** £60-£90 **D** £10.50 ✗ **LD** 20:30 **CC** MC Visa Amex DC

★★ Moorings 🛏 🛏
Gorey Pier, Gorey JE3 6EW
☎ 01534-853633 **Fax** 01534-857618
E-mail casino@itl.net

Situated beneath Mont Orgueil Castle overlooking the harbour and the sandy beach of Grouville Bay. 16 bedrs, all ensuite, 🐾 ⫶⫶ 20 ⊞ SB £37-£54 DB £72-£104 HB £317-£382 L £12.50 L ♥ D £18.50 ✕ LD 22:15 ℂℂ MC Visa Amex JCB

★★ Sarum 🛏
19-21 New St John's Road, St Helier JE2 3LD
☎ 01534-758163 **Fax** 01534-731340
E-mail welcome@jerseyweb.demon.co.uk
Closed Nov-Mar
49 bedrs, all ensuite, ④ ⊡ P 6 ⊞ SB £28-£56 DB £46-£100 HB £204-£400 L £12 D £13 ✕ LD 19:45 ℂℂ MC Visa Amex JCB ⪫ 🖾 ⅃
See advert on opposite page

★★ Savoy
Rouge Bouillon, St Helier
☎ 01534-727521 **Fax** 01534-768480
61 bedrs, all ensuite, ⊡ ⫶⫶ 150 P 70 ⊞ SB £21-£40 DB £42-£74 HB £196-£308 L ♥ D £11 D ♥ ✕ LD 20:00 ℂℂ MC Visa Amex DC JCB ⪫ 🖾 ⅃

★★ ✤ White Heather
Rue de Haut, Millbrook,
St Lawrence JE3 1JQ
☎ 01534-720978 **Fax** 01534-720968
Closed Dec-Feb
33 bedrs, all ensuite, ⫶⫶ 80 P 12 ⊞ Rest Resid SB £25-£36 DB £42-£64 HB £168-£245 D £9 ✕ LD 19:30 ℂℂ MC Visa DC ⅃
See advert on this page

Facilities for the disabled

Hotels do their best to cater for disabled visitors. However, it is advisable to contact the hotel direct to ensure it can provide a particular requirement.

DOUGLAS 10A4

Pop. 19,900. Ferry service to Heysham and steamer service to Liverpool (peak season only). London 198, Castletown 10, Peel 11, Ramsey 15 **EC** Thu **see** Villa Marina Gdns, Lighthouse, Manx Museum and Art Gallery, House of Keys and Tynwald, Tower of Refuge, St George's Church, Derby Castle Aquadrome and Solarium. TT Races June, Manx Grand Prix Sept ℹ Harris Promenade 01624-686766

★★★ Ascot

7 Empire Terrace, Douglas
☎ 01624-675081 **Fax** 01624-661512
45 bedrs, all ensuite, 🗟 ☎ ⅲ 100 ⊕ ℂℂ MC Visa Amex

★★★ ✦ Castle Mona

Central Promenade, Douglas IM2 4LY
☎ 01624-624540 **Fax** 01624-675360
98 bedrs, all ensuite, 🗟 ☎ ⅲ 200 **P** 85 ⊕ **SB** £48-£58.50 **DB** £62.50-£64 **HB** £224 **L** £10 **D** £13 **D** � ✕ **LD** 21:45 ℂℂ MC Visa Amex 🔝

★★★ ✧ Empress

Central Promenade, Douglas IM2 4RA
☎ 01624-661155 **Fax** 01624-673554
102 bedrs, all ensuite, ♀ ☎ ⅲ 150 ⊕ **SB** £72.50 **DB** £85 **HB** £350 **L** £8.50 **L** � **D** £14.95 **D** � ✕ **LD** 22:45 ℂℂ MC Visa Amex DC 🔝 ▦ ▦

★★★ Welbeck ⅋

Mona Drive, Douglas
☎ 01624-675663 **Fax** 01624-661545
E-mail welbeck@isle-of-man.com
27 bedrs, all ensuite, 🗡 ☎ ⅲ 60 ⊕ Resid **SB** £38-£53 **DB** £55-£82 **L** � **D** £14 ✕ **LD** 20:30 ℂℂ MC Visa Amex

★★ ✦ Rutland

Queens Promenade, Douglas
☎ 01624-621218 **Fax** 01624-611562
Closed Nov-Mar
60 bedrs, all ensuite, ♀ ☎ ⅲ **SB** £25.50 **DB** £51 **HB** £227.50 **L** � **D** £9.50 ✕ **LD** 19:30 ℂℂ MC Visa 🔝

PORT ERIN 10A4

Pop. 1,800. Castletown 7, Douglas 13 ℹ Town Hall 01624-832298

★★★ Cherry Orchard

Bridson Street, Port Erin IM9 6AN
☎ 01624-833811 **Fax** 01624-833583
E-mail enquiries@cherry-orchard.com

31 bedrs, all ensuite, 🗟 🗡 ☎ ⅲ 300 **P** 80 ⊕ **SB** £46.50-£53.50 **DB** £63-£77 **L** � **D** £15.75 **D** � ✕ **LD** 21:45 ℂℂ MC Visa Amex DC 🔝 ▦ ▦ ⚓

★★★ ✦ Port Erin Royal

Promenade, Port Erin IM9 6LH
☎ 01624-833116 **Fax** 01624-835402
80 bedrs, all ensuite, 🗟 ☎ ⅲ 200 **P** 100 ⊕ **SB** £37.50-£42.50 **DB** £60-£70 **HB** £273-£308 **D** £11.95 ✕ **LD** 20:30 ℂℂ MC Visa 🔝 ▦ ⚓
See advert on this page

★★ ✦ Port Erin Imperial

Promenade, Port Erin IM9 6LH
☎ 01624-832122 **Fax** 01624-835402
51 bedrs, all ensuite, ☎ ⅲ 100 **P** 100 ⊕ Resid **SB** £34.50-£39.50 **DB** £54-£64 **HB** £245-£280 **D** £11.95 ✕ **LD** 20:30 ℂℂ MC Visa 🔝 ▦ ⚓
See advert on this page

SANTON   10A4

★★★★ Mount Murray Country Club
Santon IM4 2HT
☎ 01624-661111 **Fax** 01624-611116

Countryside location yet close to air and seaports.
Two restaurants, two bars, 18 hole golf course,
driving range, leisure club, indoor pool, squash,
sports hall.
90 bedrs, all ensuite, 🔲 ⚲ 🔢 ⠿ 300 **P** 400 ⏏
SB £49.50-£79 **DB** £69.50-£99 **L** £13.50 **L** 🍵 **D** £14.95
D 🍴 ✕ **LD** 21:45 Restaurant closed D Sun **CC** MC
Visa Amex DC 🔲 🔲 🔲 🔲 🔲 🔲 🔲 🔲 ⠪

SPENCER'S

The British Golf Directory

Courses where you can turn up and play

This new Spencer's guide provides full details of golf courses the length and breadth of Britain. All are courses where you can turn up and play, from municipal courses to some of the grandest in the land. You don't need to be members or pay membership fees. Just the rate for the round.

Whether you are an old hand or one of the new wave of golf enthusiasts you will find Spencer's Directory an invaluable companion - for your home, for your car or for your holidays.

With full-colour throughout it's easy-to-use, highly practical and perfect for browsing.

Each entry has a full quarter-page, with a description of the course, and information on yardage, par, standard scratch score, directions and green fees. There's also a full-colour route-planning and map section - a feature of all Spencer's titles.

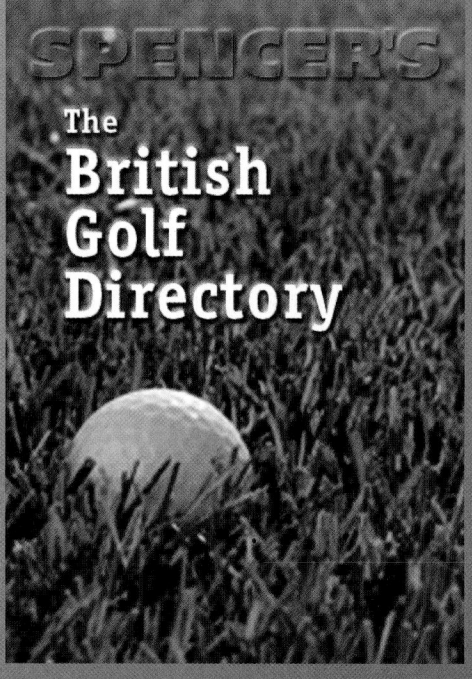

Format:	210x148mm
No. of pages:	112pp
ISBN:	1 900327 51 1
Price:	£4.99
Publication date:	April 2000

West One
PUBLISHING

West One Publishing
Kestrel House, Duke's PLace
Marlow, Bucks SL7 2QH

tel: 01628 487722

www.WestOneWeb.com

SPENCER'S

Labels For Less

Famous brands and labels at discount prices

Labels for Less is a revolutionary and colourful new guide to discount shopping.

For keen shoppers everywhere, it offers comprehensive coverage of over 1300 factory shops and factory outlet villages. Wherever you travel you will be able to find a factory shop nearby. It's essential reference for home, car and holiday.

Perfects, slight seconds and clearance lines, all at bargain prices, make Labels For Less the most exciting and rewarding guide to shopping around. For each outlet there's full information on products, labels and discounts. Plus details of locations, transport, parking, opening hours, credit cards and restaurants.

Every entry is in colour, maximising the impact and highlighting the discounts and brands each outlet features. 20 pages of mapping make route-finding easy.

Format:	210x148mm
No. of pages:	480pp
ISBN:	1 900327 35 X
Price:	£13.99
Publication date:	November 1999

West One Publishing
Kestrel House, Duke's PLace
Marlow, Bucks SL7 2QH

West One
PUBLISHING

tel: 01628 487722

www.WestOneWeb.com

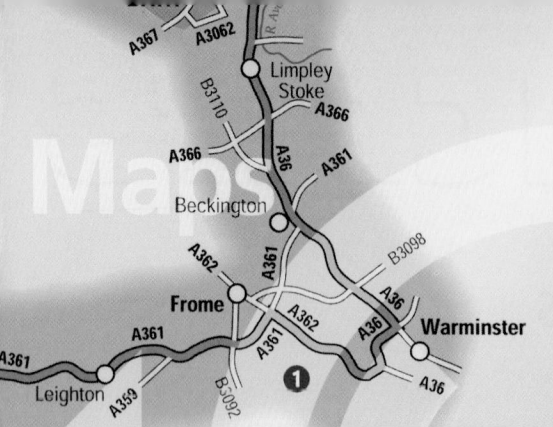

www.WestOneWeb.com

West One

Key to Maps

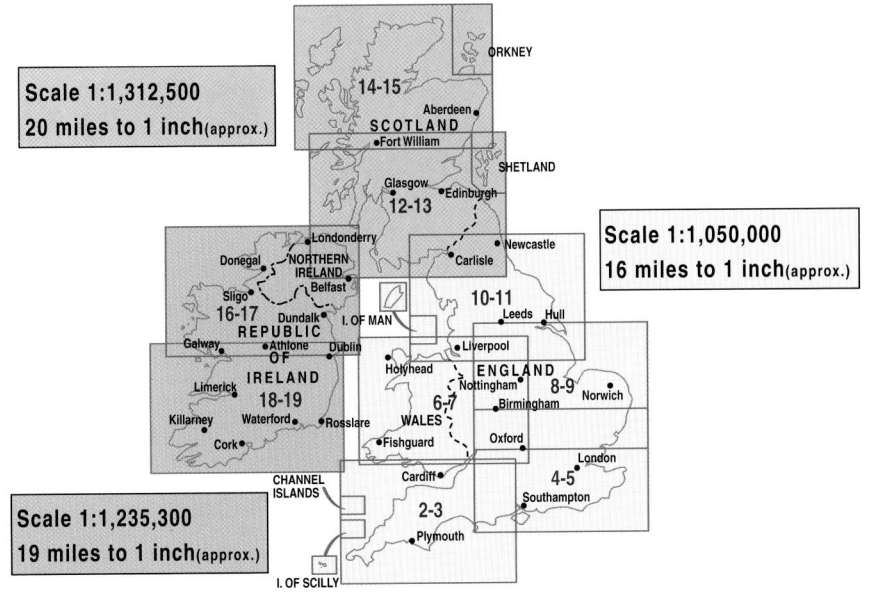

Scale 1:1,312,500
20 miles to 1 inch (approx.)

Scale 1:1,050,000
16 miles to 1 inch (approx.)

Scale 1:1,235,300
19 miles to 1 inch (approx.)

Legend

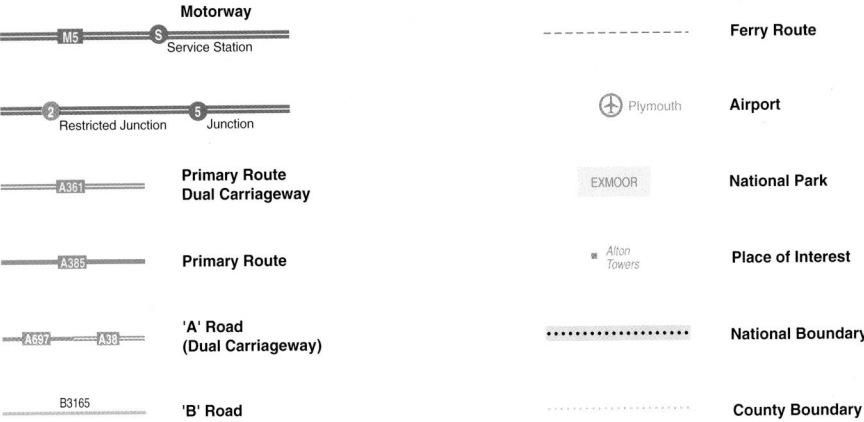

Motorway — Service Station	Ferry Route
Restricted Junction — Junction	Airport (Plymouth)
Primary Route Dual Carriageway (A361)	National Park (EXMOOR)
Primary Route (A385)	Place of Interest (Alton Towers)
'A' Road (Dual Carriageway) (A697, A38)	National Boundary
'B' Road (B3165)	County Boundary

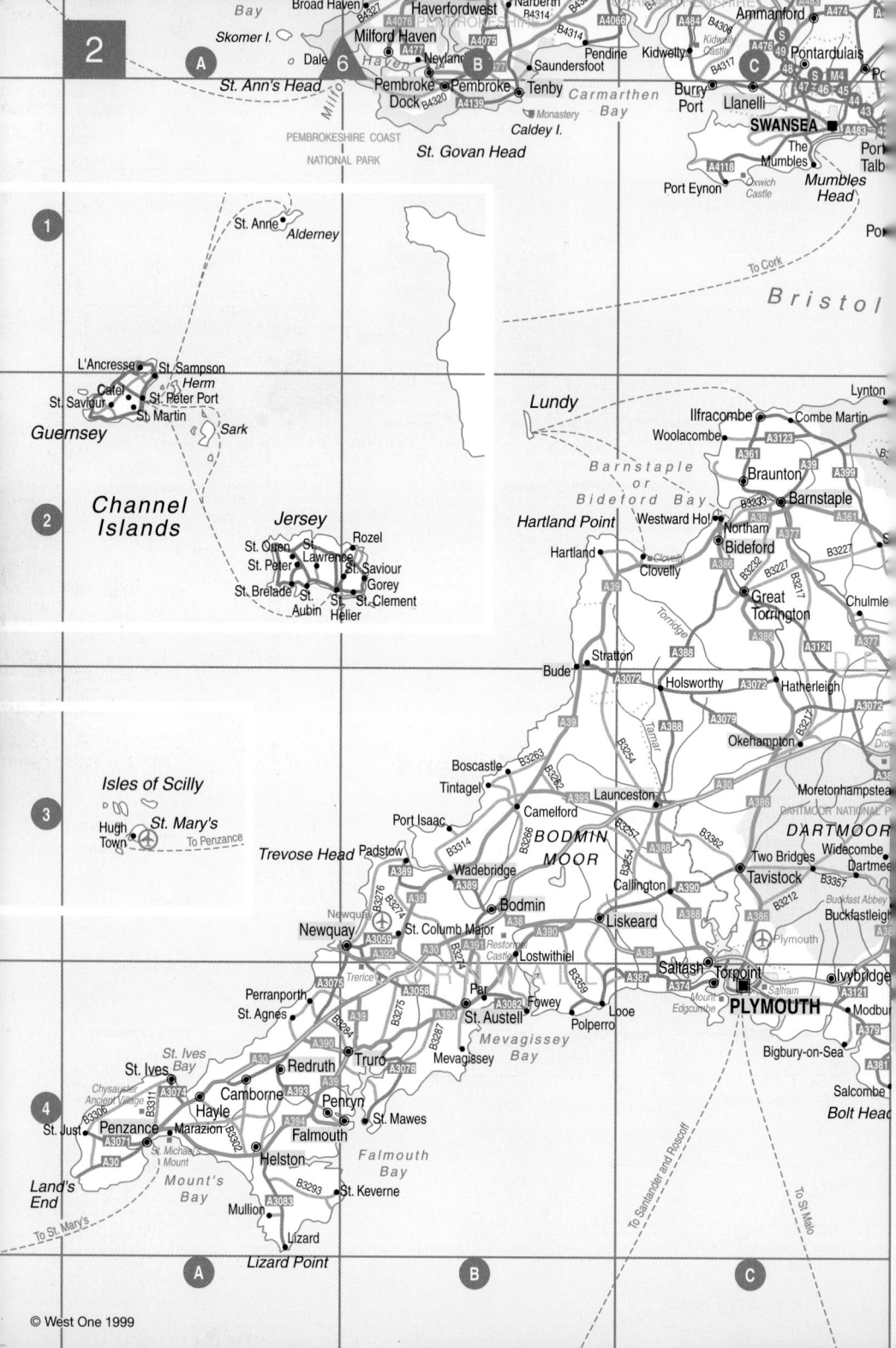

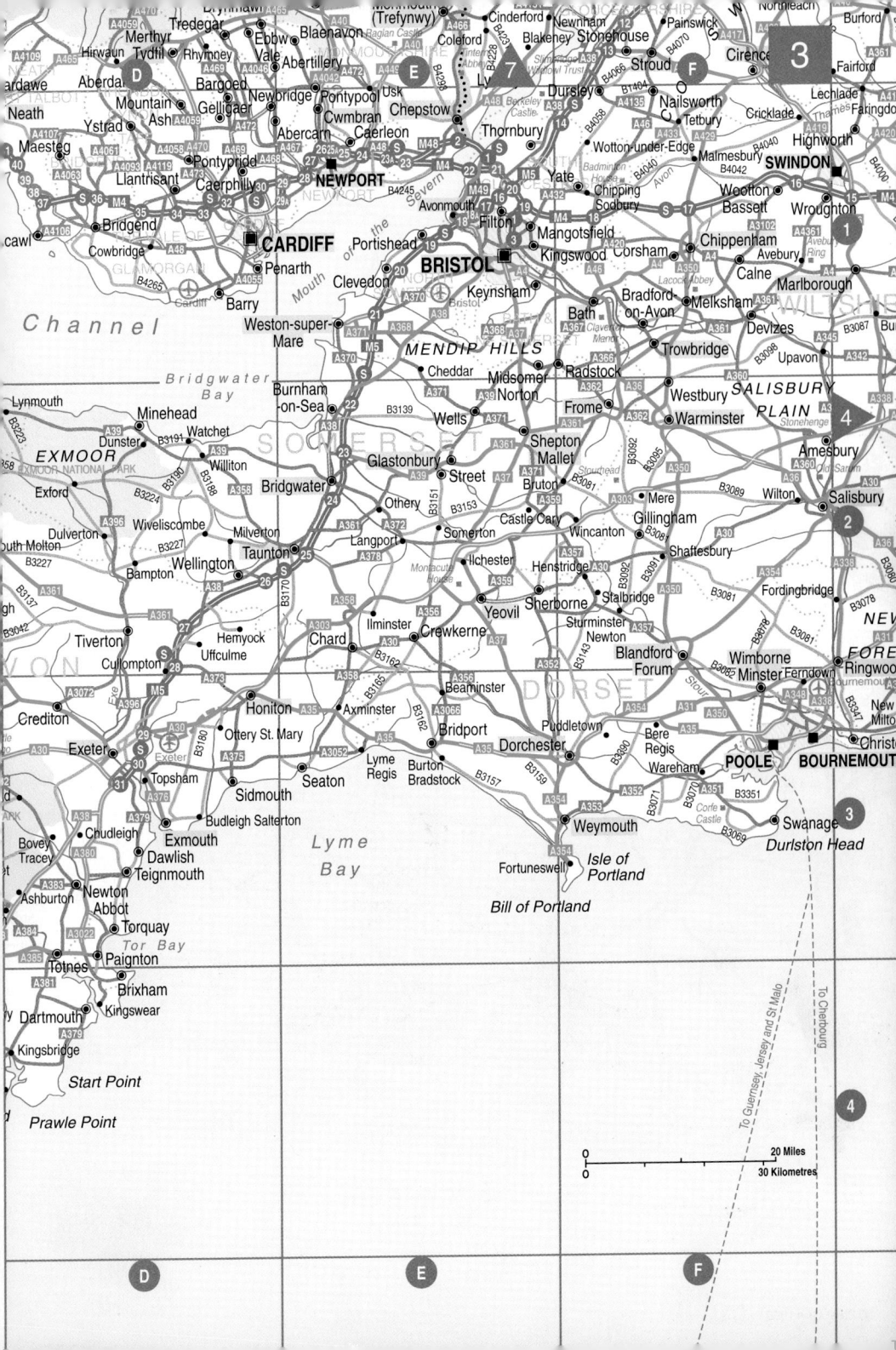

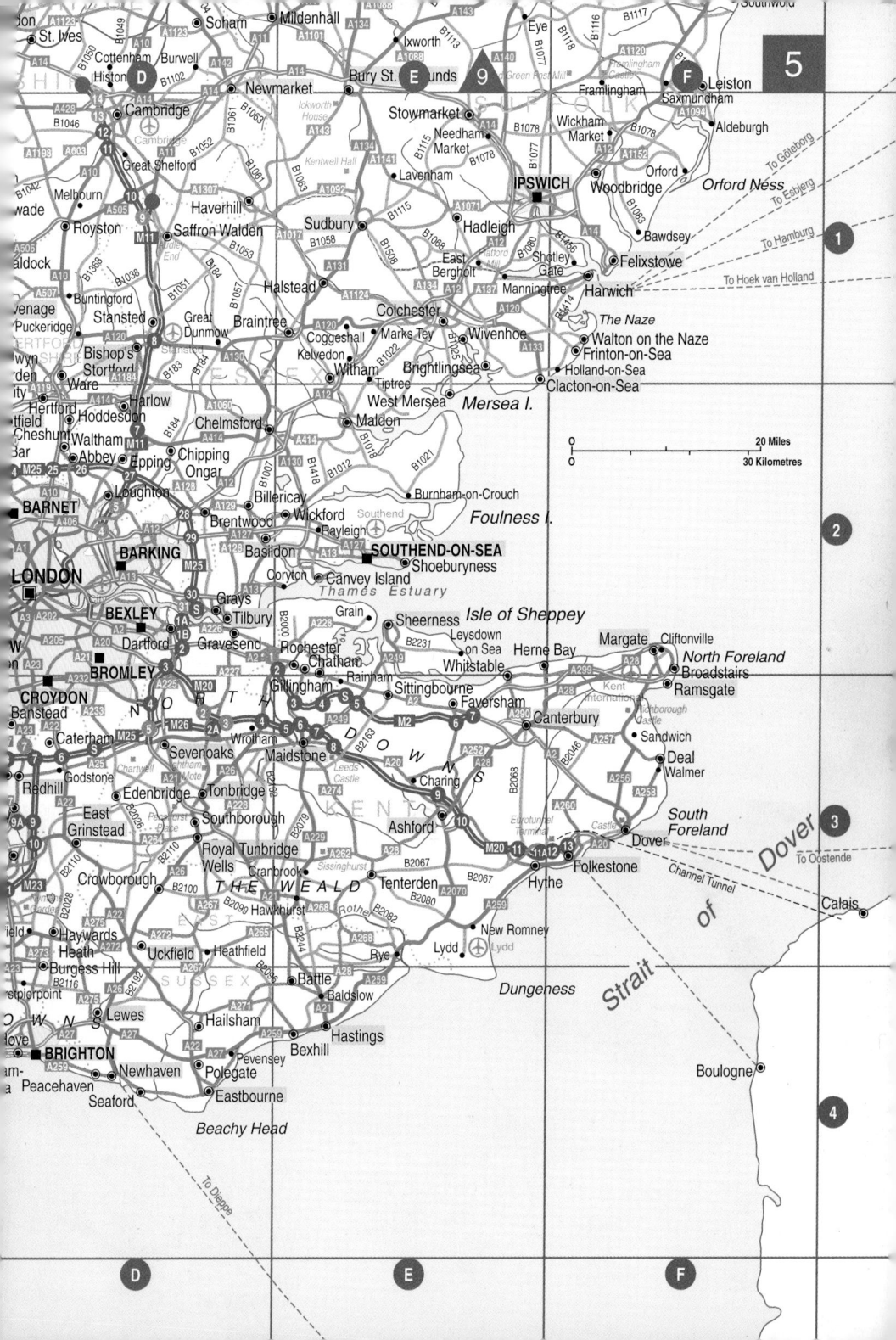

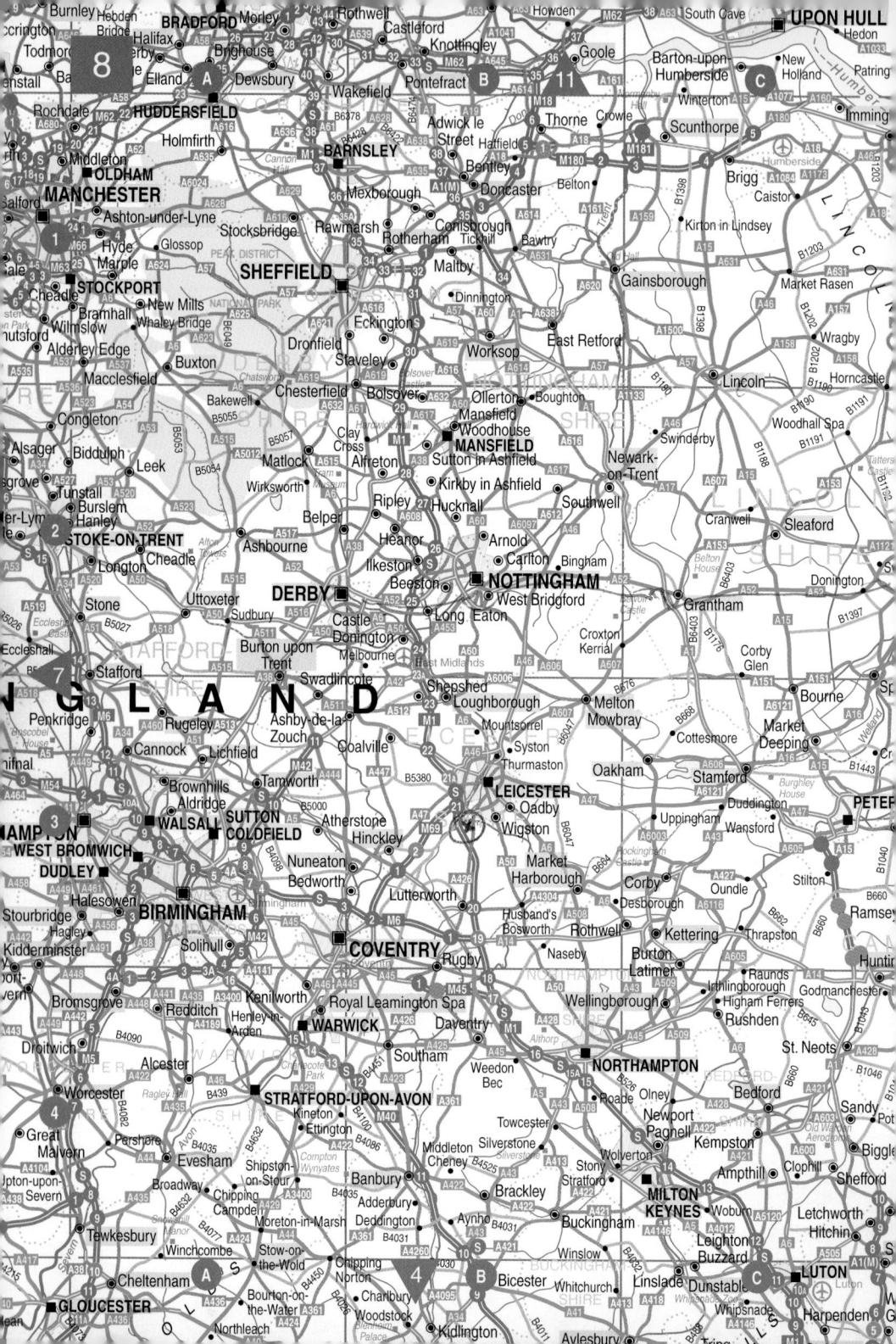

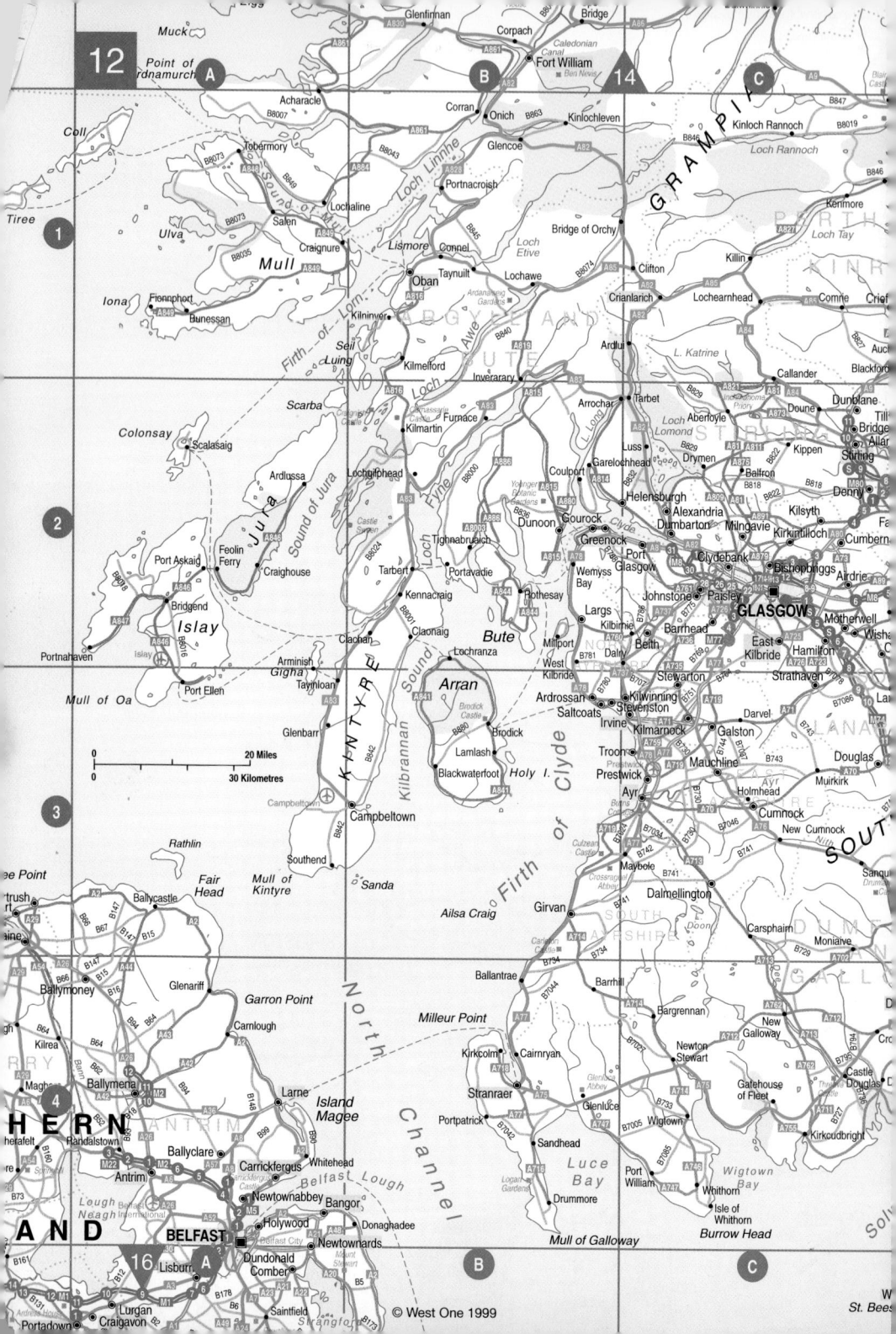

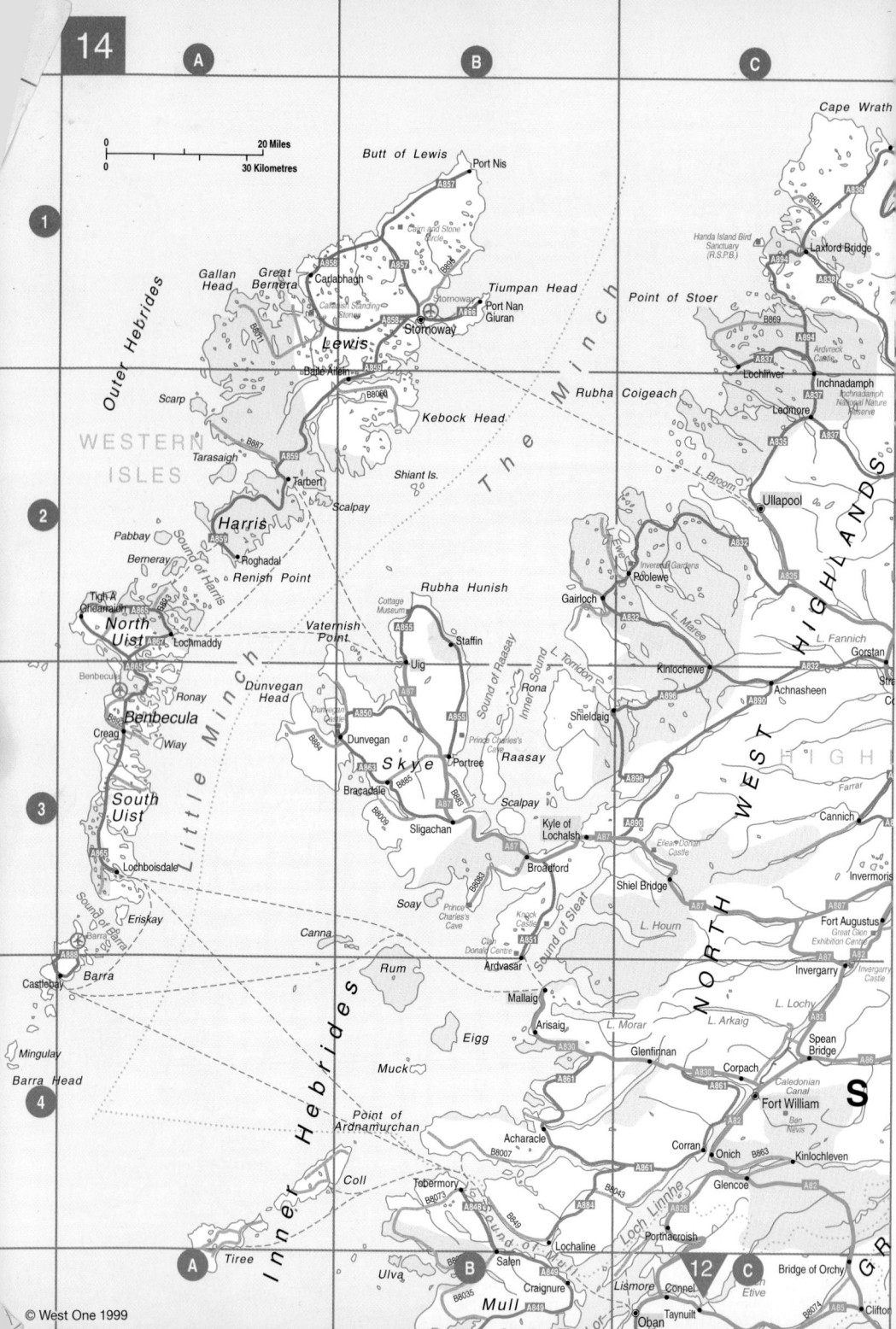

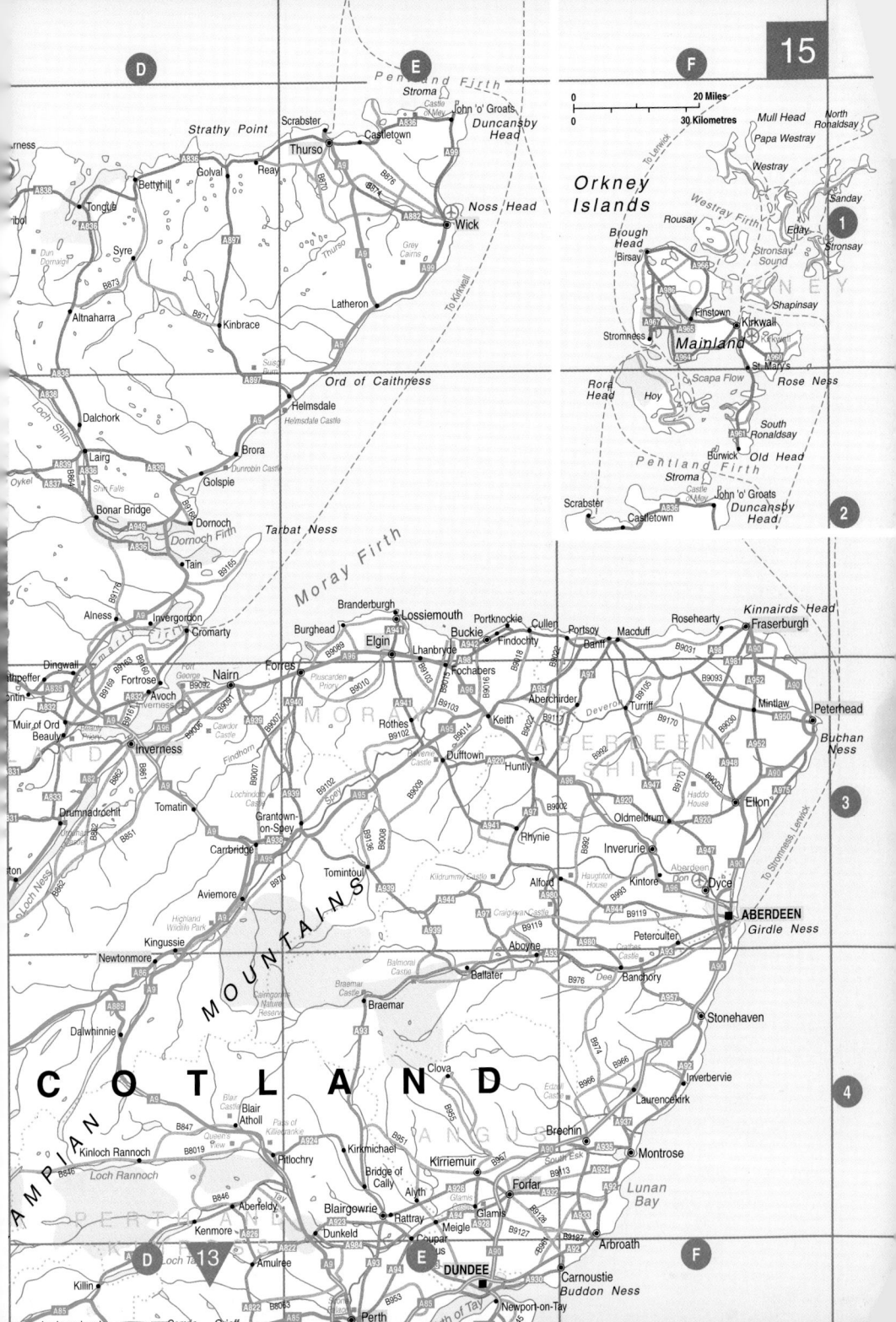

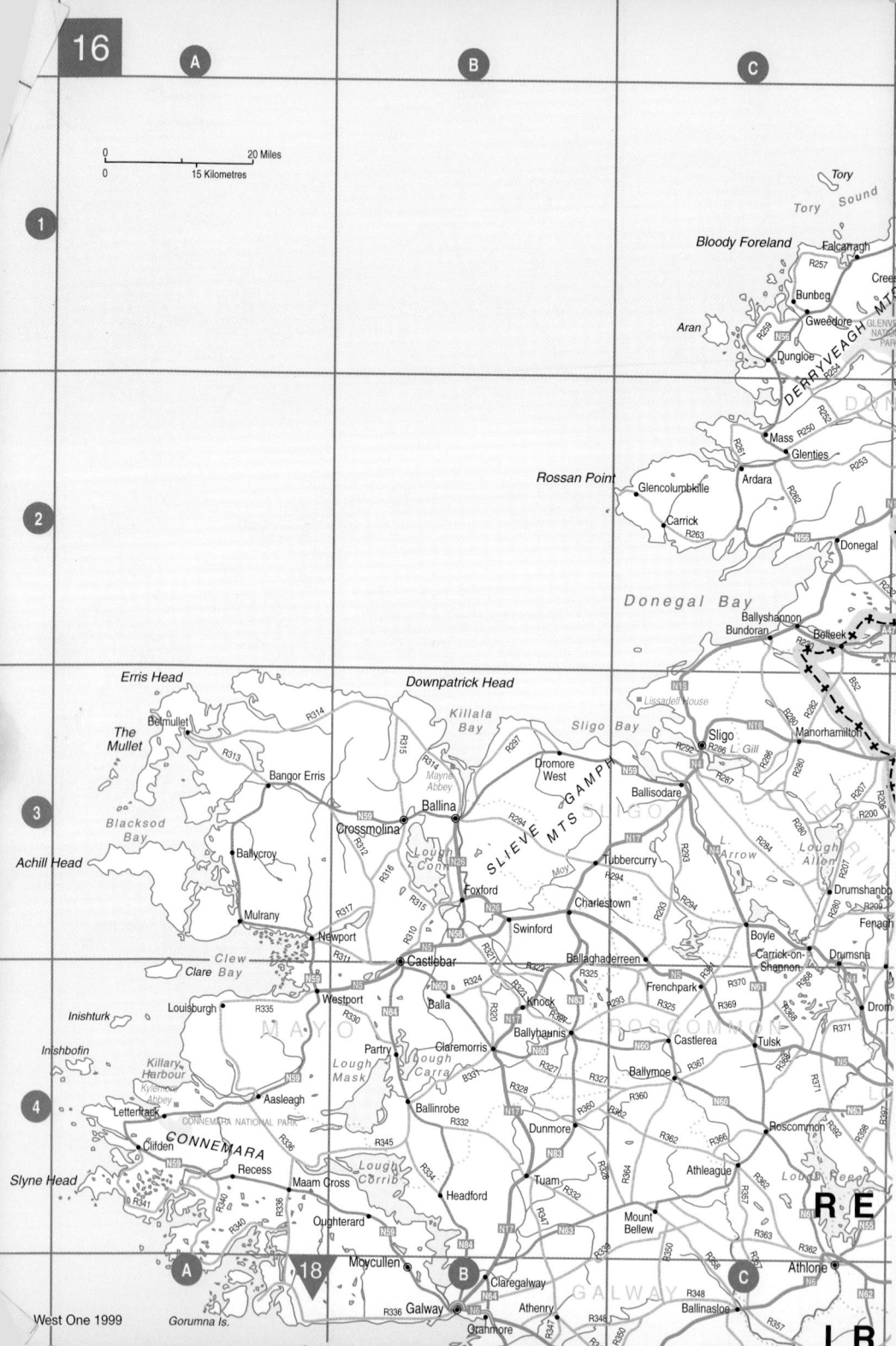

West One 1999

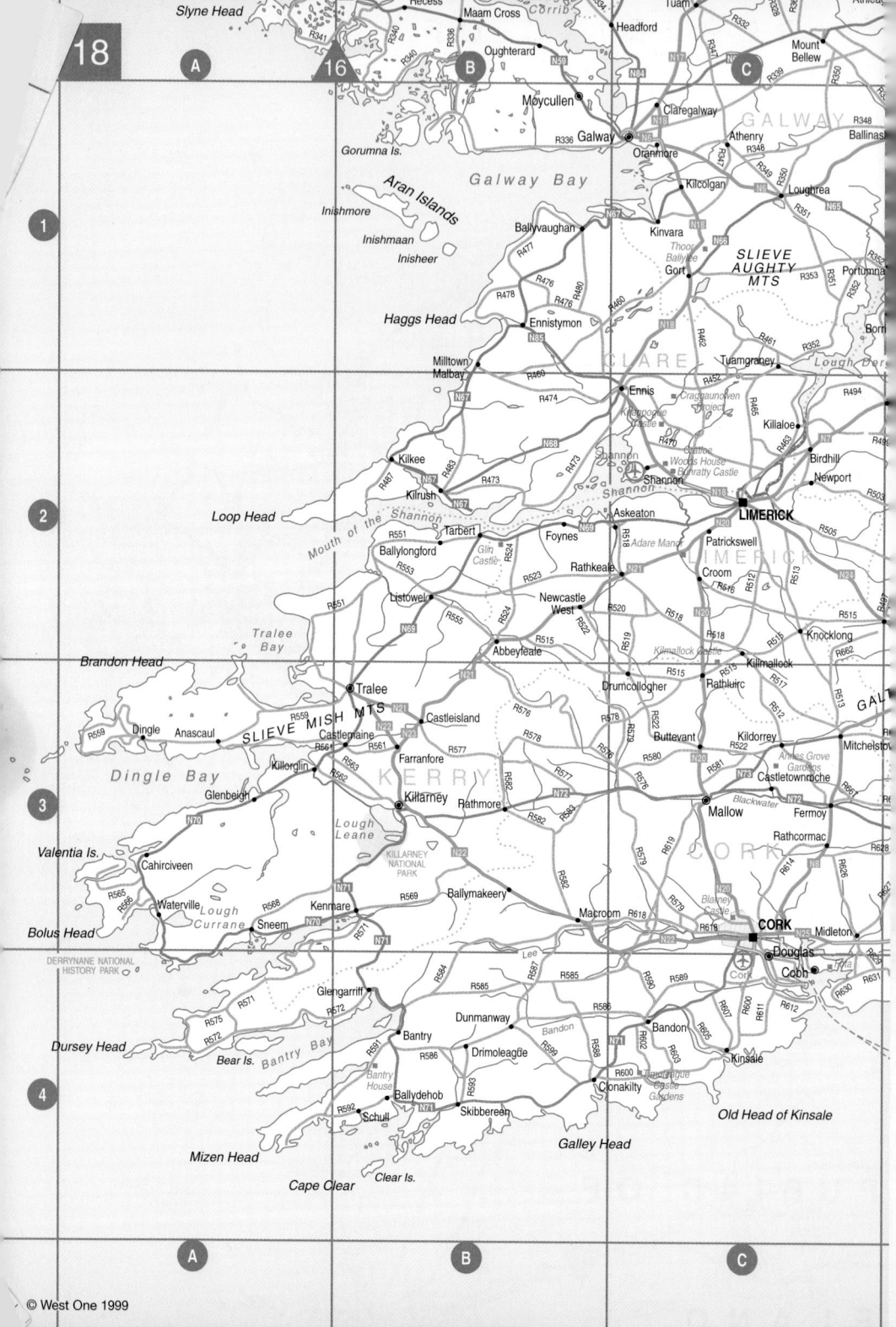

INDEX TO GREAT BRITAIN

Abbreviations of County and new Unitary Authority names used in this index.

Aber	= Aberdeenshire	Guer	= Guernsey	Oxon	= Oxfordshire
Arg	= Argyll & Bute	Hants	= Hampshire	Pemb	= Pembrokeshire
Brid	= Bridgend	Herts	= Hertfordshire	S Lan	= South Lanarkshire
Bucks	= Buckinghamshire	High	= Highland	S York	= South Yorkshire
Camb	= Cambridgeshire	IoM	= Isle of Man	Shrop	= Shropshire
Corn	= Cornwall	IoW	= Isle of Wight	Som	= Somerset
Derb	= Derbyshire	Jer	= Jersey	Staf	= Staffordshire
Dor	= Dorset	Linc	= Lincolnshire	Suff	= Suffolk
Dur	= Durham	Med	= Medway Towns	W Isl	= Western Isles
E York	= East Riding of Yorkshire	New	= Newport	W York	= West Yorkshire
G Man	= Greater Manchester	Norf	= Norfolk	Wrek	= The Wrekin
Glos	= Gloucestershire	North	= Northamptonshire		

A

Aberaeron 6 B3
Abercarn 3 E1
Aberchirder 15 F3
Aberdare 6 C4
Aberdaron 6 B2
Aberdeen 15 F3
Aberdyfi 6 C3
Aberfeldy 12 C1
Aberfoyle 12 C2
Abergavenny 7 D4
Abergele 6 C1
Aberporth 6 B3
Abersoch 6 B2
Abertillery 7 D4
Aberystwyth 6 C3
Abingdon 4 B2
Abington 13 D3
Aboyne 15 E4
Accrington 10 C4
Acharacle 12 A1
Achnasheen 14 C3
Acle 9 F3
Adderbury 4 B1
Adwick le Street 11 D4
Airdrie 12 D2
Alcester 4 A1
Aldeburgh 5 F1
Alderley Edge 7 E1
Aldermaston 4 B3
Aldershot 4 C3
Aldridge 7 F2
Alexandria 12 C2
Alford (Aber) 15 F3
Alford (Linc) 9 D1
Alfreton 8 B2
Allendale Town 10 C1
Alloa 13 D2
Alness 15 D2
Alnwick 13 F3
Alsager 7 E1
Alston 10 B1
Altnaharra 15 D1
Alton 4 B3
Altrincham 10 C4
Alyth 13 D1
Amble 13 F3
Ambleside 10 B2
Amersham 4 C2
Amesbury 4 A3
Amlwch 6 B1

Ammanford 6 C4
Ampthill 4 C1
Amulree 13 D1
Andover 4 B3
Annan 10 A1
Anstruther 13 E2
Appleby in Westmorland 10 B2
Arbroath 13 E1
Ardlui 12 C1
Ardlussa 12 A2
Ardrossan 12 B3
Ardvasar 14 B4
Arisaig 14 B4
Armadale 13 D2
Arminish 12 A2
Arnold 8 B2
Arrochar 12 B2
Arundel 4 C4
Ashbourne 7 F1
Ashburton 3 D3
Ashby-de-la-Zouch 7 F2
Ashford 5 E3
Ashington 13 F3
Ashton-under-Lyne 10 C4
Askrigg 10 C2
Aspatria 10 A1
Atherstone 7 F2
Atherton 10 B4
Attleborough 9 E3
Auchterarder 13 D1
Auchtermuchty 13 D1
Avebury 4 A2
Aviemore 15 D3
Avoch 15 D3
Avonmouth 3 E1
Axminster 3 E3
Aycliffe 11 D2
Aylesbury 4 C2
Aylsham 9 E2
Aynho 4 B1
Ayr 12 C3
Ayton 13 E2

B

Bacup 10 C4
Baile Ailein 14 B2
Bakewell 7 F1
Bala 6 C2
Baldock 4 C1
Baldslow 5 E4
Balfron 12 C2

Ballantrae 12 B4
Ballater 15 E4
Bamburgh 13 F3
Bampton 3 D2
Banbury 4 B1
Banchory 15 F4
Banff 15 F2
Bangor 6 C1
Banstead 5 D3
Bargoed 3 D1
Bargrennan 12 C4
Barking 5 D2
Barmouth 6 C2
Barnard Castle 10 C2
Barnet 5 D2
Barnoldswick 10 C3
Barnsley 11 D4
Barnstaple 2 C2
Barrhead 12 C2
Barrhill 12 B4
Barrow-in-Furness 10 A3
Barry 3 D1
Barton-upon-Humberside 11 E4
Basildon 5 D2
Basingstoke 4 B3
Bath 3 F1
Bathgate 13 D2
Battle 5 E4
Bawdsey 5 F1
Bawtry 11 E4
Beaconsfield 4 C2
Beaminster 3 E3
Beattock 13 D3
Beaulieu 4 B4
Beauly 15 D3
Beaumaris 6 C1
Beccles 9 F3
Bedale 11 D2
Bedford 4 C1
Bedlington 13 F4
Bedworth 8 B3
Beeston 8 B2
Beith 12 C2
Belford 13 F3
Belper 7 F1
Belton 11 E4
Bentley 11 D4
Bere Regis 3 F3
Berkhamsted 4 C2
Berwick-upon-Tweed 13 E2

Bethesda 6 C1
Bettyhill 15 D1
Betws-y-coed 6 C1
Beverley 11 E3
Bewdley 7 E3
Bexhill 5 E4
Bexley 5 D2
Bicester 4 B1
Biddulph 7 E1
Bideford 2 C2
Bigbury-on-Sea 2 C4
Biggar 13 D3
Biggleswade 4 C1
Billericay 5 D2
Billingham 11 D2
Billingshurst 4 C3
Bingham 8 B2
Bingley 10 C3
Birkenhead 10 B4
Birmingham 7 F3
Birsay 15 F1
Bishop Auckland 11 D1
Bishop's Castle 7 D3
Bishop's Stortford 5 D1
Bishop's Waltham 4 B4
Bishopbriggs 12 C2
Blackburn 10 B4
Blackford 12 C1
Blackpool 10 B3
Blackwaterfoot 12 B3
Blaenau Ffestiniog 6 C1
Blaenavon 7 D4
Blair Atholl 15 D4
Blairgowrie 13 D1
Blakeney (Glos) 7 E4
Blakeney (Norf) 9 E2
Blandford Forum 3 F2
Blaydon 10 C1
Blyth 13 F4
Bo'ness 13 D2
Bodmin 2 B3
Bognor Regis 4 C4
Boldon 11 D1
Bolsover 8 B2
Bolton 10 B4
Bonar Bridge 15 D2
Bootle 10 B4
Boroughbridge 11 D3
Borth 6 C3
Boscastle 2 B3
Boston 9 D2
Bothel 10 A1

Boughton 8 B2
Bourne 8 C3
Bournemouth 4 A4
Bourton-on-the-Water 4 A1
Bovey Tracey 3 D3
Bracadale 14 B3
Brackley 4 B1
Bracknell 4 C2
Bradford 10 C3
Bradford-on-Avon 3 F1
Braemar 15 E4
Braintree 5 E1
Bramhall 7 E1
Brampton 10 B1
Branderburgh 15 E2
Brandon 9 E3
Braunton 2 C2
Brechin 13 E1
Brecon 7 D4
Brentwood 5 D2
Bridge of Allan 12 C2
Bridge of Cally 13 D1
Bridge of Earn 13 D1
Bridge of Orchy 12 B1
Bridgend (Arg) 12 A2
Bridgend (Brid) 3 D1
Bridgnorth 7 E3
Bridgwater 3 E2
Bridlington 11 F3
Bridport 3 E3
Brigg 11 E4
Brighouse 10 C4
Brightlingsea 5 E1
Brighton 5 D4
Bristol 3 E1
Brixham 3 D4
Broad Haven 6 A4
Broadford 14 B3
Broadstairs 5 F2
Broadway 4 A1
Brodick 12 B3
Bromfield 7 D3
Bromley 5 D2
Bromsgrove 7 E3
Bromyard 7 E3
Brora 15 D2
Brough 10 C2
Broughton in Furness 10 A2
Broughton 13 D3
Brownhills 7 F2

Bruton 3 F2
Brynmawr 7 D4
Buckfastleigh 2 C3
Buckhaven 13 D2
Buckie 15 E2
Buckingham 4 B1
Buckley 7 D1
Bude 2 B2
Budleigh Salterton 3 D3
Builth Wells 7 D3
Bunessan 12 A1
Bungay 9 F3
Buntingford 5 D1
Burbage 4 A3
Burford 4 A2
Burgess Hill 5 D3
Burghead 15 E2
Burnham Market 9 E2
Burnham-on-Crouch 5 E2
Burnham-on-Sea 3 E2
Burnley 10 C3
Burntisland 13 D2
Burry Port 2 C1
Burslem 7 E1
Burton Bradstock 3 E3
Burton Latimer 8 C3
Burton upon Trent 7 F2
Burwell 9 D4
Burwick 15 F2
Bury St Edmunds 9 E4
Bury 10 C4
Bushey 4 C2
Buxton 7 F1

C

Caerleon 3 E1
Caernarfon 6 B1
Caerphilly 3 D1
Cairnryan 12 B4
Caister-on-Sea 9 F3
Caistor 11 F4
Callander 12 C1
Callington 2 C3
Calne 4 A2
Camberley 4 C3
Camborne 2 A4
Cambridge 5 D1
Camelford 2 B3
Campbeltown 12 B3
Cannich 14 C3
Cannock 7 F2
Canonbie 10 B1

Canterbury 5 E3
Canvey Island 5 E2
Capel Curig 6 C1
Cardiff 3 D1
Cardigan 6 B4
Carlabhagh 14 A1
Carlisle 10 B1
Carlton 8 B2
Carluke 12 C2
Carmarthen 6 B4
Carnforth 10 B3
Carnoustie 13 E1
Carnwath 13 D3
Carrbridge 15 D3
Carsphairn 12 C3
Castle Cary 3 E2
Castle Donington 8 B2
Castle Douglas 12 C4
Castlebay 14 A4
Castleford 11 D
Castletown (High) 15 E1
Castletown (IoM) 10 A4
Catel 2 A2
Caterham 5 D3
Catterick Camp 10 C2
Chandler's Ford 4 B3
Chard 3 E2
Charing 5 E3
Charlbury 4 B1
Chatham 5 E2
Chatteris 9 D3
Cheadle (G Man) 10 C4
Cheadle (Staf) 7 F2
Cheddar 3 E1
Chelmsford 5 D2
Cheltenham 7 E4
Chepstow 3 E1
Chertsey 4 C3
Chesham 4 C2
Cheshunt 5 D2
Chester 7 D1
Chesterfield 8 B1
Chester-le Street 11 D1
Chichester 4 C4
Chippenham 3 F1
Chipping Campden 4 A1
Chipping Norton 4 A1
Chipping Ongar 5 D2
Chipping Sodbury 3 F1
Chirk 7 D2
Chorley 10 B4
Christchurch 4 A4
Chudleigh 3 D3
Chumleigh 2 C2
Church Stretton 7 D3
Cinderford 7 E4
Cirencester A2
Clachan 12 B2
Clacton-on-Sea 5 E1
Claonaig 12 B2
Cleator Moor 10 A2
Cleethorpes 11 F4
Cleobury Mortimer 7 E3
Clevedon 3 E1
Cleveleys 10 B3
Clifton 12 C1
Cliftonville 5 F2
Clitheroe 10 C3
Clophill 4 C1
Clova 15 E4
Clovelly 2 C2
Clun 7 D3
Clydebank 12 C2
Coalville 8 B2
Cockburnspath 13 E2
Cockermouth 10 A1
Coggeshall 5 E1
Colchester 5 E1

Coldstream 13 E3
Coleford 7 E4
Colne 10 C3
Colwyn Bay 6 C1
Combe Martin 2 C2
Comrie 12 C1
Congleton 7 F1
Conisbrough 11 D4
Coniston 10 B2
Connel 12 B1
Consett 10 C1
Contin 15 D3
Conwy 6 C1
Corbridge 10 C1
Corby Glen 8 C2
Corby 8 C3
Corpach 14 C4
Corran 12 B1
Corsham 3 F1
Corton 9 F3
Corwen 7 D2
Coryton 5 E2
Cottenham 9 D4
Cottesmore 8 C3
Coulport 12 B2
Coupar Angus 13 D1
Coventry 7 F3
Cowbridge 3 D1
Cowdenbeath 13 D2
Cowes 4 B4
Craighouse 12 A2
Craignure 12 A1
Crail 13 E1
Cranbrook 5 E3
Cranleigh 4 C3
Cranwell 8 C2
Craven Arms 7 D3
Crawley 5 D3
Cray Cross 8 B2
Creag 14 A3
Crediton 3 D3
Crewe 7 E1
Crewkerne 3 E2
Crianlarich 12 C1
Criccieth 6 B2
Cricklade 4 A2
Crieff 12 C1
Crocketford 12 C4
Cromarty 15 D2
Cromer 9 F2
Crook 10 C1
Crosby 10 B4
Crowborough 5 D3
Crowland 8 C3
Crowle 11 E4
Croxton Kerrial 8 B2
Croydon 5 D3
Cuckfield 5 D3
Cullen 15 E2
Cullompton 3 D2
Cumbernauld 12 C2
Cumnock 12 C3
Cupar 13 D1
Cwmbran 3 E1

D

Dalbeattie 12 C4
Dalchork 15 D2
Dale 4 A4
Dalkeith 13 D2
Dalmellington 12 C3
Dalry 12 C2
Dalton-in-Furness 10 A3
Dalwhinnie 15 D4
Darlington 11 D2
Dartford 5 D2
Dartmeet 2 C3
Dartmouth 3 D4

Darvel 12 C3
Darwen 10 B4
Daventry 4 B1
Dawlish 3 D3
Deal 5 F3
Deddington 4 B1
Denbigh 7 D1
Denny 12 C2
Derby 7 F1
Desborough 8 B3
Devizes 4 A3
Dewsbury 11 D4
Didcot 4 B2
Dinas-Mawddwy 6 C2
Dingwall 15 D3
Dinnington 11 D4
Diss 9 E3
Dolgellau 6 C2
Dollar 13 D2
Doncaster 11 D4
Donington 8 C2
Dorchester (Dor) 3 F3
Dorchester (Oxon) 4 B2
Dorking 4 C3
Dornoch 15 D2
Douglas (IoM) 10 A4
Douglas (S Lan) 12 C3
Doune 12 C2
Dover 5 F3
Downham Market 9 D3
Droitwich 7 E3
Dronfield 8 B1
Drummore 12 B4
Drumnadrochit 15 D3
Drymen 12 C2
Duddington 8 C3
Dudley 7 E3
Dufftown 15 E3
Dulverton 3 D2
Dumbarton 12 C2
Dumfries 10 A1
Dunbar 13 E2
Dunblane 12 C2
Dundee 13 D1
Dunfermline 13 D2
Dunkeld 13 D1
Dunoon 12 B2
Duns 13 E2
Dunstable 4 C1
Dunster 3 D2
Dunvegan 14 B3
Durham 11 D1
Durness 14 C1
Dursley 3 F1
Dyce 15 F3
Dyffryn 6 B1

E

Ealing 4 C2
Eardisley 7 D3
Easington (Dur) 11 D1
Easington (E York) 11 F4
Easingwold 11 D3
East Bergholt 5 E1
East Cowes 4 B4
East Dereham 9 E3
East Grinstead 5 D3
East Kilbride 12 C2
East Linton 13 E2
East Retford 8 B1
East Wittering 4 C4
Eastbourne 5 D4
Easter Quarff 13 F2
Eastleigh 4 B3
Ebbw Vale 7 D4
Eccleshall 7 E2
Eckington 8 B1
Edenbridge 5 D3

Edinburgh 13 D2
Egham 4 C2
Egremont 10 A2
Elgin 15 E2
Elland 10 C4
Ellesmere Port 7 D1
Ellesmere 7 D2
Ellon 15 F3
Ely 9 D3
Emsworth 4 B4
Epping 5 D2
Epsom 4 C3
Eribol 14 C1
Eston 11 D2
Eton 4 C2
Ettington 4 A1
Evesham 4 A1
Exeter 3 D3
Exford 3 D2
Exmouth 3 D3
Eye 9 E3
Eyemouth 13 E2

F

Fairford 4 A2
Fakenham 9 E2
Falkirk 13 D2
Falmouth 2 B4
Fareham 4 B4
Faringdon 4 A2
Farnborough 4 C3
Farnham 4 C3
Farnworth 10 C4
Faversham 5 E3
Fawley 4 B4
Felixstowe 5 F1
Felton 13 F3
Feolin Ferry 12 A2
Ferndown 4 A4
Ffestiniog 6 C2
Filey 11 F2
Filton 3 E1
Findochty 15 E2
Finstown 15 F1
Fionnphort 12 A1
Fishguard 6 A4
Fleet 4 C3
Fleetwood 10 B3
Flint 7 D1
Fochabers 15 E3
Folkestone 5 F3
Fordingbridge 4 A4
Forfar 13 D1
Formby 10 B4
Forres 15 D3
Fort Augustus 14 C3
Fort William 14 C4
Fortrose 15 D3
Fortuneswell 3 F3
Fowey 2 B4
Framlingham 9 F4
Fraserburgh 15 F2
Fridaythorpe 11 E3
Frinton-on-Sea 5 F1
Frodsham 7 E1
Frome 3 F2
Furnace 12 B2

G

Gainsborough 11 E4
Gairloch 14 B2
Galashiels 13 E3
Galston 12 C3
Garelochhead 12 B2
Garstang 10 B3
Gatehouse of Fleet 12 C4
Gateshead 11 D1

Gelligaer 3 D1
Gillingham (Dor) 3 F2
Gillingham (Med) 5 E2
Girvan 12 B3
Gisburn 10 C3
Glamis 13 D1
Glasgow 12 C2
Glastonbury 3 E2
Glenbarr 12 A3
Glencoe 12 B1
Glenfinnan 14 C4
Glenluce 12 B4
Glenrothes 13 D2
Glossop 10 C4
Gloucester 7 E4
Godalming 4 C3
Godmanchester 8 C4
Godstone 5 D3
Golspie 15 D2
Golval 15 D1
Goodwick 6 A4
Goole 11 E4
Gorey 2 B2
Goring 4 B2
Gorstan 14 C2
Gosforth 11 D1
Gosport 4 B4
Gourock 12 B2
Grain 5 E2
Grangemouth 13 D2
Grange-over-Sands 10 B3
Grantham 8 C2
Grantown-on-Spey 15 E3
Grasmere 10 B2
Gravesend 5 D2
Grays 5 D2
Great Driffield 11 E3
Great Dunmow 5 D1
Great Malvern 7 E4
Great Shelford 5 D1
Great Torrington 2 C2
Great Yarmouth 9 F3
Greenlaw 13 E3
Greenock 12 B2
Greenod 10 B2
Gretna 10 B1
Grimsby 11 F4
Guildford 4 C3
Guisborough 11 D2
Gutcher 13 F1
Guyhirn 9 D3

H

Haddington 13 E2
Hadleigh 5 E1
Hagley 7 E3
Hailsham 5 D4
Halesowen 7 F3
Halesworth 9 F3
Halifax 10 C4
Halstead 5 E1
Haltwhistle 10 B1
Hamilton 12 C2
Hanley 7 E1
Harlech 6 C2
Harleston 9 E3
Harlow 5 D2
Haroldswick 13 F1
Harpenden 4 C2
Harrogate 11 D3
Harrow 4 C2
Hartland 2 B2
Hartlepool 11 D1
Hartley Wintney 4 B3
Harwell 4 B2
Harwich 5 F1
Haslemere 4 C3
Hastings 5 E4

Hatfield (Herts) 4 C2
Hatfield (S York) 11 E4
Hatherleigh 2 C3
Havant 4 B4
Haverfordwest 6 A4
Haverhill 5 D1
Hawarden 7 D1
Hawes 10 C2
Hawick 13 E3
Hawkhurst 5 E3
Hawkshead 10 B2
Haworth 10 C3
Haydon Bridge 10 C1
Hayle 2 A4
Hay-on-Wye 7 D4
Haywards Heath 5 D3
Heanor 8 B2
Heathfield 5 D3
Hebden Bridge 10 C4
Hedon 11 F4
Helensburgh 12 C2
Helmsdale 15 E2
Helmsley 11 D2
Helston 2 A4
Hemel Hempstead 4 C2
Hemyock 3 D2
Henley-in-Arden 7 F3
Henley-on-Thames 4 B2
Henstridge 3 F2
Hereford 7 E4
Herne Bay 5 E2
Hertford 5 D2
Hetton-le-Hole 11 D1
Hexham 10 C1
Heysham 10 B3
High Wycombe 4 C2
Higham Ferrers 8 C4
Highworth 4 A2
Hillswick 13 F1
Hinckley 8 B3
Hindhead 4 C3
Hirwaun 6 C4
Histon 9 D4
Hitchin 4 C1
Hoddesdon 5 D2
Hodnet 7 E2
Holbeach 9 D2
Holland-on-Sea 5 F1
Holmfirth 10 C4
Holmhead 12 C3
Holsworthy 2 C3
Holt 9 E2
Holyhead (Caergybi) 6 B1
Holywell 7 D1
Honiton 3 D3
Hook 4 B3
Hope 7 D1
Hopton 9 F3
Horden 11 D1
Horley 5 D3
Horncastle 8 C1
Horndean 4 B4
Hornsea 11 F3
Horsham 4 C3
Houghton le Spring 11 D1
Hounslow 4 C2
Hove 5 D4
Howden 11 E4
Hoylake 10 A4
Hucknall 8 B2
Huddersfield 10 C4
Hugh Town 2 A3
Hungerford 4 B3
Hunmanby 11 E3
Hunstanton 9 D2
Huntingdon 8 C4
Huntley 7 E4
Huntly 15 E3

Prestwick 12 C3
Preteigne 7 D3
Princes Risborough 4 C2
Prudhoe 10 C1
Puckeridge 5 D1
Puddletown 3 F3
Pudsey 11 D3
Pulborough 4 C4
Pwllheli 6 B2

Q

Queensferry 7 D1

R

Radstock 3 F1
Rainham 5 E3
Ramsey *(Camb)* 8 C3
Ramsey *(IoM)* 10 A4
Ramsgate 5 F3
Rattray 13 D1
Raunds 8 C4
Ravenglass 10 A2
Rawmarsh 11 D4
Rawtenstall 10 C4
Rayleigh 5 E2
Reading 4 B2
Reay 15 D1
Redcar 11 D2
Redditch 7 F3
Redhill 5 D3
Redruth 2 A4
Reepham 9 E2
Reigate 5 D3
Rhayader 6 C3
Rhosneigr 6 B1
Rhos-on-Sea 6 C1
Rhuddlan 6 C1
Rhyl 6 C1
Rhymney 7 D4
Rhynie 15 F3
Richmond 10 C2
Rickmansworth 4 C2
Ringwood 4 A4
Ripley 8 B2
Ripon 11 D3
Roade 4 B1
Robin Hood's Bay 11 E2
Rochdale 10 C4
Rochester 5 E2
Roghadal 14 A2
Romsey 4 B3
Rosehearty 15 F2
Ross-on-Wye 7 E4
Rothbury 13 F3
Rotherham 11 D4
Rothes 15 E3
Rothesay 12 B2
Rothwell *(North)* 8 C3
Rothwell *(W York)* 11 D4
Royal Leamington Spa 7 F3
Royal Tunbridge Wells 5 D3
Royston 5 D1
Rozel 2 B2
Rugby 8 B3
Rugeley 7 F2
Runcorn 7 E1
Rushden 8 C4
Ruthin 7 D1
Ryde 4 B4
Rye 5 E3

S

Saffron Walden 5 D1
Salcombe 2 C4
Sale 10 C4
Salen 12 A1

Salford 10 C4
Salisbury 4 A3
Saltash 2 C4
Saltburn-by-the-Sea 11 E2
Saltcoats 12 B3
Sandbach 7 E1
Sandhead 12 B4
Sandhurst 4 C3
Sandness 13 F2
Sandown 4 B4
Sandringham 9 D2
Sandwich 5 F3
Sandy 4 C1
Sanquhar 12 C3
Saundersfoot 6 B4
Saxmundham 9 F4
Scalasaig 12 A2
Scalby 11 E2
Scalloway 13 F2
Scarborough 11 E2
Scrabster 15 E1
Scunthorpe 11 E4
Seaford 5 D4
Seaham 11 D1
Seascale 10 A2
Seaton 3 E3
Sedbergh 10 B2
Sedgefield 11 D1
Selby 11 D3
Selkirk 13 E3
Selsey 4 C4
Settle 10 C3
Sevenoaks 5 D3
Shaftesbury 3 F2
Shanklin 4 B4
Shap 10 B2
Sheerness 5 E2
Sheffield 11 D4
Shefford 4 C1
Shepshed 8 B3
Shepton Mallet 3 E2
Sherborne 3 E2
Sheringham 9 E2
Shiel Bridge 14 C3
Shieldaig 14 B3
Shifnal 7 E2
Shipley 10 C3
Shipston-on-Stour 4 A1
Shoeburyness 5 E2
Shoreham-by-Sea 4 C4
Shotley Gate 5 F1
Shotts 12 C2
Shrewsbury 7 D2
Sidmouth 3 D3
Silloth 10 A1
Silsden 10 C3
Silverstone 4 B1
Sittingbourne 5 E3
Skegness 9 D2
Skelmersdale 10 B4
Skipton 10 C3
Sleaford 8 C2
Sligachan 14 B3
Slough 4 C2
Soham 9 D3
Solihull 7 F3
Somerton 3 E2
South Cave 11 E3
South Hayling 4 B4
South Molton 2 C2
South Queensferry 13 D2
South Shields 11 D1
Southam 4 B1
Southampton 4 B4
Southborough 5 D3
Southend 12 A3
Southend-on-Sea 5 E2

Southport 10 B4
Southwell 8 B2
Southwold 9 F3
Sowerby Bridge 10 C4
Spalding 8 C2
Spean Bridge 14 C4
Spennymoor 11 D1
Spilsby 9 D2
St Agnes 2 A4
St Albans 4 C2
St Andrews 13 E1
St Anne 2 A1
St Asaph 7 D1
St Aubin 2 A2
St Austell 2 B4
St Bees 10 A2
St Boswells 13 E3
St Brelade 2 A2
St Clears 6 B4
St Clement 2 B2
St Columb Major 2 B3
St David's 6 A4
St Helens 10 B4
St Helier 2 A2
St Ives *(Camb)* 9 D4
St Ives *(Corn)* 2 A4
St Just 2 A4
St Keverne 2 A4
St Lawrence 2 A2
St Martin 2 A2
St Mary's 15 F1
St Mawes 2 B4
St Neots 4 C1
St Ouen 2 A2
St Peter 2 A2
St Peter Port 2 A2
St Sampson 2 A2
St Saviour *(Guer)* 2 A2
St Saviour *(Jer)* 2 B2
Staffin 14 B2
Stafford 7 E2
Staines 4 C2
Stalbridge 3 F2
Stalham 9 F2
Stamford Bridge 11 E3
Stamford 8 C3
Stanhope 10 C1
Stanley 11 D1
Stansted 5 D1
Staveley 8 B1
Stevenage 4 C1
Stevenston 12 B3
Stewarton 12 C3
Stilton 8 C3
Stirling 12 C2
Stockbridge 4 B3
Stockport 10 C4
Stocksbridge 11 D4
Stockton-on-Tees 11 D2
Stoke Ferry 9 D3
Stokenchurch 4 B2
Stoke-on-Trent 7 E1
Stokesley 11 D2
Stone 7 E2
Stonehaven 15 F4
Stonehouse 7 E4
Stony Stratford 4 B1
Stornoway 14 B1
Stourbridge 7 E3
Stourport-on-Severn 7 E3
Stow 13 D2
Stowmarket 5 E1
Stow-on-the-Wold 4 A1
Stranraer 12 B4
Stratford-upon-Avon 4 A1
Strathaven 12 C3
Strathpeffer 15 D3
Stratton 2 B2

Street 3 E2
Stromness 15 F1
Stroud 7 E4
Sturminster Newton 3 F2
Sudbury *(Derb)* 7 F2
Sudbury *(Suff)* 5 E1
Sullom 13 F1
Sumburgh 13 F2
Sunderland 11 D1
Sutterton 9 D2
Sutton Coldfield 7 F2
Sutton in Ashfield 8 B2
Sutton on Sea 9 D1
Swadlincote 7 F2
Swaffham 9 E3
Swanage 4 A4
Swansea 2 C1
Swinderby 8 C2
Swindon 4 A2
Swineshead 8 C2
Syre 15 D1
Syston 8 B3

T

Tadcaster 11 D3
Tain 15 D2
Tamworth 7 F2
Tarbert *(Arg)* 12 B2
Tarbert *(W Isl)* 14 A2
Tarbet 12 C2
Tarporley 7 E1
Taunton 3 E2
Tavistock 2 C3
Tayinloan 12 A3
Taynuilt 12 B1
Teignmouth 3 D3
Telford 7 E2
Tenbury Wells 7 E3
Tenby 2 B1
Tenterden 5 E3
Tetbury 3 F1
Tewkesbury 7 E4
Thame 4 B2
The Mumbles 2 C1
Thetford 9 E3
Thirsk 11 D2
Thornaby-on-Tees 11 D2
Thornbury 3 E1
Thorne 11 E4
Thorney 8 C3
Thornhill 13 D3
Thornton 10 B3
Thrapston 8 C3
Thurmaston 8 B3
Thursby 10 B1
Thurso 15 E1
Tickhill 11 D4
Tigh A Ghearraidh 14 A2
Tighnabruaich 12 B2
Tilbury 5 D2
Tillicoultry 13 D2
Tintagel 2 B3
Tiptree 5 E1
Tiverton 3 D2
Tobermory 12 A1
Todmorden 10 C4
Toft 13 F1
Tomatin 15 D3
Tomintoul 15 E3
Tonbridge 5 D3
Tongue 15 D1
Topsham 3 D3
Torpoint 2 C4
Torquay 3 D3
Totnes 3 D3
Totton 4 B4
Tow Law 10 C1
Towcester 4 B1

Tranent 13 D2
Trecastle 6 C4
Tredegar 7 D4
Tregaron 6 C3
Tring 4 C2
Troon 12 C3
Trowbridge 3 F1
Truro 2 B4
Tunstall 7 E1
Turriff 15 F3
Two Bridges 2 C3
Tynemouth 11 D1
Tywyn 6 C2

U

Uckfield 5 D3
Uffculme 3 D2
Uig 14 B2
Ullapool 14 C2
Ulsta 13 F1
Ulverston 10 B3
Upavon 4 A3
Upper Largo 13 D2
Uppingham 8 C3
Upton-upon-Severn 7 E4
Usk 7 D4
Uttoxeter 7 F2

V

Ventnor 4 B4
Voe 13 F1

W

Wadebridge 2 B3
Wainfleet All Saints 9 D2
Wakefield 11 D4
Wallasey 10 B4
Wallingford 4 B2
Walmer 5 F3
Walsall 7 F2
Waltham Abbey 5 D2
Walton on the Naze 5 F1
Wansford 8 C3
Wantage 4 B2
Ware 5 D1
Wareham 3 F3
Warminster 3 F2
Warrington 10 B4
Warwick 7 F3
Washington 11 D1
Watchet 3 D2
Watford 4 C2
Watton 9 E3
Weedon Bec 4 B1
Wellingborough 8 C4
Wellington *(Som)* 3 D2
Wellington *(Wrek)* 7 E2
Wells 3 E2
Wells-next-the-Sea 9 E2
Welshpool (Y Trallwng) 7 D2
Welwyn Garden City 4 C2
Wem 7 E2
Wemyss Bay 12 B2
Wendover 4 C2
West Bridgford 8 B2
West Bromwich 7 F3
West Kilbride 12 B2
West Mersea 5 E2
Westbury 3 F2
Weston-super-Mare 3 E1
Westward Ho! 2 C2
Wetherby 11 D3
Weybridge 4 C3
Weymouth 3 F3
Whaley Bridge 7 F1
Wheatley 4 B2
Whipsnade 4 C1

Whitburn 13 D2
Whitby 11 E2
Whitchurch *(Bucks)* 4 B1
Whitchurch *(Hants)* 4 B3
Whitchurch *(Shrop)* 7 E2
Whitehaven 10 A2
Whithorn 12 C4
Whitley Bay 11 D1
Whitstable 5 E2
Whittington 7 D2
Whittlesey 8 C3
Wick 15 E1
Wickford 5 E2
Wickham Market 5 F1
Widecombe 2 C3
Widnes 7 E1
Wigan 10 B4
Wigston 8 B3
Wigton 10 A1
Wigtown 12 C4
Williton 3 D2
Wilmslow 7 E1
Wilton 4 A3
Wimborne Minster 4 A4
Wincanton 3 F2
Winchcombe 4 A1
Winchester 4 B3
Windermere 10 B2
Windsor 4 C2
Winsford 7 E1
Winslow 4 B1
Winterton 11 E4
Winterton-on-Sea 9 F2
Wirksworth 7 F1
Wisbech 9 D3
Wishaw 12 C2
Witham 5 E1
Withernsea 11 F4
Witney 4 B2
Wiveliscombe 3 D2
Wivenhoe 5 E1
Woburn 4 C1
Woking 4 C3
Wokingham 4 C2
Wolverhampton 7 E2
Wolverton 4 B1
Woodbridge 5 F1
Woodhall Spa 8 C2
Woodstock 4 B2
Woofferton 7 E3
Woolacombe 2 C2
Wooler 13 E3
Woore 7 E2
Wootton Bassett 4 A2
Worcester 7 E3
Workington 10 A1
Worksop 8 B1
Worthing 4 C4
Wotton-under-Edge 3 F1
Wragby 8 C1
Wrexham 7 D1
Wrotham 5 D3
Wroughton 4 A2
Wroxham 9 F3
Wymondham 9 E3

Y

Yarmouth 4 B4
Yate 3 F1
Yeadon 10 C3
Yeovil 3 E2
York 11 D3
Ystrad 3 D1

INDEX TO IRELAND

SPENCER'S

The British Golf Directory

Courses where you can turn up and play

This new Spencer's guide provides full details of golf courses the length and breadth of Britain. All are courses where you can turn up and play, from municipal courses to some of the grandest in the land. You don't need to be members or pay membership fees. Just the rate for the round.

Whether you are an old hand or one of the new wave of golf enthusiasts you will find Spencer's Directory an invaluable companion - for your home, for your car or for your holidays.

With full-colour throughout it's easy-to-use, highly practical and perfect for browsing.

Each entry has a full quarter-page, with a description of the course, and information on yardage, par, standard scratch score, directions and green fees. There's also a full-colour route-planning and map section - a feature of all Spencer's titles.

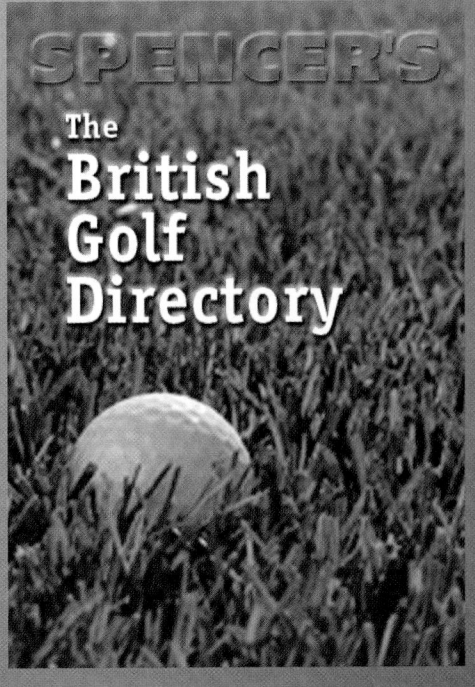

Format:	210x148mm
No. of pages:	112pp
ISBN:	1 900327 51 1
Price:	£4.99
Publication date:	April 2000

West One Publishing
Kestrel House, Duke's PLace
Marlow, Bucks SL7 2QH

West One PUBLISHING

tel: 01628 487722

www.WestOneWeb.com

SPENCER'S

Labels For Less

Famous brands and labels at discount prices

Labels for Less is a revolutionary and colourful new guide to discount shopping.

For keen shoppers everywhere, it offers comprehensive coverage of over 1300 factory shops and factory outlet villages. Wherever you travel you will be able to find a factory shop nearby. It's essential reference for home, car and holiday.

Perfects, slight seconds and clearance lines, all at bargain prices, make Labels For Less the most exciting and rewarding guide to shopping around. For each outlet there's full information on products, labels and discounts. Plus details of locations, transport, parking, opening hours, credit cards and restaurants.

Every entry is in colour, maximising the impact and highlighting the discounts and brands each outlet features. 20 pages of mapping make route-finding easy.

Format:	210x148mm
No. of pages:	480pp
ISBN:	1 900327 35 X
Price:	£13.99
Publication date:	November 1999

West One Publishing
Kestrel House, Duke's PLace
Marlow, Bucks SL7 2QH

West One PUBLISHING

tel: 01628 487722

www.WestOneWeb.com

Distance Chart

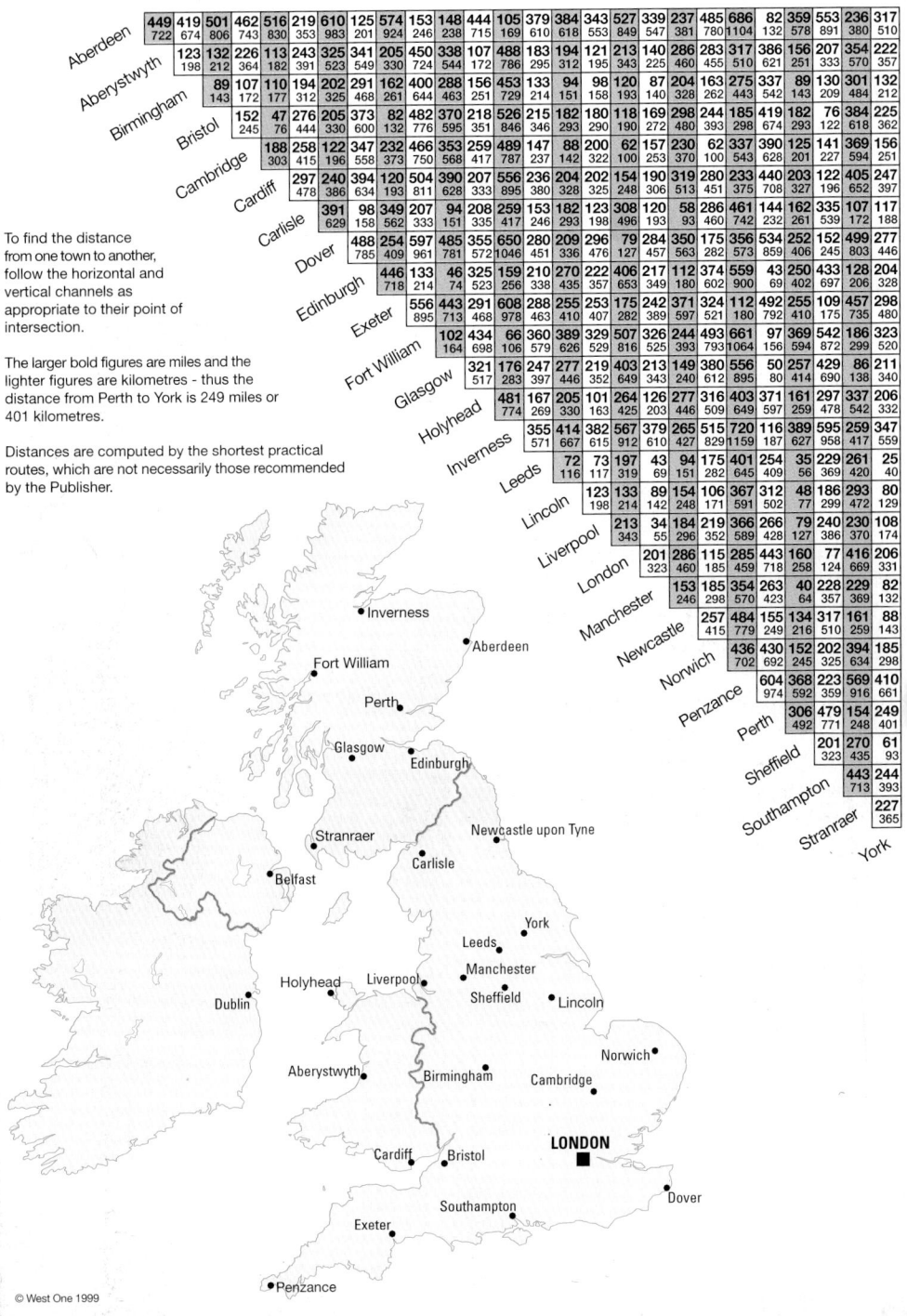

To find the distance from one town to another, follow the horizontal and vertical channels as appropriate to their point of intersection.

The larger bold figures are miles and the lighter figures are kilometres - thus the distance from Perth to York is 249 miles or 401 kilometres.

Distances are computed by the shortest practical routes, which are not necessarily those recommended by the Publisher.

© West One 1999

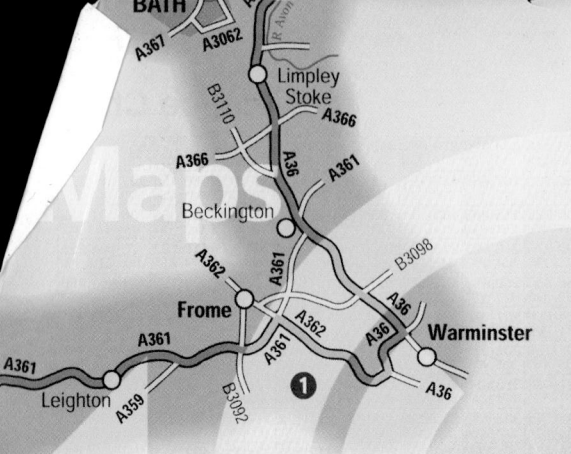

Maps

Beckington

Frome

Leighton

Warminster

Leisure

Travel

Shoppin

www.WestOneWeb.com

West One